online

encyclopedia

LONDON, NEW YORK, MELBOURNE,
MUNICH, and DELHI

REVISED EDITION 2011
Project editors Suchismita Banerjee, Ashwin Khurana
Editor Parameshwari Sircar

Project designer Romi Chakraborty
Designers Govind Mittal, Pooja Pawwar,
Pushpak Tyagi, Satish Chandra Gaur

Production editors Andy Hilliard, Sunil Sharma
Production controller Charlotte Oliver
Jacket designer Laura Brim
Jacket editor Matilda Gollon

Design development manager Sophia M. Tampakopoulos Turner
Managing editor Linda Esposito
Managing art editor Jim Green
Category publisher Laura Buller

FIRST EDITION 2003
Project editors Fran Baines, Sarah Goulding,
Clare Lister, Jayne Miller, Sue Nicholson, Karen O'Brien,
Mariza O'Keeffe, Katherine Pearce, Jane Yorke
Editors Jo Bourne, Catherine Bradley Janet Sacks
US editors Christine Heilman, Madeline Farbman, Beth Sutinis

Project designers Ann Cannings, Alex Menday,
Owen Peyton Jones, Smiljka Surla, Yumiko Tahata
Designers Peter Bailey, Jim Green, Bob Gordon, Adrienne
Hutchinson, Rebecca Johns, Joanne Little, Philip Lord, Becky Painter

Picture researchers Sarah Pownall, Alison Prior, Fran Vargo
Picture librarian Sarah Mills
Cartographer Simon Mumford
Managing editor Camilla Hallinan
Managing art editor Sophia M. Tampakopoulos Turner

Contributors and Consultants Simon Adams, Dr Kim Bryan, Andy Catling, Ian Chilvers, Peter Chrisp,
Clive Gifford, Dr. Sue Davidson, Dr. Roger Few, Dr. Linda Gambrell, David Glover, David Goldblatt,
Dr Jen Green, Dr. John Haywood, Adam Hibbert, Elaine Jackson, Robin Kerrod, Claire Llewellyn,
Dr. Jacqueline Mitton, Ben Morgan, Peggy Morgan, Philip Parker, Steve Parker Alison Porter,
Janet Sacks, Keith Shadwick, Dr. Tim Shakesby, Professor Robert Spicer, Philip Steele,
Dr. Richard Walker, Jude Welton

First American Edition published as e.encyclopedia in 2003
This edition published in 2011

Published in the United States by DK Publishing, Inc.
375 Hudson Street, New York, New York 10014

11 12 13 14 15 10 9 8 7 6 5 4 3 2 1
179076-02/11
Copyright © 2003, 2006, 2011 Dorling Kindersley Limited

A Cataloging-in-Publication record for this book
is available from the Library of Congress.

ISBN 978-0-7566-7310-9

Color reproduction by MDP, UK
Printed and bound in China by Toppan

Discover more at
www.dk.com

online

encyclopedia

Fischer Middle School
Indian Prairie School District #204
1305 Long Grove Dr.
Aurora, IL 60504

CONTENTS

MEASUREMENTS AND ABBREVIATIONS						
METRIC		**US CUSTOMARY**		**DATES**		
mm	millimeter	in	inches	c.	circa (about)	
cm	centimeter	ft	feet	BCE	before the Common Era	
m	meter	yd	yards			
km	kilometer			CE	Common Era	
sq km	square kilometer	sq miles	square miles	b.	born	
km²	square kilometer	miles²	square miles	d.	died	
km/h	kilometers per hour	mph	miles per hour	r.	reigned	
°C	degrees Celsius	°F	degrees Fahrenheit			
g	grams	oz	ounces			
kg	kilograms	lb	pounds	**billion = thousand million**		

FROM THE BOOK TO THE NET AND BACK AGAIN

The *online encyclopedia* has its own website. When you look up a subject in the book, the article gives you key facts and displays a keyword that links you to a wealth of extra information online. Just follow these easy steps.

 Enter this website address

Address : @ http://www.encyclopedia.dkonline.com

 Find the keyword in the book

You can use only the keywords from the book to search on our website for the specially selected links. The keywords are displayed in grey circles.

3 **Enter the keyword, eg astronauts**

astronauts

Be safe while you are online:

- Always get permission from an adult before connecting to the Internet.

- Never give out personal information about yourself.

- Never arrange to meet someone you have talked to online.

- If a site asks you to log in with your name or email address, ask permission from an adult first.

- Do not reply to emails from strangers – tell an adult.

Parents: Dorling Kindersley actively and regularly reviews and updates the links. However, content may change. Dorling Kindersley is not responsible for any site but its own. We recommend that children are supervised while online, that they do not use chat rooms, and that filtering software is used to block unsuitable material.

SPACE

When you look up at the night sky, the blackness you see is space. It is the great void, or emptiness, in which Earth, the Moon, the Sun, and the stars travel. Space is totally silent, and most of it is incredibly cold—around 454°F below zero (−270°C). It is also called outer space.

WHERE DOES SPACE BEGIN?
From Earth, space begins at the outer edge of our planet's atmosphere. There is no clear line between the atmosphere and space—the atmosphere gradually fades away until it merges into space about 300 miles (500 km) above Earth. However, there are tiny traces of atmosphere even farther out than this.

WHERE IS EARTH IN SPACE?
Earth is a tiny speck of matter in space. It is one of nine planets that circle around the Sun. In turn, the Sun is one of several hundred billion stars, which together form a great star "island" in space called the Milky Way Galaxy. There are billions of galaxies in space. Together, all the galaxies and the enormous voids between them make up the Universe.

HOW MUCH SPACE IS THERE?
Astronomers believe that space is infinite—it has no edge or boundary. Earth's nearest neighbor in space, the Moon, is 238,900 miles (384,400 km) away on average. The Sun is 93 million miles (150 million km) away. Most other stars in the Milky Way are between a million and a billion times more distant than the Sun. Other galaxies are millions of times farther still.

WHAT IS A LIGHT-YEAR?
A light-year is a unit for measuring distances in space. It is the distance that light travels in a year— about 5.9 trillion miles (9.5 trillion km). Proxima Centauri is the closest star to the Sun. It lies about 4.2 light-years away from Earth, which means that its light takes 4.2 years to reach us.

WHAT CAN WE SEE WHEN WE LOOK INTO SPACE?
Without a telescope, we can see about 2,500 stars on a really dark night. We often see the Moon, and sometimes the planets Mercury, Venus, Mars, Jupiter, and Saturn, as well as comets. The farthest thing we can see with just our eyes is the Andromeda Galaxy.

THE MILKY WAY ►
This pale band of light in the night sky is the Milky Way. Its light comes from hundreds of billions of stars in our galaxy. Billions more stars are hidden behind giant, dark clouds of dust and gas.

space

SPACE TIMELINE

150 CE	Ptolemy claims Earth at center of Universe
1543	Copernicus puts Sun at center of Universe
1609	Galileo first to use a telescope to study space
1687	Newton publishes the laws of gravity
1781	Herschel discovers the planet Uranus
1846	Galle discovers the Neptune
1926	Goddard launches first liquid-fueled rocket
1930	Tombaugh discovers the planet Pluto
1957	First satellite, *Sputnik 1*, orbits Earth
1961	Yuri Gagarin becomes first person in space
1965	*Mariner 4* sends back pictures of Mars
1969	*Apollo 11* makes the first manned Moon landing
1981	First launch of space shuttle
1990	Launch of Hubble Space Telescope
1998	International Space Station construction begins

◄ JOURNEY INTO SPACE
This powerful rocket launch vehicle, Ariane, sends satellites and other spacecraft into space to explore the stars and planets and view Earth from space.

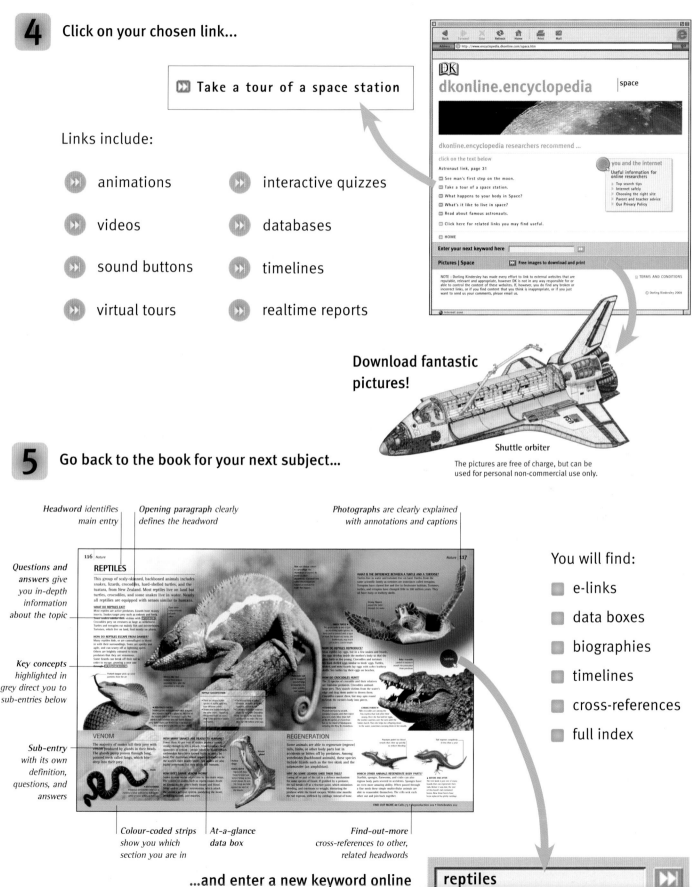

4 Click on your chosen link...

⏩ **Take a tour of a space station**

Links include:

⏩ animations

⏩ interactive quizzes

⏩ videos

⏩ databases

⏩ sound buttons

⏩ timelines

⏩ virtual tours

⏩ realtime reports

Download fantastic pictures!

Shuttle orbiter
The pictures are free of charge, but can be used for personal non-commercial use only.

5 Go back to the book for your next subject...

Headword identifies main entry

Opening paragraph clearly defines the headword

Photographs are clearly explained with annotations and captions

Questions and answers give you in-depth information about the topic

Key concepts highlighted in grey direct you to sub-entries below

Sub-entry with its own definition, questions, and answers

Colour-coded strips show you which section you are in

At-a-glance data box

Find-out-more cross-references to other, related headwords

You will find:

▢ e-links

▢ data boxes

▢ biographies

▢ timelines

▢ cross-references

▢ full index

...and enter a new keyword online

reptiles ⏩

GALAXIES

A galaxy is a vast collection of stars, gas, and dust spinning in space and held together by gravity. All the stars in the sky belong to our own galaxy, the ►► MILKY WAY .

SPIRAL GALAXY ▲

HOW MANY DIFFERENT GALAXIES ARE THERE?
The Universe contains a hundred billion galaxies, and there are four main types. Spiral galaxies have a central bulge of stars, with other stars in a pattern of curved arms. Barred spirals have arms coming from a bar through their center. Ellipticals are round or oval, with no spiral arms. An irregular is a galaxy with no special shape. The largest galaxies in a ►► GALAXY CLUSTER are mostly spirals and ellipticals.

WHAT ARE ACTIVE GALAXIES?
A few galaxies, called active galaxies, create huge amounts of energy. At their center, they have a massive black hole that generates a trillion times more power than our Sun and spits out jets of electrically charged particles. Quasars and radio galaxies are both types of active galaxies.

▲ IRREGULAR GALAXY

▲ BARRED SPIRAL GALAXY

GALAXY TYPES
Early last century, the astronomer Edwin Hubble put galaxies into groups according to their shape.

galaxies

WHEN GALAXIES COLLIDE ►
Galaxies sometimes collide with one another. The larger Cartwheel Galaxy shown here was once an ordinary spiral galaxy. But some 300 million years ago, a smaller galaxy passed through it, breaking up its spiral arms and producing a ring of new stars.

▲ ELLIPTICAL GALAXY

MILKY WAY

Our home in the Universe is the Milky Way Galaxy. It is a barred spiral galaxy that contains our Sun and 200 billion other stars, among vast clouds of dust and gas. The Milky Way measures about 100,000 light-years

◄ **ABOVE THE SPIRAL**
Viewed from above, the Milky Way Galaxy would look like a slowly spinning pinwheel firework, with spectacular spiral arms.

HOW DOES THE MILKY WAY LOOK FROM EARTH?
Earth sits out near the end of one of the Milky Way's spiral arms, so we have an excellent view of the rest of our galaxy. From Earth, the Milky Way appears as a pale band of light across the night sky. It is a flat spiral, and we see it from the side, so it seems long and thin to us. The dark rifts in the Milky Way are huge dust clouds that hide the stars behind them.

GALAXY CLUSTERS

A galaxy cluster is a large number of galaxies that are grouped together in space. The Virgo Cluster, for example, contains at least 2,000 galaxies.

WHAT IS THE LOCAL GROUP?
Our Milky Way Galaxy belongs to a galaxy cluster called the Local Group. It contains about 30 galaxies, including our near neighbors, the Andromeda Galaxy and the Magellanic Clouds, which we can see with the naked eye. Most of the galaxies are ellipticals or irregulars.

MAPPING THE UNIVERSE ►
A supercluster is a group of clusters. This computer-generated map shows the superclusters of galaxies that make up our part of the Universe. They are separated by vast empty spaces called voids.

COMA CLUSTER ►
A view of the Coma Cluster, which contains up to 3,000 galaxies. It lies about 300 million light-years away, in the constellation Coma Berenices. Most of the objects in this picture are galaxies.

FIND OUT MORE ►► Earth 16 • Solar System 14 • Space 10 • Stars 24–25 • Sun 15

ROCKETS

Spacecraft are launched into space by rockets—the only engines powerful enough to overcome Earth's gravity and lift objects into space. Most spacecraft use launch vehicles with several linked rocket units, or stages.

HOW DO ROCKETS WORK?

Rockets burn fuel mixtures called ▶▶ PROPELLANTS. The burning fuel creates a stream of hot gases that shoots out of the rocket's exhaust nozzle. The backward force of the gas jet gives the rocket a forward force called thrust. The rocket's forward thrust propels the spacecraft into space.

PROPELLANT

Rocket propellants contain fuel and oxidant. The fuel needs oxygen to burn, and the oxidant provides the oxygen. Most engines can take the oxygen they need from the Earth's atmosphere, but in airless space, a rocket has to carry its own oxygen supply.

WHAT KINDS OF PROPELLANTS DID ROCKETS USE?

Most rockets burn liquid propellants, and some burn solid propellants. The space shuttle main engines burned liquid hydrogen and liquid oxygen. Its booster rockets burned solid propellants. When a shuttle lifted off, almost 90 percent of its weight was propellant.

Upper stage burns for about 4 minutes after ignition

rockets

Core stage burns for about 5 minutes after ignition

Four boosters burn for about 2 minutes after ignition

SOYUZ LIFTOFF ▶
The Russians have used the same kind of Soyuz rocket to launch spacecraft since 1967.

FIND OUT MORE ▶▶ Elements 160–161 • Engines 198–199 • Forces 164 • Space Travel 30

SATELLITES

A spacecraft that travels in a steady path, or orbit, around Earth is called a satellite. Satellites receive and send on communication and navigation signals, watch the weather, survey the land, and study space.

HOW DO SATELLITES STAY UP IN SPACE?

Satellites stay in orbit because of their speed. A satellite in orbit about 190 miles (300 km) above Earth must travel at a speed of 17,500 mph (28,200 km/h) to stay in space. This speed is called its orbital velocity. There are several types of ▶▶ SATELLITE ORBIT.

Payload module contains scientific instruments

◀ INTEGRAL SATELLITE
Launched into orbit in 2002, Integral is an astronomy satellite that studies sources of gamma rays in space. Its elliptical orbit takes it as far as 93,000 miles (150,000 km) above Earth.

Service module contains spacecraft electronics

Solar panels provide electrical power

SATELLITE ORBITS

Satellites travel around Earth in elliptical (oval) orbits, over the Equator, over the poles, or on paths in between.

DO SATELLITES EVER RETURN TO EARTH?

Low-flying satellites may fall back to Earth after only a few months because they pass through traces of air in the upper atmosphere, which slow them down. High-flying satellites can stay in space forever.

Highly elliptical orbit

Geostationary orbit

Equatorial orbit

satellites

Polar orbit

◀ ORBITS
Satellites fly around Earth in different orbits. In a geostationary orbit, a satellite hovers over one fixed place as Earth rotates.

FIND OUT MORE ▶▶ Mass Media 298–299 • Telecommunications 192–193 • Weather 50

SPACE OBSERVATORIES

A spacecraft launched to observe the Sun, stars, and remote galaxies is called a space observatory. The HUBBLE SPACE TELESCOPE was the first really important space observatory.

Sunshade protects the telescope from direct sunlight

Radio antenna sends information to Earth and receives instructions

WHY ARE OBSERVATORIES LAUNCHED INTO SPACE?
Earth's moving atmosphere bends and distorts the light from distant stars and galaxies. In space, observatories can see far more clearly. They can also pick up radiation (such as X-rays) that we cannot detect on Earth because it is absorbed by molecules in the atmosphere.

Solar array provides electrical power

HUBBLE SPACE TELESCOPE

Launched from the Space Shuttle *Discovery* in 1990, the Hubble Space Telescope (HST) orbits about 370 miles (600 km) above Earth. It sends back some of the most detailed images of the Universe ever seen.

space observatory

Body tube houses reflecting telescope

HOW DOES THE HST WORK?
The HST is a reflecting telescope—it uses mirrors to gather and focus light. The focused light is fed to electronic cameras and infrared detectors to create images. The main sensors are CCDs (charge-coupled devices), similar to the ones used in digital cameras.

▲ HUBBLE'S VIEW
This Hubble image shows a mass of gas and dust called the Cone Nebula. It is silhouetted by intense light from hot stars behind.

Aft (rear) shroud houses cameras

FIND OUT MORE ▶▶ Astronomy 11 • Light 178–179 • Observatories 12

INTERPLANETARY SPACECRAFT

Dish antenna directs radio communications toward Earth

Gold foil protects instruments and electronics

Exploring the planets and other bodies in the Solar System are interplanetary spacecraft. They carry advanced cameras and other instruments to detect radiation, magnetism, and tiny particles of matter.

spacecraft

WHERE HAVE INTERPLANETARY SPACECRAFT BEEN?
The first spacecraft were sent to explore the Moon, then the closest planets, Venus and Mars. Spacecraft have now visited all the planets and explored moons, comets, and asteroids. Some fly by their targets but others go into orbit around them or even land. A few release a separate ▶▶ PROBE.

◀ CASSINI SPACECRAFT
Launched in 1997, the *Cassini* spacecraft went into orbit around Saturn in 2004 to explore the planet and its moons.

Rocket motor propels spacecraft

PROBES

A probe is a part of a larger spacecraft that is released to drop into the atmosphere or to the surface of a planet or a moon.

WHAT IS THE HUYGENS PROBE?
The *Cassini* orbiter carried a probe called *Huygens*. In 2005 *Huygens* parachuted down through the atmosphere of Titan, Saturn's largest moon, sending back information as it fell to the surface.

▲ VIKING LANDER ON MARS
Two landers touched down on Mars in 1976, taking photos and monitoring the weather.

KEY INTERPLANETARY MISSIONS		
DATE	MISSION	TARGET
1959	Luna 2	First to photograph far side of Moon
1965	Mariner 4	First close-up images of another planet (Mars)
1973	Pioneer 10	First close-up of Jupiter
1976	Viking 1, 2	First to land on Mars
1986	Voyager 2	First to explore Uranus and Neptune
1986	Giotto	First close encounter with a comet (Halley's)
2000	NEAR	First to land on an asteroid (Eros)

SPACE TRAVEL

People began traveling in space in 1961 in tiny spacecraft called capsules, which were launched from Earth by powerful rockets. Russian crews still travel in this kind of craft, in *Soyuz* capsules. From 1981 to 2010, the Americans had reusable rocket-planes called space shuttles.

Apollo spacecraft carried astronauts

Third-stage engine propelled spacecraft to the Moon

Second-stage engines lifted rocket 115 miles (185 km) above ground

First-stage engines lifted rocket 40 miles (65 km) off the ground

UNITED STATES

HOW DO HUMANS SURVIVE IN SPACE?

There is no oxygen in space, so all crewed spacecraft carry a life-support system. This supplies air for people to breathe. The system also includes equipment to keep the air at a comfortable temperature and pressure and to remove carbon dioxide and odors.

HOW DOES SPACE TRAVEL AFFECT PEOPLE?

When people travel in space, they seem to become weightless. This often makes them feel sick. Their bodies do not have to work as hard, because they are not fighting gravity to sit or stand up. If they stay in space for a long time, the weightlessness makes their muscles start to waste away. Exercise and a special diet help to combat these effects.

WHAT IS THE FARTHEST ANYONE HAS TRAVELED IN SPACE?

Astronauts on the ▶▶ **APOLLO PROJECT** traveled to the Moon, about 239,000 miles (385,000 km) away. Russian cosmonaut Valeri Poliakov traveled a distance of about 174 million miles (280 million km) around Earth while in the Mir space station.

◄ SATURN V LAUNCH
The Saturn V rocket was used for all the Moon landing missions in the 1960s and 1970s. At liftoff, the thrust was more than the combined thrust of 30 jumbo jets taking off.

MISSION CONTROL ▶
All US manned space missions are under the control of Mission Control at the Johnson Space Center in Texas.

APOLLO PROJECT

In the space race of the 1960s, the US Apollo Project beat the Soviet Union by landing the first astronauts on the Moon. The first Moon landing, by *Apollo 11*, took place on July 20, 1969, when Neil Armstrong and Buzz Aldrin became the first humans to set foot on another world.

WHAT WAS THE APOLLO SPACECRAFT LIKE?

The *Apollo* spacecraft was launched from Earth by the *Saturn V* rocket. On the launch pad, the whole assembly stood 365 ft (111 m) tall. The spacecraft itself weighed 50 tons (45 metric tons). It was made from three main modules (sections). The command module for flight control housed the three-person crew. The service module carried equipment, fuel, and a rocket motor. The lunar module detached from the craft and landed two astronauts on the Moon's surface.

▲ LUNAR MODULE
Apollo 11's lunar module, *Eagle*, orbited the Moon during the first Moon landing mission.

▲ MAN ON THE MOON
Buzz Aldrin walked on the Sea of Tranquillity during the two hours he spent on the Moon's surface.

▲ SPLASHDOWN
Three giant parachutes slowed the falling Apollo command module for a gentle splashdown in the Pacific Ocean.

HOW MANY APOLLO LANDINGS WERE THERE?

There were six Moon landings, beginning with *Apollo 11* in July 1969 and ending with *Apollo 17* in December 1972. During the missions, 12 astronauts explored the lunar surface for a total of over 80 hours and brought back nearly 880 lb (400 kg) of Moon rock and dust for examination on Earth.

space travel

FIND OUT MORE ▶▶ Moon 17 • Rockets 28 • Space Shuttle 32

ASTRONAUTS

Anyone who travels in space is called an astronaut. The Russians call their space travelers cosmonauts. Most astronauts stay in space for only a few days, but some remain there for months in the International Space Station (ISS).

WHAT KINDS OF TASKS DO ASTRONAUTS PERFORM?
On missions into orbit, a commander and pilot fly the spacecraft. On past missions, specialists have made observations, carried out experiments, and, if necessary, performed ▶▶ EXTRAVEHICULAR ACTIVITIES (EVAs).

HOW DO ASTRONAUTS TRAIN FOR THEIR MISSIONS?
Pilots and commanders have flight training in jet planes and flight simulators. Mission specialists rehearse mission procedures and experiments. They may train for EVA submerged in water tanks, where conditions are similar to the weightlessness of space.

Helmet with gold-coated visor to reflect light and heat

Portable life-support system in backpack provides oxygen, water (to cool the suit), and electricity. It will keep an astronaut alive for up to 8 hours

Space gloves are heated to keep astronaut's fingers flexible in extreme cold

Tool clips for attaching drills, screwdrivers, and wrenches

astronauts

Backpack control box

Astronaut's cage

One of two spinning wheels

▲ MULTI-AXIS WHEEL
Astronauts are whirled around to prepare their bodies for the strange sensations of space flight.

▲ FIRST PERSON IN SPACE
Cosmonaut Yuri Gagarin made one orbit of Earth in a *Vostok* capsule on April 12, 1961.

▲ SUITED FOR SPACEWALKING
A spacesuit is a multilayer garment that provides an astronaut with pressurized oxygen and protection from the hazards of space—extreme heat and cold, radiation, and meteorite particles.

EXTRAVEHICULAR ACTIVITIES

Any work that astronauts perform outside a spacecraft is called extravehicular activity (EVA) or spacewalking. On EVA, astronauts wear protective spacesuits. Usually, they are attached to the spacecraft by a safety tether. In 1982, astronauts tried out a jet-propelled backpack called a manned maneuvering unit (MMU).

WHY DO ASTRONAUTS NEED TO LEAVE A SPACECRAFT?
One major job for spacewalking astronauts has been to help rescue and repair satellites. On some missions, shuttle astronauts have carried out in-orbit servicing on the Hubble Space Telescope, replacing faulty or outdated equipment. Astronauts may also carry out space construction work. Lengthy EVAs are helping to assemble the International Space Station (ISS) from parts ferried into orbit by other vehicles.

WORKING IN SPACE ▶
An astronaut is at work on the ISS, high above Earth. The tools he uses are tethered to his suit so they don't float away, and he, in turn, is tethered to the craft.

NASA PROJECT PATCH

MMU

LANDMARK EVAs			
DATE	MISSION	ASTRONAUT	EVA
1965	Voskhod 2	Alexei Leonov	1st spacewalk (10 min)
1969	Apollo 11	Neil Armstrong	1st Moonwalk (2 hr 30 min)
2001	ISS	Jim Voss	Longest spacewalk (8 hr 56 min)

FIND OUT MORE ▶▶ Forces 164 • Space Observatories 29 • Space Stations 33

SPACE SHUTTLE

The USA created the space shuttle as a reusable space vehicle for astronauts and cargo. Five shuttles flew between 1981 and 2010. Each main craft was a winged ▸▸ORBITER. For launch, an external fuel tank and two solid rocket boosters (SRBs) were attached.

HOW DID THE SHUTTLE OPERATE?

At liftoff, the orbiter's main engines and the SRBs all fired together. Two minutes later, the SRBs separated and parachuted back to Earth to be used again. About six minutes later, the external fuel tank separated and broke up in Earth's atmosphere. The winged orbiter used its orbital maneuvering system (OMS) to reach the correct orbit.

Crew compartment provided two levels of living space—the flight deck and mid-deck

Payload (cargo)

Delta wing was aerodynamically shaped so orbiter could glide through Earth's atmosphere

Pods housing OMS engines and fuel tanks

Three Shuttle main engines (SMEs) used for liftoff, burning liquid hydrogen and liquid oxygen

Payload bay

Payload bay doors opened to release the payload

▲ SHUTTLE FLIGHT PATTERN
The space shuttle lifts off (top). The external tank and boosters were jettisoned, or cast off, before the orbiter reached orbit (middle). After its mission, the orbiter returned to Earth unpowered, like a glider. It landed on a runway, and used a parachute as a brake (bottom).

◄ SPACE SHUTTLE ORBITER
The orbiter was about 121 ft (37 m) long and had a wingspan of nearly 79 ft (24 m).

WHAT DID THE SHUTTLE CARRY?

The shuttle has carried parts of the International Space Station (ISS) into orbit. It has also carried some new satellites into orbit, and equipment to repair existing satellites. Other payloads (cargo) have included space laboratories, telescopes, and smaller spacecraft that went on to explore the solar system.

ORBITER

This was the main part of the space shuttle that carries the crew and payload. It was thrust into space by rockets, operated as a spacecraft in space, reentered Earth's atmosphere, and landed as a glider.

◄ AFT (REAR) FLIGHT DECK
The astronaut on the right is the flight engineer at his computer in the aft flight deck. The instrument console is on the left. Another astronaut is entering from the forward flight deck, or cockpit, where the commander and the pilot fly the shuttle.

WHAT WAS THE ORBITER MADE OF?

The orbiter was designed to withstand harsh conditions in space. The main structure was built from strong aluminum. For protection against heat, it was covered in insulating materials, such as thick ceramic tiles. Fuel cells combined hydrogen and oxygen to provide electrical power and water for drinking and washing.

LANDMARK ORBITER MISSIONS			
DATE	MISSION	ORBITER	EVENT
1981	STS-1	Columbia	First Shuttle mission
1995	STS-71	Atlantis	First linkup with Russia's space station Mir
1998	STS-88	Endeavour	First International Space Station mission

Space Shuttle

SPACE STATIONS

In a space station, a large crewed spacecraft orbiting Earth, astronauts can live and work in space for long periods. The ▶ INTERNATIONAL SPACE STATION (ISS) is the biggest structure ever to be built in space.

▲ **MIR**
Russia's Mir space station is shown docked (linked) with a US Space Shuttle. Launched in 1986, Mir was permanently crewed by two or three cosmonauts, plus guests from dozens of nations. Mir fell back to Earth in 2001.

WHAT ARE SPACE STATIONS USED FOR?
Astronauts carry out research in space stations. They examine the behavior of materials and living things in a microgravity (near-weightless) environment. They also study the effect of space flight on the human body.

Thermal panels control temperature

Solar panels power ISS

Truss acts as framework for ISS

Research laboratories

Resupply orbiter docks with ISS

External equipment platform

◀ **THE ISS**
Due for completion in 2011, the International Space Station is the biggest, most complex space station ever. With a length of 240 ft (73 m) and width of 356 ft (109 m), it will have a mass of nearly 450 tons (400 metric tons).

HOW ARE SPACE STATIONS BUILT?
Early space stations such as Russia's Salyuts and the US Skylab were built on Earth and launched into orbit as complete units. Larger stations such as Mir and the ISS are assembled in orbit from modules (sections) that are ferried up from Earth one at a time.

▲ **SKYLAB**
Skylab was a US space station launched in 1973. Three three-man crews worked in Skylab for 28, 59, and 84 days. It was allowed to fall back to Earth in 1979.

INTERNATIONAL SPACE STATION

The ISS has been built from more than 100 separate main parts, and is a global research center in space. The United States, through the National Aeronautics and Space Administration (NASA), provided most of the station hardware and was in charge of construction. Russia, Europe (through the European Space Agency), Japan, and Canada also supplied major units.

WHAT IS IT LIKE INSIDE THE ISS?
Up to six astronauts live on the ISS at one time. They have one-person booths or sleeping stations, located around the habitable modules. There are two space toilets but no shower. Instead, crew members wash with special wipes and a water jet. Four main laboratories are the places where astronauts carry out scientific research. Work takes up to 10 hours on weekdays. the rest of the time is spent on meal breaks, exercise, and recreation.

▲ **EVA ON THE ISS**
Robot arms on the shuttle and the ISS connect new sections of the station, but spacewalking astronauts are needed to complete the job. More than 850 hours of extravehicular activity (EVA) will be required before assembly of the station is complete. Afterward, astronauts will have to make regular EVAs to carry out maintenance and repairs.

space stations

EARTH

PLANET EARTH

Planet Earth is a dense, rocky ball about 7,920 miles (12,750 km) across. It is one of eight planets circling our local star, the Sun. Earth is the only planet we know of that supports life. From space, its surface looks blue and cool, but inside it is so hot that rock can melt.

YOUNG PLANET
Around 4.5 billion years ago, the young Earth was bombarded from space by huge rocky meteorites and asteroids. Molten (liquid) rock from the Earth's fiery center erupted from thousands of volcanoes. As Earth slowly began to cool, clouds of gas and water vapor escaped from cracks in the crust (the planet's thinner, outer layer) and formed the first atmosphere. The water vapor eventually formed the oceans.

HOW WAS EARTH FORMED?
The Sun began to form around 5 billion years ago out of a cloud of whirling dust and gas in space. As it formed, the Sun's gravity gradually pulled the dust and gas into lumps, which became the planets. At first, Earth was a ball of molten rock. Its surface rock slowly began to cool and harden around 4 billion years ago.

IS EARTH THE SAME ALL THE WAY THROUGH?
Our planet is made of four main layers. The outer layer is called the crust. Below is the mantle, which is solid near the top and molten below. Temperatures become hotter near Earth's center. The outer core is a mass of molten rock. The temperature of the inner core is up to 8,492°F (4,00°C).

Planet Earth

EARTH'S ATMOSPHERE
Earth's atmosphere is a layer of gases about 430 miles (700 km) thick. Without the atmosphere, there could be no life on Earth. It protects us from harmful rays in sunlight and prevents our planet from becoming too hot or too cold.

Crust

Atmosphere

Mantle

Molten outer core

Solid inner core of white-hot nickel and iron

▲ EARTH'S STRUCTURE
The crust is made up of oceanic crust, below the oceans, and continental crust, which carries Earth's land. It is Earth's thinnest layer, at only 4–43 miles (6–70 km) thick. The mantle, at 1,800 miles (2,900 km) deep, is the thickest layer. The outer core is around 1,240 miles (2,000 km) thick. The inner core at the center of Earth is about 1,702 miles (2,740) across.

FIND OUT MORE ▸▸ Asteroids 23 • Atmosphere 49 • Solar System 14 • Volcanoes 44

HOW DOES EARTH SUPPORT LIFE?

Earth is just the right distance from the Sun so that temperatures are neither too hot nor too cold for living things to survive. Earth's atmosphere and oceans also help to control temperatures. And Earth has air and water— both vital for life.

HOW DOES EARTH MOVE THROUGH SPACE?

Earth takes one year, or 365.242 days, to orbit, or travel, around the Sun. At the same time, it spins on its axis (an imaginary line joining the North and South poles). As it spins, Earth is tilted on its axis at an angle of 23.5°. This tilt produces the ▶▶ SEASONS.

Continent (large area of land)

Ocean

◀ EARTH'S OCEANS
Earth's oceans cover almost two-thirds of its surface, making the planet look blue from space. The oceans formed 4.5 billion years ago, as Earth's surface cooled.

5.0 billion years ago	The solar system begins to form from gas and dust swirling in space.
4.6 billion years ago	Earth begins to form as a ball of molten rock.
4.5 billion years ago	Volcanoes erupt gas and steam to form the oceans, and molten rock.
4.2 billion years ago	Earth's surface cools and the hard outer crust forms.
3.6 billion years ago	The first continents form; life begins on Earth.

DAY AND NIGHT ▶
Earth spins around on its axis once every 24 hours. This brings day to the regions facing the Sun and night to those facing away from the Sun.

Axis

North Pole

South Pole

Direction of Earth's spin

Equator

Sun's rays

▲ EARTH'S ORBIT AND THE SEASONS
When the North Pole tilts toward the Sun, regions in the northern hemisphere have summer while the southern hemisphere has winter (1). As Earth continues in its orbit, the seasons change to fall in the northern hemisphere and spring in the southern hemisphere (2). When the South Pole tilts toward the Sun, the southern hemisphere has summer and it is winter in the north (3). This gradually gives way to fall in the southern hemisphere and spring in the northern hemisphere (4) as Earth continues around the Sun.

SEASONS

Seasons are regular weather patterns in different places on Earth's surface caused by the planet's tilt. At any time, one hemisphere (half of Earth above or below the equator) leans toward the Sun, exposing it to more of the Sun's light and heat and bringing warm summer days. The other half tilts away and has winter.

DO ALL PARTS OF EARTH HAVE SEASONS?

Most regions experience seasonal change throughout the year. However, the seasons are least noticeable in tropical regions near the equator (an imaginary line around Earth's middle) because the equator does not tilt away from the Sun for part of the year.

▲ THE CHANGING SEASONS
Temperate lands lying between tropics and poles have four distinct seasons. In spring, days become warmer and longer and new leaves sprout on trees. Summer is the warmest season. In fall, the days grow cooler and shorter. Winter is the coldest season.

▲ SEASONS IN THE TROPICS
Regions on or near the equator are hot and wet all year. Farther north and south of the equator are tropical grasslands (above). These are always hot but have distinct wet and dry seasons.

FIND OUT MORE ▶▶ Climate Zones 63 • Life on Earth 70–71 • Oceans 40–41 • Weather 50

EARTH SCIENCES

Earth science is the study of our planet's physical characteristics, from earthquakes to raindrops, and floods to fossils. It contains many branches, such as ▸▸ GEOLOGY and oceanography (the study of the world's oceans).

WHY IS EARTH SCIENCE USEFUL?

Earth science affects our everyday lives. For example, meteorologists study the weather and watch for dangerous storms. Hydrologists study water and warn of floods. Seismologists study earthquakes and try to predict where they will strike. Geologists study rocks and help to locate useful minerals.

HOW DO EARTH SCIENTISTS WORK?

Earth scientists mainly work "in the field"—climbing mountains, exploring the seabed, crawling through caves, or wading in swamps. They measure and collect samples (such as rocks or river water), then they record their findings on charts and maps.

Earth sciences

EXTREME CONDITIONS ▸
Volcanologists study volcanic eruptions at close quarters, wearing tough suits and helmets to protect them from the heat and deadly fumes.

◂ EARTH SCIENCE FROM SPACE
The TOPEX/Poseidon satellite circles Earth 800 miles (1,300 km) above the planet's surface. It uses special sensing equipment to collect information about the oceans, which it then sends back to scientists on the ground.

GEOLOGY

Geology is the study of the rocks that form the planet's surface. Geologists examine rocks to find out about the history of the Earth and how Earth was formed.

HOW DO GEOLOGISTS DATE ROCKS?

Rocks are dated using several methods. Geologists called stratigraphers study the distribution and order of rock layers, or strata. The youngest rocks are usually found in layers near the surface; older rocks lie deeper below. Some rocks contain radioactive elements that can be dated because they decay, or change, at a particular rate.

HOW DO FOSSILS HELP TO DATE ROCKS?

Fossils (remains or prints of living things preserved in certain types of rock) tell scientists the relative age of that rock—that is, whether it is older or younger than other rocks. This helps scientists to figure out the history of rock formation in different areas. The first fossils were formed around 3,600 million years ago.

▲ DRAGONFLY FOSSIL
Most fossils are of small, shelled sea creatures. Fossils of mammals and insects, such as this dragonfly, are much rarer.

FIND OUT MORE ▸▸ Earthquakes 43 • Fossils 76 • Nuclear Energy 167 • Rocks 46–47

CONTINENTS

Dry land covers just under one-third of Earth's surface. It is made up mostly of seven huge landmasses called continents, plus many smaller islands. The largest continent, Asia, is 16,838,000 sq miles (43,608,000 sq km). The smallest continent, Australia, is 2,968,124 sq miles (7,686,850 sq km).

ALFRED LOTHAR WEGENER
German, 1880–1930
Scientist Alfred Wegener put forward the idea of drifting continents in 1919. He noticed that the shapes of continents fitted together like a giant jigsaw puzzle, which suggested they had once been joined. His ideas were not generally accepted until the 1960s.

HAVE EARTH'S CONTINENTS ALWAYS LOOKED THE SAME?
The world looked very different millions of years ago, when all the continents were joined in one huge block of land, or supercontinent, which we call Pangaea. This was surrounded by a vast ocean, called Panthalassa. Over millions of years, Pangaea split into smaller continents, which drifted across Earth's surface.

WHY DO EARTH'S CONTINENTS MOVE?
The continents (and oceans) rest on top of giant slabs called ▸▸ TECTONIC PLATES which make up Earth's outer crust. These plates float like rafts on the hot, semi-liquid mantle below the crust. Slow-moving currents deep inside Earth send the plates (and the land or ocean that rests on them) slowly moving across the surface of the planet.

220 MILLION YEARS AGO — 180 MILLION YEARS AGO — 65 MILLION YEARS AGO

◂ **MOVING CONTINENTS**
Pangaea slowly split into two huge landmasses—Laurasia and Gondwanaland. Later, as the Atlantic Ocean was formed, these broke up into separate, smaller continents. Over millions of years, the continents slowly drifted to their present positions, and they are still moving today.

TECTONIC PLATES

Earth's outer crust is split into seven large tectonic plates and about twelve smaller ones. Studying plate tectonics (plate movement) helps scientists to understand why earthquakes strike and volcanoes erupt and how mountains form.

WHAT DO TECTONIC PLATES DO?
As the plates slowly drift across the planet's surface, they may slide past each other, grind against one another, pull apart, or all three. The boundary between two tectonic plates is called a plate margin. Mountains, earthquakes, and volcanoes usually occur at plate margins, where Earth's crust is thinner than in the center of the plates.

Ocean trench forms where one plate sinks below another

Mid-ocean ridge (undersea mountain range) forms when plates pull apart

Transform fault (a crack in the surface rock) forms where plates slide past one another

Long mountain chains buckle up along fault lines where two plates collide

Molten rock rises from the mantle, creating new plate material

Subduction zone where a denser oceanic plate sinks below continental crust on adjoining plate

▴ **PLATE BOUNDARIES**
Volcanoes and earthquakes are common in zones of active plate movement. The plates are still drifting very slowly, at around 1–8 in (2–20 cm) a year.

▴ **WORLD-SIZED PUZZLE**
Earth's tectonic plates fit together like the pieces of a jigsaw puzzle. Oceanic plates make up most of the sea floor. Earth's continents are embedded in continental plates. Some plates carry both land and sea.

continents

WHAT HAPPENS WHERE PLATES MEET?
When plates carrying continents collide, the land may crumple up and form a massive mountain range. If one plate is forced under the other, oceanic crust sinks into the mantle and melts. Where plates pull apart, molten rock rises up from inside Earth. This cools and adds new material to the plates.

FIND OUT MORE ▸▸ Earthquakes 43 • Mountains 45 • Rocks 46–47 • Volcanoes 44

OCEANS

Earth's five oceans (the Pacific, Atlantic, Indian, Southern, and Arctic) are constantly moving as tides rise and fall and winds whip up ▶▶ WAVES and help to drive ocean currents. The oceans are major sources of minerals and food.

OCEAN LIFE ▶
The oceans are home to a huge variety of plant and animal life. Microscopic plants drift in the sunlit surface waters, forming the basis of most of the ocean food chain. They provide food for tiny animal plankton, which are eaten by fish, which, in turn, are eaten by larger predators, such as sharks.

◀ SUNLIT ZONE
0–650 ft (0–200 m)
The oceans' sunlit waters, just below the surface, are home to most plant and animal life, including plankton, jellyfish, flying fish, shoaling fish, tuna, swordfish, and sharks.

◀ TWILIGHT ZONE
650–6,500 ft (200–2,000 m)
Below the sunlit waters, the light begins to fade until, at 3,280 ft (1,000 m), it is completely dark. Marine life includes lantern fish, squid, shrimp, and deep-diving sperm whales.

◀ ABYSSAL AND HADAL ZONE
6,500–33,000 ft (2,000–10,000 m)
The deepest parts of the ocean are near freezing and pitch-black. Marine life includes gulper eels, anglerfish, and rattail fish.

WHY IS THE SEA SALTY?

Sea water contains traces of minerals washed from the land by rivers. These dissolved minerals are mainly chloride and sodium, which together make salt. Most oceans contain about one part salt for every 35 parts water. The world's saltiest sea, the Dead Sea, contains around one part salt for every five parts water, making it seven times saltier than the rest of the world's oceans.

WHAT CAUSES THE OCEAN CURRENTS?

Water in the oceans is constantly moving in huge, slow circles called gyres. Prevailing (regular) winds blowing across the oceans start currents near the water's surface, which may flow for thousands of miles. Warm surface currents are heated by the Sun. Some warm currents affect the climate of the land that they flow past. For example, the Gulf Stream keeps northern ports ice-free in winter. There are also cold currents deep in the oceans that flow from the poles and across the ▶▶ OCEAN FLOOR toward the equator.

▼ OCEAN SURFACE CURRENTS
The world's oceans are interlinked in one continuous expanse of water. Winds disturb this water, forming currents. On this map, warm surface currents are shown in red. Cold currents are in blue.

oceans

OCEAN FLOOR

The ocean floor has landscapes as dramatic and varied as those of Earth's continents. Some parts have deep chasms, or towering cliffs, or volcanoes. Other places are vast, featureless plains. Many features of the ocean floor are caused by movements of the tectonic plates that form Earth's crust.

ARE THE OCEANS EXPANDING?

Some of the oceans are expanding, as molten rock wells up at the edges of tectonic plates to make new crust (a process known as sea spreading). In the Atlantic Ocean, new crust is forming along the Mid-Atlantic Ridge, which runs down the ocean's center. The Atlantic is growing about 1 in (2.5 cm) wider each year.

▼ FEATURES OF THE OCEAN FLOOR
The vast, flat plain at the bottom of the oceans is dotted with isolated mountains called seamounts, which were probably once volcanic islands. Ridges form where magma (hot, molten rock) rises from below the crust, then cools and hardens.

Continental slope

Continental shelf (a ledge of land around each continent)

Sediment fan

Submarine canyon

Seamount

Guyot (flat-topped mountain, eroded by waves)

Rising magma

Abyssal plain (the flat expanse of ocean floor)

Ocean trench

Mid-ocean ridge

WAVES

The surface of the sea is never completely still, even in calm weather. Winds ruffle the surface to form ripples. If the wind keeps blowing strongly, the ripples grow into waves. As the waves approach land, their size and strength increase until they break onto the shore, to build up beaches or wear away coasts.

WHAT IS A TSUNAMI?

Tsunamis are giant waves usually caused by undersea earthquakes or volcanic eruptions. Far out to sea, tsunamis are not so noticeable. However, as they reach land, they can tower up to 250 ft (75 m) high. Giant tsunamis have smashed ports and even drowned whole islands. Tsunamis are sometimes wrongly called "tidal waves," but they are not caused by tides.

▼ BREAKING WAVES
Waves may travel great distances across the ocean, but the water in each wave stays in the same place, moving around in circles. As a wave reaches the shore, the circulation of water at the bottom of the wave is blocked by the seabed and the top spills over.

Spilling breaker—a type of tall, tumbling wave that breaks on a shallow beach

Crest (top of a wave)

Spray thrown up as crest tumbles over and breaks onto the shore

FIND OUT MORE ►► Coasts 59 • Continents 39 • Fish 112–113 • Fishing 67

ISLANDS

An island is an area of land smaller than a continent and entirely surrounded by water. Islands range from single rocks to huge landmasses, such as the island of Greenland. There are two main types of island—continental islands and oceanic islands. Islands are also found in rivers and lakes.

islands

WHAT IS A CONTINENTAL ISLAND?
Continental islands are found in shallow seas off large landmasses. They were formed when rising seas (for example, at the end of an ice age) cut off part of the land from a continent. Great Britain is an example of a continental island.

▼ AN ISLAND IS BORN
In November 1963, sailors saw a plume of smoke and ash rising from the sea off Iceland during an undersea volcanic eruption. A day later, as the eruption continued, lava broke the surface to form land. The new island was named Surtsey, after the Norse god of fire.

▲ OCEANIC ISLAND
Oceanic islands are often far from the mainland. From above, they look like tiny specks in a vast, glittering ocean. Many tropical oceanic islands have coral reefs fringing their bases, or barrier reefs separated from the main island by a lagoon.

HOW ARE VOLCANIC ISLANDS FORMED?
Volcanic islands are formed in different ways. One way is by volcanic activity on the seabed, often near the boundaries of the tectonic plates that form Earth's crust. Where two plates pull apart, lava erupts to form an undersea ridge. Layers of lava build up until a ridge breaks the sea's surface to form an island. Sometimes a whole chain of volcanic islands, called an island arc, is formed in this way. Some island arcs contain thousands of islands.

HOW DO CORAL REEFS FORM?
A coral reef is formed from the hard, shelly remains of coral polyps. These tiny creatures live in large colonies on rocks in shallow, sunlit water, such as the top of a seamount. When they die, their chalky, tube-shaped skeletons remain, and new, young coral grows on top. The coral skeletons build up over many years until they reach the sea's surface, forming a reef.

WORLD'S LARGEST ISLAND ▼
Greenland, in the Arctic Ocean, is the world's largest island, at 0.85 million sq miles (2.2 million sq km). As huge as it is, few people live there because it is almost permanently covered in snow and ice.

FORMATION OF A CORAL ATOLL

A fringing coral reef forms in the shallows around the base of a seamount, or volcanic island, in warm tropical waters.

A barrier, or offshore, reef is formed as the coral slowly builds up, while the cone is worn away or covered by rising sea levels.

A ring-shaped coral atoll with a central lagoon is all that remains after a seamount is submerged.

ARCTIC OCEAN

Greenland

PACIFIC OCEAN

ATLANTIC OCEAN

FIND OUT MORE ▸▸ Cnidarians 103 • Oceans 40–41 • Volcanoes 44

EARTHQUAKES

Earthquakes are vibrations triggered by sudden rock movements deep underground, which cause Earth's surface to shake. Major earthquakes can shatter whole cities, killing people and bringing buildings and bridges crashing down.

WHAT CAUSES EARTHQUAKES?
Earthquakes are caused by the movements of the huge tectonic plates that make up Earth's outer crust. Driven by currents in the semi-molten layer below the crust, the plates slowly drift over Earth's surface and collide, grind together, or pull apart. Most earthquakes occur on fault lines—cracks in Earth's crust where two plates meet and grind together.

Shifting tectonic plates send vibrations or shock waves through the ground

Epicenter

Shock waves grow fainter farther from the epicenter, and destruction on Earth's surface is less severe

Shock waves travel outward from the focus

Focus

▲ SEISMIC WAVES
Most earthquakes begin deep underground at a point called the focus. As the rocks shatter at the focus, shock waves called seismic waves radiate outward in all directions. The point on Earth's surface directly above the focus is called the epicenter. This is where most damage occurs.

▲ EARTHQUAKE DAMAGE
Most earthquakes last only a few seconds, but the destruction they cause can take years to clear up. The shaking can cause certain types of soil to liquefy (turn to mud), making buildings sink or fall. An earthquake in Kobe, Japan, in 1995, damaged many of the city's roads.

WHAT HAPPENS DURING AN EARTHQUAKE?
As tectonic plates grind together at a fault line, the rocks on either side stretch to absorb a certain amount of pressure. If the pressure becomes too great, the rocks shatter, releasing shock waves that shake the surface. Buildings then sway and topple, and fires may start as gas and electricity lines are ripped apart.

WHERE DO MOST EARTHQUAKES STRIKE?
Most earthquakes, and also volcanic eruptions, occur on or near the edges of Earth's tectonic plates. They are most common in the "Ring of Fire," the name given to the edge of the vast Pacific Plate that lies beneath the Pacific Ocean. Japan, the Philippines, New Zealand, and the western coastline of North and South America all lie in this major fault zone.

HOW ARE EARTHQUAKES MEASURED?
The study of earthquakes is called seismology. Scientists measure and record earthquakes using devices called seismometers. The size of an earthquake is measured according to its magnitude (the size of the shock waves and the energy produced) or its effects.

◄ THE SAN ANDREAS FAULT
The San Andreas region on the western coast of North America lies on the "Ring of Fire." Rocks are cracked and buckled along a fault line where two plates meet.

earthquakes

FIND OUT MORE ▶▶ Continents 39 • Earth Sciences 38 • Planet Earth 36–37 • Volcanoes 44

VOLCANOES

A volcano is a vent or weak spot in Earth's crust through which magma (hot, melted rock) escapes as ▶▶ **LAVA** . In some places, lava oozes slowly out of the ground. In others, there is a violent eruption.

A cloud of gas, steam, and rock fragments bursts out of the volcano

Magma is forced up the main vent and through narrower side vents called branch pipes

Magma chamber forms deep underground beneath Earth's crust

Red-hot lava flows down the side of the volcano

HOW DOES A VOLCANO ERUPT?

A volcano erupts when magma wells up from deep inside Earth. In violent eruptions, the magma fills a hollow chamber below a vent blocked by cooled and hardened rock. Gas and water mingle with the magma, forming an explosive mixture. The pressure builds up in the chamber until the magma, gas, and steam are forced upward and blast through the vent.

ARE ALL VOLCANOES DANGEROUS?

There are around 25 major volcanic eruptions on land every year and thousands of minor ones, many of which take place under the sea. Active volcanoes are those that may erupt at any time. Dormant (sleeping) volcanoes have not erupted for centuries but may still do so. Extinct volcanoes are no longer likely to erupt.

Layers of ash and lava build up to form a volcanic mountain

◀ **A VIOLENT ERUPTION**
Violent eruptions fling out red-hot lumps of rock and scorching ash, which cool to form a distinctive cone-shaped mountain.

volcanoes

▲ **CLOUD OF ASH**
The eruption of Mount St. Helens, Washington, sent a cloud of fine ash 13 miles (20 km) into the sky.

▲ **FOUNTAIN OF FIRE**
Some volcanoes with narrow vents shoot jets of magma up to 660 ft (200 m) into the sky, splattering the surrounding land.

▲ **AFTERMATH**
A huge flow of lava can destroy everything in its path, like this village near Mount Kilauea Volcano in Hawaii.

LAVA

Lava is the name given to magma once it has reached the Earth's surface. Lava may be thick and sticky or thin and runny, depending on the minerals the lava contains and the temperature and pressure when it was formed.

ARE VOLCANOES ALL THE SAME SHAPE?

Volcanoes are different shapes depending on the type of lava and shape of their vents. Shield volcanoes have broad, shallow cones and are made of runny, flowing lava. Fissure volcanoes are long cracks in the crust. Violent eruptions usually produce steep-sided conical mountains. Composite cones are built up from alternate layers of lava and ash.

Magma | Vent

SHIELD VOLCANO

Magma | Fissure

FISSURE VOLCANO

Magma | Vent | Ash | Lava | Branch pipe

COMPOSITE CONE VOLCANO

MOUNTAINS

A mountain is a steep-sided mass of rock, rising at least 2,000 ft (600 m) above sea level. Mountains are found on land and under the sea. Some are isolated peaks, but most are found in a ▶▶ RANGE .

Mauna Kea

HOW ARE MOUNTAINS FORMED?
Mountains are formed by movements of the huge tectonic plates that make up Earth's crust. Fold mountains are formed when plates collide. Block mountains occur when a slab of land is forced upward. Volcanic mountains are built up from layers of cooled and hardened lava and ash.

ARE MOUNTAINS STILL GROWING?
Some relatively young mountains are still rising, as colliding plates continue to force the land at their edges upward. At the same time, mountains are constantly eroded by ice, rain, and the wind.

WHY ARE MANY MOUNTAINS SNOW-CAPPED?
Mountaintops are cold because the thin air high up does not hold the Sun's heat well, and the temperature falls 1.8°F (1°C) for every 500 ft (150 m) of height. It is therefore cold enough to snow over high peaks (even on the equator), and since the temperature rarely rises above freezing, the snow never melts.

▲ MOUNTAINS AT SEA
Some of the world's tallest mountains lie mostly underwater, with only their summits breaking the surface. Mauna Kea in Hawaii rises 33,480 ft (10,205 m) from the ocean bed, which makes it taller than Mount Everest.

MOUNTAIN BUILDING

Faults (cracks) occur near the edges of plates

A rift valley forms when a block of land between two faults sinks down

A fold mountain forms where rock is compressed, crumpled, and forced upward

A block mountain forms when a block of land between two faults is pushed upward

Mount Everest is the world's highest mountain, at 29,028 ft (8,848 m) above sea level

Cornices are overhanging masses of snow that build up on ridges, blown by the wind

mountains

THE HIMALAYAS ▶
The Himalayas are fold mountains that formed as the plate carrying India collided with that carrying southern Asia. These mountains are still rising, by about 3.3 ft (1 m) every 1,000 years.

RANGES

Most mountains are found in groups called ranges, such as the Jura Mountains in Europe and the Sierra Nevada Mountains of California. Often, a series of ranges is connected in a larger chain of mountains called a cordillera.

WHERE IS THE WORLD'S LONGEST MOUNTAIN CHAIN?
The longest mountain chain on land is the Andes, which runs for 4,470 miles (7,200 km) down the western edge of South America. An undersea mountain chain called the Mid-Atlantic Ridge is even longer. It stretches 7,000 miles (11,300 km) down the center of the Atlantic Ocean.

▲ ANDEAN PEAKS
The Andes Mountains were formed when one of the Earth's tectonic plates, the Nazca Plate, collided with the plate carrying South America, slowly pushing up the rocks into a series of high, jagged peaks.

ROCKS

Earth's crust is made of rock, and rock is made of natural substances called ▶ **MINERALS**. There are three main types of rock—sedimentary, igneous, and metamorphic rock. Each type is produced in different ways. The oldest rocks on Earth were formed over 4.25 billion years ago.

WHAT ARE IGNEOUS ROCKS?

Igneous rocks form when magma (molten rock) rises from deep underground and cools and solidifies at or near Earth's surface. Igneous rock that forms under the ground may later reach the surface because of geological upheaval. It may also be exposed as the rocks above are worn away.

Basalt, an igneous rock, is the most common rock on Earth's surface

Hexagonal columns formed when the molten basalt lava flow cooled, contracted, and split

Igneous rocks lava forms extrusive igneous rockss

Glaciers erode rock and carry fragments downhill

Rivers wear away rock and carry rock fragments and sediment to the sea

Metamorphic rock melts and may rise to Earth's surface as magma

Heat and pressure can alter sedimentary and intrusive igneous rocks

Sedimentary rocks form from layers of sediment on lake and ocean beds

▲ THE ROCK CYCLE

The rocks that form Earth's crust are continually destroyed and remade in an endless process called the rock cycle. Rock is formed by melting; by cooling and solidifying; by changing through heat and pressure; by weathering and erosion; and by compression and cementation.

WHAT ARE SEDIMENTARY ROCKS MADE OF?

Sedimentary rocks are made of fine rock particles that have been worn away and then carried by rivers, glaciers, or the wind and collect in lakes and oceans. The tiny fragments are then compressed (squashed) and cemented together to form sedimentary rock in a process called lithification.

HOW ARE METAMORPHIC ROCKS CREATED?

Metamorphic rocks are formed when existing rocks are changed underground by great heat or pressure, or both. When volcanoes erupt and when mountains are formed by the movement of Earth's tectonic plates, rocks are heated and squeezed. The minerals in the rocks are then changed, forming metamorphic rocks.

IGNEOUS ROCK

Igneous or volcanic rock includes granite (above) and basalt.

SEDIMENTARY ROCK

This rock includes sandstone (above), limestone, and chalk.

METAMORPHIC ROCK

Metamorphic rock includes marble (above), slate, and schist.

◄ THE GIANT'S CAUSEWAY
Made up of hexagonal (six-sided) columns of the igneous rock basalt, this famous rock formation is found in Northern Ireland.

MINERALS

Rocks are made of natural, nonliving chemical substances called minerals. Some rocks contain only one mineral. For example, marble is made of the white mineral calcite. Most rocks, however, contain ▶ CRYSTALS of several different minerals.

WHAT ARE THE MOST VALUABLE MINERALS?

Some of the most valuable minerals are ores—minerals that contain metals such as gold, iron, and aluminum. Of these, gold is the most precious because it is soft and easy to work and does not tarnish. Other minerals are prized as ▶ GEMSTONES. Fossil fuels, such as coal, produce energy. Minerals such as sulfur and mica are used in industry. Granite and sandstone are used as building stones.

rocks · Gold · Quartz

▲ GOLD ORE
In most ores, metals are found mixed with other substances. However, gold occurs in a pure form in rocks such as quartz, as shown above.

CRYSTALS

Crystals are solid, regular, geometric shapes formed by most minerals. They have smooth surfaces (called faces), straight edges, and symmetrical corners because they are built up from a regular framework of atoms (tiny particles) called a lattice.

HOW DO CRYSTALS FORM?

Crystals form as a molten solid (such as molten rock) cools, or as liquid evaporates (turns into water vapor) from a solution that contains a dissolved mineral. A crystal grows as more and more atoms attach to the basic lattice. Slow-growing crystals are larger than those that form quickly.

Pyramid-shaped amethyst crystals

AMETHYST CRYSTALS ►
These purple crystals are a type of quartz. They formed in hot water, rich in the mineral silica.

GEMSTONES

About 50 of the 3,000 minerals found on Earth are prized as gemstones. Although they may not shine in their natural state, they can be cut and polished to form sparkling stones. Diamonds, the hardest minerals on Earth, are made of pure, crystallized carbon and are among the world's most prized gemstones.

WHERE ARE GEMSTONES FOUND?

Many gemstones are found in mountainous regions, usually in rocks that have been subjected to great heat or pressure. They are also found in the sediment on lake and river beds. Diamonds are often mined from rocks found deep underground.

▲ RUBY RED
Rubies are made of a mineral called corundum. Rare, deep-red rubies are precious stones, as are diamonds and emeralds.

FIND OUT MORE ▶▶ Atoms 157 • Chemistry 162 • Erosion 55 • Ice 58 • Volcanoes 44

SOIL

Soil is one of Earth's most precious resources. It provides the support and nourishment that plants need in order to grow. In turn, plants provide food for animals and people. As well as rock fragments, ▶▶SOIL LAYERS contain air, water, and plant and animal remains.

▲ CLAY
Clay soils are usually sticky and waterlogged.

HOW IS SOIL FORMED?

Soil is formed as rock is broken up by ice, frost, wind, and water. Plants take root among the rock fragments and bind them together. When plants die, they fertilize the soil. Soil takes many years to form, but it can be destroyed very quickly by bad farming methods, such as deforestation (clearing the land of trees).

ARE THERE DIFFERENT TYPES OF SOIL?

There are three main types of soil—clay, sandy, and loamy. There are also other types of soil, depending on the type of underlying rock and the climate and vegetation. Loams are a mixture of clay, sand, and silt, and are more fertile than other soils.

◄ SAND
Sandy soils are loose and dry.

▲ PEAT
Acidic peaty soils are made up of rotting plants.

▲ CHALK
Chalky soils are thin and dry.

◄ LIFE IN THE SOIL
A small patch of soil just 1 sq yd (1 sq m) in area can hold a billion living things. These include insects, spiders, worms, centipedes, mites, fungi, and tens of thousands of bacteria (shown magnified).

soil

◄ BORDER ZONE
Soil forms a vital zone above rock in which living things can grow.

HOW DO LIVING THINGS HELP THE SOIL?

Living things play an important role in helping to recycle nutrients (nourishing minerals) that enrich the soil. When plants and animals die, their remains are broken down by scavenging creatures, such as beetles, microscopic bacteria, and fungi. This releases minerals into the soil. The minerals fertilize plants so they can grow, and so the cycle of life begins again.

Grass   Wildflowers   Roots   Humus   Decomposing leaf

◄ BUSY BURROWERS
Earthworms and other burrowing animals such as moles, mice, and rabbits make their homes underground, in the topsoil. Their tunnels allow air and water to enter the soil, which helps to enrich it. Up to one million earthworms live in just 0.4 sq miles (1 sq km) of soil.

SOIL LAYERS

Soil scientists divide the soil into layers from the surface down to the underlying bedrock. This is called a soil profile. The layers in a soil profile are known as horizons. The depth of each horizon varies among different types of soil.

HOW MANY SOIL LAYERS ARE THERE?

A layer of dark, fertile humus made of rotting plants lies at the soil's surface. Underneath, the topsoil contains plant roots, and plant and animal remains that bacteria and fungi are helping to rot down. The subsoil contains fewer plant and animal remains but has plenty of minerals washed down from the layers above. Below are rock fragments, then solid bedrock.

◄ SOIL PROFILE
This slice of soil from surface to bedrock shows its five layers.

Humus

Topsoil (A horizon) often rich in humus and minerals

Subsoil (B horizon) poor in humus, rich in minerals

Weathered rock fragments (C horizon) little or no plant or animal life

Bedrock (D horizon)

FIND OUT MORE ▶▶ Erosion 55 • Microorganisms 85 • Plants 88–89 • Rocks 46–47

Most life on Earth depends on the atmosphere, a bubble of gases around our planet. This bubble, extending about 430 miles (700 km) into space, protects us from meteorites and warms Earth's surface. It includes the ▸▸OZONE LAYER, which shields us from the Sun's harmful rays.

FIVE ATMOSPHERE LAYERS

5. EXOSPHERE
Situated 280–560 miles (450–900 km) above Earth's surface, the exosphere is the atmosphere's outer layer, on the edge of space.

4. THERMOSPHERE
The thermosphere extends 50–280 miles (80–450 km) into space and contains the ionosphere, a layer of electrically charged particles from which radio waves for communications can be bounced back to Earth.

3. MESOSPHERE
The mesosphere is 30–50 miles (50–80 km) above Earth's surface. Meteors (fragments of rock and dust from space) burn up here, creating shooting stars.

2. STRATOSPHERE
Lying 7–30 miles (12–50 km) above Earth's surface, the stratosphere is a calm layer above the winds and weather. The lower stratosphere contains the ozone layer.

1. TROPOSPHERE
Extending about 7 miles (12 km) into space, the troposphere contains 75 percent of the air and water in the atmosphere.

DOES THE ATMOSPHERE REMAIN THE SAME FROM EARTH TO SPACE?

Earth's atmosphere contains five main layers—the troposphere, stratosphere, mesosphere, thermosphere, and exosphere. The main gases in the atmosphere are nitrogen (78 percent) and oxygen (21 percent). There are also small amounts of argon, carbon dioxide, and water vapor.

WHAT IS ATMOSPHERIC PRESSURE?

Atmospheric (air) pressure is the force produced by air as it pushes against its surroundings. This force is over 14 lb per sq in (1 kg per sq cm). We cannot feel it, however, because the air presses evenly from all directions, and our body fluids press outward. Air pressure is greatest at sea level and decreases with altitude.

Dark cloudtops silhouetted against light from the setting Sun mark the edge of the troposphere—the layer in which Earth's weather occurs

Dense, dusty air in the lower part of the atmosphere appears red

Sun

Thinner, dust-free air higher in Earth's atmosphere appears blue

OZONE LAYER

A layer of ozone gas in the stratosphere protects us from harmful ultraviolet (UV) rays in sunlight. UV rays can cause skin cancer, eye damage, and other health problems in humans and animals. In the 1980s, scientists discovered that the ozone layer is getting thinner and that so-called "holes" (areas containing less ozone) were appearing over Antarctica and the Arctic each spring.

WHAT IS CAUSING HOLES IN THE OZONE LAYER?

Chemicals called CFCs (chlorofluorocarbons), used in the manufacture of refrigerators and aerosol sprays, are causing the holes in the ozone layer. CFCs collect in the upper atmosphere, where they destroy ozone. During the 1990s, the holes steadily got bigger. Most countries have now stopped using CFCs, which should prevent the damage from getting worse.

atmosphere

The ozone hole as recorded in September 2000 measured 11 million sq miles (28 million sq km)

OZONE LOSS ▶
The hole over Antarctica is shown in this false-color image of Earth taken by satellite. Yellow indicates the thinnest ozone covering, blue indicates the thickest.

Antarctica shown here in dark yellow beneath the ozone hole in pale yellow

FIND OUT MORE ▸▸ Human Impact 64–65 • Space 10 • Weather 50

WEATHER

Weather is what is happening in the atmosphere now, at any place on Earth's surface. It includes the temperature and whether it is wet and windy, or dry and calm.

WHAT CAUSES THE WEATHER?

The Sun provides the energy that drives Earth's weather. The Sun heats the air in various parts of Earth's atmosphere by different amounts. Masses of warm and cold air then move from place to place, creating winds. Winds bring sunny, wet, or stormy conditions. People find out the type of weather to expect in a ▸▸ FORECAST.

▲ MORNING MIST
Fog over the Golden Gate Bridge in San Francisco, California, usually burns away quickly in the heat of the morning Sun. Weather conditions can change daily, hourly, or even from minute to minute.

weather

FORECASTS

A weather forecast is a prediction of weather conditions over a particular area, either for a few days (called a short-range forecast), or for several weeks (called a long-range forecast). The people who study the weather and make weather forecasts are called meteorologists.

WHY DO WE NEED WEATHER FORECASTS?

Weather forecasts help people to plan—what to wear, when to travel, or which products to stock in supermarkets. Forecasts are especially important for farmers, builders, sailors, and anyone else who works outdoors. Sometimes an accurate forecast may mean the difference between life and death.

◄ MAPPING THE WEATHER
Weather experts monitor the movements of air masses and clouds using satellite images. The images are colored by computer to pick out the movement of clouds. This false-color satellite image shows winds spiraling over the Atlantic Ocean, indicating unsettled, stormy weather.

Winds swirl around an area of low pressure, created when a mass of warm air is forced upward by a mass of cold air

Low-level clouds are shown in yellow; high-level clouds appear white

STORM TRACKING ►
A meteorologist tracks a storm using images taken by satellite. Weather centers issue weather warnings to all regions in the storm's path.

Image of spiraling winds photographed by a weather satellite is displayed on a computer screen

Supercomputers condense the huge amount of data from satellites

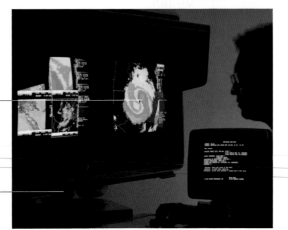

HOW DO EXPERTS PREDICT THE WEATHER?

Meteorologists receive information about air temperature, wind speeds, clouds, and rainfall from over 50,000 weather stations worldwide—on land and on ships and buoys at sea. The data is fed into huge computers that produce charts and forecasts. These are used, with satellite images, to predict the weather.

HOW DO WEATHER SATELLITES WORK?

Weather satellites carry two types of sensors. An imager takes photographs of movements in Earth's atmosphere. A sounder reads the temperature of the air and clouds.

FIND OUT MORE ▸▸ Atmosphere 49 • Climate 62 • Rain 52–53 • Winds 51

WINDS

Winds are moving currents of air, which can blow over a small local area or over a much larger region. Global winds help to moderate temperatures worldwide by carrying warm air away from the tropics and cold air from the poles. Winds bring changing weather conditions, such as clear, sunny skies or torrential ▶▶|**MONSOON** rain. Strong winds can bring storms and hurricanes.

WHY DO WINDS BLOW?

Winds are caused when the Sun heats air masses in different parts of the world unevenly. Air warmed by the Sun becomes less dense, or lighter, and rises. This creates an area of low pressure where there is less air pressing down on Earth. Because air always flows from a region of high pressure to one of low pressure, cooler air flows in to fill the space left by the rising air. This is a wind.

WHAT FORCES AFFECT THE WORLD'S WINDS?

Regular wind patterns across Earth's surface are affected by the planet's spin. This is called the Coriolis effect. In the northern hemisphere, the Coriolis effect causes winds to swirl clockwise. In the southern hemisphere, it causes winds to spin counterclockwise. The speed and direction of the wind are also affected by air currents blowing over natural features, such as mountains.

winds

GLOBAL WINDS
Three main belts, or bands, of prevailing winds blow on either side of the equator. In the Tropics, trade winds blow from the northeast or southeast toward the equator. In temperate zones, the prevailing winds are westerlies (blowing from the west). Cold easterly winds (from the east) blow in the polar regions.

Earth's spin

Winds blow around the globe in six main circular movements, called cells

Polar easterlies

Westerlies

In each cell, warm air rises from below, then cool air blows in to take its place

Trade winds

Equator

Trade winds

Westerlies

Polar easterlies

◀ **WINDY WEATHER**
Light breezes rustle leaves and twigs. In stronger gusts, whole branches sway. Strong, powerful winds may snap or uproot trees and cause widespread damage. The wind that blows most often in a particular area is called a prevailing wind.

MONSOONS

Monsoon winds are massive winds that bring heavy, seasonal rain to subtropical regions, such as southeast Asia and India, in summer. In winter, they bring dry, cooler weather. Monsoon winds are the strongest in Asia, but they also blow in West Africa, northern Australia, and parts of North and South America.

WHY DO MONSOONS CHANGE DIRECTION?

Monsoon winds change course because of seasonal temperature differences between the land and the sea. Water absorbs heat more slowly than dry land but holds the heat for longer. This makes the sea cooler than the land during the summer, and warmer during the winter. The difference in temperature causes monsoon winds to blow onshore (from sea to land) in summer, and offshore (from land to sea) in winter.

▲ **MONSOON RAIN**
The monsoon brings much-needed water to regions such as Bangladesh, in Asia, after a long, dry season. Sometimes, the rains are too heavy, washing away crops and homes and causing widespread flooding.

FIND OUT MORE ▶▶| Asia 260–261 • Atmosphere 49 • Rain 52–53 • Storms 54

RAIN

Earth is unusual among the planets in our Solar System in having an atmosphere that contains moisture. Moisture in the air gathers in ▸▸ CLOUDS and eventually falls as ▸▸ SNOW, ▸▸ HAIL, sleet, or rain. Any kind of falling moisture is called precipitation.

Storm clouds contain billions of tiny water droplets, which make them dark and gray

rain

WHY DOES IT RAIN?

The Sun's heat causes moisture from oceans and lakes to evaporate into the air, forming water vapor. The vapor rises, cools, and condenses (turns into a liquid) into tiny water droplets, which form clouds. If the clouds continue to absorb moisture, they become saturated. The water droplets in the clouds collide and become bigger and heavier until the air can no longer support them. Then they fall as rain.

DO SOME PARTS OF THE WORLD RECEIVE MORE RAIN THAN OTHERS?

Around the world, rainfall patterns vary widely. In some regions, rain falls almost daily. In deserts, it may not rain for years. The tropics are generally wet, while the polar regions are dry because moisture there is locked up in the form of ice.

Water droplets too heavy to float in the air fall to the ground as rain

◀ RAINBOW

A rainbow forms when sunlight passes through falling raindrops. The light is refracted (bent and split) into the seven colors that make it up—red, orange, yellow, green, blue, indigo, and violet.

RAINSTORM ▶

Dark storm clouds release lashing rain in hilly country. The water collects in lakes in the lowlands below. Raindrops falling from storm clouds can be ³/₁₆ in (5 mm) wide.

Rays of sunlight gleam through a gap in the clouds

THE WATER CYCLE

The water on Earth is constantly recycled between the oceans, land, and atmosphere. The water cycle, or hydrological cycle, is driven by the Sun's heat.

Life-giving rain feeds streams, rivers, and lakes. It waters plants so they can grow, and gives animals and people vital moisture.

Rain and snow fall on high ground

Water evaporates (turns into water vapor) from lakes and rivers in the Sun's heat

Water vapor is given out by plants

Clouds form as water vapor cools and condenses into tiny water droplets

Water stored in the ocean evaporates and rises into the atmosphere

Rain falls over the ocean

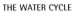

Groundwater flows into rivers or the ocean

Water seeps into rock creating groundwater (underground water)

Surface water flows back to the ocean

CLOUDS

Clouds are visible masses of moisture, made up of tiny ice crystals or water droplets, which are so light that they float. Clouds form in the troposphere (the lowest layer of Earth's atmosphere) when water vapor rising high into the sky cools and condenses.

▼ CLOUDS
There are three main types of cloud: cirrus (meaning curl or wisp of hair), cumulus (meaning heap), and stratus (meaning layer). Other clouds are mixtures of these three types. Clouds are made of ice or water, depending on their height above the ground.

CIRRUS   CUMULUS   STRATUS   STRATOCUMULUS

HOW DO CLOUDS FORM?
When the Sun shines on seas and lakes, some of the water in them evaporates into the warm air. If air currents blow the warm air over land and it rises over mountains, or if cold air pushes beneath the warm air and forces it upward, then the warm air cools. Cold air cannot hold as much moisture as warm air, so the water vapor condenses to form clouds.

WHY ARE CLOUDS DIFFERENT SHAPES?
The way clouds form depends on their height above the ground and on the movement of air. Wispy cirrus clouds form high in the troposphere. They are made of ice crystals drawn into strands by the wind. Rapidly rising pockets of warm air cause fluffy, mid-level cumulus clouds to form. Low-lying stratus clouds are formed by air that rises slowly over a large area.

◄ SNOWFLAKES
Every snowflake has a different hexagonal (six-sided) structure. Different-shaped snowflakes form at various temperatures and heights in the atmosphere.

Stellar (star) snowflake with six sides

Some stellar snowflakes can grow as large as 2–3 in (5-cm) wide

SNOW

Snow falls in cold weather when ice crystals formed high in clouds freeze together and drop to the ground as millions of tiny snowflakes. Sleet is a mixture of rain and snow, or partly melted snow.

WHY DOES IT SNOW?
Snow forms in clouds high in the atmosphere, where it is so cold that water droplets freeze into ice crystals. The ice crystals collide and stick together to make bigger crystals. When the crystals get too heavy to float, they fall to the ground as snowflakes. When snow falls, the air is just cold enough to let the flakes drift to the ground before they melt.

HAIL

Hailstones are ice pellets that grow from ice crystals formed in freezing storm clouds and then plummet to the ground. Large hailstones can shatter glass, dent car roofs, and ruin crops.

HOW DOES HAIL FORM?
Hail forms in cumulonimbus (storm) clouds that contain powerful, vertical air currents. Water droplets in the clouds freeze and are whirled up and down. Each time a hailstone is tossed upward to the frozen cloudtop, a new layer of ice forms around it. The ice builds up, layer by layer, until the hailstone becomes too heavy to remain airborne and falls to earth.

LAYERS OF ICE ▶
Layers of ice are clearly visible inside this grapefruit-sized hailstone. Hailstones this size are rare, but marble-sized ones are fairly common.

FIND OUT MORE ▶▶ Atmosphere 49 • Climate 62 • Ice 58 • Rivers 56–57 • Weather 50 • Winds 51

STORMS

A storm is a bout of severe weather, with strong winds roaring at more than 55 mph (88 km/h), lightning flashes, thunder, and heavy rain. **HURRICANES** and tornadoes are whirling storms that can wreck whole towns.

storms

▲ TORNADOES
Tornadoes are dark, whirling columns of air that form beneath thunderclouds. Some produce winds of up to 280 mph (450 km/h), which can demolish houses and lift whole trains into the air.

WHAT CAUSES LIGHTNING?
Inside black thunderclouds, ice crystals and water droplets are whirled about and clash together, producing tiny electric charges. Positive charges build up at the top of the cloud, negative charges at the base. The ground below the thundercloud is also positively charged. When the difference between the charges gets big enough, the charge is unleashed inside the cloud as sheet lightning, or to the ground as forked lightning.

WHAT CAUSES THUNDER?
When lightning surges through the air, it instantly heats the air to around 45,000°F (25,000°C). The heated air expands and sends a shock wave through the air, which we hear as a clap of thunder.

HURRICANES

Also called a typhoon or cyclone, a hurricane is a powerful, revolving storm that strikes in the tropics. It can cause great damage when it sweeps inland.

HOW DO HURRICANES FORM?
Hurricanes form over tropical oceans in humid weather, usually in the summer and fall months. Warm air charged with moisture from the sea starts to spiral upward around a calm area called the eye. Cool air is then sucked into the center, taking the place of the warm air, and fueling the storm.

◄ HURRICANE FRAN
Hurricanes are so huge, they can easily be seen from space. This colored satellite image shows Hurricane Fran approaching the North American mainland from the Caribbean Sea in 1996.

Spiral bands of rain surround the eye

The eye of the hurricane is a calm area in the middle, up to 30 miles (50 km) across

Whirling winds around the eye may reach speeds of up to 200 mph (360 km/h)

LIGHTNING STRIKES ►
Forked lightning takes the quickest path to the ground, often running down trees and tall buildings.

FIND OUT MORE ▸▸ Climate 62 • Rain 52–53 • Weather 50 • Winds 51

EROSION

Erosion is the wearing down and the carrying away of the Earth's rock by the action of wind and moving water. Erosion happens fastest on steep hillsides after heavy rain, when ▸▸ LANDSLIDES sometimes strike.

HOW DOES EROSION HAPPEN?
Rocks are gradually broken down into smaller pieces by the wind, rain, snow, and frost. For example, when water freezes in rock cracks, the water expands, slowly widening the cracks and fracturing the rock. The fragments of weathered rock are then blown away by the wind or carried away by water in the form of streams and rivers, ice in glaciers, or waves pounding coasts.

WIND EROSION ▶
Top-heavy pinnacles called hoodoos are created in deserts where sand-filled winds scour rocks. Wind is the main cause of erosion in dry, desert areas. Extreme desert temperatures, with scorching days and freezing nights, also cause rocks to crack. If heavy rain falls after a long drought, flash floods then sweep away loose soil and rock.

erosion

▲ GLACIAL EROSION
Wide U-shaped valleys were formed by glaciers during past ice ages, when ice covered much of northern Europe. Glaciers are huge, slow-moving rivers of ice, which carry boulders and stones on their sides and bases. This load scrapes away at the rock below, shaping the landscape.

▲ WATER EROSION
The Colorado River, in the western United States, has worn away rock to create narrow gorges and steep-sided canyons. Erosion is greatest after heavy rain. The eroded rock, gravel, and silt are carried along in the river water, then deposited in lakes, at deltas, or in the sea.

LANDSLIDES

Weathering and erosion usually wear away landscapes fairly slowly. A landslide occurs when a huge mass of rock and soil suddenly breaks off a hillside, engulfing everything in its path. Landslides can cause great destruction and can even wipe out whole towns.

WHAT CAUSES LANDSLIDES?
Landslides often strike after heavy rain or snow has fallen. Loose soil and rocks begin to trickle downhill; then gravity takes over and the whole hillside slips away. Landslides are common on slopes where the vegetation has been removed by tree felling or farming. Without tree or plant roots to anchor the soil, heavy rain easily washes it away. Landslides, mudflows, and avalanches are called mass wasting. Mass wasting is sometimes triggered by a volcanic eruption or by an earthquake.

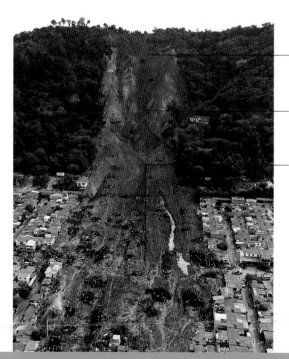

Forested hillside was swept away as the landslide gathered force

Trickling earth and pebbles may dislodge large boulders, causing further destruction

Rocks and earth finally come to rest on flatter ground

◀ DESTRUCTIVE SLIDE
The landslide shown here caused a roaring tide of earth and rocks to bury several streets in the town of Santa Tecla, El Salvador, in Central America. The landslide was set off by a minor earthquake. In 1970, a landslide set off by a major earthquake buried the town of Yungay in Peru, killing 18,000 people.

FIND OUT MORE ▸▸ Coasts 59 • Ice 58 • Rivers 56–57 • Rocks 46–47

RIVERS

A river is a natural channel down which water flows to the sea or a ▶▶ LAKE . Throughout history, rivers have provided water for drinking, farming, and industry, and offered food, transportation, and recreation. Some of the world's largest cities have grown up on river banks.

HOW DO RIVERS BEGIN?
Rivers usually begin as a trickle of water high in hills or mountains. Some come from rainwater or melting snow. Most emerge from underground streams, formed after rain or snow seeps into the ground then bubbles back to the surface. As the water flows downhill, the trickle swells into a stream and then, as side streams called tributaries join it, into a wider river.

WHAT IS A RIVER'S LOAD?
As a river flows, it carries along material, or debris, called its load. A river's load includes rocks, stones, and other large particles, which are washed along the riverbed. Finer particles float in the water.

HOW DO RIVERS SHAPE THE LANDSCAPE?
A river's load scours the riverbed, deepening its channel. The speed of the flowing water erodes the river's banks, making it wider. As the river winds through the landscape, it gradually carves out deep valleys in solid rock and deposits huge amounts of debris to form a fertile plain. In places where the river flows over soft limestone, water seeps into the rock, slowly dissolving it and forming tunnels and caves.

Wide looping meanders form on gentle slopes in broad valleys

RIVER FEATURES ▶
At its upper level, a river is small and rushes along its course. Farther downstream, as the land becomes less steep, the river's flow is less turbulent. Tributaries join it, increasing its volume of water. Lower down, the river flows more slowly over flatter ground, carving wide valleys and forming loops called meanders.

◄ RAPIDS AND WATERFALLS
Rapids are formed on a river's upper course on steeply sloping ground, where the river water tumbles over hard rocks and boulders, which are not easily worn away. A waterfall is created when a river wears away soft rock on its bed but leaves a shelf of hard rock above.

River bank is eroded on the outer side of each bend, making the channel deeper and wider

River branches into separate braids or channels on flatter ground

Islands may form if higher ground is cut off when a river flows around it

Sediment is deposited where the river slows and drops its load

WHAT IS AN ESTUARY?

As a river flows into the sea, it often widens and forms a broad inlet called an estuary. The sea's tides carry salty seawater upriver to mix with the fresh river water. The salt makes tiny particles of clay in the fresh water clump together and sink, often causing sediment to build up at the river's mouth.

HOW ARE DELTAS FORMED?

A delta is an area of flat, fertile land at a river mouth. Deltas form when a slow-moving river deposits its load of sediment as it reaches the ocean. The sediment slowly builds up and dries out, forcing the river to split into separate channels.

▲ RIVER MOUTH
Marshes and swamps often form at river mouths, where the river flows over low-lying land. These wetland habitats provide a haven for wildlife, especially birds.

rivers

MISSISSIPPI DELTA ►
A false-color satellite image of the Mississippi River delta shows land in light blue, water in dark blue, and sediment in green. The delta has a ragged coastline shaped like a bird's foot. Other deltas have curved, fan-shaped coastlines.

LAKES

A lake is an expanse of water that forms inland where water collects in a hollow in the ground and cannot drain away through the rock below. Most lakes are fed by rivers and, to a lesser extent, rainfall.

HOW DO LAKES FORM?

Small lakes called tarns form in mountains where glaciers gouge out bowl-shaped hollows. Water collects in the craters of inactive volcanoes to form volcanic lakes. The world's largest lake, the Caspian Sea, lies in a hollow created by geological upheaval. Artificial lakes called reservoirs are created by dams.

LIFE OF A LAKE ►
This lake lies in a lush, green valley and is filled up by river water from the surrounding hills. Lakes like this do not last forever and eventually dry out. They are slowly filled in by sediment dumped by a river, or disappear when there is less rainfall. What is left of the lake then forms a swamp, marsh, or bog.

FIND OUT MORE ►► Early Farming 364–365 • Erosion 55 • Oceans 40–41 • Rocks 46–47

CAVES

Caves are hollow spaces carved into hillsides or underground by the action of water and the wind. On coasts, pounding waves sometimes hollow out caves in the bases of cliffs.

caves

Point bar built up by sediment deposited on an inside bend, where the river flows more slowly and drops its load

HOW ARE CAVES FORMED?

Caves are most common in limestone rock. Rainwater, which contains a weak acid, dissolves the soft limestone and seeps into cracks, eventually carving out channels that widen into tunnels and caves. Caves are also found in glaciers and in cooled volcanic lava.

◄ STALACTITES AND STALAGMITES
Water dripping from the ceiling of limestone caves contains dissolved minerals, such as calcite. Over thousands of years, tiny deposits of calcite build up on cave roofs to form hanging spiky columns called stalactites, and on the ground below to form stalagmites.

FIND OUT MORE ►► Ice 58 • Rocks 46–47 • Volcanoes 44

ICE

At the poles and on high mountains, vast areas are covered in ice—in rivers of ice called glaciers, and in layers of ice called ice sheets or ice caps. Ice is a major force of erosion on land, where glaciers gouge deep valleys in the landscape.

HOW DO GLACIERS FORM?

Glaciers form when more snow falls each winter than melts each summer. As the snow builds up, the top layers press down on the layers below and turn them to ice. When enough ice has formed, the glacier's great weight and gravity set it moving slowly downhill, at a rate of about 3.3 ft (1 m) a day. The glacier continues to advance as long as more snow is falling at its top than ice is melting at its tip.

WHAT ARE ICE CAPS?

Ice caps are vast, domed sheets of ice that cover the land in the polar regions. They are formed as snow builds up year after year, creating a thick layer of ice. Three-quarters of the world's fresh water is locked up in the polar ice caps. The ice cap covering Antarctica at the South Pole is over 2.5 miles (4 km) deep.

GLACIAL EROSION ▶
Over thousands of years, as the base of the glacier scrapes over rock, it gouges out a wide, U-shaped valley. It may also carve sharp peaks called horns on mountains, and scoop rounded hollows called cirques or corries out of rock. Small lakes or tarns are often left in cirques when the glacial ice has melted.

Glacial ice can be more than half a mile (1 km) deep

A lateral moraine, or heap of rock and debris, is pushed along at the glacier's sides

Deep crevices, or fissures, form where the ice cracks as it moves

Meltwater trickles from the tip, or snout, of the glacier

ice

◀ ICEBERG
Icebergs form where glaciers and ice caps meet the ocean. Huge chunks of ice "calve," or break off, and fall into the water. Ocean currents may then carry the floating ice to warmer waters, where it can endanger shipping. In 1912, the luxury liner *Titanic* was sunk by an iceberg, and more than 1,500 people drowned.

The sea's surface may freeze if the water temperature drops to 28°F (–2.2°C), forming pack ice

The largest icebergs are the size of small countries and can tower 525 ft (160 m) above sea level

Waves and ocean currents sculpt the iceberg into pinnacles and crags above sea level and into deep caves below

Around one-ninth of an iceberg shows above the sea's surface; the rest lies underwater

FIND OUT MORE ▶▶ Antarctica 276 • Erosion 55 • Mountains 45 • Prehistoric Life 77

COASTS

Coasts are border zones where the land meets the ocean. There is about 312,000 miles (502,000 km) of coastline worldwide. **▶▶ TIDES**, waves, and currents endlessly wear away at the land to form a variety of coastal landscapes, from sheer cliffs and rugged headlands to sandy coves and wide, lonely mudflats.

HOW DO WAVES CHANGE COASTAL LANDSCAPES?
Pounding waves continually hurl sand, pebbles, and boulders against rocky coastlines, scouring away the land. As waves wear away coastal cliffs, the coastline gradually moves inland. Elsewhere, however, tides and rivers deposit sand, mud, and pebbles to build new land in the form of river deltas, beaches, and spits.

TIDES

Once or twice daily, coastlines are washed by the tide—a regular rise and fall in sea level. Some coastlines experience powerful tides, with rises and falls of 50 ft (15 m) or more a day. On other shores, the water level changes by only a few inches, so the tide is barely noticeable.

WHAT CAUSES TIDES?
Tides are caused mainly by the pull of the Moon's gravity on Earth. This gravitational pull creates a bulge of water, or a high tide, on the sea's surface. As Earth spins around eastward on its axis, the bulge moves westward, causing a high tide in different parts of the world.

WHY ARE SOME TIDES STRONGER THAN OTHERS?
Extra-strong tides called spring tides occur twice a month, when the Sun and Moon line up so that their combined gravitational pull produces an even bigger bulge on the ocean's surface. Weak tides called neap tides also occur twice every month, when the Sun and Moon are at right angles to Earth and their pulls largely cancel each other out.

▲ SALT MARSH
Formed on flat land at river mouths, salt marshes are regularly covered by tides.

▲ FJORD
Fjords form where glaciers gouge out valleys that are later flooded by the sea.

▲ SPIT AND LAGOON
A sandy spit may form where waves deposit sediment, with a calm lagoon behind.

▲ SEA STACKS
The Twelve Apostles rock formation in Victoria, Australia, was created by waves scouring away the bases of cliffs to form caves. In time, the cave roofs collapsed, forming arches of rock. Eventually, the tops of the arches crumbled, leaving behind a series of isolated pillars called stacks.

▲ LOW TIDE
Boats lie stranded on the shore at low tide, when the harbor at Polperro in Cornwall, Great Britain, empties of water. The tides follow a 28-day cycle, linked to the Moon's orbit around Earth.

▲ HIGH TIDE
At high tide, boats bob on the waves as water fills the harbor. Tides rise and fall once or twice every 24 hours and 50 minutes, so high and low tides occur 50 minutes later each day.

FIND OUT MORE ▶▶ Forces 164 • Moon 17 • Oceans 40–41 • Sun 15

ENERGY RESOURCES

Energy is the force that makes things work. Over many years, people have learned to produce energy from various sources, such as by burning ⏩ FOSSIL FUELS and using ⏩ NUCLEAR and ⏩ RENEWABLE ENERGY technology.

WHAT IS FUEL?

Fuel is something that can be burned to produce energy in the form of heat or power. Fuels include coal, oil, natural gas, and wood. Humans have been burning wood for warmth, and to light homes and cook food, since civilization began. However, in some parts of the world, so many trees have been cut down for fuel that firewood is now scarce.

◀ USING ENERGY
A city blazes with light. In developed countries, people consume vast amounts of energy in their daily lives.

FROM WOOD TO FIRE ▶
Wood provides fuel for cooking in a remote part of China. Firewood is the main source of fuel for half the world's population.

FOSSIL FUELS

Fossil fuels are made of the fossilized remains of living things that died millions of years ago. Coal, oil, and gas are the most important fossil fuels. Today, they provide most of the world's energy.

HOW DID OIL AND NATURAL GAS FORM?

Oil is formed from the remains of tiny plants and animals that were buried and squashed on the seabed. Natural gas forms in a way similar to oil and is found trapped in underground reservoirs.

HOW ARE FOSSIL FUELS USED TO PRODUCE ENERGY?

Power plants burn fossil fuels to heat water and produce steam. The steam pushes around turbines in a generator, which then spin a series of magnets, creating an electric current. Oil refineries process oil to make fuel to run cars, trains, ships, and aircraft.

HOW OIL FORMS

Plant and animal remains — New layers of sediment — Oil and gas rigs — Fuels collect under solid rock

1. Decaying plants and animals sink to the sea floor and are buried by layers of sediment.

2. Heat and pressure increase as the sediments sink. The organic remains become oil and gas.

3. Gas and oil rise through porous (holey) rock and collect below a layer of solid rock.

Coal is formed over millions of years from rotting plant material that accumulated in warm, muddy swamps

Moist, fibrous peat formed as rotting plant remains were buried and squashed. Peat gives off heat when burned

Lignite, or brown coal, is found nearest Earth's surface. This low-grade fuel contains up to 60 percent carbon, along with plant remains and moisture

Bituminous coal is found deeper underground. This better-quality solid fuel contains more than 80 percent carbon and is most commonly used in industry

Hard, black anthracite is found the deepest underground. Made from more than 90 percent carbon, it burns the best and is used in industry and to heat homes

energy resources

▲ COAL FORMATION
Plant remains decay to make brown, crumbly peat when they are buried and squashed. Over many thousands of years, more layers build up on top, and heat and pressure convert the remains first to lignite, then to bituminous coal, and finally to anthracite, the highest grade of coal.

NUCLEAR ENERGY

In the 1930s, scientists discovered that huge amounts of energy could be produced by splitting atoms (tiny particles) of a rare mineral called uranium. The technology was first used to make nuclear bombs. Later, it was used to generate electricity.

WHAT ARE THE ADVANTAGES AND DISADVANTAGES OF NUCLEAR ENERGY?

Nuclear fuel does not release the same polluting gases as fossil fuels, and does not use up the Earth's natural resources. However, uranium and other nuclear materials are radioactive—they give off radiation that can harm living things. This means that great care must be taken when they are processed and transported. Nuclear fuel is also difficult to dispose of safely once used.

▲ THE CHERNOBYL DISASTER
In 1986, a nuclear reactor in Chernobyl, Russia, caught fire and exploded, releasing a cloud of radiation. This image shows the extent of the contamination six days after the accident.

RENEWABLE ENERGY

Renewable energy is generated using the power of natural forces such as sunlight. Fossil fuels release harmful waste gases when burned, and they cannot be replaced when their limited supplies are used up. Renewable energy, however, will not run out and produces little pollution.

WHAT ARE THE SOURCES OF RENEWABLE ENERGY?

Most of the energy on Earth comes from the Sun. Solar power uses the energy in sunlight directly. Moving water (in the form of waves, tides, and flowing rivers) and the wind also contain energy that can be used to spin turbines to generate electricity. Geothermal energy taps heat from inside Earth.

SOLAR POWER ▶
Each curved dish at a solar power station focuses radiation from the Sun onto a thermoelectric generator. A computer steers the dishes so they always turn to face the Sun during the day.

WHAT ARE THE ADVANTAGES AND DISADVANTAGES OF RENEWABLE ENERGY?

Renewable energy will last as long as the Sun shines, winds blow, waves crash, and rivers flow. These technologies are safe to use and do not pollute the environment. However, renewable energy plants can be expensive to build and may not produce enough energy to meet local requirements.

▲ WIND POWER
Windmills have been used to power machines for centuries. The spinning blades of modern wind turbines turn a shaft, which generates electricity.

▲ HYDROELECTRIC POWER
Fast-flowing river water can be used to spin turbines that work electricity generators. A dam above the hydroelectric plant controls the flow of water.

▲ GEOTHERMAL POWER
Geothermal power plants, such as this one near natural hot springs in Iceland, pipe heat from the Earth's hot interior and use it to generate electricity.

FIND OUT MORE ▶▶ Atoms 157 • Engines 198–199 • Fossils 76 • Industry 204 • Nuclear Energy 167

CLIMATE

Every part of the world has its own climate—a characteristic pattern of weather over a long period of time. A region's climate affects the types of plants and animals found there, and also how people live—for example, the types of houses they build and the clothes they wear.

WHAT AFFECTS AN AREA'S CLIMATE?

An area's climate is affected by three main factors—its latitude (distance north or south of the equator), its height above sea level, and its distance from the sea. Tropical regions around the equator have a hot climate. Temperatures cool toward the poles. The climate is also cooler on high mountains. Seas and oceans generally make coastal climates mild and wet.

WHY DO TROPICAL REGIONS HAVE HOT CLIMATES?

Because Earth is a globe with a curved surface, the Sun's rays strike parts of its surface at different angles. Regions on or near the equator have a hot climate because the Sun's rays beat down on them more directly and the rays are more concentrated than at regions near the poles.

WHAT IS A CONTINENTAL CLIMATE?

Regions in the center of continents usually have more extreme weather than regions near the coast, with hot summers and cold winters. Land surfaces heat up and cool down more quickly than large areas of water, such as oceans. Areas farther inland therefore experience extreme temperature variations between summer and winter.

climate

▲ GLOBAL TEMPERATURES

This map of air temperatures shows the world's three main climate zones. The warmest tropical regions, on and near the equator, are shown in deep red and orange. Temperate regions farther from the equator are shown in yellow. These areas are usually mild, with warm summers and cool winters. The coldest areas, near the poles, are shown in blue.

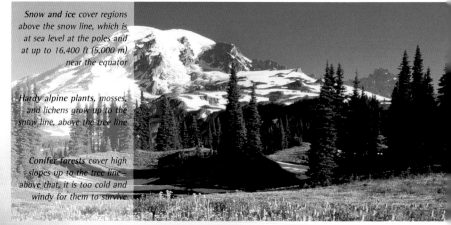

Snow and ice cover regions above the snow line, which is at sea level at the poles and at up to 16,400 ft (5,000 m) near the equator

Hardy alpine plants, mosses, and lichens grow up to the snow line, above the tree line

Conifer forests cover high slopes up to the tree line—above that, it is too cold and windy for them to survive

▲ MOUNTAIN CLIMATE

Mountain regions have a cooler climate than lowland areas because the thin air at high altitudes absorbs less of the Sun's heat. High peaks in the path of moist winds are also wetter than lowland regions.

Rain-bearing clouds blowing from the ocean make coastal regions generally wetter than areas farther inland

Growing cumulus clouds indicate changeable weather, characteristic of coastal, or maritime, climates

Trees bend toward the land, battered by strong winds blowing in off the sea and the salt spray that burns off the growth on the seaward side

Vegetation flourishes in the mild, wet climate

◄ COASTAL CLIMATE

The ocean heats up more slowly than the land, but retains its warmth for longer. Moist sea breezes rising over the ocean and blowing inshore bring rain and cool the land in summer, but warm it in winter, so coastal climates are generally wet and mild.

FIND OUT MORE ▶▶ Mountains 45 • Planet Earth 36–37 • Soil 48 • Winds 51

CLIMATE ZONES

Earth has three main climate zones—tropical, temperate, and polar. These zones can be further divided into smaller zones, each with its own typical climate. A region's climate, together with its physical characteristics, determines its plant and animal life.

WHAT IS A MICROCLIMATE?

A small area with a different climate to its surroundings is said to have its own microclimate. Examples include a city or a rooftop garden. The temperature in cities may be around 11°F (6°C) warmer than the surrounding countryside because buildings and paved streets hold the Sun's heat longer than vegetation. Artificial heating in buildings also contributes to higher city temperatures.

climate zones

■ POLAR AND TUNDRA	■ TEMPERATE FOREST	■ DRY GRASSLAND
■ BOREAL FOREST	■ MEDITERRANEAN	■ TROPICAL GRASSLAND
■ MOUNTAIN	■ DESERT	■ TROPICAL RAINFOREST

▲ EARTH'S MAJOR CLIMATE ZONES
These are many ways to classify climate. Most methods (including the one shown here, which divides Earth's surface into nine different climate zones) use a combination of temperature and rainfall.

LOUIS AGASSIZ
Swiss, 1807–1873
Naturalist Louis Agassiz studied glaciers and the effects of ice erosion in areas where glaciers no longer existed. He put forward the theory that much of Europe and North America was once covered by ice sheets. Through his work, the idea of "ice ages" became generally accepted.

HAS THE EARTH'S CLIMATE CHANGED OVER TIME?

Over the past two million years, Earth's climate has slowly changed. Long, cold periods called ice ages, or glacials, have been interspersed with warmer periods. The last ice age ended about 10,000 years ago. At its height, all of northern Europe and parts of North America, Siberia, New Zealand, Tasmania, and the southernmost tip of South America were covered by ice sheets up to 3,300 ft (1,000 m) thick.

WILL EARTH'S CLIMATE CHANGE IN THE FUTURE?

Some scientists believe that Earth will enter another ice age in a few thousand years. However, almost all scientists believe that pollution caused by human activities is slowly causing the planet to grow warmer—a phenomenon called global warming.

CLIMATE ZONE CLASSIFICATION

POLAR AND TUNDRA
Polar climates are cold and dry, with long, dark winters. In the tundra (a treeless region bordering the Arctic), temperatures rise above freezing for only a few months each year.

BOREAL FOREST
Boreal (cold coniferous) forests lie south of the tundra, stretching across much of northern Canada, Scandinavia, and Russia. Temperatures fall below freezing for 4–6 months a year.

MOUNTAIN
On mountains, the temperature decreases with altitude (height), and many high peaks are always covered in snow. Mountain climates are usually wetter and windier than lowland regions.

TEMPERATE FOREST
Temperate climates have warm summers and cool winters with year-round rain or snow. Temperate forests are characterized by deciduous trees, which lose their leaves during the winter.

MEDITERRANEAN
A Mediterranean climate is found in regions bordering the Mediterranean Sea, and in Australia and California. It is characterized by hot, dry summers and cool, wet winters.

DESERT
Earth's deserts are hot and dry year-round, and usually receive less than 10 in (250 mm) of rainfall a year. Deserts form inland in Asia and Australia but not so much elsewhere where other factors come into play.

DRY GRASSLAND
Dry grasslands are found in the center of continents where temperature variations are extreme. They have hot summers, cold winters, and little rainfall, so very few trees can grow there.

TROPICAL GRASSLAND
Tropical grasslands, such as the African savanna, lie between desert areas and tropical rainforests. The climate is hot all year, but with a distinct wet season and dry season.

TROPICAL RAINFOREST
Tropical rainforests are found in regions near the equator. Here, the climate is hot and wet all year, with temperatures remaining at around 80–82°F (27–28°C).

FIND OUT MORE ▸▸ Habitats 82–84 • Human Impact 64–65 • Winds 51

HUMAN IMPACT

Nearly seven billion people live on planet Earth. As the population grows, we are taking more and more land to live and using more of the world's natural resources. Many human activities also produce ▸▸ POLLUTION , which is damaging the Earth's environment.

HOW DOES FARMING CHANGE THE LANDSCAPE?

Since farming began, 10,000 years ago, many wild landscapes have been transformed to create fields for planting crops and raising animals. Swamps and coastal marshes have been drained. Forests have been felled and grasslands have been plowed. However, removing tree and plant roots that help to bind the soil can make the soil loose and crumbly. High winds may then blow it away, or heavy rain may wash it into rivers. In some areas, soil erosion has turned fertile farmland into barren wastes.

WORKING FACTORIES ▶
During the manufacturing process and when they burn fossil fuels, factories such as this chemical plant may release gases that harm the environment. Although they are expensive to install and run, "clean" technologies that reduce pollution are now available and should become more common in the future.

HOW DOES INDUSTRY AFFECT THE LANDSCAPE?

In the 1700s, the dawn of the industrial age revolutionized methods of manufacturing and made them more efficient. Since then, factories have been built all over the world. Factories consume huge amounts of natural resources and energy, and many give off chemical waste, which creates problems such as air and water pollution, and ▸▸ GLOBAL WARMING .

WHAT CHALLENGES FACE THE HUMAN POPULATION?

One of our main challenges is to find the right balance between using and conserving Earth's natural resources. The human species dominates Earth in a way that no species has done before. Our demands for fuel, water, land, and food are beginning to place a strain on the planet's limited resources. What makes us different from other species, however, is our ability to recognize these global problems and our inventiveness in doing something about them.

◀ TAMING THE LAND
Crop fields stretch to the horizon on the North American prairies, where wild grasslands were once home to thousands of plant and animal species. All over the world, wild land is brought under cultivation to grow food, or bulldozed to build houses, factories, roads, and railroads.

▼ GROWING CITIES
In 1900, only 10 percent of the world's population lived in cities. Today that figure is around 50 percent. All over the world, cities have mushroomed as more and more people have moved in to find work.

POLLUTION

All over the world, factories, power plants, farms, businesses, and homes produce huge amounts of pollution by releasing chemicals and other substances that pollute, or dirty, the natural environment. As people's use of energy and other resources grows, the Earth is becoming more polluted.

human impact

WHAT ARE THE MAIN CAUSES OF POLLUTION?
Industrial waste, sewage, and chemical pesticides from farms seep into streams and rivers. Cars, factories, and power plants burning fossil fuels give off fumes that pollute the air. Chemicals called CFCs (chlorofluorocarbons), used to make refrigerators and aerosol sprays, destroy the ozone layer, which protects us from harmful sunlight. Household and other waste buried underground pollutes the land.

HOW LONG DOES POLLUTION LAST?
Some kinds of pollution quickly disperse on the wind or are diluted by water. Other types, such as radioactive waste, stay poisonous for thousands of years. Plastics and other domestic garbage that are buried underground in landfill sites may take many years to rot away completely.

WHAT CAN BE DONE TO REDUCE POLLUTION?
Around the world, scientists are investigating the damage caused by pollution. Governments have introduced controls that curb the pollution produced by industry and farms, and restrict the development of land, especially in rural areas. Everyone can help to reduce pollution by using energy carefully, and by recycling glass bottles, cans, plastic, and paper so that they can be reused. This helps to save precious natural resources and cuts down on waste and litter.

▲ OIL SPILLS
Accidental oil spills from damaged tankers can kill thousands of seabirds, fish, and other marine life. The world's oceans are also polluted by industrial waste and sewage dumped at sea.

▲ CITY SMOG
Car exhausts are a major source of pollution. They belch fumes into the air that sometimes form a dense, choking smog.

▲ ACID RAIN
Acid rain harms trees, poisons wildlife, and can even erode stone. It is formed when poisonous gases released from vehicles and power plants mix with moisture in the air, forming a weak but damaging acid.

GLOBAL WARMING

Global warming is the slow and steady rise in Earth's temperature caused by a buildup of "greenhouse gases" in the air due to pollution. Some experts predict temperatures will rise by 2.5–8.1°F (1.4–4.5°C) this century.

WHAT IS CAUSING GLOBAL WARMING?
Global warming is caused by the increased level of carbon dioxide and other greenhouse gases in the atmosphere. These gases are released from car exhausts and when fossil fuels are burned in factories and power plants. Greenhouse gases also include CFCs from aerosols and old refrigerators, and methane from swamps, gas pipes, and rotting garbage.

HOW WILL GLOBAL WARMING AFFECT EVERYDAY LIFE?
Global warming will melt some of the polar ice caps, bringing greater risk of floods to low-lying and coastal regions worldwide. Heat waves, droughts, hurricanes, and torrential rain will become more common. To prevent global warming, many countries are now trying to reduce their output of carbon dioxide and use renewable energy sources.

Greenhouse gases encircle the planet and stop some of the Sun's heat from escaping

Escaping heat

Sun's rays

Trapped heat

Atmosphere

◄ THE GREENHOUSE EFFECT
Greenhouse gases occur naturally in the atmosphere. When the greenhouse effect is working normally, the gases trap some of the Sun's heat, making Earth's surface warm enough for life to flourish.

FIND OUT MORE ▶▶ Energy Resources 60–61 • Industrial Revolution 418–419 • Population 218–219 • Transportation 200–201

FARMING

Thousands of years ago, people began farming the land to grow grain crops, such as wheat, and rearing animals for their meat, milk, and other products. Today, many farmers use modern techniques and equipment to produce bumper crops.

CATTLE RANCHING ►
The world's largest herds of beef cattle are found in North and South America, where there are plenty of wide, open grasslands for the cattle to graze. On these South American grasslands, cowboys called gauchos still round up cattle on horseback.

WHICH KINDS OF ANIMALS ARE DOMESTICATED?
Middle Eastern farmers began rearing herds of sheep and goats around 10,000 years ago. The most common domesticated animals today are cattle, goats, and pigs. However, a wide range of animals including deer, ducks, turkeys, and even ostriches are now reared for their meat, milk, or eggs.

◄ MECHANIZED FARMING
Modern combines perform two jobs: harvesting cereal crops and threshing the grain to separate the husks containing the seeds from the stems. Farmers use different machines to plow, sow, and reap, and to spray fields with fertilizers and chemicals to control weeds and pests.

farming

HOW HAVE MODERN CROPS BEEN DEVELOPED?
Today's crops are descended from wild plants that produced seeds or fruits that could be eaten. Early cereal crops had small grains and therefore produced low yields. However, new scientific methods can generate disease-resistant plants, or crops with specific characteristics.

WHAT ARE STAPLE FOOD CROPS?
Staple foods form the main part of people's daily diet. They include the cereal crops wheat, corn, and rice. Wheat is eaten by around 35 percent of the world's population every day. The grain is eaten whole or ground into flour, which is then used to make bread or pasta. Corn is grown in temperate, tropical, and subtropical countries. It is eaten as a vegetable, ground into flour or cornmeal, or used to make cooking oil.

WHERE IS RICE GROWN?
Over 90 percent of the world's rice is grown in Asia and eaten by the people living there. Rice is also grown in the United States, mainly for export. In the United States, growing rice is highly mechanized. In Asia, the work of sowing, planting out the seedlings, and harvesting is usually done by hand.

WHAT IS ORGANIC FARMING?
Many farmers spray fields with chemical pesticides and use chemical fertilizers to protect and enrich their crops. Organic farmers prefer to use natural farming methods. They enrich the soil with manure, compost, or seaweed, and use pest-eating insects or companion planting (for example, planting onions with carrots to reduce such pests as carrot fly). Organic farmers also allow pigs and chickens to roam in fields or yards instead of keeping them in crowded pens or cages.

RICE FARMING ►
Rice is the main food for over half the world's population. It is grown in flooded fields called paddies in countries such as Thailand, China, Japan, and Indonesia.

Terraces are cut into hillsides so farmers can cultivate more land

Paddy fields are flooded for most of the growing season because rice, a swamp plant, grows with its roots in water

FIND OUT MORE ►► Agricultural Revolution 412 • Early Farming 364–365 • Genetic Engineering 210–211 • Southeast Asia 270–271

FISHING

Fish are an important food, so fishing is a major industry in many countries. However, overfishing has resulted in dwindling fish stocks in the world's oceans.

WHAT IS OVERFISHING?
Overfishing refers to the decreasing number of fish as the breeding population are fished faster than they are replaced. Many overfished species, such as cod, may eventually die out. Overfishing is happening because of the demand for fish to feed the world's population, and the efficiency of the modern fishing industry.

WHAT METHODS ARE USED BY THE FISHING INDUSTRY?
Modern fishing fleets work both in coastal waters and far out at sea, using sonar devices to locate shoals of fish, and a variety of lines, traps, and nets. Different kinds of floating nets are used to catch fish at the surface and in mid-waters. Bag-shaped trawl nets, dragged along the seabed, capture bottom-dwellers.

▲ THAI FISH FARM
Fish farms, where salmon, trout, catfish, crayfish, and shrimp are reared in pens, ponds, and cages, are becoming more important as the world's seas are fished out.

▲ TUNA FISHING
Frozen tuna are piled on a harborside in Tokyo, Japan. Other commercially fished species include herring, mackerel, and anchovies. An incredible 110 million tons (100 million metric tons) of fish are caught annually, along with other aquatic life, such as squid, crabs, and shrimp.

fishing

FIND OUT MORE ▶▶ Endangered Species 124 • Fish 112–113 • Oceans 40–41

FORESTRY

Forestry is the management of forests with the aim of harvesting their produce, which includes timber, fuel wood, charcoal, resin, rubber, and pulp for paper. Trees also yield food in the form of fruits, nuts, and oils.

WHAT ARE THE MAIN USES OF TIMBER?
Wood is an amazingly versatile material, which can be put to thousands of different uses. As well as being burned for fuel, timber is also used in buildings and to make furniture and tools. Hardwoods, such as teak and mahogany, are prized for their beautiful grain and toughness. Fast-growing softwoods, such as pine, are used mainly for making wood pulp for paper.

RUBBER PLANTATION ▶
A sticky sap called latex lies below the bark of rubber trees. Latex becomes stretchy as it dries and, when treated, turns into rubber. Rubber trees are farmed on large rubber plantations in countries such as Malaysia (right).

Sticky sap, or latex, oozes out when the bark is cut

Small boats keep the floating logs on course

Logs are bundled into rafts to keep them together

forestry

Collecting cup is sometimes made out of a halved coconut

Slit is made at an angle in the bark of the tree

◀ LOGGING INDUSTRY
Mature trees are felled with chainsaws or giant shearing blades. The logs are then trucked or floated downriver to a mill, where they are sawn into timber of different lengths. Lumber-producing countries include Canada, Russia, and Finland.

WHAT IS DEFORESTATION?
In well-managed forests, trees are cut down singly or in strips so that the forest has time to grow back. However, many of the world's forests are now being destroyed by large-scale logging, or deforestation. As the demand for palm oil grows, palm oil plantations in Indonesia are fast replacing rainforests and causing catastrophic damage to ecosystems.

FIND OUT MORE ▶▶ Habitats 82–84 • Industry 204 • Trees 94–95

NATURE

LIFE ON EARTH

Planet Earth is home to trillions of organisms (living things), including animals and plants. They are found on land, in lakes, rivers, and oceans, as well as in the air. Scientists use ▶ CLASSIFICATION to show how different species, or types, of organisms are related.

WHAT DO ALL LIVING THINGS HAVE IN COMMON?

All organisms need food for the energy required to live and grow. They all excrete (get rid of) waste products, and detect changes in their surroundings and respond to them. All living organisms follow a ▶ LIFE CYCLE of growth and development, reproduction, and death.

CAN LIFE EXIST WITHOUT SUNLIGHT?

Sunlight is essential for most life forms on Earth to exist. Plants use energy from sunlight to convert water and carbon dioxide gas into food. This releases essential, life-giving oxygen into the atmosphere. Virtually all other organisms rely on plants for energy to keep them alive. Even meat-eaters indirectly absorb vegetation from their plant-eating prey.

HOW DOES THE MOVEMENT OF EARTH AFFECT LIFE ON OUR PLANET?

Earth's rotation every 24 hours produces day and night. Some animals are active in the daytime, others at night. Without sunlight, plants stop making food and releasing oxygen. The annual movement of Earth around the Sun creates the seasons. Living things are more active in spring and summer.

◄ DOLPHIN FISH
These ocean-living dolphin fish, or mahi mahi, swim in large groups called shoals. They feed on smaller fish and shrimp. Fish are well adapted to life in water. They have gills for absorbing oxygen from water, and their streamlined bodies dart easily through rivers, lakes, and oceans.

AFRICAN ELEPHANTS ►
The largest of all land animals is the African elephant. Its massive body is supported by four pillarlike legs. Elephants have long, flexible trunks that raise water and food to the mouth and spray water over their bodies. Long, curved tusks are used for defense.

LIFE CYCLES

Every living thing goes through a sequence of changes called its life cycle. Initially it grows and develops, gradually changing shape and getting larger. Once it is fully mature, it reproduces. Finally, it dies, and is replaced by its offspring.

WHICH ORGANISMS LIVE LONGEST?

Elephants can live to the age of 70, and humans can live for more than 100 years. Some giant tortoises live for more than 150 years, but certain plants live for much, much longer. The Californian bristlecone pine tree is thought to live to 4,900 years old, and the Californian creosote bush may be 12,000 years old.

DO ALL PLANTS HAVE A ONE-YEAR LIFE CYCLE?

Annual plants, such as sunflowers, live and die within one year, but their seeds survive the winter. Biennial plants, such as carrots, flower and produce seeds in their second year and then die. Perennial plants, including oak trees, live for several years—some flower yearly, some only once in their life cycle.

5. Seeds are scattered as the flower withers

1. Seed germinates and a root and shoot appear

2. Leaves form and a stem grows

4. Reproduction occurs and the flower produces seeds

3. Flower begins to form and upward growth slows

▲ PLANT LIFE CYCLE
The life cycle of this sunflower is completed in one growing season. Each seed contains an embryo plant and its food store, and germinates (sprouts) in the spring. The young plant grows rapidly, developing first a stem and leaves, and then flowers. In summer, the flowers produce seeds, which fall to the ground ready to sprout next year.

life on Earth

CLASSIFICATION

Scientists use classification to name living organisms. They sort them into groups by looking for any similarities or differences that indicate how closely related they are.

HOW DOES CLASSIFICATION WORK?

Organisms are sorted into groups ordered by size. The smallest, the species, contains organisms that breed together. Related species form a genus; several genera make a family. Linked families form an order; several orders make a class. A phylum contains a few classes. Phyla make up the largest group, the kingdom.

WHAT ARE THE FIVE KINGDOMS OF LIVING THINGS?

Organisms are divided into five kingdoms. Monerans include simple, single-celled organisms such as bacteria. Protists are mostly single-celled and include protozoa and algae. Fungi include mushrooms and molds. Plants include flowers, trees, and ferns. Animals include lions, lizards, and lice.

CLASSIFYING A TIGER

KINGDOM	Animalia (animals)—organisms made of many cells that obtain energy from food.
PHYLUM	Chordata (chordates)—mostly vertebrates, such as birds and mammals.
CLASS	Mammalia (mammals)—vertebrates that have hair and feed their young with milk.
ORDER	Carnivora (carnivores)—hunting mammals that have gripping, cutting teeth.
FAMILY	Felidae (cats)—carnivores with sharp claws that can be retracted (drawn in)..
GENUS	Panthera (big cats)—large cats that roar, including lions, leopards, and tigers.
SPECIES	*Panthera tigris* (tiger)—big cat with a striped coat, found in Asia.

PANTHERA TIGRIS ▼
A species name has two parts— generic (*Panthera*) and specific (*tigris*).

▼ THE FIVE KINGDOMS
The photographs below illustrate one species from each of the five kingdoms.

ANIMAL (LION)

PLANT (RHODODENDRON)

FUNGUS (MUSHROOM)

PROTIST (PROTOZOA)

MONERAN (BACTERIA)

FIND OUT MORE ▶▶ Algae 87 • Animals 96–97 • Planet Earth 36–37 • Fungi 86 • Microorganisms 85 • Plants 88–89

BIOLOGY

The study of life and living things is called biology. Scientists who study biology are known as biologists. The main branches of biology are zoology (the study of animals), botany (the study of plants), and ▶▶ MICROBIOLOGY (the study of tiny organisms).

WHAT EXACTLY DO BIOLOGISTS STUDY?
Biologists study even more specialized branches within zoology, botany, and microbiology. Cell biology, for example, involves studying one of the smallest units of a living thing. Anatomy, on the other hand, looks at the complete structure of organisms, whereas physiology is the study of how organisms work.

DO BIOLOGISTS ONLY STUDY STRUCTURE?
As well as learning about an organism's structure, biologists discover how an organism reproduces and grows, how it behaves, where it lives, and how it interacts with other organisms. In this way, today's biologists build up a complete picture of the biology of an organism. At one time, scientists knew little more about living things than what they looked like.

Tubelike stamen is the male reproductive structure that produces pollen grains

▲ RED HIBISCUS
This tropical flowering plant has a trumpet-shaped flower and yellow brushlike anthers (male sex organs) that surround five red platelike stigmas (female sex organs). Biologists have discovered that as hummingbirds feed on hibiscus nectar (sugary liquid), they transfer dusty pollen from the anthers to the stigmas. If fertilization occurs, the plant makes seeds and reproduces.

biology

▲ STUDYING ANIMAL BEHAVIOR
Zoologist Dr. Jane Goodall takes notes as she watches one member of a group of chimpanzees in Gombe Stream National Park, Tanzania, Africa. Goodall has spent many years studying chimpanzee behavior.

MICROBIOLOGY

Microorganisms are living things that are too small to be seen with the naked eye. Microbiology is the study of these microorganisms, which include bacteria and some fungi.

WHAT DO MICROBIOLOGISTS DO?
Some microbiologists are interested in microorganisms that cause diseases in animals and plants. Some specialize in those microorganisms that may be useful for the manufacture of drugs, or food, such as bread. Others study microorganisms that recycle essential nutrients on Earth and in its atmosphere.

HOW DO ELECTRON MICROSCOPES WORK?
Electron microscopes work by passing a beam of tiny particles called electrons through, or across the surface of, a specimen, and onto a screen. This produces a greatly magnified image. Scanning electron microscopes produce a three-dimensional image that can be captured in a photograph called an SEM.

◄ ELECTRON MICROSCOPE
A scientist looks at a scanning electron microscope screen that displays a magnified image of a specimen. He can see in detail the specimen's external features.

▲ MICROORGANISM
This SEM shows a ribbonlike trypanosome and a human blood cell magnified 4,500 times. This microorganism, found in African tsetse fly saliva, infects human blood, causing sleeping sickness.

FIND OUT MORE ▶▶ Animals 96–97 • Flowering Plants 92–93 • Microorganisms 85

CELLS

The tiniest living unit that exists is a cell. Cells are the building blocks of all organisms. Most cells have a nucleus containing a set of building blocks called ▶▶GENES.

ARE THERE DIFFERENT TYPES OF CELL IN THE SAME ORGANISM?

Most organisms consist of many different types of cell, each with a specific role to play. Cells with a similar task, such as muscle cells in an animal, are organized into a group. This group, called a tissue, carries out a particular function, such as bending a leg.

HOW DO PLANT AND ANIMAL CELLS DIFFER?

Both plant and animal cells have a nucleus and a plasma membrane and contain cytoplasm. Plant cells, however, have a fluid-filled vacuole and green structures called chloroplasts. Chloroplasts make food using sunlight energy in a process called photosynthesis. Animal cells must absorb food to survive.

cells

Vacuole stores watery cell sap that gives cell its shape

Cytoplasm is the jellylike liquid inside cell

Chloroplast (green) captures sunlight needed to make food

Nucleus is the cell's control center

Cell wall

Plasma membrane is pushed up against the cell wall

▲ PLANT CELL
This cross-section of a leaf cell shows how the vacuole (blue) sap pushes cytoplasm (yellow-green) against the cell wall (brown). This gives the cell its shape.

Nucleus is surrounded by a double membrane

Cytoplasm is the area of a living cell, outside the nucleus, enclosed by the cell membrane. It contains organelles (specialized structures within a cell) that help the cell to function

Plasma membrane is the thin barrier that surrounds a cell

ANIMAL CELL ▶
Unlike plant cells, which have a rigid outer wall, animal cells are more fluid in shape.

▲ ONION BULB CELLS
These magnified cells from an onion bulb have been stained red. Boxlike cell walls have formed around the mature cells.

▲ CELL DIVISION IN AN ONION'S ROOT TIP
These onion cells (blue) are dividing in a process called mitosis. The cells' 16 chromosomes (black) also divide and separate, so that each new cell gains a complete set. Mitosis allows an organism to grow or repair itself.

GENES

The features of living things are controlled by their genes. The genes inside an organism's cells contain the instructions to make proteins, which build that cell and control the way it works. Genes are inherited by offspring from their parents.

WHAT IS DNA?

Genes are made of a chemical substance called deoxyribonucleic acid (DNA). It is stored in the nucleus of all cells. DNA holds instructions for making the proteins needed for the growth and development of new organisms. It also passes on genetic information to the next generation.

WHAT IS A CHROMOSOME?

Inside a cell's nucleus, DNA is packaged into long, threadlike structures called chromosomes. They are visible only under a microscope when the cells divide. During cell division, chromosomes shorten and thicken, then split into identical halves, one for each new cell. Chromosome numbers vary between species.

▲ GENE DIFFERENCES
These two hamsters differ because each has different versions of the genes that control fur pattern and color. Otherwise they look very similar because most of their genes are identical.

living things gradually change over many generations in a process called evolution. This allows organisms to fully adapt to their surroundings, and gives rise to new species, while others may become extinct. The driving force for evolution is ►► NATURAL SELECTION.

SPURGE   CACTUS

▲ CONVERGENT EVOLUTION
This is the evolution of similar features in unrelated species living in similar conditions. Spurge and cactus are unrelated plants with thick, spiny water-holding stems to help them survive in dry places.

WHAT IS THE EVIDENCE FOR EVOLUTION?
Evolutionary clues are found in fossils, the ancient remains of organisms. Creatures alive today share some characteristics with fossil ancestors, but have evolved new ones as well. Fossils also show that millions of living and extinct species evolved from a few simple organisms that lived billions of years ago.

HOW DO NEW SPECIES EVOLVE?
A species is a group of similar living things, such as lions, that can breed together. If a group of individuals within a species becomes separated from all the other groups of that species, they can no longer breed with them. In time, the group evolves separately and becomes increasingly different. Eventually, it is so different that it becomes a new species.

HOW LONG DOES EVOLUTION TAKE?
Evolution is a continuous process of change. In a stable environment, evolution can cause change, which can be very rapid in small organisms, while in others it may take thousands of years. ►► HUMAN EVOLUTION from an apelike ancestor took millions of years and gave rise to several different species, not just our own.

Phiomia was as big as a modern horse and had pillarlike legs and a short trunk. Sharp tusks were used for fighting and gathering food

Moeritherium, an early elephant, had a bulky body, short legs, and a long upper lip. It lived in Africa, and is thought to have bathed in lakes and rivers and fed on water plants

MOERITHERIUM
50 MILLION YEARS AGO

PHIOMIA
35 MILLION YEARS AGO

NATURAL SELECTION

Living things produce more offspring than they need to replace themselves. Only the few that are well adapted to their particular environment will survive. Thanks to this natural selection, the features needed to survive are passed on to their offspring and become more widespread, so a species gradually evolves.

HOW DOES A WELL-ADAPTED INDIVIDUAL SURVIVE?
Certain individuals have features that let them compete better for food, water, shelter, or mates. These fitter individuals are more likely to survive, breed, and pass on their advantageous features to their offspring. In this way, natural selection makes it possible for only the fittest to survive. Naturalist Charles Darwin believed that this is how species evolve over time.

evolution

CHARLES DARWIN
English, 1809–1882
Between 1831 and 1836 naturalist Charles Darwin sailed around the world, describing the animals and plants he saw. This trip convinced him that living things evolved, even though most scientists believed that they remained the same. In 1859, he published his theories in On the Origin of Species.

▲ RED CRAB SURVIVAL RACE
This forest-dweller releases many tiny eggs into the sea. After a month in the water, they race to the forest. Many die en route.

WETLANDS

Wherever salt or fresh water cannot easily drain, a wetland forms. Wetlands cover over 6 percent of Earth's surface. They include marshes, swamps, waterlogged forests, peat bogs, and river deltas.

WHY ARE WETLANDS IMPORTANT?
Many wetlands contain a large diversity of species, including birds, mammals, reptiles, insects, amphibians, and plants. Wetlands also serve as nurseries where young fish and other aquatic animals grow and develop.

WHAT ARE MANGROVE SWAMPS?
These are the salt-water wetlands, populated by mangrove trees, found along tropical coastlines. Mangrove swamps teem with life, and they also help to protect the coastline from tropical storm damage.

HOW DOES A PEAT BOG DIFFER FROM A SWAMP?
Peat bogs form in cool, wet places where a lake fills with soil and vegetation. Swamps are found in places such as river deltas, where water moves slowly enough to create permanent flooding. Plentiful vegetation provides food and homes for swamp animals.

▲ FLAMINGOS
These tropical wetland birds live on salty lakes and lagoons. They pump water through their beaks, filtering out shrimp and other small aquatic animals for food.

FORESTS

Habitats dominated by trees and shrubs are called forests. They include tropical rainforests, cool-climate coniferous forests, and temperate broad-leaved forests. These habitats all teem with life.

▲ THREE-TOED SLOTH
This South American mammal spends most of its days hanging upside down from the branches of rainforest trees.

WHY ARE RAINFORESTS SO FULL OF LIFE?
Evergreen trees continuously grow and provide food in the constant warm and wet climate of tropical rainforests. A huge variety of animals feed and shelter at all levels, from the forest floor to its canopy. Tropical rainforests contain half of all animal and plant species. Yet they cover only about 10 percent of the Earth's surface.

Stag beetles use their massive jaws to fight over mates and territory

▲ STAG BEETLES
These fighting stag beetles live in broad-leaved forests. As young larvae, they feed on rotting wood. As adults they feed upon the sap of tree trunks.

GRASSLANDS

Wherever it is too dry for forests to grow, or too wet for deserts to form, grasslands appear. The two main types are the tropical African savanna and temperate grasslands, such as the South American pampas.

HOW DO GRASSES SURVIVE GRAZING?
Grasses can withstand constant grazing because they sprout from the bottom, not from the tips. The more they are eaten, the more they grow. Grasslands support a wide variety of animals that eat grasses, as well as those that prey on grass-eaters.

HOW CAN SO MANY PLANT-EATING SPECIES LIVE IN THE SAVANNA?
The African savanna supports many species of plant-eaters, some of which eat different parts of grasses, while others eat different savanna plants. Zebras, for example, eat the coarse, tough tops of grasses, while wildebeest prefer their leafy, middle parts.

WHY DO MANY SMALLER GRASSLAND ANIMALS LIVE UNDERGROUND?
There are few trees in the grasslands to provide shelter, so burrowing protects the animals from enemies. Burrows also protect against extreme weather conditions.

▲ AFRICAN SAVANNA
The hot African savanna is home to vast herds of grazing animals, including these wildebeest and zebra. They in turn are hunted by predators such as lions and leopards.

FIND OUT MORE ▶▶ Deserts 84 • Mountains 84 • Polar Habitats 84

DESERTS

This dry and hostile habitat often receives less than 4 in (10 cm) of rain each year. Deserts are very hot by day, but cooler at night. Few animals and plants have adapted to survive these difficult conditions.

HOW DO DESERT PLANTS SURVIVE?
Some plants, such as cacti, have deep, wide-spreading roots to reach available water, and small leaves and waterproof skins that limit evaporation. Others spend most of their life cycle as seeds. When rare rains arrive, they sprout, flower, and produce seeds within two weeks. This event is called a desert bloom.

Straplike leaves absorb water vapor

▲ WELWITSCHIA
This plant grows in the extremely dry Namib Desert. It survives by using its large leaves to absorb condensation from fog that rolls off the nearby ocean at night.

Stinger at the end of jointed flexible tail is used for self-defense and to kill prey

▲ SCORPION
Like many desert animals, this scorpion is active at night, when temperatures are lower. Once a scorpion has detected its prey, it grips and then stings it.

MOUNTAINS

Land that is 1,970 ft (600 m) or more above the sea is a mountain. The higher you climb, the thinner the air, the lower the temperature, and the faster the wind speed. Only the toughest species survive.

WHAT ARE MOUNTAIN ZONES?
Mountains have various zones of vegetation. Deciduous woodlands cover the foothills. These rise up to coniferous forests, which can survive the colder, windier conditions. Above the tree line (where trees can no longer grow) is an alpine meadow of hardy plants. Next is bare rock, capped by a snow field.

WHICH ANIMALS LIVE ON MOUNTAINS?
Each vegetation zone has its typical species. Woodlands and forests provide habitats for grazers, such as deer and birds. Meadows are home to rodents and rabbits and, in summer, insects and the birds that eat them. Goats and sheep live on the rocky crags, and birds of prey circle above, in search of food.

Snow field at the top of a mountain is too cold and windy for most living things

▲ EDELWEISS
Short, tough plant species, such as this Swiss edelweiss, can survive in the alpine meadow. Here above the tree line, winds are fierce and biting, and soils are thin and rocky.

POLAR HABITATS

Cold, icy polar habitats exist at the Earth's North and South poles. Polar regions have short summers and long, harsh winters. Only animals that have adapted—with thick fur, for example—survive there.

▲ WALRUSES
These marine mammals live in herds in Arctic coastal waters. Walruses are tough-skinned, with a thick layer of blubber (fat) to protect them from the cold.

DO THE ARCTIC AND ANTARCTICA DIFFER?
The Arctic surrounds the North Pole and is a frozen ocean. Animals such as polar bears and arctic foxes live on the ice sheet. Antarctica surrounds the South Pole, is a frozen continent, and has few animals. The ocean around it is rich in nutrients and supports fish, seabirds, seals, and whales.

Chinstrap penguins gather on an iceberg in Antarctica

▲ PENGUINS
Several species of penguin live, feed, and breed in and around Antarctica. Their dense waterproof feathers and layers of fat help to keep them warm.

FIND OUT MORE ▶▶ Coasts 59 • Ice 58 • Mountains 45

MICROORGANISMS

Any living thing that is invisible to the naked eye and can be seen only under a microscope is called a microorganism. They include ▸▸ BACTERIA , protists, and some fungi, such as yeasts. ▸▸ VIRUSES are usually included, but they are not really living organisms.

WHAT IS A PROTIST?

This is a single-celled organism found in the sea, fresh water, soil, and in or on other living things. Animal-like protists, called protozoa, get their energy by eating food. They include ciliates— protists that move by beating hairlike fibers called cilia. Some protozoa cause diseases such as malaria. Plantlike protists, called algae, make their food by photosynthesis, and include ocean phytoplankton and green pond algae.

Mouth of Didinium opens wide to swallow prey whole

Paramecium is covered with cilia that beat rhythmically to make it move

Didinium moves by beating two rows of cilia

▲ DIDINIUM
Fresh water ciliate protist *Didinium* can kill and eat other protists bigger than itself. Here, it attacks *Paramecium*, another ciliate, immobilizing it with an explosive dart.

Needlelike mouthpart sucks up blood into this yellow fever mosquito

microbes

◄ YELLOW FEVER MOSQUITO
This tropical mosquito pierces human skin to feed on warm blood. It carries a virus that causes yellow fever, which is sometimes passed on as a mosquito feeds and can be fatal.

VIRUSES

Only a very powerful microscope can show the minute chemical package known as a virus. Many viruses cause disease. Viruses are active only once they have infected a living animal, plant, or bacterial cell.

HOW DO VIRUSES REPRODUCE?

A virus invades a living cell, hijacks its genes, and forces it to produce many new virus particles. These new particles then break out of the cell. Viruses are not regarded as living things because they cannot reproduce alone.

▲ COMMON COLD VIRUS
This is an adenovirus, one of the viruses that cause the common cold. Like all viruses, it consists of a thread, DNA or RNA, which carries the infection instructions. This is surrounded by a protective protein coat, which can be seen here.

BACTERIA

LOUIS PASTEUR (1822–1895)
French scientist Louis Pasteur founded the science of microbiology. He proved that microorganisms cause infectious diseases, developed vaccines, and discovered pasteurization (the heat-killing of bacteria in food).

The most abundant organisms on Earth, bacteria are found on land, in water, and in the air. Bacteria consist of one tiny cell. They have a protective cell wall, but, unlike other cells, lack a nucleus.

ARE ALL BACTERIA HARMFUL?

While some bacteria are harmful, such as those that cause diseases, others are useful. These include bacteria in our intestines that supply us with vitamins, those that are used to make foods, and soil bacteria that recycle nutrients from dead animals and plants.

Bacteria grouped together at the tip of a needle

BACTERIA ON NEEDLE ▶
This scanning electron micrograph (SEM) shows the tiny size of these rod-shaped bacteria (orange). They are clustered on the tip of a syringe needle, normally used for giving injections.

FIND OUT MORE ▸▸ Biology 72 • Cells 73 • Life on Earth 70–71

FUNGI

Neither plants nor animals, the fungi kingdom includes toadstools, puffballs, and some ▸▸MOLDS. Fungi feed on living or dead organisms by making them rot. Fungi are visible only when spore-bearing fruiting bodies form.

HOW DO FUNGI FEED?

Fungi absorb nutrients from plant or animal matter around them, which may be living or dead. They produce long, slender threads called hyphae that spread through their food. The hyphae release enzymes that break down the food into substances that the fungi can easily absorb.

HOW DO FUNGI REPRODUCE?

Most fungi reproduce by releasing tiny spores that then germinate (sprout) and grow into a new fungus. The spores are produced by, and released from, a fruiting body that is visible above the ground. Some fungi drop spores, which are blown away by the wind. Others shoot them out in an explosive burst.

ARE MUSHROOMS AND TOADSTOOLS THE SAME?

Toadstools are brightly colored and poisonous to eat, but mushrooms are usually edible and dull in color. Both toadstools and mushrooms are fruiting bodies (spore-bearing structures) produced by fungi. They belong to the same group, the Basidiomycetes, so scientists make no distinction between the two.

fungi

DON'T EAT! ▶
The bright red color of these fly agaric toadstool caps warns animals that they are poisonous. The caps, which are supported by stalks, produce spores. These spores are released from downward-hanging plates, or gills.

▲ **PUFFBALL**
When the puffball is mature, it forms in the top. The slightest knock then causes the puffball to shoot clouds of spores into the air.

▲ **BUDDING YEAST CELLS**
Yeasts reproduce by budding. New cells grow out like bubbles from parent cells, then separate.

> **FUNGI CLASSIFICATION**
>
> Scientists are continually revising the classification of the fungi kingdom (with more than 100,000 species), but currently they divide it into three groups:
> • Pin molds (Zygomycota);
>
> • Yeasts, molds, morels, and truffles (Ascomycota, or spore-shooters);
> • Smuts, rusts, jellies, mushrooms, and brackets (Basidiomycota, or spore-droppers).

MOLDS

Fungi called molds produce the woolly or furry growths found on rotting foods, such as bread and fruit. The growths are formed by threadlike hyphae that grow upward and release spores from their tips. These spores then sprout on other foods.

IS MOLD USEFUL?

Some molds are useful. *Penicillium*, for example, is a common blue mold that grows on fruit. It produces an antibiotic called penicillin, which is used to kill bacteria that cause harmful diseases. *Penicillium* molds are also used to flavor some cheeses.

◀ **BREAD MOLD**
Pin molds grow on starchy foods, such as bread, in a mass of gray hyphae with black tips that release spores. The spores float to other pieces of bread. Unseen here are hyphae growing into the bread and absorbing its nutrients.

PENICILLIN TABLETS ▶
This dish shows bacteria growing on agar jelly. The white tablets contain penicillin. Clear areas around the tablets show where penicillin has killed some of the bacteria.

ALGAE

Algae are plantlike organisms that make food by photosynthesis. All algae contain chlorophyll, which is green, but many are colored brown or red by other pigments. Most algae live in water.

ARE ALGAE AND SEAWEED THE SAME THING?
All seaweeds are algae, but not all algae are seaweeds. Seaweeds are easily visible, made of many cells, and grow in the sea. There are red, brown, and green forms. Many algae, such as diatoms, are microscopic and consist of a single cell.

DIATOMS ►
These single-celled algae float in the surface waters of oceans and lakes. Each species has its own distinctively patterned, glasslike outer casing.

Air bladders keep fronds floating near sea's surface

DO ALGAE LIVE ONLY IN WATER?
Most species of algae live in the sea, in lakes, or in ponds. Some single-celled green algae live in moist conditions on land, such as on tree trunks, on the surface of the soil, or on damp brickwork. Others live inside lichens.

◄ BLADDER WRACK
This seaweed, like many others, grows close to the seashore. Its leaflike fronds are anchored to rocks by a rootlike structure, or holdfast. Slimy mucus stops the fronds from drying out when they are exposed at low tide.

algae

BLADDER WRACK

ALGAE CLASSIFICATION

40,000 species of plantlike organisms. Single-celled types:
• Golden algae • Yellow-green algae • Diatoms • Dinoflagellates.

Multicellular types:
• Brown seaweeds • Red seaweeds and green algae (both seaweeds and single-celled forms).

▲ RED SEAWEED
Smaller than other seaweeds, red seaweeds contain a pigment that lets them photosynthesize in the dim light of deeper waters.

FIND OUT MORE ▶▶ Life on Earth 70–71 • Microorganisms 85

LICHENS

A lichen is not a single organism, but a combination of a fungus and a green alga. Lichens exist in extreme climates, from dry deserts to the icy Arctic. They grow on surfaces such as rock, bark, and soil.

FOLIOSE LICHEN

lichens

HOW DO FUNGI AND ALGAE LIVE IN LICHENS?
The fungus forms an outer layer that protects the alga beneath from drying out and shields it from harmful amounts of light. The alga makes its own food by photosynthesis, and shares it with the fungus. In return, the fungus supplies the alga with essential minerals, such as nitrogen. This beneficial relationship between two different species is called symbiosis.

▲ REINDEER EATING LICHEN
In the cold, harsh conditions of the Arctic tundra, lichens are an important source of food for grazing reindeer. In winter, they reach lichens by scraping away snow with their hooves.

FRUTICOSE LICHEN

▲ LICHENS
Two of the three main types of lichen—fruticose (shrubby) and foliose (leafy)—are seen here growing on tree bark. The third type is crustose (flat and crusty).

FIND OUT MORE ▶▶ Life on Earth 70–71

PLANTS

Plants are one of the five kingdoms of living things. They are made up of many cells and are usually rooted in soil. Their green leaves capture sunlight to make food by ▸◂ PHOTOSYNTHESIS, providing food either directly or indirectly for most other living things on Earth, as well as life-giving oxygen.

Leaf uses sunlight to make food for the seedling

GROWING PLANT ▶
An underground woodland scene reveals an oak seedling growing from a split acorn (oak seed). Although small, the seedling already shows the main features of a plant, including roots, a stem, buds, and leaves. Most species of plants, including flowering plants, grow from seeds. Each seed contains an embryo plant with its own food supply.

CAN PLANTS MOVE?
Plants cannot move around like animals, but they still show movements. Shoots grow; leaves turn toward the Sun. If a plant has flowers, they open and close. Climbing plants have fine tendrils, or stems, that reach out until they find something firm to grip onto.

WHICH ARE THE BIGGEST PLANTS?
Trees are the biggest of all plants. They grow so large because they are supported by a woody trunk that increases in width as the tree grows taller. The tallest tree, and the biggest living thing, is the Californian coast redwood, which reaches over 360 ft (110 m).

Leaf litter (dead leaves) rots on woodland floor and releases nutrients for plants

Stem supports the leaves, buds, and other parts above ground

Roots take in water and minerals for the growing oak seedling from the soil

Oak seed splits open as the embryo plant grows

PLANT CLASSIFICATION

So far, scientists have identified over 300,000 species of plants. These are divided into two groups:
• Plants that reproduce using spores, including mosses, ferns, horsetails, and four other phyla.
• Plants that reproduce using seeds, including flowering plants and conifers.

▲ ROOT HAIRS
Magnified 200 times here, root hairs are tiny projections from a plant's root. They provide a massive surface area through which the root can quickly and efficiently absorb essential water and minerals.

WHY DO PLANTS HAVE ROOTS?
Plants have roots for two main reasons. Roots anchor the plant in the soil, and prevent it from being blown away by strong winds. They also take up water and minerals, such as nitrogen and sulfur, from the soil. Plants need water to replace that lost by **▶▶ TRANSPIRATION**, and minerals to make substances essential for life.

HOW DO PLANTS DEFEND THEMSELVES?
Plants cannot escape from hungry plant-eaters, but they have evolved a wide range of defenses. Some have thorns or spines that cut into an animal's skin and will pierce its mouth if eaten. Others produce chemicals that taste terrible and may be poisonous. Some have tiny hairs on their leaves that stop leaf-eating insects from reaching the leaf's surface.

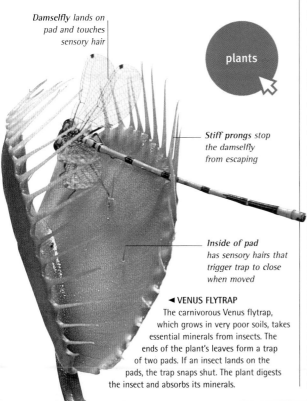

Damselfly lands on pad and touches sensory hair

plants

Stiff prongs stop the damselfly from escaping

Inside of pad has sensory hairs that trigger trap to close when moved

◀ VENUS FLYTRAP
The carnivorous Venus flytrap, which grows in very poor soils, takes essential minerals from insects. The ends of the plant's leaves form a trap of two pads. If an insect lands on the pads, the trap snaps shut. The plant digests the insect and absorbs its minerals.

PHOTOSYNTHESIS

Animals have to find and eat food, but plants are able to make their own by using sunlight energy. This process, called photosynthesis, provides plants with the energy and raw materials for growth.

WHAT HAPPENS IN PHOTOSYNTHESIS?
The leaves of plants trap sunlight energy, which changes carbon dioxide gas and water into an energy-rich food called glucose. Glucose provides the plant with energy, and is also used to make substances such as cellulose, which forms the plant's cell walls.

Leaf absorbs sunlight

MAKING GLUCOSE ▶
Leaf cells absorb sunlight energy during photosynthesis. They use it to turn carbon dioxide, from the air, and water, absorbed by the roots, into glucose molecules. Oxygen is released as a waste product.

Glucose is carried away

Water enters via the stem from the roots

Carbon dioxide enters from the air

Oxygen escapes into the air

▲ CHLOROPLASTS
The green structures seen in this microscopic view of leaf cells are chloroplasts. They contain chlorophyll, a green pigment that traps sunlight energy.

TRANSPIRATION

Leaves constantly lose water by evaporation through tiny pores, or stomata, that also let carbon dioxide into, and oxygen out of, the leaf. This water loss, called transpiration, creates a force that helps draw up more water from the roots.

WHAT IS THE VASCULAR SYSTEM?
Water and nutrients are moved through a plant by its vascular system. This consists of two types of microscopic tubes—xylem and phloem. Xylem carries water and minerals from the roots to the rest of the plant. Phloem carries nutrients, such as glucose, from where they are made to other parts of the plant.

PINEAPPLE SAGE

Water escapes from the leaves

Leaf stalk carries water into the leaf

Roots absorb water from the soil

Water is drawn up xylem vessels in the stem

▲ STOMA AT NIGHT
Seen in microscopic view, this stoma (pore) in the leaf's surface is surrounded by two guard cells. At night, these guard cells close the stoma.

▲ STOMA IN DAYLIGHT
During the day, the guard cells open the stoma. This lets carbon dioxide enter the leaf and allows water vapor to escape, during transpiration.

▲ TRANSPIRATION STREAM
Water lost from leaves by transpiration is replaced by water from the roots. An unbroken column of water flows from the roots up to the leaves.

FIND OUT MORE ▶▶ Flowering Plants 92–93 • Non-Flowering Plants 90–91 • Trees 94–95

NON FLOWERING PLANTS

Mosses, ferns, and their relatives are plants that do not produce flowers but reproduce by means of ▶▶ SPORES. Most live in shady or damp habitats. ▶▶ CONIFERS are non flowering plants that reproduce by making seeds.

Sporophyte releases spores that grow into a new moss

HOW DO FERNS GROW?

The stem, or rhizome, of a fern grows horizontally through the soil. Tiny curled-up fronds (leaves) grow from small buds on the rhizome. The buds unroll and the frond expands. The fronds of some ferns grow 20 ft (6 m) long, but others reach only ½ in (13 mm).

HOW DOES MOSS LIVE WITHOUT ROOTS?

Most mosses grow in short clumps, or cushions. They do not have true roots, but short, slender growths, called rhizoids. Rootlike rhizoids anchor moss to soil, rock, or bark, but do not draw up water. Instead, leaves absorb moisture in the air.

TREE FERN ▶
Dicksonia antarctica is a large tree fern that grows on cool, shady forest floors in Australia. Tree ferns have a large, fibrous trunk, topped with a crown of fronds (leaves). This species can grow 3–10 ft (1–3 m) tall.

Young bud unfurls into a frond, or branched leaf

non flowering plants

◀ LIVERWORT
This plant is closely related to mosses, and is found only in moist habitats. It grows on soil, trees, and wet rocks. The leaves of some species have a waxy coating to reduce water loss.

▲ MOSS REPRODUCTION
The leafy tips of mosses produce male and female sex cells. Male sex cells swim through water on the surface of the plant to reach and fertilize female cells. Fertilization produces a stalked sporophyte, or spore capsule, that scatters spores into the air.

Tree fern fronds can grow 5–8 ft (1.5–2.5 m) long

CLASSIFICATION OF NON FLOWERING PLANTS

There are 11 main divisions of non flowering plants:
• Liverworts • Mosses
• Hornworts • Whisk ferns
• Club mosses • Horsetails

• Ferns • Conifers • Cycads
• Ginkgo • Gnetophytes. The last four form a group called gymnosperms—they produce seeds instead of spores.

SPORES

Non flowering plants reproduce by releasing large numbers of tiny spores. These minute organisms consist of one or a few cells inside a tough coat.

WHY IS SPORE DISPERSAL IMPORTANT?

Many non-flowering plants rely on wind to carry their reproductive spores as far away as possible. This reduces competition with the parent plant for light, water, and important nutrients. If a spore lands in a damp place, it germinates (sprouts) and grows into a new plant.

FERN SPORES ▶
Fern spores develop in protective caps called sori (singular sorus). Sori are attached to the underside of fronds. Large ferns make and release millions of spores each year.

Sorus

INSIDE A SORUS ▶
Each sorus contains a cluster of spore-producing sporangia. In dry conditions, sporangia open and scatter their spores.

Sporangium

CONIFERS

Trees and shrubs whose seeds develop in woody cones are called conifers. The 550 species include pines, firs, and cedars. Conifers form dense forests in colder, northern regions. Most keep their leaves all year long.

▲ PINE FOREST
The branches of pines and many other conifers slope downward. This helps winter snows to slide off, preventing damage to the tree.

▲ STONE PINE CONE
Seeds mature inside the female cone, protected by its scales. In warm, dry conditions, the cone opens to release its seeds.

PINE SEEDS

HOW DO CONIFERS PRODUCE SEEDS?

Conifers have male and female cones. The male cones release pollen grains (male sex cells), which are blown by the wind. If pollen lands on the female cones, it fertilizes the female egg cells. The fertilized eggs develop into seeds. After one or two years, when the seeds have matured, the female cone opens up. It drops winged seeds, which germinate wherever they land if conditions are favorable.

WHY DO SOME CONIFERS HAVE NEEDLE-SHAPED LEAVES?

Leaves shaped like needles help conifers survive in cold, harsh climates. The leaves are tough and coated with a waxy outer coat, or cuticle. The narrow shape, toughness, and cuticles all help the leaves withstand high winds and extreme temperatures. They also reduce water loss.

DO OTHER PLANTS HAVE CONES?

A group of plants called cycads have large seed-producing cones that can grow to more than 22 in (55 cm) long. They have sturdy trunks topped by long, divided leaves, and look more like palm trees than conifers. Cycads grow in tropical and subtropical regions. They are descended from a group of plants that flourished 250 million years ago. Today, there are 140 species of cycads.

Male cones are soft, and drop off after shedding pollen

SCOTS PINE ▶
Pine trees, like most conifers, are evergreen and keep their leaves throughout the year. The long, spiky needles stay on the tree for at least two years.

Female cones are woody, and open to release their seeds

FIND OUT MORE ▶▶ Climate 62–63 • Habitats 82–84 • Plants 88–89 • Trees 94–95

FLOWERING PLANTS

This is the most abundant and widespread group of plants on Earth. Flowering plants are found in most habitats, from deserts to polar regions, and include species of trees, shrubs, and herbs. The flowers are the reproductive structures that produce new plants.

Sticky stigma receives pollen during pollination

Petals are often brightly colored

Anther covered by pollen

Ovary contains the ovum, or female sex cell

flowering plants

◄ INSIDE A FLOWER
The petals protect the flower, and also attract pollinating animals. The anthers, carried by filaments, produce pollen. Pollen grains contain male sex cells. The stigma and ovary form the female part of the flower.

WHAT IS INSIDE A FLOWER?
The male sex organs (anthers and filaments) surround the female sex organs (ovaries). Flower parts are arranged in rings from the outer petals to the inner ovary. Their purpose is to encourage ▸▸ POLLINATION so that ▸▸ SEEDS can be made.

WHY ARE GRASSES SO IMPORTANT?
The 8,000 species of grasses are plants with small flowers. Grasses provide food for many grazing animals, including buffalo and zebra. Grasses can also provide food such as grains as rice, wheat, and corn.

TYPES OF FLOWERING PLANTS

There are some 250,000 species of flowering plants. These make up over 80 percent of all plants on Earth, and are divided into two groups:
• The 70,000 species of monocots, include grasses, lilies, irises, orchids, and palms.

• The 180,000 species of dicots include roses, magnolias, cacti, daisies, and lupins, and most types of tree.

MONOCOTS AND DICOTS

Flowering plants are divided into two groups. Monocots have one cotyledon (seed leaf), which is the food store of a seed. They also have leaves with parallel veins, and flower parts in multiples of three. Dicots have two cotyledons, leaves with branching, netlike veins, and flower parts in groups of four or five.

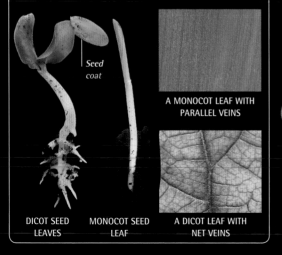

Seed coat

A MONOCOT LEAF WITH PARALLEL VEINS

A DICOT LEAF WITH NET VEINS

DICOT SEED LEAVES

MONOCOT SEED LEAF

HOGWEED

FLOWER TYPES ▶
Some plants have one flower each. Others have groups of flowers, called flower heads. Hogweed has small flowers arranged in umbrella-like clusters, called umbels. The head of a sunflower is made up of many tiny flowers grouped together. Mullein flowers are arranged in a tall spire.

SUNFLOWER

MULLEIN

POLLINATION

The transfer of pollen from a male anther to a female stigma is called pollination. If male and female sex cells from the same species come together, fertilization takes place and seeds are made. Pollination occurs in various ways, such as by wind or by animals.

▲ INSECT POLLINATION
Yellow pollen sticks to this bee's legs as it feeds on nectar. It will be passed to the next flower it visits.

WHAT IS NECTAR?
Many flowers attract pollinating animals with a sweet, sugary liquid called nectar. If an animal feeds on the nectar, it picks up pollen and carries it to other flowers that it lands on.

WHAT IS WIND POLLINATION?
Pollination in some flowers occurs when pollen is blown from other flowers by the wind. Animal-pollinated flowers are strongly scented and brightly colored, but the flowers of wind-pollinated plants, such as grasses, are often small, with no petals.

FERTILIZATION

When a pollen grain lands on a stigma of the same species, it grows a tube into the ovule (seed-forming structure). A male sex cell travels down the pollen tube and fertilizes the ovum (female sex cell) to produce an embryo plant.

Stigma — *Pollen*
Style — *Pollen tube*
Ovary — *Ovule*
Ovum (female sex cell) — *Male nucleus*

◄ POLLEN GRAIN
The spikes on this pollen grain help it stick to animals. Each grain contains a male sex cell that fertilizes the female ovum.

SEEDS

If fertilization occurs in a flowering plant, a seed forms inside the flower's ovary. The seed consists of a tiny embryo plant, a food store for the embryo, and a protective coat.

WHAT IS A FRUIT?
As the seeds of plants develop, the ovary surrounding the seed develops into a fruit, such as a tomato or a pea pod. Fruits protect seeds, and help disperse them away from the parent plant so that new plants have enough water and light to grow.

First leaves make food using sunlight energy

◄ WIND DISPERSAL
Dandelion seeds hang from parachute-like fruit. When blown by the wind, the parachutes float off into the air and carry the seeds far from the parent plant.

BEAN SEEDLING ►
Just a few days after germination, the bean seedling's roots have grown down into the soil, and its shoot has grown upward toward the Sun.

Seed

Roots take in water and minerals from the soil

RASPBERRY　　　**LOVE-IN-A-MIST**

▲ SEED DISPERSAL IN FRUIT
The seeds of juicy fruits, such as raspberries, are dispersed in droppings of fruit-eating animals. The seeds of dry fruits, such as love-in-the-mist, are spread by wind, by sticking to animal coats, or by the fruit bursting open.

WHAT IS GERMINATION?
The first growth stage of an embryo plant from a seed is called germination. When there is enough sunlight and water, the seed germinates (sprouts), and the embryo plant starts to grow. Until it develops leaves, the seedling depends on the seed's food store.

FIND OUT MORE ►► Life on Earth 70–71 • Non Flowering Plants 90–91 • Plants 88–89 • Trees 94–95

TREES

These tall, seed-producing plants have a single woody stem, called a trunk, which supports their great weight. They live for many years and do not die in winter. The largest group of trees is broad-leaved trees.

WHY ARE TREES SO IMPORTANT?
Trees release oxygen into the atmosphere for other organisms to breathe in. The roots of trees bind soil together, preventing it from being washed away. Trees also provide food and habitats for many animals, and wood for fuel, lumber, and many other products.

HOW DO TREES GROW?
Trees grow in two ways. Special cells at the tips of twigs divide, making the twigs grow. Also, a layer of cells under the bark, the cambium, divides, widening the trunk and branches. The new cells that the cambium makes form a visible ring inside the trunk.

WHAT ARE BROAD-LEAVED TREES?
Unlike conifers, with their needle-shpaed leaves, these trees have wide, flat leaves. Many are ▶▶ DECIDUOUS TREES that lose their leaves in fall, but the broad-leaved trees of a tropical rainforest are evergreen. The mass of leaves of adjacent trees form a ▶▶ CANOPY.

▲ EVERGREEN RAINFOREST
The Amazon rainforest is the largest in the world. It contains about one-fifth of all flowering plant species.

Heartwood contains mostly dead cells

Sapwood is made up of living cells and carries water and minerals

Growth ring indicates one year's growth

Cambium

Phloem carries food up or down the trunk

Fibrous bark consists of dead cells and protects the trunk

INDIAN BEAN TREE
(SIMPLE LEAF)

HERCULES CLUB
(COMPOUND LEAF)

▲ TYPES OF LEAVES
Broad-leaved trees have one of two types of leaves. A simple leaf is undivided and has its own leaf stalk. A compound leaf is divided up into several smaller leaflets that are attached to the main leaf stalk.

trees

◀ TREE TRUNK CROSS-SECTION
The inside of a tree trunk has rings of outer sapwood and inner heartwood. Both consist of strength-giving cells called xylem. Sapwood xylem also carries water and minerals up the tree. Outside the sapwood are phloem cells, which carry food, surrounded by bark.

TREE CLASSIFICATION

Trees are divided into three groups: broad-leaved trees, palms, and conifers.
• Broad-leaved trees are the largest group, with over 10,000 species. They are dicot flowering plants, and the veins in their leaves branch out like a net.
• Palm trees, with about 2,800 species, are monocot flowering plants. The veins in their leaves are always parallel.
• Conifers, with 550 species, have cones instead of flowers.

DECIDUOUS TREES

Trees that lose their leaves in the fall are called deciduous. They grow in temperate places that have warm summers and cool or cold winters.

WHY DO THESE TREES SHED THEIR LEAVES?

When trees shed their leaves, they stop growing. This helps them conserve energy during winter, when there is not enough sunlight to make food. Shedding leaves also helps trees save water, since it stops water from evaporating.

WHY DO DECIDUOUS LEAVES CHANGE COLOR?

In summer, these leaves are packed with the green pigment (coloring) chlorophyll, which captures sunlight energy. In fall, chlorophyll breaks down and is reabsorbed by the tree, revealing previously hidden pigments, such as reds, yellows and oranges.

CHANGING LEAF COLOR ▶
The leaves of deciduous trees turn from green to orange, yellow, or red with the coming of fall, or in very dry weather conditions.

PERSIAN IRONWOOD LEAVES

▲ **DECIDUOUS TREE IN SUMMER**
This lime tree is bathed in summer sunshine. The tree uses its mass of green leaves to trap sunlight energy to make food.

DECIDUOUS TREE IN AUTUMN ▲
In fall, temperatures are lower and there is less daylight. The lime tree's leaves turn orange or brown and start to drop.

Sunlight filters through to reach the forest floor

Palm tree has broad, branched leaves

CANOPY

The upper part of the trees in any forest or woodland is called the canopy. It is made up of their branches, twigs, and leaves. Tropical rainforest trees form a dense canopy that is home to many animals.

WHY ARE RAINFOREST TREES SO TALL?

In hot, steamy rainforests, the tightly packed trees grow rapidly and to great heights. This is because they are all competing for sunlight. The taller the tree, the more light its leaves will receive. Some trees can reach heights of up to 200 ft (60 m).

WHAT IS AN EPIPHYTE?

An epiphyte is a plant that grows on a larger one without harming it. Many epiphytes live high up in the rainforest canopy, firmly anchored by their roots to tree trunks and branches. In the canopy, epiphytes receive much more light than the plants on the forest floor, and more rainwater.

◀ **REACH FOR THE SUN**
This is the view that someone standing on the rainforest floor would see when looking upward. A palm tree in the shrub layer uses its large leaves to trap sparse sunlight filtering down through the canopy above.

LAYERS OF A RAINFOREST

Rainforests are made up of distinct layers. In the emergent layer, the very tallest trees stick out from the canopy. Beneath the canopy is an understory of smaller trees and a shrub layer of big-leaved plants that can live in low-light conditions. Below this is the dark forest floor, where there are fewer, smaller plants.

Emergent layer

Canopy

Understory

Shrub layer

Floor

Evergreen, broad-leaved tree

Canopy

FIND OUT MORE ▶▶ Flowering Plants 92–93 • Non Flowering Plants 90–91 • Plants 88–89

ANIMALS

Animals are grouped into two main types—vertebrates, with an inner skeleton, including a backbone, and invertebrates, without a backbone. As many as ten million species (different kinds) of animals—all with their own modes of ▶ BEHAVIOR —live on Earth.

WHICH FEATURES DO ALL ANIMALS HAVE IN COMMON?

All animals have bodies made up of many different cells and eat other organisms to survive. Unlike plants or fungi, which are rooted in one place, animals move around to find food, escape from enemies, and find a mate. Almost all animals breathe oxygen, either from the air or from water.

WHAT IS THE WORLD'S FASTEST ANIMAL?

The world's fastest animal is the peregrine falcon, which can exceed 125 mph (200 km/h) when diving through the air after prey. The fastest powered flight is that of the spine-tailed swift, at up to 105 mph (170 km/h). The quickest animal in water is the sailfish, which can swim at up to 68 mph (109 km/h).

WHAT ARE WARM-BLOODED ANIMALS?

Warm-blooded animals are those that generate their own body heat from food. Birds and mammals are warm-blooded. All other animals, including fish, reptiles, amphibians, and insects, are cold-blooded. Their body temperatures rise and fall with the temperature of their surroundings. These animals are less active in cold weather but require less food.

HOW BIG DO ANIMALS GROW?

Some animals grow to enormous sizes. The world's biggest animal, the blue whale, may reach 90 ft (27 m) long and weigh almost 165 tons (150 metric tons). On the other hand, some animals are too small to be seen with the naked eye. The world's tiniest animals are creatures called mesozoans. They consist of fewer than 50 cells and measure less than ¹/₅₀ in (0.5 mm) long.

▲ CHAMELEON
A chameleon is camouflaged to blend in with its surroundings and moves around slowly to avoid detection by its predators and prey. To feed, the chameleon shoots out its tongue at a lightning-fast speed to hit insects before they have time to react.

animals

CHEETAHS ▶
The cheetah is the world's fastest land animal, capable of speeds of up to 60 mph (96 km/h) in short bursts. It hunts by ambush, creeping as close as it can to its prey before rushing in for the kill.

Muscles drive the animal forward after prey

Long legs increase stride and speed

▲ COLD SHOWER
The Asian elephant is the world's second-largest land animal (the African elephant is the largest). Like all mammals, it is warm-blooded. Due to their size, elephants can have trouble keeping cool. One solution is to seek water. Elephants also flap their ears to cool the blood flowing through them.

◀ WORKING TOGETHER
Leaf-cutter ants live in colonies of closely related individuals, all hatched from eggs laid by a single queen. Most become worker ants.

BEHAVIOR

In order to survive, all animals must eat and avoid being eaten. They are also driven to reproduce so their species does not die out. Most animal behavior is geared to these basic goals. Some behavior is learned; the rest is controlled by instinct.

HOW DO ANIMALS DEFEND THEMSELVES?

Animals behave in many different ways to escape danger. Some are camouflaged to blend in with their surroundings. Behavior such as staying still completes their disguise. Some species defend themselves with more complex behavior, such as pretending to be injured or dead. Hedgehogs and armadillos roll into a ball to ward off predators.

HOW IMPORTANT IS INSTINCT?

Instinct plays a major part in the behavior of animals, especially animals that are not reared by their parents. For example, when danger threatens, snails instinctively withdraw inside their shells. Animals also learn by trial and error, repeating actions that are productive and abandoning ones that are not.

▲ PUFFERFISH
Pufferfish defend themselves by inflating their bodies with water. Along with their spines, this makes them harder for bigger fish to swallow. Many other species are also covered with spines to protect them from even the largest of predators.

▼ IMPRINTING
Baby birds such as goslings (young geese) instinctively follow the first animal they see after hatching. This is usually their own mother, but goslings have also been known to waddle around after humans and dogs.

WHY DO ANIMALS FOLLOW REGULAR CYCLES?

All animals follow regular cycles to help them survive. Many creatures are active by day, when their senses work best. Others come out at night to avoid predators, or take advantage of feeding opportunities. Most animals also follow yearly cycles, usually bearing young when food is abundant.

CLOWNFISH ▶
Clownfish hide from their enemies among the stinging tentacles of sea anemones. The fish's skin releases chemicals that stop the anemone's cells from firing. Clownfish are found in tropical seas around the world.

FIND OUT MORE ▶▶ Biology 72 • Life on Earth 70–71

FEEDING

All animals must eat other organisms to survive. Animals can be divided into two main groups, according to their feeding habits: ▶▶CARNIVORES (meat-eaters) and ▶▶HERBIVORES (plant-eaters).

WHAT IS AN OMNIVORE?

Most animals eat either meat or plants, but omnivores eat both. The word omnivore means "everything-eater." Bears and pigs are omnivores—so are humans. In our diet we carry on the traditions of our early ancestors, who killed game and also gathered berries and nuts.

GRIZZLY BEAR ▶
Bears eat many foods, including fruit, nuts, roots, honey, carrion (dead animals), small mammals, and salmon, as shown here.

WHAT IS FILTER-FEEDING?

This feeding method works by sifting large amounts of small organisms from water. It is a bit like using a sieve to catch prey. Filter-feeders come in a variety of shapes and sizes—barnacles, flamingos, and baleen whales (including the blue whale) all feed in this way.

◀ SCAVENGERS
Hyenas and vultures are scavengers—meat-eaters that get their food from the abandoned kills of others. This zebra was killed by lions, which have already eaten their fill and left.

feeding

CARNIVORES

Most carnivores are predators—animals that hunt other animals for food. Predators usually have sharp teeth, claws, or beaks to tear apart their prey. Animal flesh is nourishing, so predators do not have to kill very often. Meat is also easy to digest.

HOW DO PREDATORS KILL THEIR PREY?

Top predators such as lions, sharks, and eagles rely on strength and speed to overcome their victims. Smaller or weaker hunters may rely on stealth or special techniques to capture prey. Some predators, such as wolves, hunt in packs. Spiders spin webs to tangle up victims. Rattlesnakes kill their prey with venom.

TOOTHY GRIN ▶
A shark's teeth are sharp and pointed to rip prey to pieces. They grow in rows and are continually shed and replaced. Some species may go through as many as 30,000 teeth in a lifetime. Not all sharks are predators—the largest, the whale shark, is a filter-feeder.

HERBIVORES

The jaws, teeth, and stomachs of herbivores are designed to tackle tough plant food. Compared with meat, plants are not very nourishing, so many herbivores spend long hours feeding.

Toucan's bill is extra-large for probing through vegetation

◀ TOUCAN
Some birds, such as the toucan, specialize in eating fruit. Packed with sugars, fruit is much more nourishing than leaves and far easier to digest. However, it is also more scattered and harder to find. Many fruit-eating birds sometimes have to eat insects. It is only in tropical rainforests that birds can find fruit year-round.

HOW DO HERBIVORES DIGEST THEIR FOOD?

Plants contain tough cellulose, which is hard to digest. Many herbivores' stomachs are filled with microbes, which break down cellulose. Some plant-eaters, such as cattle, have stomachs with several chambers. After passing through some chambers, food is returned to the mouth for more chewing to help break it down.

HOW DO HERBIVORES AVOID CARNIVORES?

Herbivores do not need quick wits to capture their food, but they must be swift or have some means of defense to avoid being eaten by predators. Many are camouflaged to blend in with their surroundings, so that hunters do not notice them. Others have tough skin, spines, or even poison to put off enemies.

FIND OUT MORE ▶▶ Digestion 144–145 • Plants 88–89 • Teeth 143

Animals use their senses to find out about the world around them. Most have the same five senses as humans, but some have extra senses, such as **ECHOLOCATION** .

DO ANIMALS HAVE BETTER SENSES THAN US?
Many animals have far sharper senses than humans. Sight is our most important sense, but birds such as falcons have much sharper vision. Some insects can detect ultraviolet light, which we cannot see. A bloodhound's nose is many times more sensitive than a human's. Bats, whales, and elephants can detect very high or low sounds that we cannot hear.

Nostrils pick up scent to lead cat to prey

Whiskers enable the cat to feel movement even in total darkness

NIGHT PROWLER ▲
Many nocturnal predators, including cats, have a reflective layer at the back of their eyes, which helps to gather light.

Lens focuses light onto sensitive cells to help form a clear image

Antenna detects scent particles floating in the air

◄ COMPOUND EYES
Insects such as flies have huge compound eyes made up of many lenses. Each lens may be used to build up a larger picture. Although compound eyes do not provide increased clarity, they are extremely sensitive to movement.

Hairlike projections increase the sense of touch

CAN ANIMALS SEE AT NIGHT?
Some animals can see quite clearly at night even when there is no moon. The large eyes of nocturnal hunters, such as owls, are designed to make the most of very dim light. Many animals active at night also have extremely good senses of hearing and smell.

WHICH ANIMALS HAVE EXTRA SENSES?
Some aquatic animals, including sharks, can pick up tiny electrical signals given off by their prey. It is believed that many migratory animals can detect Earth's magnetic field to help find their way.

senses

Forked tongue picks up scent particles

TASTING THE AIR ►
Snakes pick up scent particles in the air with their flickering tongues. These reptiles do not have ears, but their sensitive skin can detect vibrations passing through the ground.

Heat-sensitive pits work like extra eyes

SEEING WITH SOUND ►
Insect-eating bats have very sensitive hearing that allows them to hunt and navigate in darkness using echolocation. They make high-pitched sounds, then swivel their ears to pinpoint the source of echoes, which lead them to their prey.

ECHOLOCATION

Bats, whales, and dolphins, which hunt in darkness or murky water, make sounds, then listen for echoes to track their prey. The same technique helps them to navigate and avoid collisions with objects.

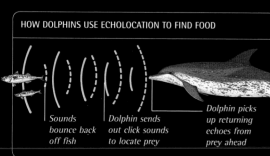
HOW DOLPHINS USE ECHOLOCATION TO FIND FOOD

Sounds bounce back off fish

Dolphin sends out click sounds to locate prey

Dolphin picks up returning echoes from prey ahead

HOW DOES ECHOLOCATION HELP WITH HUNTING?
Hunting bats and dolphins make streams of clicking sounds, which spread out through the air or water. The sound vibrations bounce back off objects such as flying insects or shoaling fish. The hunter uses its sharp hearing to listen for the returning echoes. These allow it to pinpoint the whereabouts of its victims, so that it can home in on its prey.

Moths and other insects make up most bat prey

FIND OUT MORE ▶▶ Ear 141 • Eye 140 • Mouth 142 • Nose 143

COMMUNICATION

Animals communicate with their own kind or other species to coordinate the search for food, attract mates, bring up young, or escape from danger. Various species send signals using sight, sounds, body language, touch, scent, complex chemicals, or a combination of all of these.

WHEN DO ANIMALS USE VISUAL SIGNALS?
Close-range visual signals are used to send a variety of messages, such as "Food is near" or "Keep away!" Birds from peacocks to robins attract mates using bright colors. Fireflies do the same with light. The white flash of a fleeing rabbit's tail warns others of danger.

WHY DO ANIMALS COMMUNICATE WITH SOUND?
Sound signals carry over considerable distances and give information immediately. Songbirds and howler monkeys call to establish territories. Whales, frogs, and crickets sing to attract a mate. Vervet monkeys warn others of different enemies by using different sounds.

▲ SNAKE MIMIC
Visual signals can be used for defense. This hawkmoth caterpillar has evolved a tail that looks like a snake's head. Predators are scared off by the disguise, even though the caterpillar is harmless.

communication

DO ANIMALS ALWAYS TELL THE TRUTH?
When animals communicate with their enemies, their messages are not always truthful. Dogs, cats, and other animals raise their hackles, arch their backs, or puff themselves up to look bigger. Opossums play dead to fool their enemies. Some animals mimic (copy) the appearance of dangerous creatures.

WHY DO ANIMALS USE PHEROMONES?
Animals use scent signals called pheromones to affect the behavior of others. These complex chemicals, which include hormones, are most often transferred by air. Female moths release pheromones to attract males. In ant, bee, and termite colonies, the queen releases pheromones to convey all sorts of messages to the rest of the colony.

▲ BODY LANGUAGE
A wolf can give over 20 different messages by raising or flattening its ears, back, tail, and neck hairs, or by baring or hiding its teeth.

◄ COMPLEX COMMUNICATION
Intelligent mammals such as chimpanzees communicate with others using sounds, scent, touch, body language, and facial expressions. Chimps can even be taught to communicate with humans using sign language.

▲ CHEMICAL CONTROL
Pheromones released by a queen bee prevent other fertile females from developing. If the queen is removed and the pheromones are no longer present, new queens are reared. One of these will eventually take over the hive.

FIND OUT MORE ►► Senses 99 • Sound 176–177

REPRODUCTION

All animals produce offspring so their species can continue. Some animals reproduce sexually, by mating with a partner; others reproduce asexually, without mating. Animals grow up in different ways, including by ▸▸ METAMORPHOSIS. Care of offspring varies—some young fend for themselves.

Snake egg
has leathery,
waterproof shell

Baby snake looks
like tiny version
of the adult

HOW DO ANIMALS ATTRACT MATES?
During the breeding season, animals advertise their readiness to mate by using special calls, scents, and other signals. Some animals use elaborate displays or courtship rituals to woo a wary mate. A few creatures, such as earthworms, are hermaphrodites (both male and female), which makes it easier to find a mate.

PUMA FAMILY ▼
Female mammals care for their young and feed them on a rich, nutritious food—milk. Some mammal babies take only a few weeks to grow up. Puma cubs stay with their mother for two years, learning how to hunt for themselves.

BORN INDEPENDENT ▲
Young snakes are on their own from the moment they hatch. Snakes lay large numbers of eggs so that at least some of their offspring make it to adulthood.

reproduction

◄ ASEXUAL REPRODUCTION
A sea anemone divides to form two individuals. Some insects, such as aphids, can also reproduce asexually, when their unfertilized eggs develop into young.

WHY DO SOME ANIMALS GIVE BIRTH RATHER THAN LAY EGGS?
Animals born live are more likely to survive than those that hatch out of eggs. While developing inside their mother, babies are at less risk of being eaten than eggs.

WHY LOOK AFTER YOUNG?
Animals care for offspring to improve their chances of survival. More of these babies survive to adulthood than those whose parents leave them to fend for themselves.

4. New adult
emerges after
one week

1. Adult 7-spot
ladybug lays
groups of eggs
on leaves

▲ LADYBUG LIFE CYCLE
Like all beetles, ladybugs go through complete metamorphosis, changing directly from their larval to their adult form.

3. Dormant
(sleeping) pupa
formed by each larva
a month after hatching

2. Larva hatches
after a week

METAMORPHOSIS

Some baby animals are miniature copies of their adult relatives, but some look nothing like their parents. They go through an amazing transformation, known as a metamorphosis, before they reach adulthood.

WHAT IS COMPLETE METAMORPHOSIS?
Complete metamorphosis is the change in one step from larva to adult. Moths and butterflies undergo complete metamorphosis. Their caterpillars feed and grow, then enter a resting stage as pupae. Inside the pupal case, the caterpillar transforms into a winged adult. The way tadpoles become frogs is also complete metamorphosis.

Emerging
dragonfly
breaking out
of its old skin

Empty case
left behind
on plant stem

EMERGING DRAGONFLY ►
Young dragonflies shed their skin several times as they grow, emerging from their last molt as adults. Gradual change like this is called incomplete metamorphosis.

FIND OUT MORE ▸▸ Amphibians 114–115 • Insects 110–111 • Mammals 120–123

INVERTEBRATES

About 95 percent of all animals are invertebrates—animals without bones—and many are tiny or even microscopic.

Hard exoskeleton

Anus
expels waste

invertebrates

HOW DO ANIMALS SURVIVE WITHOUT BONES?
Insects, crustaceans, and many other invertebrates have a hard outer case called an exoskeleton. This protects them against blows and predators, and keeps them from drying out. Slugs, leeches, and jellyfish have soft bodies and no exoskeleton. The pressure of fluids inside their bodies maintains their shape.

Tube feet
pass food to the mouth and help the animal move

DO INVERTEBRATES' EXOSKELETONS GROW?
The hard exoskeletons of insects and creatures such as crabs do not grow with the rest of the body. As the animal grows, its exoskeleton gets too tight—so it sheds it from time to time. Underneath is a new, slightly bigger, and looser case. The animal pumps itself up with fluid before the case has time to harden.

INSIDE A SEA URCHIN ▶
Like most invertebrates, sea urchins have relatively complex internal organs. Food is broken down using five teeth contained in a central structure known as Aristotle's lantern, before passing into the intestine.

Hemal system
transports blood around the body

Tooth

Muscles
operate the movement of the teeth

Intestine
digests food

▼ INVERTEBRATE GROUPS
Invertebrates include more than 30 different phyla (major groups) of animals. Some of the most important ones are shown here.

ECHINODERMS
6,000 species include starfish, sea urchins, and sea cucumbers.

CNIDARIANS
10,000 species include corals, sea anemones, and jellyfish.

SPONGES
10,000 species include tube sponges and glass sponges.

INSECTS
800,000 species include beetles, flies, and ants.

MOLLUSKS
70,000 species include slugs, snails, mussels, and squid.

ANNELID WORMS
9,000 species include earthworms and leeches.

FIND OUT MORE ▶▶ Crustaceans 109 • Insects 110–111 • Mollusks 106

VERTEBRATES

All vertebrates have an inner skeleton, including a skull, backbone, and ribs. These complex animals vary in size from less than 0.4 in (1 cm) to over 100 ft (30 m) long.

vertebrates

WHAT DOES THE SKELETON DO?
The skeleton is a strong frame that supports the body and anchors the muscles. Bones such as ribs protect the heart and other delicate parts, and the skull shields the brain. Most vertebrates have bony skeletons, but shark skeletons are rubbery cartilage.

HOW MANY LIMBS DO VERTEBRATES HAVE?
Most vertebrates apart from fish have four limbs. In birds and bats, the front limbs evolved (developed) into wings for flying. A fish's limbs are its fins, which vary in number between species. Snakes evolved from four-legged ancestors millions of years ago.

▲ PYTHON SKELETON
Like all vertebrates, snakes have a skull, backbone, and ribs. The backbone is made of many individual bones called vertebrae.

▼ VERTEBRATE GROUPS
Fish are the largest vertebrate group, with more species than all the other groups put together.

REPTILES
8,000 species include crocodiles, lizards, snakes, and turtles.

BIRDS
9,500 species include eagles, gulls, parrots, ducks, and perching birds.

MAMMALS
5,000 species include tigers, rodents, bats, whales, and primates.

AMPHIBIANS
6,000 species include frogs, toads, newts, and salamanders.

FISH
29,000 species include bony fish, sharks, rays, and lampreys.

FIND OUT MORE ▶▶ Animals 96–97 • Skeleton 130–131

Jellyfish, sea anemones, and CORALS, along with tiny freshwater animals called hydras, all belong to the same phylum (group)—the cnidarians. All cnidarians are simple aquatic invertebrates with stinging tentacles, which they use to capture prey. Some are venomous and have been known to kill people.

Bell contains digestive cavity and provides propulsion

Fringing tentacles trail behind the bell but do not contain stinging cells

Arms filled with stinging cells that paralyze or kill prey

HOW DO JELLYFISH MOVE THROUGH THE WATER?
Jellyfish swim using a kind of jet propulsion. They contract their hollow, saucer-shaped bodies (called bells) to force water out, which propels them forward. Their long. tentacle-like arms, which trail out behind them, are used to sting and capture prey.

SEA ANEMONE ►
Sea anemones have soft, cylindrical bodies topped with a crown of stinging tentacles. Most sea anemones are no bigger than a man's hand, although the largest may grow up to 3 ft (90 cm) across.

cnidarians

▲ SEA NETTLE
Jellyfish tentacles are armed with stinging cells known as cnidoblasts. The stings of most jellyfish produce nothing more than a painful welt in humans.

CNIDARIAN CLASSIFICATION

The phylum (group) Cnidaria contains about 10,000 species, divided into three classes:
• Hydrozoans (including hydras, the Portuguese man-of-war, and fire corals)
• Anthozoans (including all other corals, and sea anemones)
• Scyphozoans, (jellyfish)

HOW DO SEA ANEMONES FEED?
Sea anemones capture food with their tentacles, then pass it to the mouth in the middle of the tentacle crown. Sea anemones spend their adult lives attached to rocks on the seabed or in pools on the shore. Some sea anemones have a muscular collar, which they can pull over their tentacles if threatened.

CORAL

Tropical coral reefs are the ocean's richest habitats, but the creatures that create them are surprisingly small. They look like tiny sea anemones but have chalky skeletons.

STAGHORN CORAL ►
Hard coral polyps emerge to feed at night, when most of the fish and other creatures that might eat them are inactive or asleep. If they are threatened, the polyps quickly withdraw into their stony shells. They reemerge once the danger has passed.

WHAT IS A POLYP?
A polyp is an individual coral animal. It looks like a miniature sea anemone, and feeds on the tiny plants and animals, known as plankton, that float in seawater. Most coral polyps live in communities that slowly build up to form reefs. These reefs provide homes for all sorts of other sea-living creatures.

HOW DO CORAL REEFS FORM?
Coral reefs are made from the skeletons of coral polyps. Most coral polyps have a hard, chalky body case that protects the soft parts inside. When they die, the chalky skeletons remain. Over thousands of years, they build up on top of one another to form a reef that may stretch for hundreds of miles.

FIND OUT MORE ►► Islands 42 • Australasia and Oceania 272–273

ECHINODERMS

Starfish, brittle stars, sea urchins, and sea cucumbers all belong to the family of echinoderms. These slow-moving, headless invertebrates are the only animals with bodies based on a five-pointed structure. All echinoderms live in salt water.

Tiny tube feet cover the arms – up to 2,000 in some species

Skeleton made of tiny chalky fragments called ossicles

Mouth on the underside of the body

HOW DO STARFISH FEED?

Starfish feed by turning their stomachs inside out over their victims. They then ooze digestive juices, which dissolve their prey. Most starfish eat shellfish such as mussels. They move in search of food using the tiny, flexible tube feet that protrude from their underside.

WHAT HAPPENS WHEN A STARFISH LOSES A LIMB?

Starfish that lose limbs can grow new ones in their place. If a severed limb contains certain cells, it too can survive and will eventually grow into a whole new starfish. Losing a limb may help a starfish escape from a predator's clutches. Brittle stars are so called because their limbs break off easily.

▲ SPINY STARFISH
Starfish have a central body with limbs that radiate outward like spokes on a wheel. Most starfish have five limbs, although some have more.

echinoderms

◄ SEA URCHIN
Sea urchins live on the seabed or buried in sand. Like starfish, they have many tiny tube feet, which they use for crawling and feeding. Sea urchins are well protected by their sharp spines.

Tentacles have evolved from tube feet

Anus discharges waste

Tube feet pass algae and animals to mouth

Spines of some species are poisonous

◄ SEA CUCUMBER
These echinoderms can measure up to 3 ft (1 m) long. They live on the sea floor and feed on decaying matter. After a meal, a sea cucumber pulls its tentacles into its mouth to wipe them clean.

ECHINODERM CLASSIFICATION

The phylum of Echinodermata includes about 6,000 species, divided into six classes:
• Sea lilies and feather stars • Starfish • Brittle stars and basket stars • Sea cucumbers • Sea urchins • Sea daisies

FIND OUT MORE ►► Invertebrates 102

SPONGES

These animals look like plants or fungi, but they are actually simple invertebrates. Most sponges dwell in salt water, spending their lives attached to rocks or reefs.

HOW DO SPONGES FEED?

Sponges feed by drawing seawater in through pores in their surface and then filtering out tiny organisms. Sponges lack the obvious body parts most animals have. They have no heart or other organs of any description. Sponges' bodies are stiffened by tiny grains of limestone, silica, or a fiber called spongin.

YELLOW TUBE SPONGES ►
Sponges exist in a wide variety of colors and may be shaped like fingers, chimneys, or vases. They range in size from less than 4 in (10 cm) to more than 3 ft (1 m) long.

SPONGE CLASSIFICATION

This phylum includes about 5,000 species, divided into four classes:
• Calcareous sponges • Glass sponges • Demosponges (including the familiar bath sponge and tube sponges) • Sclerosponges

sponges

WORMS

Earthworms are the most familiar worms, but there are thousands of other types of these soft, legless creatures. Some are microscopic, others grow to several yards long. Earthworms and roundworms are tube-shaped. Flatworms are shaped like leaves or ribbons.

WHERE DO WORMS LIVE?

Worms live on land and in water and can be found in virtually every habitat on Earth. Earthworms live in the soil. Leeches and bloodworms inhabit ponds and rivers. Most ribbon worms and some flatworms live in the oceans. Ragworms and lugworms are found on the seashore. Some worms are ▶▶ PARASITES that live on or inside other animals.

HOW DO WORMS SENSE THEIR SURROUNDINGS?

Some flatworms have very simple eyes—known as eyespots—that can detect light, but most worms are blind. Their most important sense is touch. The earthworm's skin picks up vibrations caused by sounds or movements. Some predatory worms have sensitive tentacles on their heads, which help them to capture their food.

POLYCLAD FLATWORM ▲
Most non parasitic flatworms hunt or scavenge for food. Flatworms are a major group of worms that includes tapeworms and flukes.

◄ EARTHWORM
Earthworms aerate and enrich the soil as they burrow through it. They feed on plants and animals, or their rotting remains.

WORM CLASSIFICATION

There are over 100,000 species of worm in three main phyla:
- Flatworms (includes turbellarians, tapeworms, and flukes)
- Segmented worms, or annelids (includes earthworms, lugworms, ragworms, and leeches)
- Roundworms (includes threadworms and pinworms)

Saddle holds fertilized eggs after mating

Mucus keeps the body moist

Segments expand and contract to help the worm move

Tail is always longer than head end

Horny cuticle protects the body from damage

Mouth sometimes contains teeth to grind food

Anus expels solid waste

◄ CLOSE-UP
Tiny bristles on the front part of an earthworm help it to grip the soil as it moves. The worm propels itself forward by elongating and contracting its body segments.

ROUNDWORM ►
These worms are also known as nematodes. Some species contain more than 27 million eggs at any time, and lay more than 200,000 in a single day.

PARASITES

Parasites live on or inside other animals or plants, called their hosts. They feed on the blood or tissues of their host, or steal its food. Some parasitic worms in people survive without their host even noticing. Others can cause serious diseases.

HOW DO LEECHES FEED?

Leeches use suckers on their head and tail to latch on to animals, including humans, in order to suck their blood. They inject a chemical that keeps the host's blood flowing freely. This lets them feed until they are bloated; then they drop off. Leeches lurk in ponds, streams, and other wet places.

Hooks fix onto the host's gut

WHERE DO TAPEWORMS LIVE?

Tapeworms live in the guts of animals such as pigs, cats, and humans. The host becomes infected when it eats food containing tapeworm eggs or young. Inside the gut, the worm feeds on the host's half-digested food. As it matures, the worm produces small packages of eggs, which pass out of the victim's body.

Suckers create a strong grip

worms

◄ CAT TAPEWORM
Tapeworms attach themselves to their host's intestines using hooks and suckers on their heads. This species reaches 2 ft (60 cm) long. Some tapeworms can grow up to 100 ft (30 m) long.

FIND OUT MORE ▶▶ Ecology 80 • Invertebrates 102 • Soil 48

MOLLUSKS

Soft-bodied invertebrates, mollusks include slugs, snails, octopuses, squid, clams, and mussels. Most mollusks have ▸▸ SHELLS to protect them.

▲ GIANT AFRICAN SNAIL
Gastropods such as snails glide along on a trail of slime oozing from an area by their broad, muscular foot. The distinct head often carries two pairs of tentacles. The longer set may bear eyes on the tips. Gastropods live mainly in water, but also in a variety of land habitats.

▼ OCTOPUS IN ACTION
Cephalopods such as octopuses and cuttlefish are stealthy hunters. Octopuses creep along the seabed or lie in wait for fish and crabs. They pounce on their prey, seize it with their suckered arms, and paralyze it with poisonous saliva.

MOLLUSK CLASSIFICATION
There are over 51,000 mollusk species split into several major classes:
• Gastropods (the largest class) include slugs, snails, winkles, whelks, and limpets • Bivalves include scallops, clams, and oysters • Squid, octopuses, cuttlefish, and nautilus are cephalopods • Smaller groups include tusk shells and chitons (oval mollusks with jointed plates)

WHAT FEATURES DO MOLLUSKS HAVE IN COMMON?
As well as a shell, most mollusks have a muscular foot for creeping or burrowing. Some also have a head with sense organs. The soft body includes lungs or gills for breathing, and digestive and reproductive parts, all enclosed by a skinlike organ called the mantle.

HOW DO MOLLUSKS FEED?
Most mollusks have a rasping tongue called a radula, armed with tiny teeth. This scrapes tiny plants and animals off rocks or tears food into chunks. Bivalves, such as oysters and mussels, filter food particles from the water with their gills.

HOW DO MOLLUSKS REPRODUCE?
Mollusks reproduce sexually. Slugs and snails are hermaphrodites (possessing both male and female organs), but they must still mate to fertilize their eggs. Most aquatic mollusks lay eggs that hatch into small, free-swimming larvae called veliger.

Eyes, similar to human eyes, give excellent vision

Tentacles coordinated by a powerful brain

Shell can snap shut at the first sign of danger

Muscles hold shell open for feeding

Eyes along the edge of the shell look out for predators

shells

Suckers allow the octopus to grab slippery prey

Sensors on the arms taste what they touch

QUEEN SCALLOP ▲
Like all bivalves, the queen scallop has a two-part shell. Most bivalves live attached to rocks or in burrows on the seabed. They take in water using a muscular tube called a siphon, and remove food particles with their gills.

SHELLS

Mollusk shells come in many shapes and sizes, but most have the same, simple function—providing somewhere to hide in times of danger. In land mollusks, the shell also helps to prevent the moist, soft-bodied creature from drying out.

NAUTILUS SHELL ▶
The nautilus is a cephalopod (a relative of squid and octopuses) with a many-chambered shell. The mollusk lives only in the shell's largest outer chamber. The smaller inner chambers are used to control the animal's buoyancy. The spiraling form can be seen clearly in this cut-away shell.

Buoyancy chamber

Outer chamber contains the living animal

WHAT ARE MOLLUSK SHELLS MADE OF?
Mollusk shells are made of a chalky material called calcium carbonate. The shell has three layers for extra strength: a tough outer layer, a chalky middle layer, and a shiny inner layer, next to the animal's skin. The shiny layer in some bivalve mollusks is known as mother-of-pearl.

HOW DO MOLLUSKS MAKE SHELLS?
A mollusk's mantle (skin) releases liquid shell materials, which harden on contact with water or air. Gastropod and nautilus shells grow from their outermost edge. As the mollusk grows, its shell develops more whorls (single turns in a spiral shell) or chambers. In bivalves, new shell material is deposited on the edge that is farthest from the hinge.

FIND OUT MORE ▸▸ Invertebrates 102

ARTHROPODS

Centipedes, millipedes, insects, crustaceans, and arachnids, including spiders, all belong to a super-group of invertebrates called arthropods. Arthropods are more numerous and varied than any other animal group.

WHAT FEATURES DO ARTHROPODS SHARE?

All arthropods have bodies divided into segments and covered with a hard ▸▸EXOSKELETON. This tough casing is made of a protein called chitin, which is also found in human fingernails. The armor is flexible at joints on the legs, which makes arthropods nimble.

WHAT IS THE DIFFERENCE BETWEEN A CENTIPEDE AND A MILLIPEDE?

Centipedes are active hunters, while most millipedes eat plant matter. Also, centipedes have two legs per body segment. Millipedes have four. Centipedes and millipedes are collectively known as myriapods.

DO ALL CENTIPEDES HAVE ONE HUNDRED LEGS?

The word centipede means "100 legs," but some centipedes have fewer than 100 legs, and others have more. Similarly, the word millipede means "1,000 legs," but in fact no millipede has more than 750 legs.

ARTHROPOD CLASSIFICATION

Arthropods make up the largest phylum (group) in the animal kingdom. There are more than 900,000 named species divided into 13 classes:
- Crustaceans • Insects • Arachnids • Centipedes • Millipedes
- Sea spiders • Pauropods • Symphylans • Springtails • Proturans
- Two-pronged bristletails • Three-pronged bristletails • King crabs

---

◀ PILL MILLIPEDE
With their tough, rounded bodies, millipedes make difficult prey. The pill millipede has an extra trick to deter predators—it rolls into a ball when attacked. Some millipedes defend themselves with poisons, such as quinone and cyanide, produced by glands between their segments.

GIANT CENTIPEDE ▲
Centipedes paralyze or kill their prey with poison, injected by fanglike claws just behind the mouth. There are over 3,000 species of centipede. The largest live in the tropics and may grow up to 12 in (30 cm) long—large enough to kill a mouse.

Long antenna
helps the lobster navigate on the seabed

First leg,
or cheliped, is modified to carry a pincer

Short antenna
feels objects close to the mouthparts

Pincers,
used to grab food and for defense

Carapace
protects most of the vital organs

EXOSKELETON

An arthropod's exoskeleton is a protective case and an anchor point for muscles. As well as being tough, it is waterproof, helping these creatures to survive in even the harshest habitats.

Walking legs
are jointed in several places

HOW DO ARTHROPODS GROW?

In order to grow, arthropods have to molt (shed their exoskeletons) every so often. They then expand their bodies before their new casing hardens. Arthropods are vulnerable while molting, so they look for a safe place to hide before they begin.

arthropods

WHERE DO ARTHROPODS LIVE?

Arthropods occur in virtually every habitat, from the cold ocean depths to the hottest deserts. They can live through extremes that would kill most vertebrates. Scorpions, for example, can survive being frozen solid.

▲ LOBSTER
The lobster's hard exoskeleton supports and protects its body. Even delicate parts, such as the legs and antennae, are completely encased. The North Atlantic lobster is the world's heaviest arthropod, weighing up to 44 lb (20 kg).

Tailpiece
moves to propel the lobster

FIND OUT MORE ▸▸ Invertebrates

ARACHNIDS

A large group of eight-legged arthropods, arachnids include spiders, scorpions, ticks, and mites. All scorpions and spiders are meat-eating hunters. Ticks and mites are tiny creatures with sucking or biting mouthparts. Most ticks live as parasites on animals or plants.

HOW DO SPIDERS SPIN SILK?

Spiders produce liquid silk from glands inside their abdomens. Structures called spinnerets squeeze out the silk, which the spider then pulls into long threads with its legs. Most spiders use silk to spin webs and catch flying prey. Some spiders hunt without using webs.

HOW DO SCORPIONS KILL THEIR PREY?

Scorpions use their pincers to catch and kill prey. They pounce on insects, spiders, and even mice and lizards, then use their pincers to tear them to pieces. The poisonous sting is only used to kill powerful victims that put up a fight. Scorpions hunt at night and use mainly touch and smell to sense their prey.

◀ PROTECTIVE MOTHER
The female scorpion carries her babies on her back for two to three weeks to protect them from predators. After their first molt (shedding of skin), the young leave their mother to hunt on their own. Male and female scorpions court by performing a synchronized dance. After mating, the eggs develop inside the mother's body, so she gives birth to living young.

▲ MEAL MITE
Some mites are so small that they cannot be seen with the naked eye. This photograph of a meal mite was taken with an electron microscope and magnified many thousands of times. Meal mites feed on cereals and are often found in kitchens. The long hairs help the mite to sense its surroundings.

arachnids

ARACHNID CLASSIFICATION

Almost all arachnids live on land. The class Arachnida includes about 95,000 species, divided into 10 orders:
• Scorpions • Pseudoscorpions • Spiders • Mites and ticks
• Harvestmen (daddy long legs) • Whip scorpions • Microwhip scorpions • Solifugids (sun spiders) • Ricinuleids • Amblypygids

◀ TARANTULA
Spiders kill or paralyze their prey by biting it with poisoned fangs. Then they inject digestive juices into it. Tarantulas are active hunters, pouncing on prey rather than catching it in a web. Most tarantulas live in South and Central America.

Forward-facing eyes make it easier to judge distances

Jointed legs enable spider to move quickly

Mouthparts suck up juices of half-digested prey

Grasshopper immobilized by spider's venom

Pedipalps, used as feelers

FIND OUT MORE ▶▶ Arthropods 107 • Invertebrates 102

CRUSTACEANS

These invertebrates include crabs, barnacles, ▸◂ KRILL, and woodlice. They are sometimes called the insects of the sea, because they are the most numerous ocean arthropods. All crustaceans have hard skin, gills, and two pairs of antennae.

WHERE DO CRUSTACEANS LIVE?
Most crustaceans live in the ocean—although some species live in freshwater, and woodlice and a few crabs live on land. Prawns and shrimp swim freely in open water. Barnacles live attached to rocks, harbor walls, or the sides of ships.

Legs
drawn inside
shell at the first
sign of danger

WHAT DO CRUSTACEANS EAT?
Many crustaceans are scavengers, feeding on scraps and dead creatures. Crabs, shrimp, and prawns search for food mainly at night and hide in crevices by day. Some crabs and lobsters are active predators, seizing prey in their powerful claws. Barnacles filter tiny creatures from the water using their hairy legs. Woodlice munch on plant remains.

ARE BABY CRUSTACEANS LIKE THE ADULTS?
Most crustaceans hatch from eggs into nauplius larvae, which do not resemble their adult form at all. These tiny creatures float near the ocean surface, where they feed and grow. They molt their hard skin several times before becoming adults.

◂ **HERMIT CRABS**
These creatures wear empty mollusk shells for protection from predators. When they outgrow one shell, they simply move into another.

▲ GOOSE BARNACLES
These crustaceans extend their slender legs to trap tiny floating creatures for food. As adults, they live fixed to one spot.

▼ NAUPLIUS LARVAE
Most young crustaceans float freely near the ocean's surface. Creatures that live in this way are known as plankton. The word plankton means "wanderer."

Antenna
helps feel the way
in murky water

crustaceans

SHRIMP

CRAB

COPEPOD

CRAB LARVAE

CRUSTACEAN CLASSIFICATION

Crustaceans make up the second-largest class in the animal kingdom. They include about 58,000 species, split into eight sub-classes:
• Lobsters, crabs, prawns, shrimp, and woodlice • Barnacles
• Seed shrimp • Fish lice • Copepods • Branchiopods •
Cephalocarids • Mystacocarids

KRILL

Krill are small, pinkish, shrimplike creatures found in the oceans in huge numbers. They form an important part of the marine food chain and are the main diet of many larger sea creatures.

ARE KRILL UNDER THREAT?
Krill are extremely numerous and there is no threat of their dying out. However, they are being taken from the ocean in increasing amounts by fishermen. As krill disappear, the animals that feed on them suffer. Krill trawling in the Antarctic has had a major effect on penguin numbers.

Baleen plates
keep krill in but
let water out

WHAT DO KRILL EAT?
Krill feed on plankton—such as animal larvae (young) that float with the ocean currents. They, in turn, are eaten by everything from penguins to whales. Some whales migrate thousands of miles from warmer waters just to feed on seasonal swarms of krill.

◂ **KRILL NUMBERS**
Krill sometimes occur in such huge numbers near the ocean's surface that their rosy color appears to turn the water red.

HUMPBACK WHALE ▸
Humpback whales sieve up to 2 tons (2 metric tons) of krill from the water in a single feeding session, using fringed baleen plates in their mouths.

Head

Large compound eyes
give wide field of vision

Thorax (middle
section of the body)

Wings held together at
rest—unlike dragonflies'
wings, which are
held open

Long, delicate
legs have
several joints

Abdomen is
long and slender
to balance insect
when flying

Claspers are used by
male to hold female
during mating

INSECTS

The most numerous animals on Earth, insects form about 75 percent of the animal kingdom. Around 800,000 species have been identified, but there may be up to 10 million. Insects are six-legged invertebrates with powerful sense organs, including ▸▸ ANTENNAE. Some live in ▸▸ COLONIES.

WHY ARE INSECTS SO SUCCESSFUL?

The main reason for insects' success is their variety. There are so many species that there is almost nowhere on land they cannot live, and almost nothing they cannot eat. Their small size enables them to go almost anywhere in search of food. Many insects can fly, which makes it easy for them to colonize new places.

▲ BEDBUG
Various insects feed on blood, including head lice, mosquitoes, and fleas. The bedbug lives in mattresses and emerges when it feels the heat of a body. Its mouthparts are adapted to pierce skin and suck up blood.

▲ DAMSELFLY
Like all adult insects, damselflies have three-part bodies, with a head, thorax, and abdomen. Damselflies and dragonflies form a very ancient group of insects. Giant dragonflies flew in swampy forests 350 million years ago, before dinosaurs existed.

INSECT CLASSIFICATION

- Insects have thrived on Earth for over 400 million years. The insect world is divided into 29 groups, called orders.
- The largest order, the beetles (Coleoptera), contains more than 370,000 species.

- Other major orders are moths and butterflies (Lepidoptera, 165,000 species), bees, wasps, and ants (Hymenoptera, 198,000 species), flies (Diptera, 100,000 species), and bugs (Hemiptera, 80,000 species).

ANTENNAE

The main sense organs of most insects are the antennae (feelers) on their heads. These often long and slender projections are covered with tiny sensitive hairs. As well as feeling, the antennae are also used for smelling, and sometimes for taste and hearing, too.

Club-shaped antennae, different from the feathery antennae of a moth

BUTTERFLY SENSES ▸
Long antennae and large compound eyes help butterflies to sense the world around them.

WHAT DO INSECTS USE THEIR ANTENNAE FOR?

Insects use antennae to find food and detect enemies. Lice, fleas, and other insects that feed on other animals use their antennae to sense the body heat or moisture of their victims. Some male insects have especially sensitive antennae, which can pick up scents called pheromones given off by females (their mates).

WHAT OTHER SENSES DO INSECTS HAVE?

Many insects have compound eyes, with dozens of lenses that work together to form a detailed picture. Some also have sensitive bristles on their abdomens, which detect air currents caused by moving predators or prey. Insects' eardrums may be on their legs or body. Some insects, such as flies, have taste organs on their feet.

HOW DO INSECTS DEFEND THEMSELVES?

Many insects are camouflaged (naturally disguised), so that predators do not see them. Some species are armed with stingers or foul-tasting poison. Many of these have bright colors, such as black-and-yellow stripes, to warn enemies away.

WHAT DO INSECTS EAT?

Insects eat a huge range of foods. Around half are plant-eaters, feeding on leaves, roots, seeds, nectar, or wood. Praying mantises are predators, hunting other small creatures. Fleas and lice are parasites, eating the flesh or blood of larger animals without killing them.

Compound eye made of dozens of six-sided lenses

Antenna

Wing covered with thousands of tiny, overlapping scales

Pupal case in which the butterfly pupated (changed) from a caterpillar

MONARCH CATERPILLAR ▶
Many insect larvae (young) look very different from the adults. Moth and butterfly larvae are known as caterpillars. These feed on leaves, building up a lot of weight in a relatively short time. They then stop feeding and develop a solid body case in which they pupate (change) into their adult body shape.

insects

◀ MONARCH BUTTERFLY
After metamorphosis (the change from larva to adult), an adult monarch butterfly emerges from its pupal case and slowly pumps up its wings. Like all butterflies, the monarch butterfly feeds on nectar produced by flowers.

Feathery antennae

Elytron (wing case) fully open and raised

Back wings unfold

◀ COCKCHAFER BEETLE
In beetles such as this cockchafer, the front wings have evolved into tough, rounded cases called elytra. These protect the delicate back wings from damage when the beetle is on the ground. The elytra are lifted out of the way as the beetle takes off and flies.

WHERE DO INSECTS GO IN WINTER?

Many adult insects die off in winter. Their eggs or young survive in sheltered places and emerge in spring. Some insects survive the cold by hibernating. Others, such as monarch butterflies, migrate long distances to avoid the winter chill.

HOW DO INSECTS AFFECT HUMANS?

Plant-eating insects can harm crops and fruit trees. Wood-munching termites destroy homes and furniture, while biting insects can spread disease. However, many insects are helpful to humans—for example, honeybees make honey, ladybugs eat aphids (which damage garden plants), and silkworms produce silk.

COLONIES

Most insects live solitary lives, but termites, ants, and some wasps and bees live together in large colonies. Members cooperate in building the nest and finding food.

HOW DO SOCIAL INSECTS RAISE THEIR YOUNG?

Most insects take little or no care of their young, but social insects are an exception. Workers carefully guard the young and bring them food. Worker wasps bring chewed-up insects for their grubs (larvae). Honeybee grubs are fed on honey. These young insects grow up in a nursery at the heart of the nest.

TERMITE QUEEN WITH SOLDIERS AND WORKERS ▶
Each insect colony contains several different castes, or ranks. The queen's job is to lay eggs—queen termites are so full of eggs they cannot move. Large numbers of non-breeding female workers tend to the eggs and maintain the nest. Many insect colonies also have a defensive caste of soldiers, armed with huge jaws or poison.

FIND OUT MORE ▶▶ Arthropods 107 • Reproduction 101 • Senses 99

FISH

Fish are aquatic animals with an inner skeleton, including skull, ribs, and backbone. Most fish have bony skeletons, but shark and ray skeletons are made of rubbery cartilage. Fish extract oxygen from the water using ▶▶ GILLS, and swim using their tail and fins. A fish's skin is covered with tough scales.

WHERE DO FISH LIVE?

Superbly adapted to life in water, fish are found throughout the world's oceans, from warm tropical seas to icy polar waters. Some fish dwell near the surface. Others live in the depths, where some use ▶▶ BIOLUMINESCENCE. Fish are also found in freshwater habitats such as rivers, lakes, and swamps.

FISH CLASSIFICATION

- There are over 29,000 species of fish—more than half of all the world's vertebrates. Fish divide into three major groups.
- The first group, and by far the largest, contains the bony fish. There are more than 25,000 species alive today.
- The second group contains the 600 species of cartilaginous fish—sharks and rays.
- The smallest group, with about 60 species, is also the most primitive. Its member, the lampreys, have skeletons but no jaws.

Dorsal fin
provides stability, keeping the fish upright as it swims through the water

Tail
is swept from side to side to propel the fish forwards

◀ GREAT WHITE SHARK
Sharks include the biggest and most fearsome fish of all. The great white shark is the largest predatory fish, growing up to 23 ft (7 m) long. The whale shark, which is a filter feeder, is even bigger. It can grow to 60 ft (18 m) in length and weigh up to 23 tons (21 metric tons).

Pectoral fin
controls direction—it is held flat when swimming in a straight line

GILLS

Like all animals, fish need a constant supply of oxygen to survive. They do not breathe air but extract dissolved oxygen from the water using their gills—feathery organs located behind the eyes and supplied with many tiny blood vessels.

HOW DO FISH BREATHE UNDER WATER?

Water containing dissolved oxygen is drawn in through the fish's mouth, to pass over four or five sets of gills on either side of the head. The gill arches hold delicate, flaplike membranes with very thin walls. Oxygen passes through these membranes into the fish's bloodstream, to be distributed around the body.

HOW GILLS WORK

Water exits body through gill slits

Water enters through the mouth

Oxygen is absorbed from the water, through the gill membranes

DO ANY FISH LIVE ON LAND?

No fish live on land, but some can survive out of water for years. For example, when the pool or lake where they live dries up, African lungfish can survive while buried in the mud, extracting oxygen from the air.

▲ MUDSKIPPER
Mudskippers come out onto muddy shores to graze algae. They keep their gills puffed out with water, returning every so often for a refill. Mudskippers wriggle over the mud using their pectoral fins.

Long snout allows the moorish idol to reach morsels of food in crevices

▲ YELLOWHEAD JAWFISH
Some species of fish protect their eggs by incubating them in their mouths. Before setting off to feed, this male yellowhead jawfish will spit his mate's eggs out into his burrow, to keep them safe.

HOW DO SHARKS HUNT?
Predatory sharks detect prey with the aid of keen sensors, which can pick up tiny traces of blood from several miles away. They home in on victims using electrosensors that detect tiny charges given off by the prey's muscles. At close range, sharks use their eyesight to target prey.

Powerful suction around the mouth

LAMPREY ►
Although lampreys are jawless fish, they still have plenty of bite. Inside their suckerlike mouth are rings of sharp, rasping teeth for ripping into the flesh of their victims.

ARE THERE ANY PARASITIC FISH?
Lampreys are parasites. They attach themselves to larger creatures using their suckerlike mouth and drink their blood. Lamprey saliva contains a natural anticoagulant that prevents a victim's blood from clotting, so that the lamprey can continue to feed.

Anal fin provides stability, like the dorsal fin

◄ MOORISH IDOLS
Most fish that live on tropical coral reefs are colorful and have striking markings. Coral reefs are very crowded places. Scientists think that the bright colors and patterns may help fish to recognize others of their own kind.

BIOLUMINESCENCE

Little light from the surface reaches the twilight zone in the ocean depths below 660 ft (200 m). However, over 1,000 species of fish that live there are bioluminescent— able to produce their own natural light.

fish

WHAT IS THE PURPOSE OF BIOLUMINESCENCE?
Bioluminescence has several uses. Deep-sea anglerfish dangle a glowing lure in front of their jaws to attract prey. Other species use light to identify mates. A few even use it for camouflage—lights on the underside of the body help fish blend in with the small amount of light filtering down. Many fish nearer the surface have light-colored bellies for the same reason.

DEEP-SEA ANGLERFISH ►
A deep-sea anglerfish glows like an underwater light bulb. In some species, bioluminescence is caused by a chemical reaction in which energy is released as light. Other species are illuminated by glowing bacteria in their skin, and some have glands called photophores which can be switched on and off like miniature flashlights.

FIND OUT MORE ▶▶ Cnidarians 103 • Fishing 67 • Oceans 40–41

Large, bulging eyes help tree frog spot approaching predators

Eardrum hidden beneath skin

AMPHIBIANS

Frogs, toads, salamanders, newts, and the strange, wormlike caecilians are all amphibians—a group of small, generally moist-skinned vertebrates. The word amphibian, meaning "living two lives," refers to the fact that most amphibians spend part of their lives in water and part on land.

CAN AMPHIBIANS BREATHE THROUGH THEIR SKIN?
Yes, they can. Oxygen from the air or water can pass through the moist skin of amphibians to enter the blood. Many young amphibians also have feathery gills to extract oxygen from water, but later lose these and develop lungs. Some axolotl salamanders keep their gills throughout life.

Contrasting colors stand out like a warning flag

Sticky fingers give tree frogs greater grip

▲ RED-EYED TREE FROG
Frogs and toads are tailless and have long hind legs. The most widespread amphibians, they are found in many habitats, including rainforests, woodlands, mountains, and deserts.

▲ SALAMANDER
Newts and salamanders have long tails and lizardlike bodies. They feed on slugs, insects, and other small animals. Some species, such as this fire salamander, have poison glands on their heads.

HOW DO AMPHIBIANS DEFEND THEMSELVES AGAINST PREDATORS?
Most amphibians hop or crawl to the safety of the nearest water when danger threatens. Some also have glands in their skin that ooze poisonous or foul-tasting fluids when they are attacked. The common toad and a few other species confuse predators by puffing themselves up to look bigger.

WHAT IS A CAECILIAN?
Caecilians are long, slender amphibians found in hot countries. Almost all live underground, where they burrow through the soil using their wedge-shaped heads. Like other amphibians, caecilians are predators that hunt worms, insects, and other small soil-dwellers. Most caecilians are legless, but some have tiny limbs.

▲ CAECILIAN
Most caecilians live in leaf litter or soil. Because of their secretive habits, they are rarely seen and hard to study. Caecilians have poorly developed eyes and are also known as blindworms.

◄ POLAR BEAR CUBS SUCKLING
At birth, young mammals are fairly weak and defenseless. One or both of the parents, and sometimes other adults, takes care of the young until they are weaned and able to find food for themselves. The babies learn survival skills from the adults and often by playing with others of their own age.

MAMMAL CLASSIFICATION

- Mammals make up the vertebrate class Mammalia. There are about 4,500 species split into three main groups.
- The first group—the monotremes—is also the smallest, with five species.
- The second group contains the marsupials, with 331 species in all.
- The third group contains all placental mammals and is split into 17 orders. Rodents make up the largest order.

HOW DO MAMMALS REPRODUCE?
All mammals reproduce sexually—sperm from the male fertilizes the female's egg. In some mammal species, males establish breeding territories, where they put on displays for the females, showing that they are healthy and strong. In others, the males fight for the right to mate. Many male hoofed mammals have horns or antlers, which they crash or lock together in tests of strength.

WHY IS BEING WARM-BLOODED USEFUL?
Mammals maintain a constant body temperature, which lets them stay active in any weather. Maintaining body temperature takes up a lot of energy, so mammals need large quantities of food. To help reduce the amount of food they must find, mammals in cold environments have thick fur or fatty blubber to retain body heat. Some go into ▶▶ HIBERNATION to survive winter.

HIBERNATION

Many mammals, such as bats and dormice, survive winter in cool and polar lands by entering a deep sleep called hibernation. This strategy helps to conserve energy that would otherwise be lost in the struggle to keep warm and find scarce food.

mammals

◄ SURVIVING THROUGH SLEEP
A dormouse passes the winter in a snug ball of grass and bark in its underground nest. Not dead but simply saving energy, it lives on stored fat and wakes when temperatures rise again in spring.

WHAT CHANGES HAPPEN DURING HIBERNATION?
Heartbeat, breathing, and other body processes slow down, and the animal's temperature drops so that it feels cold to the touch. When the weather warms again in spring, these processes are reversed, and the mammal wakes up to resume active life.

WHAT OTHER TYPES OF ANIMAL HIBERNATE?
Hibernation is very common among cold-blooded animals, such as amphibians, reptiles, and insects, that live in cold or temperate regions. In deserts and other barren places, some animals enter a similar state, called estivation, to survive drought.

FIND OUT MORE ▶▶ Marsupials 123 • Monotremes 123 • Primates 122 • Rodents 122

PRIMATES

These mostly tree-living mammals are divided into two groups. Prosimians, or primitive primates, include lemurs, lorises, and tarsiers. Anthropoids, or higher primates, include marmosets, apes, monkeys, and humans. Primates range in size from mouse lemurs weighing 3½ oz (100 g) to gorillas, which are 2,000 times heavier.

WHAT FEATURES DO ALL PRIMATES SHARE?

Primates are intelligent mammals. As well as hairy bodies, most have long arms and opposable thumbs and big toes, which enable them to grasp branches. Primates' eyes face forward, giving them binocular vision, which helps them judge distances as they swing through the trees. Their main senses are sight and touch; hearing and scent are less important.

WHY DO MANY PRIMATES LIVE IN GROUPS?

By living in groups, primates can defend large feeding territories and are more likely to spot predators than they would be on their own. Group living also helps with raising young. Primate babies take a long time to grow up—three to five years in apes such as chimpanzees. Having other adults around helps the mothers and gives the babies added protection.

◄ CHIMP CRACKING NUTS

Apes are the largest and most intelligent primates. Some apes use tools. Chimpanzees, for example, use stones as weapons or to crack nuts, moss to soak up water, and sticks to probe for insect food.

▲ PREHENSILE TAIL

Many South American monkeys, such as this red howler, have a grasping tail. African and Asian monkeys' tails are not prehensile.

RODENTS

With around 2,000 species, rodents make up the largest group of mammals. The smallest rodents weigh just a few ounces. The largest, South America's capybara, is the size of a large dog. All rodents have chisel-like incisor teeth at the front of their jaws to gnaw food.

WHERE ARE RODENTS FOUND?

Rodents can survive almost anywhere except the sea. Marmots and lemmings inhabit snowy mountains and Arctic wastes, while jerboas and gerbils live in deserts. Rats and mice have colonized our towns and cities. Different rodents are adapted for climbing, swimming, burrowing, or gliding through the air.

WHAT DO RODENTS EAT?

Most rodents are plant-eaters, searching out food with their sensitive noses and long whiskers. Razor-sharp incisor teeth make short work of nuts and seeds. Some rodents carry food in cheek pouches.

▲ BABY HOUSE MICE

Rodents breed very quickly. Mice can produce up to 50 offspring in a year, which grow up so fast that they themselves are ready to breed in six weeks. Rodent populations multiply quickly when food is plentiful.

◄ BUSY BEAVER

Beavers fell trees with their teeth to dam rivers and form lakes. They build a home called a lodge in the middle of the lakes, where they can rear their young in safety. The lodge's entrance is under water.

MARSUPIALS

The group of marsupials includes kangaroos, wallabies, opossums, gliders, and wombats. All marsupials are born early and complete their development in their mother's pouch or clinging to her fur.

▼ NEWBORN JOEY
A young kangaroo, or joey, is born after just 4–5 weeks. Blind and hairless, the tiny baby crawls up its mother's fur to her pouch and clamps on to her nipple.

◄ JOEY IN THE POUCH
The fully developed joey begins to leave its mother's pouch at six months old, but hops back in at the first hint of danger. It becomes independent when one year old.

WHERE DO MARSUPIALS LIVE?

Most marsupials live in Australia and surrounding islands, but some are found in South America, and one, the Virginia opossum, lives in North America. Marsupials multiplied and evolved into all sorts of species in Australia because there were no placental mammals there to compete with them.

WHAT DO MARSUPIALS EAT?

Many marsupials are plant-eaters. Kangaroos and wombats feed mostly on grasses, while koalas eat leaves. Some gliders feed on nectar from flowers. Tasmanian devils are solitary and nocturnal, preying on rabbits, chickens, and other small animals. Virginia opossums are omnivorous, eating fruit, eggs, insects, and other small creatures.

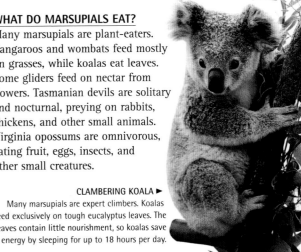

CLAMBERING KOALA ►
Many marsupials are expert climbers. Koalas feed exclusively on tough eucalyptus leaves. The leaves contain little nourishment, so koalas save energy by sleeping for up to 18 hours per day.

MONOTREMES

The small group of egg-laying mammals contains just five species—the duck-billed platypus and four species of echidnas. Monotremes are found only in Australia and on the island of New Guinea. These secretive, burrowing creatures are rarely seen.

mammals

WHAT DO MONOTREMES FEED ON?

Monotremes eat invertebrates, which they search for at night. Echidnas, also known as spiny anteaters, feed on termites and other insects. They slurp them up with their long, sticky tongues. Platypuses hunt under water, searching out worms, crustaceans, and insects with their soft, sensitive beaks.

STRANGE COMBINATION ►
The platypus has a ducklike beak, a molelike body, webbed feet, and a beaverlike tail. When the first stuffed specimens reached Europe in the late 1700s, people thought they were fakes.

▼ SPINY ARMOR
The echidna bristles with defenses against its enemies. Male echidnas and platypuses also have spurs on their legs.

HOW MANY EGGS DO MONOTREMES LAY?

Platypuses and echidnas lay between one and three soft-shelled eggs. Female echidnas incubate their eggs in pouches on their abdomens. The platypus curls around her eggs in her burrow. When the eggs hatch, after about 10 days, the babies feed on milk seeping from patches on the mother's abdomen. The young become independent after four or five months.

Long snout used for probing into termites' nests

FIND OUT MORE ►► Feeding 98 • Reproduction 101 • Vertebrates 102

ENDANGERED SPECIES

All over the world, plant and animal species are now at risk of ▶▶ **EXTINCTION** because of changes humans are causing to the environment. Experts estimate that up to 30,000 of these endangered species may now be dying out each year—including many that have not yet been identified.

WHAT IS THE WORST PROBLEM FACING WILDLIFE?

The greatest single threat to the world's wildlife is habitat loss—destruction of the wild places where animals live. In many regions, forests are felled, marshes drained, and grasslands cleared to build roads, towns, mines, and dams. Pollution from towns, farms, and factories also poisons wildlife on land and at sea.

WHY ARE ISLAND SPECIES ESPECIALLY AT RISK?

Island species are at greater risk than most because many are found nowhere else. Their populations are often very small, so they are more easily affected by new threats. Many island animals are not used to predators. When new creatures such as cats or rats are brought to islands, they can devastate wildlife.

▲ SPOTTED OWL
Spotted owls are at risk because the North American forests where they live are being cut down. Tropical rainforests hold a huge variety of plants and animals, but these are also disappearing fast.

Each tusk is made of ivory worth thousands of dollars on the black market

BURNING IVORY ▶
These elephant tusks were confiscated from poachers and are being destroyed so they cannot be sold. Although elephants are protected by law, there is a large illegal market for ivory, so elephants remain in constant danger.

EXTINCTION

Extinction occurs when all the members of a species die out. Extinction is a natural process that has happened throughout the 3.5 billion years that life has existed on our planet—but now many creatures are dying out at once because of humans.

WHAT ARE MASS EXTINCTIONS?

Mass extinctions occur when large numbers of species die out at once due to rapid changes in the environment. Around 65 million years ago, a mass extinction wiped out the dinosaurs. Now experts fear that humans are causing a new wave of extinctions.

◀ DEAD AS A DODO
Dodos were large flightless birds that once lived on islands in the Indian Ocean. They became extinct by 1800 because sailors hunted them for food.

HOW DO INTRODUCED SPECIES THREATEN WILDLIFE?

When new animals are brought into an area, they can sometimes take over habitats. If they are stronger or breed faster than local species, they may out-compete them for food. New predators often multiply rapidly and start killing local wildlife. Creatures that cannot escape, such as flightless birds, are especially at risk.

endangered species

FIND OUT MORE ▶▶ Dinosaurs 78–79 • Evolution 74–75 • Habitats 82–84 • Human Impact 64–65

CONSERVATION

Governments, wildlife organizations, scientists, and ordinary people do a wide range of conservation work to protect wild places and all the species living there. We all depend on plants and animals for food, clothing, and medicines. In addition, plants provide life-giving oxygen. It makes sense to protect the natural world.

▲ SAFE FROM POACHERS
An endangered black rhino suckles her calf in the Ngorongoro Reserve in Tanzania, Africa. Tourist fees help pay the park's costs. Around 10 percent of the Earth's land area is now protected by reserves.

Calf stays with mother until more than a year old

WHAT IS THE BEST WAY TO SAVE WILDLIFE?
Preserving natural habitats protects all of the animals and plants that live in them. All over the world, large areas of wilderness are now protected as national parks and reserves, where harming wildlife is illegal. Types of forestry and farming that harvest resources without damaging the environment are also important. So is legislation against pollution.

HAS CONSERVATION SAVED WILDLIFE IN THE PAST?
Without conservation, there would be a lot less wildlife around. In the second half of the 20th century, conservationists helped stop large-scale hunting of whales, allowing their populations to recover. Huge areas of rainforest and other habitats have also been protected, saving many species from extinction.

conservation

WHAT ACTION CAN BE TAKEN TO SAVE SPECIES ON THE BRINK OF EXTINCTION?
The Convention for International Trade in Endangered Species (CITES) restricts trade in threatened wildlife. In addition, many zoos run captive breeding programs to save rare animals. In most countries, it is illegal to harm or disturb rare species.

Herdsman guards his cattle from lions and other predators

MASAI HERDSMAN WITH CATTLE HERD ▶
Farm animals, such as cattle, compete with wild animals for food. As the number of people on the planet grows, so more and more land is taken over by farming. This leaves less space for wildlife to live in.

▲ BACK TO THE WILD
The Arabian oryx had been hunted to the brink of extinction by the 1970s. The last few individuals were taken to zoos and bred. In the 1980s, a small number were reintroduced to Oman—where 300 live today.

HOW DO CAPTIVE BREEDING PROGRAMS WORK?
As a first step, scientists find out about the needs of the endangered species, so that suitable conditions can be provided. Next, zoos lend each other animals for breeding. If the program is successful, some of the offspring may be reintroduced to the wild.

HOW CAN ORDINARY PEOPLE HELP CONSERVATION?
One way to help is to join a large organization such as the World Wide Fund for Nature (WWF) or Greenpeace. Membership fees are used to pay for conservation work or to save areas of natural habitat. You can also join local wildlife groups to conserve habitats near your home.

FIND OUT MORE ▶▶ Farming 66 • Fishing 67 • Forestry 67 • Habitats 82–84 • Human Impact 64–65 • Plants 88–89

HUMAN BODY

BODY

A human body is made up of 100 trillion ▸▸CELLS of different types. Similar cells are grouped to form tissue, and tissues form ▸▸ORGANS. Using modern ▸▸IMAGING technology, we can look into the body and see it work.

WHAT MAKES HUMANS SPECIAL?

Humans are unique in the animal world. We are the only mammals to walk on two legs, our brains are unusually large, and our skin is almost hairless. Yet in most ways we are just like other mammals, with two pairs of limbs, two eyes and ears, and the usual mammalian internal organs.

WHY ARE WE ALL DIFFERENT?

Apart from identical twins, no two people in the world are alike. We differ in many subtle ways because we each have a unique set of genes, inherited from our mother and father. Our genes control the way we grow and develop from embryos into adults.

CELLS

The microscopic units that make up all living things are called cells. In the body, there are hundreds of different types of cell, each designed to perform a specific task.

WHAT CONTROLS CELLS?

Most cells have a control center called a nucleus. The nucleus holds the DNA, which makes up the genes. Depending on the type of cell, certain genes are switched on or off. The active genes send instructions out of the nucleus, controlling all the chemical reactions that happen in the rest of the cell.

WHAT IS TISSUE?

Cells of the same type are often grouped together in a pattern, to form tissue. Muscle is made up bundles of muscle cells. Skin consists of sheets of skin cells. Blood is a liquid tissue of cells suspended in a watery fluid. There are four main types: epithelial tissue, connective tissue, muscular tissue, and nervous tissue.

The brain controls the body's activity and produces thought and emotion

Tongue

MRI BODY SCAN ▶

This magnetic resonance imaging (MRI) scan shows the insides of a nine-year-old boy. It was produced using a scanning machine containing giant magnets, which cause atoms in the body to release radio waves that the scanner detects. This image of the whole body is made up of a number of MRI scans taken down the length of the body and then put together.

The bones of the skeleton support the body and give it shape

The lungs take in oxygen from the air

The liver is a large organ that processes body chemicals

◀ FIBROBLAST CELLS

These cells are called fibroblasts and are found in connective tissue, which holds together and supports the body's organs. This picture has been colored to show each cell's nucleus (in blue) and cytoplasm, or body (in orange).

Vertebrae make up the backbone

The bladder is the organ where urine is stored until released during urination

Muscles (in blue) enable the body to move

ORGANS

Tissues are grouped together into larger structures called organs, which carry out specific tasks. The heart, for instance, is an organ designed to pump blood.

WHAT ARE ORGANS MADE OF?
Every organ contains several different tissues. The stomach, for example, consists mostly of muscle cells, which contract to churn food around. The inner lining of the stomach is made of epithelial tissue, which is continually worn away and replaced. There are also glands that secrete digestive juices; blood vessels; nerves; and connective tissue to hold it all together.

HOW DO ORGANS WORK TOGETHER?
Organs work together in teams, called systems, to carry out major tasks. For instance, the stomach, intestines, and pancreas are part of the digestive system, breaking down food into molecules the body can absorb. Some systems work together—the skeletal and muscular systems combine to enable us to move.

BODY SYSTEMS	
Integumentary system	Hair, skin, and nails protect the body from germs, injury, heat loss, and drying out.
Skeletal system	A framework of bones and connective tissues that supports the body and, with muscles, enables it to move.
Muscular system	The system of muscles (involuntary and voluntary) that contract to make the body move.
Nervous system	The brain, nerves, sense organs, and related tissues enable the body to detect and respond to changes.
Endocrine system	A system of glands that regulates body processes by secreting chemicals, called hormones, into the blood.
Circulatory system	The heart and blood vessels transport blood to the body's cells to deliver nutrients and remove waste.
Lymphatic system	A system that returns body fluids to the bloodstream via nodes, where the fluids are screened for germs.
Immune system	An internal defense mechanism, consisting of cells and tissues that destroy invading germs and abnormal cells.
Respiratory system	The lungs and airways leading to the lungs, which take oxygen into the body and expel carbon dioxide.
Digestive system	The mouth and most of the abdominal organs work to break down food into molecules the blood can absorb.
Urinary system	The kidneys remove unwanted chemicals from the blood and expel them via the bladder and urethra.
Reproductive system	The organs involved in sexual reproduction—the penis and testes in men; ovaries, uterus, and vagina in women.

IMAGING

Modern imaging techniques enable doctors to see inside the body without cutting it open. There are many different techniques, each suitable for looking at particular tissues or processes.

DO X-RAYS SHOW ONLY BONES?
No, X-rays can also be used to look at soft tissues, such as the breast or blood vessels, to check if they are healthy. For blood vessels, a harmless dye that absorbs X-rays is first injected into the vessels—X-rays will then show their outline. This type of image is called an angiogram.

WHAT IS A CT SCAN?
A computed tomography (CT) scan is a computer-generated image built from X-ray beams. A machine slowly moves over the area of the body, taking X-ray pictures from many angles. A computer then analyzes the X-rays to build up a detailed cross-section of the body, including its soft tissues.

HOW IS ULTRASOUND USED?
Ultrasound scanning is one of the most common imaging techniques. High-frequency sound waves are bounced off internal organs and the pattern of echoes is displayed on a TV screen. Ultrasound scanners are good for studying moving liquids, such as blood or fluid in the uterus (womb).

▲ PET SCAN OF THE BRAIN
Positron emission tomography (PET) uses injected radioactive substances to reveal activity in organs and tissues. The colored areas above show the parts of the brain used during speech.

◄ ULTRASOUND OF A FETUS
Ultrasound scanners are routinely used to monitor unborn babies, to check their growth and the development of organs, such as the heart and lungs.

X-RAY OF BROKEN ARM ▲
This X-ray shows badly fractured (broken) radius and ulna bones of the forearm. X-rays are a form of radiation that passes through soft parts of the body, but shows up dense material such as bones and teeth.

FIND OUT MORE ▶▶ Cells 73 • Genetics 209 • Mammals 120–123

Cranium
(skull)

Mandible
(lower jaw)

Clavicle
(collarbone)

Cervical
(neck)
vertebrae

Scapula
(shoulder
blade)

Sternum
(breastbone)

Ribs

Humerus
(upper arm
bone)

Pelvis
(hipbone)

Lumbar
(lower back)
vertebrae

Radius
(thumb side
forearm bone)

Ulna
(forearm bone)

Carpals
(wrist bones)

Metacarpals
(palm bones)

Phalanges
(finger
bones)

Femur
(thighbone)

skeleton

Patella
(kneecap)

Tibia
(shinbone)

Fibula
(calf bone)

Metatarsals
(foot bones)

Tarsals
(ankle bones)

Phalanges
(toe bones)

SKELETON

The skeleton is the inner framework of ▸▸**BONES** that supports and gives shape to the human body. It also protects some of the soft organs of the body—for example, the skull surrounds the brain. Muscles and ligaments pull on the bones of the skeleton at ▸▸**JOINTS** to make the body move.

HOW STRONG ARE BONES?
Weight for weight, bone is five times stronger than steel, but it is very light. The skeleton makes up only one-sixth of an adult's weight. The skull, in particular, is very strong, because it has to protect the brain and sense organs, such as the eyes, ears, and nose.

ARE BONES DRY?
Dead bones are dry and brittle, but living bones feel wet and a little soft. They are also slightly flexible, so they can absorb pressure. Like most parts of the body, bones have a network of blood vessels and nerves running through them, and they bleed when broken. Up to one-third of the weight of a living bone is water.

The lower jaw, or mandible is the only large freely moving bone in the skull

The cranium, the part of the skull that protects the brain, is made up of eight bones fused tightly together

HOW DOES A SKELETON GROW?
A newborn baby has more than 300 bones, but many are made of a soft, rubbery material called cartilage instead of bone. Up until the late teens, as a child grows the cartilage lengthens and turns into bone, and some bones fuse together. By adulthood, there are just 206 bones in the skeleton.

SKULL BONES ▲
This colored X-ray of the skull has an image of the brain placed over it to show the fit. The skull is made up of 22 separate bones all locked together by immovable joints, except for the lower jaw.

GROWING HANDS ▶
The first X-ray shows the gaps between the bones in a baby's hand that are filled with cartilage. By age 20, the finger bones have grown longer and ossified (turned to bone).

The fingers are now made of mature, hard bone

Cartilage outline is just visible

◀ **THE HUMAN SKELETON**
Each bone in the body has a scientific name, but many also have everyday names. The largest is the femur, or thighbone, and the smallest are the tiny ossicle bones in the inner ear. More than half the bones of an adult's skeleton are in the hands and feet.

HAND OF A
ONE-YEAR-OLD

HAND OF A
20-YEAR-OLD

This strong yet flexible material is a living tissue, made up of bone cells embedded in a matrix of fibers. Bone is not solid—blood vessels and nerves run through tunnels within it, and some areas are a honeycomb of small spaces. In the center of many bones is a cavity packed with a jellylike substance called bone marrow.

WHAT IS BONE MADE OF?

The hard matrix of bone is made of crystals of calcium phosphate and other minerals, and fibers of protein called collagen. The minerals make bone hard, while the collagen fibers are arranged lengthwise to make bone flexible. Both are produced by cells called osteocytes, found throughout the matrix.

Compact bone

Spongy bone

▲ SECTION THROUGH A BONE
This femur has been cut to show its different layers. Because this is not a living bone, the hollow center has no bone marrow in it.

◄ COMPACT BONE
Densely packed, concentric rings of minerals and collagen give compact bone immense strength. Blood vessels run through tunnels in the center of each set of rings.

SPONGY BONE ▲
A honeycomb of struts and spaces makes spongy bone lightweight yet resilient. Bone marrow fills the spaces.

WHAT DOES BONE MARROW DO?

Bone marrow makes millions of blood cells every second to replace old, worn-out blood cells, which the body destroys. There are two types of marrow: red and yellow. Red marrow makes blood cells. Yellow marrow is mainly a fat store, but it can turn into red marrow if the body needs extra blood cells. At birth, nearly all bone marrow is red. During the teens, much of it turns into yellow bone marrow.

JOINTS

Bones connect at joints. Different types of joint allow different movements. Joints are often held together by straps of tough fibrous tissue, called ligaments, and the muscles that cross the joint.

HOW DO DIFFERENT JOINTS WORK?

Most joints are free-moving. These are called synovial joints, and they allow varying degrees of movement. Hinge joints, like those in the fingers, knees, and elbows, can only bend and straighten. Others, such as the ball-and-socket joints in the shoulders and hips, allow movement in all directions.

WHY DON'T BONES RUB AGAINST EACH OTHER?

In synovial joints, the bone endings are covered with a smooth, glossy material called hyaline cartilage, which is slippery yet hard-wearing. This cartilage allows the bone ends to slide smoothly past each other. Also, a capsule of fluid surrounds the joint. The fluid lubricates the joint, reducing friction just as oil helps the movement of a bicycle chain.

Synovial fluid (blue) allows the joint to move more freely

Cartilage (pink) lines the surfaces where the bones meet

The shoulder is a ball-and-socket joint, which allows the greatest range of movement

BALL-AND-SOCKET JOINT

The elbow is a hinge joint, allowing the arm to bend and straighten

HINGE JOINT

A column of 24 vertebrae holds the trunk upright, but twists and bends to allow movement

◄ ARM MOVEMENT
The joints in the shoulder, elbow, and wrist work together to give the arm an amazing range of movement.

KNEE JOINT ►
Synovial fluid and cartilage ease movement where the femur (thigh bone) and tibia (shin bone) meet.

FIND OUT MORE ►► Circulation 134 • Growth 149 • Muscle 132

MUSCLE

Body movement is brought about by muscle, a tissue that can contract. There are three main types: skeletal muscle, smooth muscle, and cardiac muscle. Most muscle is made of elongated cells called ▶▶ MUSCLE FIBERS .

WHAT ARE INVOLUNTARY MUSCLES?

Smooth muscle and cardiac muscle are involuntary—they work automatically, without our conscious control. Smooth muscle is found in the walls of the intestines, stomach, esophagus, and other organs. It contracts slowly and rhythmically to push food through the digestive system. Cardiac muscle is found in the heart and works continuously without tiring.

HOW DO MUSCLES WORK WITH BONES?

Skeletal muscles move bones by pulling on them. Because we control this movement, they are called voluntary muscles. Muscles can pull but not push, so skeletal muscles are often arranged in pairs that pull bones in opposite directions.

MUSCLE FIBERS

Individual muscle cells are called muscle fibers. Skeletal muscle is made up of thousands of muscle fibers arranged in parallel bundles. Each fiber is thinner than a hair and can measure up to 12 in (30 cm) long.

Frontalis
wrinkles forehead and lifts eyebrows

Orbicularis oculi closes eyelids

Orbicularis oris purses the lips

Sternocleidomastoid twists and bends neck

Biceps brachii bends arm

SKELETAL MUSCLES ▶
The body has some 640 skeletal muscles, accounting for about 40 percent of body weight. Skeletal muscles are attached to bones by tough fibrous connections called tendons.

Pectoralis major swings the arm

TYPES OF MUSCLE FIBER

The three main types of muscle fiber work in very different ways. Smooth muscle can contract for prolonged periods. Skeletal muscle contracts quickly and powerfully, but only for short periods of time. Cardiac muscle contracts rhythmically and continually without tiring.

▲ SMOOTH MUSCLE
Smooth muscle has spindle-shaped fibers that overlap. It contracts about 50 times more slowly than skeletal muscle.

▲ SKELETAL MUSCLE
Skeletal muscle contains very long, slender muscle fibers arranged in parallel, which give it a striped appearance.

▲ CARDIAC MUSCLE
The short, branching fibers of cardiac muscles interconnect. They are packed with energy-producing mitochondria.

HOW DOES A MUSCLE CONTRACT?

A muscle fiber is made up of myofibrils, which are made of thinner strands called myofilaments. When myofilaments are stimulated by a nerve impulse, they slide over each other, shortening the muscle. The more signals there are, the more the muscle contracts, until it shortens to as little as 70 percent of its relaxed length.

muscle

External oblique twists trunk and bends it sideways

Adductor longus pulls the leg inward toward the body

FIND OUT MORE ▶▶ Body 128–129 • Heart 135 • Lungs 137 • Skeleton 130–131

SKIN

An outer covering of skin protects the body from injury, germs, water loss, and sunlight. Skin is also an important sensory organ, full of receptor cells sensitive to touch, heat, cold, and pain.

WHAT MAKES SKIN TOUGH?

Skin gets its strength from a supple outer layer called the epidermis, made largely of dead cells packed with a hard protein called keratin. The epidermis is continually wearing away and renewing itself. Its bottom layer of living cells keeps dividing, producing new cells that slowly move to the surface. As they travel up, they flatten, harden, and die.

WHAT'S UNDER THE EPIDERMIS?

Beneath the epidermis is the dermis, a layer of tissue containing blood vessels, nerves, sensory receptors, sweat glands, and hair roots. Under the dermis is a layer of fat cells that cushions the skin and traps heat deep within the body.

HOW DOES SKIN CONTROL BODY TEMPERATURE?

When the body is hot, sweat glands secrete a watery fluid onto the skin. The water draws heat from the skin as it evaporates. At the same time, blood vessels in the skin widen to release excess heat. When the body is cold, the skin's blood vessels narrow to reduce heat loss, and tiny muscles pull hairs erect, trapping warm air over the skin.

Skin surface is made up of dead, flattened cells from the epidermis

Epidermis cells continually divide to produce new skin cells

Dermis is a layer of living tissue below the epidermis, full of blood vessels and sensory receptors

Melanocyte cells in this area at the base of the epidermis produce melanin—the pigment that gives skin its color and filters out ultraviolet light

▲ A CROSS-SECTION THROUGH THE SKIN
This highly magnified image shows the layers in healthy skin. The top of the epidermis (red) is made up of flattened dead cells full of keratin. Surface cells continually flake away.

WHY DOES SKIN COLOR VARY?

Skin color comes from the pigment melanin, made by cells called melanocytes in the epidermis. Everyone has the same number of melanocytes, but they are much more active in people with dark skin. Melanocytes also become more active after exposure to the sun, producing pigment to protect the skin from damage from the sun.

Hair follicles are rooted deep in the dermis

◄ FINGERNAILS
Nails are made of overlapping plates of dead cells filled with the protein keratin. Keratin is tough and waterproof and is also found in hair and skin. Nails protect the sensitive tips of the fingers and toes.

▲ SWEAT
Droplets of sweat cover the skin on the back of a hand. The fluid is produced in sweat glands in the dermis, and rises up through pores onto the surface of the skin. Sweat lowers the body's temperature by using its heat to evaporate.

skin

BEARD STUBBLE ►
These shafts of hair from a man's beard have been shaved short. Hair is found all over the body to protect the skin and help us feel things that come near to the skin's surface. It is made of dead cells and keratin, and can grow up to ½ in (1 cm) a month.

Hair shaft

FIND OUT MORE ►► Body 128–129 • Circulation 134 • Growth 149

CIRCULATION

The heart, ➡ BLOOD, and blood vessels make up the circulatory system, which supplies the body with oxygen and nutrients, removes waste, distributes heat, and fights disease.

The aorta is the body's biggest artery

Heart

The vena cava is the main vein taking blood to the heart

Veins are shown in blue

Arteries are shown in red

ARE ARTERIES AND VEINS DIFFERENT?
Arteries carry blood from the heart, while veins bring it back. Arteries have thicker walls than veins, to withstand the force of the blood pumping directly out of the heart.

WHAT ARE CAPILLARIES?
About 98 percent of blood vessels are microscopically thin vessels, called capillaries, that form a network between arteries and veins. Their walls are only one cell thick, so that chemicals can pass between the blood and the body's tissues.

◀ CIRCULATORY SYSTEM
The heart pumps blood continually around the circulatory system. Arteries and veins divide into ever finer branches as they reach throughout the body.

BLOOD CELLS ▶
An adult has about 5 quarts (liters) of blood. Blood cells are made inside bones, and every second, 2 million red blood cells are made and the same number are destroyed.

BLOOD

A liquid tissue, blood consists of trillions of cells suspended in a watery liquid called plasma. Blood is the body's transportation system, keeping all tissues and organs supplied with the chemicals needed for life and removing waste. Plasma makes up 55 percent of blood, and red cells around 44 percent. White cells account for less than 1 percent of blood.

WHAT DO RED BLOOD CELLS DO?
Red blood cells pick up the life-giving gas oxygen in the lungs and release it throughout the body. A single drop of blood contains about five million of these tiny cells. Each cell is packed with the bright red protein hemoglobin, which binds with oxygen and then releases it where it is needed.

WHY DO WE HAVE WHITE BLOOD CELLS?
White blood cells destroy germs and damaged tissue. A drop of blood contains about 7,000 white cells, and there are many different types. Some patrol the body like soldiers, swallowing germs. Others produce chemicals, called antibodies, that stick to germs and so make them easier to kill.

◀ BLOOD CLOT
When the skin is cut, a tough protein called fibrin (shown in gray) forms a tangle of solid fibers that traps blood cells and seals the wound.

White blood cells are round with tiny projections on the surface to help them stick to germs

Red blood cells are flexible so they can squeeze through capillaries

circulation

FIND OUT MORE ➡➡ Respiration 136 • Skeleton 130–131

HEART

Blood is driven around the body by the heart, a powerful muscular pump that never stops beating. The heart is a dual pump. The left side sends blood to the body, while the right sends blood only to the lungs.

WHAT'S INSIDE THE HEART?

There are four chambers in the heart: two on the left and two on the right. The top chambers, called atria, are holding stations for incoming blood. The bottom chambers, called ventricles, pump blood out of the heart. It is the contractions of the atria and ventricles that make the sound of the ▶ HEARTBEAT.

WHAT IS THE HEART MADE OF?

The heart consists mostly of cardiac muscle, a special type of muscle that contracts rhythmically of its own accord. A tough membranous bag, called the pericardium, surrounds the heart, and a smooth membrane, called the endocardium, lines the inner surface.

FEEDING THE HEART ▶
This angiogram shows the network of blood vessels on the surface of the heart that keep it supplied with oxygen and nutrients. The large vessels are the coronary arteries, which branch out from the aorta to give the cardiac muscle a direct supply of oxygen-rich blood.

heart

Superior vena cava *carries used blood into the right atrium*

Aorta *carries fresh blood to most of the body*

Semilunar valves

Bicuspid valve

Right atrium *receives blood from the main veins*

Tricuspid valve

Right ventricle *receives blood from the right atrium and pumps it to the lungs*

Inferior vena cava *carries blood from the lower body*

Pulmonary artery *takes blood from the right atrium to the lungs*

Left atrium *receives fresh blood from the lungs*

Pulmonary veins

INSIDE THE HEART ▶
A system of valves ensures that blood follows a one-way route through the heart, to the lungs and back, and then out through the aorta to the body.

Descending aorta *takes blood to the lower body*

Cardiac muscle

The septum is *the sturdy muscular wall between the two sides of the heart*

Left ventricle *receives blood from the left atrium and pumps it to the body*

HEARTBEAT

One complete contraction of the heart is called a heartbeat. Each heartbeat involves a sequence of events, with different parts of the heart contracting at different times. The rhythmic "lub-dub" noise of the heartbeat is the sound of valves snapping shut.

HOW IS THE HEARTBEAT CONTROLLED?

A small patch of modified cardiac muscle, the sinoatrial node, is the heart's pacemaker. It sends out a wave of electricity to make the heart's walls contract about 70 times a minute. However, nerve signals from the brain can speed it up during exercise or stress, if necessary.

Right atrium fills *with used blood from the body*

Oxygen-rich blood *fills the left atrium*

Semilunar valves

CLOSED VALVE
The semilunar valves close to prevent backflow.

Right atrium *contracts*

Left atrium *contracts*

Tricuspid and bicuspid valves *open*

Full ventricles

▲ STAGE 1—THE HEART RELAXES
As the heart relaxes and the atria fill up with blood, the semilunar valves shut, making the "dub" beat.

▲ STAGE 2—THE ATRIA CONTRACT
The atria contract to push blood into the ventricles. Valves between the atria and ventricles are pushed open.

Oxygen-rich blood flows *to upper and lower body*

OPEN VALVE
The force of blood rushing through opens the valve.

Semilunar valves *open*

Tricuspid and bicuspid valves *snap shut*

Contracted ventricles

▲ STAGE 3—THE VENTRICLES CONTRACT
The ventricles contract to force blood out. The valves between the atria and ventricles shut to make the "lub" beat.

FIND OUT MORE ▶▶ Lungs 137 • Muscle 132 • Respiration 136

RESPIRATION

The process of taking in oxygen and expelling carbon dioxide is called respiration. When you breathe in, oxygen from the air enters the bloodstream. When you breathe out, waste carbon dioxide is removed.

respiration

HOW DOES AIR REACH THE LUNGS?

Air enters the body through the nose and mouth and travels to the pharynx (throat). The pharynx splits into the esophagus for food, and the trachea (windpipe) for air. The trachea leads to the chest, where it divides into two branches, or bronchi, one to each lung.

▲ CILIA IN THE NOSE
Tiny beating hairs, called cilia, line the inside of the nose. The cilia clean, warm, and moisten the air to protect the sensitive airways of the lungs.

HOW DO THE AIRWAYS STAY CLEAN?

The inner lining of the airways constantly produces a sticky fluid, called mucus, to trap particles of dirt. The mucus is always moving. In the nose, it is pushed by cilia toward the back of the throat, where it is swallowed. Mucus also moves up from the airways of the lungs to the throat to be swallowed.

Pharynx (throat)

The epiglottis
swings down to cover
the larynx when we
swallow, to keep food
out of the air passages

Vocal cords
in the larynx (voice
box) produce sound

The trachea
(windpipe) is made
up of rings of
cartilage that hold
the air passage open

Pulmonary vessels
run throughout the lungs,
bringing blood from the
heart to pick up oxygen,
then taking it back to the
heart to be pumped around
the body

RESPIRATORY SYSTEM ►
The respiratory system is made up of many organs, including the lungs, nose, mouth, and airways leading to the lungs, and the network of blood vessels running through the lungs.

Bronchi
divide again and
again, to form a
network of ever
smaller airways

Heart

The diaphragm
is a dome of muscle
between the chest and
the abdomen

HOW SOUND IS MADE IN THE LARYNX

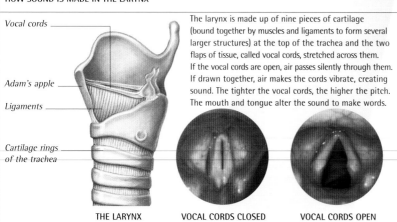

Vocal cords

Adam's apple

Ligaments

Cartilage rings
of the trachea

The larynx is made up of nine pieces of cartilage (bound together by muscles and ligaments to form several larger structures) at the top of the trachea and the two flaps of tissue, called vocal cords, stretched across them. If the vocal cords are open, air passes silently through them. If drawn together, air makes the cords vibrate, creating sound. The tighter the vocal cords, the higher the pitch. The mouth and tongue alter the sound to make words.

THE LARYNX   VOCAL CORDS CLOSED   VOCAL CORDS OPEN

WHY DO WE NEED TO BREATHE?

Breathing is essential to keep us alive, because every living cell in the body needs a continual supply of oxygen. Inside each cell, oxygen combines with food molecules in a chemical reaction called oxidation, which releases energy. This energy powers every process in the human body.

FIND OUT MORE ►► Cells 73 • Mouth 142 • Nose 143 • Sound 176–177

LUNGS

The main organs of the respiratory system are the lungs—two large organs that expand and contract. Each has a network of airways that end in tiny pockets called alveoli, where oxygen enters the blood and carbon dioxide leaves—a process known as ▶▶ GAS EXCHANGE.

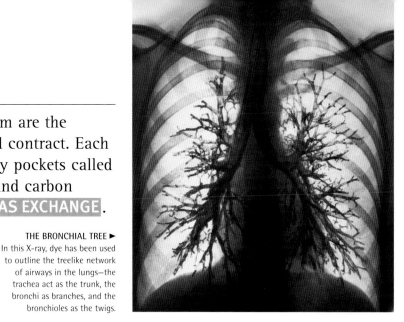

THE BRONCHIAL TREE ▶
In this X-ray, dye has been used to outline the treelike network of airways in the lungs—the trachea act as the trunk, the bronchi as branches, and the bronchioles as the twigs.

WHAT MAKES THE LUNGS EXPAND AND CONTRACT?
The lungs rely on surrounding muscles to make them expand and contract. Muscles between the ribs pull the rib cage up and out, making the chest expand and drawing air in, or relax to squeeze the lungs and force air out as the rib cage falls down and in. At the same time, the diaphragm (a dome of muscle beneath the lungs) contracts to suck air into the airway, or relaxes and rises up to push air out.

HOW IS OUR BREATHING CONTROLLED?
The respiratory center of the brain regulates our breathing, even while we sleep, with the help of receptors in some of the large arteries. The receptors monitor the level of carbon dioxide in the blood, which rises when we are active, and tell the brain if we need to breathe faster to get rid of the carbon dioxide.

Ribs provide a flexible framework for the lungs, protecting them, yet allowing them to expand and contract

Intercostal muscles move the ribs, making the lungs expand or contract

HOW BREATHING WORKS

Trachea carries inhaled air to the lungs

Muscles contract to raise the rib cage up and outward

Lungs expand, sucking air in

Diaphragm contracts and pulls downward

▲ INHALATION (BREATHING IN)
To inhale, the intercostal muscles contract, and the diaphragm moves down, making the chest expand. Air is sucked into the lungs, because the pressure in the airways is less than it is outside.

Exhaled air is pushed out through the nostrils or lips

Exhaled air is pushed up the trachea to the throat

Muscles relax and rib cage moves downward and inward

Lungs shrink and squeeze air out

Diaphragm relaxes and springs upward

▲ EXHALATION (BREATHING OUT)
When the intercostal muscles and diaphragm relax, we exhale. The ribs fall downward and inward, and the diaphragm springs back into a dome shape, gently squeezing the lungs and pushing air out.

GAS EXCHANGE

The passing of gases from the air into the blood, and from the blood back to the air, is called gas exchange. It takes place in the lungs, in tiny air pockets called alveoli.

WHAT ARE ALVEOLI?
Alveoli are like tiny bags of air with walls so thin that gases can pass through them. There are around 300 million alveoli in the lungs. Together they provide an area about as big as a tennis court for gas exchange.

HOW DOES OXYGEN GET INTO THE BLOOD?
Oxygen passes through the walls of the alveoli and the surrounding blood capillaries into the blood. The oxygen enters red blood cells and binds to a chemical called hemoglobin. Carbon dioxide passes out of the plasma (the watery part of blood) to enter the alveoli.

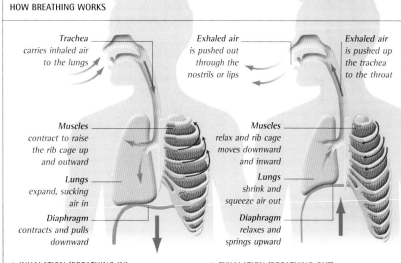

Terminal bronchiole surrounded by blood capillaries

Cluster of alveoli

Capillaries (red and blue) cover the alveoli, bringing carbon dioxide from the body and taking back oxygen

ALVEOLI ▶
Alveoli are clustered together, like a bunch of grapes, at the end of a bronchiole no wider than a hair.

lungs

FIND OUT MORE ▶▶ Brain 139 • Circulation 134 • Mouth 142 • Muscle 132 • Nose 143

Brain

Spinal cord

NERVOUS SYSTEM

The brain, nerves, and spinal cord make up the nervous system. It processes information from the sense organs and controls conscious "voluntary" actions, such as walking, and "involuntary" processes we are not aware of, like reflexes and breathing.

WHAT IS A NERVE?

Nerves are the cables of the nervous system. Each nerve is packed with hundreds of wirelike cells called neurons, which carry electric signals to and from the brain. The brain and spinal cord form the central nervous system, and the nerves outside them are the peripheral nervous system.

HOW DO NEURONS WORK?

Neurons work like wires, transmitting electric signals. When the neuron is resting, there is very little elctrical activity. If triggered, a nerve impulse rushes to the end of the cell, where a chemical called a neurotransmitter passes the signal to the next neuron across a gap, or synapse.

Spinal cord is the nervous system's main highway and runs through a tunnel in the vertebrae

◀ A NETWORK OF NERVES
Nerves branch from the brain and spinal cord, forming a treelike network that runs throughout the body.

The cerebrum is the largest part of the human brain, and is responsible for voluntary actions, thought, language, and consciousness

The cerebral cortex is the folded surface of the cerebrum where information is processed

nervous system

The hypothalamus is a tiny region in the center of the brain that controls hormone levels and regulates sleep, temperature, and body water levels

◀ MOTOR NEURON
All neurons are similar in structure to this motor neuron. The cell body contains the nucleus that controls the cell. Filaments called dendrites branch out from the cell body and pick up signals from other neurons. The nerve fiber, or axon, takes the signal and passes it on to other neurons, muscles, or glands.

Axon
(nerve fiber)

Cell body

Nucleus

Dendrite

ARE ALL NEURONS THE SAME?

There are three main types of neurons. Sensory neurons carry incoming signals from sense organs to the central nervous system. Motor neurons carry outgoing signals from the brain to the body, usually to muscle cells. Association neurons form a complex maze of connections in the brain and spinal cord, linking sensory neurons to motor neurons.

WHAT IS A REFLEX ACTION?

Reflex actions are involuntary—they happen before you have time to think. When they happen, a nerve signal takes a shortcut through the spinal cord, rather than involving the brain. If we touch a very hot object, a sensory neuron sends a signal shooting from the hand to the spinal cord. There an association neuron transmits the signal to a motor neuron, which tells a muscle in the arm to move the hand.

◀ NERVE JUNCTION
This highly magnified image shows the junction, or synapse, between two nerve cells. In the blue cell, a nerve signal has stimulated the release of chemicals called neurotransmitters (pink circles). The neurotransmitters cross the gap and bind to the pink receptor nerve cell to pass on the signal.

FIND OUT MORE ▶▶ Muscle 132 • Respiration 136

BRAIN

The largest organ in the nervous system is the brain. It controls vital involuntary processes, such as breathing, as well as our thoughts, emotions, memories, and sensations. Brain scans can monitor brain activity, called ▶▶ **BRAINWAVES**.

▲ NEURONS IN THE BRAIN
Brain cells send signals to each other via spindly connections. Each cell has an average of 10,000 connections, which change as the brain learns and adapts.

The cerebellum is involved in the involuntary control of balance and posture, especially during movement

WHY IS THE HUMAN BRAIN SPECIAL?
Relative to body weight, the human brain is one of the largest in the animal kingdom. Its surface, the cerebral cortex, is also the wrinkliest. During human evolution, the cerebral cortex grew, and so became wrinklier to fit inside the skull. The large cortex, site of unique abilities such as language, is probably what makes humans unusually intelligent.

WHAT IS THE BRAIN MADE OF?
The brain contains more than 100 billion neurons and a multitude of helper cells, which nourish and support the neurons. The cells are organized into different areas, the largest of which is the cerebrum. The whole brain is surrounded by protective membranes and cushioned by fluid-filled hollows.

◄ BRAIN SCAN
This MRI scan shows how the brain fills the space inside the skull. The cerebrum takes up most of the room, and accounts for nearly 70 percent of the weight of the nervous system.

HOW DOES THE BRAIN WORK?
Scientists used to think that each part of the cerebral cortex carried out a specific function. Recent research has shown the brain to be more complicated. During speech, for instance, large areas of the cerebral cortex work together in an ever-changing pattern.

◄ PET SCANS OF THE BRAIN
Active parts of the cerebral cortex show as flashes of color in a PET scan. Scientists use these scanners to carry out research into how the brain works.

LISTENING

IN CONVERSATION

The brain stem is an extension of the spinal cord and controls vital involuntary functions such as breathing and heart rate

brain

Spinal cord

BRAINWAVES

Doctors can monitor a person's brain by looking at brainwaves, the pattern of electrical activity produced by all the brain's neurons. There are three main types of wave: alpha, beta, and delta. They are detected by an EEG (electroencephalograph).

IS THE BRAIN ACTIVE WHEN WE SLEEP?
The brain is always active, but the level of activity varies. In deep sleep, when delta waves occur, the brain is working but at its least active. During dreams, the eyes dart around, and the brain produces alpha waves and is just as active as during waking hours.

WAVE PATTERNS ►
When a person is awake but resting, the brain produces a regular pattern of medium-length waves—alpha waves. When alert and concentrating, the brain produces shorter, quicker waves—beta waves. During deep sleep, very long, slow delta waves occur.

ALPHA: AWAKE BUT RESTING

BETA: ALERT AND CONCENTRATING

DELTA: SLEEPING DEEPLY

FIND OUT MORE ▶▶ Nervous System 138 • Skeleton 130–131

EYE

Our eyes create our sense of vision. They take in light rays, focus them to create an image, and convert this image into a stream of billions of nerve impulses that travels to the brain. The impulses are interpreted in different parts of the brain, but come together to create the detailed, color, 3-D image we "see."

Pupil _____

Iris _____

WHAT IS THE PUPIL?

The pupil is a hole that lets light enter the eye. It appears black, because light passes straight through it without being reflected. Around the pupil is the iris, a circle of colored muscle that controls the pupil's size. In dim light the pupil widens to take in extra light. In bright light it shrinks to protect the nerve cells at the back of the eye.

HOW THE EYE FOCUSES

The eye has a curved, transparent lens that bends light rays to create an image. The eye focuses images on the retina, just as a projector focuses images on a screen. To keep the image sharp, the lens changes shape. Muscles around the lens make it fatter for nearby objects and thinner for distant objects.

Cornea

Retina

Light rays reflected from the tree enter the eye

Elastic lens changes shape to focus light clearly on the retina

WHY DO WE HAVE TWO EYES?

Each eye sees the world from a different angle, creating slightly different pictures. The brain combines these two pictures into a single, three-dimensional image. This is called binocular vision. Seeing in 3-D helps you to judge the distance and size of objects much more easily.

HOW DO WE SEE IN COLOR?

The cells in the retina that are sensitive to light are called rods and cones. Rods work best in dim light, but cannot see color. Cones can detect colors in bright light. There are three types of cones, and each type is sensitive to one of the primary light colors— red, blue, or green. By combining information from all three, we are able to see all the colors of the rainbow.

THE EYE'S EXTERIOR ▶
Most of the eyeball lies inside the eye socket; only the iris and pupil of the eye can be seen. The surface of the eye is kept moist with tears, and blinking keeps the eye clean as tears are washed across the surface.

The iris _____
is a ring of colored muscle that changes the size of the pupil

The cornea _____
is the curved front of the eye, which helps focus light

The lens _____
is an elastic, transparent disk that changes shape to adjust the eye's focus

Ciliary muscles *control the shape of the lens*

INSIDE THE EYE ▶
There are two cavities in the eye. The smaller cavity in front of the lens contains a watery substance, called aqueous humor. The larger cavity behind the lens contains a jellylike substance, called vitreous humor. This fluid fills the eye and creates the pressure that maintains the eye's shape. Blood vessels nourish the cells of the retina.

Optic nerves _____
cross and divide to take signals from both eyes to each side of the brain

Left visual cortex _____
processes signals from the left side of both eyes

◀ MRI SCAN
The two optic nerves cross over just behind the eyes and run deep into the brain. Each contains about a million nerve fibers leading from rods and cones in the retina. The left side of the brain processes signals from the left side of each retina; the right side of the brain processes signals from the right side of each retina.

FIND OUT MORE ▶▶ Brain 139 • Color 180 • Lenses 181 • Light 178–179 • Nervous System 138

EAR

The ear is the organ of hearing and balance. The outer ear collects sound and directs it to the sensory structures deep inside the skull.

HOW DOES SOUND TRAVEL THROUGH THE EAR?

Sound travels into the ear as vibrations in air. The eardrum picks up the vibrations and transmits them to tiny bones in the middle ear. These bones pass the vibrations to the fluid-filled cochlea in the inner year.

Outer ear

The middle ear has three tiny bones that carry vibrations to the inner ear

The inner ear is made up of the tiny organs that detect sound, balance, and movement

The eardrum passes vibrations to tiny bones inside the middle ear

Ear canal

INSIDE THE EAR ▲
Sound vibrations push the eardrum against the bones of the middle ear, which pass the signals to the inner ear.

WHAT HAPPENS IN THE COCHLEA?

Sound vibrations travel along the cochlea's spiral, fluid-filled tube, creating waves of pressure. These stimulate tiny hair cells on a structure called the organ of Corti, which sends signals to the brain.

HOW DO EARS HELP US BALANCE?

The semicircular canals contain fluid that moves whenever the head moves, making tiny blobs of jelly swing and sway and triggering nerve cells. There are also two fluid-filled chambers, called the utricle and saccule, which contain blobs of jelly that sway with gravity, telling the brain which way is up and down.

Semicircular canals contain balance receptors

Saccule and utricle detect gravity

Nerve fibers carry signals to the brain

Cochlea contains receptor cells that detect vibrations

INNER EAR ▲
The inner ear consists of the semicircular canals; the saccule and utricle, which detect movement; and the cochlea, which contains the sound receptors.

The retina is a layer of light-sensitive cells lining the back of the eye

The optic nerve contains nerve cells carrying signals from the retina to the brain

eye

◄ RODS AND CONES
Magnified thousands of times, this picture shows rods (in blue) and a shorter cone (in green) in the retina. Each retina has more than 100 million rods and up to 7 million cones. The cones are concentrated mainly in an area called the fovea, in the middle of the retina. The fovea creates a detailed image of whatever the eyes are looking at directly.

ear

FIND OUT MORE ▶▶ Brain 139 • Sound 176–177

Parotid salivary gland
lies in front of the ear

Salivary duct
opens into
the cheek

Tongue
moves food
during chewing
and swallowing

Teeth
cut and
grind food

Sublingual
salivary gland
is located under
the tongue

Submandibular
salivary gland
lies deep in
the mouth

Epiglottis

Larynx

Esophagus
leads to the
stomach

▲ INSIDE THE MOUTH
The mouth is a complex collection of
muscles, glands, and other structures that work
together smoothly. The tongue alone contains
18 interwoven muscles, which makes it
amazingly flexible. Its flexibility is essential for
speech, chewing, and swallowing.

mouth

MOUTH

Food enters the body through the
mouth. The mouth is the first part
of the digestive system, where food
is mashed and moistened, so that it
can be swallowed. The mouth also
plays an essential role in speech
and breathing.

WHY IS THE MOUTH ALWAYS WET?
Saliva contains chemicals that kill bacteria, and it
flows constantly into the mouth to help keep it free
of disease. The mouth's inner lining also secretes
a lubricating fluid called mucus. Saliva and mucus
both moisten food, making it easier to swallow.

WHAT HAPPENS TO FOOD IN THE MOUTH?
The front teeth cut up food, and the tongue and
cheek muscles push it between the back teeth, where
it is ground by the lower jaw. Saliva softens and
moistens food and washes over ▶▶ TASTE BUDS
in the tongue so that flavors can be identified. The
digestive process also begins in the mouth—saliva
contains chemicals that break down some foods.

TASTE BUDS

Our sense of taste comes from tiny,
onion-shaped clusters of cells called taste
buds. Most taste buds are scattered across
the surface of the tongue, where there are
around 10,000, but they are also found
in the roof of the mouth and the throat.

WHAT CAN THE TONGUE TASTE?
The tongue is sensitive to five basic tastes: salty,
sweet, bitter, acidic (sour), and umami (savory). The
chemicals that cause these tastes dissolve in saliva on
the tongue and seep into the taste buds, where they
trigger receptor cells that send signals to the brain.

TONGUE TASTE MAP ▶
Until recently, it was
thought that a specific area
of the tongue was sensitive
to a particular taste. It is
now understood that a taste,
such as bitter, can be located on
different parts of the tongue.

The surface of
the muscular tongue
is covered by tiny
bumps called papillae

Taste buds contain
25–30 receptor cells

◀ SURFACE OF THE TONGUE
The surface of the tongue is
covered by tiny bumps, called
papillae, which give it a rough
texture to grip food. Most are
small filiform papillae (shown in
blue) that have a sense of touch.
Scattered among these are larger
fungiform papillae (shown in
pink), which contain taste buds.

Saliva pours into the
gap between papillae

▶ TASTE BUDS
This magnified view of papillae
on the tongue shows the taste
buds in their sides. Each taste bud
has a tiny opening, or taste pore,
to let in the dissolved flavors of
food and drink.

FIND OUT MORE ▶▶ Brain 139 • Digestion 144–145 • Respiration 136

TEETH

Anchored firmly in the jawbones are the teeth. Our teeth are used to tear, chop, and grind food to make it soft enough to swallow and easier to digest.

The crown of a tooth is the part above the gum

Enamel

Dentine

Pulp cavity containing blood vessels and nerves

Roots secure teeth in the jawbones

WHAT ARE TEETH MADE OF?
The white, outer shell of a tooth is made of enamel, the hardest substance in the body. Under the enamel is a softer substance called dentine, and inside this is the soft, living heart of the tooth, called the pulp cavity.

WHY DO TEETH DECAY?
If teeth are not properly cleaned, a mixture of bacteria and food, called plaque, builds up on them. As the bacteria feed on the sugary food debris, they produce an acid that dissolves the calcium minerals in enamel and dentine, forming a cavity. If the sensitive dentine layer is exposed, hot and cold foods can cause pain.

INSIDE A TOOTH ►
Beneath the hard outer surface, dentine forms the body of a tooth. Nerves (green) and blood vessels (red and blue) run through the tissue of the pulp cavity and out through root canals at the base of the tooth.

teeth

PLAQUE ►
A sticky deposit called plaque builds up on teeth that are not cleaned regularly. Plaque consists of mucus, food debris, and bacteria that cause tooth decay.

◄ ORAL X-RAY
This X-ray shows all the teeth in an adult's mouth in one picture. It reveals their long roots, usually hidden beneath the gums. The white areas in the crowns are fillings. There are four main types of tooth, each suited to a particular task. Incisors (1) bite and chew; canines (2) pierce and tear; premolars (3) and molars (4) crush and grind.

Plaque (yellow) has built up on the enamel (gray) of this tooth

FIND OUT MORE ►► Digestion 144–145 • Microorganisms 85

NOSE

The main entrance to the body's airways is the nose. It also contains our smell sensors. The outer part of the nose is made mostly of a rubbery tissue called cartilage.

The olfactory bulb carries signals from smell receptor cells to the brain

The olfactory epithelium is a small patch of tissue containing smell-sensitive cells

Nasal cavity

Cartilage

WHY DO WE BREATHE THROUGH THE NOSE?
Breathing through the nose helps to protect the tissues of the lungs from germs, dirt, and very dry or cold air. The moist lining of the nasal passages warms and moistens air. Sticky mucus traps particles of dust, soot, and bacteria. Tiny beating hairs, called cilia, drive the mucus toward the throat to be swallowed.

▲ SMELL RECEPTORS
This magnified view shows a tangle of cilia (microscopic hairs) emerging from a smell receptor cell in the nose.

Hairs in the nostrils filter out large particles

HOW DOES THE NOSE DETECT SMELLS?
In the roof of each nostril is a patch of nerve endings, called the olfactory epithelium, covered by mucus. Odor molecules dissolve in the mucus and stimulate the nerve endings, which send signals to the olfactory bulb and the brain. We can recognize more than 10,000 smells and detect just a few molecules of some odors in a breath of air.

nose

INSIDE THE NOSE ►
Inside the nose is the hollow nasal cavity where air is warmed, moistened, and cleaned before it continues on its way down the pharynx (throat) to the lungs.

FIND OUT MORE ►► Brain 139 • Digestion 144–145 • Respiration 136

DIGESTION

The process of breaking down food into molecules the body can absorb is called digestion. The digestive system begins with the mouth and involves many organs in the abdomen. The digestive organs produce **▸▸ ENZYMES** which break down food chemically.

HOW DOES THE STOMACH WORK?
The stomach is a stretchy, muscular bag that stores food and churns it around until it is a thick liquid. Glands in the lining of the stomach secrete gastric juice, which contains pepsin and hydrochloric acid. Pepsin is an enzyme that digests protein molecules; hydrochloric acid kills germs and helps pepsin work.

WHERE DOES FOOD GO AFTER THE STOMACH?
Food is squirted from the stomach into the small intestine. Here it mixes with digestive juices from the liver and pancreas. Bile from the liver breaks up fat. Pancreatic juice neutralizes stomach acid and contains enzymes that digest carbohydrates, proteins, and fats.

▲ VILLI IN SMALL INTESTINE
Fingerlike villi line the inside of the small intestine, giving it a velvety texture and increasing the area for absorbing food.

WHY IS THE SMALL INTESTINE SO LONG?
The small intestine measures 21 ft (6.5 m) and is the main organ of digestion and absorption. As food moves slowly along the great length of the intestine, it has plenty of time to break down properly. The size of the small intestine also maximizes the area of inner lining that food passes and the absorbtion of nutrients.

HOW IS FOOD ABSORBED?
The lining of the small intestine is covered with microscopic projections called villi which dramatically increase its surface area. Molecules of nutrients dissolve in fluids in the intestine and pass into the villi. From there, nutrients pass through the thin walls of the blood vessels in the villi, and into the body.

DIGESTIVE SYSTEM ▸
The job of the digestive system is to turn the food we eat into material that the body can use for energy, growth, and to repair itself. It is a long system of different organs, each section working in a slightly different way to extract nutrients and water from food until only waste remains.

The tongue
tastes food and moves it around in the mouth and down the throat

Salivary glands
produce saliva to moisten food so that it travels comfortably down the throat

Teeth
cut and chew food into small pieces

The esophagus
takes swallowed food to the stomach

The stomach
churns food into a thick liquid and produces acid and an enzyme that digests protein

The liver
produces bile, which breaks down fats

The gall bladder
stores bile and releases it into the small intestine

The pancreas
produces enzymes that digest fat, protein, and carbohydrate in the small intestine

The small intestine
is where most digestion and nutrient absorption take place

The large intestine
is about 5 ft (1.5 m) long and absorbs water from the undigested remains of food

The appendix
is a small dead-end tube with no function

The rectum
stores undigested waste (feces) until it can be expelled

THE TIMETABLE OF THE DIGESTIVE SYSTEM

An average meal takes between 18 and 30 hours to pass through the digestive system, depending on the amount and type of food. Meals rich in carbohydrates (such as sugar and starch) are digested quickest, and fatty foods take longest.

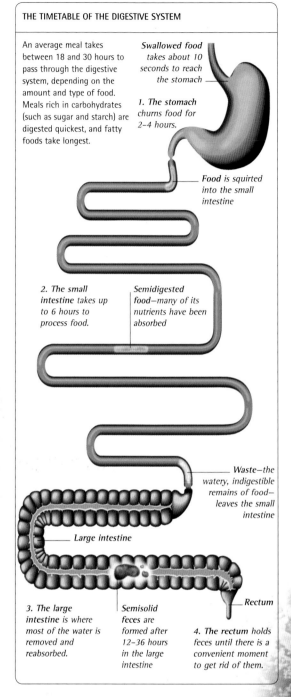

Swallowed food takes about 10 seconds to reach the stomach

1. The stomach churns food for 2–4 hours.

Food is squirted into the small intestine

2. The small intestine takes up to 6 hours to process food.

Semidigested food—many of its nutrients have been absorbed

Waste—the watery, indigestible remains of food—leaves the small intestine

Large intestine

Rectum

3. The large intestine is where most of the water is removed and reabsorbed.

Semisolid feces are formed after 12–36 hours in the large intestine

4. The rectum holds feces until there is a convenient moment to get rid of them.

WHY DON'T THE DIGESTIVE ORGANS DIGEST THEMSELVES?

The lining of the stomach and intestines secretes a thick, slippery liquid called mucus, which helps food slide along and protects the digestive organs from acid and enzymes. Even so, the intestinal lining does gradually wear away, but it continually renews itself by producing new cells, just as skin does.

HOW DOES FOOD MOVE ALONG THE DIGESTIVE SYSTEM?

The esophagus, stomach, small intestine, and large intestine all have muscular walls. When these muscle walls contract, the hollow organ narrows, pushing the food forward. The contraction happens in waves that move along the organs. This action is called peristalsis.

WHAT HAPPENS IN THE LARGE INTESTINE?

Undigested leftovers pass into the large intestine, which absorbs water and minerals. Harmless bacteria flourish in the waste and produce some vitamins, which are also absorbed. The semisolid wastes (feces) collect in the rectum before being expelled.

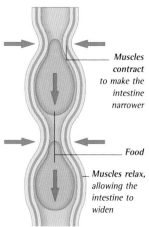

Muscles contract to make the intestine narrower

Food

Muscles relax, allowing the intestine to widen

▲ PERISTALSIS
The muscular walls of most sections of the digestive system contract in a wavelike pattern, known as peristalsis, to push food through.

BACTERIA IN THE LARGE INTESTINE ▶
This image shows rod-shaped bacteria (in pink) on the surface of the large intestine. Billions of useful and harmless bacteria live in the large intestine. This is one of the most common species, which helps release vitamins from food.

ENZYMES

Most chemical reactions in living organisms are controlled by enzymes. There are many types, each suited to a particular task.

HOW DO ENZYMES WORK?

Enzymes are catalysts, which means that they speed up the rate of a chemical reaction. The molecules of each enzyme have a very particular shape which enables them to bind to a specific molecule in the body and make it react.

WHICH ORGANS MAKE DIGESTIVE ENZYMES?

The salivary glands, stomach, pancreas, and small intestine all produce digestive enzymes. These enzymes break down proteins, carbohydrates, and fats into the units they are made up of—amino acids, sugars, and fatty acids. These tiny units are so small they can pass into the villi lining the intestine.

◀ ENZYMES IN THE PANCREAS
This magnified view shows granules of enzymes (in yellow and orange) made by the pancreas. These will be released into the small intestine to help the digestion of food.

digestion

LIVER

A vital organ, the liver carries out hundreds of essential chemical processes, adjusts the levels of many substances in the blood, and produces a digestive juice called bile. The liver is the body's heaviest organ, weighing about 3½ lb (1.5 kg).

WHAT IS INSIDE THE LIVER?
The liver is made up of thousands of lobules—tiny hexagonal units about $1/25$ in (1 mm) wide. Each is surrounded by a network of incoming blood vessels. Blood filters through the lobule and drains away through a vein in the middle.

HOW DOES BLOOD GET TO THE LIVER?
Unlike other organs, the liver receives blood from two major blood vessels. The hepatic artery brings oxygen-rich blood from the heart. The hepatic portal vein brings blood rich in digested nutrients from the intestine. This means excess nutrients can be removed and stored before blood circulates around the body.

WHY IS THE LIVER A FACTORY?
The liver carries out so many tasks that scientists compare it to a chemical factory. It filters blood from the intestines and removes excess food and iron for storage or for conversion into other substances. It also removes debris, destroys poisons, worn-out blood cells, and alcohol, and manufactures vitamin A and many other chemicals vital to the body.

▼ LIVER CELLS
This magnified view shows red blood cells flowing through spaces between the cells in a liver lobule. As the blood filters through the lobule, the liver adjusts the levels of many different chemicals.

Red blood cells
pass through channels
called sinusoids

SCAN THROUGH THE ABDOMEN ►
This MRI scan shows a vertical slice through the back of the abdomen. Seen from the front, the liver is on the left and the stomach is on the right. This view shows a section of one end of the liver, making it look smaller than it is.

The liver is not seen in full in this image, which shows a cross-section of the back part of the liver

Kidneys lie beneath the ribs at the back of the abdomen

Vertebrae of the spine

liver

Liver fills the upper-left area of the abdomen

Intestines show up only partially on this scan

Vena cava carries blood to the heart

Aorta carries blood out of the heart

Vertebra

Stomach

▲ HORIZONTAL CROSS-SECTION THROUGH THE BODY
This scan shows a horizontal slice through the abdomen and gives an impression of the liver's size. The liver is the largest organ in the body and takes up most of the space in the upper abdomen, just below the ribs. The blue "hole" in the liver is the inferior vena cava—one of the body's largest veins.

WHAT IS BILE?
The liver makes a greenish-brown liquid called bile, which is stored in a pouch called the gall bladder and emptied into the small intestine, where it makes fats mix with water and so helps digestion. Bile consists of water, bile salts, acid, cholesterol, and a pigment called bilirubin, which gives feces their color.

FIND OUT MORE ▶▶ Circulation 134 • Digestion 144–145

KIDNEYS

The kidneys are two bean-shaped organs at the back of the abdomen that filter and clean the blood, removing chemical wastes and excess water. Wastes drain out of the kidneys as urine.

Stomach

Left kidney

WHAT IS INSIDE A KIDNEY?
Each kidney contains about a million tiny filtering units called nephrons. Blood flows through a kind of filter at the top of each nephron, and water and small molecules pass through it into a long tube. In the tube useful substances such as glucose and salt are then reabsorbed, and what is left over forms urine.

WHY DOES BLOOD NEED CLEANING?
If the kidneys did not filter the blood, chemical wastes would build up in the body and become poisonous. The kidneys also control the level of water in the blood by varying how much water is reabsorbed in the nephrons. If we drink a lot, the kidneys can excrete the excess to stop the blood from becoming diluted.

WHERE DOES WASTE GO?
Urine from each kidney drains through a tube called a ureter and collects in the bladder. As the bladder fills, its muscular wall stretches. When it is full, receptors in the wall send a signal to the brain and trigger the urge to urinate. During urination the muscles that close the bladder exit relax to release the urine.

kidneys

▲ A FULL BLADDER
In this X-ray, dye is used to show urine from the kidneys draining through the ureters to a full bladder. An adult bladder can hold about 1 pint (0.5 liter) of urine.

FIND OUT MORE ▶▶ Brain 139 • Circulation 134

HORMONES

Hormones are control chemicals that trigger major changes in the body. They control many important functions, including body chemistry, growth and sexual development, and the body's response to stress.

HOW DO HORMONES WORK?
Hormone molecules travel in the blood looking for specific cells which they bind onto. This triggers a chain of chemical reactions and changes the cell's job. Some hormones work by switching genes on or off.

PITUITARY GLAND ▶
This 3-D CT reconstruction shows the pituitary gland at the base of the brain. The pituitary gland produces hormones and controls other hormone glands in the body.

hormones

The pituitary gland is about the size of a pea

HORMONAL GLANDS AND THEIR FUNCTIONS			
Pituitary gland	A key gland that releases nine hormones that control body functions or trigger other glands.	Parathyroid glands	Four small glands that work with the thyroid gland to balance levels of calcium in the blood.
Pancreas	Secretes insulin and glucagon, which control the level of sugar in the blood.	Pineal gland	Secretes melatonin, a hormone that controls the daily rhythm of sleep and waking.
Adrenal gland	Secretes epinephrine, which helps the body cope with fear or excitement, and steroids.	Ovaries (in females)	Make estrogen and progesterone, which control the development and function of the sex organs.
Thyroid gland	Secretes thyroxine, which speeds up the rate of body chemistry.	Testes (in males)	Secrete testosterone, which controls the development and function of the male sex organs.

FIND OUT MORE ▶▶ Cells 73 • Growth 149 • Reproduction 148

The umbilical cord carries food and oxygen to the baby from the placenta— the organ inside the womb that links the baby to the mother's blood supply

REPRODUCTION

New life is created by reproduction. The mother and father produce sex cells, which join to form an embryo. These sex cells also determine the child's ▸▸ **HEREDITY**.

WHERE DO SEX CELLS FORM?

Male cells are called sperm. They are produced by the million in the testes—a pair of ball-shaped glands that hang outside the body in the scrotum. A female sex cell is called an ovum (plural ova). A woman's ova form before she is born, in two organs called ovaries, in her abdomen.

HOW DOES AN EMBRYO FORM?

Sperm and ova come together as a result of sexual intercourse (sex). During sex, a man places his penis inside a woman's body. Sperm leave the penis and swim into the woman's reproductive organs. If the ovaries have released an ovum, a sperm cell may fuse with it and form an embryo. This is called fertilization.

Sperm attach to the ovum and try to enter it

▲ **HUMAN FETUS**
At five months old, the human fetus weighs under 1 lb (500 g) but has fully developed lips, eyes, fingers, and toes. The mother can feel movements of the fetus inside the uterus (womb).

WHERE DOES THE EMBRYO DEVELOP?

The embryo develops inside an organ called the uterus (womb). It sinks into the soft lining of the uterus and absorbs food from the mother through an organ called the placenta, which develops from the embryo. The uterus has a very stretchy wall so that it can expand as the baby grows.

◀ **OVUM AND SPERM**
When sperm cells find an ovum, they try to break through its coat. The first to get through fertilizes the egg and the rest die. Nuclei from the sperm and the ovum then fuse to make a single nucleus.

Ovum—ova are the largest cells in the human body

reproduction

HEREDITY

The process of inheriting characteristics from parents is called heredity. Many of our characteristics are passed on through genes— instructions made up of DNA molecules in our chromosomes.

HOW ARE GENES INHERITED?

People inherit half their genes from their mother and half from their father. The genes are passed on in chromosomes carried by sperm and ova. The chromosomes interact with each other in different ways, so children from the same parents may share characteristics, but are also very different. Apart from identical twins, everyone has a unique set of genes.

HOW DO GENES AFFECT CHARACTERISTICS?

Genes determine most of your physical characteristics, such as eye color. Eye color is controlled by only a handful of genes, but other characteristics, such as height, involve lots of genes. Genes can also affect mental characteristics such as personality and intelligence, but these are heavily influenced by your experiences as well. The study of genes and how they affect you is called genetics.

▲ **CHROMOSOMES OF A WOMAN**
Chromosomes are microscopic threads in our cell nuclei. Each one contains a long DNA molecule. We have 46 chromosomes in 23 pairs. One of each pair comes from our mother and the other from our father.

The sex chromosomes are the only chromosomes that differ between men and women

GROWTH

It takes nine months for an embryo to grow into a baby inside its mother's uterus (womb). After birth, the baby keeps growing for another 20 years, changing all the time. Growth is quickest in the first few years of life.

HOW DOES A BABY GROW?

An embryo begins life as one cell. It divides repeatedly, changing shape to form a ball of cells. After four weeks it has the early stages of a brain and spinal cord. At six weeks it has the flap-like beginning of limbs and its heart starts beating. At 12 weeks it looks like a miniature baby.

WHAT HAPPENS AS CHILDREN GROW?

Children change shape as they grow because parts of the body grow at different speeds. The brain grows quickest at first, which is why babies have such large heads. Muscles and bones grow later on. The rate of growth slows down during childhood, but shoots up again at puberty.

HOW DO GIRLS CHANGE AT PUBERTY?

The period when a child changes into an adult is called puberty. For girls, puberty usually begins between 10 and 12 years. They grow taller, their breasts develop, and their hips widen. Hair grows under the arms and around the groin. Girls' ovaries start to release ova each month and they have periods.

WHAT HAPPENS WHEN PEOPLE GROW OLD?

After early adulthood, the body gradually begins to decline. The skin loses its elasticity, muscles get weaker, and internal organs become less efficient. Certain diseases become more common as we get older, including heart disease and cancer. Aging is a very slow process, and most people lead active lives well into their 70s and 80s.

BABY TEETH ▲
A human has two sets of teeth in their lifetime. At about six months old, the first set, called baby teeth, begin to appear. Baby teeth start to fall out when we are about six years old, as permanent teeth, shown here in green, grow up beneath them. In adult life, most people have a full set of 32 permanent teeth.

This vertebra (colored red) has shrunk and become wedge-shaped

▲ OSTEOPOROSIS
A natural part of aging is a condition called osteoporosis, which makes bones become weaker and more brittle. Some people with osteoporosis shrink in height or become hunched because the bones of their spine lose shape and crumble.

This bacterium is multiplying by dividing in two

ACNE BACTERIA ▶
During puberty, many people get a rash of reddish pimples, called acne, especially around the face. Acne develops because the sex hormones released during puberty make the skin oilier. Bacteria get trapped in plugs of oil at the base of hairs, making the skin become inflamed.

HOW DO BOYS CHANGE AT PUBERTY?

Boys go through puberty later than girls—between 12 and 14 years. They shoot up in height, and their shoulders and chests get broader. Hair starts to grow on the face, under the arms, around the groin, and sometimes on the chest. The voice gets deeper, and the testes start to make sperm.

AGING SKIN ▶
These hands of a child and an elderly person show the effects of aging on the skin. The outer layer of skin becomes thinner and loses the protein fibers that make it elastic, causing it to wrinkle. Harmless dark spots also often appear, the result of the overproduction of melanin.

growth

BRAIN AND SKULL DEVELOPMENT

NEURAL NETWORK — *Neuron*

Gaps between the bones of a baby's skull allow the head to grow

AT BIRTH
A baby's brain has a full set of brain cells, but there are few connections between them. The brain grows quickly in the first two years.

NEURAL NETWORK

Skull plates are now fixed at the sutures

AT SIX YEARS
The brain is nearly adult size, but continues to change and learn by growing new connections between the brain cells.

NEURAL NETWORK

The facial bones are now mature

AT 18 YEARS
The brain is fully formed and brain cells have formed billions of complex connections, but we still continue to learn.

FIND OUT MORE ▶▶ Hormones 147 • Skeleton 130–131 • Skin 133 • Teeth 143

HEALTH

Being healthy means being free of disease or injury and able to lead a fulfilling, active life. Many factors contribute to a person's health, including genes, the environment, ▸▸ NUTRITION, lifestyle, and luck.

WHAT ARE THE MAJOR HEALTH ISSUES IN THE WORLD TODAY?

In poor countries, dirty water and lack of adequate food are among the main causes of poor health. Infectious diseases such as malaria and AIDS are also major problems, especially in countries that cannot afford modern drugs and medical equipment. In rich countries, health problems are more often caused by people's lifestyle.

CLEAN WATER ▸
A supply of clean drinking water, such as this pump in Cambodia, is vital for good health. In places without a modern sewage system, germs from sewage often contaminate the drinking water supply and cause diseases such as typhoid and cholera.

health

HOW DOES LIFESTYLE AFFECT HEALTH?

The affluent lifestyle of people in rich countries can increase the risk of serious diseases. Heart disease, obesity (excessive storage of fat), and strokes (blood clots in the brain) are all more common in people who do little exercise or eat too much rich food. Health problems caused by tobacco, alcohol, and drug abuse are common in both rich and poor countries.

LIFE EXPECTANCY

These United Nations figures show average life expectancy for babies born from 2005-2010. The life expectancy of people living in the wealthy countries of the world is almost three times that of people in the poorest.

THE TOP FIVE COUNTRIES	THE BOTTOM FIVE COUNTRIES
Japan 82.6 years	Liberia 41.8 years
Iceland 81.8 years	Sierra Leone 41.3 years
Switzerland 81.7 years	Mozambique 41.2 years
Australia 81.2 years	Zambia 38.6 years
Spain 80.9 years	Angola 38.2 years

Sweets, oils, and candies are rich in fats and sugars that contain useful nutrients but should only be eaten in small quantities

Milk, cheese, butter, and yogurt are good sources of calcium

Meat, eggs, fish, and nuts are rich in protein, vitamins, and minerals, but some kinds of meat contain large amounts of fat, which can cause health problems if eaten in large quantities

Fruit is a good source of water, fiber, and vitamins and contains natural sugars that give us a burst of energy

Vegetables contain vitamins and minerals and are rich in fiber

Bread, potatoes, rice, and pasta are mostly carbohydrate and are the body's main source of energy

NUTRITION

The process of supplying the body with the nutrients (foods) it needs to stay alive is called nutrition. Eating a variety of foods—a balanced diet—is an important part of keeping healthy.

WHAT IS A BALANCED DIET?

A balanced diet includes a mixture of carbohydrates, proteins, fats, vitamins, minerals, and fiber. Sweets and fast foods usually contain too much carbohydrate and fat, and little of the fiber needed to keep the digestive system healthy. Fast food that does not contain fresh ingredients is often low in vitamins and minerals.

WHAT IS MALNUTRITION?

Malnutrition means "bad nutrition." This can happen when a person has too little of certain types of food. Lack of protein, for example, can cause stunted growth. Malnutrition can also occur if the diet has excessive amounts of some types of foods—too much fat and sugar, for example, can result in obesity.

WHY IS OBESITY A PROBLEM?

Obesity is increasingly common in wealthy countries. It can lead to medical problems, including diabetes, heart disease, stroke, and high blood pressure. Excess weight can also put strain on the body, causing back pain, shortness of breath, and arthritis.

◂ FOOD PYRAMID
The food pyramid shows the proportions and range of food types that make up a healthy diet. It is important to eat plenty of fresh fruit and vegetables and to reduce the intake of saturated fats and sugar.

DISEASE

Anything that damages the body or how it works can be called a disease. Some diseases are caused by microscopic organisms (germs), others by injury, poisons, or the body itself. Nearly all diseases can be treated by modern ►► **MEDICINE** to some extent.

WHAT ARE BACTERIA AND VIRUSES?
The most common infectious diseases are caused by bacteria and viruses. Bacteria are single-celled organisms that live outside our cells. They multiply in body fluids and wounds. Many are killed with drugs called antibiotics. Viruses are microscopic particles with their own genetic material. They live in our cells and take them over, but cannot survive without them.

PNEUMONIA BACTERIA ►
Pneumonia is a lung disease which can be caused by bacteria or a virus. This electron micrograph shows pneumonia-causing bacteria (shown in pink) on the tiny hairs (green) that line the lungs' airways. Pneumonia can affect anyone, but people who are sick and so have a weakened defense system are particularly vulnerable.

◄ HIV
The virus that causes AIDS (acquired immune deficiency syndrome) is called HIV (human immunodeficiency virus). The virus invades cells of the immune system, making it more difficult for the body to defend itself from the virus and other diseases.

This image clearly shows the surface of the virus. The glycoprotein complex that sticks out enables the virus to attach to and fuse with target cells, such as white blood cells, and then initiate an ongoing and infectious cycle.

WHAT ARE GENETIC DISEASES?
Genetic diseases, such as cystic fibrosis and muscular dystrophy, occur when a person inherits a particular gene or combination of genes that is harmful. Sometimes the harmful genes are passed on unknowingly by unaffected parents; in other cases the gene changes at conception to become abnormal.

WHY DO SOME PEOPLE SUFFER FROM ALLERGIES?
The body has sophisticated defenses for attacking germs, called the immune system, but sometimes the system attacks the wrong targets—people have an allergic reaction when the immune system is triggered by harmless substances like pollen and dust.

WHAT IS CANCER?
There are many different types of cancer, but what they all have in common is that cells start to divide uncontrollably, forming a tumor. The tumor may then prevent part of the body from working normally. This is sometimes caused by agents called carcinogens, such as sunlight or tobacco smoke.

disease

MEDICINE

The study and treatment of disease is called medicine. Modern medicine aims to prevent and cure disease where possible. Some diseases, such as diabetes, are incurable, but medical treatment can still relieve symptoms and improve a patient's quality of life.

CAN DISEASES BE PREVENTED?
Many infectious diseases are prevented by vaccination, which protects the body from specific germs. Screening programs can detect the early stages of diseases such as cancer. A healthy lifestyle can also help prevent conditions such as heart disease.

HOW ARE DISEASES TREATED?
The body can cope with most illnesses itself, without medical help. We recover from a sore throat, for example. For major problems, a range of treatments can be used, such as drugs, surgery, or radiotherapy the killing of harmful cells using radiation).

Femur

Blood flow in this femoral artery has stopped just above the knee

Femoral artery with normal blood flow

BLOCKED ARTERY ►
X-rays are one of the many medical imaging techniques that doctors use to investigate and diagnose disease. This X-ray reveals a blockage in a major artery (yellow) in a person's leg.

PERIODIC TABLE

The periodic table is a simple list of all the elements. The elements are arranged by their atomic number. The information given for each element includes atomic number, symbol, name, and mass number. The vertical columns of the table are called groups, and the horizontal rows are called periods.

WHY ARE ELEMENTS IN A GROUP SIMILAR?
The chemical properties of an element depend on the number of electrons in its outer shell. Elements in the same group have the same number of outer electrons. For example, all the elements in Group 1 (alkali metals) have one electron in their outer shells. They are all silvery white, highly reactive metals.

HOW DOES THE PERIODIC TABLE WORK?
The periodic table sets out the elements in a way that highlights similarities and trends in their properties. Elements in the same group (column) have similar properties. The properties change gradually along periods (rows) in the table—elements on the left are metals, elements on the right are nonmetals. As you move across periods, the atomic number increases. Also, at the start of a period, elements have one electron in their outer shell—by the end, they have eight.

79
Au
Gold
197

The atomic number is the number of protons in the nucleus

The symbol is used as shorthand for the element in chemical equations

The mass number gives the number of protons and neutrons in the nucleus. The mass numbers given on this page are for the most common isotope (form) of the element

KEY
- Alkali metals
- Alkali-earth metals
- Transition metals
- Rare earths
- Radioactive rare earths
- Other metals
- Semimetals
- Non-metals
- Noble gases
- Hydrogen does not belong to any one group
- Undefined

1 H Hydrogen 1																	2 He Helium 4
3 Li Lithium 7	4 Be Beryllium 9											5 B Boron 11	6 C Carbon 12	7 N Nitrogen 14	8 O Oxygen 16	9 F Fluorine 19	10 Ne Neon 20
11 Na Sodium 23	12 Mg Magnesium 24											13 Al Aluminum 27	14 Si Silicon 28	15 P Phosphorus 31	16 S Sulfur 32	17 Cl Chlorine 35	18 Ar Argon 40
19 K Potassium 39	20 Ca Calcium 40	21 Sc Scandium 45	22 Ti Titanium 48	23 V Vanadium 51	24 Cr Chromium 52	25 Mn Manganese 55	26 Fe Iron 56	27 Co Cobalt 59	28 Ni Nickel 58	29 Cu Copper 63	30 Zn Zinc 64	31 Ga Gallium 69	32 Ge Germanium 74	33 As Arsenic 75	34 Se Selenium 80	35 Br Bromine 79	36 Kr Krypton 84
37 Rb Rubidium 85	38 Sr Strontium 88	39 Y Yttrium 89	40 Zr Zirconium 90	41 Nb Niobium 93	42 Mo Molybdenum 98	43 Tc Technetium 97	44 Ru Ruthenium 102	45 Rh Rhodium 103	46 Pd Palladium 106	47 Ag Silver 107	48 Cd Cadmium 114	49 In Indium 115	50 Sn Tin 120	51 Sb Antimony 121	52 Te Tellurium 130	53 I Iodine 127	54 Xe Xenon 132
55 Cs Cesium 133	56 Ba Barium 138	57-71	72 Hf Hafnium 180	73 Ta Tantalum 181	74 W Tungsten 184	75 Re Rhenium 187	76 Os Osmium 192	77 Ir Iridium 193	78 Pt Platinum 195	79 Au Gold 197	80 Hg Mercury 202	81 Ti Thallium 205	82 Pb Lead 208	83 Bi Bismuth 209	84 Po Polonium 209	85 At Astatine 210	86 Rn Radon 222
87 Fr Francium 223	88 Ra Radium 226	89-103	104 Rf Rutherfordium 261	105 Db Dubnium 262	106 Sg Seaborgium 268	107 Bh Bohrium 264	108 Hs Hassium 267	109 Mt Meitnerium 268	110 Ds Darmstadtium 281	111 Rg Roentgenium 281	112 Cn Copernicium 285	113 Uut Ununtrium 284	114 Uuq Ununquadium 289	115 Uup Ununpentium 288	116 Uuh Ununhexium 293	(117) (Uus) (Ununseptium) (not known)	118 Uuo Ununoctium 294

57 La Lanthanum 139	58 Ce Cerium 140	59 Pr Praseodymium 141	60 Nd Neodymium 142	61 Pm Promethium 145	62 Sm Samarium 152	63 Eu Europium 153	64 Gd Gadolinium 158	65 Tb Terbium 159	66 Dy Dysprosium 164	67 Ho Holmium 165	68 Er Erbium 168	69 Tm Thulium 169	70 Yb Ytterbium 174	71 Lu Lutetium 175
89 Ac Actinium 227	90 Th Thorium 232	91 Pa Protactinium 231	92 U Uranium 238	93 Np Neptunium 237	94 Pu Plutonium 244	95 Am Americium 243	96 Cm Curium 247	97 Bk Berkelium 247	98 Cf Californium 251	99 Es Einsteinium 254	100 Fm Fermium 257	101 Md Mendelevium 258	102 No Nobelium 255	103 Lr Lawrencium 256

elements

▲ PERIODIC TABLE
Russian chemist Dimitri Ivanovich Mendeleev (1834–1907) drew up the first periodic table in 1869. Gaps in Mendeleev's table suggested the existence of elements that were not known at the time. The missing elements have all since been discovered—for example, scandium, gallium, and germanium.

WHAT IS AN ISOTOPE?
All elements have several forms called isotopes. Each isotope of an element has the same atomic number, but a different atomic mass. In carbon, 99 percent of the atoms are isotope carbon 12, and 1 percent are carbon 13. Both isotopes have six protons, but carbon 12 has six neutrons, while carbon 13 has seven.

WHY IS THE PERIODIC TABLE USEFUL?
Scientists can tell a great deal about the properties of an element, even before they do experiments—by looking at its position in the periodic table. They can decide whether it will be a metal or a nonmetal, judge how well it will conduct electricity, and predict how it will react with other elements.

FIND OUT MORE ▶▶ Alloys 174 • Atoms 157 • Electricity 182 • Heat 168–169 • Materials 170 • Matter 156

pH 14

*Caustic soda
(oven cleaner)
Caustic soda reacts with
fat and grease marks, and
destroys skin and flesh.*

pH 11

*Milk of magnesia
This alkali is used to cure
indigestion—it neutralizes
the acid in your stomach.*

pH 9

*Liquid soap
All cleaning products are
bases. Like most bases,
soap feels slippery.*

pH 7.5

*Blood
Medical injections contain
chemicals called buffers to
match the pH of blood.*

pH 6–7

*Pure water
Pure water is neutral—
it is neither an acid nor
a base.*

pH 4

*Oranges
Oranges are mildly acidic,
which is why they taste
slightly sharp.*

pH 3

*Vinegar
The acid in vinegar kills
bacteria, so it is used in
pickling to preserve food.*

pH 2

*Lemon juice
Lemons taste sour because
they contain citric acid.
Acid means "sour" in Latin.*

pH 1

*Hydrochloric acid
This is a strong, corrosive
acid. It eats through most
metals in a fizzing reaction.*

CHEMISTRY

Chemistry is the science of matter. Scientists study chemicals, their properties, and ▸▸REACTIONS. ▸▸BIOCHEMISTRY is the chemistry of living things.

WHAT IS A CHEMICAL?

Chemicals are the basic types of matter. The elements, such as hydrogen and oxygen, are chemicals. So are the compounds, such as water, that are made when atoms of different elements join. Our bodies, food, and the clothes we wear are all made from chemicals.

WHAT ARE CHEMICAL PROPERTIES?

The properties of a chemical describe what it does to other chemicals. Oxygen, for example, makes iron rust, or oxidize, so oxygen is an oxidizing agent.

WHY ARE SOME CHEMICALS DANGEROUS?

Our bodies contain tens of thousands of chemicals that mix and react to give us energy and keep us alive. Toxic (poisonous) chemicals interfere with these reactions. Some chemicals are also corrosive—they eat through solid material.

◂ **THE pH SCALE**
The pH scale is a measure of acidity. Very strong acids have a pH of 1, neutral chemicals are pH 7, and strong bases, or alkalis, are pH 14.

STRONG REACTION ▸
Chemists use experiments to find out how chemicals react when they are mixed in different ways. Some chemicals react strongly, bubbling, burning, or even exploding. Other chemicals do not react at all.

Vapor escapes into the atmosphere

Two liquids react in a flask

CHEMICAL REACTIONS

A chemical reaction happens when two or more chemicals combine to make new chemical compounds. Many reactions release heat—for example, burning.

WHAT ARE ACIDS AND BASES?

Acids are chemicals that react with metals. Strong acids, such as sulfuric, nitric, and hydrochloric acid, are very corrosive. A base is a chemical that neutralizes an acid. When acids and bases react, they form chemicals called salts. Alkalis are bases that dissolve in water.

◂ **GRAPHITE**
Graphite is a form of pure carbon. The carbon atoms in graphite are bonded in sheets that slide over each other easily. This is why a graphite pencil leaves black marks.

DIAMOND ▸
The carbon atoms in diamond are bonded in a strong 3-D network. This makes diamond the hardest material on Earth.

chemistry

BIOCHEMISTRY

Biochemistry studies the molecules in living things, including plants, animals, and the human body. These molecules are all compounds of the element carbon.

WHY IS LIFE BASED ON CARBON?

Carbon atoms can link to each other (and to other elements) in many, many ways, including rings and chains of any length. This enormous variety means carbon is the perfect main building block for the complicated molecules of life.

FIND OUT MORE ▸▸ Elements 160–161 • Materials 170 • Matter 156

PHYSICS

Physics is the study of the forces, the energy, and the matter that make up the Universe and everything in it. ▶APPLIED PHYSICS uses the discoveries of physics in medicine, engineering, and other practical situations.

WHAT DO PHYSICISTS STUDY?
Physicists investigate what atoms are made of, how materials behave, and the forces that keep planets in orbit. They also study heat, light, sound, electricity, and magnetism. They try to discover the basic laws that matter and energy obey. Discoveries are usually written down as scientific ▶EQUATIONS.

WHAT ARE PHYSICAL PROPERTIES?
Physical properties are features that can be measured as numbers—length, weight, and volume, for example. Other physical properties include hardness, density, elasticity (how flexible a material is), conductivity (how well it conducts electricity or heat), and reflectivity (how much light it reflects).

HOW DO PHYSICISTS WORK?
There are two main types of investigation in physics. Experimental physicists work in laboratories, designing experiments to measure physical properties and processes. Theoretical physicists work with ideas, equations, and models to uncover new laws of physics that can explain or predict the results of experiments.

ROLLER COASTER ▲
Designers used physics to make sure this roller coaster is safe, but also fun. They use the basic laws of motion to predict the forces you will experience at every loop and turn of the ride.

EQUATIONS

An equation is a short way to write a scientific idea. For example, the density of a material is a measure of how tightly packed the matter inside it is. The equation density=mass/volume says that an object's density is its mass divided by its volume.

SIR ISAAC NEWTON
English, 1642–1727
Isaac Newton made some of the most important scientific and mathematical discoveries of all time. His laws of motion and theories of gravity explain how all objects from atoms to planets move. His theories of optics (light) show that white light is made of a spectrum of colored light.

WHAT DO EQUATIONS TELL US?
An equation states that the amount to the left of the equals sign is the same as the amount on the right. Letters are used for physical properties—in the equation F=ma, F is force, and ma means mass (m) multiplied by acceleration (a). Some equations show the results of an experiment, and others show the predictions of a theory.

$$d = 0.7v + 0.07v^2$$

▲ STOPPING DISTANCE
This equation shows how the stopping distance (d) of a braking car depends on its speed, or velocity (v). The distance has two parts. $0.7v$ (0.7 times the speed) is the distance traveled while the driver is reacting (the thinking distance). $0.07v^2$ is the distance traveled during braking. The symbol ^{2} means the number multiplied by itself.

APPLIED PHYSICS

Applied physicists use the basic laws of the physical world to design useful tools and techniques for many areas of science and technology, including medicine, astronomy, meteorology, materials science, and information technology.

physics

◀ MRI SCAN
With an MRI (magnetic resonance imaging) scan, a doctor can look inside the body without surgery. MRI is based on the magnetic properties of atomic nuclei, discovered by physicists.

HOW IS PHYSICS USED IN MEDICINE?
Physics has been used to develop many valuable medical instruments and techniques. Scanners, X-ray machines, and laser surgery are based on discoveries made by physicists. So are heart monitors and radiation treatment for cancer.

FIND OUT MORE ▶▶ Energy 166 • Forces 164 • Matter 156 • Measurements 155

FORCES

When you strike a ball with a bat, stretch a rubber band, or lift a suitcase, you are applying a force. All forces are pushes and pulls. Some forces can act over long distances—for example, the force of ▸▸ GRAVITY pulls you down when you jump from a high diving board.

WHAT CAN FORCES DO?

Forces change motion and shape. The force of a foot kicking a ball speeds the ball up. The force of a parachute on a skydiver slows the skydiver down. The force of a string on a whirling ball constantly changes the direction of motion, keeping it moving in a circle. Combinations of forces applied to materials can stretch, twist, and crush them.

HOW CAN YOU MEASURE A FORCE?

Forces are measured by their effects. Spring balances are used to measure the effect of forces. The stronger the force applied to a spring, the more it is stretched. The amount the spring is stretched from its normal size is proportional to the force applied to it. The unit of measurement of force is called a newton. One newton of force increases the speed of a one-kilogram mass by one meter per second every second.

WHAT ARE BALANCED FORCES?

Two forces are balanced when they are equal in size and opposite in direction. If the balanced forces are applied to an object, they will have no effect on its motion in a straight line, but may stretch or compress it. If the forces do not act along the same line, they may cause the object to rotate.

FUNDAMENTAL FORCES		
FORCE	*EFFECTS*	*RELATIVE STRENGTH*
Gravity	Gives objects weight Holds moons and planets in their orbits	Very weak
Electromagnetic	Holds electrons in atoms and atoms in molecules Gives materials strength and shape Responsible for electricity, magnetism, light, and other forms of electromagnetic radiation	Strong
Weak nuclear	Involved in radioactivity	Weak
Strong nuclear	Holds protons and neutrons in the nuclei of atoms	Very strong

▲ IMPACT
Forces always come in pairs. As you head a soccer ball, the force on your head is opposite in direction from the force on the ball. During the impact, both the head and the ball change shape. Their motion changes in opposite ways. The ball goes away from you as your head goes back.

▲ SKYDIVERS
The force of gravity pulls these skydivers toward Earth. Their speed increases until their weight is exactly balanced by the force from the air (air resistance), which acts in the opposite direction. They continue to fall, but at a steady rate. By spreading their arms and legs, the skydivers use air resistance to steer as they fall, linking hands to make a ring.

forces

GRAVITY

Gravity is the force that acts between all objects with mass. Gravity always attracts, never repels—it is always a pull and never a push. The strength of the force of gravity increases either when mass is increased or when the distance between the objects is decreased.

WHAT IS THE DIFFERENCE BETWEEN MASS AND WEIGHT?

Mass is the amount of matter in an object. The mass of an object does not change if it is taken from Earth into space. Weight is a force. The weight of an object on Earth is the force acting on it because of Earth's gravity. On the Moon the object weighs less than on Earth since the Moon's force of gravity is less.

WHY DO THINGS FLOAT OR SINK?

If you place a block of wood in water, it displaces (pushes aside) some of the water but floats. A force in the water called upthrust acts upward on it to counter the downward pull of gravity. The upthrust equals the weight of the displaced water. When you place a heavy object in water, the weight of the displaced water, which equals the upthrust, is less than the weight of the object, so the object sinks.

FIND OUT MORE ▸▸ Atoms 157 • Earth • Matter 156 • Motion 165 • Planet Earth 36 • Space Travel 30

MOTION

From molecules in this sheet of paper, to planets in orbits, the objects around us are in constant motion. The simplest motion is in a straight line at constant speed. When the speed or direction change, scientists say that motion is accelerated.

WHAT IS ACCELERATION?

When you drop a stone, it starts from rest (speed equals zero), then speeds up as it falls. The stone is accelerating. A force is always needed to produce acceleration—in this case, it is the force of gravity. Acceleration is slowed by ▶▶ FRICTION – in this case, air resistance.

HOW IS SPEED MEASURED?

Two measurements are needed to find speed—the distance moved, and the time taken. Speed is calculated by dividing the distance by the time. If a runner covers five meters (about 5 yards) in one second, his or her speed is five meters per second. A car that travels 100 miles in two hours has an average speed of 50 miles per hour.

Pendulum

PENDULUM SWING ▲

The child on the swing is moving like a pendulum. She kicks to start. Gravity slows her down as she rises, then speeds her up again in the opposite direction. She swings back and forth until friction and air resistance eventually bring her to rest.

CIRCULAR MOTION ▶

Whirling in a circle involves constantly changing direction. The ice skater's arms fly out as she spins. By using a force to bring them straight above her head, she can increase her turning speed.

◀ COMPLEX MOTION

The complicated motion of a gymnast's front handspring combines movement in a straight line and movement in a circle.

FRICTION

The force of friction opposes motion when one surface slides, or tries to slide, over another. You feel friction as you drag your hand across a table. Friction is produced by forces between the molecules in the surfaces. Drag is the friction between a solid object and the fluid it is traveling through.

HOW CAN FRICTION BE REDUCED?

Friction between parts of machines can damage them by wear and tear. Friction also wastes energy as heat instead of movement. Friction can be reduced by using oil as a lubricant to make a slippery film between surfaces. Machines built with a streamlined shape reduce drag. Airplanes are designed to let air flow over them smoothly with the least resistance. The study of air flow is called aerodynamics.

HOW CAN WE USE FRICTION?

Friction is not always a problem—sometimes we use it to prevent or slow down motion. Without friction, your shoes would not grip the ground and you would slip and fall, and a car's wheels would spin and skid. Friction is increased by making shoe soles and tires from soft, "sticky" materials such as rubber.

motion

FRICTION BY DESIGN ▶

An athlete needs friction between the soles of his shoes and the road to run. Without friction, his feet would slide in place.

Soft rubber soles grip the ground

Grooves channel water away

FIND OUT MORE ▶▶ Atoms 157 • Forces 164 • Materials 170

ENERGY

Without energy, the world would be lifeless, dark, and still. When something has energy, it can do work and bring about change. Energy produces light and movement. Energy is required to produce heat, to generate electricity, and to overcome forces such as friction.

WHAT FORMS CAN ENERGY TAKE?

Speeding cars, whizzing rockets, and wind and waves have ▶▶ KINETIC (motion) energy. A stretched rubber band has potential (stored) energy because of the forces that try to make it return to its original size. Heat is the kinetic energy of particles in materials. Light is radiation energy created by the electromagnetic force.

Kinetic energy increases with speed

Elastic energy is stored by the rope as it stretches

Gravitational potential energy increases with height above the Earth's surface

HOW DOES ENERGY CHANGE FORM?

When something happens, energy is changed from one form into another. When you climb stairs, chemical energy in your food is changed into kinetic energy by your muscles, and into potential energy as you raise your body against gravity. The amount of energy transferred is measured in ▶▶ JOULES.

◄ BUNGEE JUMP
A bungee jumper uses gravitational energy to power his dive from a bridge. As he accelerates down, gravitational energy is converted into kinetic energy. As the bungee rope begins to stretch, then slow his fall, kinetic energy is converted into elastic (potential) energy.

DOES ENERGY GET USED UP?

Energy cannot be created or destroyed; it can only change from one form to another. There is always as much energy after an event as there was before, but some of the energy may be wasted as heat that escapes into the surroundings.

KINETIC

Moving and vibrating objects have kinetic energy. The greater the moving object's mass, and the higher its speed, the more kinetic energy it has.

WHY IS IT WORSE TO CRASH AT HIGHER SPEEDS?

You might think that a 40-mph crash is twice as dangerous as a 20-mph crash. In fact, doubling the speed increases the kinetic energy by a factor of four. At 40 mph there is four times as much energy to cause damage as at 20 mph.

KINETIC ENERGY ▲
Racing cyclists convert food into muscular energy, and then into kinetic energy.

PLAYER POWER ▲
An athlete playing high-intensity sports consumes lots of calories. He can burn 1,000 calories an hour during a game. You use just 50 calories an hour watching TV.

energy ➜

JOULES

The modern international unit of energy is the joule. One joule is the energy used up when a force of one newton moves through a distance of one meter.

WHAT IS A CALORIE?

The original calorie was an old-fashioned unit of heat energy, equal to just over four joules. A different, larger unit, also called a calorie, is used today give the energy content of foods. This type of calorie is equal to 4,200 joules. An active teenager needs between 2,000 and 2,500 calories of energy a day. The body stores excess calories as fat.

FIND OUT MORE ▶▶ Forces 164 • Electricity 182 • Electromagnetism 186 • Heat 168–169 • Light 178–179 • Motion 165

NUCLEAR ENERGY

The energy that makes the stars shine and produces the heat inside a nuclear reactor is nuclear energy. It is produced by the strong force that holds protons and neutrons together inside atomic nuclei.

WHAT ARE FUSION AND FISSION?

Two kinds of reaction release nuclear energy. Fusion takes place when two light nuclei combine (fuse) to make a heavier nucleus. This is the process that powers the stars. Fission takes place when an unstable nucleus of a heavy element, such as uranium, splits in two. Fission is used in nuclear power stations.

HOW IS A NUCLEAR REACTION CONTROLLED?

The fission of ▶▶ RADIOACTIVE uranium produces nuclear energy. The process is controlled by adjusting the number of neutrons produced. Control rods that absorb neutrons are inserted between the uranium fuel rods. They are raised or lowered to maintain a steady release of energy.

Crane

Fuel rod

Water cools the fuel rods and shields workers from dangerous radiation

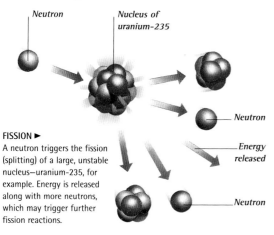

FISSION ▶
A neutron triggers the fission (splitting) of a large, unstable nucleus—uranium-235, for example. Energy is released along with more neutrons, which may trigger further fission reactions.

Neutron

Nucleus of uranium-235

Neutron

Energy released

Neutron

FUSION ▶
At the temperatures found in the interior of stars, nuclei of deuterium and tritium (forms of hydrogen) fuse to form a nucleus of helium. The fusion reaction releases a large amount of energy.

Deuterium nucleus

Tritium nucleus

Helium nucleus formed

Energy released

Neutron

NUCLEAR FUEL ▲
Rods of nuclear fuel generate heat in a nuclear reactor. The used fuel rods are still hot and highly radioactive. A remotely operated crane transfers rods from the reactor core to a water-filled cooling pond.

nuclear energy

RADIOACTIVITY

Strong forces act inside the nuclei of atoms. Some atoms are unstable—they decay (break down) over time, releasing energy as radiation. These atoms are radioactive. There are three main types of radiation—alpha, beta, and gamma.

◀ NUCLEAR WASTE
A nuclear technician checks nuclear waste storage containers for emissions of radiation. The radiation detector records the number of radioactive particles (alpha, beta, and gamma rays) penetrating the thick walls of the storage containers.

HOW IS RADIOACTIVITY USEFUL?

Radioactive substances decay over time in a predictable way. Geologists and archaeologists can date rocks by measuring the radiation they emit. In industry, radiation is used to trace underground pipes and to kill dangerous germs on food before it is packaged. In medicine, radiation treats cancer and sterilizes medical instruments.

WHY IS RADIOACTIVITY DANGEROUS?

To a living cell, an alpha particle, beta particle, or gamma ray is like a bullet from a gun. Its energy damages molecules, disrupting the cell's life processes. Long-term exposure to radiation can cause cancers, such as leukemia. Exposure to a single, large dose of radiation can produce radiation sickness and death. Radioactive material must be handled with great care.

MARIE CURIE
French, 1867-1934
Polish-born physicist Marie Curie was one of the first scientists to investigate radioactivity. She discovered the radioactive element radium. She was the first person ever to win two Nobel Prizes. Marie Curie died of leukemia caused by the radiation she worked with.

FIND OUT MORE ▶▶ Atoms 157 • Energy 166 • Energy Resources 60–61

HEAT

Everything around us contains heat. Heat is a form of energy—the energy of the random jiggling motion of particles that make up all matter. ▸▸TEMPERATURE is a measure of how hot an object is—it can be recorded using a ▸▸THERMOMETER.

HOW DOES HEAT FLOW?

Heat always flows from a higher temperature to a lower temperature. If you stand next to a hot oven, the heat from it warms you up. Different materials let heat flow through them at different rates. Metals are the best conductors (they let heat flow easily). ▸▸THERMAL INSULATORS don't conduct heat well.

WHAT ARE THE THREE TYPES OF HEAT TRANSFER?

Conduction is the transfer of heat from one molecule to another. Energetic molecules pass on heat energy when they collide with less energetic molecules. Convection is the transfer of heat through a liquid or a gas as warm fluid rises and cool fluid sinks. These movements are convection currents. Radiation is the movement of heat by electromagnetic rays. All objects emit radiation, but the hotter they are, the more radiation they give off.

▲ THERMAL IMAGING
Rescue workers use a thermal-imaging camera to search for survivors in dense smoke or under fallen rubble. A warm body shows up as a bright area in the image.

CAN WE SEE HEAT?

We cannot see heat, but we can see its effects. Convection currents rising from a hot asphalt road make the air above shimmer. A thermal-imaging camera detects radiation emitted by hot objects. Electronics convert invisible electromagnetic rays into an image on a television screen.

Eyes are hot areas because they contain lots of blood vessels

Blue and green regions are coolest

Red and yellow regions are warmest

The nose loses heat easily because it does not contain many blood vessels

THERMOGRAPH ▲
This false-color image shows the temperature differences over a man's head and shoulders. Thermal imaging cameras installed at airports can spot passengers with a fever (higher than normal temperature) who may be carrying an infectious disease. They are also used at ports to detect people smuggled in vehicles.

TEMPERATURE

Temperature tells us how hot an object is. It is a measure of how fast the particles in the object are moving. The hotter an object, the more vigorously its molecules move. Temperature is measured in degrees on a temperature scale.

WHAT IS ABSOLUTE ZERO?

If you could remove all the heat energy from an object, its molecules would be effectively stationary. The temperature at which molecules are no longer moving is called absolute zero. It is the lowest possible temperature. Absolute zero is equivalent to –459.67°F (–273.15°C).

WHERE IS THE HOTTEST PLACE IN THE UNIVERSE?

The center of the Sun is 25 million°F (14 million°C). In 2010, a laboratory in New York, USA generated temperatures 250,000 times hotter than the Sun. But even these temperatures are small in comparison to the Big Bang—this was more than 18 billion billion billon°F!

TEMPERATURE SCALE ▶
Three different temperature scales are commonly used. On the Fahrenheit scale, the temperature of melting ice is 32°F. On the Celsius scale, the melting temperature of ice is 0°C. On the Kelvin scale, ice melts at 273.15 K.

heat

25 million°F/14 million°C/
14 million K
Interior of the Sun

5,480°F/3,027°C/3,300 K
Metals are welded

1,220°F/660°C/933 K
Natural gas burns

363.2°F/184°C/457 K
Paper burns

212°F/100°C/373 K
Water boils

136.4°F/58°C/331 K
*Highest temperature on Earth,
Death Valley, California*

98.6°F/37°C/310 K
Normal body temperature

–128.2°F/–89°C/184 K
*Lowest temperature on Earth,
Antarctica*

–459.67°F/–273.15°C/0 K
Absolute zero

THERMOMETERS

The instrument for measuring temperature is called a thermometer. Most thermometers have a scale with two fixed points—the melting point of ice and the boiling point of water. All temperatures are measured against these points.

▲ GLASS THERMOMETER
This thermometer contains liquid in a glass capsule. The liquid expands when heated, and flows up the scale. This gives the temperature of the liquid.

HOW DOES A THERMOSTAT WORK?

Thermostats control the temperatures of buildings and machines. A simple room thermostat has a two-metal strip as part of a switch that turns the heat on and off. As the temperature rises, the two metals in the strip expand by different amounts. The strip bends, breaking the circuit and turning off the heat supply. As the room cools, the strip straightens, completes the circuit again, and turns the heat back on.

THERMAL INSULATORS

Any material that resists the flow of heat is a thermal insulator. Many animals keep warm because fur is a good insulator—it stops heat from flowing away from their bodies.

Stopper

Bottle

Double
walls with
vacuum
between

◀ VACUUM BOTTLE
The vacuum bottle has silvered double walls with a vacuum in between. This design prevents heat transfer by conduction, convection, and radiation.

HOW DOES A VACUUM BOTTLE WORK?

A vacuum bottle (Thermos™) is designed to keep hot food hot, or cold food cold. Double walls prevent heat flow in or out by conduction. The walls are silver-coated to reflect electromagnetic rays, reducing heat transfer by radiation. The space between the walls contains air at a low pressure (vacuum). This reduces heat transfer by convection.

FIND OUT MORE ▶▶ Atoms 157 • Circulation 134 • Energy 166 • Sun 15

MATERIALS

Any substance that is used to make something is a material. Natural materials such as stone and wood are used as they are found in nature. ▶▶ SYNTHETIC materials are made from natural materials with the help of heat and chemical reactions.

materials

WHAT ARE MATERIALS' PROPERTIES?
Materials are selected for use according to their properties (characteristics). Mechanical properties, such as strength, are important for materials used in construction. Chemical properties show if a material will react with other materials. Thermal properties show how a material conducts heat.

TENSILE TEST ▶
This machine tests the strength of the plastic toy by using a pulling (tensile) force. If the head comes off easily, the toy is a choking hazard to small children.

▲ SPIDER'S WEB
A spider weaves its web from silk fibers made from proteins called fibroin. The silk is not easily broken because it is both strong and elastic.

HOW STRONG IS A SPIDERWEB?
Millions of years of evolution have produced natural materials ideally suited to the jobs they do. A spider's web is, weight-for-weight, 10 times as strong as steel, and far more elastic. Bones, teeth, and tusks are also very strong natural materials. They can be used every day for a hundred years without breaking.

HOW ARE MATERIALS USED?
The chosen materials for a product need to be shaped and put together. Wood is shaped by sawing, planing, and drilling. It is joined with nails, screws, or glue. Metal is bent and hammered into shape—or heated until it melts, and poured into molds. Metal is joined with nuts and bolts, rivets, or by welding.

SYNTHETICS

A substance made artificially, by heat and chemical reactions, is a synthetic. It may be similar to a natural material, or have completely new properties.

WHAT WERE THE FIRST SYNTHETICS?
Heat melts sand and other minerals to make glass. The first glass bottles were made about 3,500 years ago in Ancient Egypt. The first modern synthetic was made in 1909, when Leo Baekeland, an American chemist, created a plastic called Bakelite.

WHAT IS A COMPOSITE MATERIAL?
Composite materials combine the useful properties of two or more materials in one. Steel is strong and concrete is strong, but steel-reinforced concrete is even stronger. It is used for constructing tall buildings and long bridges.

▲ HEAT-RESISTANT CLOTHING
Many natural and synthetic fibers burn easily, but the fibers used to make a firefighter's suit are heat and flame-resistant. The whole suit is coated with a thin layer of aluminum to reflect heat away from the surface, like a mirror.

▲ GLASS-REINFORCED PLASTIC (GRP) CHAIR
A GRP chair is light and tough. It is made from glass fibers in plastic. The fibers stop cracks from spreading through the material, giving it great strength.

CHANGING MATERIALS

We can use chemical reactions and heat to change materials and their properties to meet our needs. Some changes are ▶ PERMANENT, others are ▶ REVERSIBLE.

HOW DO CHEMICAL REACTIONS CHANGE MATERIALS?

Chemical reactions take place when existing bonds between atoms are broken and new bonds form. When the gas ethene is heated at high pressure, its molecules link together in long chains to make the plastic polythene. Polythene is used to make plastic dishpans, squeeze bottles, and plastic bags.

WHAT MAKES GLUE STICK?

A good glue is a substance that starts as a liquid, but transforms into a solid when exposed to air. As a liquid, the glue can flow into every nook and cranny of the surfaces where it is spread. The glue molecules form bonds with the molecules in the surfaces. As the glue sets, the surfaces are held firmly together.

changing materials

ROT AND DECAY ▶
The complex molecules in living things are decomposed by microorganisms after death.

HOW DOES HEAT CHANGE MATERIALS?

Heat makes many solids, especially metals, softer and easier to shape. As the temperature rises, most solids eventually melt to the liquid state. But some materials react differently to heat. Heat can trigger chemical reactions between mixtures. In an oven, heat changes a cake mix from a sticky liquid into a fluffy solid.

RUSTING IRON ▲
Any iron object left in a damp location becomes covered with an orange-brown substance called rust. Rusting is a chemical reaction between iron, oxygen, and water.

Fungus spores multiply on the nectarine skin, breaking down its structure as they feed

Water escapes into the atmosphere and the nectarine shrivels and rots

FRESH NECTARINE   ROTTEN NECTARINE

REVERSIBLE CHANGES

Melting and boiling are reversible changes produced by heat. Steam from a boiling kettle condenses back into drops of water when it comes into contact with a cold surface, such as a window.

◀ LAVA FLOW
Liquid lava pouring from a volcano is solid rock melted by heat from the Earth's core at about 1,300°F (700°C). The lava's surface cools first, setting into a thin skin that wrinkles as the lava moves. When it is completely cool, it sets back into solid rock.

CAN STONE MELT?

Candle wax melts at 140°F (60°C), lead melts at 621.5°F (327.5°C), and iron melts at 2,804°F (1,540°C). Even stone can melt. The material with the highest known melting temperature is the metal tungsten, which melts at 6,129°F (3,387°C). Tungsten wire is used to make the filaments of electric light bulbs and television tubes.

PERMANENT CHANGES

Burning, rusting, and cooking are permanent changes. They cannot be undone by reversing the conditions that brought them about.

HOW DOES CONCRETE CHANGE FROM A LIQUID TO A SOLID?

Concrete is a mixture of sand, gravel, cement, and water. Cement powder contains calcium oxide (lime) and silica or similar chemical compounds (substances that are two or more elements). When cement is mixed with water, the compounds react and set into a solid. The setting cement glues the sand and gravel particles together to make a permanent solid structure.

CONCRETE ▶
An electron microscope picture of setting concrete shows the changes that take place as the concrete hardens. As cement reacts with water, crystals form, bonding sand and gravel particles together.

FIND OUT MORE ▶▶ Atoms 157 • Chemistry 162 • Electricity 182 • Heat 168–169 • Matter 156 • Microorganisms 85 • Mixtures 172

MIXTURES

A mixture is a jumble of different things. Soil is a mixture of sand, clay, stones, roots, and plant and animal remains. The air is a mixture of different gases. Seawater contains a mixture of different chemical compounds in ▶▶ SOLUTION.

WHAT IS THE DIFFERENCE BETWEEN A MIXTURE AND A COMPOUND?

The components of a mixture are physically mixed together, but they have not reacted chemically. When materials react chemically, chemical bonds break and reform, producing compounds with new properties.

DO SOLIDS, LIQUIDS, AND GASES MIX?

All the states of matter can mix, with themselves and each other. Solid powders mix easily. Most rocks are a mixture of different minerals. Some liquids mix easily, and some don't. Water and alcohol mix together, but water and oil do not mix. Gases mix rapidly by ▶▶ DIFFUSION—their molecules can move between each other because gas molecules are widely spaced.

SOLUTION

A solution is a mixture in the liquid state. Molecules of one substance are dispersed (scattered) throughout molecules of another—the substance is dissolved. The amount of a substance that will dissolve in another is called its solubility.

◀ LAYERS OF OIL AND WATER
Oil and water don't mix, and therefore do not form a solution.

DIFFUSION

When two liquids or gases are in the same container, the random motion of their molecules makes them mingle together until the mixture is the same throughout. This is called diffusion.

WHAT IS A RANDOM WALK?

The movement of a single molecule in a liquid or a gas is a zigzag random walk. The molecule is continually moving and changing direction as it collides with other molecules. A group of molecules that were concentrated in one spot gradually spread apart. This explains how an odor—for example, perfume—spreads through a room.

WHY IS IT EASIER TO MIX THAN TO SEPARATE?

It couldn't be easier to mix a bucket of red balls with a bucket of white balls—just dump them together. Mixing makes the balls more jumbled. Scientists say that they have more entropy (disorder). Separating the balls is much harder. To make them ordered again—red balls in one bucket, white in another—you have to pick the balls out one at a time.

◀ LAVA LAMP
The lamp contains two liquids with slightly different densities that do not mix.

Warm bubbles rise, cool, and sink again

Liquid bubbles expand and float up

Lamp base contains an electric bulb. This heats the bubbles. The liquid closer to the heat expands, becomes less dense, and rises

WHY DON'T OIL AND WATER MIX?

Oil is insoluble (does not dissolve) in water because oil and water molecules repel each other. Cooking oil and water can be physically mixed together by shaking them vigorously in a bottle, but when the mixture is left to stand, the oil and water molecules gradually separate again. Oil is less dense (heavy) than water, so the oil floats on top of the water.

mixtures

◀ MIXING BY DIFFUSION
Crystals of potassium permanganate dissolve in water, producing a dark purple solution. Even without stirring, the purple solution spreads gradually through the clear water in the flask.

Potassium permanganate diffuses into the water

Potassium permanganate crystals

SEPARATING MIXTURES

How do we extract salt from seawater? Methods for separating a mixture depend on differences in the physical properties of its components.

Water boils at 212°F (100°C)

separating mixtures

HOW CAN SOLIDS BE SEPARATED?

Differences in size, density, solubility, and magnetic properties separate one solid from another. Adding water separates salt from sand—salt dissolves, but sand does not. ▶▶FILTRATION separates an insoluble solid (one that does not dissolve) from a liquid.

PANNING FOR GOLD ►
Gold is separated from gravel. Gold is heavier and sinks more quickly to settle in the bottom of the pan.

HOW DOES DISTILLATION WORK?

When a liquid mixture is heated, the liquid with the lower boiling point evaporates (becomes a vapor), leaving behind the liquid with the higher boiling point. Cooling condenses the vapor back to liquid. Fractional distillation separates substances one by one as the temperature rises.

Hot water vapor enters the condenser's inner tube

◄ LABORATORY DISTILLATION
In this laboratory demonstration, the solution to be distilled is boiled by a Bunsen burner. Vapor from the boiling liquid is directed into a water-cooled condenser. The condenser is angled so that gravity causes the condensed liquid (turned from vapor back to liquid by cooling) to run down into the collecting flask.

Water is drawn off from the outer tube

Vapor rises as water in the mixture boils

Sodium dichromate and water

Cold water is fed into the condenser's outer tube

Vapor condenses and liquid runs into collecting flask

HOW ARE GASES SEPARATED?

Air is separated to produce nitrogen, oxygen, and other gases by first cooling it to the liquid state at −321°F (−196°C). The liquid air is fractionally distilled. Gases may also be separated by the rate at which they diffuse through a barrier. Light molecules diffuse more quickly than heavy molecules.

Bunsen burner gives heat

FILTRATION

Filtration is a method of separating a solid from a liquid by trapping solid particles in a material that only lets the liquid through. A coffee filter separates solid coffee grounds from liquid coffee. The size of the pores (holes) in the filter paper determines which particles will pass through.

CENTRIFUGE ►
A blood sample in a microtube is placed into a centrifuge. The high-speed rotation separates the blood components into layers, ready for analysis.

WHAT IS DIALYSIS?

Your kidneys clean your blood. Waste chemicals dissolved in the blood pass through a membrane to be excreted in urine. Blood cells are too big to pass through and are retained in the body. People whose kidneys fail can be treated on a dialysis machine. This uses a synthetic membrane outside the body.

WHAT IS A CENTRIFUGE?

A centrifuge is a spinning machine, a bit like a clothes dryer, that separates materials. A mixture of liquids and solids is spun at high speed in a tube. The larger, denser particles sink and collect at the bottom. Light particles collect at the top. Blood cells are separated from plasma (the liquid part of blood) by this method.

FIND OUT MORE ▶▶ Chemical Industry 206–207 • Kidneys 147 • Matter 156 • Mixtures 172

ALLOYS

An alloy is a mixture of metals, or of metals and other substances. Mixing metals and other elements in alloys can improve their properties. The alloy bronze is a mixture of the metals copper and tin. It is resistant to water corrosion and is used in outdoor structures.

alloys

METAL TOOLS ▶
The metal for a good tool must be strong enough to take blows and hard enough to sharpen to a fine cutting edge. Modern tools are still made from iron, alloyed with carbon.

Bronze Age sickle with a wooden handle and a bronze blade

Iron Age sickle made of the metal iron, which is extracted from ores (minerals)

◀ STEEL ALLOY
The Atomium in Brussels, Belgium, is built from steel girders, which give it strength. Steel is a mixture of iron and carbon. The Atomium is covered in aluminum, which protects it from the weather. The nine spheres are arranged like the atoms in iron. There is a science museum inside the spheres.

ARE ALLOYS STRONGER THAN PURE METALS?
A pure metal has identical atoms arranged in regular layers. The layers slide over each other easily. Alloys are harder and stronger because the different-sized atoms of the mixed metals make the atomic layers less regular, so they cannot slide as easily.

DO ALLOYS MELT EASILY?
The different sizes of atoms in an alloy make their arrangement less regular than a pure metal. This makes the bonds between the atoms weaker, and lowers the melting point. Alloys that melt easily, such as ▶▶ SOLDER, have important uses.

WHO FIRST USED ALLOYS?
About 6,000 years ago, early peoples made the alloy bronze by roasting together copper and tin ores (minerals). Bronze is stronger and longer-lasting than pure copper. This period in history when bronze was the main material used is called the Bronze Age.

ALLOYS		
NAME	MAIN CONSTITUENTS	USES
Brass	copper, zinc	musical instruments, decorative items
Bronze	copper, tin	statues, bearings, coins
Cupronickel	copper, nickel	coins
Duralumin	aluminum, copper, magnesium, manganese	aircraft, bicycles
Nichrome	nickel, chromium	electrical heating elements
Steel	iron, carbon	construction, tools, vehicles
Stainless steel	iron, chromium, carbon	kitchen fixtures, cutlery, surgical equipment
Solder	lead, tin	joining metals

SOLDER

Lead is a heavy, soft metal, and melts at a low temperature, 622°F (328°C). By adding tin to make the alloy solder, the melting point is lowered further.

WHAT IS FLUX?
Flux is any substance that stops a metal from oxidizing (combining with oxygen), such as salt. Most metals oxidize in air—the process is speeded up with heat. When a plumber solders together lengths of copper pipe, he or she coats the surface with flux to stop the copper from oxidizing. Otherwise, the solder would not stick, and the pipes could not be joined.

HEATING SOLDER ▲
Solder is melted with a hot soldering iron to connect electronic components on a circuit board.

FIND OUT MORE ▶▶ Circuits 184–185 • Elements 160–161 • First Metalworkers 367

NEW MATERIALS

Materials scientists combine atoms in new ways to produce new materials with ⏩ **SMART** properties. Imagine a window that changes color to control the room temperature, or artificial arteries that pump blood around the body—these new materials are being developed, tested, and used now.

HOW ARE NEW MATERIALS MADE?
Most new materials are developed from existing materials. Scientists try out new combinations of elements. They apply heat and pressure to materials to impart new properties.

WHAT PROPERTIES SHOULD NEW MATERIALS HAVE?
Different properties are needed depending on where the materials are used. Materials for use in the human body must be nontoxic and resistant to corrosion by blood and other body fluids. New packaging materials should be cheap to produce, easy to recycle, or biodegradable.

WHY IS CARBON FIBER SO STRONG?
The latest carbon fiber sports rackets and bicycles are as light as wood but as strong as steel. Diamond is the hardest material—the bonds between its carbon atoms are strong because they are arranged in a 3-D structure like a honeycomb. Carbon fibers are strings of carbon atoms. The bonds between the atoms give the fibers strength and stiffness.

SEAGel is made from agar, obtained from red algae and kelp. It is so light that it rests on soap bubbles without popping them

LIGHTER–THAN–AIR SEAGEL SOLID ▲
This new material is a foam made from agar (jelly extracted from seaweed). It could replace plastic in packaging.

SMART MATERIALS

A material that responds to its environment, like the ch skin, is a smart material. Smart clothes could control yo temperature, light up in the dark, or even keep themselv

◀ SEE-THROUGH CLOTHING
The image on the front of this woman's coat shows what is happening in the street behind her. The coat is covered with tiny reflective beads. A TV image of the scene behind is projected onto the beads. New materials could use this method to provide camouflage for people, vehicles, and buildings.

CAN A METAL REMEMBER?
Alloys of nickel and titanium have shape The pattern of the atoms changes when is bent or twisted, but when the metal is atoms spring back into their original pos eyeglasses have frames made from memo

CAN A TELEVISION SCREEN GET ANY TH
Some new polymers (plastics) conduct el Electric currents may make them emit lig Video screens made from these polymers as thin and flexible as sheets of paper, a to ultra-thin cell phone displays. In the f be possible to spray a video screen onto

FIND OUT MORE ⏩ Chemistry 162 • Electricity 182 • Elements 160–161 • Materials 170 • Te

BAT 12,000–150,000 Hz
Bats hunt and fly at night. To help them find their way in the dark, they make a series of very high-frequency clicks (which humans cannot hear). Then they use their sensitive ears to listen for the echoes bouncing back off objects in their path.

GRASSHOPPER 7,000–100,000 Hz
To attract females, male grasshoppers make a loud rasping sound by scraping their hardened wing cases across a comblike series of pegs on their back legs. Grasshoppers have ears on their abdomens.

HOWLER MONKEY 400–6,000 Hz
The loud hooting call of a howler monkey can travel for several miles through the dense forest where it lives. A hollow space in its neck bones works like an amplifier to strengthen the call through resonance.

HUMAN 85–11,000 Hz
Human hearing is not as sensitive as that of a bat or a dog, but we do make a wide range of sounds. Using the air in our lungs, we vibrate the vocal cords in our throat to make complicated sound patterns. We cry, scream, laugh, sigh, speak, and sing.

FROG 50–8,000 Hz
A male frog croaks to attract a female. The frog puffs up a pouch of skin under its jaw. Then it forces air through its vocal cords to make them vibrate. The air in the pouch picks up the vibration and strengthens it by resonance, making the sound louder.

ELEPHANT 10–10,000 Hz
When an elephant trumpets a warning, humans can hear it. But elephants also produce low-frequency sounds that we cannot hear. Sounds that happen outside our frequency range are called ultrasonic (higher frequencies), or infrasonic (lower frequencies).

SOUND

Our world is full of sounds. Sound is a form of energy that travels as ▸▸ SOUND WAVES . As well as making and hearing sounds, we also record them. Today, many recordings are made using ▸▸ DIGITAL SOUND .

HOW ARE SOUNDS MADE?
Sound is made when something moves or vibrates. The movement sets up a sound wave in the surrounding air. Continuous sounds, such as drumming, are made when an object vibrates back and forth. A sudden clap or bang sends out a single sharp pulse of sound called a shock wave. The shock wave from an explosion can knock people over.

HOW DO MUSICAL INSTRUMENTS MAKE MUSIC?
Stringed instruments (such as violins) have a series of stretched strings, which vibrate when they are plucked or stroked. Players of wind instruments (such as flutes) blow across or into a mouthpiece to force columns of air to vibrate in tubes or pipes. Percussion instruments (such as drums) vibrate when they are struck.

WHY ARE SOUNDS DIFFERENT?
Sounds are different because sound waves have different frequencies. The frequency is the number of vibrations or sound waves produced in a second. We sometimes describe frequency as pitch. High-pitched sounds, such as from whistles, have a higher frequency (more waves per second) than low-pitched sounds, such as from bass drums.

WHAT IS RESONANCE?
A wine glass has a natural frequency at which it vibrates. A singer can break the glass by singing a note at the same frequency. Because the frequencies match, energy transfers from the sound to the glass until its vibrations become so strong it shatters. This is called resonance. Resonance is used to strengthen the sound in some types of musical instrument.

Jet engines work hardest and make most noise at takeoff

Eardrums need protection from very loud sounds

DEAFENING SOUND ▶
The sound of a jet aircraft at takeoff is millions of times louder than the quietest sounds we can hear. Very loud sounds can cause us pain and damage our ears.

◀ SOUND FREQUENCY
Frequency (the number of vibrations or waves per second) is measured in hertz (Hz). Low-pitched sounds have low frequencies; high-pitched sounds have high frequencies. There is an enormous variety of sounds in the animal world, and different types of animals make, and hear, sounds of different frequencies.

Aircraft in flight give out sound waves in all directions

SOUND WAVES

A vibrating object moves back and forth. As it moves forward, it pushes against the air around it, compressing or squashing it. As it moves backward, it lets the air spread out. These squashing and expanding movements create a sound wave.

THOMAS EDISON
American, 1847–1931

In 1877, Thomas Edison and his team invented the phonograph, the first practical device for recording and playing back sounds. This used a vibrating needle to scratch a groove into a wax cylinder.

HOW DOES SOUND TRAVEL?
The energy in a sound wave moves outward from its source, passing from air molecule to air molecule in a series of pulses called compressions (air is squashed) and rarefactions (air is spread out). Sound travels easily through air.

HOW IS SOUND RECORDED?
A microphone changes sound waves into electrical signals that rise and fall in the same pattern as the sound. Analog recordings store the pattern as a wavy groove cut into a plastic disc (record), or as a magnetic pattern on a plastic tape.

COMPRESSION   RAREFACTION

SOUND BARRIER ▲
A jet traveling faster than sound creates a loud shock wave. This is called breaking the sound barrier.

◄ SOUND WAVE
In a sound wave, a series of compressions and rarefactions carries the sound energy along.

The high points of a sound wave have the highest numbers

3 5 6 6 4 2 1 2

COUNTING WAVES ▲
In a digital recording, the pulsing pattern of each sound wave is mapped as a series of numbers.

The low points of a sound wave have the lowest numbers

DIGITAL SOUND

Sound can be recorded or transmitted as a digital signal. A digital signal holds the pattern of a sound wave as a series of numbers that can be stored on CD or digital tape, or on a computer. When the signal is played, it changes back into sound waves.

WHY IS DIGITAL SOUND BETTER THAN ANALOG?
Analog recordings rely on making an exact copy of the sound-wave pattern. But making more copies of the original recording can distort the pattern and add extra noises (hiss, for example). Because a digital recording is just numbers, it can be copied and corrected, if necessary, over and over again.

Wave height is turned into binary numbers

| 3 | 5 | 6 | 6 | 4 | 2 | 1 | 2 |

0 1 1 1 0 1 1 1 0 1 1 0 1 0 0 0 1 0 0 0 1 0 1 0

Binary numbers are shown as pits or no pits

◄ RECORDING NUMBERS
The numbers in a digital recording are stored as binary code. This is made up of just two digits, 0 and 1. Each binary number is pressed onto a compact disc (CD) as a series of pits (dents) and no pits.

HOW CAN ONE PERSON PRODUCE THE SOUND OF AN ENTIRE ORCHESTRA?
Different instruments make sounds with a mixture of different frequencies. By making sounds with the right mix of frequencies, an electronic synthesizer can imitate any instrument in an orchestra. A computer helps the player to arrange the sounds into music.

sound

FIND OUT MORE ►► Atoms 157 • Computers 190 • Ear 141 • Musical Instruments 332

LIGHT

Light is a type of energy known as electromagnetic radiation. It is given out by hot objects such as the Sun, light bulbs, and ➡ LASERS . When light hits a surface, its energy can be absorbed (soaked up), ➡ REFLECTED , or deflected by ➡ REFRACTION .

WHAT IS LIGHT?

Light is made up of little packets of energy called photons. Most of these photons are produced when the atoms in an object heat up. Heat "excites" the electrons inside the atoms and they gain extra energy. This extra energy is then released as a photon. The hotter an object gets, the more photons it gives out.

HOW DOES LIGHT TRAVEL?

Light travels as a wave. But unlike sound waves or water waves, it does not need any matter or material to carry its energy along. This means that light can travel through a vacuum—a completely airless space. (Sound, on the other hand, must travel through a solid, a liquid, or a gas.) Nothing travels faster than light energy. It speeds through the vacuum of space at 186,400 miles (300,000 km) per second.

light

◄ POLARIZING LIGHT
Bright sunlight reflected from the road dazzles our eyes. One way of cutting down the glare is to look through a polarizing filter. Light waves vibrate (shake) in all directions. A polarizing filter lets through light vibrating in only one direction, blocking out the rest and reducing glare.

WHAT ARE SHADOWS?

Light waves travel out from their source in straight lines called rays. Rays do not curve around corners, so when they hit an opaque object (one that does not allow light to pass through it), they are blocked from reaching the other side of that object. We see a dark shadow in the area from which light is blocked.

WHAT MAKES SOME MATERIALS OPAQUE?

When light falls on a material, the energy in its photons can affect the atoms in the material. In some materials, such as metal, the atoms absorb some of the photons so light does not pass through them. These materials are opaque. In other materials, such as glass, the atoms cannot absorb the photons and light passes through them. These materials are transparent.

The glass tube is full of argon gas and mercury vapour, which gives off ultraviolet radiation. This makes the phosphor coating on the tube glow

The ballast sends electricity through the tube

The screw-in base allows the bulb to fit securely in the socket

ENERGY-EFFICIENT LIGHT BULB ►
Compact fluorescent lamps (CFL) feature a spiraling glass tube full of gases, which emit ultraviolet light when electricity flows through them. This triggers a phosphor coating on the tube to shine brightly. A CFL is more energy efficient and lasts a lot longer than standard incandescent bulbs.

REFLECTION

Light rays reflect (bounce) off objects. The Moon shines because it reflects light from the Sun. Smooth surfaces, such as mirrors, reflect light in one direction.

A glass mirror is coated on one side with a thin, reflective layer of metal

The beam hits the mirror, and is reflected, just like a billiard ball bouncing off the side of a table

LAW OF REFLECTION ▶
The law of reflection says that the angle of the beam bouncing off a mirror will be equal to the angle at which it arrived.

The laser beam travels in a straight line through the air

Multiple reflections alternately flip from left to right

MIRROR, MIRROR ▶
If you stand between two mirrors that are directly across from each other, you will see reflections of your reflection vanishing off into the distance.

Boy looking in mirror

WHAT HAPPENS WHEN YOU LOOK IN A MIRROR?
At first sight, your image is identical to you. But a closer look shows that as you lift your right hand, your image raises its left. Reflection always flips an image from left to right. If you hold up a sheet of paper with writing on it, the image in the mirror shows the writing in reverse.

REFRACTION

Light travels more slowly through some materials than others. The change in speed can cause light rays to change direction. This directional change is called refraction.

◀ SEEING THINGS
Refraction makes this girl's body look closer when it is seen through the surface of the water. This is because the light rays change direction as they travel from water into air.

The laser beam leaves the block. It has moved sideways, but is still parallel to the original beam

Laser beam in air

Refracted laser beam inside plastic block

WHY IS A SWIMMING POOL DEEPER THAN IT LOOKS?
Refraction can make things look closer than they really are. The difference in speed between light traveling through water and through air means that, from the surface, a 13-ft (4-m) pool appears to be just 10 ft (3 m) deep. Glass is another material that refracts light. It is used to make eyeglasses and other lenses.

▲ REFRACTION
A laser beam is refracted (changes direction) when it passes from air into a block of transparent plastic.

LASER

A laser produces an incredibly powerful, concentrated form of light. Inside a laser, light waves are bounced back and forth between two mirrors to build up energy before being released as a narrow beam.

WHY IS LASER LIGHT SO SPECIAL?
Laser light does not spread out in the way that light from other sources does. All the light waves in laser light are precisely in step with each other. As a result, laser light can be concentrated and controlled far more accurately. It can carry television and other signals over great distances without losing quality.

Fine laser beams can be very precisely controlled

LASER EYE SURGERY ▶
Extremely fine laser beams are used to perform operations on the human eye.

FIND OUT MORE ▶▶ Atoms 157 • Color 180 • Eye 140 • Lenses 181 • Matter 156

COLOR

Light has different wavelengths, which we see as colors. The range of wavelengths we see is called the visible spectrum. We separate the colors of the spectrum by ▸▸DISPERSION.

WHAT IS THE VISIBLE SPECTRUM?
Light waves are just one type of electromagnetic wave. They belong to an electromagnetic spectrum that includes radio waves, X-rays, and gamma rays. The visible spectrum is the only part the human eye can see. To our eyes, the colors in the visible spectrum range from violet at one end to red at the other.

WHAT ARE PRIMARY COLORS?
The light-sensitive cells in the human eye react to just three types of light: red, green, and blue wavelengths. These are the three primary light colors. If all three types of wavelength enter the eye with equal strength, we see white light. When just red and green light are present, we see the mixture as yellow.

HOW MANY COLORS CAN WE SEE?
Different wavelengths of light blend to produce millions of shades of color. The human eye is able to pick out over 10 million of them—some of which can be shown by a ▸▸COLOR TREE. The amount of color we see depends on how much light there is. In dim light, we see no colors at all, only shades of gray.

Beam of white light

Some light is reflected off the bottom of the prism

Triangular glass prism

▲ PRIMARY LIGHT
The three primary light colors, red, green, and blue, combine in pairs to create secondary colors. Red and green make yellow, blue and green make cyan, and red and blue make magenta. All three together make white light.

The different wavelengths (colors) in the light beam are refracted at different angles

BENDING LIGHT THROUGH A PRISM ▲
Different wavelengths of light travel at different speeds through glass. A prism refracts (bends) the shortest wavelengths the most. We see these as violet light. The longest wavelengths are refracted the least. We see these as deep red. All the other colors are in between.

DISPERSION

When white light shines through a specially shaped piece of glass called a prism, it is separated into its different wavelengths by dispersion. The wavelengths show up as a range of colors called a spectrum. English scientist Isaac Newton first used a prism to disperse sunlight in the late 1600s.

HOW DOES A RAINBOW FORM?
Rainbows appear when there are water droplets in the atmosphere and bright sunshine at the same time. The droplets act like tiny prisms, refracting and reflecting the sunlight, and dispersing it into the colors of the spectrum. To see a rainbow, you have to be standing at a particular angle to the water droplets and the Sun.

◄ RAINBOW OF LIGHT
Sunlight is a mixture of all the colors of the spectrum—red, orange, yellow, green, blue, indigo, and violet. Some animals can see colors that we cannot see.

COLOR TREE

A color tree is one way of grading or classifying colors. Using a color tree, it is possible to describe and then match a particular shade of color (of paint or fabric, for example).

visible spectrum

On a computer, moving a slide up or down changes the level of value

Range of color shades at the highest value level

◄ THE MUNSELL COLOR TREE
This system describes a color according to three characteristics: its hue (basic color, such as blue), its chroma (strength of color), and its value (lightness or darkness). There are ten levels of value (like the trunk of a tree), going up from black to white. At each level, each hue has a range of shades, depending on how far out it is from the central trunk. Today, this system is used to specify color on computers.

HOW IS COLOR CREATED ON A COMPUTER?
Most computer drawing and graphics programs include an electronic version of a color tree for choosing colors. This may be done by selecting preset colors from a given range, or by setting the percentages of red, green, and blue in the color.

FIND OUT MORE ▸▸ Eye 140 • Light 178–179

LENSES

When you look through a magnifying glass, or take a picture with a camera, you are using a lens. A lens is a polished piece of glass or transparent plastic with curved surfaces. There are two main shapes of lenses, ▶▶CONVEX and ▶▶CONCAVE.

WHAT DOES A LENS DO?

A lens changes the direction of light waves by refraction. It may form an image of a scene or an object. The image might be smaller (as in a camera), or larger (as in a microscope). Because a lens is curved, light rays strike different parts of its surface and are bent by different amounts. Depending on the lens shape, a beam of light either diverges (spreads out) or converges (concentrates).

WHAT IS THE DIFFERENCE BETWEEN A MICROSCOPE AND A TELESCOPE?

A microscope makes a tiny, nearby object look much bigger. A telescope makes a large, distant object or scene appear much closer and brighter. In both instruments, light from the object passes through two or more lenses to form an image. The shapes of the lenses and the distances between them alter the image that is produced.

▲ MAGNIFIED IMAGES

Optical microscopes use beams of light, but electron microscopes use beams of electrons to give much greater magnification. This image of a silverfish has been magnified thousands of times.

Eyepiece lens views the magnified image

Image of bacteria magnified 400 times their real size

Focusing knob adjusts the distance between the specimen and the objective lens

Objective lenses of different powers view the specimen at different magnifications

Specimen (object to be viewed) is mounted on a glass slide

Mirror reflects light onto and through the specimen

OPTICAL MICROSCOPE ▶

Optical microscopes use light to magnify an image up to 2,000 times. Light from a brightly lit specimen (object) is captured and concentrated by a powerful objective lens to produce a magnified image. The eyepiece lens may then magnify the image further.

CONVEX LENS

This type of lens is thicker in the center than at the edge. Parallel rays of light entering it on one side will converge (meet) at a particular spot on the other side of the lens. Magnifying glasses and microscopes use convex lenses.

lenses

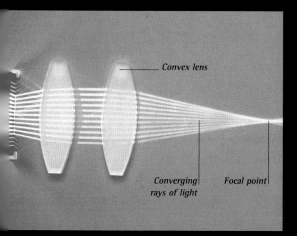

Convex lens

Converging rays of light

Focal point

◀ CONVERGING RAYS

Diverging (spreading) light rays are made parallel by the first convex lens. The second convex lens angles the parallel rays so that they converge—meet or focus—at a certain point, called the focal point.

HOW DOES A MAGNIFYING GLASS WORK?

A magnifying glass makes an object look bigger. Holding it close to an object makes a virtual image of the object form on the same side of the glass as the object. When you look through the magnifying glass, this virtual object seems to be larger than the real one. The thicker the lens, the larger the virtual image.

CONCAVE LENS

A concave lens is thinner at the center than at the edge. Parallel light rays passing into one side of the lens diverge (spread out) as they emerge from the other side.

HOW DO CONCAVE LENSES HELP YOU SEE?

If you are nearsighted, your eye lens focuses a scene just in front of the retina in your eye and the image you see is blurred. A concave lens spreads out the light rays before they enter the eye, so that they are focused on the retina and the image is sharp.

DIVERGING RAYS ▶

Diverging light rays are made parallel by a convex lens. But when the parallel light rays pass through a concave lens, they diverge (spread out) again.

Concave lens

Diverging rays of light

FIND OUT MORE ▶▶ Eye 140 • Light 178–179

ELECTRICITY

A lightning strike demonstrates the incredible energy of electricity. This intense flash of heat and light is created naturally by static electricity. We use this same electric force to provide a clean, controllable power supply to our homes, farms, factories, and cities.

Lightning flash heats the surrounding air to 54,000°F (30,000°C)

electricity

WHAT IS ELECTRICITY?

The electrons and protons inside every atom carry a property called an electric charge. Electrons have a negative charge and protons a positive charge. These charges either attract or repel each other. Unlike (opposite) charges attract, and like (the same) charges repel. The force they do this with is called electricity.

ELECTRIC LIGHTNING ▶
The buildup of electric charge in a storm cloud creates an opposing charge in the ground. Eventually, a gigantic electric spark leaps between the two charges in a spectacular release of energy.

HOW MANY FORMS OF ELECTRICITY ARE THERE?

Electricity comes in two forms—as electric current when electric charges flow along wires in a circuit, and as static electricity, when electric charges do not move. Normally, most materials are neutral (have no charge). But if a material gains or loses large numbers of electrons, it becomes charged with static electricity.

Lightning stroke between cloud and ground may be up to 9 miles (14 km) long

HOW DO MATERIALS BECOME CHARGED?

Materials can become charged with static electricity by ▶▶ INDUCTION or by friction. When two materials rub together, friction transfers electrons from one to the other. This gives one material a negative charge, and the other a positive charge. A nylon comb gains a negative charge when it is pulled through hair.

◀ PLASMA GLOBE
A charged metal ball causes electrons to separate from gas atoms inside a glass sphere. The gas gives out light as electrons flow through it.

ELECTROSTATIC INDUCTION

Electric induction is the process by which a charged object can charge another object without touching it. A charged nylon comb, for example, will attract scraps of paper, even though the scraps are not charged themselves.

▼ USING ELECTROSTATICS
By making the car body and the paint sprayer oppositely charged, paint drops are attracted into all the bumps and hollows of the surface to be painted.

Charged nylon comb attracts paper scraps

Cap
Rod
Gold leaf
Scale

HOW DOES INDUCTION WORK?

When the comb is brought close to the paper, the negative charge on the comb repels electrons in the paper to the side farthest away from the comb. This creates a positive charge (fewer electrons) on the side of the paper facing the comb. Positive and negative attract, so the paper is pulled toward the comb.

◀ GOLD LEAF ELECTROSCOPE
Electric charge can be measured by an electroscope. One of the simplest is a gold-leaf electroscope. A charged object held near the cap repels like charges to the far end of a metal rod, onto a thin sheet of gold. The charges on the gold leaf and the rod repel each other, and the leaf rises. The amount by which it rises can be measured against a notched scale.

FIND OUT MORE ▶▶ Atoms 157 • Circuits 184–185 • Forces 164 • Motion 165

MAGNETISM

Magnetism is an invisible force that attracts or repels some materials, such as iron and steel, but not others, like plastic and silver. In a magnetic material, the atoms line up in groups or regions called ▸ MAGNETIC DOMAINS.

WHAT ARE MAGNETIC POLES?
Every magnet has a north magnetic pole and a south magnetic pole. These are the places where the magnetic force is strongest. The laws of magnetism are that like (the same) poles repel each other, and unlike (opposite) poles attract each other.

WHAT ARE MAGNETIC MATERIALS?
The elements iron, nickel, and cobalt are magnetic materials—they can be magnetized by another magnet. But in their pure form they easily lose their magnetism by heat or hammering. Permanent magnets are made from mixtures of these elements with others, such as steel (iron and carbon), for example.

▲ MAGNETIC EARTH
Earth's magnetic poles attract particles from the Sun that glow when they reach the atmosphere. Earth's magnetic north and south poles are close to its geographical north and south poles.

HOW DOES A MAGNETIC COMPASS WORK?
Earth's core acts as a gigantic magnet with a vast ▸ MAGNETIC FIELD. In a magnetic compass, the northern end of the compass needle always points in the direction of Earth's north magnetic pole. Its other (southern) end always points south.

magnetism

Horseshoe magnet

Magnetic domains are lined up in the two poles

Keeper

Keeper

◀ MAGNETIC POWER
To keep a magnet strong, place a keeper between its poles when it is not in use. A keeper is a piece of soft iron. The poles magnetize the keeper, which in turn keeps the poles' domains pointing in the same direction.

MAGNETIC DOMAINS

Every atom in a piece of iron is a tiny permanent magnet. These tiny magnets group together in magnetic regions called domains. If the north–south magnetic poles of these domains all point in different directions, they cancel out each other's magnetism.

WHAT MAKES A PERMANENT MAGNET?
In a permanent magnet, the magnetic poles of the domains point in the same direction, so their magnetic fields reinforce one another. Magnetic material can be magnetized by stroking it with a magnet to line up the domains. Heat or hammering shakes the domains out of position, and the material loses its magnetism.

MAGNETIC FIELD

A magnet creates a force in the space around it. The area in which the force operates is the magnetic field. A magnetic field can be imagined as lines of force that spread out from the magnet's poles.

HOW CAN A MAGNETIC FIELD BE SEEN?
If iron filings are sprinkled around a magnet, they will line up along the lines of force of its magnetic field. The pattern made by the filings always shows the lines of force looping outward between the magnet's north and south poles. The magnetic field gets weaker as it gets farther away from the magnet.

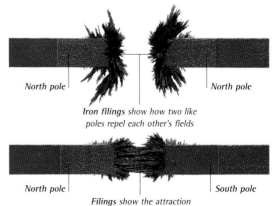

North pole   North pole

Iron filings show how two like poles repel each other's fields

North pole   South pole

Filings show the attraction between unlike poles

MAGNETIC POLES ▲
Iron filings can be used to show the repulsion between two like poles, and the attraction between unlike poles.

CIRCUITS

An electric current flows in a loop, powering bulbs or other electric ▸◂ **COMPONENTS** . The loop is an electric circuit. A circuit is made up of various components linked together by wires. The current is driven around the circuit by a power source, such as a ▸◂ **BATTERY** .

Plastic
does not carry current and can be used to separate different parts of the circuit

WHAT IS AN ELECTRIC CURRENT?

Electric current is a flow of electric charge (usually in the form of electrons) through a substance. The substance or conductor that an electric current flows through is often metal wire, although current can also flow through some gases, liquids, and other materials.

PINBALL MACHINE ▶
A pinball machine uses components wired in to parallel circuits to produce light, sound, and movement from electricity. Switches control the circuits—when a switch is off, no current flows. The steel ball turns on switches so that bells ring, lamps flash, and springs and flippers move.

Electrons flow from negative terminal on battery, to each bulb in turn

Positive terminal

Electrons flow back to positive terminal

Bulbs dimly lit

SERIES CIRCUIT

Negative and positive terminals wired to both bulbs

Battery

Bulbs brightly lit

PARALLEL CIRCUIT

circuits

Flat disk
operates a switch when it is hit

▲ IN SERIES AND IN PARALLEL

Circuits can be wired in two ways. In a series circuit, current flows to each bulb in turn. Both bulbs are dimly lit. In a parallel circuit, the current divides and flows directly to both bulbs at the same time. The bulbs are then brighter.

WHEN DOES CURRENT FLOW IN A CIRCUIT?

Current only flows when a circuit is complete—when there are no gaps in it. In a complete circuit, the electrons flow from the negative terminal (connection) on the power source, through the connecting wires and components, such as bulbs, and back to the positive terminal.

WHAT MAKES CURRENT FLOW IN A CIRCUIT?

When a wire is connected to battery terminals, electrons flow from negative to positive. Unlike (opposite) charges attract, like (same) charges repel. Electrons have a negative charge—they are repelled from the negative and attracted to the positive.

BATTERY

A battery is a compact, easily transportable source of electricity. When a battery is connected in a circuit, it provides the energy that drives the electrons along in a current. Batteries contain chemical substances that react together to separate positive and negative charges.

Zinc electrode becomes negatively charged

Wires carry current in circuit

Copper electrode becomes positively charged

Sulfuric acid

Bubbles show chemical action

◀ SIMPLE BATTERY CELL
A simple cell can be made by putting zinc and copper electrodes into a liquid electrolyte, such as sulfuric acid.

WHAT IS INSIDE A BATTERY?

A battery is made of one or more sections or cells. Inside each cell, two chemically active materials called electrodes are separated by a liquid or paste called the electrolyte. Small batteries may have just one cell. Large, powerful batteries may have six cells.

HOW DOES A BATTERY CELL WORK?

Inside a cell the electrolyte reacts with the electrodes, causing electrons to move through the electrolyte from one electrode to the other. One electrode gains a negative charge and the other a positive charge. The two electrodes are the positive and negative terminals.

Bulb inside
bumper unit
lights up when
the ball activates
a switch

Decorative
metal ring
bounces ball
away

Heavy steel ball
operates switches
with its weight, or by
completing a circuit

COMPONENTS

The different objects that make up a circuit
are called components. A circuit must have
a power source, such as a battery, and the
current flows through a conductor, such
as a wire. Bulbs, buzzers, and motors are
components that change electricity into
light, sound, and movement.

WHAT IS A CONDUCTOR?
A material that carries a current well is called a
conductor. Metals are good conductors because metal
atoms readily release electrons to carry the current.
Silver and copper are the best conductors, and most
electric wires are made from copper. To prevent
electric shocks, wires are covered
with an insulator.

◄ HEART PACEMAKER
The battery and other components
of an artificial heart pacemaker
send electric pulses through wires
to a patient's heart to keep it
beating steadily. A pacemaker is
put in when the heart does not beat
steadily by itself.

WHAT IS AN A INSULATOR?
Some materials do not carry current well. They are
said to resist (oppose) the flow of current. Materials
that do this are called insulators. Plastics, glass, rubber,
and ceramics are all good insulators. Insulators are
used to cover wires and components to prevent electric
shocks, and to stop currents from flowing.

HOW DOES A SWITCH WORK?
Switches are like gates that control the flow of
electricity in a circuit. When a switch is open, it
creates a gap in the circuit and current will not flow.
When it is closed, it completes the circuit, and current
flows through it. Switches are used in parallel circuits
to turn different parts of the circuit on and off.

HOW IS ELECTRICITY SUPPLIED?
Most of the electricity we use in our homes and
workplaces is produced by machines in power stations
called generators. Generators send the electric current
through a huge network of circuits and wires and into
houses, offices, and other buildings.

POWER INSULATORS ▶
Electricity travels around the country in wires called power lines. Giant
ceramic insulators prevent the current from flowing to the ground.

CIRCUIT DEFINITIONS	
Voltage	is the energy given to each unit of charge that flows in a circuit
Current	is the amount of electric charge flowing past a point in a circuit each second
Wattage	is the amount of electrical energy a circuit uses each second

FIND OUT MORE ▶▶ Chemistry 162 • Electricity 182 • Electricity Supply 187 • Electromagnetism 186

Crane jib
moves magnet
into place

electromagnet

Electromagnet
hangs from
chains

Cable carries
electric current

ELECTROMAGNETISM

An electric current produces magnetism, and a magnet can produce an electric current. The two forces are so closely connected that scientists talk about the single force of electromagnetism. Without it, we would not have an electricity supply, or ►► ELECTRIC MOTORS.

HOW DOES ELECTRICITY CREATE MAGNETISM?

Each electron is surrounded by a force called an electric field. When an electron moves, it creates a second field—a magnetic field. When electrons are made to flow in a current through a conductor, such as a piece of metal or a coil of wire, the conductor becomes a temporary magnet—an electromagnet.

◄ METAL DETECTOR
A metal detector makes use of electromagnetic effects to find metal land mines hidden under the soil. Wire coils in the detector produce a changing magnetic field, which induces (causes) electric currents to flow in the metal land mines. These in turn produce magnetism that can be sensed by the detector.

Iron and steel scrap
is attracted by the
magnet when it is on

◄ ELECTROMAGNET
Unlike permanent magnets, electromagnets can be switched on and off. This is useful in a junkyard, where a powerful electromagnet separates iron and steel scrap from other materials.

Nonmagnetic scrap
is left behind

HOW DOES MAGNETISM PRODUCE ELECTRICITY?

If a coil of wire is placed near a magnet with an unchanging magnetic field, nothing happens. But if the magnetic field is changed, by moving the magnet back and forth or spinning the wire, the changing magnetic field produces an electric current in the wire.

WHAT DO GENERATORS DO?

Generators supply us with most of the electric current we use. They turn mechanical energy (movement) into electrical energy. Inside a generator, a coil of wire is spun inside a powerful magnetic field. This creates an electric current in the wire. A large generator can produce enough electricity to run an entire city.

ELECTRIC MOTORS

Electric motors are machines that turn electrical energy into mechanical energy to do work. Electric motors can be small, like the motor that turns the fan in a hair dryer, or huge, like the engine that drives a train.

HOW DO ELECTRIC MOTORS WORK?

A current turns a conductor into an electromagnet. If the current is reversed, the electromagnetic poles will reverse, too. When the electromagnet is placed near a fixed magnet, the two sets of poles repel and attract each other. This produces a force that makes the conductor rotate (spin) at high speed. This turns a shaft, which then drives a machine.

▲ MICRO MOTOR GEARS
In 1960, engineer William McLellan built a motor the size of a period on this page from 13 separate parts. Today, engineers are working on motors thousands of times smaller. The gears in this picture are magnified 200 times.

ELECTRICITY SUPPLY

Electricity has revolutionized the way we use energy. It can be generated in large **POWER STATIONS** far away from towns and cities, and distributed cleanly to homes, offices, and factories through a network of power lines.

HOW ARE MOST GENERATORS POWERED?
To make electricity, the coils inside a generator are turned by turbines. Most large generators are powered by turbines spun around by high-pressure steam. The steam is produced in boilers heated by fossil fuels (or in a nuclear reactor). Water turbines are also used to turn the generators in hydroelectric power stations.

WHAT IS THE POWER GRID?
From the power stations, electricity is fed into a vast network of cables and wires called the power grid. Electricity travels through the grid into almost every room in the system. Controlling the power in the grid is complex. Engineers must try to make sure that enough power is available whenever it is needed.

POWER GRID ▶
Electricity generated by the power stations is fed into a grid of interconnecting power lines. These take the energy wherever it is required. When you switch on a light, you have no way of knowing which power station the electricity came from.

electricity supply

WHAT IS ALTERNATING CURRENT?
Current is produced in two forms: direct current (DC) and alternating current (AC). Direct current (produced by batteries) only flows in one direction. Alternating current (produced by power stations) switches back and forth, reversing direction regularly. An AC current switches back and forth 50 or 60 times a second.

▲ NIGHT LIGHTS
This night-time satellite photograph shows the artificial light produced on Earth by electric road and building lights. North America, Europe, India, China, and Japan are the most brightly lit regions. Over time, this map will change as countries increase—or decrease—their electricity output.

POWER STATIONS

Power stations work day and night to produce the electricity that provides us with heat and light, and drives all kinds of machines, from hair dryers and refrigerators to televisions and trains.

HOW DOES ELECTRICITY GET FROM THE POWER STATION TO US?
Electricity from a power station is boosted from 25,000 volts to 400,000 volts to travel along power lines. But the voltage must be lowered before it is safe to use. Transformers reduce the voltage in stages to different levels to supply factories, subways, farms, hospitals, offices, homes, and highways.

ENERGY EVERYWHERE

POWER STATION
A large, coal-fired power station like this may produce a continuous flow of up to 1,000 MW (megawatts) of electricity. That's enough power to light 20 million light bulbs, or meet all the power needs of a small city.

POWER LINES
Electric current is carried around the country by power lines. Most power lines are slung high above the ground, on tall metal pylons. In towns or cities, the lines may go underground. Power lines carry electricity at 400,000 volts—thousands of times greater than the voltage received in our homes.

SUBSTATION
At various stages along the way, the power lines feed into substations. These contain transformers and heavy-duty switching gear that reduce (lower) the voltage to safer levels and direct power to where it is needed.

FACTORIES
Large industrial plants such as this chemical factory use tremendous amounts of electrical energy. Many have their own dedicated power stations.

HOMES
Electric power travels from substations to homes through underground cables or lightweight overhead lines. For domestic use, voltage is reduced to 110 volts. Each house has its own meter to record the amount of electrical energy used.

FIND OUT MORE ▶▶ Circuits 184–185 • Electricity 182 • Engines 198–199

ELECTRONICS

Electronic circuits operate nearly every modern machine—microwave ovens, cars, and computers. In an electronic circuit, an electric signal carries information. Signals are controlled and changed by components made from materials called ▶▶ SEMICONDUCTORS.

WHAT IS AN ELECTRIC SIGNAL?
A signal is a current or voltage change that carries information. Changes can represent instructions, numbers, sounds, or pictures in the form of a code. A digital signal is either on or off. An analog signal is continuously flowing electricity, which increases and decreases to represent the information.

WHAT ARE ELECTRONIC COMPONENTS?
Electronic circuits use components (parts) to control electric signals. These include resistors, capacitors, diodes, and transistors. Resistors control how much current flows through them, capacitors store electric charges and release them when necessary, and diodes let current pass through in only one direction.

WHAT IS A TRANSISTOR?
Transistors are electronic components that can change and control electronic signals. A transistor can work as a switch—turning a signal on or off— or as an amplifier—increasing the current or voltage in a circuit.

Volume control

Connecting wires

Loudspeaker *gives out sound*

Capacitors *store high voltages*

electronics

◀ RADIO
This colorful X-ray picture shows the electronic components of a radio through its casing. The radio receives radio waves from a radio station, translates them into an electric current, and then turns them into sounds, which are produced by its loudspeaker.

Microchip

Printed circuit board

SEMICONDUCTORS

A semiconductor is a material that conducts electricity less well than a metal, but better than an insulator, and can act as both a conductor and an insulator. The chemical elements silicon and germanium are the most important semiconductors for making electronic components.

HOW DOES A SEMICONDUCTOR CONDUCT ELECTRICITY?
The current in a semiconductor is carried by positive holes and by negative electrons. A hole is an empty space left in the orbit of an atom when an electron has escaped. Holes move through a semiconductor in the opposite direction from electrons, hopping from atom to atom.

FIND OUT MORE ▶▶ Circuits 184–185 • Elements 160–161 • Sound 176–177 • Telecommunications 192–193

MICROCHIPS

A microchip is an electronic device built as a single unit from many miniature components—mainly transistors. It is plugged in to a socket on a printed circuit board to connect it to other components.

WHAT DO MICROCHIPS DO?

Each kind of microchip performs a different task, and is identified by a code number. Some microchips work with analog signals (a microchip with code 741 is an analog amplifier). Others work with digital signals—to act as ▸▸ **LOGIC GATES** , or to get digital sound from a CD.

CIRCUIT BOARDS ▲
These technicians are checking the quality of circuit boards before final assembly. Individual microchips are linked on circuit boards to form electronic devices, such as computers.

◄ CERAMIC CAPSULE
A microchip is encased in an insulating capsule. This capsule has a transparent cover—the chip is inside. It is a charged-coupled device (CCD) used to take images in digital cameras.

A single CCD is a grid of a million or more transistors

Metal pins plug in to a socket on a circuit board

◄ SILICON WAFER
Hundreds of identical copies of a microchip are made on a slice of pure silicon. The circuits are tested and faulty units rejected. Those that work are linked by gold wires to pins and sealed in their capsules (cases).

HOW ARE MICROCHIPS MADE?

Microchips are made by building up electronic circuits in a tiny wafer (slice) or pure silicon in a complicated layer-by-layer process. The different circuit components are produced by doping (treating) areas of the silicon with different chemicals.

WHAT IS BINARY CODE?

Digital microchips send and receive digital electronic signals in binary code. All information is represented by on/off signals. These signals are processed by the transistors on microchips. When a switch is on, it is the digit 1; when it is off, it is the digit 0. The binary code for the letter "a" on a keyboard is 01100001.

LOGIC GATES

A logic gate is a digital circuit that makes a simple decision. Logic gates include AND, OR, NOT, NOR, and NAND gates. Logic gate circuits can be made with individual transistors, or formed on microchips.

HOW ARE LOGIC GATES USED?

You can link logic gates to make complex decisions, or perform difficult calculations. For example, a washing machine can be designed to start only when a program has been selected AND the door is closed AND the water supply is on.

LOGIC GATES ▶
A logic gate may have one or two inputs, and an output. Whether the output is on (1) or off (0) depends on the state of the inputs according to the logic set out in the tables.

microchips

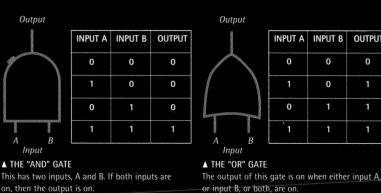

Output

INPUT A	INPUT B	OUTPUT
0	0	0
1	0	0
0	1	0
1	1	1

A *B*
Input

▲ THE "AND" GATE
This has two inputs, A and B. If both inputs are on, then the output is on.

Output

INPUT A	INPUT B	OUTPUT
0	0	0
1	0	1
0	1	1
1	1	1

A *B*
Input

▲ THE "OR" GATE
The output of this gate is on when either input A, or input B, or both, are on.

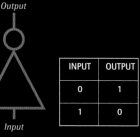

Output

INPUT	OUTPUT
0	1
1	0

Input

▲ THE "NOT" GATE
This gate has only one input. The output is on when the input is not on.

FIND OUT MORE ▸▸ Computers 190 • Electronics 188

COMPUTERS

An electronic machine that uses binary code to store and process data is a computer. Binary code can represent numbers, text, sounds, pictures, and movies. This data is stored in the computer's memory and on magnetic disks, CD-ROMs, and DVDs.

WHAT IS A MICROPROCESSOR?

A microprocessor is a computer's brain. It is an integrated circuit made of millions of transistors. It carries out the instructions (the programs) that make a computer operate. Everything the computer does is broken down into simple steps. The power of a microprocessor is measured by how fast it carries out these instructions.

WHAT IS MEMORY?

Data is stored in binary code on microchips. They are made up of millions of transistors that are on or off– 1 or 0 in binary code. The capacity (size) of a memory chip is measured in megabytes (MB). One byte is an eight-digit binary number. One megabyte is just over one million bytes of information.

HOW IS VIRTUAL REALITY CREATED?

Virtual reality controls what you see, and responds to your movements and actions. When you wear virtual reality goggles, the scene you see changes as you move. Sensors on special gloves, or a body suit, allow you to interact with the scene by pointing or touching. Sounds increase the experience of reality.

▲ VIRTUAL REALITY
Virtual reality goggles feed slightly different images to the right and left eyes to create a realistic 3-D scene. These goggles help architects visualize plans.

Read/write head finds data stored on disk

Liquid crystal monitor screen

Screen displays output on a grid of almost one million colored dots (pixels)

Magnetic disk

Arm moves to retrieve data

Track selector mechanism

Motherboard holds the microprocessor and other components that operate the computer

▲ HARD DISK DRIVE
The computer's hard disk is the main storage area for programs, documents, images, and other files. It can hold dozens of gigabytes of data (billions of binary numbers). Information is written (put on) and read (taken off) by electromagnetic heads that swing over the disk surfaces as they spin at high speed.

computers

Keyboard used to input letters and other characters

Disk drive reads and writes disks

Touchpad moves the pointer around the screen, like a mouse

▲ LAPTOP COMPUTER
All the components of a personal computer can be built into a convenient folding package the size of a book. Some laptops use wireless technology to interact with printers, scanners, and other devices by radio waves. Through wireless telephone links, you can log on to the Internet to send emails from your laptop.

FIND OUT MORE ▸▸ Electronics 188 • Robots 194

NETWORKS

A network is formed when people, places, or things are linked together. A rail network links towns and cities. A computer network links computers.

◄ NETWORK CONTROL
The global telephone system is the largest communications network on Earth. Engineers at this telecommunications control center maintain network links and control the flow of information.

WHAT IS THE TRAVELING SALESMAN PROBLEM?
A network of roads connects the towns that a traveling salesman must visit. How does he work out the shortest route to take so that he visits each town only once? This is a difficult mathematical puzzle. The same problem faces engineers designing efficient communications networks.

FIND OUT MORE ▸▸ Internet 191 • Telecommunications 192–19⬛

INTERNET

The global computer network connecting computers by telephone cables, optical fibers, and microwaves is called the Internet. The Internet provides almost instant electronic communication around the world.

TIM BERNERS LEE
British, 1955–
MARC ANDREESSEN
American, 1971–

Tim Berners Lee invented the World Wide Web as a source of information for scientists in the 1980s. In 1993, Marc Andreessen developed the first browser program (Mosaic) with text, pictures, and hypertext links.

HOW DOES THE INTERNET WORK?
Every computer linked to the Internet has an address. This is its IP number. When you send a message or request information on the Internet, your computer sends packets of data with the sender's and receiver's addresses attached. Special computers called servers and routers direct the data through the Internet.

WHAT IS THE WORLD WIDE WEB?
The World Wide Web is a library of billions of pages of information, including ▸▸ SEARCH ENGINES, stored on servers connected to the Internet. The pages are written using hypertext, which links them. A program called a browser on your computer uses a web address (URL) to request a page. The request is routed through the Internet to the correct server, and the page is sent back to your computer.

USES FOR THE INTERNET
We are always finding new ways to use the Internet, from swapping text messages between messenger programs to playing online computer games. Video phone calls, shown above, are becoming popular, allowing people to see and talk to each other over distances.

WHAT IS HYPERTEXT?
Web pages are written using hypertext. Hypertext links one web page to another. Web pages contain text prepared in a computer language called HTML. Hypertext links special words or phrases to other sections of the document, or to other documents. Clicking on a link takes you to the linked page.

SEARCH ENGINES

If you need to find information on the World Wide Web, you use a program called a search engine. When you enter keywords, the search engine (located on a server) makes a hypertext list of Web pages that have the words you are looking for.

◄ FIBER OPTICS
An optical fiber is a hair-thin strand of very pure glass. It carries computer data as pulses of laser light. Reflections stop the light from escaping through the fiber, so it emerges at the far end almost as bright as it went in.

Optic fiber directs light along its length by internal reflection

HOW DOES A SEARCH ENGINE RANK PAGES?
Entering the words "team sports" will produce a list of millions of results from a search engine. The engine tries to place the most relevant pages at the top of the list. Different engines do this in different ways. For example, the engine may check if all the words appear or how many times they appear.

FIND OUT MORE ▸▸ Computers 190 • Light 178–179 • Telecommunications 192–19⬛

TELECOMMUNICATIONS

Telecommunications are messages carried around the world in seconds by electric signals and waves from the ►► ELECTROMAGNETIC SPECTRUM . They include radio and television broadcasts, and telephone conversations.

HOW DOES A TELEPHONE WORK?

A telephone has a microphone and an earpiece. The microphone converts sound into an electric signal. The signal travels at the speed of light along wires, through optical fibers, or via microwaves. A network connects the phones. The earpiece contains a loudspeaker. This changes the signal back into sound.

HOW DOES A RADIO WORK?

Radio broadcasts are made from a central transmitter. Sound signals from microphones in the radio studio are combined with radio waves broadcast from an antenna. Your radio at home has a receiver that separates the sound signal from the radio signal and sends it to a loudspeaker. This is the sound you hear.

HOW DOES A TELEVISION WORK?

An analog television transmitter sends pictures and sounds as a pattern of radio waves through cables. ►► DIGITAL BROADCASTS transmit the sounds and pictures in binary code through cables and satellites.

HOW DOES A CELL PHONE WORK?

A cell phone sends and receives signals using microwaves. A phone has a range of only a few miles, so land-based aerials are used. The area that each aerial covers is called a cell. A phone exchanges signals with the nearest aerial. As you move from cell to cell, the phone changes aerials. The aerials are connected to the global telephone network.

GUGLIELMO MARCONI
Italian, 1874-1937
Scientist and inventor Guglielmo Marconi made the first radio transmissions in 1894. His transmitter rang a bell 30 ft (10 m) away. By 1901, he had developed his invention and made the first wireless transmission across the Atlantic Ocean from England to Canada. Marconi was awarded the Nobel Prize for Physics in 1909.

◄ COMMUNICATIONS SATELLITE
A satellite bounces telecommunications signals from one side of Earth to another. The satellite travels in a geostationary orbit so that it stays over the same point on Earth's surface at all times.

telecoms

TELEPHONE TOWER ►
The BT tower in London, England, provides telecommunications links into and out of the city. It is an electronic communications center for radio and television broadcasting, telephone services, and digital computer data transmissions.

◄ HIDDEN CELL-PHONE MAST
To create an effective cell-phone network, phone masts are built at regular intervals. In some locations, masts ruin attractive views of the countryside or historic buildings. This mast has been disguised as a tree.

Aircraft warning beacons flash on the top and sides of the tower at night

Dish-shaped microwave antennae point toward similar dishes on masts in other cities

ELECTROMAGNETIC SPECTRUM

Electromagnetic rays are waves of electromagnetic force that travel at the speed of light. The full range of rays make up the electromagnetic spectrum.

WHAT ARE RADIO WAVES?

Electrons produce radio waves as they vibrate. They are low-frequency, long-wavelength waves. Radio broadcasts use the lower-frequency range of radio waves, and television broadcasts use the higher range.

HOW ARE DIFFERENT WAVE BANDS USED?

Waves are grouped in wave bands by frequency. Low- to medium-frequency wave bands travel far, and are used for shipping signals. High-frequency waves are used for radio and telephones. The ultra-high to extremely high-frequency bands carry huge amounts of information, including TV, cell phone, and radar signals, and microwave communications.

ELECTROMAGNETIC SPECTRUM ▶
The spectrum arranges the waves according to frequency (number of waves passing a point per second) and wavelength (the distance between the crest of one wave and the crest of the next).

DIGITAL BROADCASTS

Have you seen television pictures as clear as computer graphics? In a digital broadcast, sounds and pictures are converted into streams of binary numbers. The result is higher-quality reception, and many more channels.

▲ DIGITAL BROADCASTING
A TV cameraman records a soccer game to be broadcast digitally. The image is created with 30 still pictures (frames) each second. Only the changes from frame to frame are transmitted.

HOW DOES DIGITAL TV WORK?

Digital TV converts sounds and images into binary code. The code is carried on electromagnetic waves. Digital pictures are clearer because binary code can be compressed (made smaller) to send lots more information about the picture to the receiver. Broadcasters can also send more channels this way.

Gamma rays have wavelengths of up to about 0.01 nm (1 nanometer [nm] = one billionth of a meter)

▲ GAMMA RAYS
Nuclear reactions and radioactive decay emit these high-energy rays.

X-rays 0.001–10 nm

▲ X-RAYS
X-rays go through materials that block light, such as clothing and skin.

Ultraviolet rays 10–390 nm

▲ ULTRAVIOLET RAYS
These dangerous rays from the Sun can damage your skin.

Visible light 390–7000 nm

Infrared rays 700 nm–1 mm

▲ INFRARED
Night-vision cameras detect infrared rays to see missiles in the dark.

▲ RADAR
Radar systems transmit radio waves to detect moving ships and aircraft.

Microwaves 0.3 m–0.001 m

Radio waves 1 mm–1 km+

▲ RADIO WAVES
Radio waves are used for radio, TV, telephone, and satellite communication.

FIND OUT MORE ▶▶ Home Entertainment 351 • Internet 191 • Media 298–299 • Networks 191 • Satellites 28 • Sound 176–177

ROBOTS

Robots are automatic machines. Some robots can perform mechanical and repetitive jobs faster, more accurately, and more safely than people. Robots can also handle dangerous materials and explore distant planets.

WHAT CAN ROBOTS DO?

Robots can sense and respond to their surroundings. They can handle delicate objects or apply great force—for example, to perform eye operations guided by a human surgeon, or to assemble a car. With **▸▸ ARTIFICIAL INTELLIGENCE**, robots will also be able to make decisions for themselves.

HOW DO ROBOTS SENSE?

Electronic sensors are a robot's eyes and ears. Twin video cameras give the robot a 3-D view of the world. Microphones detect sounds. Pressure sensors give the robot a sense of touch, to judge how hard to grip an egg. Built-in computers send and receive information with radio waves.

Limbs moved by pipes and pistons

HUMANOID ROBOT ▶
This humanoid robot has been built for the entertainment industry. Dressed as pirates or cowboys, robots like this are performers in theme park attractions.

Joints move like a human's

▲ ROBOTS IN MEDICINE
Monitoring progress on a TV, a skilled surgeon performs an operation by remote control. Robot instruments carry out his actions on the patient.

robots

Movements controlled by a computer

ARTIFICIAL INTELLIGENCE

Artificial intelligence attempts to create computer programs that think like human brains. Current research has not achieved this, but some computers can be programmed to recognize faces in a crowd.

◀ ROBOT CLEANER
This robot vacuum cleaner finds its own way around as it cleans your home. With three computers, and over 70 sensors, it plans an efficient route, remembering where it has been and deciding where to clean next.

CAN ROBOTS THINK?

Robots can think. They can play complex games, such as chess, better than human beings. But will a robot ever know that it is thinking? Humans are conscious—we know we are thinking—but we don't know how consciousness works. We don't know if computers can ever be conscious.

WILL ROBOTS TAKE THE PLACE OF PEOPLE?

Robots have replaced people performing repetitive jobs, and dangerous jobs, such as bomb disposal. In the future, robots may do housework and other jobs for us. But will robots replace people in jobs that need kindness or creativity? It's hard to imagine a robot teacher or dancer.

FIND OUT MORE ▸▸ Computers 190 • Industry 204 • Machines 196–197

NANOTECHNOLOGY

A nanometer is one billionth of a meter. This is about a million times smaller than the period on this line. Nanotechnology aims to make tiny machines measured in nanometers.

WHAT IS A NANOMACHINE?

A nanomachine is built from individual atoms, like the parts of a tiny construction kit, with atomic wheels and motors. A nanomachine will make other products from atoms, such as nanovehicles to transport drugs through the body's blood stream. Vast armies of nanomachines might even assemble ▶ CARBON COMPUTERS, atom by atom.

WHAT IS SELF-ASSEMBLY?

Nanomachines will be designed to build and copy themselves. They will be self-assembling in a way similar to the molecules that make up living things. To build a large structure, such as a car, billions of nanomachines will be organized to work together.

Red blood cells

Nanorobot powered by a propeller

NANOTECHNOLOGY IN MEDICINE ▲
This imaginative artwork shows how nanotechnology might work in medicine. Tiny nanorobots the size of cells are programmed to travel through the bloodstream, finding and repairing defects in the body's organs and tissues.

NANOTECHNOLOGY BEARING ▶
Before complete nanomachines and robots can be constructed, scientists will build basic machine components, such as levers, gears, bearings, and motors, all at a nano scale. This computer design shows how a frictionless bearing might be assembled from individual atoms.

ARE THERE ANY DANGERS ASSOCIATED WITH NANOTECHNOLOGY?

One danger is that self-assembling nanomachines could multiply and spread out of control, damaging natural materials. They would have to be programmed so that they could not escape into the environment in this destructive way.

CARBON COMPUTER

At an atomic scale, scientists think carbon will have better electrical properties than silicon for making computers. A computer processor could be made by linking individual carbon atoms. Only nanomachines could work at this scale.

HOW COULD NANOTECHNOLOGY BUILD A CARBON CAR?

Nanomachines could make things, such as carbon cars, by linking carbon atoms one at a time into the diamond structure. These new cars will be many times stronger, yet lighter, than existing versions made with titanium, aluminum, and steel. A carbon car built by nanomachines would be light enough to lift with one hand.

◀ NANO FLY
Using nano components built from carbon and other atoms, it might be possible to build intelligent robot insects such as this fly—pictured on a computer key. Tiny machines like this could be used for police surveillance.

WHAT HAS NANOTECHNOLOGY ACHIEVED SO FAR?

Nanotechnology is still at a very early stage, but some progress has been made. Simple wheels, axles, and gears have been produced. Scientists have already manipulated individual carbon atoms to produce nano-scale numbers and lettering.

FIND OUT MORE ▶▶ Atoms 157 • Machines 196–197

MACHINES

From can openers to cranes, machines make work easier. Simple machines include ▸❙ LEVERS , ▸❙ PULLEYS , ▸❙ INCLINED PLANES , and ▸❙ GEARS . They transfer force and movement from one place to another, often magnifying the force or the movement at the same time.

Load lifted by the digger

WHAT IS MECHANICAL ADVANTAGE?
The mechanical advantage of a machine is the amount that it magnifies (increases) a force to overcome a load. Nutcrackers have a mechanical advantage of about five. The force you use to squeeze the handles is magnified five times—making it strong enough to crack even the hardest nut.

HOW IS A MACHINE'S EFFICIENCY MEASURED?
The efficiency of a machine is the ratio of the work output to the work input. If the machine is perfect, then all the work (energy) that you put in (the effort) is used to move the load. It would be 100 percent efficient. In reality, a machine always wastes some energy as a result of friction between its parts.

INDUSTRIAL DIGGER ▶
A complicated machine, such as this digger, is built from many simple machines that work together—the digger arms are levers, and the teeth on the bucket are inclined planes. The driver operates the machine to move a load far beyond his own strength.

machines

Arms raise or tip the bucket

Effort
Load

Fulcrum

Effort

▲ FIRST-CLASS LEVER
These pliers are a pair of first-class levers. The fulcrum is between the load and the effort. The effort is magnified because the load is closer to the fulcrum.

LEVERS

A lever is a rod or bar that turns on a pivot (the fulcrum). The effort applied at one place moves a load at another place via the fulcrum. There are three different types of levers, each with the effort, load, and fulcrum in different places.

WHAT ARE THE DIFFERENT CLASSES OF LEVER?
The three classes of levers are suitable for different jobs. In a first-class lever, such as a seesaw, the effort and load are on opposite sides of the fulcrum. In a second-class lever, such as a bottle opener, the fulcrum is at one end, the effort at the other, and the load in between. In a third-class lever, such as chopsticks, the fulcrum and the load are at either end, with the effort in between.

WHAT IS A WHEEL AND AXLE?
The steering wheel of a car works like a circular lever—it magnifies a turning force. Your hands·on the wheel move through a much larger distance than the axle (the steering column). The turning effort is magnified to produce enough force to steer the car wheels. A crank is a turning handle that works in a similar way, to raise a heavy bucket of water up a well, for example.

Effort
Fulcrum
Load
Effort

▲ SECOND-CLASS LEVER
These nutcrackers have the fulcrum at one end, the effort at the other, and the load between—ideal for cracking open a nut.

Pistons apply the effort to lift the load

Oil pressure pushes the piston along a hydraulic cylinder

Wide wheels are needed to cross rough ground

Fulcrum
Effort
Effort
Load

◀ THIRD-CLASS LEVER
In chopsticks, the effort is between the fulcrum and the load. The effort is reduced by this lever, but the movement is magnified. With small movements of the hand, you can pick up anything from a grain of rice to a large nut–but you can't crack the nut.

PULLEYS

A pulley is a grooved wheel that a rope or belt runs over. A single pulley changes the direction of a force, without changing its size—for example, to raise a flag up a pole by pulling down on the rope.

WHAT IS A BLOCK AND TACKLE?

A block and tackle is two sets of pulleys linked by a single rope. Pulling the rope draws the block and tackle together. This magnifies the effort put in so that you can lift or lower a heavy load—a car engine, for example. Block and tackle pulley systems have been used for centuries to raise sails and shift cargo on sailing ships.

Effort

Upper pulley block

A single length of rope runs over four pulleys. The mechanical advantage of this pulley system means it can lift a load that is four times bigger than the effort applied

Lower pulley block

BLOCK AND TACKLE ▶
A block and tackle is a pulley system designed to lift a large load with a smaller effort. The crane on the far right is equipped with a block and tackle to move heavy loads, such as steel plates, into position on a construction site.

Load

INCLINED PLANES

The first construction machine was probably the inclined plane. Early builders raised loads such as blocks of building stone by pushing them gradually up a slope. The more gradual the slope, the easier it is to raise the load, but the farther you have to travel to get to the top.

Cab where the driver operates controls

WHY DOES A SLOPE MAKE IT EASIER TO RAISE A LOAD?

When you push a load up a slope, the weight of the load is shared between your effort and the slope. You do not have to lift the whole weight at once. However, although the effort is smaller, the distance moved is greater. If you climb a zigzag path up a mountain, each step is easier, but you take many more steps to reach the top than if you follow a steeper but more direct route to the top.

WHAT IS A WEDGE?

A wedge is a movable inclined plane. As it is pushed forward, it pushes a load sideways. The sharper the wedge, the farther it has to be pushed to produce the same sideways movement, but the greater the sideways force it applies. The blade of an ax is a wedge that produces a splitting force as it cuts into hard materials, such as wood, rock, or ice.

◀ INCLINED PLANE
This road follows a zigzag path up a hillside. The distance traveled is greater than following the direct route to the top, but the slope is gentler, so less effort is needed.

GEARS

Gears are toothed wheels that transfer turning motion and forces from one place to another, such as from a car engine to the car wheels. The gear teeth mesh (fit together) so that as one gear turns, it forces its neighbor to turn in the opposite direction.

WHAT IS A GEAR RATIO?

If two gears have the same number of teeth, then they turn at the same rate and with the same force. If one gear has twice the number of teeth as the other, the gear with more teeth rotates at half the speed of the other gear, but with twice the force.

WATCH GEARS ▶
The gears in this watch carry the turning force from the spring inside the watch to the hands on its face. The gear ratios make each hand turn at the correct rate to keep time.

FIND OUT MORE ▶▶ Engines 198–199 • Forces 164 • Motion 165

ENGINES

A machine that converts energy from a fuel to do work is an engine. Steam engines were the first engines for transportation and industry. Internal combustion engines power road vehicles and many trains. Jet engines power aircraft, and ▶ **TURBINES** drive ships.

WHAT IS A HEAT ENGINE?

Most engines convert heat energy into motion. The heat comes from burning a fuel such as coal, gasoline, or hydrogen gas. The heat makes a gas, such as air, expand rapidly. In a piston engine, the expanding gas pushes a piston down a cylinder. The piston moves down on the power stroke, which drives the machine. The amount of fuel an engine uses to run for a given time is called its ▶ **FUEL CONSUMPTION**.

WHAT IS AN INTERNAL COMBUSTION ENGINE?

In this engine, fuel is burned in a cylinder. The cylinder draws in air and fuel through a valve as the piston moves down. As the piston moves up, it compresses the air and fuel, making them heat up. The fuel combusts (explodes), and the gases from the explosion push the piston down, producing power.

HOW DOES A STEAM ENGINE WORK?

In a steam engine, fuel is burned outside the cylinder. Coal heats water in a boiler, which makes steam. Steam is fed into the cylinder, where it expands and pushes the piston. The piston pushes a rod connected to a crank to turn a wheel.

◀ **STEAM ENGINE**
The first steam engines pumped water from deep mines. Scottish engineer James Watt (1736-1819) introduced many improvements to the steam engine. His ideas led to efficient steam engines that could power factories and drive heavy locomotives, such as this one from Harbin, Manchuria, China.

Crankshaft turns the wheels

Piston drives the crankshaft as it is forced down by expanding hot gases

Air intake draws in air needed for fuel to burn. A filter traps dust and dirt

Cylinder where the fuel is ignited

Valves open to let fuel and air mixture into cylinder and to let exhaust gases out

Camshaft controls the opening and closing of the valves

Sparkplug ignites the fuel and air mixture

GASOLINE ENGINE

Gasoline engines are internal combustion engines. Most modern gasoline engines work on a four-stroke cycle. Fuel and air are drawn into the cylinder; the mixture is compressed and ignited. The expanding gases push down the piston. As the piston descends, power is applied to the crankshaft, and finally the exhaust gases are forced out. Each cylinder operates out of step with the others, so the four work in sequence. This produces a continuous output of power so that the car runs smoothly.

Inlet valve

Piston

Crankshaft

Sparkplug

Ignition system causes a spark

INTAKE STROKE
The inlet valve opens. Fuel and air are drawn into the cylinder as the piston descends.

COMPRESSION STROKE
The mixture of fuel and air is compressed as the piston rises. Then the spark plug ignites the mixture and it explodes.

HOW DOES A JET ENGINE WORK?

Air entering the front of the engine is compressed by rotating blades and fed to a combustion chamber. Jet fuel injected into the chamber mixes with the compressed air, and burns at a high temperature. This makes a jet of gas shoot from the rear of the engine at such speed that it thrusts the aircraft forward.

Belt drives the alternator to charge the battery

FRANK WHITTLE
English, 1907–1996
Engineer Frank Whittle proposed the idea for jet aircraft in 1928. But it was not until 1937 that he built the first successful engine. His ideas were developed in World War II, and the first Whittle engine jet fighters flew in 1944.

ENGINE DEVELOPMENT

c 60 CE	Steam powers an engine
1698	First practical steam engine
1765– 1790	James Watt improves steam engines
1804	First steam locomotive
1876	First internal combustion engine
1903	First gas turbine
1937	First jet engine

◄ CAR ENGINE
In this high-performance, six-cylinder car engine, the power strokes from the pistons take place in sequence. The power is transferred smoothly through the crankshaft to the transmission and wheels.

Hot gases expand and force the piston down

Exhaust valve

Crankshaft rotates

POWER STROKE
The hot gases expand, which forces the piston down, transferring power to the crankshaft.

EXHAUST STROKE
The exhaust valve opens. The exhaust gases (waste gases) are forced out of the cylinder as the piston rises.

TURBINES

A turbine is an engine that has a set of blades or paddles rotated by a moving liquid or gas. Turbines are used in hydroelectric power stations and ships.

WHAT ARE THE DIFFERENT TYPES OF TURBINES?

Water mills and windmills are examples of water and air turbines. They are not heat engines because they do not rely on heat to produce motion. Gas and steam turbines are powerful heat engines—the turbine blades are spun by hot gases from burning fuel, or by high-pressure steam from a boiler. They are used to drive large ships and turn power station generators.

WHAT MAKES A TURBINE TURN?

The flowing gas or liquid pushes the turbine blades, spinning the shaft. The turbine is connected to a generator. In a modern turbine, the angled blades have a shape similar to aircraft wings to maximize the force generated. The fluid may pass through two, three, or more sets of blades arranged in sequence, to convert as much energy as possible to motion.

▲ STEAM TURBINE
This turbine rotor is spun by high-pressure steam. It turns a generator to produce electricity at a power station. The rotor blades are arranged in stages. Multistage turbines are the most efficient because they take all the energy produced by the steam.

FUEL CONSUMPTION

A vehicle's fuel consumption is measured by how much fuel it uses to travel a certain distance. The fuel consumption of a car depends on its engine power, its weight, its aerodynamics (how smoothly it moves through the air), its speed, and how it is driven.

HOW CAN ENGINE EFFICIENCY BE IMPROVED?

The more fuel a car needs to work, the less engine-efficient it is. Scientists are developing cars that use less fuel, and therefore do not waste energy or pollute the air. They are also making cars that use different sources of energy, such as solar panels, electric motors, or hydrogen fuel, which is pollution-free.

▼ ELECTRIC CAR
Solar panels in this car's roof feed power to its batteries. Electric cars do not pollute city streets with exhaust fumes.

engines

FIND OUT MORE ►► Electromagnetism 186 • Energy 166 • Human Impact 64 • Machines 196–197 • Rockets 28 • Transportation 200–201

TRANSPORTATION

Many people live in one place, but work in another. At local supermarkets, people buy products from other countries. Modern transportation—the movement of people and ▶▶FREIGHT by land, sea, and air—lets us travel all over the world with great speed.

▲ CYCLE PATH
In some cities, special cycle paths keep cyclists and motor vehicles in separate lanes, making cycling safer and more enjoyable.

WHAT IS A TRANSPORTATION SYSTEM?
Road, rail, sea, and air transportation link together to make an integrated system. A package sent from London can be delivered 24 hours later to an address in Chicago. A van driver picks up the package and takes it by road to the airport. The freight plane flies overnight to the US. Its cargo is sorted, and the package travels onward by road once again.

▼ AIR TRAFFIC
Demand for air travel is so great that a busy airport can operate flights every minute, 24 hours a day. This can create disturbing noise pollution for people living along the flight path. Night flights are restricted, or banned completely, at many airports.

HOW EFFICIENT ARE DIFFERENT FORMS OF TRANSPORTATION?
The most fuel-efficient way to transport people and goods is by sea, but travel times are long. Rail is the next most efficient, and safe. Flying is fastest but least efficient. The best transportation for short trips is cycling or walking—both are pollution-free, keep you in shape, and help you avoid congestion.

WHAT IS A SCIENTIST'S ROLE IN TRANSPORTATION?
Scientists and engineers seek solutions to transport problems. They try to reduce ▶▶CONGESTION and pollution and improve ▶▶ROAD SAFETY. They also work with governments to introduce scanning equipment to improve security and stop the smuggling of illegal goods across borders.

Flight deck, where the pilot and co-pilot fly the plane

Fuselage (aircraft body) is made from strong but lightweight alloys such as aluminum

transport

Turbofan engines power the plane at more than 500 mph (800 km/h)

Ground crew guides plane into its docking bay

HOW ARE AIRCRAFT CONTROLLED IN THE AIR?
The pilot and crew use flight deck computers to fly the plane, and radar screens to show their position and weather conditions ahead. Air traffic controllers on the ground give pilots permission to take off and land, issue flight paths, and make sure that no aircraft come within 10 miles (16 km) of one another horizontally, or 1,000 ft (310 m) vertically.

CONGESTION

Congestion occurs when too many vehicles use the same route at the same time, and traffic slows or comes to a halt. One solution is to build more roads, but some people argue that the number of vehicles grows to fill the roads available. An alternative is to encourage people to use public transportation.

TRANSPORT FIRSTS	
3200 BCE	Wheels
3000 BCE	Sailing ships
1803	Steam train
1807	Steamboat
1839	Bicycle
1885	Car
1903	Airplane
1947	Supersonic flight
1952	Commercial passenger flight

WHAT IS GRIDLOCK?

The streets in many cities are laid out on a grid. At busy times, traffic may stop as traffic jams form at intersections. This is called gridlock. Gridlock may be avoided by synchronizing traffic signals from one street to the next, and by introducing one-way systems.

WHY IS PUBLIC TRANSPORTATION IMPORTANT?

Public transportation is more efficient and less polluting than private cars. Underground rail can transport two million people in and out of a city each day, but two million cars can block the roads. City planners also encourage people to use trams, bicycles, buses, light rail, and riverboats to reduce congestion.

▲ TRAFFIC JAM
Managing traffic flow at peak periods and dealing with incidents, such as crashes, are challenging problems for transportation planners. Engineers are developing ways to avoid jams—charging road tolls to discourage drivers, introducing in-car navigation systems to warn drivers of jams ahead, and installing synchronized traffic signals.

FREIGHT

When goods are being transported, they are called freight. Almost everything you purchase—clothes, electronics, food, and books—has been brought to the store from elsewhere.

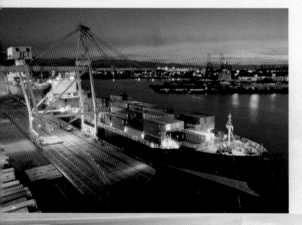

◄ LOADING CONTAINERS
A huge crane called a derrick loads containers onto the ship. The crew makes sure the ship doesn't tilt during loading. They chalk numbers on the floor of the ship so they know where to place the different containers.

HOW IS A CONTAINER SHIP LOADED?

Container ships are loaded at special container ports. The containers are easily transferred from road to rail to ship because each container is a standard size, 8 ft by 8 ft by 40 ft (2.5 m by 2.5 m by 12 m). They stack together like bricks. The largest container ship can carry 4,000 containers.

▼ CRASH-TEST DUMMIES
New car models are crash-tested in laboratories before they go into production. Dummies in the car show what happens to passengers in a crash. The impact forces in the crash are monitored with sensors inside the dummies and by high-speed videos.

ROAD SAFETY

Scientists are always looking for ways to improve safety on the roads so that fewer people are hurt or killed in accidents. Millions of people are injured each year in road crashes around the world, but many more injuries are not reported.

HOW CAN ROAD SAFETY BE IMPROVED?

Driving too fast is a major cause of accidents. Speed increases the severity of accidents. Nine out of ten collisions with a pedestrian at 40 mph (64 km/h) are fatal, but less than one in ten are fatal at 20 mph (32 km/h). Speed bumps and traffic islands help to keep speeds down. Police patrol cars equipped with radar equipment stop speeding vehicles, encouraging drivers to obey speed limits. Electronic signs on freeways tell drivers about road conditions ahead.

FIND OUT MORE ▶▶ Engines 198–199

CONSTRUCTION

From houses and skyscrapers to bridges and highways, our environment is constructed from many different materials. Architects design structures to look good and fulfill a purpose— ▶▶ ENGINEERS make structures work.

HEMISPHERIUM ▲
An architect explores his new designs inside a virtual reality dome. He uses a joystick to navigate round the view.

WHAT DOES AN ARCHITECT DO?

An architect's job is to design and plan new buildings and structures. Architects must consider the building's use, the choice of materials, and the building's environment. Plans show the exact position and construction of every detail, even the electric sockets.

HOW ARE BUILDING MATERIALS CHOSEN?

Most large structures are built with concrete and steel. Concrete is used in huge quantities to make solid foundations. Concrete walls, columns, and arches are reinforced with steel to make them stronger. Wood is still used for many smaller buildings, particularly in ▶▶ MODULAR CONSTRUCTION . It is light yet tough.

HOW IS A ROAD BUILT?

The first stage is planning. The route must not destroy important landscapes or buildings. The design depends on the terrain the road crosses. Tunnels are needed through hills, and bridges across rivers. The site is cleared, foundations are dug, and a stable stone base is laid. The road is paved with concrete or asphalt.

SKYSCRAPER CONSTRUCTION ▶
When a new building is built in a busy city, the construction company plans carefully so that they do not disrupt the traffic and trade nearby. This skyscraper in Hong Kong's financial district will be 88 stories high when complete.

Giant tower cranes
lift building materials

Scaffolding
at the top of the building provides a platform for materials and construction workers to build higher

Concrete core
reinforced with steel rods

Empty shell
does not contain fittings or fixtures, such as carpets, yet

Temporary structures
around the main building contain equipment, cafeterias, and restrooms for construction workers

Fence
seals off construction site for safety

MODULAR CONSTRUCTION

Large parts of modern buildings can be built away from the site, then delivered for assembly. The modules fit together in a preplanned way. Modular construction reduces construction costs and the time spent at a construction site.

WHAT ARE BUILDING SYSTEMS?

As well as the foundations, walls, and roof, the parts or systems that go into making a building include the heating, lighting, plumbing, and ventilation systems. Usually, these systems are installed when the main structure is complete, but some modules arrive with bathrooms and electrical wiring intact.

▲ MICROFLATS
These modular microflats in Tokyo, Japan, were built to save space in the city. They are cheaper because they are smaller than most houses, and easier to build.

ENGINEERING

An engineer applies the principles of science to the design of structures and machines. Structural engineers, for example, make calculations to predict the stability of structures. Civil engineers plan the construction of railroads, roads, and dams.

▼ BRIDGES
These bridges are some of the most beautiful engineering structures. They are carefully designed to carry heavy loads and survive bad weather.

ARCH BRIDGE

CABLE-STAYED BRIDGE

CANTILEVER BRIDGE

SUSPENSION BRIDGE

Concrete and steel frame will be covered with glass so that it looks attractive.

construction

HOW DOES A BRIDGE CARRY A LOAD?
A straight beam bends in the middle as it supports a load. A beam bridge can carry a load over a narrow gap, but a longer bridge needs a stronger shape. An arch supports the load from beneath—it directs the force around the curve to push against the ground at both sides. A suspension bridge supports a load from above, with cables.

HOW HIGH CAN A SKYSCRAPER GO?
The Burj Khalifa in Dubai opened in 2010. It stands at a height of 2,717 ft (828 m) and is the tallest skyscraper in the world. Engineers could build even taller structures, but higher buildings cost more money and need to be made safe.

WHAT IS THE BEST SHAPE FOR A DAM?
A dam holds back water in a river to form an artificial lake. Water pressure increases with depth, so the greatest pressure on the dam is at its base—the dam wall is much thicker at the bottom than at the top.

▲ CURVED DAM
The curved shape of this concrete dam gives it strength. The water pressure is directed around the curve, which pushes against the high ground at either side, so the ground takes some of the pressure away from the dam.

HOW IS A TUNNEL BORED?
Tunnels are cut with tunnel boring machines (TBMs), burrowing through the ground. As their cutting blades turn, the machines move forward at an average rate of about 1 mph (1.6 km/h). Engineers line the tunnel behind the TBMs with reinforced concrete rings to prevent the roof and walls from collapsing.

▲ TUNNEL DIGGING
Each of the six TBMs used to dig the Anglo-French Channel Tunnel was pushed forward on rails with a force of over 400 tons. As the TBM worked, conveyor belts following behind carried away 1,000 tons of clay and rubble each hour.

FIND OUT MORE ▶▶ Architecture 328–329 • Computers 190

INDUSTRY

Industry is a general term meaning the businesses and organizations that provide the goods and services we need. There are primary industries, such as agriculture and mining, manufacturing industries, and service industries, such as tourism and banking.

WHAT ARE PRIMARY INDUSTRIES?
Primary industries supply us with food and with the ▶▶ RAW MATERIALS we need to clothe and house ourselves, and to make all the other things we use. For example, agricultural and fishing industries produce food. Forestry supplies wood for making paper and construction. Oil drilling and mining extract fuels to supply energy and materials.

WHERE ARE INDUSTRIES LOCATED?
Industries develop wherever their supplies are found. Steelmaking and shipbuilding, for example, need raw materials. Steel plants are often built near coal mines, which supply the fuel they need to produce the steel. Some other industries need lots of workers, so they are often located where labor costs are low.

WHAT IS A COTTAGE INDUSTRY?
A cottage industry is run by an individual or a family, often from their home. Before the Industrial Revolution, most industries were cottage industries. Family names such as Weaver and Potter identified the family trade. Today, there are new kinds of cottage industry in which home-based workers use computers and the Internet to supply their customers.

▲ **TEA PRODUCTION**
Growing tea is an agricultural industry. Tea leaves are picked by hand, so it is labor-intensive—it needs a lot of workers. Many such jobs in agriculture are now done by machine.

AUTO INDUSTRY ▶
The auto industry is now one of the biggest industries in the world. Each day, thousands of cars roll off the production lines of car plants around the world.

Robot arms, guided by computers, assemble car bodies

Partially completed cars move steadily along the production line

Modern cars consist of a steel shell to which all the other parts are attached

RAW MATERIALS

Raw materials are the natural sources of fuel and manufacturing materials used by industry. For example, oil supplies energy and also chemicals for making plastics. Metal ores give us metals such as iron. Clay makes pottery, and sand makes glass.

HOW ARE RAW MATERIALS USED?
Many raw materials have to be processed using force, heat, or chemical reactions. Iron ore rock is crushed, then heated with coke (a form of carbon) in a blast furnace. Chemical reactions with the coke and air reduce the ore to liquid iron, which flows from the bottom of the furnace and hardens as it cools.

WHAT ARE BY-PRODUCTS?
A by-product is any material that is left over from an industrial process. The slag (crumbled rock) left behind when iron is extracted from iron ore can be used for road building. Useful amounts of gold, silver, and platinum are left behind as by-products of copper production.

▲ **OPEN-PIT MINING**
An open-pit mine is a gaping hole in the ground where raw materials are dug. Coal, metal ores, and stone are all used as raw materials for industry.

industry

FIND OUT MORE ▶▶ Energy Resources 60–61 • Farming 66 • Fishing 67 • Forestry 67 • Materials 170 • Rocks 46–47

MANUFACTURING

From ankle socks to aircraft, almost everything we use has been manufactured. Manufacturing is the process of making products from materials. It may be done by hand, or by computer-controlled ▸▸ PRODUCTION LINES.

WHERE DO NEW PRODUCTS COME FROM?

Product development begins with an idea—such as a new design for a running shoe or an electronic game. If the idea is accepted, working samples are made and tested. The samples are shown to the public to get their reaction. If it seems that enough people would buy it, the product is put into production.

▼ **TEXTILE MANUFACTURING**
At one time, all textiles (fabrics) were spun and woven by hand. Today, machines do the same job in a fraction of the time it once took, and produce a vast variety of fabrics—from cotton and silk to nylon string and carpeting.

HENRY FORD
American, 1863–1947
The son of a farmer, Henry Ford founded the Ford Motor Company in 1903 and introduced production-line methods to car manufacturing. For the first time, cars became generally affordable. The first type of car produced in this way was the Model T. Ford. Ford said his customers could have any color of car, "so long as it was black."

WHAT IS MASS PRODUCTION?

A product is mass-produced when identical copies of it are made in vast numbers by machines. Once, all books were copied by hand. The printing press made it possible for books to be printed quickly and easily, so books became cheaper and more widely available.

PRODUCTION LINE

A production line is a system for mass producing a complicated product efficiently. The idea was first used by Henry Ford as a way of making cars quickly and cheaply, so more people could buy them.

manufacturing

HOW DOES A PRODUCTION LINE WORK?

On a production line, every stage in the making of a product is a separate workstation. Workers (or machines) at each station do the same task over and over again as partly made products move along a line from station to station. This means that many more products can be completed each day than if groups of workers made one complete product at a time.

▲ **AUTOMATED PRODUCTION**
In a bottling factory, bottles are sterilized, filled, and capped by machines. Human workers watch over the process in case there is a problem. People are still better at solving problems than machines.

WHAT IS QUALITY CONTROL?

Things can go wrong in a complicated production process. Machines break down, the materials may not be available, or they may be the wrong kind. Such problems can lead to faulty products, which must not be allowed to leave the factory or customers will be disappointed. Quality control makes sure that every finished product is of a sufficiently high standard.

FIND OUT MORE ▸▸ Changing Materials 171 • Materials 170 • Robots 194

CHEMICAL INDUSTRY

Plastics, ▸▸ AGROCHEMICALS, ▸▸ PHARMACEUTICALS, paints, and detergents are just a few of the products of the chemical industry. Chemicals are manufactured in huge chemical plants or extracted at ▸▸ OIL REFINERIES.

chemical industry

Derrick
supports the drill and the drill string (the pipes that lead down to the drill head in the seabed)

Communication towers keep the rig in constant touch with the mainland

Rig platform
supports the derrick, as well as offices, cafeterias, recreation rooms, and sleeping quarters for the workers

WHAT DOES A CHEMICAL PLANT DO?
Chemicals found in nature, such as salt, sulfur, nitrogen, and natural gas, are the raw materials of the chemical industry. At a chemical plant, these materials are mixed, heated, and refined. The chemical reactions that take place transform the raw materials into acids, alkalis, and other valuable chemical compounds.

HOW ARE ACIDS AND ALKALIS USED?
Sulfuric acid is made from sulfur, air, and water. It is the biggest single product of the chemical industry. It is used in batteries, dyes, detergents, fertilizers, and synthetic fibers. Other acids make rocket fuel, varnish, and explosives. Sodium carbonate is a common alkali used to make both soap and glass, for example.

▲ OIL REFINERY
Oil refineries break down crude (untreated) oil into many of the chemical compounds used by the chemical industry. A refinery operates around the clock—at night, its illuminated pipes, tanks, and towers look like a small city.

DRILLING FOR OIL ▶
Crude oil is extracted from under the seabed by offshore oil rigs. These enormous platforms are the largest sea-based structures in the world. Anchored to the seabed, the rig supports the drill and all the machinery needed to run the drilling operation.

Massive legs
support the platform. They may stand directly on the seabed, or may be filled with air to provide a floating base that is anchored to the seabed

OIL REFINERY

Crude oil from oil fields around the world is shipped to refineries. The thick, black crude is not a single substance, but a mixture of many different carbon compounds (groups of atoms). At the refinery, the compounds are separated by fractional distillation.

WHAT IS FRACTIONAL DISTILLATION?
At a refinery, crude oil is heated until it boils and turns into a mixture of vapors. Different compounds in the vapors cool and condense at different levels inside a tall distillation tower, allowing them to be separated out. Heavy industrial fuels condense at the bottom of the tower, lighter petroleum fuel at the top.

WHAT CAN WE MAKE FROM OIL?
Using further treatments, lighter compounds can be turned into important fuels, such as gasoline and kerosene for motor vehicles and aircraft. They can also make fibers and plastics, solvents for paints, inks, adhesives, cosmetics, and pharmaceuticals. Heavier molecules are used for lubricant oils and bitumen.

AGROCHEMICALS

Plants need minerals from the soil to grow well. But repeated use of soil drains the minerals from it and fewer crops are produced. The farming industry uses agrochemicals to help improve the quality of the soil, and also to fight off the insect pests, diseases, and weeds that would otherwise destroy their crops.

WHAT IS ORGANIC FARMING?
Because of the effect of artificial sprays and fertilizers on the environment, organic farmers choose not to use them. Instead, they use animal manure and compost, and rotate their crops with beans and peas to replace nitrogen in the soil. They also control pests with natural methods, such as planting onions between carrots to discourage carrot fly.

▲ CROP SPRAYING
Fruit trees in an orchard are sprayed with pesticides to control insects and other pests that would damage the fruit or the trees. At the same time, care has to be taken not to kill helpful insects, such as bees.

WHAT ARE SELECTIVE WEEDKILLERS?
In the past, farmers tried to kill weeds with sea salt and other common chemicals. But these substances killed crops as well. Modern herbicides (weedkillers) are organic chemicals designed to limit weed growth. Many are selective, which means that they kill the weeds but do little harm to the crop.

PHARMACEUTICALS

A pharmaceutical is any substance used to treat or prevent disease. Since ancient times, people have experimented with plants as medicines, often poisoning themselves, but sometimes finding substances with real benefits—aspirin, for example. Today, the pharmaceutical industry is based on stricter scientific methods.

HOW ARE NEW DRUGS DEVELOPED?
Now that biochemists understand the chemicals in living cells, they can design molecules to combat illness. Molecules can be made in a laboratory and tested on cells in a culture (in vitro). Successful compounds are then tested on animals (in vivo).

HOW ARE NEW DRUGS TESTED?
When a drug has been tested in a laboratory, it is given to patients in tests called clinical trials. In these, some patients are given the new drug while others receive a placebo (a fake medicine). Because the patients do not know which one they have received, the test will show if the drug has a genuine effect.

DRUG MANUFACTURE ▲
This mold is used for shaping tablets (pills). Pills contain the drugs prescribed for patients by doctors. Each drug is made into a pill with a different shape, color, size, or pattern. This makes it less likely that the wrong pill will be taken by mistake.

◄ TAKING DRUGS
Most types of drug are taken orally (by mouth) in the form of tablets or pills, or as powders. Some drugs are swallowed in liquid form, and some are injected using a hypodermic syringe. Some drugs can also be absorbed through the skin.

FIND OUT MORE ▸▸ Atoms 157 • Cells 73 • Chemistry 162 • Farming 66

BIOTECHNOLOGY

The use of microbes (micro-organisms) to produce and process materials is called biotechnology. Bacteria and yeasts are used to produce products, such as yogurt, cheese, and wine, by ▶▶ FERMENTATION.

SIR ALEXANDER FLEMING
Scottish, 1881–1955
Fleming won the Nobel Prize for Medicine in 1945 for the discovery of penicillin. While searching for compounds that would kill bacteria without harming the body, he noticed that bacteria cultured (grown) in a glass dish had died around spots of mold. The mold had blown in through a window. Fleming extracted the antibiotic substance from the mold and called it penicillin.

HOW DO WE USE MICROBES?
Microbes are like tiny chemical factories. They make chemicals called enzymes (biological catalysts) to break down chemicals in their surroundings for food. As microbes feed and multiply, they produce chemical by-products. Yeast cells make an enzyme that turns sugar into alcohol.

◀ **PENICILLIN GROWTH**
This macrophotograph (close-up) shows a disk-shaped culture (growth) of the green penicillin mold growing on agar jelly in a glass petri dish. Penicillin is an antibiotic substance made by the mold *Penicillium notatum*. It was among the first antibiotics to be discovered, and is still widely used to treat infections.

WHAT ARE ANTIBIOTICS?
Some microbes produce chemicals that kill disease-spreading bacteria. These chemicals are antibiotics. They either destroy the bacteria completely, or stop it from multiplying. The first antibiotic, penicillin, was made from a mold that grows on bread. Its antibiotic action was discovered by chance in 1928.

FERMENTATION

Fermentation is the action of yeasts and bacteria on the sugars in fruit, grains, milk, and other food. Yeast cells added to bread dough feed on its natural sugars, turning them into carbon dioxide and water. This makes the dough rise to make light, fluffy bread.

◀ **CHEESE MAKING**
The type of cheese made depends on the variety of microbes added, and the conditions of fermentation. As the milk curdles, the curds are separated from the whey. This batch will become Baby Swiss cheese.

HOW IS MILK TURNED INTO CHEESE?
An enzyme called rennin is added to milk. It ferments the milk sugars to produce lactic acid. The acid separates the milk into solid curds and liquid whey. The curds are pressed into cheeses. Microbes continue to work in the cheese as it ages, making its flavour stronger and changing its texture.

HOW ARE GRAPES MADE INTO WINE?
Natural yeast on grape skins ferments the fruit sugars to produce alcohol. Fermentation stops after 10 to 30 days, when all the sugars have been used up, or when the alcohol content is 12 to 15 percent, which stops yeast cells from working. The wine is sealed in barrel. If it is exposed to the air, the alcohol is oxidized to acetic acid (vinegar), and the wine turns sour.

Carbon dioxide gas produced during fermentation gives champagne its fizz

Yeast cells sink downwards

▲ **YEAST**
This electron microscope picture shows individual yeast cells. Some of the cells are reproducing by budding (producing two cells from one).

◀ **WINE MAKING**
In the traditional champagne method for making sparkling (fizzy) wine, the wine continues to ferment after it has been bottled. The bottles are turned upside down to allow the yeast to settle onto the cork. Finally, the cork is loosened briefly, and the gas pressure shoots the sediment (settled particles of yeast) from the bottle.

biotechnology

GENETICS

Genetics is the study of how living things pass their features from one generation to the next. Your sex and your chances of developing certain diseases are fixed by your genes.

Hydrogen atom (white)

Oxygen atom (green)

genetics

Carbon atom (pink)

Nitrogen atom (blue)

Phosphorus atom (orange)

DNA DOUBLE HELIX ►
This 3-D computer graphic shows a section of the double helix (spiral) of DNA. Individual atoms are shown as colored balls. These atoms form into groups to create different bases. The two strands of the helix are linked by bases.

FRANCIS CRICK
English, 1916–
JAMES WATSON
American, 1928–

In 1953, inspired by scientist Rosalind Franklin, Crick and Watson built a DNA double helix (spiral) model. They linked the strands of the helix with A, T, C, and G molecules.

WHAT IS THE GENETIC CODE?
The genetic code has four letters, A, T, C, and G. These letters represent groups of atoms called bases, spaced out along the DNA molecule. The makeup of living things is fixed by the order of these bases. Words in the code are three letters, such as TCA. Genes are like long sentences written with these words.

WHAT IS A GENOME?
A genome is the sequence of all the letters of the genetic code in the DNA of a particular organism. The ▶▶ HUMAN GENOME has about three billion letters. Scientists have developed special techniques for sequencing (reading) DNA, with the help of powerful computers.

HUMAN GENOME PROJECT

The aim of the Human Genome Project is to produce the complete sequence of the genome of the human being.

HOW WILL THE HUMAN GENOME BE USED?
Scientists are using results of the Human Genome Project to study genetic diseases (those that may be inherited), such as cystic fibrosis. By identifying the gene, they should be able to diagnose a disease much earlier, and design more effective treatments. Knowing part of the genome means that scientists can already identify an individual's ▶▶ DNA FINGERPRINT.

◄ **HUMAN GENOME**
Each of the wells in this tray contains a different fragment of human DNA. It takes 60 of these trays to hold a complete human genome.

DNA FINGERPRINT

Except for identical twins, everyone's DNA is different. By scanning about 10 sections (each about 500 letters long) of your DNA, scientists can create your DNA fingerprint.

DNA FINGERPRINT ▲
The pattern and the strength of the bands on this chart represent the DNA sequences of samples taken from individuals.

CAN DNA PROVE WHO COMMITTED A CRIME?
The chance of two individuals having the same DNA sequence in 10 scanned sections is incredibly small. If DNA found at a crime scene—in a hair, for example—matches a sample from a suspect to this degree, then it is proved "beyond reasonable doubt" that the hair is the suspect's.

FIND OUT MORE ▶▶ Cells 73 • Genetic Engineering 210–211 • Reproduction 148

GENETIC ENGINEERING

Genetic engineering is the manipulation of genes of living things. Scientists can now insert genes from one organism into another. They do this to grow ▸▸GM FOOD. They can also ▸▸CLONE embryos that provide ▸▸STEM CELLS to repair damaged body tissue.

genetic engineering

WHAT IS GENETIC VARIATION?

The differences between species and between individuals are explained by the differences in their genes. Sexual reproduction, which randomly mixes genes from parents in their children, produces variation from generation to generation.

HOW CAN WE MANIPULATE GENES?

When dog breeders select puppies with short tails to breed from, they are manipulating the gene for tail length. The gene for short tails is passed on, and the gene for long tails dies out. Now, scientists can select and move genes between organisms in the laboratory. A gene for disease resistance can be "snipped out" from the DNA of one plant and inserted into another.

MICROBE COLONY ▲
Genetic engineering is commonly performed on microbes grown in the laboratory, such as on this fungus. Genes are inserted into microbes to make them produce substances to treat disease.

GM FOOD

The first genetically modified (GM) food went on sale in 1994. It was a variety of tomato called Flavr Savr. The gene that makes the tomato soften had been changed to make it ripen more slowly, so that it would develop more flavor.

GM seedling tolerates pesticides and herbicides

◄ GM OR NOT?
GM crops, such as these tomatoes, look just like traditional varieties. The changes produced by gene manipulation are subtle. Genetic modification is more likely to be used to affect the crop's disease resistance or shelf life than its appearance.

Soil with natural nutrients

ARE GM CROPS SAFE?

Some farmers are not eager to grow GM crops. One worry is that genes introduced into the crop will transfer to other species. Another concern is that herbicide- and pesticide-resistant crops encourage farmers to use too many of these chemicals, which might damage wildlife.

GENETICALLY MODIFIED PLANT ►
This GM seedling has had genetic material from another species inserted into its genetic code. Scientists perform genetic modification on plants to make them more resistant to disease, pests, pesticides, and even bad weather conditions.

WHAT WAS THE GREEN REVOLUTION?

In the 1960s, scientists tried to breed crops to match conditions in developing countries. The aim was to reduce food shortages by introducing productive crops that were disease resistant. In India, crop production increased, but in other places, the new crop varieties needed fertilizers that farmers could not afford.

CLONES

Clones are different individuals with the same genes. Clones are common in nature—a bacterium clones itself by splitting in two, producing two identical bacteria. Now scientists have developed artificial cloning techniques that work with mammals.

HOW ARE ANIMAL CLONES PRODUCED?

The first clone made with DNA from an adult animal was Dolly the sheep in 1997. DNA was taken from an adult sheep (Dolly's biological mother) and inserted into an egg cell (with its own DNA removed) from another sheep. The cell started to divide, and the embryo was taken and put into the womb of a third sheep—Dolly's surrogate (birth) mother. Animal clones could be used for medical research.

Leaves designed to grow using less fertilizer

HOW ARE BANANAS CLONED?

Many plants propagate (reproduce) vegetatively (without sex). Each new plant has the same DNA as the parent and is therefore a clone. On a plantation all the banana plants are clones of their parents.

DOLLY THE SHEEP ▲
Dolly's biological mother was six years old when her DNA was cloned to produce Dolly. Sheep can live for 11 to 12 years, but Dolly died when she was six.

COULD HUMAN BEINGS BE CLONED?

In principle, humans could be cloned in the same way as Dolly, perhaps to help a person unable to have a child in any other way. But as with other aspects of genetic engineering, human cloning is controversial, and has already been banned in many countries.

◄ **INTRACYTOPLASMIC SPERM INJECTION (ICSI)**
ICSI is used to help couples who have difficulty conceiving a baby. The father's sperm is injected into an egg from the mother. In cloning, the procedure is different. Instead of injecting sperm, the nucleus of the egg cell is removed and replaced with the nucleus of a mature cell from the mother. Sperm is not needed.

STEM CELLS

The starter cells in an embryo are called stem cells. As the embryo grows, stem cells change to become the different cells needed in the body, such as nerve cells and blood cells.

HOW CAN STEM CELL RESEARCH HELP PEOPLE?

Stem cell research is investigating the use of stem cells to repair damaged or diseased tissue. For example, the body cannot repair or replace nerve cells damaged by disease or injury. Transplanted stem cells could be grown to develop into new nerve cells to treat Parkinson's and Alzheimer's diseases.

WHY IS THERE CONCERN ABOUT IT?

Stem cell research is controversial because the cells are taken from human embryos that have been fertilized in the laboratory. To avoid rejection of the cells, the embryo should ideally have been cloned using the patient's DNA. Many people have concerns about using human embryos in this way.

▲ **STEM CELL RESEARCH**
This electron microscope image shows stem cells from an adult's bone marrow. These are the only kind of stem cells that occur in an adult's body. These stem cells change to produce different blood cells, but only embryo cells can produce all the different cells that make up a human being.

FIND OUT MORE ▶▶ Cells 73 • Farming 66 • Genetics 209 • Growth 149 • Nervous System 138 • Reproduction 148

PEOPLE and PLACES

PHYSICAL WORLD

Despite being called Earth, more than two-thirds of our planet's surface is covered in water. The rest consists of seven vast expanses of land called continents. The largest of these is Asia, followed by Africa, North America, South America, Antarctica, Europe, and Australasia. They contain an amazing variety of landscapes—mountains, deserts, tropical rainforests, woodlands, and polar ice.

▲ **PYRENEES MOUNTAINS**
The Pyrenees stretch for 270 miles (435 km) between the Bay of Biscay and the Mediterranean Sea in western Europe. Like other mountains, the Pyrenees were formed by movements in the Earth's crust, causing the land above

ELEVATION

	over 13,000 ft (4,000 m)
	6,500–13,000 ft (2,000–4,000 m)
	3,300–6500 ft (1,000–2,000 m)
	1,600–3,300 ft (500–1,000 m)
	800–1,600 ft (250–500 m)
	300–800 ft (100–250 m)
	0–300 ft (0–100 m)
	below sea level

SEA DEPTH

	0–800 ft (0–250 m)
	800–6,500 ft (250–2,000 m)
	6,500–13,000 ft (2,000–4,000 m)
	below 13,000 ft (4,000 m)

physical world

▲ **NORTHERN HEMISPHERE**
Most of the land on Earth is concentrated in the northern hemisphere, although Europe and North America are the only continents that lie entirely in the north.

◄ **SOUTHERN HEMISPHERE**
Oceans dominate the southern hemisphere. Australia and Antarctica are the only continental landmasses that lie entirely in the south.

◄ **THE AMAZON**
The Amazon River is the largest river in the world, measuring 4,001 miles (6,439 km). It carries more water than any other river and drains 2,500,000 sq miles (6,475,000 sq km)—about 40 percent—of the land in South America.

SAHARA DESERT ▶
The world's largest hot desert is the Sahara, which stretches from the Atlantic Ocean in the west, all the way across North Africa to the Red Sea in the east.

◀ IGUAÇU FALLS
Lying between Argentina and Brazil, the Iguaçu Falls have two main sections, each containing hundreds of waterfalls separated from each other by rocky islands. The name Iguaçu comes from the Guarani Indian word meaning "great water."

PHYSICAL WORLD

Longest river: Nile
4,160 miles (6,695 km)

Largest lake: Caspian Sea
143,243 sq miles
(371,000 sq km)

Highest point: Mt. Everest
29,035 ft (8,850 m)

Lowest point: Dead Sea
−1,285 ft (−392 m)

Largest ocean: Pacific Ocean

Largest desert: Sahara
3,263,400 sq miles
(9,065,000 sq km)

Largest island: Greenland
839,852 sq miles
(2,175,219 sq km)

Coldest inhabited place:
Verkhoyansk, Siberia
−94°F (−70°C) in January

Hottest inhabited place:
Baghdad, Iraq,
110°F (43°C), July/August

Wettest inhabited place:
Buenventura, Columbia,
2,651 in (6,734 cm) of rain per year

Driest place: Aswan, Egypt,
1 1/8 in (2.9 cm) of rain per year

▲ WATERY WORLD
Seventy-one percent of our planet is covered with water in the form of oceans, seas, lakes, and rivers. The tallest mountain, the deepest trench, and the longest mountain range are all found under the ocean.

VOLCANOES ▶
Volcanoes such as Kilauea on the island of Hawaii in the Pacific Ocean erupt when plumes of hot magma rise up from the Earth's mantle and explode as lava. Some volcanoes erupt regularly, but others can lie dormant for many years before they erupt, often with tremendous force.

FIND OUT MORE ▶▶ Continents 39 • Mountains 45 • Oceans 40–41 • Planet Earth 36–37 • Rivers 56 • Volcanoes 44

POLITICAL WORLD

The world today is divided into 195 independent nations, differing from each other in size, shape, population, people, language, government, culture, and wealth. World maps are always changing, as new countries emerge from colonial rule or old ones divide or fall apart. In 1950, there were only 82 independent nations, the rest being colonies or dependencies waiting to gain their independence.

political world

POLITICAL WORLD

Largest country: Russian Federation 6,592,735 sq miles (17,075,200 sq km)

Smallest country: Vatican City 0.17 sq miles (0.44 sq km)

Longest border: US–Canada 5,526 miles (8,893 km)

Country with most neighbors: China (14),

Oldest country: San Marino, 301 CE

Youngest country: Kosovo (disputed), 2008

▲ FLAGS
Every nation has its own unique flag, which often represents the history or geography of that country in some way. For instance, the 13 stripes of the US flag represent the 13 colonies that first formed the United States, while the 50 stars stand for each of the current 50 states.

◀ UNGUARDED BORDER
Some border posts, such as this one between Cambodia and Vietnam, are unguarded, since the two countries are at peace and their people can travel freely between them. Most international borders are agreed by both sides, with one-sixth formed by rivers, and many more formed by lakes, mountain ridges, or seas. Some, notably those in the Sahara, are just straight lines across the ground.

THE WORLD ▲
Every part of Earth's land surface belongs to or is claimed by one country or another, with the exception of Antarctica, where territorial claims have been set aside by international treaty (a formal agreement).

US-MEXICO BORDER ▶
The international border linking San Diego, California, with Tijuana, Mexico, is crossed by thousands of workers every day. Both countries are part of a free-trade area, but their long, joint border is heavily policed to prevent immigrants from Mexico entering the US illegally in order to seek work and a better standard of living.

GUARDED BORDER ▶
Some borders are disputed and heavily guarded, such as this one between North and South Korea, which was the scene of fierce fighting between the two nations in 1950–53.

FIND OUT MORE ▶▶ Eastern Asia 268–269 • Nations 312 • Politics 306–307 • Social Equality 304–305 • War 313

POPULATION

People have lived on Earth for two million years. For most of that time, the population has remained small, as the number of births has roughly equaled the number of deaths. Improved medicine and health care, better sanitation, improved farming methods producing more and better food, and less physical work have all led to fewer infant deaths and more people living longer. This has caused a massive increase in population over the last 150 years. Today, the world's population is nearly 7 billion, and is rising at a rate of about one million a week.

POPULATION

Top five biggest cities and populations:
> Tokyo, Japan 33.8 million
> Seoul, South Korea 23.9 million
> Mexico City, Mexico 22.9 million
> New Delhi, India 22.4 million
> Mumbai, India 22.3 million

Country with smallest population:
> Vatican City 826

Most densely populated country:
> Monaco
> 42,840 people per sq mile
> (16,477 people per sq km)

Least densely populated country:
> Greenland 0.067 people per sq mile (0.026 people per sq km)

Country with highest birth rate:
> Niger
> 52 per 1,000 population

Country with lowest birth rate:
> Japan
> 7 per 1,000 population

Country with highest death rate:
> Swaziland
> 31 per 1,000 population

Country with lowest death rate:
> United Arab Emirates
> 2 per 1,000 population

Country with the highest life expectancy:
> Andorra (83)

Country with the lowest life expectancy:
> Swaziland (32)

Richest country (highest GNP*):
> United States $10,207 billion

Poorest country (lowest GNP*):
> Tuvalu US$21 million

*GNP = Gross National Product

▲ MULTICULTURAL SOCIETY
A busy street in a large European city such as Amsterdam, the Netherlands, shows just how multiracial most cities and countries now are. Immigration, international travel, trade, and tourism have all contributed to this great change.

WORLD POPULATION ▶
The world's six billion people are not evenly distributed around the planet, but concentrated in areas where the climate is suitable and the land habitable. This concentration of people is measured by population density, which is the average number of people living in each square mile.

◀ SOWETO TOWNSHIP, SOUTH AFRICA
An estimated two million people live in Soweto. Originally little more than tin shacks for mine workers, better suburbs have gradually grown, but overcrowding, poverty, and crime are still major problems.

HONG KONG, CHINA ▶
Cities such as Hong Kong have solved the problem of limited space by building up rather than out. This has led to a growing number of so-called megacities, with populations of more than ten million. However, overcrowding, pollution, and a lack of open space make such cities unpleasant to live in.

population

REFUGEES ▶
Poverty drives many people, such as these Albanians, to flee their country in search of jobs and a better life elsewhere.

FIND OUT MORE ▶▶ Architecture 328–329 • Human Impact 64–65 • International Organizations 434 • Social Equality 304–305

PHYSICAL FEATURES

VICTORIA FALLS
Major waterfalls, such as the Victoria Falls on the Zambezi River in Africa, are clearly labeled on the maps in this section. In real life, they are dramatic natural features, but on a large-scale continental map, they are sometimes too small to pinpoint precisely.

GREAT BARRIER REEF
The Great Barrier Reef is the largest living thing in the world and consists of millions of tiny coral polyps. It runs for about 1,240 miles (2,000 km) along the coast of Queensland, northeast Australia. Major natural features like this are labeled on the maps in this section.

MOUNT KILIMANJARO
Tall mountain ranges are marked on maps in white. Individual peaks, such as Mount Kilimanjaro in Tanzania, Africa, are marked with a special triangular symbol. See the map key on the opposite page for an example.

LAKE CHAD
Rainfall over the land is collected in lakes or underground chambers and drains into the ocean via rivers. Major rivers and large lakes, such as Lake Chad in central Africa, are colored blue and clearly labeled on the maps here. See the map key on the opposite page for an example.

NAMIB DESERT
Many parts of the world are covered by hot, dry deserts such as the Namib Desert in southern Africa. Deserts often contain sandy soil that can support few plants other than cacti. They are labeled on the continental maps in this section.

PACIFIC OCEAN
Seventy-one percent of the world's surface is covered by water, mainly in the form of vast oceans such as the Pacific, the largest ocean in the world. The oceans are colored blue on the maps here, and are all labeled.

MAPPING

A map is a picture that represents a particular part of the Earth's surface, usually from above and at a reduced size. It can show the whole world, a single country, or the street where you live. Unlike a photograph, a map can give different kinds of information, such as place names, the elevation of the land, or the borders between countries.

THE NEW WORLD ▶
This map of the New World was drawn in 1584, just 62 years after Ferdinand Magellan completed the first circumnavigation of the world. European mapmakers used their imagination as much as anything when compiling maps, since many parts of the world, such as Australia, the Arctic, and Antarctica, were unknown to them, and many coastlines had yet to be fully explored.

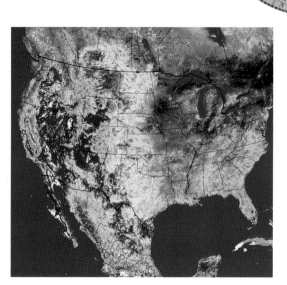

◀ MODERN TECHNOLOGY
Today, cartographers (mapmakers) use sophisticated satellite imaging to accurately map the world. This map of the United States was created from a satellite photograph and clearly shows the contours and vegetation of the land.

TIME ZONES ▼
The world is divided into 24 time zones, starting with Greenwich Mean Time (GMT) on the prime meridian. Countries to the east of this line are ahead of GMT, those to the west are behind. The 180° line of longitude is called the International Date Line. Places just west of this line are one day ahead of places to the east.

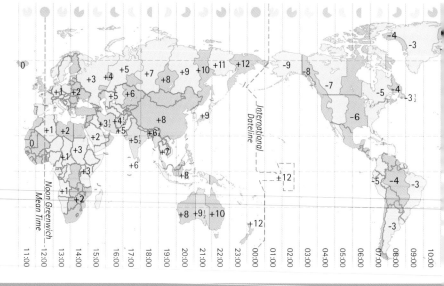

HOW TO USE THE MAPS

This section of the encyclopedia looks at the world and its people. The world has been divided into its seven continents, and each continent is featured with its own map and photographs. Following each continental spread are illustrated double pages that look at each continent in more detail.

LATITUDE AND LONGITUDE

Latitude Imaginary lines drawn around the world to make a grid tell us exactly how far north, south, east, or west anywhere on Earth is. Horizontal lines of latitude run from east to west, parallel to the Equator which runs around the middle of Earth, and is given the value 0°. All other lines of latitude are numbered in degrees north or south of it. They measure how far north or south a place is.

North Pole 90°N
Equator 0°
South Pole 90°S

Lines of latitude are measured from the center of the Earth

One degree of latitude is about 70 miles/113 km

Longitude Vertical lines of longitude run between the North and South Poles. The prime meridian (numbered 0°) runs through Greenwich, England, and all other lines of longitude are numbered in degrees east or west of this line. The line opposite the prime meridian on the other side of the world is numbered 180°. Lines of longitude measure how far east or west a place is.

180°

Lines of longitude divide the world up into segments

Prime Meridian 0°

Lines of longitude are measured from the center of the Earth

CONTINENTAL MAP ►

This map of Africa shows what the continental maps in this section look like. Physical features, such as mountains, deserts, rivers, lakes, seas, and oceans are all labeled. Countries, capital cities, and other major towns are also marked on the maps.

ELEVATION

- over 13,125 ft (4,000 m)
- 6,500–13,125 ft (2,000–4,000 m)
- 3,300–6,500 ft (1,000–2,000 m)
- 1,600–3,300 ft (500–1,000 m)
- 800–1,600 ft (250–500 m)
- 300–800 ft (100–250 m)
- 0–300 ft (0–100 m)
- below sea level

MAP KEY

Congo	River
Lake Turkana	Lake
Kilimanjaro △ 5,895 m (19,340 ft)	Mountain with height in meters
	International border
⦿ LUANDA	Capital city
○ Benghazi	Major town

GLOBE LOCATOR ►

Each of the seven continental map pages has a locator globe showing where in the world the continent is located. The continent is marked in red, the rest of the world in green.

REGION LOCATOR ►

On the regional pages following each continental page, the location of the region is marked on a locator map: red for the region and green for the rest of the continent.

North and West Africa highlighted red

Rest of Africa colored green

mapping

FIND OUT MORE ►► Exploration 400–401 • Habitats 82–84

NORTH AMERICA

North America is a continent of enormous diversity, with vast mountain ranges, huge, flat, grassy plains, hot deserts, and frozen ice caps. In the south lie the tropical islands of the Caribbean and the rainforests of Central America. To the far north, a polar ice cap 2 miles (3 km) thick covers most of Greenland. Most North Americans live in large cities in the East, and on the West Coast. The Great Plains and deserts west of the Mississippi River are sparsely populated, as are the forests and frozen wastes of northern Canada and Alaska.

ARCTIC OCEAN

Arctic Circle

Bering Strait

Beaufort Sea

Queen Elizabeth Islands

Bering Sea

Aleutian Islands

Yukon

Brooks Range

ALASKA (US)

Mt McKinley 20,321 ft (6,194 m)

Alaska Range

Anchorage

Victoria Island

Great Bear Lake

Mackenzie Mountains

Mackenzie

YUKON TERRITORY

NORTHWEST TERRITORIES

Great Slave Lake

Slave

Athab

Kodiak Island

Coast Mountains

Gulf of Alaska

ROC

C A N

PACIFIC OCEAN

Queen Charlotte Islands

BRITISH COLUMBIA

ALBERTA

Reinde La

Fraser

Edmonton

SASKATCHEW

Saskatch

Vancouver Island

Vancouver

Calgary

Reg

Saska

Seattle

WASHINGTON

Portland

Salem

OREGON

Boise

IDAHO

MONTANA

Snake

WYOMING

UNITED

Sacramento

Reno

San Francisco

NEVADA

San Jose

Salt Lake City

UTAH

Denver

COLORA

O F   A M

Las Vegas

Colorado

Central Valley

CALIFORNIA

Los Angeles

San Diego

Tijuana

Mexicali

ARIZONA

Phoenix

Albuquerq

NEW MEXICO

El Pa

Rio Gr

Ciudad Juárez

N

Hermosillo

Chihuahu

Lower California

M

Tropic of Cancer

Sierra Madre Occiden

Guadalaja

▲ ROCKY MOUNTAINS
Running down the western side of North America from the Arctic in the north, to Mexico in the south, the Rocky Mountains formed about 80-55 million years ago. As they are relatively young, the Rockies have not yet worn down, giving them a craggy appearance.

▲ HOCKEY
Hockey is Canada's favorite sport, with millions of people watching every major game live or on television. Teams of skaters use long, curved sticks to try to get a hard rubber disk, called a puck, into the opposing team's goal. The Canadian men's and women's teams both won gold medals in the 2002 Winter Olympics.

◄ PRAIRIES
The Great Plains, or prairies, of central Canada and the US lie between the Rocky Mountains and the Mississippi River valley. Vast herds of buffalo once roamed these grassy plains, but today they are largely agricultural, producing wheat in the north and corn farther south.

Map Labels

Greenland
(Denmark)

Baffin
Bay

Davis Strait

Baffin Island

NUUK

UNAVUT

*Labrador
Sea*

Hudson Strait

Ungava
Peninsula

Hudson
Bay

NEWFOUNDLAND
& LABRADOR

St. John's

Newfoundland Cape
Race

St. Pierre
& Miquelon
(France)

ANITOBA

QUEBEC

Laurentian Mountains

PRINCE
EDWARD
ISLAND

NEW
BRUNSWICK

Lake
Winnipeg

Albany

Quebec

Halifax
NOVA
SCOTIA

ONTARIO

Thunder Bay

MAINE

Montreal

nnipeg

*Great
Lakes*

Lake
Superior

OTTAWA

NEW HAMPSHIRE

MINNESOTA

MICHIGAN

Lake
Huron

Boston

Cape Cod

VERMONT

RTH
KOTA

WISCONSIN

Toronto

NEW
YORK

Lake
Ontario

MASS.

RHODE IS.

Lawrence

STATES

Minneapolis

Milwaukee

Detroit

Lake
Erie

CONNECTICUT

DAKOTA

Chicago

Cleveland

PENNSYLVANIA

New York

NEW JERSEY

Lake Michigan

IOWA

OHIO

Philadelphia

RASKA

Des Moines

INDIANA

Columbus

DELAWARE

Omaha

Indianapolis

WEST

WASHINGTON D.C.

Missouri

Ohio

VIRGINIA

MARYLAND

ERICA

ILLINOIS

VIRGINIA

Kansas City

*ATLANTIC
OCEAN*

KANSAS

MISSOURI

KENTUCKY

NORTH

Cape
Hatteras

Nashville

CAROLINA

OKLAHOMA

ARKANSAS

TENNESSEE

SOUTH

Arkansas

CAROLINA

ahoma
City

Memphis

Atlanta

GEORGIA

Red River

Little
Rock

MISSISSIPPI

ALABAMA

Dallas

Brazos

Jackson

Jacksonville

EXAS

LOUISIANA

FLORIDA

Austin

New Orleans

Tallahassee

Houston

*Mississippi
Delta*

Tampa

BAHAMAS

San Antonio

Miami

NASSAU

Rio Grande

*Gulf of
Mexico*

Straits of
Florida

HAVANA

CUBA

Monterrey

Santa Clara

Santiago
de Cuba

HAITI

SANTO
DOMINGO

ICO

Cayman Islands
(U.K.)

PORT-AU-PRINCE

DOMINICAN
REPUBLIC

San Luis Potosí

JAMAICA

KINGSTON

*Caribbean
Sea*

eón

Bay of
Campeche

Mérida

Yucatan
Peninsula

elia

MEXICO CITY

Puebla

BELIZE

BELMOPAN

HONDURAS

apulco

GUATEMALA

San Pedro Sula

GUATEMALA CITY

TEGUCIGALPA

NICARAGUA

SAN SALVADOR

EL SALVADOR

MANAGUA

SAN JOSÉ

PANAMA CITY

PANAMA

COSTA RICA

*SOUTH
AMERICA*

Tropic of Cancer

Anguilla (U.K.)

British Virgin
Islands (U.K.)

Virgin Islands
(U.S.)

ST. KITTS &
NEVIS

ANTIGUA &
BARBUDA

Turks &
Caicos
Islands
(U.K.)

Puerto
Rico
(U.S.)

Guadeloupe (France)

DOMINICA

Montserrat
(U.K.)

Martinique (France)

ST. LUCIA

BARBADOS

ST. VINCENT & THE
GRENADINES

GRENADA

Netherlands
Antilles
(Neth.)

Aruba
(Neth.)

TRINIDAD
& TOBAGO

PORT-OF-SPAIN

North
America

Statue of Liberty

▲ **STATUE OF LIBERTY, NEW YORK**
The Statue of Liberty was erected in 1886 and stands 305 ft (93 m) tall in
New York Harbor. It was the first thing millions of immigrants saw as they
sailed into New York in the 1800s and 1900s to start a new life. The
statue has become a symbol of freedom and opportunity.

Junkanoo Festival

JUNKANOO FESTIVAL ►
Extravagant carnivals, such as the
Junkanoo Festival in the Bahamas,
are held throughout the Caribbean.
People dress up in flamboyant
costumes, stage elaborate parades,
and dance in the street in the days
before Lent, the 40-day period of
fasting and restraint leading up to
the Christian holiday of Easter.

North America Facts

NORTH AMERICA

Total land area:
9,358,340 sq miles
(24,238,000 sq km)

Total population: 501 million

Number of countries: 23

Largest country: Canada
3,855,171 sq miles
(9,984,670 sq km)

Smallest country: St Kitts & Nevis
101 sq miles (261 sq km)

Largest country population:
United States 310 million

Largest lake: Lake Superior,
Canada/US 32,151 sq miles
(83,270 sq km)

Longest river:
Mississippi-Missouri
3,710 miles (5,969 km)

Highest point: Mt.McKinley
(Denali), Alaska 20,322 ft
(6,194 m)

Major deserts: Great Basin,
Mojave, Sonoran, and
Chihuahuan deserts

Largest island: Greenland
839,852 sq miles
(2,175,219 sq km)

0 km   400   800

0 miles   400   800

FIND OUT MORE ►► American Revolution 414 • Colonial America 409 • Competitions 354–355 • Early Americans 380

CANADA, ALASKA, AND GREENLAND

Northern North America is occupied by Canada, the second-largest country in the world, the US state of Alaska, and the Danish self-governing territory of Greenland. Much of Greenland is covered by ice, and all these regions are sparsely populated, although there are several large cities in Canada. These are mainly in the south of the country and on the Pacific coast near the stunning Rocky Mountains. Huge oil and mineral reserves have brought wealth to both Canada and Alaska.

▲ TRANS-ALASKAN PIPELINE
The Trans-Alaskan pipeline runs 789 miles (1,270 km) from the oilfields of Prudhoe Bay in the Arctic Ocean, south to the ice-free port of Valdez. The pipeline is raised on stilts above the ground to allow migrating moose and caribou to pass underneath it, and to stop the oil from freezing.

HOW DID ALASKA BECOME PART OF AMERICA?
Alaska was part of Russia until 1867, when it was sold to the US for $7.2 million. Most Americans thought this was a huge waste of money until gold was discovered there in 1896, attracting many people hoping to make their fortune. The discovery of oil in the Arctic Ocean in 1968 brought great wealth to the state, and tourism is also a major source of income.

▼ NATIVE PEOPLES
The Aleut and the Inuit, the native peoples of Alaska and northern Canada, respectively, have adapted to their harsh environment, combining modern technology with a traditional lifestyle of hunting and fishing.

FISHING, NEWFOUNDLAND ▶
Fishing has traditionally been a major industry of Newfoundland, with huge stocks of fish once found off the east coast. But overfishing has greatly reduced these stocks, and catches are now severely restricted.

Sled races between rival teams are fiercely contested

Alaska

Team of huskies pulls a sled across the ice

WHO ARE CANADA'S NATIVE PEOPLES?
The First Nations and the Inuit peoples lived in Canada long before Europeans began settling there in the 17th century. They number about 900,000 people, or 4 percent of the population, and have kept many of their traditional customs and traditions. In 1999, the self-governing Inuit homeland of Nunavut was created in northern Canada.

WHAT IS LIFE LIKE IN GREENLAND?
Greenland is the world's largest island, but has a population of less than 60,000 because its climate is so harsh and cold. Most live in small settlements along the coast, making a living from catching fish, shrimp, and seals. There is a small network of roads, but dogsleds and planes are more reliable than cars for getting around.

Greenland

CANADA, ALASKA, & GREENLAND	
ALASKA (US STATE)	
Capital city: Juneau	
Area: 570,374 sq miles (1,477,268 sq km)	
Population: 699,000	
Official state language: English	
Major religion: Christian	
Currency: US dollar	
CANADA	
Capital city: Ottawa	
Area: 3,854,670 sq miles (9,984,670 sq km)	
Population: 34 million	
Official languages: English and French	
Major religion: Roman Catholic	
Currency: Canadian dollar	
GREENLAND	
Capital city: Nuuk (Godthab)	
Area: 839,852 sq miles (2,175,219 sq km)	
Population: 56,000	
Official language: Greenlandic and Danish	
Major religion: Lutheran	
Currency: Danish krone	

▼ NIAGARA FALLS
About 48 million gallons (180 million liters) of water plunge over Niagara Falls every minute. The falls are 190 ft (58 m) high, and lie between lakes Erie and Ontario on the border between the US and Canada.

WHY IS CANADA BILINGUAL?

Until the middle of the 18th century, large parts of eastern Canada were ruled by France, and many French people settled there, mainly in Quebec. Today, one-quarter of Canadians speak French as their first language. Canada is officially bilingual and recognizes both English and French as its official languages, but some French speakers in Quebec want to leave Canada and set up their own independent state.

▲ TORONTO, CANADA
The Toronto skyline is dominated by the CN Tower, currently the world's third-tallest free-standing structure at 1,822 ft (555 m). Toronto is Canada's biggest city and its main commercial and industrial center.

Rainbows often form in the mist

▲ BANFF, CANADA
Spectacular scenery like this is one of the reasons Canada is such a popular tourist destination. Banff National Park, in Alberta, is in the majestic Rocky Mountains.

Canada

HOW DO CANADIANS COPE WITH THE COLD?

One-third of Canada lies within the Arctic Circle, and much of the land is permanently frozen. Farming in the north is therefore impossible, and food supplies are flown in from outside. Houses are built on stilts above the snow, and pipes are heavily insulated against the cold. Farther south, large cities such as Montreal and Toronto have underground shopping centers so that shoppers can stay inside during winter.

FIND OUT MORE ▶▶ Canada 417 • Fishing 67

EASTERN US

The eastern half of the US is the most heavily populated part of the country, with many Americans living in the large cities along the east coast. The national capital, Washington, D.C., is located here, as are the thirteen original states that founded the country in 1776. To the north, the St. Lawrence River and the Great Lakes separate the region from Canada.

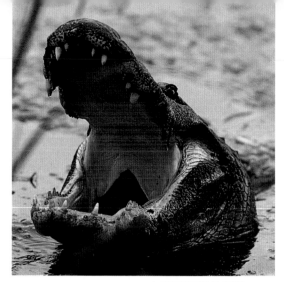

▲ EVERGLADES, FLORIDA
During the wet summer months, alligators, snakes, and other inhabitants of the Everglades can move freely throughout the national park. In contrast, the dry winter months reduce their habitat to the areas around the few remaining water holes.

WHO IS THE CAPITAL NAMED AFTER?

Washington, D.C. ("D.C." stands for "District of Columbia") is named after George Washington, commander-in-chief of the American army in the Revolutionary War against Great Britain, and first president of the US. Washington is the political capital of the US, and the home of the American president.

WHAT ARE THE EVERGLADES?

This huge expanse of marsh and swampland in southern Florida is a haven for many rare creatures, such as the Florida panther and the manatee. Drainage programs to create more land for building and farming threaten to reduce the size of the Everglades and destroy the habitat of these creatures forever.

WHY IS THE US KNOWN AS A "MELTING POT"?

The US calls itself a melting pot of different peoples because, over the centuries, people from all over the world have come to the US, settling alongside the original American Indian population. Some came as slaves from Africa, others fled religious or political persecution in Europe, and many more escaped poverty to start again. The US is proud of its rich mix of peoples, although racial tension and segregation continue to be major problems.

◀ FALL LEAVES, NEW ENGLAND
The large deciduous forests that cover much of New England turn vibrant shades of red, orange, and yellow during the fall. Tourists come here to see this spectacular display of color, as well as to fish, hike, ski, or just enjoy the scenery.

▼ NEW YORK CITY
The Manhattan skyline in New York is one of the most famous in the world, with huge skyscrapers towering over the city's streets. New York is the business center of the US, as well as its cultural capital.

WHAT IS THANKSGIVING?

The first Thanksgiving feast was held in 1621 as a gesture of friendship between the Pilgrim Fathers (immigrants from England) and American Indians, after their first successful joint harvest. Ever since, Americans have celebrated Thanksgiving in November with a traditional meal of turkey and pumpkin pie.

WHY IS THE US SO POWERFUL?

The economic strength and wealth of the US have made it the most powerful nation on Earth. It uses its huge wealth to maintain vast armed services and employ the latest military technology, making it the world's only superpower. US companies dominate the international economy, while American popular music and movies have a major impact on global culture.

SHUTTLE, FLORIDA ►
The Kennedy Space Center at Cape Canaveral, Florida, is the launch site for the space shuttle and the rest of the US space program. Staff members have to check the runway for stray alligators and bobcats before the shuttle can land safely after its mission.

External fuel tank and solid rocket booster lift shuttle into space

Space shuttle, or orbiter, has three main engines and carries seven crew members

USA

Discovery

eastern US

WHY DO ROCKETS BLAST OFF FROM FLORIDA?

NASA (the National Aeronautics and Space Administration) blasts its rockets, shuttles, and satellites into space from Cape Canaveral on the east coast of Florida. The site was chosen because it enjoys year-round good weather, and its remoteness means that few people are disturbed by the noise of a launch.

WHAT HAPPENS WHEN THE MISSISSIPPI FLOODS?

The flooding of the Mississippi inundates farmland and towns, kills livestock, and causes huge financial losses. Intensive cultivation and deforestation have worsened the problem. In 2005, Hurricane Katrina destroyed the levees (dykes) protecting New Orleans, Louisiana, and the river flooded 80 percent of the city, causing great loss of life.

▲ THE GREAT LAKES
The five Great Lakes—Superior, Michigan, Huron, Ontario, and Erie—mark the border between the US and Canada. The lakes are linked by the St. Lawrence Seaway to the Atlantic Ocean, so cargo can be carried far inland.

USA

Capital city: Washington, D.C.

Area: 3,717,792 sq miles (9,629,091 sq km)

Population: 310 million

Dominant language: English

Major religion: Protestant

Currency: US dollar

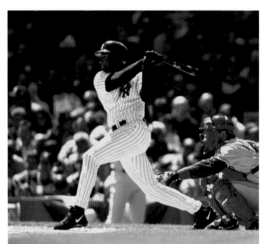

NEW YORK YANKEES ►
Major League baseball teams such as the New York Yankees have a huge following throughout the country. The game is one of the most popular spectator sports in the US, along with football and basketball.

THE CAPITOL, WASHINGTON, D.C. ▲
The Capitol building in Washington, D.C., is the home of Congress, the United States legislature. Congressmen and senators represent every state and region of the US and meet to pass laws and oversee the president and the Supreme Court. The president of the US lives a short distance away on Pennsylvania Avenue in the White House.

FIND OUT MORE ►► American Revolution 414 • Colonial America 409 • Space Shuttle 32

WESTERN US

Beyond the Mississippi valley, the western US rises gently through the vast expanses of the Great Plains until it reaches the Rocky Mountains. The land then drops down again to the coastal ranges and plains of the Pacific coast, where there are forests, orchards, and farms, as well as deserts and rocky, flat-topped hills. Most people live in the southwestern states, or in cities along the Pacific coastline.

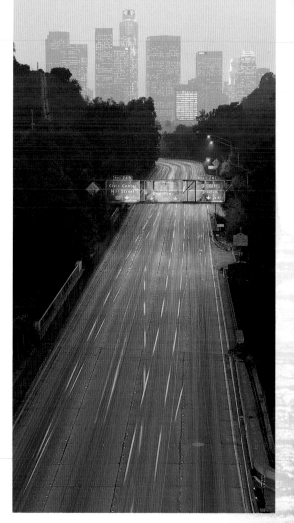

LOS ANGELES ►
The best way to get around most American cities is by car. Freeways such as this six-lane highway in Los Angeles carry thousands of cars every day. Combined with sun, heat, and fog, their pollution produces the brown smog for which LA is famous.

◄ SAN FRANCISCO
Cable cars run throughout the hilly California city of San Francisco. The cars fasten on to a constantly moving wire cable, gripping it tightly on the way up a hill, and then releasing it to glide down the other side.

HOW FERTILE IS THE WEST COAST?
The Pacific coast is hugely productive. Its soils are rich, its rivers provide extensive irrigation, and the sun shines all year. Apples are grown in Washington State, while California produces vegetables and citrus fruit, as well as Napa Valley grapes that make some of the best wines in the world.

▼ YOSEMITE NATIONAL PARK
The first national park to be created in the US was Yosemite, in central California. Its scenery is spectacular, with towering cliffs, tumbling waterfalls, and more than 2,000 varieties of plants and animals, including brown bears.

WHY DOES LOS ANGELES HAVE TROUBLE WITH POLLUTION?
Los Angeles is the center of a sprawling, developed area with a total population of 15 million people. Public transportation is limited, so everyone travels by car. As the city is sandwiched between the coast and a ring of surrounding mountains, air pollution is extremely high.

DO AMERICAN INDIANS HAVE THEIR OWN LAND?
The American Indians who once wandered freely across the whole of the US, hunting buffalo and living off the land, now live mainly on reservations. Here, they control their own affairs, but the land is often poor and jobs scarce, so many leave the reservations to live and work elsewhere.

WHY IS THE PACIFIC COAST A DANGEROUS AREA TO LIVE IN?
The San Andreas, San Fernando, and Santa Monica fault lines cause frequent earth tremors and sometimes earthquakes, especially in the San Francisco area. Long periods without rain often lead to serious bush fires that threaten the West Coast's big cities, and flooding is a major problem because of sinking coastal areas.

WHAT IS DEATH VALLEY?

Sheltered by mountains from the Pacific coastline are some of the driest, hottest regions of North America. One of these, Death Valley in California, has very little rainfall, and temperatures that soar to 134°F (57°C). Its landscape is bleak but magnificent, attracting tourists to see its many canyons and strange rock formations.

RODEO ▲
The vast cattle ranches that stretch from Montana down to Texas still need cowboys to watch over their cattle, although today, trucks and even helicopters are used alongside horses. Traditional cowboy skills are still celebrated at rodeos and stampedes.

◄ MONUMENT VALLEY
Millions of years of erosion have created the amazing cliffs and rock pinnacles of Monument Valley in northern Arizona. The area is a center of Navajo culture. It has also served as the backdrop for many movies.

George Washington   *Thomas Jefferson*   *Abraham Lincoln*

Theodore Roosevelt

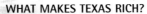

WHAT MAKES TEXAS RICH?

The wealth of Texas comes mainly from oil, which was discovered there in 1901. As well as being the second-largest oil-producing state in the US after Alaska, Texas is rich in iron ore, magnesium, uranium, and other minerals. Cattle ranching and cotton farming also help make it one of the wealthier states.

MOUNT RUSHMORE ▲
The faces of four great US presidents gaze out from a granite cliff on Mount Rushmore in South Dakota. The four faces, each about 60 ft (18 m) high, were carved between 1927 and 1941 by 400 workers.

CAN YOU SEE THE GRAND CANYON FROM SPACE?

The Grand Canyon is the largest land gorge on Earth, and is easily visible from space. The canyon runs through northern Arizona and is more than 1 mile (1.6 km) deep and 277 miles (446 km) long. It was formed by the Colorado River cutting through a rocky plateau for over a million years, exposing at its lowest point some of the oldest rocks in North America.

western US

FIND OUT MORE ▸▸ American Indians 408 • Earthquakes 43

MEXICO, CENTRAL AMERICA, AND THE CARIBBEAN

From the high, snowy mountains and hot, arid deserts of northern Mexico, south to the lush tropical forests of Nicaragua's Atlantic coast, this is a region of great contrasts. Central America consists of seven small countries on the thin land bridge between Mexico and South America. To its east lie the beautiful tropical islands of the Caribbean Sea.

TELESCOPES, MEXICO ►
The clean air and high altitude of the Sierra Madre in Mexico make it an ideal location for radio telescopes. They tune in to radio waves from Space, which are then converted into electronic images.

CARIBBEAN ISLANDS ►
The sandy beaches of the Caribbean islands are popular destinations for tourists avoiding winter in the US or Europe. Cruise ships also visit the many islands, their passengers helping to support local economies.

◄ MEXICAN CIVILIZATIONS
The Aztec Empire, conquered by Spaniards in 1521 CE, was the last in a series of great civilizations going back 2,700 years. This statue of a warrior was carved by the Toltecs who lived from 950–1150 CE.

PANAMA CANAL ►
More than 50 miles (80 km) long, the Panama Canal connects the Atlantic and Pacific Oceans. More than 14,000 ships a year sail through it, from tankers and cargo vessels to cruise liners.

Mexico

WHAT REMAINS OF MAYA AND AZTEC CIVILIZATIONS?
The Mayan and Aztec empires no longer exist, but both civilizations have left behind the ruins of many amazing buildings. Mayan temples and cities can be found in the forests of Mexico, Guatemala, and Belize, and ancient Aztec remains are still being uncovered beneath the buildings of Mexico City.

WHAT IS THE DAY OF THE DEAD?
Every year, on November 1, Mexicans honor their dead family and friends in a celebration called the Day of the Dead. They believe death is a part of life and should be celebrated. They decorate the streets with flowers and hang up ghoulish papier-mâché skeletons. Families gather together to pray to the dead and visit family graves.

DO NATIVE PEOPLES STILL LIVE IN CENTRAL AMERICA?
Native peoples lived in Central America for thousands of years until Europeans conquered the region during the 16th century. As a result, many people today are mestizos (of mixed European and Native American descent). Native peoples themselves make up less than 10 percent of the total population.

DIA DE LOS MUERTOS ▼
On the Day of the Dead, people dress up as skeletons and dance in huge parades. At home, families make small altars, which they decorate with flowers, candles, food, and photographs of those they want to remember.

▲ CARIBBEAN BANANAS
Caribbean islands such as Dominica, St. Lucia, and St. Vincent are heavily dependent on the export of bananas to the US and Europe for their income. The loss of these markets to cheaper bananas from Central America threatens many farmers' livelihoods.

WHAT ARE THE CARIBBEAN'S BIGGEST EXPORTS?

The Caribbean islands export sugar, bananas, tobacco, coffee, rum, and, more recently, illegal drugs. But the biggest exports are people and culture. Poverty led many islanders to migrate to the US or Europe, taking with them an extraordinarily vibrant culture.

WHY ARE THERE SO MANY ISLANDS IN THE CARIBBEAN?

The eastern Caribbean islands sit on the edge of a small plate (section) of the Earth's crust surrounded by bigger plates. As these plates were forced into each other over millions of years, they created a chain of volcanic islands. Most of the volcanoes are now extinct, but some, such as Soufrière Hills volcano in Montserrat, have erupted recently.

WHY ARE MANY CENTRAL AMERICAN COUNTRIES POOR?

In recent years, Central American nations have lost income as the prices for exports of coffee, bananas, and other cash crops have fallen. At the same time, they borrowed money from abroad to pay for new roads, hospitals, and other projects, leaving them heavily in debt. Political instability and civil war have helped keep countries in this region very poor.

WHAT IS LIFE LIKE IN MEXICO CITY?

Life is tough in Mexico City, as housing is often poor and earthquakes are a constant threat. The city is home to more than 20 million people, making it one of the largest cities in the world. It is very polluted because a ring of mountains surrounds it, trapping polluted air from cars and factories.

Central America

Caribbean

MEXICO CITY ►
Despite being a huge, bustling city, the lack of environmental controls and poor public transportation give Mexico City one of the worst air-qualities of any city in the world. Children sometimes have to wait until after the rush hour to go to school, to avoid car fumes.

NORTH AMERICA	
MEXICO	
Capital: Mexico City	
CENTRAL AMERICA	
GUATEMALA	
Capital: Guatemala City	
BELIZE	
Capital: Belmopan	
EL SALVADOR	
Capital: San Salvador	
HONDURAS	
Capital: Tegucigalpa	
NICARAGUA	
Capital: Managua	
COSTA RICA	
Capital: San José	
PANAMA	
Capital: Panama City	
CARIBBEAN ISLANDS	
CUBA	
Capital: Havana	
BAHAMAS	
Capital: Nassau	
JAMAICA	
Capital: Kingston	
HAITI	
Capital: Port-au-Prince	
DOMINICAN REPUBLIC	
Capital: Santo Domingo	
ARUBA	
Capital: Oranjestad	
PUERTO RICO	
Capital: San Juan	
ST. KITTS & NEVIS	
Capital: Basseterre	
ANTIGUA & BARBUDA	
Capital: St. John's	
GUADELOUPE	
Capital: Basse-Terre	
DOMINICA	
Capital: Roseau	
MARTINIQUE	
Capital: Fort-de-France	
ST. LUCIA	
Capital: Castries	
BARBADOS	
Capital: Bridgetown	
ST. VINCENT & THE GRENADINES	
Capital: Kingstown	
GRENADA	
Capital: St. George's	
NETHERLANDS ANTILLES	
Capital: Willemstad	
TRINIDAD & TOBAGO	
Capital: Port-of-Spain	

FIND OUT MORE ►► Astronomy 11 • Aztecs 403 • Continents 39 • Islands 42 • Maya 381

SOUTH AMERICA

The triangular continent of South America stretches from north of the equator almost down to the Antarctic Circle. It contains three very different landscapes. In the west, the Andes tower 22,833 ft (6,959 m) high, forming a backbone down the entire length of the continent, along the Pacific Ocean coast. Dense rainforests in the humid Amazon valley and along the Caribbean coast cover much of the north and northeast. In the south, windswept grasslands and dry pampas roll down to the cold, rocky point of the continent at Cape Horn.

◄ ATACAMA DESERT
The Atacama Desert in northern Chile is the driest place on Earth—in places, it has not rained at all for a century. When rain does fall, devastating flash floods are often the result. There are huge deposits of copper under the sun-baked rocks and shifting sands.

▲ SÃO PAULO, BRAZIL
One of the biggest cities in the world and also one of the fastest-growing, greater São Paulo has a population of around 20 million people. Because much of the interior of South America is uninhabitable, all its biggest cities are on the coast. Many people move to these cities in search of work and a better standard of living.

PERUVIAN TEXTILES ►
The hand-woven, brightly colored woolen textiles worn by these Peruvian women are based on traditional Indian designs that have been handed down through the generations.

▲ THE ANDES
The world's longest mountain chain, the Andes, runs 4,505 miles (7,250 km) down the western edge of South America. Its steep slopes are terraced to grow barley, potatoes, and wheat on its colder, upper slopes, and coffee, tobacco, and corn on the warmer, lower slopes.

RAINFOREST TOUCAN ▶
The Amazon rainforest covers an area the size of Australia. It is also home to the greatest variety of wildlife on Earth, including this fruit-eating Toco toucan.

South America

SOUTH AMERICA
Total land area: 16,886,000 sq miles (7,835,000 sq km)

Total population: 386 million

Number of countries: 12

Largest country: Brazil 3,286,469 sq miles (8,511,965 sq km)

Smallest country: Suriname 63,039 sq miles (163,270 sq km)

Largest country population: Brazil 192 million

Largest lake: Lake Titicaca, Bolivia/Peru 3,220 sq miles (8,340 sq km)

Longest river: Amazon, Brazil 4,049 miles (6,516 km)

Highest point: Cerro Aconcagua, Argentina 22,833 ft (6,959 m)

Major deserts: Atacama Desert, Chile

Largest island: Tierra del Fuego 18,140 sq miles (47,000 sq km)

◀ AIRCRAFT PRODUCTION
Now one of the world's major industrial nations, Brazil produces a wide range of goods, including aircraft, cars, and computers, but borrowing money to modernize its industry has caused massive debt.

GOLD MINER, BRAZIL ▶
South America has vast reserves of gold, silver, iron, copper, and manganese. Working conditions in the mines are often harsh and primitive, with little help from machines. This Brazilian gold miner is resting on the bags of excavated dirt from the mine that he will carry to the sifters, who sort through it for gold nuggets.

PATAGONIAN ICE FIELDS ▶
At the southern tip of South America, Patagonia is close to Antarctica and has extreme weather. Here, it is very cold, wet, and windy. Glaciers carve out huge valleys in the mountains and the sea is full of icebergs. Cruise ships sail along the many inlets and channels, carrying tourists to see this spectacular landscape.

FIND OUT MORE ▶▶ Exploration 400–401 • Habitats 82–84 • Industry 204

One of the two mountain peaks that overlook this high city

NORTHERN SOUTH AMERICA

Spanish influence remains strong in the four countries in this region that were once Spanish colonies (Peru, Ecuador, Colombia, and Venezuela). The others were colonized by Britain (Guyana), the Netherlands (Suriname), and France (French Guiana)—the last European colony. The people are a mix of native peoples, Europeans, and descendants of African slaves.

◄ MACHU PICCHU, PERU
The ancient ceremonial site of Machu Picchu, high up in the Andes in Peru, was never discovered by the Spanish conquerors and gradually fell into ruin. It was found in 1911 and is now a major tourist sight.

SALT MINING, COLOMBIA ►
Along Colombia's flat Caribbean coast, workers remove sand to create tidal pools, which are flooded at high tide. The sun dries them out, leaving sea salt behind.

Below these houses there are terraces, built against the mountainside, for farming

More than 3,000 steps connect the different levels

Temples, homes, and other ceremonial buildings are built around a central square

WHAT IS LATIN AMERICA?
South America, Mexico, Central America, and the Caribbean islands where Spanish is spoken (Cuba, Puerto Rico, and Dominican Republic) are called Latin America. People here speak the Latin-based languages spanish and Portuguese, which they learned from the invaders who settled here in the 16th century. Culture, language and religion still link Latin America, Spain and Portugal.

HOW DO PEOPLE MAKE A LIVING IN THE ANDES?
Most people in the Andes are farmers. Because fertile land is scarce, they cut terraces into the steep hillsides. Crops are chosen to suit either the hot, humid climate of the lower slopes or the cooler climate higher up. Animals such as the llama and alpaca are also kept for food and wool, which is used for clothing.

HAVE NATURAL RESOURCES HELPED NORTHERN SOUTH AMERICA?
This region has immense oil and mineral wealth: the oil reserves in Venezuela are the biggest outside the Middle East, and Colombia produces over half the world's emeralds. But despite this wealth, public services have been neglected, and many people remain poor because the dangerous mining work is low-paid.

ARE ECUADOR'S MANGROVE SWAMPS IN DANGER?
The mangrove swamps of Ecuador's Pacific coast teem with shrimp, and are a vital source of food, firewood, and timber for local people. Shrimp are Ecuador's second-biggest export after oil, but while large shrimp farms have created much-needed jobs, they are slowly destroying the environment on which they depend.

northern South America

▲ TOMATO HARVEST, ECUADOR
The hot, humid coastal plain of Ecuador has an ideal climate for growing tomatoes and other important crops, such as bananas, coffee, and cocoa, which are produced on an industrial scale for export.

WHAT IS HAPPENING TO SOUTH AMERICA'S RAINFORESTS?

About 30 percent of all the world's plant and animal species live in the Amazon rainforest in Brazil, as do many native Indian tribes. Since 1970, vast swaths of forest have been cut down for timber, or to clear land for cattle pasture or new roads. Similar problems are also facing the forests of Colombia and Ecuador.

WHAT REMAINS OF THE INCA CIVILIZATION IN SOUTH AMERICA?

The Spanish destroyed the Inca Empire in the 1530s, but many buildings and some towns survived, such as the hilltop city of Machu Picchu. In the Peruvian Andes, 6–8 million Indians still speak Quechua, the Inca language.

WHAT ARE THE LOST WORLDS OF VENEZUELA?

More than 100 flat-topped sandstone hills called tepuis tower up to 3,300 ft (1,000 m) above Venezuela's rainforests. They are called "lost worlds" because their remoteness has meant that some unique animals and plants have evolved there.

HOW DO THE OTAVALO INDIANS MAKE A LIVING?

Ecuador's Otavalo Indians have adapted to modern life and are one of wealthiest groups of Indians in South America. They weave colorful ponchos, blankets, and rugs, which are in great demand in the US and Europe. The income this generates enables the Otavalo to continue their traditional way of life.

◄ BOGOTÁ, COLOMBIA
The Colombian capital of Bogotá lies on a plateau in the eastern Andes and has a cool, damp climate. The city is the financial center of the country and is home to about 7.3 million people.

▲ ROCKETS, FRENCH GUIANA
French Guiana, the only remaining European colony in South America, is home to the European Space Agency launch site. From here, *Ariane* rockets carry satellites into space.

Llama carries heavy loads at high altitudes

Quechua Indian woman wearing a distinctive hat with a four-quarters-of-the-world design

◄ PERUVIAN WOMAN
The Quechua Indians keep llamas and alpacas—close relatives of the camel—which thrive in the high Andes of Peru and Bolivia. Alpacas are kept for their long, soft wool, and llamas carry loads and provide wool, milk, and meat.

NORTHERN SOUTH AMERICA

PERU
Capital city: Lima
Area: 496,141 sq miles (1,285,000 sq km)
Population: 28.8 million
Official languages: Spanish and Quechua
Major religion: Roman Catholic
Currency: New sol

ECUADOR
Capital city: Quito
Area: 109,483 sq miles (283,560 sq km)
Population: 13.6 million
Official language: Spanish
Major religion: Roman Catholic
Currency: US dollar

COLOMBIA
Capital city: Bogotá
Area: 439,733 sq miles (1,138,910 sq km)
Population: 45 million
Official language: Spanish
Major religion: Roman Catholic
Currency: Colombian peso

VENEZUELA
Capital city: Caracas
Area: 352,143 sq miles (912,050 sq km)
Population: 27.9 million
Official language: Spanish
Major religion: Roman Catholic
Currency: Bolívar

GUYANA
Capital city: Georgetown
Area: 83,000 sq miles (214,970 sq km)
Population: 769,000
Official language: English
Major religion: Christian
Currency: Guyana dollar

SURINAME
Capital city: Paramaribo
Area: 63,039 sq miles (163,270 sq km)
Population: 471,000
Official language: Dutch
Major religions: Hindu, Protestant, Roman Catholic, and Muslim
Currency: Suriname dollar

FRENCH GUIANA
Capital city: Cayenne
Area: 34,749 sq miles (90,000 sq km)
Population: 222,000
Official language: French
Major religion: Roman Catholic
Currency: Euro

FIND OUT MORE ▶▶ Exploration 400–401 • Habitats 82–84 • Human Impact 64–65 • Incas 402

SOUTHERN SOUTH AMERICA

Brazil is the giant of South America, occupying almost half the continent and containing more than half its people. Once-rich Argentina has been impoverished by corrupt government, and all six countries in this region have had long periods of military or dictatorial rule in recent years, although all now have elected governments.

HOW LONG IS THE AMAZON RIVER?

The Amazon River is 4,049 miles (6,516 km) long, which makes it the longest river in South America and second-longest in the world after the Nile. It flows from the Peruvian Andes eastward across Brazil to the Atlantic Ocean. The Amazon carries one-fifth of the world's fresh water and discharges so much water into the Atlantic that seawater 110 miles (180 km) out to sea is still only slightly salty.

WHAT ARE THE PAMPAS?

The Pampas are vast, fertile grasslands that stretch across Argentina and Uruguay. This land is ideal for growing wheat and other cereals and for feeding vast herds of sheep and cattle, all of which are extremely important to the two national economies. Gauchos (cowboys) rode the pampas for 300 years, working on cattle ranches, but there are few left now, since their role has largely disappeared.

▲ GAUCHOS
These cowboys look after cattle on ranches. The name comes from a South American Indian word for "outcast," because they used to live outside towns and cities and beyond the law.

◄ FAVELAS, BRAZIL
Living conditions are poor in the crowded favelas, or slums, that surround the main cities of Brazil. Many inhabitants suffer from bad health due to inadequate drainage and sanitation.

AMAZON RIVER ►
The Amazon is an important waterway for Brazil. Ships can travel inland as far as Manaus, about 995 miles (1,600 km) from the ocean, and floods deposit fertile silt on the land.

WHAT ARE FAVELAS?

The favelas are the sprawling shanty towns around most of the big cities in South America, notably Rio de Janeiro and São Paulo in Brazil. Overcrowding and the lack of affordable housing in the cities force poor people to build their own homes from scrap metal and junk. The favelas have little running water or sanitation. Recent self-help schemes have begun to introduce some basic amenities, but progress is slow.

DO NATIVE INDIANS STILL LIVE IN THE RAINFORESTS?

There were once more than two million native Indians living in the Amazon rainforest, but today only about 240,000 survive. Most of them were wiped out by Western diseases such as influenza and measles. Deforestation, farming, and gold prospecting are a threat to the habitat of many tribes, although some, like the Xingu, now live in protected areas.

KAYAPO INDIAN ►
The headdress of this Kayapo Indian elder from the Amazon rainforest is made of feathers from the macaw and the stork. Unfortunately, both birds are now endangered species in Brazil.

▲ CAR INDUSTRY, BRAZIL

Brazil is a major industrial nation, producing iron, steel, computers, aircraft, and cars, such as this Volkswagen/Audi assembly line at San Jose dos Pinhais. The country is also rich in minerals and is a major exporter of coffee, sugar, and other products.

WHAT IS SOUTH AMERICA'S MOST SOUTHERLY TOWN?

The town of Ushuaia lies at the southern tip of Argentina, so close to the Antarctic that it is bitterly cold for much of the year. The town is situated on a chain of islands called Tierra del Fuego, or "land of fire" in Spanish, named after the Indian fires seen there by the first explorers. Once a port for whaling ships, Ushuaia is now a bustling, modern town.

WHY HAVE SO MANY EUROPEANS SETTLED IN ARGENTINA?

About 98 percent of the population of Argentina is descended from European settlers. This includes the descendants of the two million people who came from Italy to escape poverty in the years before World War I, and many people from Wales. Immigrants were attracted by the relative wealth of the country and the almost unlimited areas of fertile land for farming.

WHAT IS THE NATIONAL DANCE OF ARGENTINA?

The tango began in the slums of the Argentinian capital, Buenos Aires, in the late 1800s, but is now danced worldwide. It is a passionate dance for two people and has a distinctive stop–start rhythm. It was traditionally accompanied by a type of concertina known as a bandoneon, together with a piano and a violin.

◄ SANTIAGO, CHILE

Although the Chilean capital of Santiago is a rich and modern city, wealth is unevenly distributed and one-third of all Chileans live at or below the poverty line.

BRAZILIAN SOCCER ►

Soccer is an all-consuming passion for Brazilians. From an early age, Brazilians play on every back street and open space, and players like Pelé, Ronaldo, and Ronaldinho are national heroes. In 2002, Brazil won the World Cup for a record fifth time.

southern South America

SOUTHERN SOUTH AMERICA

BRAZIL

Capital city: Brasília

Area: 3,268,470 sq miles (8,511,965 sq km)

Population: 191 million

Official language: Portuguese

Major religion: Roman Catholic

Currency: Real

CHILE

Capital city: Santiago

Area: 292,258 sq miles (756,950 sq km)

Population: 16.6 million

Official language: Spanish

Major religion: Roman Catholic

Currency: Chilean peso

BOLIVIA

Capital city: La Paz (administrative); Sucre (judicial)

Area: 424,162 sq miles (1,098,580 sq km)

Population: 9.5 million

Official languages: Spanish, Quechua, and Aymara

Major religion: Roman Catholic

Currency: Boliviano

ARGENTINA

Capital city: Buenos Aires

Area: 1,068,296 sq miles (2,766,890 sq km)

Population: 39.5 million

Official language: Spanish

Major religion: Roman Catholic

Currency: Argentine peso

PARAGUAY

Capital city: Asunción

Area: 157,046 sq miles (406,750 sq km)

Population: 6.4 million

Official language: Spanish

Major religion: Roman Catholic

Currency: Guaraní

URUGUAY

Capital city: Montevideo

Area: 68,039 sq miles (176,220 sq km)

Population: 3.5 million

Official language: Spanish

Major religion: Roman Catholic

Currency: Uruguayan peso

FIND OUT MORE ▶▶ • Dance 336–337 • Endangered Species 124 • Politics 306–307 • South American Independence 420

AFRICA

Africa is the second-largest continent in the world after Asia. More than one billion people live there—nearly one in seven of the world's population. The majority of Africans are Muslim or Christian, although there are many local religious beliefs and customs. Most people live in small towns or villages, where they grow crops, tend livestock, and sometimes work in tourism and other industries. Rapid population growth means that people often need to move to cities in search of food or work. They also move to escape the civil wars, droughts, and famines in rural areas.

Ceuta (Spain)
Melilla (Spain)
ALGIERS
Tangier
Madeira (Portugal)
RABAT
Fès
Oran
Constantine
TUN
Casablanca
Oujda
Kairouan
MOROCCO
Atlas Mountains
TUNIS
Marrakech
Canary Islands (Spain)
LAAYOUNE
ALGERIA
Ahaggar
WESTERN SAHARA (disputed)
Sahara
Tropic of Cancer
MAURITANIA
MALI
NIGER
NOUAKCHOTT
Taoudenni Basin
Senegal
Niger
Sahel
CAPE VERDE
DAKAR
SENEGAL
BAMAKO
OUAGADOUGOU
NIAMEY
Maradi
PRAIA
BANJUL
GAMBIA
BURKINA FASO
Kano
BISSAU
GUINEA-BISSAU
GUINEA
BENIN
NIGERIA
CONAKRY
CÔTE D'IVOIRE
(IVORY COAST)
GHANA
TOGO
Niger
ABUJA
FREETOWN
SIERRA LEONE
YAMOUSSOUKRO
Oyo
Ibadan
Lagos
MONROVIA
Cotonou
LOMÉ
PORTO-NOVO
Adamaw
Highlan
LIBERIA
Abidjan
ACCRA
Port Harcourt
Douala
Gulf of Guinea
MALABO
EQUATORIAL GUINEA
YAOUN
SAO TOME & PRINCIPE
Equator
SÃO TOMÉ
LIBREVILL
GABO

ATLANTIC

OCEAN

Cabind (Angola

Namibian elephants

Nomad with a camel train crossing the desert

DISAPPEARING WILDLIFE ▼
These Namibian elephants, like much of Africa's wildlife, are in danger of extinction from hunters who kill the animals for their ivory, hides, or meat. Game reserves now protect these creatures, and tourists can see them in their natural habitat.

SAHARA DESERT ▲
Africa has three huge deserts: the Kalahari and Namib in the south, and the Sahara in the north. The Sahara is the world's largest desert, and few animals other than camels can survive its intense heat.

JOHANNESBURG ▼
This is the commercial and industrial capital of South Africa and the center of its gold and diamond production. Despite the city's great wealth, many of its inhabitants still live in primitive shanty towns around its edge, because housing is scarce and wages are low.

Namib

NORTH AFRICAN MARKETS ▲
Markets like this one in Morocco are called souks and are the bustling heart of every town in North Africa. Here, farmers sell vegetables and fruit, while traders sell a variety of items, from natural dyes, herbs and spices, and rolls of cloth, to fine silver jewelry and handcrafted leather goods.

Paintings of houses decorate this Ndebele home

NDEBELE STYLE ▲
The Ndebele people of South Africa are renowned for their distinctive sense of color and pattern. Their houses are brightly decorated with strong, geometric shapes. The women are responsible for the upkeep of their houses, and they repaint the walls each spring.

VICTORIA FALLS ▶
In its long course from Zambia down to the Indian Ocean, the Zambezi River plummets 354 ft (108 m) at Victoria Falls. This magnificent waterfall creates so much noise and spray that local people call it "the smoke that thunders." The falls were officially named after Queen Victoria by British explorer David Livingstone, who became the first European to see them in in 1855, during her reign.

FIND OUT MORE ▶▶ Age of Empire 422–423 • Christianity 288 • Islam 290 • Local Religions 283 • Medieval Africa 394–395

NORTH AND WEST AFRICA

The Sahara desert is vast and covers most of north and west Africa, stretching from the Atlantic Ocean in the west to the Red Sea in the east. Few people live in this desert area, which separates the Arab and Berber peoples of the north coast from the mainly Black African peoples to the south. Most of the 290 million Africans who inhabit this region live on the narrow coastal plain where the climate is milder.

WHAT INFLUENCE HAS ISLAM HAD?
During the 7th century CE, Arabs from the Arabian peninsula swept across north Africa, bringing their new religion of Islam with them. Today, most north and west Africans are Muslims, speak a common Arabic language, and share a culture based on the Islamic faith. Every town has at least one mosque, where the faithful are called to prayer.

WHO LIVES IN THE SAHARA?
Few people live in the Sahara because it regularly has temperatures of over 122°F (50°C) and water is very scarce. People such as the Tuareg have learned how to survive in these extreme conditions, and live by trading salt and other goods across huge distances. Camels are their transportation and also provide milk, meat, and hides. However, long droughts and other hardships have led many to give up desert life.

DATES FROM ALGERIA ▶
The giant date palm is found near the oases (watering holes) scattered across the hot, dry Sahara, and its sweet fruit is known as the "bread of the desert." Highly nutritious, dates provide food for people and animals, while every part of the palm tree itself has some use.

WHAT IS DESERTIFICATION?
The growth of the world's deserts is called desertification. This occurs when people extract too much groundwater and divert river water to towns and industries, and also due to overgrazing. Good farmland turns into wasteland, causing famine. Crops still grow but the soil becomes infertile. As plants die, the soil turns to dust. With the Sahara spreading south, huge areas are under threat.

▲ CAIRO, EGYPT
The Egyptian capital of Cairo is the largest city in Africa, and has a population of about 7 million people. This huge, modern city on the Nile River is also the site of historic monuments built during its long history, such as the colossal statue of Rameses II.

◀ MINARET
Beside every mosque is a thin minaret, or tower, from which the *muezzin* (crier) calls all Muslims to prayer five times a day. Minarets are often beautifully decorated with engravings and elaborate stone work. They are usually the tallest buildings in a Muslim town.

TUAREG NOMADS ▶
The Tuareg are a nomadic (wandering) tribe who live in the Western Sahara. In the past, they traveled in great camel trains that crossed the desert to the Mediterranean, carrying slaves, ivory, gold, and salt. Today, some still follow this way of life, but most have now become settled farmers.

Distinctive blue robes are specially dyed

north Africa

◄ **FISHING ON THE NILE**
The Nile is a rich source of food for Egyptians. Fishermen use a traditional single-sail, flat-bottomed boat called a felucca, which can navigate the sandbanks and strong currents of this wide river.

west Africa

◄ **MARKET LIFE, IVORY COAST**
Throughout West Africa, women grow crops and prepare food, both to feed their families and to sell in the local street markets. This woman from the Ivory Coast has dried fish to sell. Others sell dates, groundnuts, and palm oil.

WHY DO SO MANY PEOPLE LIVE NEAR THE COAST?

Most of the people of this region live on the land alongside the Mediterranean Sea and Atlantic Ocean. The climate here is warm and wet in winter and hot and dry in summer, which is better for farming than the desert interior. Many crops can be grown here, from citrus fruits and dates, to olives and tomatoes.

WHAT CAN YOU BUY IN A SOUK?

The colorful and busy souks (markets) of Morocco and Tunisia sell anything from traditional goods and handicrafts such as jewelry, leather, handwoven carpets, and embroidered clothes, to fresh meat, fish, vegetables, and household items. A souk is vital to the economy of a town, and is also a meeting place for workers, farmers, and traders coming in from the countryside.

WHY IS THE NILE SO IMPORTANT?

The Nile, the world's longest river, is an essential part of Egyptian life. When it floods in the summer, it brings vital water and rich mud from the highlands of Ethiopia and Sudan to its deserts, creating a fertile valley for crops. It also provides drinking water for those who live alongside it, and money from tourists who visit the many ancient sites along its banks.

WHAT IS UNUSUAL ABOUT THE MOROCCAN CITY OF FEZ?

Fez has hardly changed for centuries. Like all medieval Islamic cities, the old town of Fez was built according to Islamic principles. The mosque is in the center, each religious and ethnic group has its own quarter, and the streets are narrow enough to give shade and wide enough for two fully laden camels to pass through.

ABU SIMBEL, EGYPT ►
The magnificent temple of Abu Simbel was built during the reign of Pharaoh Rameses II more than 3,200 years ago. During the 1960s the rising waters of Lake Nasser behind the new Aswân Dam threatened the temple, so it was dismantled and rebuilt at a higher and safer location.

▲ **DOGON VILLAGE, MALI**
Many African people build their homes from whatever local materials are at hand. The Dogon of Mali, for instance, construct tall, thin houses from local sandstone topped with conical reed roofs. This village is surrounded by stone walls for defense, and the only entrance is through a narrow doorway.

NORTH & WEST AFRICA	
CAPE VERDE	
Capital city: Praia	
Population: 498,700	
SENEGAL	
Capital city: Dakar	
Population: 12.2 million	
GAMBIA	
Capital city: Banjul	
Population: 1.7 million	
GUINEA-BISSAU	
Capital city: Bissau	
Population: 1.6 million	
GUINEA	
Capital city: Conakry	
Population: 9.8 million	
SIERRA LEONE	
Capital city: Freetown	
Population: 5.6 million	
LIBERIA	
Capital city: Monrovia	
Population: 3.8 million	
IVORY COAST	
Capital city: Yamoussoukro	
Population: 20.6 million	
GHANA	
Capital city: Accra	
Population: 23.3 million	
TOGO	
Capital city: Lomé	
Population: 6.5 million	
BENIN	
Capital city: Porto-Novo	
Population: 8.7 million	
BURKINA FASO	
Capital city: Ouagadougou	
Population: 15.7 million	
MALI	
Capital city: Bamako	
Population: 12.7 million	
MAURITANIA	
Capital city: Nouakchott	
Population: 3.2 million	
MOROCCO	
Capital city: Rabat	
Population: 31.6 million	
ALGERIA	
Capital city: Algiers	
Population: 34.3 million	
TUNISIA	
Capital city: Tunis	
Population: 10.3 million	
LIBYA	
Capital city: Tripoli	
Population: 6.3 million	
EGYPT	
Capital city: Cairo	
Population: 81.5 million	

FIND OUT MORE ►► Ancient Egypt 370–371 • Islam 290 • Islamic Civilization 386–387 • Medieval Africa 394–395

EAST AND CENTRAL AFRICA

Central Africa is a hugely fertile region, with abundant grasslands, vast tropical rainforests, and many rivers and lakes. Both Niger and Chad are mostly desert, however, and in recent years, Lake Chad has shrunk to one-tenth of its former size as the rivers that feed it have dried up. Although many of the countries have great agricultural and mineral wealth, political instability and civil wars have kept people in this region in great poverty.

▲ RWANDAN REFUGEES
Since 1993, at least one million lives have been lost and many more people injured in fighting between the majority Hutu and minority Tutsi tribes in Burundi and Rwanda. The conflict has ruined both countries' economies and created nearly two million refugees.

HOW CAN THE ANIMALS BE PROTECTED?
Governments have established huge national parks and wildlife reserves, such as the Masai Mara in Kenya and the Serengeti in Tanzania. Here, tourists can go on a safari to view the animals in their natural habitat, contributing much-needed income to both local and national economies.

WHAT IS THREATENING AFRICA'S WILDLIFE?
Africa has an amazing variety of wildlife, but in recent years, many species have come under threat from hunters. Elephants are prized for their ivory tusks, black rhinoceroses for their horns. These and other species are now threatened with extinction, while some species have been lost forever.

NIGER RIVER ▲
The Niger River flows east through Guinea, Mali, and Niger before turning south into Nigeria and the Gulf of Guinea. It is a means of transportation for people living along its banks.

▼ GORILLAS
The gorillas that live in the forests of Rwanda, Uganda, and elsewhere in East Africa are in danger of extinction, especially from hunters. Their habitat is threatened by farming, although some are now protected in national parks.

east Africa

SCALE

0 km 200 400
0 miles 200 400

Europe

N

North Cape

Barents Sea

Ostrov Kolguyev

Arctic Circle

Ural Mountains

EUROPE

Total land area: 4,053,309 sq miles
(10,498,000 sq km)

Total population: 831.4 million

Number of countries: 44

Largest country: Russian
Federation (European section)
1,527,341 sq miles
(3,955,818 sq km)

Smallest country: Vatican City
0.17 sq miles (0.44 sq km)

Largest country population:
Russian Federation (whole
country) 141.9 million

Largest lake: Ladoga, Russian
Federation 7,100 sq miles
(18,390 sq km)

Longest river: Volga, Russian
Federation 2,290 miles
(3,688 km)

Highest point: El'brus, Caucasus
Mountains, Russian
Federation 18,510 ft (5,642 m)

Murmansk

Kola Peninsula

White Sea

Archangel

Northern Dvina

R U S S I A N

Lapland

FINLAND

Gulf of Bothnia

Tampere

Turku • **HELSINKI**

Åland

Lake Onega

Lake Ladoga

Vologda

Perm'

F E D E R A T I O N

▲ **FLAMENCO DANCER, SPAIN**
Spain is famous for flamenco
dancing, which developed over
several centuries from Andalusian,
Gypsy, and Moorish roots. It
became popular in the early
19th century. Europe is a small
continent, but its many countries
reflect a rich mix of cultures
and traditions.

Gotland

psala

OCKHOLM

DEN

Saint Petersburg

ESTONIA

TALLINN

Yaroslavl'

Ufa

Kazan'

Baltic Sea

LATVIA

RÍGA

European Plain

Nizhniy
Novgorod

Ul'yanovsk

Samara

Orenburg

60°

LITHUANIA

Vitsyebsk

MOSCOW

Central Russian Upland

Volga Uplands

Volga

Ural

RUSS.
FED.
Kaliningrad

ansk

VILNIUS
Kaunas

MINSK

BELARUS

Homyel'

Voronezh

50°

Bydgoszcz

the European

Brest

Pripet Marshes

Don

▲ **OLIVE GROVES, GREECE**
Much of Europe has rich,
fertile soils, and more than half the land is
used for farming. Olive trees grow
around the Mediterranean, where
the summers are hot and dry.

POLAND

nan

Łódź

roclaw

WARSAW

Bug

Vistula

Dnieper Lowlands

Kharkiv

Volgograd

Kraków

KIEV

Dnieper

Dniester

Dnipropetrovs'k

Astrakhan'

L'viv

UKRAINE

Chernivtsi

Donets'k

Rostov-na-Donu

Caspian Sea

SLOVAKIA

Carpathian Mountains

RATISLAVA

BUDAPEST

MOLDOVA

CHISINAU

Odesa

Sea of Azov

Stavropol'

50°

UNGARY

Cluj-Napoca

Crimea

ROMANIA

Simferopol'

C a u c a s u s

BELGRADE

Brasov

BUCHAREST

Constanta

Black Sea

El'brus
5,642 m
(18,510 ft)

*The Matterhorn in
Switzerland has a
pyramid-shaped peak*

AJEVO

SERBIA

Danube

BULGARIA

Varna

40°

MONT.

KOS.

PRISTINA

Balkan Mts.

Burgas

CA

RANA

KORE

SOFIA

MACEDONIA

TURKEY

ALBANIA

Aegean Sea

40°

GREECE

Piraeus • **ATHENS**

Peloponnese

▲ **THE ALPS ►**
The Alps, Europe's highest mountains,
sweep from the southeastern corner of
France through Switzerland and Italy, and
into Austria. Over millions of years, ice has
molded the scenery, carving peaks, ridges,
waterfalls, and basins filled with lakes.

Crete

Irákleio

Sea

30°

FIND OUT MORE ▶▶ Architecture 328–329 • Christianity 288 • Dance 336–337 • Mountains 45 • World War II 432–433

SCANDINAVIA AND ICELAND

Scandinavia, the most northerly region in Europe, is made up of Norway, Sweden, Denmark, and Finland. Together with the volcanic island of Iceland, this is a sparsely populated land of mountains, pine forests, and unpolluted lakes. In the far north, snow falls for six months of the year. Parts of Scandinavia are highly industrialized, but agriculture is important in Denmark and parts of Finland, where the flatter land is more suitable for farming.

WHY IS TIMBER SO IMPORTANT TO FINLAND?
Trees are Finland's most important natural resource. About three-fourths of the country is covered in forests of pine, spruce, and birch. The softwood timber they provide supplies the building and furniture industries, and accounts for about a third of the country's exports. In addition, Finland is the world's largest producer of plywood, wood pulp, and paper.

▲ TIMBER STACK, FINLAND
Finland is a forested country, and timber is its largest industry. As old trees are felled, new ones are planted, creating sustainable forests.

DO SCANDINAVIANS HAVE A GOOD STANDARD OF LIVING?
The people of the region enjoy high living standards. All Scandinavian countries have small populations, and provide good child-care facilities, schools and universities, and health care for all. With low levels of unemployment, these services are funded through high taxation.

DO SCANDINAVIANS PROTECT THE ENVIRONMENT?
People in Scandinavia value their unspoiled country and work hard to protect it. They avoid pollution by recycling waste materials and making use of natural sources of energy. Electricity is generated by wind power in Denmark, geothermal power in Iceland, and hydroelectric power across the whole region.

▲ WINTER SNOW, NORWAY
Log cabins, made of horizontal logs with a sloping roof, are built to withstand heavy winter snowfalls.

WHERE DO MOST SCANDINAVIANS LIVE?
Most Scandinavians live in the south of the region, away from the harsh northern climate. Towns, cities, roads, and railroads have been built on flat land in valleys, beside lakes, and along coasts. Many coastal towns, including all the capital cities, are important ports. Scandinavia has so many lakes and rivers that boats are a vital form of transportation for people and their goods.

Scandinavia

Glass walls make the most of the sun's warmth and light

◄ SCANDINAVIAN HOUSE
Scandinavia is famous for its architectural design. Local materials, such as timber and glass, are used to create modern, well-insulated homes that sit in harmony with the environment. Many houses are powered by solar panels that transform sunlight into heat.

Colorful houses and market stalls line the harbor front

▲ COPENHAGEN, DENMARK
Copenhagen, the capital of Denmark, lies on the coast of the island of Sjaelland. It is the largest city in Scandinavia and a busy trading center. Many old buildings and historic churches line its canals, alleyways, and pedestrianized streets.

▲ FROZEN COAST, SWEDEN
Winters are extreme in northern Sweden, where there are six months of snow. The freezing temperatures cause the sea in the Gulf of Bothnia, which divides Sweden and Finland, to ice over.

WHERE IS THE LAND OF THE MIDNIGHT SUN?

The far north of Scandinavia is known as the land of the "Midnight Sun." In midsummer, the sun never sets, and there are 24 hours of daylight. During midwinter, the sun hardly rises and there are just a few hours of natural daylight. The darkness has an effect on some of the population, who suffer from seasonal affective disorder, or SAD.

WHAT IS LAPLAND?

Lapland is a region that stretches across the northernmost parts of Norway, Sweden, and Finland, deep inside the Arctic Circle. The Sami people have lived in Lapland for centuries, surviving the long, harsh winters by herding reindeer for meat, milk, and skins. Today, the Sami still keep their own language and customs, but increased development is threatening their traditional way of life.

Reindeer feed on lichens under the snow

Sami herders wear thick boots and traditional dress

REINDEER HERDER, LAPLAND ▲
The Sami people live in the inhospitable Arctic region of northern Scandinavia. For thousands of years, they have raised reindeer for their meat and rich, creamy milk.

SCANDINAVIA & ICELAND
DENMARK
Capital city: Copenhagen
Area: 16,639 sq miles (43,094 sq km)
Population: 5.5 million
Official language: Danish
Major religion: Evangelical Lutheran
Currency: Danish krone
FINLAND
Capital city: Helsinki
Area: 130,127 sq miles (337,030 sq km)
Population: 5.3 million
Official languages: Finnish and Swedish
Major religion: Evangelical Lutheran
Currency: Euro
ICELAND
Capital city: Reykjavik
Area: 39,768 sq miles (103,000 sq km)
Population: 317,400
Official language: Icelandic
Major religion: Evangelical Lutheran
Currency: Icelandic króna
NORWAY
Capital city: Oslo
Area: 125,181 sq miles (324,220 sq km)
Population: 4.8 million
Official language: Norwegian
Major religion: Evangelical Lutheran
Currency: Norwegian krone
SWEDEN
Capital city: Stockholm
Area: 173,731 sq miles (449,964 sq km)
Population: 9.2 million
Official language: Swedish
Major religion: Evangelical Lutheran
Currency: Swedish krona

▲ GEOTHERMAL POOL, ICELAND
Bathers on the volcanic island of Iceland swim in the warm, mineral-rich waters of a natural, geothermal pool. The nearby power station uses the underground heat to power its turbines and produce electricity.

HOW DOES ICELAND USE ITS ACTIVE VOLCANOES?

Iceland has more than 100 volcanoes. At least 20 of these are active and could erupt at any time. The underground heat created by volcanoes is known as geothermal power and is used to produce electricity. Geothermal power stations are clean, cheap, and also provide hot water and heating. Together with the electricity from water-powered stations, they supply all of Iceland's energy needs.

Steam billows from the pool's warm water

Iceland

Deep sheltered water makes a natural harbor for ships and boats

NORWEGIAN FJORD ▶
Norway's west coast is heavily indented with long, deep inlets called fjords. These were carved out by glaciers during past ice ages. Today, the fjords shelter villages and towns and make perfect natural harbors.

FIND OUT MORE ▶▶ Energy Resources 60–61 • Forestry 67 • Vikings 388 • Volcanoes 44

BRITISH ISLES

The British Isles is made up of two separate nations: The United Kingdom of Great Britain and Northern Ireland (the UK) and the Republic of Ireland. These islands have a rugged coastline and a varied landscape of mountains, moorlands, marshes, and fertile, rolling farmland. In past centuries, Britain controlled a vast empire, and so English is now spoken around the world.

◄ LONDON EYE
The London Eye, a huge wheel standing 443 ft (135 m) high, gives passengers a 360° panoramic view of London and its landmarks, including St. Paul's Cathedral, Buckingham Palace, and the Houses of Parliament.

The Eye is over 200 times the size of a bicycle wheel

32 glass capsules carry up to 15,000 passengers a day

WHY IS LONDON A LEADING FINANCIAL CENTER?
The city of London is home to the country's banking and financial services. London is conveniently located halfway between the important financial centers of Tokyo and New York, and more currency changes hands in London each day than in any other city.

▲ CITY OF LONDON, ENGLAND
London is a historic, multicultural city and a leading financial center. It remains the ruling capital of the UK in spite of some devolved powers passing to the new Scottish Parliament and the Welsh National Assembly.

◄ TRINITY COLLEGE, DUBLIN, IRELAND
Ireland's most famous university is a well-known landmark in the Irish capital. In the past, its graduates often had to leave the country to find jobs elsewhere. Although many graduates still choose to stay and find work in Ireland, the country's growing debt will likely lead to an escalation in unemployment. Graduates, then, will look for employment in other parts of the world.

British Isles

WHAT IS GREAT BRITAIN?
The countries of England, Scotland, and Wales make up the island known as Great Britain. Wales was united with England in 1536 and Scotland in 1707. All three nations have separate identities, customs, and traditions. English remains the main language, but Welsh is widely spoken in Wales, and Gaelic is spoken by some people in Scotland.

WHY IS IRELAND KNOWN AS THE EMERALD ISLE?
Ireland was named the "Emerald Isle" because of its lush, green hills. Pastures thrive in the mild, wet climate and provide grazing for breeding cattle and racehorses. Since joining the European Union in 1973, Ireland's largely agricultural society has become a modern, technologically advanced economy based on industries such as finance, electronics, and tourism.

IS THE UK A MULTICULTURAL SOCIETY?
The UK is home to a multicultural population, where one in 20 people are from ethnic minorities. Since the 1950s, many people from the country's former colonies in Africa, India, and the Caribbean have settled in the UK. Recent refugees from the world's trouble spots have also brought with them their culture and traditions. This multiracial population is largely integrated into British life.

▲ MILLENNIUM STADIUM, CARDIFF, WALES
Wales's new national stadium is a highly visible icon in its capital, Cardiff. Built to seat up to 74,000 spectators, the stadium has a retractable roof and hosts many big sporting events.

WHY DO SO MANY TOURISTS COME HERE?

Over 23 million tourists visit the British Isles each year, attracted by their history and heritage. Visitors flock to the medieval cities of Oxford and Cambridge, the Roman city of Bath, Shakespeare's home town of Stratford-upon-Avon, and the beautiful scenery of Ireland, Wales, and the Scottish Highlands. Royal palaces and traditions are also a major attraction.

HOW HAS THE DECLINE IN NORTH SEA OIL AFFECTED JOBS IN SCOTLAND?

After rich reserves of oil and natural gas were found under the North Sea in the 1960s, the energy industry boosted the Scottish economy by creating work on oil rigs and in refineries. With reserves now running low, employment is in decline. However, developing industries such as petrochemicals, electronics, and textiles are creating new jobs.

◄ NEWCASTLE, ENGLAND
Northern towns like Newcastle and Manchester have been transformed by wealthy investors turning industrial buildings into businesses and homes. This has created vibrant, lively cities in which to live and work.

HOW DO THE WELSH CELEBRATE THEIR CULTURAL HERITAGE?

Welsh people celebrate their ancient culture in annual arts festivals called eisteddfods, where poets, dramatists, performers, and choirs compete with each other. The Welsh are renowned for their singing, and male-voice choirs can be found in factories, villages, and towns. The country's national sport is rugby, and the Welsh team now plays in the Millennium Stadium, which opened in Cardiff in 1999.

◄ WELSH FARM
The cool, wet climate and hilly landscape of Wales make it unsuitable for growing crops. Instead, sheep are reared on remote farms throughout the country, and Welsh lamb, fattened on the lush pasture, is highly prized.

BRITISH ISLES	
REPUBLIC OF IRELAND	
Capital city: Dublin	
Area: 27,135 sq miles (70,282 sq km)	
Population: 4.4 million	
Official languages: Irish, English	
Major religion: Roman Catholic	
Currency: Euro	
UNITED KINGDOM	
Capital city: London	
Area: 94,525 sq miles (244,820 sq km)	
Population: 61.4 million	
Official language: English	
Major religions: Anglican and Roman Catholic	
Currency: Pound sterling	

HIGHLAND GAMES, SCOTLAND ►
Scotsmen in traditional tartan kilts participate in a tug of war. Scotland has a strong sense of national identity, which is kept alive by customs such as these Highland Games. Scottish kilts are pleated skirts made of the special tartan that belongs to each family "clan" or tribe.

▼ SCOTTISH LOCH
The spectacular scenery of the Scottish Highlands attracts many tourists to the north of the country. Beautiful lochs, empty hills, and romantic castles make up for the region's cool, damp summers and long, harsh winters.

FIND OUT MORE ►► Age of Empire 422–423 • Energy Resources 60–61 • Farming 66 • International Organizations 434

WESTERN EUROPE

Many countries of Western Europe combine successful industry with abundant agriculture and a booming tourist trade. As a result, most people here enjoy high living standards. The region, which has a long history, includes world-famous cities, such as Paris and Rome, and a landscape of rolling farmland, high mountains, and a beautiful coastline along the Mediterranean Sea.

western Europe

▲ THE ALGARVE, PORTUGAL
The villages and beaches of Portugal's Algarve coast are a magnet for European tourists. Portugal is one of the poorer countries in this region, so tourism provides a welcome economic boost.

WHY DO TOURISTS FLOCK TO THE REGION'S BEACHES?
Every year, millions of tourists travel to the beaches of the Mediterranean Sea to enjoy the sunny climate, warm waters, and beautiful scenery. Tourism has led to heavy development along many parts of the coast, such as the Algarve in Portugal, the Costa del Sol in Spain, and the Riviera in Italy and France.

WHY IS FISHING UNDER THREAT IN SPAIN AND PORTUGAL?
Fishing is at risk in Spain and Portugal because years of overfishing in the North Atlantic Ocean, and recent marine pollution, have reduced fish stocks to an all-time low. In 2002, a vast oil spill in northwest Spain brought fishing there to a halt. Both countries have well-developed fishing industries—Spain has the largest fishing fleet in Europe—that provide the fish for paella and other popular regional dishes.

FRENCH VINEYARDS ▶
French pickers empty baskets of grapes ready for winemaking. France's first vines were planted by the Romans about 2,000 years ago. Since then, the country has become one of the world's leading wine producers.

◀ TOUR DE FRANCE
The world-famous cycle race, the Tour de France, celebrated its centennial in 2003. Riders cover about 3,000 miles (4,800 km) of beautiful French countryside in grueling one-day stages in a contest that lasts three weeks.

▲ VENICE CANALS, ITALY
Venice is one of Europe's most beautiful cities. Every year, thousands of tourists visit its palaces, churches, and galleries, and take a boat ride on its canals.

WHAT DO FARMERS GROW IN ITALY?
Italian farmers grow lots of cereals, fruit, vegetables, and vines. Agriculture is very important to Italy's economy and, although most farms are small and family-run, the country is a leading producer of oranges, lemons, wine, olives, and olive oil. The best farming region lies in the north, in the flat, fertile valley of the Po River. Higher land offers pasture for cows and sheep, whose milk makes delicious cheeses.

WHY IS FRANCE FAMOUS FOR FOOD AND WINE?
A range of climates and landscapes enable France, Western Europe's largest country, to produce many different foods, including wheat, sunflowers, olives, grapes, and dairy products. These foods help to make the regional dishes, cheeses, and wines for which France is famous. The country's vineyards produce a quarter of all the world's wine.

▲ THE ACROPOLIS, ATHENS, GREECE
Just as in ancient times, the Acropolis dominates the city of Athens. The rocky hill is crowned by the ruins of the Parthenon temple, which is more than 2,400 years old.

▲ ROMANIAN FARMERS
Hay is harvested on this Romanian farm as it has been for centuries. Romania is a rich farming country—wheat, corn, potatoes, and fruit are all grown on its fertile land.

WHICH COUNTRY IS MADE UP OF 2,000 SCATTERED ISLANDS?
Hundreds of small Greek islands dot the Aegean and Ionian Seas. Every year, more than nine million tourists visit Greece for its warm blue waters, beautiful scenery, ancient ruins, and sunny climate. Demand for hotels and restaurants has made tourism more profitable than the more traditional farming and fishing.

WHY ARE CARS OFTEN BANNED FROM ATHENS?
In order to protect the ancient buildings of Athens from damaging lead fumes, cars are sometimes banned from the streets of the Greek capital. Traffic produces toxic fumes that create a thick smog of air pollution. This obscures the view of the Acropolis and the Parthenon, Athens' most famous ancient ruins, and destroys the carving on their marble sculptures.

WHICH TWO COUNTRIES ARE SEPARATED BY THE RIVER DANUBE?
Bulgaria and Romania are divided by the Danube River, which forms a border between them. The fertile plain on each side of the river is used as farmland for grazing sheep, goats, and cattle, and for growing crops like sunflowers, wheat, corn, potatoes, and fruit.

▲ LESBOS HARBOUR, GREECE
Fishing boats shelter in this harbor on the Greek island of Lesbos. Fishing is an important part of the Greek islands' economy, and fresh fish features on the menu of every restaurant.

◀ THERMAL SPRINGS, BUDAPEST, HUNGARY
Many baths and spas are built around Hungary's warm natural springs, whose mineral waters are believed to cure bathers of their ailments. Some bathe for so long that they have time to play a game of chess!

WHICH COUNTRY IS FAMOUS FOR ITS HOT SPRINGS?
Hungary is famous for its thermal springs. These warm mineral waters rise naturally from the ground and are said to have medicinal properties. Baths and spas have been built over the hot springs since Roman times.

SOUTHEAST EUROPE

ALBANIA
Capital city: Tirana
Area: 11,100 sq miles (28,748 sq km)
Population: 3.1 million
Official language: Albanian

BOSNIA & HERZEGOVINA
Capital city: Sarajevo
Area: 19,741 sq miles (51,129 sq km)
Population: 4.6 million
Official languages: Bosnian, Serbian, Croatian

BULGARIA
Capital city: Sofia
Area: 42,822 sq miles (110,910 sq km)
Population: 7.6 million
Official language: Bulgarian

CROATIA
Capital city: Zagreb
Area: 21,831 sq miles (56,542 sq km)
Population: 4.4 million
Official language: Croatian

GREECE
Capital city: Athens
Area: 50,942 sq miles (131,940 sq km)
Population: 11.2 million
Official language: Greek

HUNGARY
Capital city: Budapest
Area: 35,919 sq miles (93,030 sq km)
Population: 10 million
Official language: Hungarian

KOSOVO (DISPUTED)
Capital city: Pristina
Area: 4,212 sq miles (10,908 sq km)
Population: 2.1 million
Official languages: Albanian, Serbian

MACEDONIA
Capital city: Skopje
Area: 9,781 sq miles (25,333 sq km)
Population: 2 million
Official languages: Macedonian, Albanian

MONTENEGRO
Capital city: Podgorica
Area: 5,332 sq miles (13,812 sq km)
Population: 622,300
Official language: Serbian

ROMANIA
Capital city: Bucharest
Area: 91,699 sq miles (237,500 sq km)
Population: 21.5 million
Official language: Romanian

SERBIA
Capital city: Belgrade
Area: 29,905 sq miles (77,453 sq km)
Population: 7.3 million
Official language: Serbian

SLOVENIA
Capital city: Ljubljana
Area: 7,820 sq miles (20,253 sq km)
Population: 2 million
Official language: Slovene

FIND OUT MORE ▶▶ Islands 42 • Olympics 356–357

EASTERN EUROPE

Once part of the former Soviet Union, the countries of eastern Europe are now independent republics. The region stretches from the Arctic in the north to the Crimea in the south, and from the Baltic Sea in the west to the Ural Mountains in the east. Much of the landscape is forested. There are also hills and lakes in the Baltic area, marshes in Belarus, and rolling plains in Ukraine and the Russian Federation.

The tower of Tallinn's Oleviste church dominates the picturesque skyline

▲ TALLINN, ESTONIA
Tallinn, the capital of Estonia, is an important Baltic port with regular ferries to Scandinavia. Its modern facilities contrast with the city's historic area, whose ancient walls, turrets, towers, and narrow, cobbled streets date back to medieval times.

WHAT ARE THE BALTIC STATES?

Latvia, Lithuania, and Estonia are known as the Baltic states because they border the Baltic Sea. Coastal ports provide access to shipping trade routes between northern and eastern Europe, but the sea ices up during the cold winter months. In summer, the long coastline attracts many tourists from Finland and Scandinavia. They come to enjoy the area's unspoiled beaches, sand dunes, and islands.

WHY WAS UKRAINE ONCE KNOWN AS A "BREADBASKET"?

Ukraine is the second largest country in Europe. It was known as a "breadbasket" because it once supplied grain to the former Soviet Union and provided this vast population with its bread. The country is covered by flat, fertile plains known as steppes. Here, large farms still produce huge quantities of wheat, corn, barley, oats, buckwheat, and rye. The Ukraine broke away from Soviet control in 1991.

▲ POTATO FARMING, UKRAINE
Potatoes, carrots, and other root crops are harvested throughout Ukraine. Vegetables form an important part of the Ukrainian diet, and the country is famous for its borscht, a rich, warming beet soup.

WHY DO MOST PEOPLE LIVE IN THE EUROPEAN PART OF THE RUSSIAN FEDERATION (RUSSIA)?

Over 100 million people live in the European part of Russia because it has a milder climate, fertile farmland, and is highly industrialized. Most people live in big cities, such as St. Petersburg and the capital, Moscow. The Russian Federation is the world's largest country. Two-thirds of it lies in Asia, but vast expanses are uninhabited because the climate is so harsh.

IS RUSSIA RICH IN NATURAL RESOURCES?

The Russian Federation has huge natural resources. The land is rich in minerals and has many mines from which diamonds, gold, nickel, copper, iron, and other metals are extracted. The country is also a leading producer of oil and gas and has enormous reserves of coal.

◀ MINING, RUSSIAN FEDERATION
Mining is important in the European part of Russia, where there are rich reserves of minerals. Some of these remain unexploited because of poor investment and a lack of technology.

eastern Europe

▲ RUSSIAN BALLET
Russia is famous for its ballet, a popular form of entertainment. The Bolshoi Ballet company of Moscow and the Kirov Ballet of St. Petersburg are renowned throughout the world.

▲ PRIPET MARSHES, BELARUS
Horses graze on the Pripet Marshes, in southern Belarus. This vast area of marshland gives way to huge forests of alder, pine, and oak, which are home to mink and deer.

WHICH PRECIOUS MATERIAL IS FOUND ALONG THE BALTIC COAST?

Two-thirds of the world's amber is found washed up on the shores of the Baltic Sea in chunks of different shapes and sizes. Amber is the fossilized sap of ancient pine trees. It forms over millions of years buried in sediments under the sea. The most sought-after amber is collected in shades of yellow, orange, or gold and is cut and polished to make jewelry.

WHICH CROPS ARE GROWN IN MOLDOVA'S FERTILE FARMLAND?

Moldova's fertile black soil enables farmers to grow a variety of crops, such as wheat, corn, and sunflowers. The country's mild climate is also well suited to growing fruit and grape vines, which are used to make wine.

This gilt-domed chapel of the czars was built in 1449

WHY DO PEOPLE VISIT THE CRIMEA IN UKRAINE?

The Crimea is a peninsula in southern Ukraine that juts into the Black Sea. The region's warm summers and mild winters attract many tourists who cram onto the crowded beaches. Holiday resorts, such as Yalta and Sevastopol, cater to visitors who come for a healthy regimen of massage, exercise, and rest.

WHERE ARE EUROPE'S LARGEST MARSHLANDS?

Vast areas in the south of Belarus are low-lying and covered by swampy marshland, fed by the Byerazino and Dnieper Rivers. The Pripet Marshes stretch over 15,500 sq miles (40,000 sq km) and form the largest expanse of wetland in Europe. The marshes and surrounding forests are a haven for wildlife, including elk, lynx, wild boar, and grouse.

▼ THE KREMLIN, RUSSIAN FEDERATION
Moscow's Kremlin, or citadel, has witnessed many political changes. Initially, it was the residence of the Russian emperors called the czars, then the headquarters of the first Communist government in 1917. Today it is the symbolic home of the new leaders of the Russian Federation.

The Cathedral of the Annunciation is situated inside Moscow's Kremlin

EASTERN EUROPE

ESTONIA
Capital city: Tallinn
Area: 17,462 sq miles (45,226 sq km)
Population: 1.3 million
Official language: Estonian
Major religion: Evangelical Lutheran
Currency: Kroon

LATVIA
Capital city: Riga
Area: 24,938 sq miles (64,589 sq km)
Population: 2.3 million
Official language: Latvian
Major religion: Lutheran
Currency: Lats

LITHUANIA
Capital city: Vilnius
Area: 25,174 sq miles (65,200 sq km)
Population: 3.4 million
Official language: Lithuanian
Major religion: Roman Catholic
Currency: Litas

BELARUS
Capital city: Minsk
Area: 80,154 sq miles (207,600 sq km)
Population: 9.7 million
Official languages: Belarusian and Russian
Major religion: Russian Orthodox
Currency: Belarusian rouble

UKRAINE
Capital city: Kiev
Area: 233,089 sq miles (603,700 sq km)
Population: 46.3 million
Official language: Ukrainian
Major religion: Ukrainian Orthodox
Currency: Hryvna

MOLDOVA
Capital city: Chisinau
Area: 13,067 sq miles (33,843 sq m)
Population: 3.6 million
Official language: Moldovan
Major religion: Eastern Orthodox
Currency: Moldovan leu

RUSSIAN FEDERATION
Capital city: Moscow
Area: 6,592,735 sq miles (17,075,200 sq km)
Population: 141.9 million
Official language: Russian
Major religion: Russian Orthodox
Currency: Russian rouble

ASIA

Asia is the world's biggest continent and covers almost a third of the Earth's land surface. The landscape includes the frozen tundra in the north, the baking deserts of the Middle East, a vast coniferous forest, and the Himalayas—the world's highest mountains. Large areas of Asia are uninhabitable, but there are the Steppes—huge grassy plains—and fertile valleys beside the Indus, the Mekong, and other mighty rivers. In the southeast of the region, there are thousands of tiny, volcanic islands, many of which are covered by tropical rainforests. Two-thirds of the world's population lives in Asia, reflecting a great variety of cultures, lifestyles, and religions.

SIBERIAN TIGER ▲
The rare Siberian tiger, the largest and most powerful of all the big cats, lives in mountain forests in eastern Russia. Up to 400 tigers are thought to remain in the wild, and they are rigorously protected.

▲ FLOATING MARKET, BANGKOK, THAILAND
Flat-bottomed boats, called sampans, are still used to transport fruit and vegetables from the countryside into the city of Bangkok, where they form a floating market. The Thai capital is built on a river, and its streets were once canals.

Fresh produce is brought in from outlying farms

▼ MOUNT EVEREST, HIMALAYAS
Standing tall at 29,035 ft (8,850 m), Mount Everest is the world's highest peak. It lies in the Himalayas, a mountain range that forms a natural barrier between the Indian subcontinent and northern Asia.

VOLCANIC ERUPTION, LUZON, PHILIPPINES ▶
The biggest-ever eruption of Mount Pinatubo in 1991 brought destruction to the island of Luzon in the Philippines. Families grabbed their belongings and fled from their homes before they were buried by ash and rocks.

ARCTIC OCEAN

Wrangel Island

Gulf of Anadyr

Anadyr'

East Siberian Sea

New Siberian Islands

Laptev Sea

...ri'sk

Central Siberian Plateau

Magadan

Yakutsk

Petropavlovsk-Kamchatskiy

Sea of Okhotsk

Kamchatka

RUSSIAN FEDERATION

...beria

Bratsk

Lake Baikal

Chita

Irkutsk

...kuznetsk

Amur

Khabarovsk

Sakhalin

Yuzhno-Sakhalinsk

Kurile Islands

Sapporo

Qiqihar

Harbin

Vladivostok

Sendai

ULAN BATOR

MONGOLIA

Gobi

Changchun

Jilin

Shenyang

Anshan

Fushun

NORTH KOREA

PYONGYANG

JAPAN

TOKYO

Nagoya

Kyoto

Osaka

Kobe

Sea of Japan (East Sea)

Baotou

BEIJING

Dalian

SEOUL

SOUTH KOREA

Hiroshima

Kitakyushu

Fukuoka

Tianjin

Shijiazhuang

Qingdao

Yellow Sea

Jinan

Lanzhou

Zhengzhou

Yellow River

Kilien Mountains

...tains

CHINA

Xi'an

Nanjing

Shanghai

...Tibet

Yangtze

Wuhan

Nanchang

East China Sea

...hasa

Chengdu

Chongqing

Mekong

Hengyang

Fuzhou

Guiyang

Ryukyu Islands

Tropic of Cancer

TAIPEI

TAIWAN

PACIFIC OCEAN

Guangzhou

...UTAN

...HIMPHU

...hati

...GLADESH

...DHAKA

Brahmaputra

MYANMAR (BURMA)

Mandalay

PYINMANA

Macao (Aomen)

Hong Kong (Xianggang)

HANOI

Hai Phong

Louangphabang

Vinh

Hainan Dao

Luzon

Philippine Sea

...ttagong

...kata

...cutta)

Chiang Mai

LAOS

VIENTIANE

THAILAND

Irrawaddy

Da Nang

South China Sea

MANILA

PHILIPPINES

RANGOON

BANGKOK

CAMBODIA

PHNOM PENH

Hồ Chi Minh

Cebu

Mindanao

Davao

Andaman Islands (India)

Gulf of Thailand

BRUNEI

BANDAR SERI BEGAWAN

Manado

Jayapura

...Jicobar Islands (India)

Andaman Sea

Taiping

MALAYSIA

Medan

KUALA LUMPUR

Borneo

Moluccas

Celebes

New Guinea

Equator

N

PUTRAJAYA

SINGAPORE

Sumatra

INDONESIA

Ambon

Makassar

Flores Sea

EAST TIMOR

DILI

...NDIAN OCEAN

Padang

Palembang

Java Sea

Semarang

Surabaya

Lesser Sunda Islands

Timor Sea

...gal

...RANGOON

JAKARTA

Bandung

Java

Red River

Bay of Bengal

Mekong

0 km 500 1,000

0 miles 500 1,000

CHINESE DRAGON ▶

Chinese New Year, China's most important festival, is celebrated in late January or early February. The festival lasts for several days and is marked by spectacular processions. Displays of dancing dragons pass through the streets, featuring huge, colorful dragon costumes like this one.

▲ HONG KONG, CHINA

Hong Kong's modern, high-rise skyline reflects the prosperous economy of this former British colony. Hong Kong was returned to communist China in 1997, and has become a special administrative region where foreign trade and enterprise are encouraged. It is an important trading and financial center.

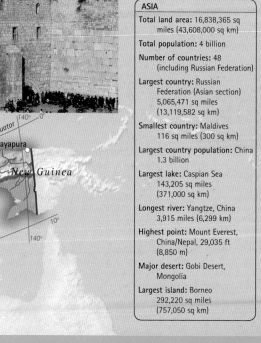

◀ JERUSALEM, ISRAEL

The historic city of Jerusalem is sacred to the Jews, Christians, and Muslims, reflecting major divisions inside Israel. For Jews the Western Wall (seen here) is the most sacred site, while the golden Dome of the Rock, also shown, is part of a Muslim shrine.

ASIA

Total land area: 16,838,365 sq miles (43,608,000 sq km)

Total population: 4 billion

Number of countries: 48 (including Russian Federation)

Largest country: Russian Federation (Asian section) 5,065,471 sq miles (13,119,582 sq km)

Smallest country: Maldives 116 sq miles (300 sq km)

Largest country population: China 1.3 billion

Largest lake: Caspian Sea 143,205 sq miles (371,000 sq km)

Longest river: Yangtze, China 3,915 miles (6,299 km)

Highest point: Mount Everest, China/Nepal, 29,035 ft (8,850 m)

Major desert: Gobi Desert, Mongolia

Largest island: Borneo 292,220 sq miles (757,050 sq km)

FIND OUT MORE ▶▶ Conservation 125 • Judaism 287 • Mountains 45 • Volcanoes 44

RUSSIAN FEDERATION AND CENTRAL ASIA

The Asian part of the Russian Federation is a land of bleak, frozen tundra and cold conifer forest. To the south and west are windswept grasslands known as the steppes, rugged, mountainous plateau, and arid deserts.

▲ REGISTAN SQUARE, SAMARKAND, UZBEKISTAN
Samarkand contains some outstanding examples of 14th-century Islamic architecture, such as this beautiful, mosaic-covered building, which is a Muslim school for training clerics.

Russian Federation

WHICH ANCIENT CITY IN UZBEKISTAN IS ON THE SILK ROAD?

The ancient Islamic city of Samarkand lies on the Silk Road, an ancient trading route that linked China with central Asia, the Middle East, and Europe. Samarkand was once the center for China's silk trade, and the manufacture of silk and cotton textiles is still the city's main industry.

◀ NOMADS, KYRGYZSTAN
The Kyrgyz people of Kyrgyzstan are nomads. They live in felt tents called yurts and move around in search of mountain pasture. Here, a woman cooks a meal outside.

▲ AFGHAN CARPET SELLERS
Carpet-makers from Uzbekistan, Turkmenistan, and northern Afghanistan use the fine wool from karakul sheep to hand-knot and weave distinctive carpets in shades of red, brown, and maroon.

HOW DO PEOPLE LIVE IN CENTRAL ASIA?

In the grasslands of central Asia, many people breed animals and move from place to place searching for fresh pasture. In Afghanistan, for example, sheep-herders are nomadic. They live in tents with very few belongings, surviving on their animals' milk, meat, and wool and selling the excess in towns and cities.

◄ NENETS PEOPLE, SIBERIA, RUSSIAN FEDERATION
The Nenets people live in a cold, inhospitable Arctic region of the Russian Federation. This Siberian community traditionally survived by herding reindeer or trapping wild animals. Today, however, the region is being developed for its huge reserves of gas.

▼ RUSSIAN SPACE CENTER, KAZAKHSTAN
A rocket is towed to the launch pad of the Russian space center at the Baikonur Cosmodrome in Kazakhstan. From here, the Russians launched the world's first artificial satellite, *Sputnik 1*, in 1957, and the first person in space, Yuri Gagarin, in 1961.

DO MANY PEOPLE LIVE IN SIBERIA?
Siberia, a vast, bitterly cold region of tundra, pine forest, rivers, and lakes, is sparsely populated. The Yakut and other native peoples survive there by hunting, fishing, and herding reindeer. Siberia stretches from the Ural Mountains in the west to the Pacific Ocean in the east. The region is rich in natural resources, such as coal, oil, gas, diamonds, and gold.

WHY IS THE ARAL SEA SHRINKING?
The Aral Sea in Uzbekistan and Kazakhstan was once the world's fourth-largest freshwater lake. Today it is shrinking at an alarming rate because the rivers that feed it, the Syr Darya and the Amu Darya, have been diverted to irrigate cotton fields. A fishing village that once stood on the lake's banks now stands 30 miles (48 km) from the shore.

◄ METAL WORKER, RUSSIAN FEDERATION
This copper foundry in western Siberia is typical of the heavy industry that has dominated the Russian economy. Many such factories are old and inefficient, and also pollute the environment.

WHERE IS THE WORLD'S LONGEST RAILROAD?
The Trans-Siberian Railroad, the world's longest continuous rail line, crosses the Russian Federation. It starts in Moscow and runs 5,870 miles (9,446 km) to the Pacific port of Vladivostok. The whole journey crosses eight time zones and takes eight days to complete.

central Asia

RUSSIAN FEDERATION & CENTRAL ASIA	
GEORGIA	
Capital city: T'bilisi	
Area: 26,911 sq miles (69,700 sq km)	
Population: 9.8 million	
Official languages: Georgian and Abkhazian (in Abkhazia)	
ARMENIA	
Capital city: Yerevan	
Area: 11,506 sq miles (29,800 sq km)	
Population: 3.1 million	
Official language: Armenian	
AZERBAIJAN	
Capital city: Baku	
Area: 33,436 sq miles (86,600 sq km)	
Population: 8.7 million	
Official language: Azerbaijani	
KAZAKHSTAN	
Capital city: Astana	
Area: 1,049,150 sq miles (2,717,300 sq km)	
Population: 15.7 million	
Official language: Kazakh	
TURKMENISTAN	
Capital city: Ashgabat	
Area: 188,455 sq miles (488,100 sq km)	
Population: 5 million	
Official language: Turkmen	
AFGHANISTAN	
Capital city: Kabul	
Area: 250,000 sq miles (647,500 sq km)	
Population: 29 million	
Official languages: Pashtu and Dari	
UZBEKISTAN	
Capital city: Tashkent	
Area: 172,741 sq miles (447,400 sq km)	
Population: 27.3 million	
Official language: Uzbek	
TAJIKISTAN	
Capital city: Dushanbe	
Area: 55,251 sq miles (143,100 sq km)	
Population: 6.8 million	
Official language: Tajik	
KYRGYZSTAN	
Capital city: Bishkek	
Area: 76,641 sq miles (198,500 sq km)	
Population: 5.3 million	
Official languages: Kyrgyz and Russian	
RUSSIAN FEDERATION	
Capital city: Moscow	
Area: 6,592,735 sq miles (17,075,200 sq km)	
Population: 141.9 million	
Official language: Russian	

FIND OUT MORE ▶▶ China's First Empire 378 • Habitats 82–84 • Islam 290 • Space Stations 33

WESTERN ASIA AND THE MIDDLE EAST

The Middle East is the name given to the area of land between the Red Sea and the Gulf, from Israel in the west to Iran in the east. Along with western Asia, much of this land is inhospitable, with dry desert in the Arabian Peninsula, and mountains in Iran and Iraq. Turkey is dominated by a high plateau, but has plenty of fertile farmland. There are snow-capped mountains in north Lebanon and Israel, which drop down to fertile plains along the coasts.

▲ SOUK STALL, SYRIA
A stall sells fresh fruit in the souk, or marketplace, of Syria's capital, Damascus. The souk's narrow, bustling alleyways are packed with workshops and stalls offering all kinds of foodstuffs and crafts.

▲ BEIRUT, LEBANON
Modern high-rise buildings stand alongside ruins in Beirut, the capital of Lebanon. This elegant city was almost completely destroyed in the civil war of 1975–89 that raged between the Christian and Muslim populations. Once a dangerous destination for visitors, the rebuilt city is now attracting increasing numbers of tourists.

HOW HAS OIL CHANGED THE GULF REGION?

The discovery of oil in the Gulf has brought enormous wealth to Saudi Arabia, Iraq, Kuwait, and other desert countries, which now supply 30 percent of the world's oil. Fleets of oil tankers have made the Gulf one of the world's busiest seaways. The presence of oil has increased this area's international importance and its influence on world affairs.

WHY IS THE MIDDLE EAST CALLED A TROUBLE SPOT?

There have been many recent conflicts in the Middle East. In 1975, Lebanon suffered a violent civil war between the Christian and Muslim populations. In 1990 and 2003, international forces led by the US invaded Iraq, eventually deposing President Saddam Hussein's regime. Today, huge tensions exist between Israelis and Palestinians, who lost their homes in 1948 when Israel was created as a homeland for the Jews.

WHICH TURKISH CITY LIES HALF IN ASIA AND HALF IN EUROPE?

Istanbul is the only city in the world to lie in two continents. Split by a narrow channel of water called the Bosporus Strait, the European and Asian parts of the city are linked by a number of bridges. Istanbul is Turkey's largest city and home to nearly 9.4 million people. Once known by the name of Constantinople, Istanbul was Turkey's capital from 330–1923 CE.

High towers, called minarets, broadcast the call for Muslims to come to prayer

Middle East

Istanbul stands on two sides of the Bosporus waterway

▲ PETRA, JORDAN
The ancient city of Petra in Jordan dates from the 4th century BCE. Its temples and other spectacular buildings were cut out of pink limestone rock deep inside a desert canyon. Bedouin nomads still travel around the Syrian Desert using camels, cars, and trucks.

◄ BLUE MOSQUE, ISTANBUL, TURKEY
Istanbul's Blue Mosque is an outstanding example of Islamic architecture. It stands in a city where East meets West: the mosque's graceful minarets and domed roof rub shoulders with bustling bazaars, designer shops, restaurants, and high-rise blocks.

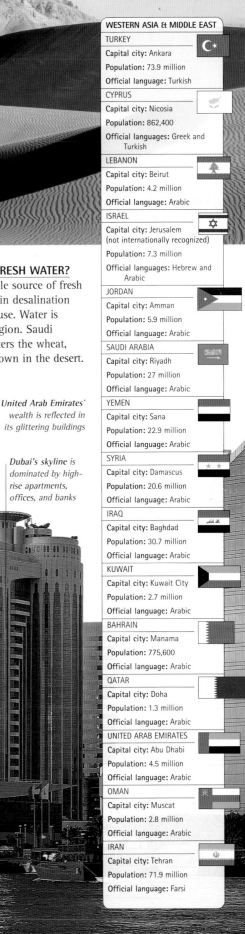

SAUDI ARABIAN DESERT ▶
Over 95 percent of Saudi Arabia is dry, inhospitable desert, where daytime temperatures reach 118°F (48°C) and plunge to near freezing at night. The extreme temperatures and wind-borne sand wear down the desert rocks. The southern desert covers 250,000 sq miles (650,000 sq km) and is the largest expanse of sand in the world.

western Asia

HOW DO DESERT COUNTRIES GET FRESH WATER?

Many desert countries have no reliable source of fresh water and have to process sea water in desalination plants for domestic and agricultural use. Water is carefully managed throughout the region. Saudi Arabia's huge irrigation program waters the wheat, fruit, and vegetable crops that are grown in the desert.

WHERE IS THE LOWEST PLACE ON EARTH?

At 1,285 ft (392 m) below sea level, the Dead Sea is the lowest place on Earth. This vast lake, 46 miles (74 km) long, lies on the border between Israel and Jordan. Its water is so salty that nothing can live in it, which is how the lake got its name. However, the mud on its shore is rich in minerals, and is said to have healing properties.

WHO ARE THE KURDS?

The Kurds are a stateless people, whose mountainous homeland of Kurdistan straddles the borders of Turkey, Syria, Iraq, and Iran. For many years, the Kurds have wanted self-government, which has led to violence and bloodshed, and with many Kurds living as refugees. However, after the Iraq War in 2003, Kurdish self-governance was established in Northern Iraq.

United Arab Emirates' wealth is reflected in its glittering buildings

Dubai's skyline is dominated by high-rise apartments, offices, and banks

▲ KURDISH REFUGEES, TURKEY
Years of dictatorship and conflict in Iraq have led to thousands of Kurds leaving the country for refugee camps in Turkey. The Kurds, who number about 25 million, are one of the largest stateless peoples in the world.

DUBAI, UNITED ARAB EMIRATES ▶
Dubai, one of the United Arab Emirates, has been rebuilt with wealth generated by oil revenues. Like other nations in the Gulf, the United Arab Emirates is a prosperous country, and most of its people enjoy a high standard of living.

WESTERN ASIA & MIDDLE EAST

TURKEY
Capital city: Ankara
Population: 73.9 million
Official language: Turkish

CYPRUS
Capital city: Nicosia
Population: 862,400
Official languages: Greek and Turkish

LEBANON
Capital city: Beirut
Population: 4.2 million
Official language: Arabic

ISRAEL
Capital city: Jerusalem (not internationally recognized)
Population: 7.3 million
Official languages: Hebrew and Arabic

JORDAN
Capital city: Amman
Population: 5.9 million
Official language: Arabic

SAUDI ARABIA
Capital city: Riyadh
Population: 27 million
Official language: Arabic

YEMEN
Capital city: Sana
Population: 22.9 million
Official language: Arabic

SYRIA
Capital city: Damascus
Population: 20.6 million
Official language: Arabic

IRAQ
Capital city: Baghdad
Population: 30.7 million
Official language: Arabic

KUWAIT
Capital city: Kuwait City
Population: 2.7 million
Official language: Arabic

BAHRAIN
Capital city: Manama
Population: 775,600
Official language: Arabic

QATAR
Capital city: Doha
Population: 1.3 million
Official language: Arabic

UNITED ARAB EMIRATES
Capital city: Abu Dhabi
Population: 4.5 million
Official language: Arabic

OMAN
Capital city: Muscat
Population: 2.8 million
Official language: Arabic

IRAN
Capital city: Tehran
Population: 71.9 million
Official language: Farsi

FIND OUT MORE ▶▶ Energy Resources 60–61 • Habitats 82–84 • Islam 290 • Mesopotamia 368 • Middle East 435

SOUTHERN ASIA

Southern Asia, home to over one-fifth of the world's population, is bordered by the sea to the south and the Himalayan mountains to the north. Dominated by the Indian subcontinent, a great variety of landscapes and climates are found throughout southern Asia, from dry, sandy deserts in the northwest, to tropical rainforests in the south. In the east, three major rivers—the Brahmaputra, the Meghna, and the Ganges—flow together toward the Bay of Bengal, where they form the world's largest delta.

▲ GANGES RIVER, INDIA
Hindus bathe in the sacred Ganges River from one or more of the 40 ghats (stone steps) along the river in Varanasi. Hindus believe that Varanasi is the earthly home of the god Shiva, creator of the world.

WHY DO HINDU PILGRIMS GATHER AT VARANASI?
The city of Varanasi is sacred to Hindus, who form 90 percent of India's population. Every year, millions of pilgrims gather on the stone steps called ghats along the high banks of the Ganges River. Here they pray, meditate, and purify themselves in the river's holy waters. The dead are cremated on funeral pyres and their ashes are sprinkled onto the surface of the water.

HOW ARE HIKERS DAMAGING THE HIMALAYAS?
The large number of hikers visiting the Himalayas each year are damaging the fragile mountain environment and threatening its ecology. Every year, 300,000 tourists visit Nepal to walk on the slopes of Mount Everest and other major peaks. These visitors erode mountain trails and often leave behind vast quantities of garbage.

southern Asia

Bangladeshi houses are raised on stilts above the floodplain

▲ FLOODING IN BANGLADESH
Water levels in Bangladesh rise 20 ft (6 m) above normal during the annual monsoon rains. Flood-waters can destroy animals, crops, and homes, and spread disease. More than 50 percent of Bangladeshis live in extreme poverty, and the country is too poor to invest in large-scale flood defenses, such as dams.

Stilts are handed down from father to son

WHY IS BANGLADESH PRONE TO FLOODING?
Large parts of central and southern Bangladesh are flat, low-lying river plains, which flood during the summer monsoon rains. In good years, the floods water the crops and fertilize the fields. In bad years, they cause devastation by surging over flood defenses and sweeping away villages, livestock, and crops.

WHICH ISOLATED COUNTRY IS RULED BY THE DRAGON KING?
Bhutan is a small Buddhist kingdom in the Himalayas, ruled by a monarch called the Dragon King. The country has little contact with the outside world, although television was introduced in 1999. Most of the population makes a living from farming.

◄ HIMALAYAN MOUNTAIN CLIMB
The Sherpa people of Nepal are skilled climbers, who act as guides and porters for the tourists and mountaineers visiting the Himalayas. Hiking provides a welcome boost to Nepal's economy.

HOW DID GREAT BRITAIN INFLUENCE INDIA?
India was a British colony from the mid-19th century until 1947, when it gained its independence. British influences can still be seen in the region today, such as the widespread use of English, the European style of architecture, the vast rail network, the passion for cricket, and in the legal and political systems.

◀ REPUBLIC DAY, INDIA
Parades in New Delhi mark the anniversary of Republic Day, when India became a republic on January 26, 1950.

WHAT IS CITY LIFE LIKE IN INDIA?
India's two largest cities are crowded, bustling places where modern high-rise office buildings stand next to ancient temples, monuments, and mosques. Calcutta is a major industrial city, and Mumbai (Bombay) is the center of India's huge film industry. As more people move from the countryside in search of work, overcrowding in the cities' slums is a growing problem.

WHICH CROP IS IMPORTANT TO SRI LANKA?
The island of Sri Lanka has over 2,000 tea plantations and is the world's largest tea exporter. The best tea grows on the hillsides in the cooler, central highlands. Tea is harvested by hand—machines would bruise the fragile leaves and spoil their delicate flavor. The leaves are then rolled, dried, and packed for export.

MUMBAI, INDIA ▶
Mumbai, on India's western coast, has a modern, high-rise skyline. Here, extreme wealth is seen alongside extreme poverty: 100,000 people live on the city's streets.

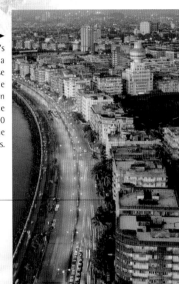

Mumbai's rich live in elegant housing that overlooks the Arabian Sea

Stilt fishing is thousands of years old

▼ FISHING IN SRI LANKA
Stilt fishing is famous in Sri Lanka. The fishermen perch on poles embedded in the seabed, and fish with a rod and line. The small fish that swim in the shallow waters are a valuable catch.

SOUTHERN ASIA

PAKISTAN
Capital city: Islamabad
Area: 310,401 sq miles (803,940 sq km)
Population: 166 million
Official language: Urdu
Major religion: Sunni Muslim
Currency: Pakistani rupee

INDIA
Capital city: New Delhi
Area: 1,269,338 sq miles (3,287,590 sq km)
Population: 1.14 billion
Official languages: Hindi and English
Major religion: Hindu
Currency: Indian rupee

MALDIVES
Capital city: Male'
Area: 116 sq miles (300 sq km)
Population: 305,000
Official language: Dhivehi
Major religion: Sunni Muslim
Currency: Rufiyaa

SRI LANKA
Capital city: Colombo
Area: 25,332 sq miles (65,610 sq km)
Population: 20.1 million
Official languages: Sinhala, Tamil, and English
Major religion: Buddhist
Currency: Sri Lanka rupee

NEPAL
Capital city: Kathmandu
Area: 54,363 sq miles (140,800 sq km)
Population: 28.8 million
Official language: Nepali
Major religion: Hindu
Currency: Nepalese rupee

BANGLADESH
Capital city: Dhaka
Area: 55,598 sq miles (144,000 sq km)
Population: 160 million
Official language: Bengali
Major religion: Muslim (mainly Sunni)
Currency: Taka

BHUTAN
Capital city: Thimphu
Area: 18,147 sq miles (47,000 sq km)
Population: 2.2 million
Official language: Dzongkha
Major religion: Mahayana Buddhist
Currency: Ngultrum

FIND OUT MORE ▶▶ Age of Empire 422–423 • Cinema 346–347 • Hinduism 286 • Winds 51

EASTERN ASIA

The harsh landscapes of Eastern Asia include remote mountains, cold deserts, and the vast, dry grasslands of Mongolia and northern China. In southeastern China, there are wide plains and valleys, watered by mighty rivers. North and South Korea form a peninsula, where the land is mountainous and thickly forested, as are the neighboring islands across the sea that make up Japan.

HOW LONG IS THE GREAT WALL OF CHINA?

The wall stretches over 3,980 miles (6,400 km) through the mountains and deserts of northern China. It is the longest structure ever built by hand. Work began over 2,200 years ago by order of the first Chinese emperor, Qin Shi Huangdi. Most of the wall we see today was built by peasants in the 15th century to keep out northern invaders.

▼ THE GREAT WALL OF CHINA
The Great Wall of China is made up of two high walls sandwiched together with earth. The top is paved with stone slabs, making a roadway about 13 ft (4 m) wide. Along its length, there are 25,000 square watch towers.

Guards sat in towers along the wall, watching for signs of danger

▲ HONG KONG, CHINA
A traditional Chinese junk sails into Hong Kong's harbor. Hong Kong is not only a leading financial center and a major manufacturer of textiles and electronics, but also one of the world's busiest ports.

WHEN WAS HONG KONG A BRITISH COLONY?

Hong Kong was returned to China in 1997, having been a British colony for 99 years. With a population of over 6.5 million people, this small territory lies in southeast China and comprises a mountainous mainland area and 236 offshore islands.

WHERE DO CHINA'S 1.3 BILLION PEOPLE LIVE?

About 80 percent of China's vast population lives in small, rural villages, and works on the land. The rest live in overcrowded cities, where housing is scarce. With the world's largest population, China has a huge task to provide all its citizens with food and education.

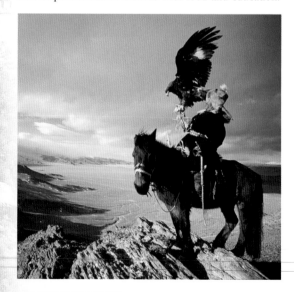

▲ MONGOLIAN HORSEMAN
Mongolians are some of the world's most accomplished horseback riders. Here, a Kazakh horseman hunts with a trained golden eagle. Kazakhs are the largest of Mongolia's ethnic minorities.

eastern Asia

◄ SHANGHAI, CHINA
International trade is transforming the east coast port of Shanghai, China's largest city. Home to more than nine million people, Shanghai is a leading industrial and commercial center with the world's busiest harbor. Its modern skyline is crowded with high-rise office buildings, convention centers, and modern shopping malls.

EASTERN ASIA
CHINA
Capital city: Beijing
Area: 3,705,386 sq miles (9,596,960 sq km)
Population: 1.3 billion
Official language: Mandarin Chinese
Major religion: Majority are nonreligious
Currency: Renminbi (called yuan)
MONGOLIA
Capital city: Ulan Bator
Area: 604,247 sq miles (1,565,000 sq km)
Population: 2.6 million
Official language: Khalkha Mongolian
Major religion: Tibetan Buddhist
Currency: Tugrik
NORTH KOREA
Capital city: Pyongyang
Area: 46,540 sq miles (120,540 sq km)
Population: 28.8 million
Official language: Korean
Major religion: Atheist
Currency: North Korean won
SOUTH KOREA
Capital city: Seoul
Area: 38,023 sq miles (98,480 sq km)
Population: 48.6 million
Official language: Korean
Major religions: Mahayana Buddhist and Protestant
Currency: South Korean won
TAIWAN
Capital city: Taipei
Area: 13,892 sq miles (35,980 sq km)
Population: 23.1 million
Official language: Mandarin Chinese
Major religion: Buddhist
Currency: Taiwan dollar
JAPAN
Capital city: Tokyo
Area: 145,882 sq miles (377,835 sq km)
Population: 127.7 million
Official language: Japanese
Major religions: Shinto and Buddhist
Currency: Yen

WHY ARE FISH IMPORTANT TO THE JAPANESE?
The mountainous islands of Japan have limited farmland, so the people depend on the sea for food. The fishing fleet, which is the largest in the world, catches about 6 million tons of fish each year. Fish is included in most Japanese cooking, and much of it is eaten raw.

A kimono is fastened by a broad sash called an obi

▲ JAPANESE CHILDREN WEARING KIMONOS
The Japanese often wear kimonos for special occasions. These traditional wide-sleeved, wraparound robes are made from colorful printed silks and tied at the back with a sash.

WHAT IS UNUSUAL ABOUT THE GOBI DESERT?
Unlike most deserts, the Gobi Desert in Mongolia has hot summers, but icy winters. The Bactrian camels that live in the Gobi have adapted by growing thick winter coats that molt in the spring. The desert, the fourth largest in the world, is made of rock and sand. It is famous for the discovery of fossilized bones and eggs of dinosaurs that lived here 85 million years ago.

WHICH STAPLE FOOD IS GROWN IN THE REGION?
Rice is the staple food of eastern Asia, and the region's farms must produce enough to feed the vast populations. The fertile, flooded rice fields of southern China produce two harvests every year. Planting and harvesting are still done by hand, and water buffalo or oxen pull farm machinery. In contrast, rice is intensively farmed in Japan with modern machinery.

◄ SEOUL, SOUTH KOREA
A busy shopping street in nighttime Seoul. South Korea's thriving capital is home to a quarter of the country's population.

WHY ARE THERE TWO KOREAS?
Korea was a single country until the end of World War II, when the north was occupied by the Russians and the south by the USA. In 1948, it was divided in two, and South Korea separated from North Korea. Hostilities between these countries led to the Korean War (1950–53). Today, South Korea specializes in producing and exporting manufactured goods. North Korea remains a politically isolated regime.

FIND OUT MORE ►► Cold War 435 • Dinosaurs 78–79 • Farming 66 • Fishing 67 • Imperial China 393

SOUTHEAST ASIA

Southeast Asia is made up of a large mainland peninsula, and a maritime area with 20,000 islands scattered through the Pacific and Indian Oceans. Much of the land in this region is mountainous and covered in dense, tropical forest.

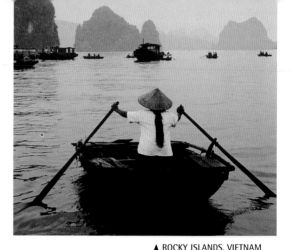

▲ ROCKY ISLANDS, VIETNAM
A Vietnamese woman rows her boat among the rocky limestone islands of Ha Long Bay. The beauty of the coastline draws many tourists to this area on the Red River delta.

HOW DOES DEFORESTATION AFFECT THE REGION?
Deforestation in Indonesia, Thailand, Burma, and Laos has destroyed the habitats of many rare plants and animals, such as tigers and wild elephants. It has also caused flooding and soil erosion. Some trees, such as teak, are logged for their timber; others are felled to create farmland, and replanting is rare. Thailand took the step of banning commercial logging in 1989.

HOW IS RICE FARMING CHANGING IN THE REGION?
In the last 20 years, rice farmers have been planting new species of high-quality rice, which produce a greater yield. These, along with new, intensive rice-planting programs and sophisticated machinery, have helped some countries, such as Indonesia, raise living standards. Indonesia is now the world's third-largest rice producer. Rice is a staple food of the region and grows well in the warm, humid climate.

WHY DOES SOUTHEAST ASIA HAVE A RICH TRADITION OF PERFORMING ARTS?
The music, dance, and drama of southeast Asia derive from the region's religious traditions. Cambodia's highly stylized classical dances are based on 12th-century Hindu dances, while much of Indonesian drama retells Hindu myths. Indonesia is also famous for its shadow puppet shows.

southeast Asia

A rich headdress and jewelry transform the dancer into a goddess or other divine being

Hand gestures convey a specific meaning

CAMBODIAN CLASSICAL DANCER ▶
In her traditional close-fitting silk costume, a dancer performs the graceful movements of a classical Cambodian dance.

Terraces were cut by hand about 2,000 years ago

Stone walls prevent major soil erosion on the hillsides

▲ RICE TERRACES, PHILIPPINES
The stone walls on these ancient rice terraces in the Philippines help to retain the water in the fields at each level. Rice has been cultivated in southeast Asia for 7,000 years.

New Zealand

◀ **GREAT BARRIER REEF, AUSTRALIA**
The Great Barrier Reef stretches for 1,242` miles (2,000 km) in the Pacific Ocean. It is a major attraction to tourists in glass-bottom boats and divers, who come to see the huge variety of wildlife. This includes 350 species of brightly colored corals, 1,500 species of fish, sea anemones, giant clams, and many different types of sponges.

WHY IS THE GREAT BARRIER REEF UNDER THREAT?

Each year, thousands of tourists visit the Great Barrier Reef, causing damage and pollution to what is the largest coral reef in the world. The fragile reef lies off the northeast coast of Australia, and is home to a huge variety of underwater life. Constructed by tiny creatures over thousands of years, the reef is also threatened by infestations of the crown of thorns starfish, which devours large areas of coral in a day.

WHO WERE THE FIRST PEOPLE IN NEW ZEALAND?

New Zealand was uninhabited until the Maori people came to settle from Pacific islands over 1,000 years ago. Later in the 19th century, European settlers arrived in the country. In recent years, there has been an influx of non-Maori Polynesians and Asians, adding to this multicultural society. Today, Maoris—the original inhabitants—make up about 12 percent of New Zealand's total population.

WHAT SIGHTS CAN YOU SEE IN NEW ZEALAND'S NATIONAL PARKS?

Nearly 13 percent of New Zealand's land lies inside national parks. The rugged mountains, huge glaciers, lakes, fjords, and forests are ideal for hiking, sailing, white-water rafting, and other outdoor pursuits. The spectacular scenery also includes active volcanoes, spouting geysers, and boiling mud pools.

GEYSERS, NEW ZEALAND ▶
Geysers are found where volcanic rocks inside the Earth heat water in underground chasms to the boiling point. It erupts as a fountain of scalding water and steam up to 1,509 ft (460 m) high.

◀ **NEW ZEALAND SHEEP**
Since the introduction of refrigerated ships, New Zealand sheep have been raised for meat. Frozen lamb is a major export to Asia, Europe, and the US.

WHY ARE THERE SO MANY SHEEP IN THE REGION?

New Zealand's damp climate and rich pasture make sheep farming the country's biggest industry. With over 44 million sheep (about 11 sheep for every person), wool and lamb are major exports. Australia is the world's chief wool-producing country. Its 120 million sheep are raised on huge farms called stations, where farmers use light aircraft to patrol up to 5,792 sq miles (15,000 sq km) of land.

FIND OUT MORE ▸▸ Cnidarians 103 • First Modern Humans 362–363 • Islands 42 • Mammals 120–123 • Polynesia 396

ANTARCTICA

The freezing, inhospitable continent of Antarctica was the last place on Earth to be explored. It is a vast, mountainous land mass at the South Pole, buried under an ice sheet up to 2.5 miles (4 km) thick, and surrounded by frozen seas.

Antarctica has no countries and no permanent population. With winter temperatures falling to –122˚F (–80˚C), its sole inhabitants are visiting research scientists.

WHO OWNS ANTARCTICA?

Antarctica does not belong to any nation, but is governed under an international treaty that bars countries from owning or exploiting its land. The 1959 Antarctic Treaty, signed by 45 nations, suspended the claims of seven countries for territory in the region. Today, Antarctica is designated as "a continent for science," and only used for peaceful purposes.

WHAT DO SCIENTISTS STUDY IN ANTARCTICA?

Scientists from all over the world visit Antarctica to study the climate, weather, geology, and wildlife of this unique region. Their research has helped to highlight global problems, such as climate change. During the summer, about 3,700 scientists work in the 46 or more scientific research stations scattered across the continent. Only about 1,200 scientists remain in winter because of the intense cold.

SOUTHERN OCEAN

South Orkney Islands
Orcadas (Argentina)
Signy (U.K.)

Sanae (South Africa)
Maitri (India)
Georg von Neumayer (Germany)
Novolazarevskaya (Russian Federation)
Cape Norvegia

Scotia Sea

Drake Passage

Capitán Arturo Prat (Chile)
General Bernardo O'Higgins (Chile)
Esperanza (Argentina)
Marambio (Argentina)
South Shetland Islands

Lyddan Island
Brunt Ice Shelf
Stancomb-Wills Glacier
Halley (U.K.)
Coats Land
Belgrano II (Argentina)

Dronning Maud Land

Palmer (U.S.)
Faraday (U.K.)
Rothera (U.K.)
San Martín (Argentina)
Jason Peninsula
Larsen Ice Shelf
Antarctic Peninsula

Weddell Sea

Mount Jackson 13,746 ft (4,190 m)

Filchner Ice Shelf
Recovery Glacier

Antarctic Circle

Alexander Island
Wilkins Ice Shelf
Smyley Island

Ronne Ice Shelf
Berkner Island

ANTARCTICA

Support Force Glacier
Pensacola Mountains

Limit of winter pack ice

Bellingshausen Sea

Peter I Island (Norway)

Limit of summer pack ice

Thurston Island

Bear Peninsula

Amundsen Sea

Carney Island

Vinson Massif 16,066 ft (4,897 m)

Ellsworth Land
Pine Island Glacier

Mount Seelig 9,915 ft (3,022 m)

Whitmore Mountains

Lesser Antarctica

Amundsen-Scott (U.S.) South Pole

Transantarctic Mountains

Beardmore Glacier
Mount Kirkpatrick 14,855 ft (4,528 m)
Nimrod Glacier
Mount Markham 14,275 ft (4,351 m)

Marie Byrd Land

Mount Sidley 13,717 ft (4,181 m)

Siple Coast

Ross Ice Shelf

Mount Siple 10,170 ft (3,100 m)
Russkaya (Russian Federation)

Roosevelt Island

Mount Liste 13,208 ft (4,026 m)
Scott Base (New Zealand)

Edward VII Peninsula

Mount Erebus 12,447 ft (3,794 m)
McMurdo Base (U.S.)

SOUTHERN OCEAN

Ross Sea

Coulman Island

Mount Minto 13,658 ft (4,163 m)
Cape Adare

Antarctic Circle

◄ PENGUIN COLONY, ANTARCTICA
Emperor penguins feed on fish and spend most of the year at sea. They come onto the ice to breed in huge colonies called rookeries.

◀ **AMUNDSEN-SCOTT BASE**
The American-owned Amundsen-Scott research station, named after two Antarctic explorers, is situated at the South Pole. It is insulated against the intense cold, and parts are built below the surface in order to conserve heat.

ANTARCTICA

Total land area: 5.4 million sq miles (14 million sq km)

Total population: no indigenous inhabitants, but there are seasonally staffed research stations

Number of countries: 0

Highest point: Vinson Massif 16,066 ft (4,897 m)

Major deserts: the continent is technically a desert

Largest island: Alexander Island

Lowest temperature on Earth: −128.6°F (−89.2°C) recorded at Vostok Station

ARCTIC

The Arctic region lies around the North Pole. It is a small, frozen ocean surrounded by the northern edges of Europe, Asia, and North America, whose flat, bleak landscape is known as the tundra. The region is a cold and hostile environment and few people live there. The Arctic Ocean, however, teems with wildlife.

◀ **POLAR BEAR ON ARCTIC ICE**
A polar bear's thick white fur protects it from the cold and provides camouflage as it hunts for seals and other animals.

WHICH ANIMALS CAN SURVIVE IN THE ARCTIC?

The Arctic Ocean is home to seals, walruses, and many species of whales, which thrive in the icy waters, protected by thick layers of blubber. In the warmer summer months, animals such as reindeer, musk oxen, hares, and Arctic foxes hunt for food on land, but they migrate south during the harsh winter.

Antarctica map labels

Limit of summer pack ice
Antarctic Circle
Asuka (Japan)
Syowa (Japan)
Thorshavnheiane
Thyer Glacier
Molodezhnaya (Russian Federation)
Mount Victor 8,491 ft (2,588 m)
Enderby Land
Mount Elkins 7,546 ft (2,300 m)
Kemp Land
SOUTHERN OCEAN
Mac. Robertson Land
Mawson (Australia)
Mount Menzies 11,007 ft (3,355 m)
Lars Christensen Coast
Cape Darnley
Lambert Glacier
Amery Ice Shelf
Mackenzie Bay
Princess Elizabeth Land
Zhongshan (China)
Davis (Australia)
West Ice Shelf
Greater
Mikhaylov Island
Philippi Glacier
Antarctica
Wilhelm II Land
Mirny (Russian Federation)
Davis Sea
Masson Island
Vostok (Russian Federation)
South Geomagnetic Pole
Shackleton Ice Shelf
Wilkes Land
Vincennes Bay
Casey (Australia)
Sabrina Coast
Cape Poinsett
Banzare Coast
Limit of summer pack ice
Terre Adélie
Cape Keltie
George V Land
Dumont d'Urville (France)
Leningradskaya (Russian Federation)
Cape Gray
Cape Hudson
Dumont d'Urville Sea
Victoria Land

Antarctica

Arctic map labels

NORTH AMERICA
ALASKA (U.S.)
Bering Strait
RUSSIAN FEDERATION
CANADA
Arctic Circle
Beaufort Sea
East Siberian Sea
Permanent pack ice
Limit of summer pack ice
ASIA
Queen Elizabeth Islands
ARCTIC
North Pole
Kara Sea
Baffin Island
OCEAN
Greenland (Denmark)
Svalbard (Norway)
Barents Sea
Baffin Bay
Greenland Sea
Arctic Circle
EUROPE
ICELAND
Limit of winter pack ice

Arctic

0 km 800
0 miles 800

FIND OUT MORE ▸▸ Canada, Alaska, and Greenland 224–225 • Habitats 82–84 • Human Impact 64–65 • Ice 58

SOCIETY and BELIEFS

RELIGION

Religion involves belief in divine beings along with a set of practices and a moral code that help to reinforce that belief. A religion's teachings, usually written down in a holy book, and its stories are intended to help people to understand the meaning of life. Each religion has its own idea of the ultimate goal of life, its own place for worshiping ▶▶ GOD or gods, its own rituals, and its own rules for living.

▲ **ILLUMINATED GOSPEL**
Before printing was invented, holy books were beautifully written out by scribes. Christian Bibles, like this 1503 New Testament in ancient Greek from Moldavia in present-day Romania, were all hand-copied in monasteries by monks.

◀ **HOLY RIVER**
The Ganges River, also worshiped as the goddess Ganga, is considered the holiest of all rivers by Hindus. Pilgrims drink, bathe, and scatter their loved ones' ashes in the sacred waters in an act of spiritual purification.

Hindu pilgrims ritually wash themselves in the Ganges during a religious festival in the holy city of Varanasi (Benares)

ARE THERE MANY RELIGIONS?

Religions are not easy to count. Islam, Judaism, and Christianity share some common origins, but are all separate. Each of these may contain more recent differences, such as Sunni and Shia Muslims, or Catholic and Protestant Christians.

GOD

Most religions believe in one god or many gods. A god is a supernatural being, with power over human lives. In some religions, believers pray to their god or gods for help. In others, they use meditation to help them focus on their duties.

DO ALL FAITHS HAVE A GOD?

Although Buddhists share common roots with Hindus, they worship no gods but instead use Buddha's teachings to encourage spiritual progress. Confucians strive for cosmic harmony by creating a society based on order and virtue. Many local religions worship spirits that inhabit the natural world around them.

WHY IS THERE SUFFERING IN THE WORLD?

Each religion has its own explanation for suffering. Often it is seen as punishment for sin, or bad behavior. People may be tricked into being bad by a devil figure, or they may be misled by their own desires. Western religions generally see suffering as the result of human failings. Eastern religions see it as the result of human ignorance.

WHO DOES NOT HAVE FAITH?
Atheists reject all belief in supernatural beings. Agnostics argue that it is impossible to know if God exists. Humanists replace faith with human reason. Many people are nonreligious, but may describe themselves as having spiritual beliefs.

HOW DO WE LEARN A RELIGION?
Young people usually learn a religion by following the same beliefs and rituals as their parents. Most religions use teachings and stories to inform children about, for example, ▶▶ CREATION . Some religions also try to convince other people to join their faith.

DO RELIGIONS HAVE ALL THE ANSWERS?
As people grow up, they start to ask all kinds of questions: "What is the meaning of life?"; "Why do people suffer?"; "Does God exist?" The world's religions have all sought in different ways to provide answers to these questions. Where Western religions tend to focus on obedience to God and salvation from sin, Eastern religions tend to focus on self-knowledge and release from the cycle of rebirth.

WHY DO PEOPLE BECOME RELIGIOUS?
The mysteries of the natural world and the Universe have inspired religious feelings throughout time. Today, science can explain much but not everything, and people still use religion to help them explain events and their place in the world.

FAITHS AND FOLLOWERS (A ROUGH GUIDE BASED ON CENSUSES)	
BELIEFS	*NUMBER OF FOLLOWERS*
Christianity	2.1 billion
Islam	1.5 billion
Nonreligious	920 million
Hinduism	900 million
Confucianism/Taoism	540 million
Buddhism	330 million
Shintoism	119 million
Sikhism	26 million
Judaism	14 million
Zoroastrianism	150,000

▲ RELIGIOUS UNITY
These religious leaders are marching for peace in the world. They include a Jewish rabbi, a Muslim sheikh, a Christian bishop, and a Japanese Buddhist monk, showing how universal goals can rise above religious differences.

CREATION

Many religions have their own story about the origins of the Universe and of humankind. Called creation stories, these often pass on ancient insights about humanity and its relation to the natural world. Some view the scientific Big Bang theory as another creation story.

HOW DID THE WORLD BEGIN?
Some religions have complex stories about the gods who gave birth to the world. Australian Aboriginal beliefs recount a Dreamtime when mythic ancestors roamed Earth, creating the landscape by their actions. Judaism and Christianity describe a world that was created in seven days by God's command.

DO RELIGIONS BELIEVE IN EVERLASTING LIFE?
Most religions follow their own calendar. The Mayan calendar of Central America predicts that the current epoch will end in 2012. Hindus and Buddhists believe that time is cyclical, so everything is reborn over and over again, including the world. Christians and Muslims believe that time is linear and that the world will end with a Day of Judgment.

▲ NAVAJO YEI RUG
The Yei figures in this American Indian rug were originally only shown during the healing Night Chant ritual, when medicine men (healer-priests) created their images on the ground with colored sand.

Yei are sacred beings, possibly ancestors, worshiped by the Navajo

FIND OUT MORE ▶▶ Southern Asia 266–267 • Universe 26

ANCIENT RELIGIONS

Some religions have died out, along with the cultures that practiced them. We know about them and their practices, such as belief in the ▶▶ AFTERLIFE , through their buildings and artifacts. Some of the best-known are from Egypt, Greece, and Mexico.

WHO WAS RA?

The Egyptian sun god Ra could be shown with the head of a falcon, a ram, or an old man. Like many long-lived religions, Ancient Egyptian beliefs combined gods from several local religions.

WHO WORSHIPED A FEATHERED SNAKE?

The Feather Serpent god, Quetzalcoatl, was worshiped for over a 1000 years by the Aztecs in Ancient Mexico. He was also the god of fertility and wind. When the Spanish conquistador Cortés landed in Mexico, the Aztec ruler believed he was returning Quetzalcoatl.

ARE THE OLD GODS STILL WITH US?

The names of the Ancient Roman and Greek gods are still used in Western naming systems. All the planets of the Solar System (aside from Earth) are named after Roman gods. The swift-footed messenger god Mercury gives his name to a silvery liquid metal.

▲ MARS, GOD OF WAR
Mars, the Roman god of war, gave his name to the fourth planet of the Solar System, the month of March, martial arts (fighting skills), and martial law (military rule).

▲ REACHING TO THE HEAVENS
Central American cultures such as the Zapotecs (forerunners of the Aztecs) built pyramid temples with stairs leading to platforms for human sacrifice (top). In Japan, Mount Fuji (above) is sacred to Shintoism.

AFTERLIFE

The idea of an afterlife—what happens to people after they die—has been around as long as the oldest religions. Ancient rulers were often buried with large numbers of useful items, such as model boats and food, to help them live on in the next world.

ancient religions

◀ EGYPTIAN MUMMY
The corpses of Egyptian nobles were mummified, so that they were preserved for the afterlife. Internal organs were carefully removed and kept in sealed jars near the body.

WHAT IS A SOUL?

Many religions believe that there is an eternal, godlike part in people, called a soul or spirit. Some religions, such as Hinduism, believe that all living things have a soul. After death, the soul returns to Earth in a new body, or goes on to inhabit heaven or hell.

WHAT WERE THE PYRAMIDS?

Some Ancient Egyptian pharaohs were buried in huge pyramids. These monumental tombs symbolically pointed to the stars to guide the pharaoh's soul on its journey to the heavens. The most famous pyramids are the three in Giza, near Cairo.

FIND OUT MORE ▶▶ Ancient Egypt 370–371 • Conquistadors 405

LOCAL RELIGIONS

Local religions are unique to tribal or cultural groups living apart from modern societies. They are not taught through texts, but through story-telling, art, songs, and ⏩ RITUALS. Many honor their ancestors as well as gods or natural spirits.

ULURU ▶
This huge red rock (also known as Ayers Rock) in the heart of the Northern Territory, Australia, is the most sacred place for the Aboriginal people.

WHY ARE SOME PLACES SACRED?
Sacred places always have a special importance to the life of the tribe. They may be a source of water, a gathering point, a site of ancestor activities, or a border with another group's territory. Sometimes they are used as burial grounds for the dead.

WHO WORSHIPS ANCESTORS?
Offering gifts and prayers to dead ancestors is a common feature of local religious ritual throughout the world, especially in Asia. The dead are believed to help their living relatives, and to intervene with the gods on their behalf.

WHAT IS A FETISH FOR?
Fetishes are portable, carved, and customized objects that are believed to be the home for a spirit or to possess magical powers. The owner of the fetish may use it to borrow the powers of that spirit or simply as protection against bad luck or bad health.

TOTEM POLE ▶
Totem poles are mainly found among the tribal peoples of the northwest coast of North America. The carvings represent the different clans (symbolized by animal spirits) to which the owner belongs.

RITUALS

Like all world religions, local religions have rituals—special performances of words and actions that help to bind the community together in a common identity. Rituals may mark a rite of passage, such as marriage, or be a call for help from the spirit world.

WHAT IS A SHAMAN?
Most local religions have a shaman, or "medicine man," who possesses secret knowledge and uses spells, rituals, and traditional knowledge of medicinal plants or animals to help those who need healing or spiritual help.

SHAMAN DANCING ▶
This Dayak shaman from Indonesia is performing a ceremonial dance. Shamans often use dance to enter altered states of consciousness in order to communicate with the spirit world.

local religions

FIND OUT MORE ⏩ Canada, Alaska, and Greenland 224–225

ZOROASTRIANISM

Zoroaster (or Zarathustra) lived around the 13th century BCE in Iran. He taught that people should choose between the opposing forces of good and evil. His teachings were highly influential on later religions.

WHAT MAKES A PARSI?

Zoroastrianism was the official religion of the Persian Empire. When that empire fell, some of its followers, after a period of much religious persecution, moved to India, where they became known as Parsis ("people from Persia"). Young Parsis are initiated into the faith at the age of seven, in a ceremony called Navjote.

HOW DO PARSIS WORSHIP?

Zoroastrian religious buildings are called Fire Temples. Zoroastrians perform prayer rituals before a sacred fire, where incense and sandalwood are burned. This is believed to represent the god Ahura Mazda, source of light and life. Zarathustra's teachings are read or sung from the sacred Avesta scripture.

NAVJOTE INITIATION ▶
A young initiate receives the kusti, or sacred thread, which is wrapped three times around the waist, and undone during prayers.

Three layers of feathers on the wings represent good words, good thoughts, and good deeds, while the three layers on the tail represent the opposite

Zoroastrianism

FARAVAHAR ▶
This symbol, known as the faravahar, represents the immortal human soul, and by extension the Zoroastrian religion. Its human face indicates its connection to humankind.

FIND OUT MORE ▶▶ Persian Empire 375 • Western Asia and the Middle East 264–265

SHINTO

Shinto ("the way of the gods") is Japan's oldest religion and centers on the worship of kami, or spirits. These are believed to inhabit any powerful or impressive natural phenomena, such as the wind or Mount Fuji.

WHEN DID SHINTO BEGIN?

No one knows how old Shinto is, for its origins lie deep in prehistory. Its main elements probably appeared from the 4th century BCE onward. Although most Shinto worship relates to earthly kami, Shinto texts written around 700 CE also mention heavenly kami, who are responsible for creating the world.

▲ MATSURI PARADE
The matsuri, or festival is a shrine's most important annual event. Local people carry an image of the local kami through the streets in a portable shrine or mikoshi. The ceremony blesses both the neighborhood and the carriers.

TORII GATE ▲
The distinctive torii arch symbolizes the border between the human world and the kami world. The best-known example is the floating torii off the island of Miyajima, near Hiroshima.

◀ AMATERASU EMERGES
The most important kami is the sun goddess Amaterasu, who is also associated with the imperial family. Here she is shown emerging from her cave and restoring sunlight to the world.

WHAT MARKS A SACRED PLACE?

Followers of Shinto consider nature to be sacred, so their places of worship are often found in beautiful natural settings. Natural sacred places are marked with a thick rope (shimenawa) tied around a tree or rock. Shinto shrines, which are built to house at least one kami, are marked by a simple torii, or gateway.

Shinto

FIND OUT MORE ▶▶ Eastern Asia 268–269 • Local Religions 283

CONFUCIANISM

Kong Fuzi ("Master Kong"), known as Confucius to Western cultures, was a wise man who lived in China from 551 to 479 BCE. His teachings focused on the proper relationships between people, including respect for one's parents and ancestors, and the creation of a harmonious society based on virtue.

Confucius carries the five classic scrolls

Confucianism

DO PEOPLE WORSHIP CONFUCIUS?

Kong Fuzi made no claim to holiness, and taught that living a good life is its own reward. After his death, his teachings were developed by his followers and spread to Korea, Japan, and Vietnam. His followers worship his soul as a great ancestor.

WHAT ARE THE FIVE CLASSICS?

Confucianism consists of five classic texts—*History*, *Poetry*, *Rituals*, *Seasons*, and the *I Ching*, or *Book of Changes*. The *I Ching* helps people cope with uncertainty by offering them the chance to predict the future.

◄ **CONFUCIAN TEMPLE**
Although Confucians do not worship gods, they honor their ancestors in temples, like this one in Taiwan.

CONFUCIUS ►
The writings of Confucius were originally intended as advice for the rulers of China. One of his most famous lines was: "Rule by the power of moral example."

FIND OUT MORE ►► China's First Empire 378

Laozi carries a scroll of the Daode Jing

DAOISM

Followers of Daoism (or Taoism), another Chinese religion, believe that humans should live in harmony with the universe. Dao ("the way") is the force that keeps the universe balanced and ordered. The best way to act or think is by following *wuwei*, or effortless action.

▲ **YIN AND YANG**
The Daoist Universe is made up of two opposite but balancing forces. Yin is female, dark, fluid, and low energy. Yang is male, fiery, solid, and high energy.

Daoism

WHO FOUNDED DAOISM?

Laozi ("the old master"), who lived in China in the 6th century BCE, wrote the *Daode Jing*, whose teachings form the cornerstone of Daoism. According to tradition, Laozi served as archivist in the royal court and knew Confucius. When Laozi decided to go on a spiritual pilgrimage, he was not allowed to leave China until he had written down all his teachings.

◄ **LAOZI ON A BUFFALO**
There are several legends about the life of Laozi, but very little is known for certain. He is said to have traveled around China on the back of a water buffalo.

WHAT IS QI?

The principle of qi lies at the root of Chinese life and belief. It is the vital substance that makes up the universe and is composed of two complementary energy forces: yin and yang. The Chinese believe that qi runs through energy lines in our bodies and that when these lines are blocked, ill health results. Acupuncture uses needles to unblock them.

FIND OUT MORE ►► China's First Empire 378

HINDUISM

Hinduism is one of the world's oldest religions and the main religious tradition of India. More a way of life than a set of beliefs, it has no individual founder. It developed slowly over a long period of time out of a variety of local religions.

WHAT IS BRAHMAN?
Many Hindus believe that beneath this variety there is one unchanging reality known as Brahman, the eternal creative force that made the Universe and to which all things return. Hindus believe that human souls are reborn in cycles of ▶▶ REINCARNATION.

DO HINDU GODS LIVE IN STATUES?
Images are powerful symbols of the presence of a god and offerings are often made before them. The most popular gods include the elephant-headed Ganesh, symbol of wealth and success, and the monkey god Hanuman, symbol of heroism and loyalty.

▲ SACRED SOUND
The sacred symbol *Om* (or *Aum*) is a mantra (repeated sound) that represents Brahman and is often used to help meditation.

SHIVA THE DANCER ▶
The god Shiva symbolizes both destruction and creation. He is shown here dancing on the body of a demon, with a hoop of flames around him to represent the energy of the Universe.

▲ FESTIVAL OF COLOR
Holi marks the start of spring. During the day, people visit and greet one another, and commemorate the mischievous pranks of the god Krishna by throwing colored water and powder over one another.

Hinduism

▲ "HAIL TO KRISHNA"
Hare Krishnas belong to a branch of Hinduism that was established in the US in the 1960s by A.C. Bhaktivedanta. They honor Krishna, one of Vishnu's incarnations, and their name comes from the devotional mantra they chant: "Hare Krishna" ("Hail to Krishna").

BRAHMA ▶
Brahma the creator (not to be confused with Brahman) has four heads, in order to see in all directions. Together with Vishnu the preserver and Shiva the destroyer, these gods are known to Hindus as the Trimurti, or "three forms."

◀ HOLY SADHU
Sadhus are wandering holy men who have cut all family ties, own nothing, and live on alms. They devote their life to gaining wisdom and achieving *moksha* (release from the cycle of rebirth).

REINCARNATION

Hindus believe that living things do not have just one life but are trapped in a cycle of death and rebirth, known as samsara. People are reborn into higher or lower social positions depending on their actions in their current life.

DID BUDDHISM LEARN FROM HINDUISM?
Buddhism is not interested in whether God exists, or how and why the world was created. Instead, it focuses on the Hindu idea of the cycle of rebirth and how to achieve nirvana, or release from this cycle, by freeing its followers from greed, hatred, and ignorance.

FIND OUT MORE ▶▶ Buddhism 289 • Southern Asia 266–267

JUDAISM

Judaism is the world's oldest religion based on belief in one God. Jews believe that God made them his chosen people and promised them a land of their own, Israel, in return for following his commandments. These are laid down in the sacred text of the ▸▸ TORAH .

The rabbi is the spiritual leader of the synagogue

A yarmulka, or kippa, is a skullcap used to cover the head as a sign of respect for God

A tallit is a prayer shawl with knotted fringes

HOW MANY TYPES OF JUDAISM ARE THERE?

Religious Jews are divided into two main groups: Orthodox and Non-Orthodox. Orthodox Jews unquestioningly obey the Torah and all its rules. Non-Orthodox Jews try to adapt Judaism to modern life. Both groups observe the Jewish ▸▸ HOLY DAYS .

HOW DO YOUNG BOYS COME OF AGE?

At the age of 13, a boy is considered an adult and becomes bar mitzvah ("son of the covenant") after a ceremony of the same name. This takes place in the place of worship, the synagogue, and is followed by a big party to celebrate the occasion.

STAR OF DAVID ▶
The six pointed Star of David was used as far back as the 14th century. The star has 12 sides, symbolizing the 12 tribes of Israel unified by King David. Today, it is the main symbol on the Israeli flag.

BAR MITZVAH ▲
When a boy attends his bar mitzvah, he reads from the Torah scroll in the synagogue for the first time.

Yad is the silver pointer used to follow the text

The Sefer Torah, or Torah scroll, is the most sacred object in Judaism

TORAH

The most sacred texts of Judaism are the first five books of the Hebrew Scriptures, which are known as the Torah or Book of Law. Orthodox tradition believes that God spoke the words of the Torah directly to Moses. Every synagogue keeps a beautifully hand-written Torah scroll in an ark (cupboard) facing Jerusalem.

IS THE TORAH JUDAISM'S ONLY SCRIPTURE?

The Hebrew Bible (known to Christians as the Old Testament) consists of the Torah and two other books: The Prophets and The Writings. The Talmud, which contains Jewish law and writings of the ancient rabbis, is also important.

Judaism

HOLY DAYS

Jewish families come together to mark major festivals throughout the year, including Yom Kippur (Day of Atonement), Pesach (Passover), and Rosh Hashanah (New Year). One of the most important commandments is to observe the Sabbath as a day of rest.

◀ LIGHTING THE MENORAH
The eight-day celebration of Hanukkah, or festival of lights, is marked by lighting one extra candle each night on the menorah (a nine-branched candlestick).

WHAT IS THE SABBATH?

The Sabbath (Shabbat in Hebrew) is the Jewish holy day. It begins at sunset on Friday and lasts until sunset on Saturday. It is a day of rest when no work—not even cooking—may be done. It honors the belief that God rested on the seventh day of Creation.

FIND OUT MORE ▸▸ Christianity 288 • Middle East 264–265 • Middle Eastern Empires 372–373

CHRISTIANITY

Christians believe in one God with three aspects: God the father, God the son (Jesus Christ), and God the Holy Spirit. Jesus's role as the Messiah, who lived around 2,000 years ago, is revealed in the ▸▸ BIBLE .

▲ THE CROSS
Jesus was nailed to a wooden cross by the Romans and left to die—a method of execution known as crucifixion.

WHY IS JESUS CALLED KING OF THE JEWS?
Judaism teaches that a Messiah, or holy king, will come to Earth to complete God's plan for humankind. Christians believe that Jesus (who was born a Jew) is this Messiah, while Jews believe he was a prophet, preparing the way for a Messiah yet to come.

WHAT DOES THE CROSS MEAN?
The cross symbolizes the death and ▸▸ RESURRECTION of Christ. Christians believe that Jesus's death brought salvation, by taking away their sins. When Christians are baptized, they are marked with the sign of the cross in remembrance of this sacrifice.

▲ ST. BASIL THE BLESSED, MOSCOW
This distinctive 16th-century Russian cathedral belongs to the Orthodox tradition of Christianity. This tradition, based in eastern Europe, split from the Roman Catholic Church, and its leader the Pope, in the 11th century.

Flag with a red cross is a symbol of Christ's resurrection

+ I + AM + THE + RESVRRECTION + AND + THE + LIFE +

Angels are God's messengers and helpers

THE RESURRECTION ▲
This 19th-century stained-glass window from Lincoln Cathedral, England, shows Jesus rising from the dead. Christians celebrate this event during the Easter festival.

Jesus rising from the tomb

Wounds on Jesus's hands and feet show where he was nailed to the cross

Christianity

RESURRECTION

Christians believe that Jesus Christ came to life three days after his death and rose up to heaven to live again at the right hand of God. His resurrection is a symbol of hope for all Christians.

HOW LONG DID JESUS LIVE ON EARTH?
Jesus Christ lived in Roman-occupied Palestine. He was the son of Mary and Joseph. He worked as a carpenter before becoming a religious teacher. His teachings upset the Roman and religious authorities, and he was executed at the age of 33.

BIBLE

The Christian scripture is called the Bible. It combines the Jewish Old Testament with the Christian New Testament that includes accounts of Jesus's teachings and those of his followers.

DO CHRISTIANS THINK THE BIBLE IS TRUE?
Many Christians regard the Bible as the sacred word of God and literally true. Others view it as a mixture of history, stories, poems, and parables that can be interpreted in a more symbolic way.

MANUSCRIPT BIBLE ▶
Before the age of printing, the Bible was carefully hand-copied in Latin or Greek, usually by monks in monasteries, and sold to rich, well-educated people.

FIND OUT MORE ▸▸ Crusades 389 • Judaism 287

BUDDHISM

Buddhism was developed in India about 2,500 years ago by Siddhartha Gautama, or Buddha ("the enlightened one"). He reinterpreted Hindu ideas about ▶ KARMA and rebirth to show how suffering could be avoided. His teachings spread throughout eastern Asia.

▲ BUDDHA'S FOOTPRINTS
This relief sculpture shows Buddha's footprints on a pillar at the Great Stupa of Sanchi, India, built by King Ashoka.

WHAT IS MEDITATION FOR?
The Buddha is believed to have found nirvana (enlightenment) while meditating under a bodhi tree. Meditation involves emptying the mind of all thoughts and distractions in order to achieve inner peace and greater understanding.

DO BUDDHISTS HAVE SACRED BUILDINGS?
Many Buddhists visit temples or shrines to pay homage to Buddha or ask for his help. The oldest style of Buddhist shrine is a stupa (a bell-shaped mound) and holds holy relics. Chinese and Japanese shrines are multistory towers, known as pagodas.

▲ BUDDHIST MONKS
These young monks from Thailand wear distinctive saffron-colored robes and live in a monastic community called the Sangha. Monks and nuns may start their training as early as five years old.

Buddhism

KARMA

Karma refers to the idea that a person's good or bad actions have consequences in this and future lives. Buddhists believe that the inequality of mankind is the result of karma accumulated over many lives, but that it is always open to change.

WHAT IS NIRVANA?
Nirvana is enlightenment, which means freedom from the cycle of rebirth and suffering, and is imagined as a blissful, everlasting state. This is reached when a person is completely free from greed, hatred, and ignorance, and attachments to the human world. Unlike Hindus, Buddhists do not believe in an everlasting individual soul.

TIBETAN PRAYER WHEEL ▶
The wheel contains hundreds of mantras (short prayers) written on a paper scroll. Spinning the wheel releases these mantras into the world.

▲ MANDALA
A mandala is an image of the heavenly realm used to help focus meditation. Monks made this mandala over many months by sprinkling colored sand on the ground. They made it for a young monk's initiation ritual and will destroy it at the end.

◀ ENLIGHTENED BUDDHA
Many statues of Buddha capture his enlightenment and usually show him sitting cross-legged or lying on his side. This 98-ft- (30-m-) high statue is one of four at Kyaikpun pagoda in Bago, Myanmar (formerly known as Burma).

FIND OUT MORE ▶▶ Southern Asia 266–267 • Hinduism 286

ISLAM

Islam means obedience to the will of Allah (God) and honors the laws and teachings revealed to his prophet Muhammad in the sacred book known as the ▶▶ QUR'AN. Followers of Islam are called Muslims ("obedient ones").

WHERE DO MUSLIMS WORSHIP?

Muslims can pray anywhere, but often gather in a mosque to pray together. A mosque usually has a minaret tower, from which a muezzin (crier) chants a call to prayer five times a day. All Muslims pray facing toward Mecca, and a small niche (mihrab) is always set into the mosque wall nearest Mecca.

WHY DO MUSLIMS PRAY TOWARD MECCA?

Mecca in Saudi Arabia is Muhammad's birthplace and the holiest city of Islam. Muslims believe that, in 610 CE, Muhammad received the first of his revelations from God on a mountain outside Mecca. All Muslims are supposed to make the ▶▶ HAJJ at least once in a lifetime,

▲ KA'BA
When Muslim pilgrims arrive in Mecca, they must walk seven times around the Ka'ba, a shrine covered in a black cloth.

WOMAN PRAYING ▶
A Muslim woman prays to Allah in a part of the mosque separated from the men. The designs on the carpet direct her attention toward Mecca, and her head is covered as a mark of respect.

▲ MOSQUE IN DJENNE, MALI
Islamic architecture tends to reflect its surroundings. This 14th-century African mosque in Djenne, once a major center of trade and learning, is built of mud and shaped like a fort.

▲ CRESCENT MOON
The hilal, or crescent moon, has become the recognized symbol of Islam. It has ancient connections with Islamic dynasties and also links the lunar calendar to Muslim religious life.

HAJJ

The Hajj is a pilgrimage to Mecca made once in every Muslim's lifetime, if it is possible. It is one of the five Pillars of Islam—which also include the statement of faith, daily worship, charity, and fasting.

WHAT IS THE KA'BA?

The Ka'ba is a holy shrine at the heart of Mecca's Sacred Mosque. Muslims believe it was originally built by Ibrahim (Abraham) on a site made holy by the first man, Adam. In the pre-Islamic period it was a shrine to 360 Arabic deities. In 630 CE, Muhammad rededicated the shrine to Allah.

QUR'AN

Also spelled Koran, this is Islam's holiest text, believed to have been revealed to Muhammad by Allah. The Qur'an unites all Muslims in a single language—they must learn Arabic to read Allah's original words.

Islam

HOW DOES THE QUR'AN SPEAK?

The Arabic name Qur'an means "the recital." Muhammad's first revelation began with the angel Gabriel's instruction, "Recite!" The verses (Ayat) and chapters (Surahs) are arranged to help reading aloud. Marks show when to breathe at the end of each verse.

DECORATED QUR'AN ▶
Many copies of the Qur'an are precious works of art, such as this 17th-century example. Making the word of Allah beautiful is an act of worship in itself.

FIND OUT MORE ▶▶ Judaism 287 • North and West Africa 240–241

SIKHISM

Sikhism was founded over 500 years ago in the Punjab region of India, by a man who became known as ▸▸ **GURU** Nanak. He taught that all religions share the same essential truth and that holiness is to be found within. Sikh literally means "disciple."

◂ THE KHANDA
The khanda symbol represents many of the core Sikh beliefs. The khanda (two-edged sword) symbolizes belief in the power of the truth. The circle is a chakram (a flat, sharp-edged weapon) that also represents unity and eternity. The curved swords stand for the warrior spirit.

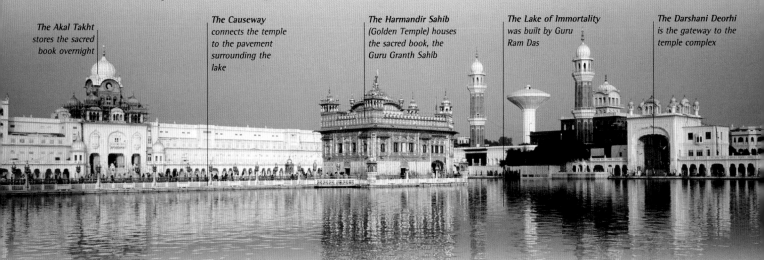

The Akal Takht stores the sacred book overnight

The Causeway connects the temple to the pavement surrounding the lake

The Harmandir Sahib (Golden Temple) houses the sacred book, the Guru Granth Sahib

The Lake of Immortality was built by Guru Ram Das

The Darshani Deorhi is the gateway to the temple complex

WHERE IS THE CENTER OF SIKHISM?
The Harmandir Sahib, or the Golden Temple, has become the symbol of the Sikh religion and their most important pilgrimage site. The fourth Guru, Ram Das, built a city and sacred lakes in Amritsar, in the Punjab, where Guru Nanak once meditated. The fifth Guru, Arjan, built the Golden Temple and collected the teachings of the Gurus into a sacred book, the Guru Granth Sahib.

HOW DO SIKHS WORSHIP?
Guru Nanak taught that "the only temple that matters is inside oneself." Sikhs pray at home, and also worship together, with hymns read from the sacred book. The focus of worship is on Nam, the divine name that lives within everyone. Sikh gurdwaras (temples) have a langar, or eating space, where Sikhs can share a communal meal with anyone who comes.

▴ GOLDEN TEMPLE, AMRITSAR
The Golden Temple, or Harmandir Sahib (House of God), has been rebuilt many times since its completion in 1601. "Sahib" is a title of respect that Sikhs use for places as well as people.

GURU

As with Hindu traditions, guru means "wise teacher," or more literally, "revealer of light and darkness." Sikhism regards its Ten Gurus as a single living spiritual flame, passed down from God, through Guru Nanak onward, and eventually reaching all Sikhs.

WHO WAS GURU GOBIND SINGH?
Guru Gobind Singh, the tenth Guru (1666–1708), founded the Khalsa, or community of Sikhs, in 1699 to protect them against religious persecution. He called for volunteers who were prepared to die for their faith. All Sikhs wear five symbols, known as the five "Ks," as a sign of their allegiance to the Khalsa. These include the kirpan (dagger) and kangha (comb).

WHERE IS THE SACRED BOOK KEPT?
The tenth Guru, Gobind Singh, appointed the sacred Adi Granth ("First Book") as his successor, so that after him there would be no more human gurus. It became known as the Guru Granth Sahib and copies are kept with great care at temples and treated with the respect a human guru would be given.

Sikhism

THE TEN GURUS ▸
This picture honors the Ten Gurus, and shows Guru Nanak (top), Guru Gobind Singh (top right), and Guru Granth Sahib (center). The boy guru is Har Krishnan, who died after defying the orders of a Mughal emperor who objected to Sikhism.

FIND OUT MORE ▸▸ Hinduism 286 • Southern Asia 266–267

PHILOSOPHY

Philosophy comes from the Ancient Greek words for "love of wisdom." It is the search for truth based on reason rather than religious teaching. Most philosophy is concerned with questions of being, knowing, and acting, such as: "Why are we here?"; "What is real?"; and "How should we behave?"

FAMOUS SAYINGS BY FAMOUS PHILOSOPHERS	
Man is the measure of all things	Protagoras c. 5th century BCE
Knowledge is power	Francis Bacon 1561–1626
I think, therefore I am	René Descartes 1596–1650
[Without] law, there is no freedom	John Locke 1632–1704
Man was born free, and everywhere he is in chains	Jean-Jacques Rousseau 1712–1778
Man makes himself	Jean-Paul Sartre 1905–1980

WHO WERE THE FIRST PHILOSOPHERS?

We do not know when philosophy began. The Western tradition originates with the writings of Ancient Greek thinkers, such as Plato and Aristotle, from 500 BCE onward. Plato and Aristotle's thoughts on logic, science, classification, ethics, and politics have guided Western thought for over 2,000 years.

IS PHILOSOPHY LIKE RELIGION?

Like religion, philosophy tries to explain the mystery of the world and of human existence. Unlike religion, which relies on faith, philosophy applies reasoned thought to its problems, such as the question of moral obligation or free will.

WHAT IS LOGIC?

In philosophy, logic is the search for a way of distinguishing good from bad reasoning. The classic example given by Aristotle shows how a conclusion may be drawn from two facts. If "Socrates is a man," and "All men are mortal," then "Socrates is mortal."

◄ HUMAN PROPORTIONS
One of philosophy's main objectives has been to understand humankind's place in the Universe. Renaissance artist Leonardo da Vinci's drawing *Vitruvian Man* showed how the arms and legs of a human figure could be fitted in a square and a circle. He believed these two shapes formed the basis of the Universe.

philosophy

SCHOOL OF ATHENS ▼
This 16th-century fresco from the Pope's library in the Vatican, Rome, was painted by the Italian artist Raphael. It shows wise men from different eras as colleagues in a timeless academy. At its center, Plato and Aristotle can be seen deep in discussion.

Socrates in animated discussion with Xenophon and Alexander the Great (in armor)

Plato points up to represent the Universe and abstract thought

Aristotle gestures down to represent the Earth and ethical thought

Flaming torch represents freedom

◄ THE STATUE OF LIBERTY
Liberty towers over New York Harbor as a symbol of liberal democracy. The ideas that inspired American independence in 1776 were developed by political philosophers such as John Locke and Jean-Jacques Rousseau.

Spiked crown represents the seven continents and seas

▲ ARJUNA AND KRISHNA
The *Bhagavad Gita* ("the Song of the Lord") features many philosophical discussions between Krishna (Vishnu in human form) and Arjuna, his close friend. Krishna's practical advice guides the soldier Arjuna in his actions.

WHY DOES TRUTH MATTER?

The question of truth—what it is and how to recognize it—is among the oldest and most controversial in philosophy. Some philosophers believe that the abstract rules of mathematics are a kind of absolute truth. Others believe there is no such thing as absolute truth, only the relative truth of individual or cultural viewpoints—that "Man is the measure of all things."

WHAT IS FREE WILL?

The question of free will—a major concern of many religions, too—revolves around the question of what controls our lives. Can we choose our own destiny, or are our actions limited by what has gone before (determinism) or by God's will (predestination)?

WHAT IS ETHICS?

Ethics, or moral philosophy, is the study of how people create moral systems and judge right and wrong behavior. Does good behavior come from duty to God or a person's own sense of how to live a proper life? Not all societies share the same ethical truth—in general, Eastern societies place more emphasis on collective duty than Western societies do.

Zoroaster (holding a celestial globe) discusses geography with Ptolemy

FIND OUT MORE ►► Ancient Greece 376–377 • Hinduism 286

SOCIETIES

Throughout time and in every part of the world, people have organized themselves into groups with common rules of living. A society is the name we give to the organization of such a group.

WHAT DO SOCIETIES HAVE IN COMMON?

Certain institutions are found in every society, such as the family, marriage, kin relationships, childcare, and division of work based on age and gender (male and female). The customs that govern social behavior vary greatly worldwide.

HOW ARE SOCIETIES ORGANIZED?

All societies are organized around an unequal division of labor and decision-making. Modern societies are expected to provide protection, law and order, economic security, and a sense of belonging to their members. Trying to understand how societies organize themselves is the goal of the ▶▶ SOCIAL SCIENCES.

◀ ONCE DIVIDED, NOW UNITED
In 1989, Germans celebrated as the Berlin Wall separating the societies of East and West Germany was torn down.

Cash suggests that society is ruled by the wealthy

Rulers appear to be the sole decision-makers

Church leaders fool those below by teaching them obedience to authority

The military protects the rulers from rebellious workers

Workers struggle to provide for the rest of society's needs

The middle class relies on workers' labor for their wealth and lifestyle

1912 AMERICAN ELECTION POSTER WOOS THE WORKERS' VOTE

▲ CAKE FOR A FEW, CRUMBS FOR THE REST
Some people think that society should work for the good of all its members. The picture illustrates that capitalist society works for the benefit of all the classes except the numerous working class which supports everyone by its labor.

DO SOCIETIES EVOLVE?

Societies usually adapt to changes around them, such as the environment or technology. Most change happens gradually, but some major events, such as war or revolution, can completely transform societies.

societies

SOCIAL SCIENCES

Social scientists study how people live together in societies. Economists study commercial activities and relate them to human behavior. Sociologists study the social structures of modern societies and relate them to human behavior. Anthropologists focus on the cultures and social structures of traditional societies.

▲ MARKING A BOY'S PASSAGE TO MANHOOD IN SOUTH AFRICA
While each society has its own customs, many celebrate the same thing in their own unique way. One of the most common customs is the "coming of age" ritual that marks a child's transition to adulthood.

▼ A GLOBAL COMMUNITY
Today, improved communications mean that very few societies are completely isolated from others. Most people—from villagers to city-dwellers—depend on economic and technological systems that connect the world, creating a global community.

WHY ARE THE SOCIAL SCIENCES USEFUL?
During the Industrial Revolution, rapid economic growth brought enormous social changes. Social sciences evolved to help explain the effects of these changes and to collect social data. Today, social scientists help us to understand complex social issues, from cultural differences to race relations.

DO OUR GENES AFFECT SOCIETY?
For many years, scientists have debated about what has more influence on society: nature or nurture, biology or culture. Sociobiologists argue that genes, which determine our physical characteristics, are responsible for most human behavior. Other scientists argue that culture is mostly responsible.

WHAT IS ANTHROPOLOGY?
Anthropology is the study of humanity. Physical anthropologists study the evolution of the human species, by looking at evidence from fossils and genes. Social anthropologists study the social behavior of living human beings.

▲ ANIMAL SOCIETIES
Ants are among many animal groups that live in societies. Because their society's "rules" are encoded in the queen ant's genes and passed down, ant societies cannot invent new rules.

MARGARET MEAD
American, 1901-1978
This pioneering anthropologist studied social behavior, especially rites of passage and child-rearing, in Samoa, New Guinea, and Bali. Her main conclusion was that personality was culturally and not biologically determined. She also analyzed US society.

FIND OUT MORE ▶▶ Culture 296–297 • Economy 302–303 • Families 300 • Genetics 209 • The State 308–309

CELEBRATING CULTURE ACROSS THE GLOBE

DAY OF THE DEAD
In this Mexican festival, held on All Souls' Day, people pray to the souls of their dead relatives, inviting them to return to the land of the living for one more celebration. These are festival-goers in Los Angeles, California, a city that has a large Hispanic American population.

MASAI DANCE
The Masai men of east Africa live in age groups called brotherhoods. The members of a brotherhood practice this Eunoto ritual, in which the men dance with straight-legged jumps. This is to mark the passage from a younger to an older brotherhood.

INDEPENDENCE DAY
Each year on the Fourth of July, Americans of all cultural backgrounds mark the anniversary of US freedom from Great Britain. Annual celebrations encourage citizens to take pride in their country's history, freedom, and prosperity.

DUSSEHRA FESTIVAL
The story of Rama's victory over Ravana, a battle between good and evil, is celebrated in this colorful Hindu festival in India. In the city of Mysore, elephants are decorated and painted, like those used in India's past to carry kings to war.

TROOPING THE COLOR
An annual parade in London marks the official birthday of Queen Elizabeth II, Britain's head of state. The time-honored rituals, uniforms, flags, and the monarch's horse-drawn carriage highlight tradition and stability.

HANDS UP
Spectators at this football game rise to their feet to send "the wave" around the stadium. Joining a large audience at sports events, or supporting a sports team, gives people a powerful sense of community.

CULTURE

Culture is made up of all the shared values, customs, and beliefs that give a society a common identity. It includes the ▸◂ LANGUAGE a society uses, along with its rituals, fashions, arts, food, stories, and lifestyles.

DO ALL MEMBERS OF A SOCIETY SHARE ONE CULTURE?
Traditional societies usually share a common culture. People who live in larger, more diverse societies share a mainstream culture, with which most people can identify. Societies may also have ▸◂ SUBCULTURES , alongside their normal cultures, often based on shared values or interests, especially among immigrants and young people.

IS THERE A GLOBAL CULTURE?
Cultures spread and influence one another as a result of increased trade and communication, and modern technology has brought the world's cultures closer than ever. Some cultural events, such as a Hollywood movie, are shared across the world—but local aspects of culture, such as language or myth, remain the most powerful cultural influences in most people's lives.

▲ AMISH CULTURE
North America's Amish people choose to separate themselves from mainstream US culture. Most Amish live without modern innovations such as electricity or engines, because their religion encourages them to question the need for change. Like their plain clothing, this sets them apart from those outside their culture.

DO CULTURES CHANGE?
Cultures emerge from the growing history and experiences of a society, or its ▸◂ TRADITION . Rapid social change and revolution can cause changes in culture. Cultures also change as people make contact with other cultures. Greater global communications and opportunities to travel allow people across the world to study and learn from other cultures.

HOW DO WE LEARN A CULTURE?
Most people grow up immersed in their culture. They absorb it from their family, through rituals and customs, through language, through the arts, through social habits, and through a shared history. People also learn about culture through school, friends, television, and books.

◂ PATCHWORK OF CULTURE
Each of these cultures is unique. Together, they build a vast global culture. A greater understanding of the world's cultures means that people can be influenced by many different ways of life.

TRADITION

Tradition generally refers to patterns of customs and beliefs that reflect a group's common identity. Tradition is passed down from one generation to the next through teaching and practice.

WHY DO WE HAVE TRADITIONS?
Traditions often come from deep-rooted beliefs, or are simply "invented" at a certain point in history. Special events, such as royal pageants in the UK, Thanksgiving Day in the US, and Bastille Day in France, help people to remember certain times and traditions, giving them a sense of a shared cultural history.

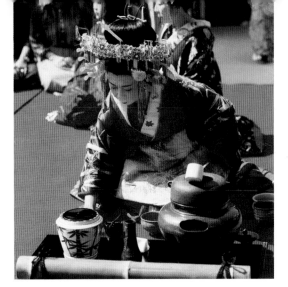

TEA CEREMONY (CHAJI) ►
A Japanese woman in traditional dress performs a tea ceremony in front of honored guests. The ceremony is highly complex with many rules to follow. Originally, this tradition was part of the formal welcoming of guests.

LANGUAGE

Each culture communicates through language—a set of words and grammar, signs and symbols. There are some 5,000 different languages in the world.

STOP SIGN ►
This stop sign gets its message across in Arabic and English. Its distinctive shape and color also help to convey the meaning.

HOW DO LANGUAGES CHANGE?
Languages evolve in the same way as cultures—through interaction with other languages. Languages adopt new words and lose old words all the time. Sometimes, old words take on new meanings. Local variations of the same language are known as dialects. These may occur when a group of speakers moves away from their homeland, such as the Spanish settlers in South America, or when they become isolated from other speakers of the same language.

SUBCULTURE

Many complex societies encourage diversity by allowing smaller groups to form their own subcultures, with their own distinct behavior, beliefs, and attitudes. Through fashion, music, and art, subcultures often influence mainstream culture.

WHAT IS GANG CULTURE?
People looking for excitement, a strong identity, and a code to live by may choose to join a gang, such as the Hell's Angels or Japanese Yakuza. Gangs usually create their own subculture, complete with dress codes, tattoos, slang, and music. These highly visible signs show the members' loyalty and pride in belonging to the gang. Mainstream music, such as "gangsta rap," is often influenced by gang culture.

WHO JOINS A SUBCULTURE?
Many people, especially younger people, choose to join a subculture to express their interests and identity. Teenagers and young adults often feel a lack of identification with the values or interests of mainstream society, so they seek out groups of like-minded people—with similar musical, sporting, or political interests—to give them a sense of belonging. Subcultures can even be based around hobbies such as folk dancing or pigeon racing.

▲ ANARCHY, MUSIC, AND FASHION
The punk subculture appealed to teenagers in the late 1970s, inspired by its raw, fast rock music and angry lyrics. Punk fashions, such as dyed hair and facial piercings, represent a rejection of mainstream cultural values, perfect for shocking or rebelling against parents and society.

GRAFFITI ▲
Gang members often use graffiti—tags (signatures) or artwork illegally sprayed on walls and other visible spots—to mark their territory. The distinctive style of graffiti artists has now crossed over into mainstream art.

FIND OUT MORE ►► Cinema 346–347 • Popular Music 334 • Societies 294–295

MEDIA

The media (sometimes called mass media) includes all the institutions and technology that communicate news and entertainment to society. They include print media (or the **PRESS**), **BROADCAST** media (or television and radio), and new media, like the Internet.

WHO PAYS FOR THE MEDIA?

Media can be state-owned, such as the British Broadcasting Corporation (BBC), or owned by a private company. Media consumers normally pay a small fee to access information, although private companies meet most of the cost by selling **ADVERTISING** space to businesses or sponsors.

WHAT EFFECTS DO MASS MEDIA HAVE?

People depend on media for everything from the latest headlines to yesterday's sports results. At its best, the media educates, provokes, and entertains. Yet mass media can also be used for propaganda purposes to sway public opinion and distort the truth.

HOT OFF THE PRESS ▶
Newspapers must be written by journalists, printed in vast quantities, and distributed—all before their news is out of date. A typical morning paper must meet a 1am deadline so that its 6am first edition hits the newsstand.

SUPERMAN

HOLLYWOOD MOVIES
The American film industry depends on popular movies, with plenty of action, comedy, or romance, to capture the interest—and ticket sales—of a global audience. Blockbusters such as the *Superman* series enable studios to cover the huge production costs of making the movies.

IS THE INTERNET DIFFERENT FROM OTHER MEDIA?

In most mass media, information flows in one direction only, from its creators to the public. The Internet, however, has created a "virtual" community that can share information, views, and experiences with each other via emails, chatrooms, and message boards. While Internet sites are not checked for accuracy or fairness, they can provide a balanced and informal alternative to the official media by letting diverse voices be heard.

◀ THE WORLD IS JUST A CLICK AWAY
Over 2 billion people worldwide use the Internet. Its technology enables us to access information wherever we find a computer, a modem, and a phone link, provided we can pay. Mobile phone technology can allow people to log on from almost anywhere.

PRESS

Newspapers, magazines, and the journalists who write for them are known collectively as the press. One in every six people reads a daily newspaper. The world's leading newspaper, Japan's *Yomiuri Shimbun*, sells over 14 million copies a day.

HOW DO PEOPLE CHOOSE A PAPER?

Readers often pick a newspaper that reflects their own interests and political views. Each newspaper has its own editorial standards, which shape how the news is presented. Some newspapers present a more serious coverage; others are more sensational. Readers may buy a different paper if it has an exclusive story.

PRESS GANG ▶
Newspapers often buy photos from paparazzi, people who take unofficial pictures of the rich and famous.

▲ SELF-POWERED RADIO
This Burundian girl lives in a refugee camp in Tanzania. As there is no school, she listens to lessons on a battery-free radio. These economical radios are solar-powered and can be charged by turning a crank.

BROADCAST

Broadcast media send information to a wide audience using advanced electronic technology. Radio was first broadcast in the 1920s, and television in the 1930s. In recent years, digital technologies have created a huge expansion in the number of channels of all kinds.

WHO LISTENS TO THE RADIO?

Radio is a truly global medium for talk, news, and music. More than 300 million battery-powered radios are sold every year, providing a cheap and accessible alternative to television. Television is often less easily available to many in developing countries, especially for those without access to electricity.

ADVERTISING

Producers of goods and services use the media to encourage people to buy their products. They buy space in any media that reach their target consumers, in order to advertise, or promote, their goods in a way that appeals to them.

DOES ADVERTISING WORK?

Although consumers rarely admit to being influenced by ads, effective advertising does increase sales. Global industry pours over $350 billion into advertising every year, with around 40 percent of the total budget dedicated to TV coverage.

ADVERTISING ICON ▶
Coca-Cola™ is one of the world's most successful products. Its soft drinks are sold almost everywhere, and its distinctive logo is recognized worldwide.

media

FIND OUT MORE ▶▶ Cinema 346–347 • Internet 191 • Printing 339 • Telecommunications 192–193

FAMILIES

The family is a basic social unit that exists in every culture, although its structure varies widely. The main purpose of families, which are usually created by marriage, is for ▸▸ PARENTING children.

WHAT IS A NUCLEAR FAMILY?

The term "nuclear family" refers to two married adults and their children. It has been the main family unit of Western society since the Industrial Revolution. Recent social changes, such as divorce and remarriage, have resulted in many single-parent and stepfamilies.

▲ IN THE FAMILY
Extended families, such as this group of yak herders in Bhutan, work together like a miniature society. They share domestic and work duties, childcare, and care of the elderly for the benefit of all the members.

WHAT ARE EXTENDED FAMILIES?

In most societies, especially in preindustrial, traditional communities, it is normal for a wide circle of relatives from one or both sides of the family to live together in the same household. This type of family is known as an extended family.

ARE ALL FAMILIES BASED ON MARRIAGE?

Most societies have an elaborate religious ritual to celebrate marriage. Some couples may choose to reject this tradition and marry in a civil ceremony. Others may choose to create a family outside marriage.

families

◂ OLDER AND WISER
Much of the world's population is living longer as healthcare improves. While many families still care for their elderly, some nations also provide some housing and financial support.

HINDU MARRIAGE ▲
A traditional Hindu marriage ceremony is not just a bond between husband and wife. Members of both families play an important part in the life of the new family afterward.

Red is the most common color for a Hindu bride

A veil of beaded strings shields the bride from evil

A sherwani is embroidered with golden thread

Groom wears an elaborate turban

PARENTING

Parents and children, whether united by birth or by adoption, share a unique bond. Parenting means providing food, shelter, and emotional support for children, as well as preparing them for a role in adult society. Sometimes children are cared for by their legal guardians.

WHY DO CHILDREN NEED PARENTS?

Children enter the world without the skills or ability to take care of themselves. Parents must protect and nurture children during their early years as they develop and grow. In later years, parents lay down guidelines for behavior, so children learn how to be responsible for themselves. As children grow older, parents continue to support them, both emotionally and financially, as they take their first tentative steps toward adulthood.

▲ CLOSE TIES
This South American girl will rely on her family's care until she reaches adulthood. In some societies, a parent's role can also extend to providing education or teaching a trade or skill.

FIND OUT MORE ▶▶ Hinduism 286 • Industrial Revolution 418–419 • Societies 294–295

CIVIL SOCIETY

Many people see themselves joined by common interests to a social network that extends beyond their immediate families. People organize themselves to promote causes and organize sports and other leisure activities.

civil society

WHY DO PEOPLE FORM SOCIETIES AND CLUBS?

Especially in wealthier societies, people have time for interests, such as sports, outside their main economic and family roles. Joining a club or society with others who share the same interests provides a common bond among people. Some groups, called charities, exist to provide support for those in need.

▲ INDIAN WOMEN'S TRADE COOPERATIVE
Wealthy people and companies sometimes use part of their wealth to set up charities called foundations. A foundation provides financial support for good causes, such as development aid or the environment.

WHAT IS VOLUNTEERING?

Clubs, societies, and charities often rely on the work of unpaid helpers, or volunteers, to achieve their goals. People volunteer because they agree with the goals of the group, and find satisfaction in helping others. Volunteering can also bring people new friendships, or improve their work skills.

▲ "FEED THE WORLD!"
In 1985, a charity called Live Aid staged twin concerts in the UK and the US to raise money for African famine victims. Millions of people pledged money during its broadcast, raising over $65 million in aid.

FIND OUT MORE ▶▶ Hinduism 286 • Societies 294–295

ECONOMY

People work together to grow things, extract raw materials from the Earth, manufacture objects that are sold to ▸▸ CONSUMERS, and help to organize our lives through services like banking. The ▸▸ PRODUCTION and distribution of all these things make up the economy.

WHAT IS SUPPLY AND DEMAND?

In an economy, there are people who supply goods and services at a cost, and people who demand those goods and services and pay for them. The laws of supply and demand try to explain how and why prices change and how producers and consumers behave. For example, if there is a lot of demand, prices increase. If supply is high, prices go down.

WHAT IS THE MARKET?

In economics, the market is a place, or a network, where buyers and sellers exchange goods and services for money. All activity in the market depends on the supply of, and demand for, these goods and services.

▲ DOMESTIC WORK
This woman in India handwashes her family's clothes in the nearest river. This kind of domestic work is not considered part of the economy.

WHAT TYPES OF ECONOMIES ARE THERE?

In traditional economies, people produce the goods they need on a small scale, and sell the surplus (what they do not need) at local trading centers, or markets. In command economies, most economic activity is controlled by the government rather than private companies or market forces. In a mixed economy, some industries are privately owned by companies and others, such as public transportation, are publicly owned and run by the government.

WHAT IS NOT PART OF THE ECONOMY?

Domestic work, such as housework, is not considered part of the economy, unless someone is paid to do it. The portion of a nation's income that is (illegally) not declared for tax is called the black economy.

Computers
store details of the best time to buy and sell stocks according to their price. This means that some trading can happen automatically

Paper slips are dropped
to the floor after being used by traders to scribble down prices of the deals they have made

NEW YORK STOCK EXCHANGE ▸
Big companies are usually owned by thousands of people, who each hold stakes in the company called stocks. Stocks are traded through a stock exchange. People invest their money in stocks to claim a portion of a company's profits if the company does well. However, they risk losing money if the company does badly and the stock price goes down.

PRODUCTION

Production involves the use of Earth's raw materials and human labor to make useful things. Every society uses its land, people, skills, and tools to make products, from gasoline to stainless steel and running shoes. In modern economies, companies aim to maximize profits by keeping their production costs down and their sales up.

WHAT IS ECONOMIC GROWTH?

An economy grows when its production increases in quantity. Growth in the economy can lead to more jobs and more income for consumers to spend. It also frees resources for other uses, such as science, the arts, or sports. However, economic growth can also create difficulties, such as environmental problems and a widening gap between rich and poor.

Video screens display the latest stock prices of different companies

Traders buy and sell stocks on behalf of companies and investors

LARGEST MANUFACTURING OUTPUT (US$ BILLION)	
USA	1,700
Japan	934
China	893
Germany	595
Italy	299
France	283
UK	270
South Korea	240

MASS PRODUCTION ▲
These cars are produced on a state-of-the-art factory production line. Automated assembly lines help to cut production costs. Sometimes producers pass these savings along to consumers in the form of lower prices, hoping to sell more cars than their competitors.

CONSUMERS

Someone who buys goods and services is called a consumer. Most people are consumers, because they need to buy basic goods, such as food, shelter, and clothing, in order to live. Producers need to predict what consumers want, so that they can make goods that will sell.

WHAT GIVES CONSUMERS POWER?

Consumers need a way to pay for goods before they can decide which goods to buy. Their buying power comes from income (wages earned by working) or investment (profits made from owning stocks or property). A wide choice of products gives consumers some power over producers, since a company will go out of business if consumers do not buy its product.

▲ CONSUMER POWER
Consumers have the most power in markets where there are many traders. It is easy to compare prices and choose between many products and prices on display, such as on a fruit and vegetable stand.

WHAT ARE CONSUMER GOODS?

Consumer goods are products manufactured to satisfy personal needs. Goods that are required for the production of other goods and services, such as paper or coal, are known as producer or capital goods. Consumer goods can include anything from clothing and CDs to children's toys and Coca-Cola™. Demand for consumer goods is often created by advertising and by technological changes.

◄ ON THE ROAD
These cars will be shipped around the world to meet consumer demand. Sometimes it is cheaper for producers to manufacture goods in one place; sometimes it is cheaper to manufacture them in several locations.

FIND OUT MORE ▸▸ Human Impact 64–65 • Industry 204 • Manufacturing 205

SOCIAL EQUALITY

Sociologists have shown that all societies are stratified or divided into layers, which may be based on class, ethnicity, or sex. As a result, some people in a society have greater advantages than others, leading to social inequality.

WHY ARE SOME SOCIETIES DIVIDED?

Some basic differences between people may affect their place in the social hierarchy. ▶︎GENDER divisions are common, because of the different roles men and women play in bearing and raising children. Other divisions come from the unequal distribution of ▶︎WEALTH, or attitudes to ▶︎ETHNICITY.

WHAT ARE THE CASTE AND CLASS SYSTEMS?

The caste system is an ancient hierarchy, where fixed social roles are inherited, practiced by followers of the Hindu religion in India. While caste positions often guarantee employment, it also means that its members are unable to improve their social status. In most other societies, people are born into a social position or class, depending on the property, employment, or wealth of their family. However, education and economic success can help people improve their social position.

CROSSING BARRIERS ▶
When people use their talents and skills to cross physical and social barriers, it provides inspiration to others. Singer Stevie Wonder and former US President Bill Clinton both overcame obstacles to achieve their success.

CAN SOCIAL DIVISIONS CHANGE?

Societies can change when the roles dividing people, such as the division of labor or job opportunities, are shared more equally. For example, peacemaking efforts between Catholics and Protestants in Northern Ireland are directed at sharing political power fairly.

HOW CAN PEOPLE BE TREATED EQUALLY?

In recent history, many societies have passed laws that prohibit discrimination against people based on race, gender, or age. These ensure that all people are treated equally by employers, governments, and other members of society. These laws have primarily been won by struggle, protest, and organization.

◀ EDUCATIONAL GOALS
All children deserve a good education to help them achieve their full potential. Many developing countries cannot afford to provide education after primary level. Often, wealthy people choose to buy a better education for their children, giving them access to a full range of activities outside the classroom, such as sports or music.

▲ BASIC NEEDS
This Peruvian boy is one of billions of people around the world who live in poverty—around a third of the world's population, according to the United Nations—without enough money to meet their basic needs. Poor people often have limited access to healthcare and education.

▲ WOMAN IN A MAN'S WORLD
Traditionally, men have monopolized jobs that required greater physical strength. However, improved technology means that there are fewer jobs that rely on muscle power alone. Women, like Space Shuttle astronaut Mary Ellen Weber, have broken barriers by choosing careers once held exclusively by men.

GENDER

Gender division is the social recognition and reinforcement of sexual differences between men and women. This might take the form of an unequal division of labor, reduced social opportunities, or social discrimination.

DO WOMEN HAVE EQUAL RIGHTS?

Although women have won important rights over the last 100 years, gender inequality is still commonplace in most parts of the world. While countries with equal rights laws have improved women's access to politics, jobs, and property, women are still not equally represented in government and business, and are often paid less for doing the same jobs as men.

WEALTH

A few people in each society earn large amounts of money, or inherit fortunes handed down through their families. Their wealth gives them access to more economic and social opportunities than others, and can give them more influence over society as a whole.

HOW DOES WEALTH DIVIDE PEOPLE?

Wealth gives people power in a society, because wealthy people can buy and use other people's time. This can be seen as a reward for individual success. However, if only the rich can enjoy such success, there can be no social equality. The numbers on the chart below illustrate the huge—and growing—gap between the world's rich and poor.

TABLE OF GLOBAL WEALTH

$ (excluding homes)	Number of people
Above $1 billion	480
$5m–$1 billion	483,000
$1 million–$5 million	6,500,000
$100,000–$1 million	25,000,000
$10,000–$100,000	180,000,000
$0–$10,000	5,700,000,000

▲ WHAT IT MEANS TO BE RICH
Wealth allows people to choose their own lifestyles, free of the limits most people face. The wealthy may also make choices that affect other people's lives, such as where to spend, donate, or invest money.

social equality

THE DIVISIONAL COUNCIL OF THE CAPE
WHITE AREA
BY ORDER SECRETARY
DIE AFDELINGSRAAD VAN DIE KAAP
BLANKE GEBIED
OP LAS SEKRETARIS

◄ ETHNIC DIVIDE
In South Africa, the white minority imposed years of enforced separation on black people, denying them basic rights. This policy, known as apartheid, ended in 1993.

ETHNICITY

Ethnicity refers to a group's distinctive culture as well as racial background. The term "race" is now considered to be an outdated concept for distinguishing groups of people who share common physical characteristics, such as black skin or blonde hair.

WHAT IS A MULTIETHNIC SOCIETY?

Societies made up of several ethnic groups, each with their own cultural traditions, are called multiethnic societies. During the 20th and 21st centuries, many multiethnic societies have searched for ways to promote respect for these different groups, often passing laws to promote equal opportunities for all.

FIND OUT MORE ▶▶ Decolonization 434 • Human Rights 317 • Societies 294–295

POLITICS

Politics is the process of obtaining and using power to shape and execute the rules that govern a society. It can involve elected politicians in a ▸DEMOCRACY, or the unelected members of a ruling elite.

WHY DO PEOPLE CARE ABOUT POLITICS?
Political decisions affect people's daily lives in two very important ways. They decide how much money the state will take from people in the form of taxes to spend on public projects such as healthcare, education, or defense. Political decisions also make the laws that affect people's lives.

▲ HEATED DEBATE
Arab Israeli and Jewish Labor Party politicians have an angry exchange in the Knesset, Israel's parliamentary chamber. Working out differences of opinion through debate can provide an alternative to violent conflict.

▲ HOUSES OF PARLIAMENT, LONDON
In the UK, government is divided into three areas: Parliament which makes laws; the judiciary ensures that the laws are applied fairly; and the executive (the Cabinet and the civil service) carry out the laws.

CAN POLITICS CHANGE SOCIETY?
Political ideas alone do not change society, but when enough people with the same ideas form a ▸PARTY, they can influence how society changes. Sometimes the process of change can be gradual; sometimes it comes from violent revolution, fueled by new political ideas. This happened in countries such as the United States, France, and Czarist Russia.

DOES EVERYONE HAVE A SAY?
There are two main types of government: democratic and authoritarian. In democratic societies, adults have a role in shaping how their country is run, by voting in free elections for a political party. This is part of their ▸CIVIL RIGHTS.

▼ INSIDE THE BUNDESTAG
In the Bundestag, or German parliament, deputies are elected by proportional representation. The Bundestag moved to Berlin in 1991, following the reunification of East and West Germany.

Cabinet members run the government

President of the chamber oversees debates

Deputies sit in party groups and vote electronically

DEMOCRACY

Democracy (from the Greek for "rule by the people") is a way that people can choose their government from a range of political parties. In republics, or countries without monarchies, the electors vote for a head of state, or president, as well as the government.

HOW MANY TYPES OF DEMOCRACY ARE THERE?

There are two main types of democracy: presidential, where voters elect a president, who then appoints the government, such as in the US or France; and parliamentary, where voters directly elect the government of their choice, such as in the UK. Sometimes a president may rule yet represent a minority party.

WHAT IS A REFERENDUM?

Some political decisions are too important to be left to elected politicians. So the issue is decided on by all voters, normally with a simple yes or no answer to a direct question. Referendums are typically used for decisions that affect basic rights, or the sovereign (independent) status of a nation.

politics

▲ NELSON MANDELA CASTING VOTE IN SOUTH AFRICA'S ELECTIONS
During elections, each citizen may vote anonymously for the candidate of their choice by marking an "X" against the candidate's name on the ballot slip and placing it in a sealed ballot box. Sometimes electors vote for individuals; sometimes they vote for parties.

CIVIL RIGHTS

Citizens of democratic societies expect equal participation in political, social, and economic life. These freedoms are called civil rights. They are meant to guarantee that society is fair to everyone.

DO DEMOCRACIES NEED CIVIL RIGHTS?

Sometimes laws that represent the will of the majority can restrict the freedom of others and exclude minorities from full political and social participation and threaten the idea of democracy. Civil rights protect the freedoms of all people within society.

MARTIN LUTHER KING
American, 1929–1968
"We know through painful experience that freedom is never voluntarily given by the oppressor; it must be demanded by the oppressed." In the 1950s and 1960s, King campaigned against racial injustice and for civil rights for all black Americans.

WOMEN DEMONSTRATING ▶
Women in Aceh, Indonesia, protest against the introduction of sweeping emergency laws by the government in 2002, issued to combat rebel groups. These laws took away many basic civil rights.

PARTY

Political parties are formed to represent different interests. These may be economic, social, or religious—each with its own ideas about how society should be ruled.

HOW ARE POLITICAL PARTIES CREATED?

A new party is created when people who share common political beliefs feel unrepresented and decide to compete for political power. They choose a name for themselves and draw up a list of their ideas, called a platform, for voters to consider. Party members normally vote to choose their leader.

◀ POLITICAL RALLY
Parties often hold large meetings, such as this convention of Democratic Party supporters in the US. The meetings help choose party leaders, reward their supporters, and publicize their interests.

THE STATE

A state is a territory ruled by a single government, and which is not subject to another power. A modern state has its own government, armed forces, and a civil service, which carries out the work of the government. The state generally manages police and other emergency services, and the departments of health, education, and ▶ WELFARE. It also has a ▶ CENTRAL BANK.

WHO WORKS FOR THE STATE?

A state employs a large workforce of civil servants to carry out its many functions. These state employees include police officers, health inspectors, teachers, and office workers. Together, they represent a large part of the total workforce. In the UK, for example, 20 percent of all workers are employed by the state.

WHY ARE STATES FORMED?

States were first created many thousands of years ago, mainly to fight wars and defend territory. Today, states do more than this. They provide a form of central control for public services, and look after the welfare of their citizens.

TOP 8 INDUSTRIALIZED STATES: ANNUAL STATE SPENDING PER CITIZEN	
Germany	$10,067
Italy	$9,189
United Kingdom	$9,037
United States	$5,908
Japan	$5,633
Canada	$5,124
France	$4,060
Russian Federation	$300

The hammer and sickle was the official symbol of the former Soviet Union

HOW DOES A STATE PAY FOR ITS SERVICES?

Each year, a government decides how much money the state will need to pay for its public services. Most of this is raised via a ▶ TAX on its citizens and businesses, but states can also charge for services—for example, through road tolls. If a state gets into debt, it may also borrow money from private corporations or from wealthier nations or from International Monetary Fund, an organization which oversees the world's financial systems.

the state

◀ STATE DEPARTMENT
In the Russian Federation, the state has a say in many aspects of society. Many civil servants work to carry out government policy in huge offices, such as this Ministry of Foreign Affairs in Moscow.

▲ ARMED FORCES
The state pays to staff and equip its armed forces. This American F-22 Raptor jet cost around $70 billion to design. Although made by a private company, the jet could not be built without state money.

▲ EDUCATION
States have funded education, from nursery schools to universities, since the 19th century. Investment in education results in a better-educated society, which in turn creates steady economic growth for the state.

▲ TRANSPORTATION
Roads and bridges are complicated and expensive to build. States pay for transportation networks, like this road system in Shanghai, China, to improve communications and to encourage more economic activity.

▲ ARTS
The Sydney Opera House in Australia was built with state money. States give money to support the arts—especially orchestras, opera and ballet companies, theater groups, and museums—as symbols of national pride.

TAX

Tax is the money that citizens and companies have to pay to the government, helping the state raise the funds it needs to operate. A state may impose direct taxes on an individual's income or property, or indirect taxes on business trade in goods and services.

WHAT ARE TAX INCENTIVES?
A state can use tax incentives to encourage its citizens to make certain economic choices. Most people try to avoid paying large amounts of tax, so a state can actually encourage participation in an activity by lowering or removing the tax on it. The opposite is true when a state raises taxes. For example, some governments impose high taxes on cigarettes and alcohol to discourage people from consuming these products, which are known to create health risks.

DO TAXES MAKE SOCIETIES MORE EQUAL?
Whether taxation can make societies more equal depends on the mix of taxes raised by the state. Progressive taxes, such as income tax, take more from the rich than the poor. Others, such as flat rate taxes, take the same amount of money from everyone. However, this has a worse impact on the poor than the rich who can afford to pay it.

▲ TAXING CONSUMERS AT THE GAS PUMP
If a government sees private car use as bad for society, it can discourage driving by raising taxes on gasoline. High gas taxes also encourage people to buy smaller cars that consume less fuel.

▲ PROVIDING FOR THE POOR
In times of economic crisis, larger numbers of people turn to the state for welfare aid. These unemployed New Yorkers lined up for a free Christmas meal during the Great Depression of the 1930s, a financial slump that began in the US and spread across the globe.

WELFARE

Welfare is the financial assistance that a country or state provides to help people in need. Government welfare support may include payments to unemployed workers or disabled people who cannot work, or social security payments for retired people. Welfare benefits can also be provided to all citizens in forms such as public education.

HAVE ALL COUNTRIES CREATED A WELFARE STATE?
Every government decides how much welfare to provide to its citizens. Politicians debate over how much a person's welfare is their own responsibility, or the responsibility of the state. Some developing countries have little money for welfare, and the needy must rely on charity for help instead.

CENTRAL BANK

A state that possesses its own currency has a central bank, which prints money. A central bank tries to regulate the state's economy by influencing interest rates. The goal is to ensure economic stability and prevent sharp swings between growth and decline.

WHAT IS INTEREST?
Interest is what money costs to borrow. People pay a price to borrow money—for example, to make a large consumer purchase—and that price is called interest. The central bank sets a basic interest rate called the base rate, which private banking companies follow when people arrange to borrow money from them.

▲ US GOLD BULLION DEPOSITORY, FORT KNOX, KENTUCKY
Different countries have different currencies, or money. One of the tasks of the central bank is to determine how much currency should be in circulation (in use) at any given time. Until 1971, the value of each US dollar in circulation was backed up by a dollar's worth of gold, some of which was stored at Fort Knox.

FIND OUT MORE ▶▶ Culture 296–297 • The Depression 430 • Economy 302–303 • The Law 310–311

THE LAW

Laws are the formal rules that society makes for itself. They are made for various reasons: for example, to settle arguments and maintain a peaceful social order. Some laws are made by governments. Others are set down by custom or religion.

Sword represents punishment for the guilty

Blindfold protects from the risk of prejudice

Scales help to weigh both sides of a dispute fairly

▲ **A SYMBOL OF JUSTICE**
Law courts across the world feature images of the Greek goddess Themis ("Justicia" in Roman religion), goddess of justice. Themis is always seen holding the scales of justice.

WHO MAKES THE LAW IN A DEMOCRATIC SOCIETY?
In a democracy, the power to make laws is held by a branch of the government called the legislature. In the legislative chamber, politicians (usually elected to represent the views of the voters) introduce new laws and debate them. Through discussion and compromise, they try to gain support for a law and organize a vote on it. The majority of members must approve a law before it can be put into effect.

CAN POLITICIANS MAKE ANY LAW THEY WISH?
Politicians in different countries have different law-making powers. In some cases, a head of state can refuse to accept a law. Sometimes, political leaders may put forward a law that would weaken rights or freedoms that have been promised to all citizens. Such laws can be challenged by citizens in ▶▶ COURT .

HOW IS CRIMINAL LAW DIFFERENT FROM CIVIL LAW?
Criminal law defines a person's responsibility toward society as a whole. Breaking a criminal law is an offense against the public good, so the state pursues criminals in the name of the public. Civil law deals with a person's responsibility toward another person. Civil laws cover agreements between people, such as property ownership, contracts, or marriage.

WHY DO PEOPLE OBEY THE LAW?
Most people obey the law because they believe it results in a peaceful society. The law is enforced by the ▶▶ POLICE . The risk of being caught by the police and punished reminds most people to obey the law. But some political activists deliberately break laws they disagree with—an act called "civil disobedience."

DO DIFFERENT COUNTRIES HAVE DIFFERENT LAWS?
Because law-making is part of national politics, most countries have very different laws. But there are also many similarities. English-speaking countries around the world share ideas laid down in the common law of Britain. French-speaking countries share parts of the law codes set down in France by Napoleon. There are also international agreements that many countries treat as laws, such as those to do with human rights.

US SUPREME COURT ▶
Most countries have a high court to make decisions about its most important legal problems. In the US, the Supreme Court is made up of nine justices. The justices hear an average of 6,500 cases a year, mostly appeals from lower courts. A majority vote decides the outcome of each case.

law

POLICE

Every modern state has created a police force to find law-breakers, charge them with crimes, and bring them to court for a trial. The police are entrusted with enforcing the law, as well as protecting the rights of citizens.

WHY DON'T CITIZENS POLICE THEMSELVES?

In small societies, rule-breakers are usually discovered and punished by their fellow citizens. In complex, mobile societies, there are often weaker social links between people. This makes it harder for communities to police themselves. Some crimes also require the work of specially trained detectives.

WHAT IS A THREAT TO PUBLIC ORDER?

One of the reasons that police forces were created—in the early 19th century—was to maintain public order Today, public order usually involves controlling large crowds or political protesters, and protecting property. Police are allowed to use force, if necessary, to maintain public order.

CAN POLICE FORCES PREVENT CRIME?

Police forces invest time in teaching citizens to prevent crimes—for example, by installing locks to stop burglars. Crimes can be prevented if the risk of being caught is increased. The percentage of crimes in which a criminal is caught varies. Generally, more resources are used to solve serious crimes than petty crimes.

CROWD CONTROL IN JAPAN
Large crowds—such as those that assemble at big sporting events, rock concerts, or a rush-hour subway platform—can be dangerous. These Japanese policemen are creating a barrier to keep a crowd back, to protect those in front from being trampled or forced onto the tracks.

▲ POLICE IN THE COMMUNITY
This US police officer addresses schoolchildren during a drug awareness and education program. These programs show children that there is an alternative to gangs and violence.

COURT

A person accused of law-breaking is tried in a court, a public hall of justice presided over by a state official called a judge. The court hears the evidence both against and in favor of the accused. If the court finds the person guilty, it can impose a penalty.

WHY DO WE HAVE JURIES?

A jury is a panel of usually 12 citizens selected from the general population. They hear all the evidence and decide whether they think an accused person is guilty or innocent. Juries represent the public during a trial, bringing with them a democratic power to balance the powers of state officials.

HOW ARE LAW-BREAKERS PUNISHED?

Different legal systems use different punishments to deter crime and discipline a law-breaker. Legal systems based on traditional rules tend to prefer penalties that cause physical injury to the guilty person (corporal punishment). Modern systems tend to prefer detention in prison or cash fines.

PRISON ►
The law sets down which types of crimes deserve shorter or longer prison terms. The risk of losing personal and economic freedoms while locked away in a prison such as this one can deter law-breaking. However, prisons can also brutalize and dehumanize inmates.

◄ COURT OF LAW
Some cases are tried in front of a panel of judges, rather than a jury of citizens. This trial of a US serviceman, accused of a crime in Japan, was too politically sensitive for a normal jury to hear.

PRISON POPULATION		
COUNTRY	PRISONERS	PER 100,000 CITIZENS
USA	2,293,000	756
Russia	891,700	629
South Africa	164,300	335
Singapore	11,800	267
UK	92,900	131
China	1,565,000	119
France	60,000	96
Germany	73,000	89
Japan	81,000	63
India	373,000	33

FIND OUT MORE ▶▶ Global Protest 316 • Human Rights 317 • Politics 306–307 • Society 294–295 • The State 308–309

NATIONS

A nation (from the Latin for "birthplace") is defined as a large group of people unified by a common language or culture. Nationalism is the belief that people sharing national characteristics should be able to form their own independent state, surrounded by a ▸▸ BORDER.

WHAT ARE NATIONS FOR?

Modern nation-states were created by nations to give people sharing a common language and cultural characteristics the right to govern themselves as they choose. Nations provide protection against external threats and can ask their citizens to perform tasks, such as military service, in return. The greater a nation's economic and military power, the more it can promote its own interests.

▲ DIALOGUE BETWEEN NATIONS
Nations sometimes make alliances with other nations to advance common causes. Here Cuba's Fidel Castro (left) meets the USSR's Nikita Khrushchev (right) to seal the friendship between their two countries.

HOW DO NATIONS FORM?

Throughout history, nations have formed in several ways. Some were established as a result of geographic isolation, such as England. Others, such as Australia, were created as the result of emigration and imperial conquest, often displacing existing nations. Others again were created from the breakup of larger empires or from peace treaties, such as Croatia. Some nations, such as the Kurds or the Palestinians, are still fighting to create their own nation-states.

◂ A NATION WITHOUT A HOME
These Kurds have no territory. Their homelands lie within the borders of five other nations.

HOW DO NATIONS DEAL WITH OTHER NATIONS?

Nations interact on many levels. Trade agreements allow businesses from different nations to buy and sell their goods and services with each other. Formal agreements, signed by political leaders or their diplomatic representatives, reinforce friendly relations and allow cooperation in different areas, such as military technology. International agreements ensure that all member nations abide by the same rules.

BORDERS

A border is a line marking where the territory of one nation-state ends and another begins. Borders are clearly marked on maps, but those between friendly nations may often be unmarked on the ground. Borders under dispute are often heavily guarded and have strictly controlled border crossings.

WHY DO NATIONS ARGUE OVER BORDERS?

Nations often contest their borders, because of the need for land and valuable raw materials, such as oil, which are important to a nation's wealth. Borders are often redrawn as a result of wars. Sometimes people end up on the wrong side of the border, such as in the former Yugoslavia, and this can lead to conflict, too.

DO NATIONS END AT THE COAST?

The open sea is considered public territory except for a strip of water extending 3 miles (5 km) from a nation's coastal shoreline. Nations seeking to mine the seafloor or fish the waters beyond these borders should have this agreed to by treaty.

nations

▲ SYMBOLIC BORDER MARKER
This Peace Arch marks the border between the US and Canada, which is unmarked for most of its 5,526-mile (8,893-km) length. The US's southern border with Mexico is more difficult to police. It is one of the busiest land borders in the world, with around 500 million people making the crossing each year.

FIND OUT MORE ▸▸ International Organizations 434 • Nationalism 421 • New World Order 314–315 • Political World 216–217

WAR

When nations fail to settle their arguments by peaceful means, they often turn to war, or the use of armed conflict. War is also caused by some states pursuing a policy of active imperial conquest. Civil war is war between people within a nation. This can happen when political or ethnic differences become too great.

DO WARS HAVE RULES?

Henri Dunant founded the Red Cross as a medical service to care for the war wounded. In 1864, the first Geneva Convention was signed, guaranteeing their protection. Later treaties attempted to minimize the suffering of war and to ensure that prisoners and civilians are treated with respect. Groups using ▸▸ TERRORISM to reach their goal do not obey rules.

HOW DO WARS END?

Wars between nations end when the leaders of one side agree to surrender to prevent further destruction. Wars also end when leaders perceive there is a military stalemate, or when they are threatened with revolt from below by their disaffected people.

▲ ARMED PROFESSIONALS
Nations at war rely on their armed forces—army, navy, and air force—to fight the opposing side. Some nations, such as the US or UK, employ professional full-time soldiers, while others, such as China or Israel, rely on conscription, or forced service.

▲ WEAPONS OF WAR
Expensive, state-of-the-art military equipment allows wealthy nations to engage in warfare far from their own borders. This Typhoon class Russian submarine is the world's largest underwater vessel. It is 558 ft (170 m) long and holds 150 crew.

TERRORISM

If a group feels it cannot achieve its goals under the normal rules of a nation or of international politics, it may resort to terrorism. Terrorists use or threaten violence to make their demands. Some groups target only political enemies; others target anybody.

HOW IS TERRORISM SET APART FROM WARFARE?

Terrorism has been around since the Jewish Zealots in the 1st century CE. Today, it can be difficult to separate terrorism from other forms of warfare. Guerrilla fighters, small bands who attack larger armies, often use terrorist tactics. Governments may also use illegal violence as part of their secret service operations.

war

▲ TERROR AGAINST TERROR
The use of terrorist tactics—surprise, boldness, and a willingness to target the innocent—is becoming increasingly common in conflicts around the globe. These Amal fighters (a Syrian-backed militia) are launching missiles into a refugee camp in Lebanon, trying to target a Palestinian terror group hiding there. Thousands of refugees with no links to terrorism have died in such attacks.

FIND OUT MORE ▸▸ New World Order 314–315 • Political World 216–217

◄ ZEMIN AND BUSH
President Jiang Zemin of China and President George W. Bush of the US met in October 2001 to improve links between their countries. During the Cold War, China and the US were enemies.

NEW WORLD ORDER

After 1945, two powerful and opposing nations emerged within the ▶▶ INTERNATIONAL COMMUNITY: the Soviet Union and the United States. When the Soviet Union fell apart in 1990 and the Cold War ended, a new order began, with the US as the world's only superpower.

WHAT IS THE NEW BALANCE OF POWER?

The US is now the world's most powerful country, giving it a leadership role in global issues. Its global leadership is balanced by regional powers, such as the nations of the European Union (EU), the Middle East (Arab League), and the Association of South East Asian Nations (ASEAN). Their relationships are marked by both cooperation and conflict.

IS THE NEW ORDER STABLE?

The Cold War order was made stable by ▶▶ SECURITY alliances between nations, to align themselves with the might of the two superpowers. Nations must now find other reasons to work together, because stability will depend on countries agreeing on shared goals.

WHAT TRENDS WILL AFFECT THE NEW ORDER?

Trends such as ▶▶ GLOBALIZATION will affect how economic power is shared between nations. Regional powers, such as the European Union, may become stronger to counter US power. Security issues such as terrorism may remain a focus worldwide.

DEVASTATION IN CHECHNYA ▶
As the Soviet Union's power crumbled at the end of the Cold War, many new conflicts emerged at its borders. In Chechnya, the new leaders in Russia waged war to stop a movement for national independence.

GLOBALIZATION

▲ FACTORIES ABROAD
Sights such as this German auto factory in Shanghai, China, are now more common. Companies can set up factories wherever there is a workforce.

Globalization has brought new wealth and new problems to the world. When the Cold War ended, a vast global economy emerged. Trade and migration between countries became easier, and big businesses set up bases across the world. The term also describes the spread of Western culture.

WHAT ARE THE RISKS OF GLOBALIZATION?

Creating a truly global market that includes every nation could make business more efficient, improving everyone's quality of life. But if some people are excluded, the gap between the rich and poor of the world could grow. Governments must also make sure that the economic power of a huge business does not undermine the rights of some sections of society.

WHEN DID GLOBALIZATION BEGIN?

The term "globalization" was first used in the 1980s, but trade on a global scale has been going on for centuries. In the 16th and 17th centuries, Portugal, Spain, the Netherlands, and Britain built up trading empires that spanned the world. The Industrial Revolution of the 19th century also helped to unite the world's markets. Global trade slowed down during the two World Wars, but began to build up again in the late 1980s, toward the end of the Cold War.

CAN INDIVIDUAL NATIONS AFFECT GLOBAL TRENDS?

Individual nations may not have much power on their own, but they can open up their economies to the world as a whole by working as part of larger organizations. Nations can also work together to agree on a set of international rules, which should apply to businesses wherever they are based.

INTERNATIONAL COMMUNITY

Representatives of the world's 193 countries meet and talk in different forums, such as the United Nations (UN) and the World Bank. These countries make up a community of nations, which can act together to deal with global problems.

UN flag's olive branches symbolize global peace

Soldiers in UN forces wear blue helmets

▼ UN PEACEKEEPERS
The United Nations Security Council can ask member nations to send troops to war zones to keep the peace. UN soldiers do not normally fight, but they do try to keep enemies apart.

WHAT ARE THE GOALS OF THE UNITED NATIONS?
The major goals of the United Nations are defined in its charter. The first is to recognize each nation's sovereignty, or the right to govern itself. The second is to encourage a policy of nonintervention in each other's affairs. The UN also seeks to prevent conflict by providing a forum for cooperation.

new world order

CAN THE COMMUNITY HELP THE WEAK?
The international community aims to maintain global peace, which is vital for social progress. It also provides aid for countries facing great difficulty, such as those devastated by famine, debt, or war. Aid might come in the form of food or medicine, or a deal to cut one nation's debt to another.

National badge shows a soldier's home nation

Vehicles painted white to show they belong to UN forces

KENYA

SECURITY

The government of every country needs a security system to protect its citizens. Governments must have the resources to defend the country from attack, and gather good information to warn against future attacks. Under the new world order, the need for global security requires nations to work together.

IS SECURITY NEEDED IN THE NEW WORLD ORDER?
After the Cold War, many nations hoped to cut military spending and put the money into social projects, such as poverty relief, instead. But the new world order created new tensions and pockets of resistance across the globe, so that defense spending started to grow again in 1995.

WHAT DOES SECURITY COST?
The cost of protecting the world by military and other means is enormous. Military spending around the world is roughly $1,200,000,000,000 (1.2 trillion) per year, or about 2.4 percent of the global economy. US spending makes up a third of the global total.

Solar panels generate power from the Sun

MILITARY SATELLITE ▶
This spy satellite is used to detect missile launches and nuclear explosions. It helps the US to find out which countries are testing or firing nuclear missiles.

Infrared sensor detects heat sources from space

FIND OUT MORE ▶▶ Cold War 435 • Industrial Revolution 418–419 • International Organizations 434 • Satellites 28

GLOBAL PROTEST

People who object to their government's policies may gather together to protest. But many issues, such as **▶▶ DEBT** and the **▶▶ ENVIRONMENT**, affect people across the globe. In the 1990s, global protest groups emerged, uniting voices of protest from all nations.

HOW DO GLOBAL PROTESTERS GET ORGANIZED?
Cheaper travel and improvements in communications, such as the development of the Internet, have made it easier for people from different countries—already united by shared opinions—to meet and plan political action or demonstrations.

WHAT CAN PROTESTERS ACHIEVE?
By questioning decisions made or actions taken by world leaders and big business, protesters can draw other people into a wider discussion of the issue. This democratic debate can influence global as well as national decisions. Protesters can also share knowledge with others about how such issues affect their own countries.

◀ ON THE MARCH
Protests can alert the wider public to issues that demand action. This protest in Seattle, in 1999, drew media attention to issues being discussed by the World Trade Organization, and inspired more people to support global protest in other countries.

WHAT ARE THE PROTESTS AGAINST?
Although global protests express many different concerns, an issue at the root of many protests is equality. For example, some protesters feel that people in poor countries are treated unfairly in the global community, because international rules are made by powerful countries to help their own economies.

DEBT

Wealthy countries have loaned money to the governments of poor countries. As a result, debt payments cost the world's poorest people US$100 million a day, on top of the cost of basic survival. This makes it difficult for the poor to escape poverty.

CAN DEBT BE CANCELED?
About five percent of the debt of developing countries has been canceled by wealthy countries. In return for this, countries in debt had to agree to open their economies to the global market. People fighting to reduce such debt want more of it canceled faster, with fewer controls placed on the countries in debt.

global protest

ENVIRONMENT

Companies desperate to compete in the global market often do not respect the environment. Protestors campaign to protect the environment from human damage—pollution or habitat destruction, and the threat of global warming—by setting up international controls.

WHAT IS SUSTAINABLE DEVELOPMENT?
In the past, Western countries have often achieved wealth by using up natural resources such as coal or forests, without considering the future effects on the environment. Sustainable development aims for growth that works with nature rather than against it—for example, replanting logging areas with new trees.

GM CROP PROTEST ▶
Greenpeace activists attack a field of genetically modified (GM) crops in the UK. They aim to persuade more people that GM plants are a hazard to the environment.

FIND OUT MORE ▶▶ Economy 302–303 • Human Impact 64–65 • New World Order 314–315

HUMAN RIGHTS

Human rights are basic rights and freedoms, to which all people are believed to be entitled. After World War II, the United Nations (UN) drew up a list of human rights to protect all citizens and promote the rights of each individual.

DOES EVERYONE AGREE OVER HUMAN RIGHTS?
Some human rights are accepted by almost all cultures and political parties, while others are still disputed. For example, rights supporting political freedoms, such as the right to vote in elections, are more widely accepted than those supporting economic and social freedoms, such as equal rights for women.

WHAT IS SOVEREIGNTY?
Nations have rights, just as citizens within nations do. The right of nations to make decisions free from outside control is called sovereignty. Sovereignty can be a barrier to ▶▶ HUMANITARIANISM, if a nation refuses to admit to its human rights problems.

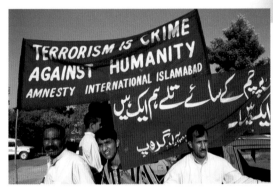

▲ **UN UNIVERSAL DECLARATION**
On December 10, 1948, world leaders announced that the UN had voted to support a single human rights law for all humanity. The Soviet Union, South Africa, and Saudi Arabia chose not to vote on this issue.

◀ **RIGHTS CAMPAIGNERS**
Groups like Amnesty International help to defend human rights worldwide. This banner was raised in Pakistan to challenge those who supported the Taliban's rule in neighboring Afghanistan.

human rights

CAN HUMAN RIGHTS ABUSERS BE PUNISHED?
International law on human rights allows the international community to punish politicians if they abuse the rights of their citizens. But many states reject this use of international law, because they suspect that it could be used to control a country, rather than to improve its human rights.

▲ **INTERNATIONAL COURT OF JUSTICE, THE HAGUE**
Nations can bring a complaint to the International Court of Justice in The Hague, in the Netherlands, about crimes committed by another nation. This 1999 sitting of the court found NATO countries not guilty of a complaint by Yugoslavia that it had been illegally bombed.

HUMANITARIANISM

The goal of humanitarianism is to put human welfare above all things. In warfare, for example, the humanitarian approach is that doctors should treat wounded enemy soldiers as well as their own, without concern for the political issues involved. Humanitarian organizations provide vital sources of aid in times of war or crisis.

WHAT IS IMPARTIAL AID?
Humanitarian organizations, such as the Red Cross, are able to enter war-torn areas to get help to the people who need it most. All sides trust them to give impartial aid during a conflict—to help any human being who needs it, whichever political side they may be on. Some humanitarian aid agencies prefer to be partial, giving aid only to the people whose political positions they share.

▲ **FOOD AID REACHES THE HUNGRY**
In 2001, wealthier countries gave food to thousands of Afghan refugees through the World Food Program. Refugees from wars or government oppression urgently require access to food, clean water, and shelter.

FIND OUT MORE ▶▶ Cold War 435 • International Organizations 434

SCULPTURE

Sculpture is three-dimensional art. Traditionally, there are two main methods: carving material such as wood or stone, and modeling forms by adding pieces of material such as clay. Modern artists have explored new materials and techniques.

Sculpture is 13 ft 6 in (4.1 m) high

The cobra is the serpent demon, representing evil

WOODEN MASK ▶
Wood is carved to make sculptures or functional objects such as this Sri Lankan dancer's mask, created from carved and painted wood.

WHAT DOES "THREE-DIMENSIONAL" MEAN?
The term refers to the three dimensions of space—length, breadth, and depth. It is a useful way of distinguishing between art such as painting, drawing, and prints, which are two-dimensional (flat), and sculpture, which is three-dimensional.

HORSES OF SAN MARCO ▼
Four life-size horses stand atop the Basilica de San Marco, Venice. They date from the 4th century BCE to the 4th century CE. They were taken to Italy from Constantinople in the 13th century.

▲ RELIEF CARVING
This detail is from an ancient Hindu relief carving cut into a massive rock in Tamil Nadu, southern India. It was made during the 7th or 8th centuries.

Material is steel mesh sprayed with expanding foam, covered with fiber-glass skin, and topped with ceramic tiles for mosaic effect

IS SCULPTURE ALWAYS VIEWED FROM ALL SIDES?
Not all sculptures are carved in the round. Relief sculptures are carved on one side only, and stand out from a background surface. Relief panels have been used since ancient times, often to decorate important buildings, such as temples and churches.

HOW IS SCULPTURE MADE?
Techniques depend upon the materials used. When carving stone or wood, the sculptor chips away with a hammer and chisel. When sculpting clay, artists may use their hands. Clay models may be cast in bronze to create a strong, permanent sculpture. Other techniques include welding metal, molding plastic or concrete, and using fiberglass.

Big face decorates most of Halpern's sculptures, often inspired by Picasso

sculpture

◀ OPHELIA, DEBORAH HALPERN, 1996
Australian artist Deborah Halpern (1957–) creates public art, sculptures created for outside. This one adds color and exuberance to city life in Melbourne.

Bronze consists of copper mixed with small amounts of lead and tin. This bronze is overlaid with gold

FIND OUT MORE ▶▶ Decorative Arts

ARTISTS

Artists are people who create art. Although some of them have no formal training, most great artists have studied art. Today, artists can study at art schools, but in the past they learned by apprenticeship, working with more experienced artists. Every culture and period of history has its great artists.

WHERE DO ARTISTS WORK?

Most artists have a studio—a room or other place where they make their art. Many also work outside. For example, landscape painters might make sketches in the open air, and complete the work in their studio. Other artists work mainly in the landscape, completing paintings outside, or creating land art within the natural environment.

HOW DO ARTISTS EARN A LIVING?

Sometimes artists receive commissions (orders) for work from a patron—an individual or an institution. Sometimes existing work is bought by an individual, an institution, or a **▶▶ GALLERY**. Earning a living as an artist is not easy. Vincent van Gogh (1853–1890), whose works now sell for vast sums of money, sold hardly any paintings during his lifetime.

▲ *SURROUNDED ISLANDS*
Christo and Jeanne-Claude surrounded these Florida islands in 1983 with floating pink fabric.

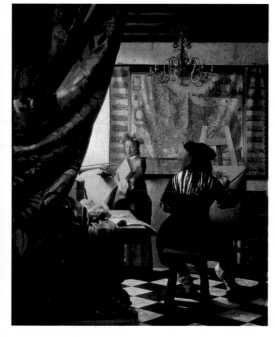

▲ *THE ARTIST'S STUDIO*, JAN VERMEER, *c.* 1665
This Dutch artist (1632–1675) gives us a glimpse of how and where he worked. Seated at his easel, he paints a female model, who poses as Clio, the muse of history.

▲ PABLO PICASSO MIXING PAINTS IN HIS STUDIO
Some artists become celebrities. One of the most versatile and influential artists of the 20th century was the Spanish painter Picasso (1881–1973), who became a world-famous personality.

▲ BARBARA HEPWORTH CARVES IN WOOD
The achievement of women artists has often been overlooked. British sculptor Hepworth (1903–1975) was one of the most famous artists of the 20th century.

GALLERIES

▲ METROPOLITAN MUSEUM
In this tour at the Metropolitan Museum in New York City, a guide shows visitors around the different galleries and explains the history of the paintings.

A gallery is an exhibition space where works of art are shown. Galleries show all kinds of art and crafts—including painting, sculpture, ceramics, installations, video, and photography. They can be public institutions (which are like museums) or privately owned.

artists

DO ALL GALLERIES BUY AND SELL ART?

Privately owned commercial galleries sell the works they exhibit. This type of gallery often specializes in certain types of art—such as contemporary art, or traditional landscape painting. Public galleries acquire works of art to add to their permanent collections— not to sell, but to show to the public.

GREAT GALLERIES OF THE WORLD	
LOCATION	*MAJOR GALLERIES*
London	National Gallery, Tate, Victoria & Albert Museum
Madrid	Prado
New York	Metropolitan Museum of Art, Museum of Modern Art
Paris	Louvre, Musée d'Art Moderne, Musée d'Orsay
Rome	Vatican Museums

FIND OUT MORE ▶▶ Drawing 322 • Painting 320–321 • Sculpture 323

PHOTOGRAPHY

The word photography comes from two Greek words meaning "light" and "drawing." Photography is the process of creating fixed images on a chemically prepared surface, or on an image sensor in a digital camera.

WHO INVENTED PHOTOGRAPHY?
Joseph Nicéphore Niépce (1765–1833) took the first photograph c. 1827. However, his process needed eight hours of exposure to light, and the picture was fuzzy. In 1837 Louis Daguerre (1787–1851) created a sharp but one-use image in a few minutes. In 1839 William Henry Fox Talbot (1800–1877) presented negative film and prints—still used in today's photography.

WHEN DID CAMERAS BECOME PORTABLE?
In the early days of photography, cameras were large and cumbersome, and pictures were made on individual glass plates. The big breakthrough came when George Eastman (1854–1932) invented flexible film. In 1888, he introduced the Kodak camera— it was small, light, and loaded with a roll of film. The craze for snapshot photography soon spread.

▲ MOTION IN PICTURES
Eadweard Muybridge (1830–1904) developed a technique for taking a rapid sequence of photographs, which revealed surprising truths about the way animals moved. Before his photographs were published, painters wrongly depicted galloping horses with all four legs outstretched.

▲ LANDSCAPE BY DENNIS STOCK
In this colored landscape, American photographer Dennis Stock (1928–) uses the effects of the stormy sky to create atmosphere. Dark foreground shadows contrast with the trees and path, which glow in shafts of light.

▲ INTERIOR BY EUGENE ATGET
The French photographer Atget (1857–1927) recorded the changing face of 19th- and 20th-century Paris in more than 10,000 photos. His work is both art and social document.

HAS PHOTOGRAPHY INFLUENCED PAINTING?
The influence has always worked both ways. In the early days of snapshots, for example, Impressionist painters were inspired by their accidental effects, such as the blurring of moving figures, and figures being cropped by the photo's edge. Photographic portraits and landscapes are often inspired by painted ones.

◄ *AFGHAN GIRL* BY STEVE MCCURRY
This photograph of an Afghan girl in a Pakistani refugee camp was taken in 1984 and appeared on the cover of *National Geographic* magazine. It shows her as ragged and scared, yet dignified, gazing directly at the photographer and the viewer. In its way, it is as unforgettable a portrait as the *Mona Lisa* by Leonardo da Vinci.

photography

WHAT DO DOCUMENTARY PHOTOGRAPHERS DO?
Since the 19th century, documentary photographers have recorded the experiences of others. Photographs of Victorian street sellers or of poverty-stricken US farmers in the Great Depression made a huge impact on public awareness. Tragic images of the Vietnam War reduced public support for the war in the US.

HOW DOES DIGITAL PHOTOGRAPHY WORK?
Today the popularity of digital cameras has grown. Using light-sensitive electronic sensors instead of film, digital cameras ensure that each picture gets the right amount of light (autoexposure) and is perfectly sharp (autofocus). The images are usually stored in removable memory cards, which can be transferred to a computer and printed out or sent over the Internet.

FIND OUT MORE ▶▶ Color 180 • Lenses 181 • Light 178–179 • Media 298–299 • Painting 320–321

DESIGN

Design is the way something is planned, arranged, and made. A designer aims to create things that look good and do their job well. Most manufactured objects—including the page you are reading, the chair you are sitting on, and the clothes you are wearing—have been designed. Increasingly, computers are used in design.

Mazes create visual intrigue and entertainment

Plants are evenly spaced within a geometric layout

▲ GARDEN DESIGN
This wonderful Renaissance garden at the Villa d'Este in Tivoli, Italy, is a strictly geometric, formal design. Garden designs may be formally planned—like this one, with fountains and mazes—or more relaxed and natural.

WHAT MAKES A GOOD DESIGN?
The successful combination of form (how good something looks) and function (how well it works) is the basis of good design. A chair, for example, should look good and be fit for its purpose—which is to provide a safe, comfortable support for a person to sit on. There are many institutions that award prizes for excellent designs.

WHY DO DESIGNS CHANGE?
Designs change as lifestyles and tastes change, and as new materials and technologies develop. For example, in the 20th century, eating styles became less formal, and people wanted convenience. At the same time, new materials such as stainless steel became available. As a result, kitchen products became more streamlined and more desirable.

Whistle is plastic bird

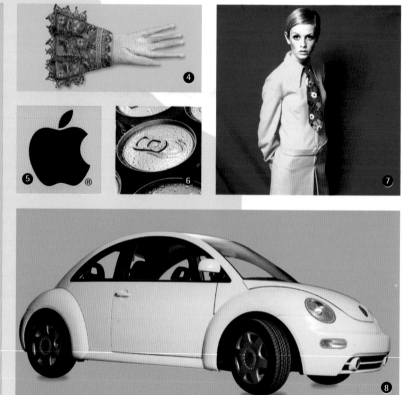

1 **Graphic design:** This movie poster was designed by Saul Bass for *Vertigo* (1958). The spiral creates a sense of vertigo (dizziness). 2 **Homeware:** This stylish kettle was designed by Michael Graves and made by Alessi in 1985. 3 **Furniture design:** Charles Rennie Mackintosh designed this elegant chair c. 1898.

4 **Fashion design:** This 16th- or 17th-century leather glove is trimmed with tapestry woven in silk and gold. 5 **Brand design:** This is the logo of Apple Macintosh, the first firm to design personal computers in bright colors. 6 **Product design:** The ring-pull for cans is convenient. 7 **Fashion design:** Twiggy models a new look in 1967. 8 **Car design:** The 1998 Volkswagen Beetle updates the original car, designed in the 1930s.

HOW OLD IS FASHION DESIGN?
Some 40,000 years ago, people sewed hides together to fit the body, using needles made from mammoth ivory and reindeer bone. This was mainly for survival, but there was also some emphasis placed on the decorative value of clothing. In many ancient cultures, such as Egypt, Greece, and Rome, fashion was linked to wealth and social status.

HOW IS A PRODUCT DESIGNED?
Designers sketch out ideas on paper, decide on materials, and then make detailed drawings. They also make sketches on a computer to create images of three-dimensional models, which the designer can then manipulate and view from all angles. Usually a prototype (trial product) is built and fully tested before being manufactured.

design

FIND OUT MORE ▶▶ Architecture 328–329 • Cinema 346–347 • Construction 202–203 • Renaissance 398 • Technology 154

DECORATIVE ARTS

In contrast to the fine arts of painting and sculpture, this term refers to the design of everyday objects that are turned into works of art. These objects are often purely ornamental. The decorative arts include textiles, jewelry, glasswork, and ceramics.

WHO ARE THE GREAT DECORATIVE ARTISTS?

The most famous is probably William Morris (1834–1896). He believed that the craftsmanship of decorative art improved the lives of those who made everyday objects and those who used them. His firm produced furniture, tapestry, stained glass, fabrics, carpets, and wallpaper—all still popular today. Other famous names include Clarice Cliff (1899–1972) and Louis Comfort Tiffany (1848–1933).

Minute hand

STARBURST WALL CLOCK, 1953 ►
This clock by American designer George Nelson has 12 colorful rays, each representing an hour.

Materials used are beech, metal, and acrylic lacquer

Shape of the vase is both beautiful and functional

Bold simplicity of line and color are part of the appeal that keeps this clock in production today

Illustration depicts one of the 12 Labors of Hercules

❶

❷

❸   **❹**   **❺**   **❻**   **❼**   **❽**

1 Ceramics: Ancient Greek painted vase. **2 Ceramics:** This Art Deco plate was hand painted by Clarice Cliff in a pattern called *Autumn*. **3 Textiles:** Finnish designer Maija Isola created this flowery fabric pattern in the 1960s. **4 Textiles:** William Morris wallpaper of the 19th century is still manufactured in the 21st.

5 Textiles: Detail from a Persian Bidjar rug c. 1890. **6 Jewelry:** Art Deco enameled brooch c. 1925. **7 Metalwork:** The *Artichoke* lampshade was designed by Paul Henningsen in 1958. Manufactured from copper and steel by Louis Poulsen, it is still popular today. **8 Glasswork:** This beautiful glass table lamp with *Poppy* motif was designed in the Art Nouveau style by American glass designer Louis Comfort Tiffany.

WHAT IS ART DECO?

This decorative style spread through all areas of decorative art between World Wars I and II—from jewelry to ceramics, from furniture to architecture. Combining varied influences from Cubist paintings to ancient Egyptian and Aztec jewelry, Art Deco's vivid style was characterized by sleek lines, bold colors, and geometric forms.

WHY IS SOME POTTERY CALLED CHINA?

People sometimes use the term china to mean crockery, but china is a special type of ceramic called porcelain. First produced in China in the 7th or 8th century, it is hard and translucent (light can shine through it). Europeans did not discover how to make it until the 18th century in Meissen, Germany, which is still famous for its china.

decorative arts

FIND OUT MORE ▶▶ Ancient Greece 376–377 • China's First Empire 378 • Sculpture 323

ARCHITECTURE

Architecture is the art of designing buildings. Architects design buildings in different shapes and sizes, from single-story houses to soaring ▸▸ SKYSCRAPERS. The combination of form and function is vital, since buildings have to be safe as well as good-looking and suitable for their purpose.

WHY DO BUILDINGS LOOK SO DIFFERENT?

The way a building looks depends on several factors: its purpose, its particular architectural style, and the materials and technology available. Domestic buildings, corporate offices, and sacred architecture, for example, have entirely different functions that are reflected in their size, form, and content.

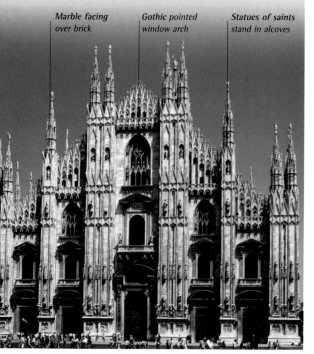

Marble facing over brick

Gothic pointed window arch

Statues of saints stand in alcoves

▲ DUOMO, MILAN
One of the world's largest cathedrals, Duomo was designed to hold 40,000 people. Begun in the 14th century, it was not finished until the 19th. The façade reflects many styles, including Gothic and neoclassical.

WHAT IS SUSTAINABLE ARCHITECTURE?

Sustainable buildings aim to be environmentally friendly. The construction and running of buildings causes pollution and uses up energy and resources. Buildings made with renewable materials, nontoxic paints, solar panels, good insulation, and even toilets that use less water all help to preserve the planet.

HOW DO ARCHITECTS WORK?

A client tells the architect about the type of building they want and how much they can pay. The architect then makes designs, and works out detailed technical drawings, often using computer programs. Engineers check the plans and any models to make sure that the building will be structurally sound.

Natural daylight reflects down into the building, which means less artificial light is needed

Central cone is made of 360 laminated glass mirrors that reflect everything around them

Cone inside the building supports the dome on top of the building (see image below)

REICHSTAG, BERLIN ▸
Germany's parliament building, the Reichstag, was partially destroyed by a fire in 1933. When it was renovated by the British architect Norman Foster in the 1990s, the use of glass symbolized the openness of democracy.

architecture

Visitors walk up the ramp that spirals up the glass dome

New glass dome rises from the shell of the 19th-century building

EXTERIOR OF REICHSTAG

SAPPORO DOME, HOKKAIDO ▶
Built by Japan for the 2002 World Cup, this futuristic stadium has a translucent domed roof made from Teflon-coated fiberglass. Its natural-turf field can be moved inside or outside by floating it on a cushion of air.

WHAT MATERIALS DO ARCHITECTS USE?

Traditional building materials are stone, wood, brick, and concrete. However, as technology develops, so do new materials. Steel and glass are commonly used. Fabrics are created by coating fiberglass with a durable plastic such as Teflon to make a membrane (skin) that can be attached to a steel framework.

WHAT DOES CLASSICAL ARCHITECTURE MEAN?

The architecture of the ancient Greeks and Romans, which was based on balanced, harmonious proportions, is known as classical architecture. It has had a huge influence on the history of Western architecture. Some modern architects still use elements of the classical tradition today.

THE CLASSICAL ORDERS

The ancient Greeks designed buildings in three orders (styles). Each had its own design rules, such as features for columns. The shaft of the column is topped by a capital.

Capital is a circle topped by a square

Shaft is fluted

DORIC

Volute (spiral scroll)

Shaft is fluted

IONIC

Acanthus leaves for decoration

Shaft is slim and plain

CORINTHIAN

▲ PARTHENON (447–432 BCE), ATHENS
This temple's Doric columns support the beams and a richly carved triangular pediment at each end of its roof. Though now in ruins, the Parthenon is the most famous example of classical architecture.

SKYSCRAPERS

The term skyscraper became popular in the US in the 1880s to describe a new type of tall office building in Chicago and New York City. They rose up to 12 stories, a startling height at the time.

WHAT IS THE WORLD'S TALLEST BUILDING?

Buildings could only rise as high as about 250 ft (75 m) until the invention of steel-frame construction. In 2010 the Petronas Towers in Kuala Lumpur, Malaysia—at 1,483 ft (452 m)—was overtaken by Burj Khalifa in Dubai, United Arab Emirates, which stands at 2,717 ft (828 m).

CHRYSLER BUILDING, NEW YORK CITY ▶
Completed in 1930, this Art Deco masterpiece was briefly the tallest building in the world at 1,048 ft (319 m). In 1931 the nearby Empire State Building overtook it, rising to 1,250 m (381 m).

FIND OUT MORE ▶▶ Ancient Greece 376–377 • Construction 202–203 • Design 326

MUSIC

Music is the art of making sounds and arranging them in an entertaining way. People create and listen to music for pleasure, celebration, and to express ideas and feelings. Types of music include classical, folk, and pop.

HOW IS MUSIC CREATED?

Instruments generate sounds, as does the human voice. Some sounds with a specific ▶▶ PITCH are called notes. These sounds are then grouped to create ▶▶ RHYTHM and ▶▶ MELODY. Some music is created spontaneously, and some is composed over many years. Musicians compose alone and in groups.

LIVE PERFORMANCE ▶
Live performance takes place on stage in front of an audience. Although more people listen to recorded music (on CD, radio, and in clubs), watching the skill of musicians playing live together creates a great atmosphere.

Double bass has four strings, but a fifth can be added to play lower notes

▲ WOODSTOCK, NEW YORK, 1969
Joe Cocker's band prepares to perform for a huge crowd at the Woodstock music festival. Around 500,000 fans attended the event, which featured 30 top bands and musicians. It was the first festival for popular music.

Plucking the strings by hand produces a stronger rhythm than using a bow

HOW DO WE REMEMBER PIECES OF MUSIC?

Music can be memorized, written down, or recorded on to a medium such as CD. There are several systems for writing music. The most common is to create a score. A score is a page with a series of five-line grids called staves. Using notation (symbols), a composer writes the melody and rhythm of a piece of music.

music

RHYTHM

The basis of all music is its beat, which divides it into units of time. Composers and musicians group these beats together, decide how long each beat is, and place accents on some for emphasis. This creates the basic rhythm of a piece of music.

WHAT ARE THE BASIC RHYTHMS?

The most basic rhythm is a group of two beats (1, 2) as in the act of walking or the sound of a heartbeat. Another basic rhythm is a group of three beats (1, 2, 3), as in a waltz. Both groups have the accent on the first beat. These two basic rhythms can be multiplied or combined to create more complex rhythms. A group of beats repeated in a regular rhythm is a bar.

Fret is wooden – pressing the string against the fret changes the pitch

▲ SNARE DRUM AND STICKS
Drummers tap rhythm with sticks, by hand, or with a foot pedal.

PITCH

Pitch is the height or depth of a particular note or sound. When two or more different notes are played at once, the sound produced is called harmony. Harmonies can change the mood of a piece of music, giving it a bright or a dark feel.

WHY ARE NOTES AT DIFFERENT PITCHES?
The pitch of a note depends on the speed its sound vibrates at: a fast speed of vibration produces a high note, a slow speed produces a low note. The rate of vibration per second is called the frequency of the note. In the West, concert pitch is the standard to which instruments are usually tuned for performance.

▲ DIDGERIDOO
The sounds made by blowing into a didgeridoo have a slow speed of vibration, creating low notes.

A letter labels each of the eight notes in this octave, which climbs from C to C—where a new octave begins at a higher pitch

◄ SCALE IN KEY OF C MAJOR
A scale shows the rising or falling pitches of notes. It usually contains one octave (eight notes). A key is a group of notes based on a particular note, such as C major.

MELODY

The arrangement of differently pitched notes one after the other creates a melody or tune. Simple melodies consist of just a few notes, but more complex ones are created using many different notes, rhythms, and harmonies. Good melodies tend to be catchy.

HOW MANY MELODIES ARE THERE?
The world never seems to run out of new tunes, although echoes of one tune often turn up in another. There are only seven notes in the Western scale, but the way notes are combined into patterns and harmonies, and grouped into rhythms, creates countless melodies. Other cultures in the world have more complex scales that create even more melodies.

▲ RAVI SHANKAR
Indian classical musicians, such as sitar player Ravi Shankar (1920–), use sets of notes called ragas, melodic scales. There are about 130 ragas. Each has its own mood.

◄ BILLIE HOLIDAY
This jazz singer (1915–1959) sang hundreds of songs. Since the songs were not her own, the melodies were often familiar to audiences. However, the way she used her voice made each song unique.

Saxophone is a woodwind instrument, not brass, because its mouthpiece is a reed

FIND OUT MORE ▶▶ Composition 333 • Musical Instruments 332 • Musicals 338 • Opera 338 • Orchestra 335 • Popular Music 334

MUSICAL INSTRUMENTS

We use a huge range of instruments to produce sounds and make music. Some are simple pieces of solid wood or hollowed-out seashells. Others are highly technical or electric. Instruments vary around the world, and each has its own character.

HOW ARE MUSICAL INSTRUMENTS CATEGORIZED?

Acoustic instruments generate sound physically and electronic instruments create sound electrically. There are four acoustic groups: percussion (hit or shaken), wind (woodwind and brass; blown), string (bowed or plucked), and keyboard (played by striking a key).

Cymbal — Tom-tom
Snare
High-hat
Floor tom
Bass drum

▲ DRUM KIT
Drums belong to the percussion family. This standard kit is used in popular music, such as jazz and rock. A drummer needs coordination and energy to hit several drums at once using different rhythms.

HOW DO INSTRUMENTS GENERATE SOUND?

An instrument creates sound when part of it vibrates rapidly. The column of air inside a wind instrument, the string of a string instrument, or the stretched skin of a drum all vibrate when played. This vibration produces sound waves in the air, which we hear as musical notes.

Tuning peg

Violin bow

◄ VIOLIN
Like most string instruments, the violin has four strings, each tuned to different notes. It is played either with a bow or by plucking it with the fingers.

▲ GRAND PIANO
When a musician hits a key, a hammer strikes a string inside the piano. The string vibrates, making a sound. In a grand piano the strings are arranged horizontally. In an upright piano they are arranged vertically, to save space.

Keyboard has 88 keys. The difference between each is called a semitone

Tuning pin adjusts the tautness of the string to produce the correct pitch

Felt-covered hammer makes the string vibrate

HOW DO ELECTRONIC INSTRUMENTS WORK?

Electronic instruments—such as electronic keyboards—do not make actual sounds in the way an acoustic instrument does. An electronic instrument produces an electric signal that is transmitted to an amplifier and then broadcast through a loudspeaker. Using a process called synthesis, electronic instruments imitate acoustic instruments or create their own sounds.

Mouthpiece — Valve

Wide, flared bell to broadcast the sound

▲ TRUMPET
This brass instrument is played by blowing air through the mouthpiece into a narrow metal tube. Pressing the valves alters the length of the column of air, producing different notes.

instruments

FIND OUT MORE ▸▸ Music 330–331 • Orchestra 335 • Sound 176–177

COMPOSITION

Most music is imagined first and then written down as a composition in a ▶SCORE. The music might be vocal or instrumental, for a single singer or a big orchestra, and might last for a few minutes or a few hours. A hit single on the charts, a movie soundtrack, and a Mozart symphony are all compositions.

WHERE DO COMPOSERS GET THEIR IDEAS?
Sometimes composers are inspired by an existing melody or just a few notes that they have heard. Sometimes composers express the mood or emotions they are feeling at that time. People, plays, poems, novels, paintings, and landscapes can all give composers ideas for music. In sacred music, inspiration is believed to come from God.

WHAT ARE THE PARTS OF A COMPOSITION?
Compositions are lyric (with words) or instrumental (without words). A song usually consists of several verses and a repeated chorus. An instrumental may have more than one movement (section). A concerto, for an orchestra and one or more soloists, usually has three movements. A symphony, a large-scale orchestral composition, has four or five movements.

WHAT COMES FIRST—WORDS OR MUSIC?
Some composers write the music first, inspiring their lyricist (songwriter) to then write the words. Other composers rely on words to give them the inspiration to write music. Words and music can also be written together by a single composer or a team of musicians.

IS ALL MUSIC COMPOSED?
Some music, such as jazz, is largely improvised (made up on the spot). The musicians often start with an agreed written melody but then individually or collectively use it as a basis to create new, unwritten music. Improvisation has always been part of folk and blues, where lyrics and melodies are often improvised.

▲ SINGER/SONGWRITER
Alicia Keys (1981–), the American rhythm and blues singer, writes the music and words to most of her own songs. Other singers, such as the jazz vocalist Ella Fitzgerald (1917-1996), were famous for interpreting other people's songs.

KEY COMPOSERS
1567–1643	● Claudio Monteverdi
1685–1750	● Johann Sebastian Bach
1685–1759	● George Frideric Handel
1756–1791	● Wolfgang Mozart
1770–1827	● Ludwig van Beethoven
1882–1971	● Igor Stravinsky

▲ MUSIC TECHNOLOGY
Computers have made composition faster. Composers can use software to notate a score instead of writing by hand. They can also record melodies using electronic instruments and build up a piece gradually.

SCORE

A score is the written document of a composition. It shows the tempo (speed), rhythm, key, and instruments. Scores used to be written out by hand, but most are now produced on computer.

WHAT ARE PARTS?
A full score is the complete composition for every musician, while the parts of a score are just those notes an individual musician or singer has to perform. The conductor uses a comprehensive copy of the entire composition, but each musician or singer only requires the part that shows their role.

composition

Rest symbol indicates that no notes are played here

Stave consists of two five-line grids. For this piece, the right hand plays the top or treble line, and the left hand plays the bottom or bass line

HANDWRITTEN SCORE ▶
This score by J. S. Bach is for a well-known piano work titled The Well-Tempered Clavier. It is a fugue written in the key of C minor. A fugue is a variation of the main melody that is played at a higher or lower pitch.

FIND OUT MORE ▶▶ Cinema 346–347 • Music 330–331 • Opera 338 • Orchestra 335 • Poetry 343

POPULAR MUSIC

Popular (pop) music is largely vocal and appeals to a mass, mainly teenage audience. Originally sold as vinyl records, music is now available as compact disks (CDs) and payable downloaded computer files or free, as streaming audio via the Internet. Its popularity is measured by ▶▶ **THE CHARTS**

Acoustic guitar was replaced with an electric guitar in Elvis's later career

Glamorous outfits, such as this satin cowboy shirt, were part of Elvis's image

popular music

WHEN DID POPULAR MUSIC BEGIN?
Popular music began in the late 19th and early 20th century when hit songs were played at music halls and distributed as sheet-music so people could play at home. From the 1930s people such as Bing Crosby and Frank Sinatra sang with swing bands. During the 1950s, rock and roll emerged with songs of rebellion and love.

WHAT STYLES OF POPULAR MUSIC ARE THERE?
The main form of popular music is pop itself. Pop bands usually have singers, guitarists, keyboard players, and percussionists. Rock music has a heavier sound and is guitar-led. Reggae from Jamaica, country from the US, and national folk music, such as rai from Algeria, are also popular around the world.

◀ POP STAR
Popular singers such as Britney Spears sell millions of copies of their records around the world and are international celebrities.

GOLD DISC ▶
A record company awards a gold-plated disc to an artist when they reach certain sales figures for an album or a single. This disc was given to the Swedish band ABBA.

THE CHARTS

The charts measure the popularity of a record by the number of copies it has sold in a given period, usually a week. Most pop musicians dream of reaching number one. Charts show top sellers, highest new entries, fastest climbers, and records on the way down.

WHY ARE THERE SO MANY CHARTS?
Music magazines, radio and television companies, and other organizations all compile their own charts. The best-known charts are the weekly charts for albums and singles, but there are also charts for different types of music, such as classical or jazz. Charts cover different regions, such as a country, and different periods, such as a month or a year.

HOW DO YOU GET TO NUMBER ONE?
A record gets to number one because it has sold more copies than any other record over a specified time. In case a record company or performer tries to influence the charts by artificially boosting sales (with reduced prices or other tricks), all charts are independently checked to ensure their accuracy.

▲ THE BEATLES AT ABBEY ROAD
The *Abbey Road* album was recorded at the Abbey Road studios in London. In 1969 it reached number one in the album charts in both the US and UK. It stayed in the UK charts for 81 weeks.

▲ ELVIS PRESLEY
Elvis Presley (1935–1977) is the most famous face of rock and roll and one of the best-selling singers of all time. He was as well known for his outrageous dancing as for his rich, distinctive singing voice. The songs Elvis sang drew on the American country and blues traditions.

FIND OUT MORE ▶▶ Composition 333 • Music 330 • Musicals 338

An orchestra is a group of musicians playing together under the direction of a conductor. The musicians perform music specially composed for specific instruments in an orchestral performance. They play as soloists, in small groups, and all together, which creates a tremendous sound.

HOW MANY MUSICIANS PLAY IN AN ORCHESTRA?
A full-scale orchestra playing a symphony includes at least 90 musicians, while a smaller orchestra playing a chamber piece ranges from 15 to 45. Sections of the orchestra can perform separately—a string orchestra, for example, includes about 60 musicians.

HOW ARE THE MUSICIANS ARRANGED?
The musicians are arranged into four sections. The strings—such as violins and cellos—sit at the front. The woodwind—such as oboes, clarinets, and bassoons—and brass—such as trumpets and French horns—sit in the middle. Percussion—such as kettledrums and a xylophone—sit at the back.

WHAT DOES A CONDUCTOR DO?
A conductor's job is to make sure that the musicians play perfectly together. A conductor keeps time using a baton (stick) to clearly count out each individual beat in the tempo (speed) the music is to be played.

▲ SIMON RATTLE
The conductor of the Berlin Philharmonic Orchestra uses hand gestures and facial expressions to show how music should be played

TWO BEATS   THREE

FOUR BEATS   FIVE

▲ BEAT PATTERNS
The conductor uses baton patterns to count out beats.

▲ GAMELAN PERCUSSION ORCHESTRA
The gamelan orchestras of Bali in Indonesia use a wide range of percussion instruments, such as gongs, chimes, marimbas, and drums, as well as strings and woodwind. They create an amazing rhythm-driven sound totally unlike that achieved by Western symphony orchestras.

Brass

Percussion, including loud drums

Woodwind

orchestra

▲ ORCHESTRA
An orchestra with every musician playing together is one of the greatest sounds in classical music.

Conductor stands on a raised platform

String section

FIND OUT MORE ►► Composition 333 • Musical Instruments 332 • Opera 338

When people move in time to music, they are dancing. As they dance, they organize their body movements into rhythmic and visual patterns. These dance patterns may be formal, with structured steps and movements, or informal, a natural style of dance known as ►►IMPROVISATION.

WHY DO PEOPLE DANCE?

People have a natural urge to move in time to music. They dance to celebrate an event, or for entertainment and relaxation. Dance is an important part of many religions. Around the world, many folk dances (popular local dances) mark the stages of life, such as birth and death.

WHAT IS CLASSICAL DANCE?

Classical dance is historic and takes many years to learn. Western classical dance is called ballet and combines dance with mime (silent acting). It began in Europe in the 15th century. Countries such as India and Thailand also have great classical dance traditions. ►►CHOREOGRAPHY is used to create classical dance.

Each mudra, or hand gesture, carries a specific meaning

WHIRLING DERVISH ►
The Sufi sect of Islam uses dance and music to worship Allah, or God. Some dancers, known as whirling dervishes, spin around in a trance to empty the mind and help them concentrate on God.

INDIAN CLASSICAL DANCE ►
Bharat natyam is a classical dance from south India. Most Indian dances act out stories from Indian mythology. The movements are often slow, graceful, and controlled.

Feet and hands are decorated with jewelry and red henna, a plant dye

DANCE SHOES

BALLET SHOES
Pointe shoes are made stiff with paper and burlap to allow ballerinas to dance on tiptoe.

FLAMENCO SHOES
Flamenco dancers wear shoes with hard soles and metal on the heels to stamp out the rhythms noisily.

IMPROVISATION

Unlike classical dance, improvised dance has no formal steps, although it can be choreographed. Improvisation is the basis of contemporary, or modern, dance. In it, dancers express their feelings in their movements to create a highly personal, natural performance.

dance

◄ CONTEMPORARY DANCE
These contemporary dancers work closely together, combining their body movements to create interesting shapes and sequences. Each time they perform this improvised dance, it will be slightly different.

Contemporary dancers often wear everyday clothes and dance in their bare feet to feel natural

WHEN DID CONTEMPORARY DANCE START?

Contemporary dance began at the start of the 20th century when US dancer Isadora Duncan (1878–1927) broke away from ballet and developed her own, more natural style. Contemporary dance has many different styles, some of them closely linked to music, such as jazz, rock and roll, and hip-hop.

CAN ANYBODY DANCE?

Anybody can dance, no matter how young or old they are, or how physically fit. People in wheelchairs can move and spin in time to the music, while those who are immobile can move their hands or heads. Deaf people can feel the vibrations of music and respond.

Choreography is the arrangement of dance steps and movements into an organized sequence (order). This means that every dancer knows exactly what steps to perform throughout the performance. Dance is usually choreographed to music.

ARE FOLK DANCES CHOREOGRAPHED?

Folk dances, such as Scottish reels and Spanish flamenco, are not choreographed. However, they do have traditional steps that have developed over centuries and have been passed down through the generations to the present day. Each dancer learns the dance by heart and knows which move to make in time to the music.

HOW ARE DANCE STEPS RECORDED?

Choreographed dance steps must be written down so that they can be remembered over time. The most common recording system, called Benesh Movement Notation, was developed in the 1940s by Rudolf and Joan Benesh. Each movement is recorded with symbols on a five-line diagram. The diagram is combined with the musical notation so that both can be read together.

HOW DOES A CHOREOGRAPHER WORK?

A choreographer works closely with a dance group to create a new dance, designing steps that show off the skills and strengths of the individual dancers. Steps are memorized by counting them out into sequences. Choreographers have usually been dancers themselves.

BENESH MOVEMENT NOTATION

Flowing line should be created from fingertips to shoulders

Back leg is raised high to create a beautiful stretch

Perfect balance is needed to hold pose

ARABESQUE

TOP OF HEAD

SHOULDER LINE

WAIST LINE

KNEE LINE

FLOOR LINE

▲ BENESH MOVEMENT NOTATION FOR ARABESQUE
1 Left hand in front, below the top of head height **2** Right foot is pointed and turned out **3** Right hand is behind, above shoulder height **4** Left knee is bent and turned out **5** Left foot is on the floor **6** Dancer is facing stage left

▲ IRISH FOLK DANCE
Folk dances, such as this Irish jig, are often performed in costumes. This dancer wears soft shoes, but some Irish dances use hard soles.

Hair must be tied back in a neat style

SWAN LAKE ►
Swan Lake (1895) is a famous ballet and was created by the French choreographer Marius Petipa, the Russian choreographer Lev Ivanov, and the music composer Pyotr Tchaikovsky. Based on a German fairy tale, it tells the story of Princess Odette, who is turned into a swan by an evil magician.

The thumb is slightly spread from the fingers for a graceful effect

The ballerinas (female ballet dancers) wear identical white costumes to help them to look like the swans in the story

A tutu is a traditional stiff skirt worn by ballerinas

Toes are pointed and feet arched to create a perfect line along the leg

FIND OUT MORE ▶▶ Composition 333 • Music 330–331 • Musicals 338

OPERA

An opera is a drama set to music. It is performed and sung by singers who act out different roles. Opera is often staged in a grand opera house or theater with lavish costumes and magnificent stage designs. The songs are full of passion and emotion. Opera began in Europe during the Renaissance.

opera

WHAT ARE THE DIFFERENT VOICES IN OPERA?
Opera is technically difficult and takes years of training. The female range covers soprano (high pitch), mezzo-soprano (middle), and contralto (low). The male voice covers tenor (high), baritone (middle), and bass (low).

WHAT ARE THE PARTS OF OPERA?
An opera opens with an overture (an instrumental piece of music). The songs sung by the soloists are arias (Italian for "air"). Recitatives are speechlike passages between arias that move the plot along. A long opera may be broken into several acts.

▼ *LA TRAVIATA*
One of the most famous operas is *La Traviata* (*The Woman Who Strayed*) written by the Italian composer Giuseppe Verdi (1813–1901). It tells the tragic love story of Violetta and Alfredo.

Leading man often has tenor voice and leading lady is usually soprano

Dance reflects opera's origins as a court event with ballet

The chorus is a group of performers who sing in unison

FIND OUT MORE ▶▶ Music 330–331 • Theater 344–345

▲ *SINGIN' IN THE RAIN*
This 1952 movie musical, starring Gene Kelly, is most famous for its title tune, *Singin' in the Rain*. During this song, Kelly sings and dances his way down a street from lamppost to lamppost in the pouring rain.

MUSICALS

Musicals are plays with song and dance. Their stories are fast-paced and dramatic, and the songs are catchy. Musicals are performed in theaters, or made into movies. These big productions need hundreds of cast and crew. A popular musical can run at a theater for many years.

WHERE DID MUSICALS ORIGINATE?
Musicals began in England in the late 19th century by combining the comic stories of operetta (short operas) with the songs and dances of the music hall. It was in the Broadway theater district of New York City in the early 20th century that musicals developed into their modern form: a highly entertaining music and dance show.

HOW ARE MUSICALS PRODUCED?
Musicals are spectacular productions with large choruses of singers and dancers. Musicals can sometimes require hundreds of extras. A composer writes the music and songs, and a choreographer creates the dance sequences. Singing and dancing coaches help the performers learn their parts. The sets built for musicals are often large and visually stunning.

musicals

FIND OUT MORE ▶▶ Cinema 346–347 • Dance 336–337

WRITING

Before writing, people had to store information in their heads. Writing was invented to record information so that it could be passed on to other people. Later it became a means of personal expression.

WILL HANDWRITING ALWAYS EXIST?
Writing has changed throughout history. Early writing was created by scratching in clay. Ancient Egyptians used reed brushes dipped in ink made of carbon, soot, or ochre. None of these forms exist today, and word processing may one day replace handwriting.

WHAT IS CREATIVE WRITING?
Creative writing is using the imagination to write stories, describe events and places, and express thoughts. It is different from writing that records facts and events, such as history or biography. Creative writing includes poems, plays, short stories, and novels, and may also include diaries.

Decorated initial with an image inside opens the page

Borders contain elaborate color illustrations, such as flowers

Latin script describes the life and death of Saint Sebastian

BOOK OF HOURS ▶
These medieval prayer books, often made by monks, were for private reading and meditation at various hours of the day. They were beautifully written on parchment (animal skin) and decorated in brightly colored inks to glorify God. This one was created in 1470 for a French noblewoman, Margaret de Foix.

This hieroglyph was carved in stone in the 7th century CE at the royal palace at Palenque, Mexico

◀ MAYAN WRITING
Mayan writing was hieroglyphic, using pictures or symbols to represent objects, ideas, or sounds. This hieroglyph shows four pictograms.

writing

WHAT IS LITERACY?
Literacy is the ability to read, write, and use language. Without this skill, people are at a disadvantage. They cannot find out information from written sources, such as books or the Internet, and they cannot fill in forms, or write letters, text messages, or emails.

FIND OUT MORE ▶▶ First Scripts 369 • Writers 348

PRINTING

Printing is the mass production of the written word. The Chinese invented wooden print blocks in the 8th century. In the West, all books were written by hand until Johann Gutenberg invented movable type around 1450.

printing

▲ EARLY PRINTING SHOP
This painting shows a 17th-century printing shop in France. The printers first arranged the type (letters) into words on a frame, then added ink. The paper and type were put into a wooden press and squeezed together by turning a screw so that the ink printed on the paper.

HOW DID PRINTING DEVELOP?
Movable metal type—letter molds that can be put together to make words, then taken apart and reused—made printing faster. Combined with the spread of literacy and the new affordability of books, this made information and literature available to the masses. Today, computers and digital technology have replaced movable type and speeded up printing again.

OLD ENGLISH   TIMES   UNIVERSE

▲ TYPEFACES
The alphabet has been designed in many different styles, known as typefaces. Historic typefaces tend to have more detail, while modern styles are simpler and easier to read. Each typeface has a name.

FIND OUT MORE ▶▶ Design 326 • Industrial Revolution 418–419 • Reformation 399

LITERATURE

Literature uses words to create works of art. It is usually written, but the earliest literature was memorized and passed on by word of mouth. Literature has different forms such as poetry, drama (plays), or ▶▶ NOVELS , and they all offer insights into people's deepest thoughts and feelings.

WHAT WERE THE FIRST WORKS OF LITERATURE?

The earliest written works were epic poems—long stories or ▶▶ MYTHS about the adventures of heroes. The Indian epics *Ramayana* and *Mahabharata* (c. 500 BCE) are still read today. Two famous Greek poems, Homer's *Odyssey* and *Iliad*, were first written down from the spoken tradition in the 8th century.

IS LITERATURE DIFFERENT AROUND THE WORLD?

Literature differs from country to country because of the language it is written in. Some forms of literature come from one country, such as Japanese haiku poetry. However, the themes of love, revenge, and death are found everywhere.

◀ *1,001 NIGHTS*
1,001 Nights (also called *The Arabian Nights*) is a collection of traditional folk tales from the Middle East. Scheherazade tells her husband, the sultan, 1,001 wonderful stories to save her life. The tale of Aladdin and his magic flying carpet is one of the stories.

The monsters seem fierce, but Max can tame them with a single look

Set design and costumes were amazing in this 1999 opera staging of the book

Max is given the name "wild thing" by his mother for being a naughty boy

The Hatter with the March Hare and Dormouse

Alice is invited to a mad tea party at the March Hare's home

◀ *WHERE THE WILD THINGS ARE*
Maurice Sendak's tale was thought to be too scary for children when it was first published in the US in 1963. In it, a boy named Max sails to the Land of the Wild Things, where he meets monsters and becomes king. However, Max's travels are imaginary, and the smell of his supper brings him back to reality.

▲ *THE ADVENTURES OF ALICE IN WONDERLAND*
This fantasy of a young girl's adventures down a rabbit hole was written by English author Lewis Carroll in 1865, and illustrated by John Tenniel. It is a witty commentary on society and education in Victorian times.

WHY DO PEOPLE WRITE LITERATURE?

Creative people who have something to say need to find a means of expression. Painters use paint, and writers use words. Authors write to inform, explore, amuse, inspire, and to tell a good story. They also write ▶▶ NONFICTION to record events and lives.

IL POSTINO ▶
Il Postino (1994) was a film of a novel called *Burning Patience* (1983), written by Chilean author Antonio Skarmeta. The story, set in Italy, tells how a humble mailman is inspired by poetry to win the woman of his dreams and to express his political beliefs.

▲ *THE TALE OF GENJI*
This early form of the novel was written by a Japanese noblewoman, Lady Murasaki, in the 11th century. It is about the life of a prince called Genji and describes the daily activities of the Japanese royal court.

NOVELS

Novels are stories in prose (not verse) that explore people and society using imaginary characters. They are structured around ▸PLOTS and are usually more than 50,000 words in length. Novels are organized into categories of fiction called ▸GENRES.

WHAT WERE THE EARLIEST NOVELS?
One of the earliest novels was *Don Quixote* (1605) by the Spanish writer Miguel de Cervantes (1547–1616). Around 100 years later, novels became popular when *Robinson Crusoe* (1719) was published. Written by English author Daniel Defoe (1660–1731), it is the story of a shipwrecked man alone on a remote island.

▲ PAPERBACKS
Most books had hard covers until the first paperback novels were published by Penguin in 1935. Paperbacks were cheap and made books more affordable.

GENRES

Genres are categories of art and culture. In literature, a love story belongs to the romance genre, and a murder story is categorized as crime. However, stories can belong to more than one genre.

WHY DO DIFFERENT GENRES EXIST?
Authors, like readers, have their favorite interests and will only write on a subject they feel connected to. Categorizing a book means that readers know what to expect and where to look for it in a bookstore or library. Changing social trends and tastes can inspire new genres.

1 CRIME **2 ROMANCE** **3 HORROR**
1 The first popular detective in fiction was Sherlock Holmes, created by Arthur Conan Doyle (1859–1930). 2 *Gone with the Wind* is a classic romance written by Margaret Mitchell (1900–1949). 3 The blood-sucking Count Dracula from Transylvania was created by Bram Stoker (1847–1912).

SCIENCE FICTION ▶
Science fiction (stories about the future and space travel) was a particularly popular genre in the 1950s. It reflected a real interest in space at the time.

PLOTS

The plot is what happens in a story. Most plots have a beginning, a middle, and an end, and contain problems that are eventually solved. Writers usually invent plots, although some authors, like William Shakespeare, may take them from history.

WHAT MAKES A GOOD PLOT?
A good plot grabs the reader's interest and captures his or her emotions right to the end. The writer uses suspense and surprise to control the pace of the plot. Sometimes flashbacks (returning to the past) gradually fill in the background to a story.

▲ *A MIDSUMMER NIGHT'S DREAM*
A Midsummer Night's Dream (c. 1595) by Shakespeare is a comedy. The plot has many fantastic and funny twists, and a happy ending.

literature

MYTHS

All cultures have myths—stories that reflect religious and social beliefs. These stories feature gods and superhumans and explore the great questions of life—such as "Where do we come from?", "Why are we here?", and "Why does evil exist?"

WHAT IS A HERO?

Mythic heroes are humans with superhuman powers, often because one of their parents was a god or goddess. They have to show tremendous courage in overcoming spiritual and physical challenges to save an individual, their family, or an entire nation.

▼ BHAGAVAT PURAN
This sacred Hindu text contains Indian history and mythology. Here the god Rama (a form of the supreme god, Vishnu) and his human wife, Sita, are seated on a five-headed serpent.

Rama's blue skin shows he is a form of the god Vishnu

Lotus flower is a Hindu symbol of divine beauty

Sita is a human form of the goddess of wealth, Lakshmi

Rama's half-brother, Lakshmana, becomes a snake to make a bed for the couple

▲ THE GREEK MYTH OF PERSEPHONE
The goddess Persephone is kidnapped and taken to the underworld. While she is gone, her mother—the corn goddess, Demeter—grieves, and the fields lie barren. In spring, Persephone returns, and so do the crops.

WHY DO MYTHS EXIST?

Although myths are old, they still appeal to us because they contain lasting truths about the way people feel. The myth of Persephone, for example, is about the annual crop cycle, but also illustrates the strength of the bond between mother and daughter.

WHAT IS THE ORAL TRADITION?

The oral (spoken) tradition is literature that has not been written down but has been passed on from one storyteller to another over many years. Myths began in this way. The oral tradition continues today with storytelling, folk tales, and children's stories.

NONFICTION

Nonfiction deals with facts and real events, and is written in prose. It includes histories, essays, travel writing, letters, biographies, and diaries. The first known work of prose was a history of the Persian wars, written by Herodotus c. 430 BCE in ancient Greece.

▲ THE DIARY OF ANNE FRANK
This young Jewish girl recorded how she and her family hid from the Nazis in Amsterdam during World War II. She gave a moving account of the difficulties of her life, but also her friendship with the son of the family hiding with them. Anne Frank died in a concentration camp in 1945.

IS ALL NONFICTION LITERATURE?

Much nonfiction is written for reference only, and so is usually not considered to be literature because the information being conveyed is more important than the literary style. Compare this with a biography, where the author's writing style and interpretation of facts are essential to the understanding of the subject.

WHY ARE DIARIES IMPORTANT?

A diary is a daily record of a person's thoughts and experiences, often not intended for publication. The great English diarist Samuel Pepys (1633–1703) wrote in code. His diary records a mixture of great public and intimate personal events and builds up a vivid picture of the times in which it was written.

▲ WILD TURKEY BY JOHN JAMES AUDUBON
Audubon (1785–1851) was an American natural history author and illustrator who wrote *The Birds of America*. His detailed observations included beautiful hand-colored engravings.

FIND OUT MORE ▶▶ Theater 344–345 • Writers 348 • Writing 339

POETRY

Poetry (verse) is literature that works through sounds and images. It was originally recited (spoken aloud) to an audience, and its rhythms and sounds affect the meaning of the words. Poetic language is concentrated (it says a lot in few words) and expresses feelings and ideas.

▲ *THE TYGER* BY WILLIAM BLAKE
Blake (1757–1827) was a painter and a poet. This powerful poem asks questions about the creation of the world and good and evil.

ARE THERE DIFFERENT TYPES OF POETRY?

The epic was the earliest known type of poetry, presenting a long narrative (story) of amazing heroic deeds. Lyric poetry, originally a song for a lyre (an ancient musical instrument), is short and often expresses the poet's own ideas or feelings. Dramatic poetry is written in the voices of different characters and can be acted.

WHAT IS THE OLDEST POEM?

The oldest written poem is the *Epic of Gilgamesh* from Babylon. It is about 4,000 years old and tells the story of a king, Gilgamesh, who was half-man, half-god. The oldest poem in English is *Beowulf*, written in the 8th century CE. This 3,000-line epic is about a Scandinavian hero, Beowulf, who saves the Danes from two monsters—Grendel and its mother.

WHAT IS METER?

Meter is the rhythm of a poem. Rhythm is created by the stressed (long) and unstressed (short) syllables (parts of a word) in a line. Short and long syllables are arranged in fixed patterns known as feet. A foot with a long and a short syllable is called a trochee. A line with ten syllables is called a pentameter.

RHYME AND METER

Tyger! Tyger! burning bright — **A** — *"Bright" sounds like "night," which is a rhyme.*
1
In the forests of the night, **A**

What immortal hand or eye **B** — *Two lines that rhyme form a pair called a couplet.*
Could frame thy fearful symmetry? **B**
2

1 This symbol shows a metric foot. This type of foot is called a trochee and contains a stressed syllable ("Ty-") and an unstressed one ("-ger").
2 This symbol shows a syllable or word that stands alone.

DO POEMS ALWAYS HAVE RHYME AND RHYTHM?

Rhyme (when words sound the same) does not always suit the subject or feeling of a poem, so many poets write poetry that does not rhyme, called blank verse. *Paradise Lost*, the epic poem by John Milton (1608–1674), does not rhyme but has a particular meter (rhythm). Poetry without meter is called free verse.

IS A VERSE THE SAME AS A STANZA?

Verse can mean poetry in general, or it can mean a paragraph of poetry, also called a stanza. Traditionally, a stanza contains no more than 12 lines. A two-line stanza is called a couplet, and a four-line couplet is a quatrain.

▲ 18TH-CENTURY HAIKU
This is a simple form of poetry from Japan that contains only 17 syllables. A haiga is a painting of the words and image of a haiku.

▲ POETRY IN PERFORMANCE
Poems are often best appreciated when read aloud. Here, English poet Benjamin Zephaniah recites his poetry at a concert. Popular music that uses the spoken word, such as rap and hip-hop, is a new type of poetry.

WHAT ARE POETIC DEVICES?

Poetic devices are the special tricks and techniques that make poetry different from everyday language. Alliteration repeats consonants, as in "slithering snake"—the repeated use of the "s" makes us think of the sound a snake makes, which strengthens the image. Other common devices are metaphor and simile, both forms of comparison. A simile uses "like" or "as": "My love is like a red, red rose." A metaphor does not: "My love is a red rose."

poetry

THERE WAS AN OLD MAN ON WHOSE NOSE MOST BIRDS OF THE AIR COULD REPOSE ... ▶
The English poet Edward Lear (1812–1888) invented nonsense poems called limericks, consisting of five lines that rhyme—usually in unexpected and amusing ways. He also illustrated his poems.

FIND OUT MORE ▶▶ Theater 344–345 • Writers 348

Theater is the performance of a drama (play) usually on a ▶ STAGE in front of an audience. The ancient Greeks were the first to build theaters where people could watch the two main types of dramas: ▶▶ TRAGEDY and ▶▶ COMEDY.

drama

WHAT WERE THE FIRST PLAYS?

The first plays developed from religious rituals where a chorus (a group of performers) recited stories of the Greek gods and heroes. In the 6th century BCE, a Greek poet, Thespis, became the first actor to recite lines by himself.

WHO IS INVOLVED IN MAKING A PLAY?

The director is the person who chooses the play and tells everyone what to do. The actors become the characters in the play by acting out the plot (story). Other people design and make the set and costumes, and create lighting and sound effects.

KABUKI ▶
Kabuki is traditional Japanese theater with an all-male cast. (Men play the female roles.) The highly dramatic plots rely on skills in dancing and singing, as well as acting.

Distinctive makeup style is called kumadori. Deep red on a white face symbolizes rage mixed with cruelty

◀ THE ZULU MACBETH
Shakespeare's *Macbeth* (1606) is updated from historic Scotland to 20th-century Africa, illustrating the timeless theme of ambition.

Assistant works on stage, performing costume transformations

A hakama is a divided skirt, worn here by a samurai (warrior). Each character has a specific costume

▲ ELIZABETHAN COSTUME
Ben Jonson's *Volpone* (1606) was one of many great English plays written during or shortly after the reign of Queen Elizabeth I (1558–1603). To conjure up the period, the designer recreates Elizabethan costumes.

WHAT IS MIME?

Mime expresses a mood or an idea through gestures and facial expressions, without using words. The well-known mime characters Harlequin and Pierrot developed in Italian theater during the 16th century, and later gave rise to the clown. In China, drama contained no words until the 19th century.

IS DRAMA ALWAYS PERFORMED IN A THEATER?

Street theater is performed in public places and is often free to those who watch. It aims to bring plays to people who would not generally get the chance to go to a theater, and is a direct way of communicating with local people about issues that affect them.

KEY PLAYWRIGHTS

16–17th century	Shak espeare (England)
17th century	Molière (France)
18–19th century	Goethe (Germany)
19th century	Wilde (England)
19–20th century	Chekhov (Russia)
19–20th century	Ibsen (Norway)
20–21st century	Miller (US)
20–21st century	Soyinka (Nigeria)

TYPES OF STAGES ►
The arena stage is modeled on the Greek theater. The thrust stage was very popular in the Elizabethan period.

TRAGEDY

A classical Greek tragedy is a serious play about the sufferings of an often mythical hero or heroine. It showed how people behaved in terrible situations, allowing the audience to face their fears in the safety of a theater.

WHY DO PEOPLE WATCH TRAGEDY?

According to the Greek scholar Aristotle (384–322 BCE), the audience shares in the sadness and fear of the characters they are watching. At the end of the play, the audience feels emotionally purified and uplifted by the release of tension. This process is called catharsis.

ARE THERE MODERN TRAGEDIES?

There are modern tragedies, but not many are similar to Greek plays. Today, tragedy is often the unhappy story of an ordinary person with many faults. The tragedy occurs not because a hero has a tragic flaw, but because beliefs or illusions are destroyed.

▲ FARCE
Noises Off (1982) by English writer Michael Frayn is a farce, a type of comedy with very silly behavior.

▲ GREEK CHORUS
In Greek tragedy, the chorus was a group of performers who spoke in unison and performed ritual dance steps together. The role of the chorus was to provide a commentary on the main action.

COMEDY

Comedy is a play that makes us laugh. It deals with people and their relationships to each other. By laughing at the actors on stage and through wit (jokes), we reach an understanding of the characters' foolishness.

IS SATIRE A TYPE OF COMEDY?

Satire is a cruel form of comedy that criticizes society by showing the weaknesses of public figures. Satire uses caricature (exaggeration of a person's character) and mockery (making fun of someone). The first great writers of satire were the ancient Romans.

STAGE

In the theater, a stage is a platform where plays are performed. The Ancient Greeks watched drama in round, open-air theaters. The Romans also had the same but unlike the Greek theaters, they were smaller and had retaining walls rather than being built into hillsides.

ARE ALL STAGES THE SAME?

The most common type is the proscenium stage, where the audience is separated from the framed, raised stage by a curtain. It was invented in Italy in the 18th century. Other stage designs try to bring the audience and actors closer by locating the stage within the audience, or having the audience surround the stage entirely.

■ STAGE   ■ AUDIENCE   ARENA   THRUST   PROSCENIUM

FIND OUT MORE ►► Opera 338 • Writers 348

Cinema is a hugely popular modern art form that uses moving pictures to tell a story. Early films were in black and white, and silent. *The Jazz Singer* (1927) was the first "talkie," and color films appeared in the 1930s. Today many movies use ⏭ SPECIAL EFFECTS.

WHERE ARE MOVIES MADE?

Movies are made in studios using sets—life-size models of buildings or places. Underwater scenes are sometimes filmed in huge tanks. Movies are also shot on location (outdoors or in a real building). Location filming in towns or cities is often done early in the morning when the streets are empty.

▲ SHOOTING A SCENE
The famous director Alfred Hitchcock (second from right) works with actor Paul Newman (left) and crew on *Torn Curtain* (1966). The camera sits on a dolly (a wheeled platform) so it can move smoothly.

WHAT DOES A DIRECTOR DO?

Directors decide which script the movie will be based on and use their personal vision to create the overall style. They advise the actors on how to play the characters and tell the camera crew when and how to film. They also choose the music for the movie.

HOW OLD IS CINEMA?

Motion pictures were invented in 1889 in the US by Thomas Edison. In 1895 in France, the Lumière brothers projected films for the first time to a paying audience. Within 20 years ⏭ HOLLYWOOD dominated the film industry around the world.

Spaceship set was amazing at the time. The director, George Lucas, drew his ideas from science-fiction books and movies

C-3PO is an android, an intelligent robot. He has a smaller companion called R2-D2

Princess Leia (Carrie Fisher) is a rebel leader fighting against the evil Galactic Empire. She is helped by the smuggler Han Solo (Harrison Ford), shown right

cinema

STAR WARS ▶
Star Wars (1977) by George Lucas, with its stunning special effects and epic story, was a landmark in cinematic history. It won seven Oscar awards and started the trend for summer blockbusters.

▲ BOLLYWOOD
Bollywood is the nickname of the Hindi film industry, centered in Mumbai (Bombay). The films are often romantic, with singing and dancing.

▲ STUNTS
Most stunts, such as fast car chases, are done by doubles of the lead actors. However, in *Crouching Tiger, Hidden Dragon* (2000), Zhang Ziyi, playing the Jade Fox, did all her own martial-arts fights.

▲ ADAPTATIONS
Many movies are based on books. *An Ideal Husband* (1999) was taken from the 1895 play by Oscar Wilde. Films that recreate a historical period are called costume dramas.

HOLLYWOOD

Hollywood—a suburb of Los Angeles—is the center of the world film industry. The Californian sunshine attracted early movie-makers, because the film they used at the time worked best in strong light. The varied landscape also provided good locations.

WHY IS HOLLYWOOD SO FAMOUS?

The big Hollywood studios controlled the industry for many years, because they not only made movies but also owned most of the US cinemas. They used their power to turn their actors into worldwide stars. Today, Hollywood studios fund and distribute movies made by smaller companies, too. While Hollywood remains dominant, other cinematic cultures, such as the Indian film industry, have a big following.

OSCAR STATUETTE ▶
This trophy is given to winners of categories (such as Best Actor) in the annual Academy Awards for film. It shows a knight with a sword standing on a film reel.

© A.M.P.A.S. ®

LEONARDO DICAPRIO · KATE WINSLET

TITANIC ▲
Titanic (1997) attracted huge audiences to cinemas and made millions of dollars. It won 11 Oscars, a record it shares with *Ben-Hur* (1959), and *Lord of the Rings: Return of the King* (2004).

SPECIAL EFFECTS

These are techniques used to create illusions (images that are not real). Hidden wires make it look like an actor is flying. A train crash can be filmed with tiny models. Most effects today are computer-generated.

WHAT WERE THE EARLY SPECIAL EFFECTS?

Moving scenery was projected on a screen behind the actors. This made it look like a car was driving along a road when, in fact, it was stationary in a studio. Another effect was to mask part of the camera, so that the same piece of film could be used twice. In this way, actors could be superimposed on backgrounds.

MAKEUP ▲
Arnold Schwarzenegger is being made up for *The Terminator* (1984). Gory face paints create a fake wound and make it look like he has robot parts beneath his skin.

▲ GENRES
Genre is a category of movies, such as Westerns. The Hollywood Western *The Magnificent Seven* (1960) was based on Japan's *The Seven Samurai* (1954) (above).

▲ SPECIAL EFFECTS
Computers have revolutionized special effects. This spectacular explosion in *The Rock* (1996) was filmed and then enhanced by computer-generated imagery to make it even more breathtaking.

▲ STUDIO SETS
A submarine enters the specially built set in the James Bond movie *The Spy Who Loved Me* (1977). This costly set recreates the inside of a warship.

FIND OUT MORE ▶▶ Animation 349 • Literature 340-342 • Musicals 338

WRITERS

Writers express themselves in words. There are many different kinds of writers—for instance, journalists who report for newspapers, and technical writers who explain how machines work. However, many of the best-known authors write fiction and are valued for the way they tell stories and how they use language.

▲ WILLIAM SHAKESPEARE
Shakespeare (1564–1616) was an English playwright and poet. His work deals with human nature so convincingly that it is understood around the world. Although his plays are around 400 years old, they are still produced today.

writers

WHAT MAKES A GOOD WRITER?
A good writer has a style of writing that grips your attention, whether in a long novel or a short poem. Style includes creation of characters, use of dialogue (conversation), descriptive language, and how a piece of work is structured. Some writers experiment with language, such as Irish author James Joyce, who invented a highly individual form of English in his novel Finnegans Wake (1939).

DO WRITERS GO OUT OF STYLE?
Different writers are appreciated at different times. In the 18th century, writers copied the style of the Greeks and Romans. The early-19th-century Romantic writers, such as the English poet John Keats (1795–1821), valued nature and personal experience. They later gave way to the Realists, such as the French writer Victor Hugo (1802–1885), who wrote about politics and the daily struggles of ordinary people.

IS WRITING FOR CHILDREN DIFFERENT?
Children's writers feature children as main characters, and write from the point of view of a child. Children's stories often appeal to the imagination and have a lot of humor. Children's authors choose subjects that are part of a child's world, such as school, as in the *Harry Potter* series by J. K. Rowling (1965–); or the family, as in *Little Women* by Louisa May Alcott (1832–1888). However, many themes of children's writing appeal to all ages, such as love, friendship, and adventure.

Manuscript was typed on a typewriter

▲ ERNEST HEMINGWAY
American author Ernest Hemingway (1899–1961) is famous for his novels and short stories. His economical style (expressing many ideas in a few words) has made him a widely admired and imitated writer.

▲ ARUNDHATI ROY
This Indian writer (1961–) won the British Booker Prize in 1997 with her first novel, *The God of Small Things*. Key literary prizes are the Nobel Prize for Literature, the Pulitzer Prize, and the Commonwealth Writers' Prize.

▲ J. K. ROWLING
English writer J. K. Rowling was a struggling author when she wrote her first *Harry Potter* novel, published in 1997. Today she has sold hundreds of millions of books globally and is a multimillionaire and celebrity.

WHAT IS A NARRATOR?
In fiction, the narrator is the person who tells the story. This can be the author or one of the characters. First-person narration is when the narrator speaks from the "I" point of view about events in which he or she has been personally involved.

WHY DO SOME WRITERS BECOME FAMOUS?
Some writers are famous because they sell lots of books. Some cause controversy (public debate). Others win prizes, such as the Nobel Prize for Literature, or have a successful movie made of their book. Writers are also promoted in schools and colleges.

Handwritten manuscript

Editing is when a writer reads back over what they have written and makes changes to improve it

Ink sketch, one of many that Hugo produced

◄ VICTOR HUGO'S DESK
French writer Hugo made sketches and notes that were the basis of his manuscripts (the final text). This manuscript records a journey on the Rhine River in Germany. It shows how he edited his work before publication.

FIND OUT MORE ►► Literature 340 • Poetry 343 • Writing 339

ANIMATION

Animation is an illusion made with a sequence of still pictures that are each slightly different. The pictures are shown quickly to give an impression of movement. Animation is often filmed at 24 frames per second (fps) and 12 fps. The main types are cel, stop-frame, and ▶◀ **COMPUTER ANIMATION**.

▲ BUILDING A MODEL
Animation models are made with clay or latex (a rubber and plastic compound). They are built up on a simple metal skeleton called an armature, which can be moved.

WHAT IS CEL ANIMATION?

An animator produces a sequence of pencil drawings on paper. These are traced onto clear sheets called cels, and colored in with paints. Each cel is placed on a background and filmed as one frame. The background remains constant while the cels are changed.

HOW DOES STOP-FRAME ANIMATION WORK?

Stop-frame animation is made using models. A miniature set is built to represent a room or a street. Puppets are placed in the set, moved small amounts, and filmed one shot at a time. Modern stop-frame animation also uses computers.

▲ *AN AMERICAN TAIL*
This 1986 feature animation was made on cel and directed by the famous US animator Don Bluth. It tells the story of Russian Jewish mice who flee to America, only to discover that cats live there, too!

animation

▲ *CHICKEN RUN*
The set for *Chicken Run* (2000), made by animation firm Aardman, was built in a warehouse. The team of 40 animators moved each model a tiny amount for each of the 24 shots needed to produce one second of film.

COMPUTER ANIMATION

Computer animation was first used in video games, but as the technology developed, it spread to movies and television for special effects and animated features. Computer animation has evolved from both cel and stop-frame animation techniques.

HOW IS COMPUTER ANIMATION MADE?

Using 3-D computer software, models can be built, colored, and animated in a virtual environment. Computer animation, unlike stop-frame animation, does not need the model to be placed in every position of a movement. Instead, key poses are set and the computer creates the positions in between.

CAN COMPUTERS ANIMATE BY THEMSELVES?

Computer software can calculate and recreate the physical movement of objects dropping, bouncing, and even knocking into each other. However, the personalities and emotions of people and creatures are too complex for a computer to understand. The human animation artist is still a vital part of the process.

ANTZ ▶
Antz (1998) by Dreamworks was the second fully computer-animated movie ever made. The characters are individually animated but the film used a crowd animation system so that scenes could contain thousands of ants.

FIND OUT MORE ▶▶ Cinema 346–347 • Home Entertainment 351

TOYS

A toy is an object that is designed to be played with. Toys are entertaining and often educational. There are traditional toys—such as dolls, balls, and kites—and high-tech toys—such as electronic robots, remote-controlled cars, and game consoles.

toys

▲ SONY "AIBO"
This battery-operated robot dog imitates real animal instincts that change over time. It can play with a ball or ask to be fed.

ANTIQUE TEDDY BEAR ▶
The German firm Steiff began making bears in 1903. Steiff bears are famous for their high quality.

WHY DO WE PLAY WITH TOYS?
Toys are fun tools for learning, and help a child to understand life and the world. Children can learn to share by having a tea party with a teddy bear, or use their imagination to transform a doll into a superhero in a fantastic adventure. Adults also enjoy toys, often because they have a hobby, such as collecting model trains or flying kites.

WHAT ARE THE OLDEST TOYS?
One of the oldest toys is the spinning top. The first tops were natural objects like shells and acorns. These later developed into clay tops like those discovered in the ancient city of Ur in Mesopotamia. Village squares in 18th-century England often featured giant tops that were played with for physical exercise. Yo-yos existed in ancient Egypt and in ancient Greece, where they were believed to bring protection from the gods.

▲ SPINNING TOP
The most common top today has a mechanical plunger. Simple tops, spun between the fingers, require more skill to set off.

FIND OUT MORE ▶▶ Musical Instruments 332

GAMES

A game can be a competition between two or more people, or played by one person, following a set of rules. Players may need skill or rely on the luck of the dice. Games are played for fun or to entertain an audience.

HOW OLD IS CHESS?
It is thought that chess began in China or India around 1,400 years ago. From there it spread to North Africa and eventually to Europe. The modern form of chess emerged in the 16th century and remains one of the world's most popular games. Today, computers can be programmed to play chess against humans.

WHO INVENTS GAMES?
Big companies employ workers to invent new games, but many games are invented by ordinary people with a good idea. An unemployed architect thought up Scrabble in 1931. Monopoly was invented in 1933 during the Great Depression by an American salesman. The dice game Yahtzee was invented in 1956 by a Canadian couple to play on their yacht.

◀ MANCALA
Mancala is thought to be the oldest board game in the world. It originated in Africa and is a complex game of counting and capturing.

Pebbles used as counters

Pieces are placed on grid lines, not inside the squares

games

▲ GO
Go is an ancient Japanese game. Played by two people, the aim is to control vacant areas of the board and capture the opponent's pieces.

CHESS ▶
Chess is played on a checkered board of 64 squares. It has 16 playing pieces per side. It is a game of war in which two players aim to capture each other's pieces and trap the opponent's king.

FIND OUT MORE ▶▶ Olympics 356–357

HOME ENTERTAINMENT

Home entertainment is how we have fun and relax at home. Today it is dominated by technology, especially television. Watching videos, playing computer games, and listening to music are all home entertainment. So are reading books, playing cards, and storytelling.

A tweeter is a small speaker for high frequencies

Main speaker carries the low (bass) and middle ranges of sound

WHAT DID PEOPLE DO BEFORE TV WAS INVENTED?

People had to make their own amusement by playing games, singing, or reading stories. The invention of the radio and the gramophone at the beginning of the 20th century meant that people could listen to music and programs at home. Just as we sit in front of the TV to watch our favorite shows, people in the past sat around the radio or listened to the gramophone.

WHAT IS HOME CINEMA?

Home cinema is an attempt to bring the look, the sound, and the excitement of movies to the home. A basic kit includes a wide-screen television, a DVD (digital video disc) player, and speakers positioned around the room to give surround sound. For a more cinematic effect, a wall-mounted digital projector and projection screen can be used instead of a TV.

▲ 1960s HOME LISTENING
Electric record players were popular and played two sizes of vinyl discs, 12-inch and 7-inch.

▲ LOUDSPEAKERS
The stylish, curved case of these music loudspeakers, made by Blueroom, is shaped to give accurate sound.

home entertainment

① ② ③ ④ ⑤

1 MP3 player stores digital music files called MP3s 2 DVDs (digital video discs) offer crystal-clear images, as in *The Matrix* (1999) 3 Digital radio produces clear, interference-free sound 4 State-of-the-art machine plays CDs, MP3s, and radio 5 Flat-screen TVs do not distort the picture like curved TVs

IS DIGITAL BROADCASTING HERE TO STAY?

Digital broadcasting has many advantages over the old analog system. Information is compressed (made smaller), producing more channels and better-quality pictures and sound. Digital technology makes TV and radio more interactive for the audience.

WHAT IS "HI-FI" MUSIC?

"Hi-fi" is short for "high-fidelity," and it refers to recorded music that is an accurate copy of the original music. High-fidelity recordings were first made using vinyl records, then magnetic tape (cassettes). They are now captured on digital media—CDs, MiniDiscs, and MP3 files.

Information screen shows which part of the system is selected

Control buttons for functions such as volume

Arrow keys for radio and TV channel navigation

◄ REMOTE CONTROL
This operates a combined system that covers music, TV, DVD, video, satellite, CD, radio—and the lights!

SUPER MARIO BY NINTENDO ►
Since his first game, *Donkey Kong* (1981), Super Mario has appeared in more than a 100 video games and starred in his own movie.

FIND OUT MORE ►► Cinema 346–347 • Sound 176–177 • Telecommunications 192–193

SPORTS

Sports are any competitive game that has set rules and involves physical exertion or coordination. There are ▸▸TEAM SPORTS, individual sports, winter sports on snow and ice, motor sports with cars and motorcycles, sports with horses and dogs, and ▸▸EXTREME SPORTS.

HAVE PEOPLE ALWAYS PLAYED SPORTS?

People of all cultures and times have played games to test skill and athleticism. Some early ball games used balls made from straw or an inflated animal's bladder. Games were often linked to social and religious rituals. The Greeks pioneered regular sporting competitions, founding their Olympic Games in 776 BCE.

WHEN DID SPORTS BECOME ORGANIZED?

The first set of rules for golf were drawn up in Scotland in the 18th century. Many other sports—such as soccer, baseball, cricket, and football—acquired formal rules from the mid-19th century onward. Some games are relatively recent—basketball was invented from scratch in 1891.

WHAT ARE PROFESSIONAL SPORTS?

In professional sports, competitors are paid prize money or salaries, or both. In amateur sports competitors are not paid. Before sports like rugby union and track and field became professional, many amateurs had to work part-time in other professions to support themselves.

▲ FORMULA ONE
The Formula One Grand Prix is the most important race in motor sports. Here, Michael Schumacher (1969–) drives his Ferrari in 2002.

▲ TIGER WOODS
Tiger Woods (1975–) has become a superstar in golf. He is the first and only player to have held all four major championship titles at once—the Masters Tournament, PGA, US Open, and British Open.

SNOWBOARDING ▲
Snowboarding was invented in the US in the 1960s, using skis tied together, with ropes attached for steering. The first custom-made snowboard, modeled on a surfboard, was built in 1966.

Snowboard size depends on the rider's height, build, and shoe size

sports

TEAM SPORTS

Team sports involve more than one person per side and require the members of a team to cooperate with one another to win the game. Nearly all team sports are ball games. Teams attract long-term interest and loyal fan support that outlasts the popularity of their individual star players.

Helmet helps prevent injury to the head when the rider falls

WHAT ARE THE WORLD'S MOST POPULAR TEAM SPORTS?

Soccer is the world's biggest team sport. Football and baseball are the most popular in the US. Hockey, cricket, and rugby are strong in other nations. Field hockey, handball, netball, and volleyball get less media coverage but are widely played.

▲ RUGBY
Rugby is a hugely popular team sport in Australia and South Africa as well as western Europe. Here, Australia (in the yellow shirts) plays South Africa at Ellis Park, Johannesburg, in 2002. South Africa won.

▲ BASEBALL
Baseball is the national sport of the US. The baseman for the New York Yankees dives to catch the ball in his mitt in a game against the Los Angeles Dodgers.

Goggles protect the eyes from the glare of the snow

▲ BASKETBALL
Michael Jordan (1963–) is often called the greatest basketball player of all time. The 6-ft-6-in (1.83-m) player was with the Chicago Bulls in 1984–1994 and 1995–1998, with a year off in between as a baseball player.

WHAT DOES A TEAM COACH DO?

A coach trains the individual players to work together as a successful team. Coaches motivate the players to keep up the discipline required during training. They also create strategies for winning. During a game, a coach may send in substitutes to replace players who are injured or playing badly.

EXTREME SPORTS

Extreme sports are events that are a deliberate extension or intensification of older games. Extreme sports are dangerous, challenging, and sometimes bizarre. They have few rules and are usually not team-based. Players use their skills to control the risks.

WHAT ARE THE X GAMES?

The X stands for extreme. The X Games began in 1995 in the US. They are now the biggest annual international event for extreme sports. Summer events are inline skating, skateboarding, stunt biking, and motocross. Winter events are snowboarding and skiing. In the past, competitions were also held for skysurfing (with parachutes), barefoot waterskiing, ice-climbing, and mountain biking in the snow.

ROCK CLIMBING ▶
France's Catherine Destivelle (1960–) climbs a steep rock cliff in Spain. Unlike traditional rock climbing, in which the climber uses safety ropes fixed in place with bolts, she has no ropes to guide her.

FIND OUT MORE ▶▶ Competitions 354–355 • Olympics 356–357

COMPETITIONS

Competitions define the highest level of achievement, and exist in every major sport. Football has the ⏩ **SUPER BOWL**; soccer has the ⏩ **THE WORLD CUP**. The most prestigious competitions attract global media coverage and huge ⏩ **SPONSORSHIP** deals.

▲ THE ASHES
This urn is given to the winner of the Ashes Test Cricket Series played biennially between England and Australia. It is said to hold the ashes of the bail used in the first Test match in 1882.

WHAT WERE THE FIRST GREAT COMPETITIONS?
Although the Oxford and Cambridge rowing race in London, England, has been running since 1829, organized sporting competitions began to develop in the late 19th century. The English Football Association Cup in soccer began in 1872. The first American National Baseball League began in 1876.

WHY ARE SOME COMPETITIONS SO FAMOUS?
Competitions become famous when they have continued for many years and have an exciting history filled with sports legends. Over time they attract loyalty and respect from fans. Some competitions have sponsorship deals and as a result receive publicity from advertisers and broadcasters.

TOUR DE FRANCE ▶
American cyclist Lance Armstrong leads the way in the Tour de France in 2000. The yellow jersey is worn by the current leader of the Tour during each of its many stages. The competition began in 1903.

THE WORLD CUP

First held in 1930, the FIFA (Fédération Internationale de Football Associations) World Cup is the most important tournament for national soccer teams. It is held every four years and has grown from just 11 teams in 1930 to 32 teams in 2010.

HOW MANY PEOPLE WATCH THE WORLD CUP?
There are seats for around one million people at a modern World Cup. It now attracts about 500 million televsion viewers around the world, although the exact figure is unknown as different sources give different figures. The 1950 final in Rio de Janeiro, Brazil, saw the biggest attendance at any football game in history—more than 200,000 people.

WHICH TEAM HAS WON THE MOST WORLD CUPS?
Brazil has won five World Cups (1958, 1962, 1970, 1994, and 2002). Italy has won the title four times (1934, 1938, 1982, 2006). Germany has won it three times (1954, 1974, 1990) and Uruguay has won it twice (1930, 1950). Spain won the title for the first time in 2010.

competitions

WORLD CUP WINNERS 2010 ▶
Iker Casillas, the captain and goalkeeper of the Spanish football team, lifts the trophy after Spain beat the Netherlands 1-0 in Johannesburg, South Africa. This was Spain's first victory at the FIFA World Cup.

SUPER BOWL

The Super Bowl is the biggest event in the American sporting year. It is a single game between the winners of the NFL (National Football League) and the winners of the AFL (American Football League) to decide the national champion.

WHEN DID SUPER BOWL START?
The NFL was started in 1920 and was the only national football league until the AFL began in 1960. In 1967, the two leagues merged for a single end-of-season playoff between the two champions. The first Super Bowl was won by Wisconsin's Green Bay Packers, who beat the Kansas City Chiefs 35–10.

WHO ARE THE BIGGEST SUPER BOWL TEAMS?
The most successful team is the Pittsburgh Steelers who have won six Super Bowls. They are followed by the Dallas Cowboys and the San Francisco 49ers, who have each won five Super Bowls. The Green Bay Packers, Washington Redskins, New York Giants, Oakland Raiders, and New England Patriots have three titles each.

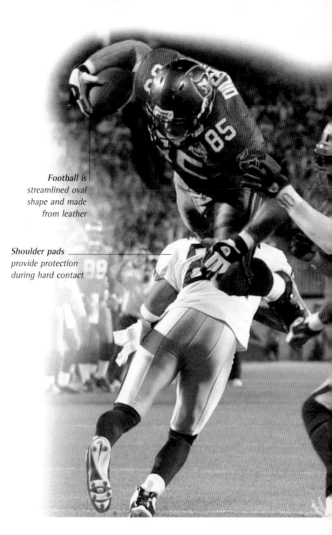

Football is streamlined oval shape and made from leather

Shoulder pads provide protection during hard contact

SUPER BOWL XXXVII ▶
The Tampa Bay Buccaneers (in white) won their first Super Bowl in San Diego, January 2003. They beat the Oakland Raiders 48–21. XXXVII is 37 in Roman numerals, and means the 37th year of the competition.

SPONSORSHIP

Big sporting events need lots of money to organize, promote, and pay prize money and salaries. Companies pay competition organizers, venues, teams, and individual sports stars to display their logos and advertising. Sponsors also use their connections with sports stars to promote their brands in the media in general.

HOW BIG ARE SPONSORSHIP DEALS?
The biggest personal sponsorship deals are with the clothing firm Nike. US golfer Tiger Woods has a deal worth $125 million over five years, and basketball star LeBron James is receiving $90 million over seven years. Nike also has the biggest deal with a team—sponsoring Brazil's soccer team for $100 million.

HOW MUCH INFLUENCE DO SPONSORS HAVE OVER SPORTING COMPETITIONS?
Many organizations now design their events to attract sponsors and TV audiences. In the US, basketball introduced a rule called the 24-second shot—a team has to shoot within 24 seconds of getting the ball. This increased the pace and excitement of the game, and made it more appealing to TV broadcasters.

▲ SERENA WILLIAMS, 2003 AUSTRALIAN OPEN CHAMPIONSHIP
In 1998 this American tennis star signed a five-year deal with clothes firm Puma for $11.7 million. The deal was dependent on her becoming one of the world's top 10 players, which she did.

FIND OUT MORE ▶▶ Olympics 356–357 • Sports 352–353

OLYMPICS

The Olympic Games are the world's biggest sporting spectacle. They are divided into a summer and winter Games, held every four years by a single city. Athletes with disabilities compete at the Paralympics. More than 10,000 athletes take part in the summer events alone.

Olympic flame has an ancient counterpart—a sacred flame lit in honor of the goddess Hera

Olympic torch was first used in modern Games in 1936, carried by runners from Greece to Berlin

olympics

◀ BERLIN OLYMPICS, 1936
The 1936 Olympics is opened as the runner lights the Olympic flame. Organized by the Nazi government, the Berlin Olympics were the first to be openly linked to political propaganda.

▲ OLYMPIC RINGS
Baron de Coubertin is said to have seen the five rings on an ancient Greek artifact. The rings symbolize the unity of the world's five continents (Europe, Asia, Africa, Oceania, and the Americas). Every national flag in the world contains at least one of the five colors.

WHO INVENTED THE MODERN OLYMPICS?
In the 19th century, archaeological discoveries revived interest in the ▶▶ ANCIENT OLYMPICS. The Greeks tried to recreate the Games in Athens in 1859 and 1870. However, the major force behind the modern Olympics was the French aristocrat Baron de Coubertin (1863–1937). In 1894 he organized an international conference in Paris to support a revival of the Games.

WHO RUNS THE OLYMPICS NOW?
De Coubertin's 1894 conference created the International Olympic Committee (IOC), which has run the Games ever since. The IOC chooses the host cities and sets the rules for competing. In recent years, its reputation has been hurt by scandals over corruption and bribery in the selection of the host cities.

WHAT IS THE OLYMPIC IDEAL?
Baron de Coubertin saw the Olympics as a place in which sporting excellence could be celebrated. The ideal was to build international understanding and cooperation. The Olympic code promotes amateurism, or performance without payment, and professionals are allowed to participate only under certain rules.

ANCIENT OLYMPICS

The ancient Olympics celebrated the god Zeus and were held every four years at Olympia, Greece. Winners received an olive wreath. The first Olympic Games are believed to have been held in 776 BCE, and the first Olympic champion was Koroibos, who won a sprint that year.

WHAT TOOK PLACE AT THE ANCIENT OLYMPICS?
The events at Olympia in 776 BCE were sprints and horse races. Later, longer races were added, including sprints wearing full armor. Chariot racing and combat sports such as boxing and wrestling were soon regular features. All events were held in a stadium. The open-air track for horse racing was called a hippodrome.

WHY DID THE ANCIENT OLYMPICS END?
The Romans conquered Greece in 146 BCE. They continued the Olympic Games, but this was disrupted by a Germanic invasion around 300 CE. The Games became part of a pagan festival until the Christian emperor Theodosius I ordered the closure of all pagan events in 393.

▲ ATHLETES WRESTLING
This carving from Athens dates from c. 510 BCE. Athletes mostly competed naked. Women were not allowed to take part or watch.

Cast-iron disks are added to central bar in increasing weights

Body suit is designed to support muscles and spine

WEIGHT LIFTING ▶
Hossein Rezazadeh of Iran lifts 260 kg (about 573 lb), more than his own body weight. He won the gold medal in the super heavyweight final in 2000.

Supports help to protect the knees from strain

IS IT EXPENSIVE TO HOST THE OLYMPICS?
The summer and winter Games each cost around $3 billion to host. Cities must house hundreds of thousands of visitors and provide security and transportation for them. The host city must also build world-class stadiums and facilities. All this bankrupted the 1976 host, Montreal. Costs are met by the income from television sponsorship and tourism.

HAVE NEW EVENTS BEEN ADDED SINCE 1896?
The Olympics have changed a great deal since 1896, when there were no women's events at all. The winter Games only began in 1924. **▶▶ TRACK AND FIELD** is the focus of the summer Games, but many events have come and gone, such as the tug-of-war. Recent additions include volleyball, canoeing, and cycling.

▲ OLYMPIC EVENTS, SYDNEY, 2000
1 Chinese gymnast Xuan Liu reaches for the asymmetric bars.
2 Liuhui Kong concentrates hard to take the gold medal for China in the men's table tennis singles final. 3 Holland's Pieter van den Hoogenband (right) and Australia's Ian Thorpe race to the finish in the 200-m freestyle swimming final. Van den Hoogenband took the gold medal.

TRACK AND FIELD

Track and field events were the core of the ancient Olympics and included running, throwing, and jumping, which combined into multi-event competitions—the pentathlon (five events) and the decathlon (ten events). Today, track and field also includes pole-vaulting, hurdling, and relay racing.

WHAT MAKES A GREAT ATHLETE?
Great athletes, like all great sports competitors, require fitness, dedication, natural ability, and luck. What lifts some athletes above others is a relentless will to win, psychological strength, and the capacity to produce their best performance under any circumstances.

HOW DO ATHLETES KEEP SETTING NEW RECORDS?
With sponsorship, athletes have more resources and time to devote to sports. High-tech running tracks, clothing, and shoes have improved performance. So have new techniques such as the flop in high jumping. However, performance-enhancing drugs damage the Olympic ideals and the competitors' health.

RELAY RACING ▶
The American team passes the baton (stick) at the 2000 Games in the 4 x 100-m relay race.

FIND OUT MORE ▶▶ Ancient Greece 376–377 • Competitions 354–355 • Sports 352–353

HISTORY

HISTORY

History is a record of what happened in the past. It is all about people—how they lived and worked, where they traveled, why they went to war, and what they thought and believed.

WHY DO PEOPLE STUDY HISTORY?

Historians work like detectives. In fact, the word history comes from the ancient Greek for "learning by enquiry". They gather ▶▶ **EVIDENCE** , search for lost treasures, and report their finds. Their studies can explain why things happen, and how change occurs.

Death mask of _____
gold, to place over
dead man's face

Detailed _____
metalwork
shows beard

DEATH MASK, GREECE ▶
This mask was found in the 1870s, in a grave at Mycenae. It was discovered by German archaeologist Heinrich Schliemann, who originally claimed that it belonged to Agamemnon, a Mycenaean king described in the poems of Homer. Experts first thought that it was from around 1200 BCE, but modern dating techniques suggest that it is older.

▲ ETRUSCAN WALL PAINTING, ITALY
The dancers in this Etruscan fresco (wall painting) look just as lively as when they were first painted, almost 2,500 years ago. To us, pictures such as this are like windows into the past.

HOW IS HISTORY USED?

History helps us to understand our own times, and to plan for the future. Learning about the past shapes our sense of who we are, and a knowledge of past injustices often inspires people to fight for change.

DO HISTORIANS AGREE WITH ONE ANOTHER?

Historians frequently have different opinions about the past, and some may also be influenced by their own religious or political views. In their studies, historians use new evidence and ideas to challenge existing theories about historical periods and events.

EVIDENCE

Anything that survives from the past can be used as evidence of what happened long ago. Some evidence comes from written documents such as letters, diaries, or government records. Other forms of evidence are still standing—such as old buildings, statues, or grand monuments—while much of it lies hidden in the ground, yet to be discovered.

◄ MAGNA CARTA, ENGLAND
This great document records an agreement made in 1215 CE between King John and a group of nobles. It sets out the laws and customs the king had to respect in dealing with his subjects. It still influences English law today.

HOW DO HISTORIANS STUDY EVIDENCE?

Historians study many different forms of evidence, preserved in libraries, archives, and museums. Often, they have to learn dead languages so that they can read and understand ancient documents. They also rely on the techniques of other subjects, such as ▶▶ **ARCHAEOLOGY** and ▶▶ **ANTHROPOLOGY** .

ARCHAEOLOGY

Archaeology involves studying the past through the analysis of physical remains. These include stone or flint objects, metal items, pottery, paintings, tools, weapons, and textiles, as well as fields, towns, and ruined buildings.

WHAT TECHNIQUES DO ARCHAEOLOGISTS USE?

Today's archaeologists locate sites using aerial photography, satellite pictures, and a satellite system called GPS. Then they excavate (dig up) the sites to uncover buried remains, and record the details of any finds using photos, drawings, charts, and maps. They scan and X-ray their finds to investigate them without harming them, and use computer modeling to create reconstructions of damaged objects and buildings.

PEWTER JUG FROM THE *MARY ROSE*, ENGLAND ▶
This jug, encrusted with barnacles, was salvaged in 1982. It is part of the remains of the wrecked English warship Mary Rose, which had been built for King Henry VIII. The ship sank in 1545.

WHERE DO ARCHAEOLOGISTS LOOK FOR REMAINS?

Archaeologists search for remains in many different places, including shipwrecks, tombs, caves, and even garbage dumps. They survey towns and villages—recording the location of all historic sites—and examine the soil to find any traces of past fires, fields, and buildings. They study animal bones and seeds to find out what people ate and what the climate was like.

Noose around neck shows Tollund Man was strangled

HOW DO ARCHAEOLOGISTS DATE THEIR FINDS?

Archaeologists have many ways of dating finds. Fragments of pottery, or coins, can show when people lived on a site, and tree rings in lumber can reveal when a building was made. These experts can also measure the level of radioactive carbon or magnetic energy in an object to calculate its age.

TOLLUND MAN, DENMARK ▲
This man was thrown into a bog around 2,000 years ago, as a sacrifice to the gods. The acidic earth in the bog preserved his body. Because of this, archaeologists have been able to work out his age, health, height, weight, and social status—and even what he ate for his last meal.

ANTHROPOLOGY

Anthropology is the study of humankind. It often focuses on people living today—especially groups that follow ancient customs and traditions, or still use ancient forms of technology. Anthropologists visit these people to ask them questions, and to observe their family life, social customs, and religious rituals. They record their songs, myths, legends, and beliefs.

HOW DOES ANTHROPOLOGY HELP HISTORY?

The study of anthropology can help historians to understand how ancient objects were used, or why ancient beliefs were so important, by comparing evidence from the past with observations made today. It is especially useful to historians investigating past civilizations that have left no written records.

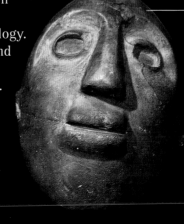

Head made of stone –face may represent an ancestor

◀ BURIAL HEAD
This head was found in a burial mound in Ohio, and dates from around 300 BCE. It was carved by descendants of the Hopewell culture. Today's anthropologists study the religious customs of present-day cultures in Ohio. Their studies help historians to understand the various uses of figures such as this one.

history

FIND OUT MORE ▶▶ Ancient Greece 376–377 • Early Americans 380 • First Metalworkers 367 • Prehistoric Pottery 367

FIRST MODERN HUMANS

Homo sapiens (modern humans) first evolved between 200,000 BCE and 100,000 BCE. They were like us, physically, and had the same brain power. They developed many skills of survival, and advanced **⤷FLINT-KNAPPING** techniques for making better tools.

WHERE DID THE FIRST MODERN HUMANS LIVE?

Most archaeologists think that *Homo sapiens* first lived in Africa, and that our direct ancestor was *Homo habilis* ("handy man"), who evolved about 2.5 million years ago. But some believe our ancestor was *Homo ergaster* ("work man"), who developed around 1.9 million years ago. This issue about where modern humans first lived and settled continues to divide opinions.

POSSIBLE ROUTE TAKEN BY MODERN HUMANS

EXTENT OF ICE SHEETS c. 10,000 BCE

▲ **THE SPREAD OF MODERN HUMANS**
The arrows on this map show how modern humans may have spread out from Africa. The dates record the age of the earliest modern human bones and tools found on each continent.

▲ **CAVE PAINTING**
This plump horse is one of more than 600 cave paintings, from c. 15,000 BCE, found in Lascaux, France. Early modern humans probably believed that animals had magical powers to protect families and tribes, or help hunters.

HOW DID MODERN HUMANS REACH OTHER AREAS?

Wandering groups of modern humans moved out of Africa, in search of food, around 125,000 BCE. They reached other continents via land bridges—areas of seabed left uncovered as the Earth's water froze during the last Ice Age (c. 70,000 BCE to c. 10,000 BCE). By c. 28,000 BCE, they had replaced all earlier *hominins* ("human like primates") or similar, including the Neanderthals.

WHO WERE NEANDERTHALS AND WHY DID THEY DISAPPEAR?

Neanderthals (*Homo Neanderthalensis*) are a closely related, but separate, species from *Homo sapiens* ("wise man"). They lived in Europe and Asia from c. 200,000 BCE to c. 28,000 BCE. The spread of modern humans may have been the cause of their extinction.

Thick ridge above brow

Smaller jaw— large jaw not needed, since today's humans do not eat tough roots and leaves

▲ **MODERN HUMAN SKULL**
The first modern humans were tall, and had slender bones, high-domed foreheads, smooth brows, and small jaws. Their muscles were not as well developed as those of the Neanderthals, and their eyesight was weaker.

◀ **NEANDERTHAL SKULL**
Neanderthals had larger brains than modern humans. Their short, stocky build and broad nose helped them to conserve body heat in Europe's chilly Ice Age climate. They relied more on strength than brain power.

*Bark made
a good container
for hazelnuts
and blackberries*

FLINT-KNAPPING

Early and modern humans used a technique called flint-knapping to make stone tools. They chipped flakes off one piece of flint (a hard, glassy stone) by striking it with another piece. This required great patience and skill. ►► ABORIGINALS still practice flint-knapping today.

*Design
resembles
leaf of a
laurel tree*

WHAT KINDS OF TOOLS DID EARLY HUMANS USE?
Early humans used five main kinds of flint tools—knives for cutting, scrapers for removing flesh from hides, burins (small, pointed tools) for carving, awls for piercing holes, and points or tips for attaching to spears. They also used flint hand-axes for chopping wood and butchering animal carcasses.

◄ CRAFTWORKER'S BURIN
This sharp-pointed flint tool, known as a burin, was made around 35,000 BCE. Burins were probably used for engraving bone or adding grooves to leather. The craftworker would guide the point using an index finger.

*Rounded
shape fits
worker's
hand*

Spur

▲ STORING FOOD
In late summer and fall, women and children gathered large quantities of nuts, fruits, and berries, then dried them over fires to preserve them for the winter. Archaeologists have found remains of food preserved 12,000 years ago.

*Bison
grazing*

FEATHERED ARROW ▲
Hunters fitted a flight of duck feathers to each arrow to make it travel farther. This way, they could attack their prey from afar.

*Hunter crawls
along ground*

CLOVIS POINT ►
Ice Age hunters in North America used a curved piece of flint, known as a Clovis point, to make a spear. Two small spurs (spikes) at the rear of the point made it easier to attach to a wooden shaft, using animal sinew or plant twine.

STALKING BISON ▲
The picture on this fragment of bone was carved in France between 15,000 BCE and 10,000 BCE. Teams of people worked together to catch large animals by herding them over cliffs or trapping them in narrow valleys.

SPEARHEAD ►
This leaf-shaped blade was once part of a hunting spear made in France between 20,000 BCE and 15,000 BCE. It is beautifully shaped, using the pressure-flaking technique developed around 35,000 BCE. This technique allowed craftworkers to shape their tools much more precisely.

ABORIGINALS

Aboriginals, also known as indigenous Australians, were the earliest inhabitants of Australia. Until the 20th century, they followed a lifestyle similar to that of earlier humans. Their skills helped archaeologists understand evidence about the distant past.

HOW DID ABORIGINALS SURVIVE?
In 10,000 BCE, sea levels around Australia rose and Aboriginal people were forced to move farther inland, where conditions were harsh. To survive, they used fire to clear bushland so that wild food plants could grow, hunted kangaroos with boomerangs, wove traps for fish, and dug grubs from deep underground.

first modern humans

◄ ABORIGINAL ART
Aboriginals created art on rocks, such as this turtle on Ubirr Rock at the Kakadu National Park in Australia's Northern Territory. Some of their paintings are more than 20,000 years old.

FIND OUT MORE ►► Africa 238–239 • Australia and New Zealand 274–275 • Evolution 74–75

EARLY FARMING

Farming began *c.* 9,000 BCE on land that became known as the ▶◀ FERTILE CRESCENT. Hunter-gatherers, who were traveling in the area in search of food, began to harvest (gather) wild grains they found growing there. They scattered spare grains on the ground to grow more food.

HOW DID FARMING CHANGE PEOPLE'S LIVES?

Before farming, people lived by hunting wild animals and gathering wild plants. When supplies ran out, these hunter-gatherers moved on. Farming meant that people did not need to travel to find food. Instead, they began to live in settled communities, and grew crops or raised animals on nearby land. They built stronger, more permanent homes and surrounded their settlements with walls to protect themselves.

Plaster spread over real human skull

Eyes made of shells from the Red Sea

MOLDED HEAD ▶
This human head statue, from around 7000 BCE, was probably made to show respect for an ancestor. Many statues like this have been found at Jericho. They give us clues as to how people in early farming communities lived.

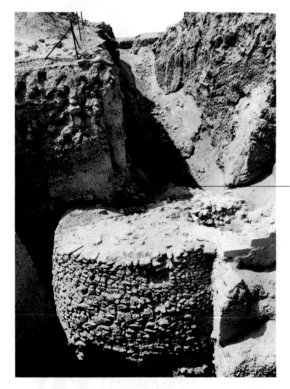

Base of round tower that formed part of Jericho's ancient walls

early farming

▲ THE WALLS OF JERICHO
The settlement of Jericho was founded c. 9000 BCE by farmers, who built walls 10 ft (3 m) thick around it, with a tower 30 ft (9 m) high. Jericho was close to a natural spring, which provided water for their fields.

WHICH PLANTS DID THE FIRST FARMERS GROW?

In the Fertile Crescent, farmers grew tall, wild grasses, including an early type of barley, and primitive varieties of wheat called emmer and einkorn. These naturally produced large grains (seeds) that were tasty and nourishing. In other parts of the world, between 8000 BCE and 3000 BCE, farmers discovered how to ▶◀ DOMESTICATE their own local plants and animals.

HOW DID PEOPLE BECOME BETTER FARMERS?

By around 8500 BCE, people were storing grains during the winter, then sowing them in specially cleared plots. By 8000 BCE, the farmers had discovered which grains gave the best yields and selected these for planting. They produced more food than they needed and were able to feed non-farmers such as craftworkers and traders. The farmers exchanged their food for various kinds of useful or decorative goods.

▼ FOOD GRAINS
Einkorn and emmer produce grains (seeds) that fall from the ear (seed head) when they are ripe. Seeing this happen probably inspired the first farmers to experiment with different methods of scattering and planting grains.

EINKORN

Ripe grains from ear of einkorn

Ear of einkorn

EMMER

DOMESTICATION

Domestication is the process of making wild plants and animals more useful to humans, through selective breeding. Farmers select and plant only the best seeds from their last crop. Wild cattle or other animals are selectively bred to make a herd docile (easy to control).

FERTILE CRESCENT

Archaeologists use the name Fertile Crescent to describe an area to the east of the Mediterranean Sea, where farming first developed. It was a crescent-shaped strip of land that stretched across the Levant region (now known as Israel, Lebanon, and Syria), and around the edges of the Tarus and Zagros mountains.

WHY DID FARMING BEGIN HERE?

The Fertile Crescent had regular rainfall, making it ideal for growing grains such as emmer and einkorn, and for raising herds of grass-eating animals such as sheep and goats. In Mesopotamia, where the soil was particularly fertile, large-scale farming became possible once irrigation methods had developed to supply the land with water.

TIMELINE OF EARLY FARMING	
9000 BCE	Wheat/barley, Fertile Crescent
8000 BCE	Potatoes, South America
7500 BCE	Goats/sheep, Middle East
7000 BCE	Rye, Europe
6000 BCE	Chickens, South Asia
3500 BCE	Horse, West Asia
3000 BCE	Cotton, South America
2700 BCE	Corn, North America

▲ HOME OF THE FIRST FARMERS
The Fertile Crescent stretched in a crescent-shaped curve from the northern tip of the Red Sea around to the Persian Gulf. Some of the world's first settlements, including Jericho, were built in this region. Important trading centers, such as Çatalhöyük, also developed nearby.

WHY WAS ÇATALHÖYÜK SO PROSPEROUS?

Çatalhöyük was founded in around 7000 BCE, and grew to be the largest settlement in the Middle East. Its wealth came from farming and trade. The farmers kept cattle and grew wheat, barley, and peas. Çatalhöyük made itself especially prosperous by controlling the trade in obsidian (a coarse, glassy rock), which came from a nearby volcano. Craftworkers used this volcanic glass to make high-quality tools.

WHAT WERE THE FIRST DOMESTICATED ANIMALS?

Dogs were the first animals to be domesticated, c. 12,500 BCE. They were descended from wild wolf cubs that had learned to live with human families, who fed and petted them. By 10,000 BCE, hunters were managing wild herds of gazelle, sheep, and goats, watching over them and killing the weakest for food. Around 7500 BCE, farmers were taking the best animals from their herds to breed them for meat and milk.

◄ HERDED ANIMALS
This seal came from the ancient city of Susa, north of the Persian Gulf, and was made around 3000 BCE. By this time, herding animals was a way of life for farmers. Cattle were also being used to prepare the land where farmers grew crops. Sheep with longer hair had been selectively bred to develop fleecy coats, which the farmers used to make wool.

Seal (stamp) engraved with rams and goats

Cutting edge of blade slices wheat and barley stalks

◄ STONE SICKLE
This sickle has a wooden handle and a sharp flint blade, carefully shaped by a stoneworker around 6,000 years ago. Farmers used sickles to cut ripe ears of grain from the stalk.

Stone is rolled back and forth to crush grains

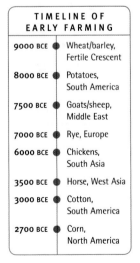

HAND MILL ►
This is a hand mill known as a quern. It consists of a curved slab of stone and a ball-shaped stone roller. Querns were used by farming women, between c. 6000 BCE and 4000 BCE, to grind grains of wheat and barley into flour.

ÇATALHÖYÜK HOMES ►
Excavation of the Çatalhöyük site found mud-brick houses closely packed together, without any streets. Access to each home was by ladders leading up to doorways on a flat roof. Rooms had hearths for heating, benches for sitting and sleeping on, and ovens for baking bread. When family members died, they were buried under the floor.

FIND OUT MORE ▶▶ Early Americans 380 • Farming 66 • Maya 381 • Western Asia and the Middle East 264–265

MEGALITHIC EUROPE

Between *c.* 3200 BCE and 1500 BCE, people in northwest Europe built monuments from massive stones known as megaliths. Some were arranged in circles or lines, pointing to the sky. Others, called ▸▸ CHAMBER TOMBS, were buried under the earth.

WHO BUILT MEGALITHIC MONUMENTS?
Megalithic monuments came in many different shapes and sizes. Most were fairly small, and could easily have been assembled by a family over a few seasons. Large monuments, like Stonehenge and Carnac, were probably built by powerful chiefs who could command their subjects to work on the monuments.

WHAT WERE STONE CIRCLES USED FOR?
Stone circles were probably used for religious ceremonies or for astronomy. Most of them line up with the Sun, Moon, and stars on special days. For example, the rising Sun shines through the center of Stonehenge, England, at midsummer, and lights up a chamber tomb in Newgrange, Ireland, at midwinter.

▲ CARNAC'S MEGALITHS
These rows of standing stones in Carnac, France, are arranged in parallel lines that run for about two-thirds of a mile (1 km) and link two stone circles. Carnac also has many separate standing stones, chamber tombs, and barrows (earth mounds).

Trilithon—a stone arch made of two upright stones and a horizontal stone on top. Five stood at Stonehenge.

▲ STONEHENGE, ENGLAND
In around 3000 BCE, workers at this site built a henge (circular ditch and earth bank) and a ring of wooden posts. In 2500 BCE, smaller bluestones, from Wales were added to the monument, and 200 years later huge 26-ton sandstone sarsens were erected there.

CHAMBER TOMBS

Megalithic tombs with several chambers (rooms) were built using massive stone slabs, then covered with an earth mound called a barrow. Each one could be used as a burial place for hundreds of years.

WHO WAS BURIED IN THE CHAMBER TOMBS?
Archaeologists are not certain for whom the chamber tombs were made, because they were robbed long ago. From their design, it seems likely that they were used to bury rich, powerful leaders, who controlled vast areas of farmland and the people living in the region.

megaliths

Vaulted roof made of strips of stone

◀ MAES HOWE TOMB
This tomb, on Mainland Island in the Orkney Islands, Scotland, was built in around 2700 BCE. The main chamber is reached through a long passageway lined with stone. Square holes in the chamber's walls lead to smaller side rooms, which were also used for burials.

FIND OUT MORE ▸▸ Rocks 46–47

PREHISTORIC POTTERY

The earliest pottery was made by Japanese fishing communities, in c. 10,500 BCE. When they cooked, people noticed that the clay soil underneath their fires baked and became hard. They soon began to shape clay into pots, cook them on bonfires, and leave them to cool.

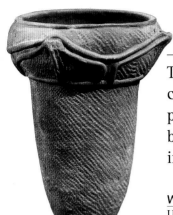

▲ JAPANESE POTTERY JAR
This rope-patterned pot was made between 10,500 BCE and 7500 BCE. A craftworker shaped it by hand using coils of clay.

WHY WERE THE FIRST POTS SO IMPORTANT?
Unlike earlier containers—made from leather, woven twigs, bark, and string—clay pots were heatproof and waterproof. They made it possible to cook soups and stews, brew drinks such as wine and beer, and store grain and oil for long periods. The remains of pots help archaeologists to identify different peoples.

prehistoric pottery

Paintwork helps place and date the urn

BURIAL URN ▲
Pottery was often used in religious rituals. This Banshan type burial urn, from China's Yangshao culture, was made in around 2500 BCE.

FIND OUT MORE ▶▶ Rocks 46–47 • Sculpture 323

FIRST METALWORKERS

From around 9000 BCE, people in different lands began to work with nuggets of soft metals, such as copper. Later, they discovered how to extract metals, such as tin, from rocks by smelting (heating). Finally, they discovered how to melt metals together to make new materials called alloys, such as bronze.

first metalworkers

SOME OF THE FIRST METALWORKERS	
9000 BCE	Hammered copper, Central Asia
5000 BCE	Gold/copper, Europe
3500 BCE	Bronze, Middle East
2300 BCE	Bronze, Europe
1500 BCE	Iron, western Asia
1000 BCE	Iron, Europe

Face perhaps represents a revered ancestor

WHAT WAS BRONZE USED FOR?
Bronze is a mixture of copper and tin. It is much harder than either metal, and can be sharpened to make a cutting edge. It was used to create more powerful and long-lasting weapons, tools, and farm implements. Craftworkers also used it to make intricate castings—objects made by pouring melted bronze into a mold.

▲ BRONZE ARCHER
This bronze statue was made in around 600 BCE on the Mediterranean island of Sardinia. Bronze was also used to make sharp arrowheads, spear tips, and sword blades.

HOW WAS BRONZE FIRST MADE?
Bronze-workers heated copper and tin in a furnace fueled by charcoal. When the two metals melted, they combined to form liquid-hot bronze, which ran down a clay pipe into containers made of clay or sand. When cold, these ingots (solid blocks of metal) were remelted and poured into different-shaped molds.

Handle at either end made vessel easier to carry

WHO MADE THE FIRST BRONZE OBJECTS?
The technique of making bronze objects—by pouring molten (melted) metal into molds—was invented in western Asia in around 3500 BCE. It was also discovered separately in China in around 2000 BCE. The Chinese bronze-makers developed their skills to create much more elaborate patterns and designs.

RITUAL VESSEL ▶
This bronze vessel was made while the Shang dynasty ruled China (1650–1027 BCE). It was used for cooking ritual meals in honor of the spirits of dead ancestors.

Leg shape possibly derived from that of an animal

FIND OUT MORE ▶▶ Alloys 174

MESOPOTAMIA

Mesopotamia is the land between the Tigris and Euphrates rivers. Farmers used the river water to irrigate fields and grow plentiful crops. Around 3500 BCE, the Sumerians of southern Mesopotamia built the world's first cities, including Ur, Uruk, and Eridu.

HOW WERE THE SUMERIAN CITIES RULED?

Mighty kings, who commanded large armies, had strong cities, great palaces, and magnificent royal tombs made. The kings were assisted by priests and well-trained scribes, who collected taxes, controlled irrigation projects, and took charge of laws governing city crafts and trade. Priests also served the gods in ziggurats (temples).

HOW WERE THE ZIGGURATS BUILT?

Mesopotamian builders built ziggurats and houses from bricks made of mud mixed with chopped straw (left to dry and harden in the sun). Teams of workmen moved huge loads of bricks using sleds on wooden rollers, or carried smaller quantities in baskets on their backs. Mud was used as a mortar to bind the bricks.

Mesopotamia

Bull's head made of gold

▼ ZIGGURAT AT UR
Ziggurats were holy "mountains," where people could get closer to the gods. The ziggurat at Ur (in modern Iraq) was built in around 2100 BCE. Originally, it had three tall terraces (raised levels), one on top of the other, which were planted with trees and flowers. A shrine to Nanna, the Moon god, stood at the top. Today, only the temple's lower section survives.

▲ QUEEN'S TREASURE
This bull's head decorates a harp from the tomb of Queen Shub-ad of Ur, who died in around 2500 BCE. The harp-player's skeleton was found close by, still holding the harp strings. She had been buried alive to entertain the queen in the afterlife.

FIND OUT MORE ▶▶ Ancient Religions 282 • Western Asia and the Middle East 264–265

INDUS VALLEY

Between around 3500 BCE and 2000 BCE, people in the Indus Valley built more than 100 towns. The largest were Mohenjo-Daro and Harappa, with populations of 40,000. These towns had large temples, granaries, brick houses, and streets laid out in neat grid patterns.

HOW DID THE PEOPLE OF THE INDUS VALLEY LIVE?

Farmers grew wheat, barley, cotton, and rice on land fertilized by yearly Indus River floods. They also raised animals. In towns, people made cloth, pottery, metalwork, and jewelry. On the coast, they went abroad to trade.

Indus Valley

CARVING OF ROYAL PRIEST ▶
This figure, carved from limestone in around 2500 BCE, was found at Mohenjo-Daro.

WHY DID INDUS VALLEY CITIES DISAPPEAR?

At Mohenjo-Daro, the Indus River changed its course, causing a water shortage. Other towns may have been destroyed by floods, disease, or invaders. But nobody knows for sure why the Indus Valley civilization collapsed.

◀ TWO-WHEELED CART
This ceramic model of a farm cart pulled by mules, from around 2500 BCE, was found in Mohenjo-Daro.

FIND OUT MORE ▶▶ Western Asia and the Middle East 264–265

FIRST SCRIPTS

Writing was invented in Mesopotamia, around 3400 BCE. Cities had grown so big that people could no longer do business by keeping every detail in their heads. Rulers needed to keep track of who had paid their taxes, which craftworkers had been given rations, and how many goods they had made.

first scripts

WHAT WERE EARLY FORMS OF WRITING LIKE?

The first writing was made up of pictograms—small pictures representing objects or expressing actions or ideas. These writing systems, which included ►► CUNEIFORM, were complicated, and few people managed to learn them.

WHERE ELSE DID PEOPLE USE PICTOGRAMS?

Different forms of picture-writing developed in Egypt, China, and Meso- (Middle) America. In the Indus Valley, scribes used pictures combined with symbols—a system that today's experts have still not explained.

Pattern of cracks on heated bone gave an answer to a question

▲ EGYPTIAN HIEROGLYPHS
These hieroglyphs form part of the *Book of the Dead*, found inscribed on the walls of the tomb of Pharaoh Rameses VI (r.1156–1148 BCE) in Egypt's Valley of the Kings.

ORACLE BONE ►
In around 1500 BCE, priests carved questions in Chinese characters into bones.

CUNEIFORM

Cuneiform is the name given to the wedge-shaped script, written using trimmed reeds, developed by scribes in Sumer around 3200 BCE. It was borrowed by other Middle Eastern peoples to write and develop their own languages, before the ►► ALPHABET was developed.

HOW WAS THE FIRST SCRIPT WRITTEN?

The first pictograms were scratched on to tablets of wet clay, using stalks from reeds that grew beside Mesopotamian rivers. The tablets were then dried in the sun to preserve the written text. Scribes (people trained to copy manuscripts) soon began to trim the reeds to make a triangular tip, which created clear, wedge-shaped marks.

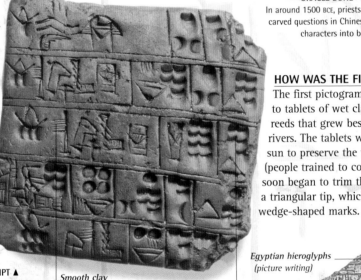

CUNEIFORM SCRIPT ▲
This Mesopotamian clay tablet, made soon after 2900 BCE, lists details of fields and crops. The cuneiform script is very neatly written, with wedge-shaped symbols formed in straight rows.

Smooth clay surface for writing on

Clear cuneiform marks left on clay

Egyptian hieroglyphs (picture writing)

ALPHABET

The world's first alphabet was invented in around 1000 BCE by the Phoenicians, who lived in the eastern Mediterranean region. Unlike pictogram scripts, the alphabet used letters that stood for individual sounds.

ROSETTA STONE ►
In 196 BCE, Egyptian scribes carved the same text in three different scripts on this stone. It was discovered in Rosetta, Egypt, in 1799, and provided the key to translating Egyptian hieroglyphs.

WHY WAS THE FIRST ALPHABET SO IMPORTANT?

The Phoenicians discovered that letters could be put together in different combinations to spell almost all known words. Alphabetic writing needed fewer than 30 letters, compared with the 600 cuneiform symbols used by Sumerian scribes, or the 5,000 characters used by Chinese scholars. This made it much easier to learn, so literacy (reading and writing) became much more widespread in societies using alphabetic scripts.

Egyptian demotic (picture-based script used for writing quickly)

Ancient Greek (written using an alphabet)

FIND OUT MORE ►► Ancient Egypt 370–371 • Writing 339

ANCIENT EGYPT

From around 3100 BCE to 30 BCE, the dry desert land of Egypt was home to an advanced civilization. The Ancient Egyptians produced massive ▸▸ **PYRAMIDS**, fabulous golden treasures, and wonderful works of art. They invented hieroglyphs, and were expert engineers.

Uraeus (cobra), symbol of Lower Egypt (in the north) _____

Vulture, symbol _____ of Upper Egypt (in the south)

Nemes _____ _headdress made_ of solid gold and bands of colored (dark blue) glass paste

WHY WERE NILE FLOODS IMPORTANT?

The Nile River flows through Egypt on its way to the sea. Every year, in July, it flooded the surrounding desert and covered the land with fertile silt (fine mud). Ancient Egyptian farmers were able to grow excellent crops on this land, including wheat, barley, grapes, figs, and many different types of vegetables.

◂ **THRESHING WHEAT**
These farmworkers are threshing wheat to separate the ripe grains from the stalks. This picture decorated the walls of an Egyptian tomb built in around 1400 BCE.

WHO DID THE EGYPTIANS WORSHIP?

The Egyptians worshiped hundreds of gods and goddesses. Gods like Osiris, ruler of the underworld, looked human. Others were shown as animals, such as the cat-goddess Bastet, who brought fertility. The most important was ram-headed Amun, king of the gods.

WHY DID EGYPTIAN CIVILIZATION LAST SO LONG?

Egypt became wealthy through farming and trade. Its power was built up by strong governments, led by ▸▸ **PHARAOHS** and staffed by well-trained scribes (officials). The nation was defended by large armies.

Golden ball representing life-giving Sun pushed along by scarab

▴ **SACRED SCARAB**
This gold bracelet, from the tomb of Amenemope, is decorated with a scarab (dung beetle) made from blue lapis lazuli, a semiprecious stone. For the Egyptians, scarabs symbolized the life-giving Sun.

PHARAOHS

Ancient Egypt was ruled by powerful kings called pharaohs, who took the roles of chief priest, war leader, and head of government. Egyptians believed that the pharaohs were living links between people and gods, and that they actually became gods after death.

WHAT DOES "PHARAOH" MEAN?

The name pharaoh came from two Egyptian words, per-aa, meaning "great house" or "palace." Later, the name for such a building was also used to refer to the king living there. It was used to show great respect.

Ancient Egypt ⬉

FUNERAL BOAT ▸
Model boats like this one were buried with the pharaohs in royal pyramid tombs.

Pharaoh's spirit carried through world of the dead

GOLDEN MASK ▸
This portrait mask covered the face of the mummified body of Pharaoh Tutankhamen (r 1333–1324 BCE). The tomb of Tutankhamen was discovered in the Valley of the Kings, Egypt, in 1922.

PYRAMIDS

Massive stone tombs protected the bodies of dead pharaohs. These pyramids represented stairways leading to the sky. They took great skill to plan and build, and were designed to keep out robbers—but no pharaoh's ▶▶ **MUMMY** has ever been found inside one.

▲ PYRAMIDS AT GIZA
These pyramids were built in around 2500 BCE for the pharaohs Khufu, Khephren, and Menkaure. They were originally covered in limestone and topped with gold. The tallest, the Great Pyramid, was 482 ft (147 m)

WHO BUILT THE PYRAMIDS?
The pyramids were constructed by teams of skilled professional builders, such as stone masons, who were paid very well for their work. During the flood season, when the Nile River washed over the farmlands, royal officials commanded peasant farmers to assist the professional workers in building the pyramids.

MUMMIFICATION

A mummy is a dead body that has been carefully preserved, or mummified. Workers removed organs that might rot, then dried the body with natron (salty crystals) and wrapped it in resin-soaked bandages.

WHY WERE PEOPLE MUMMIFIED AFTER DEATH?
Ancient Egyptians thought that people were made up of five elements. These elements were the body, its ka (spirit), ba (personality), name, and shadow. By preserving the body, the Egyptians believed that they could keep the other four elements alive. If the body decayed, to them the person would stay dead forever.

MUMMY COFFIN ▶
This wood-and-plaster coffin protected the mummified body of a man who died around 700 BCE. It is decorated with images of gods.

Collar made of gold and semiprecious stones

Magic spells written in hieroglyphs

EGYPT'S HISTORY	
5500–3100 BCE	Pre-Dynastic Period: before the time of the Pharaohs
3100–2686 BCE	Early Dynastic Period: Upper and Lower Egypt are united – Menes becomes first pharaoh
2686–2181 BCE	Old Kingdom: age of the pyramids
2181–2055 BCE	First Intermediate Period: breakdown of centralized government
2055–1650 BCE	Middle Kingdom: Egypt reunited
1650–1550 BCE	Second Intermediate Period: invasion of Hyksos people, who are then defeated
1550–1069 BCE	New Kingdom: Egypt at its greatest
1069–747 BCE	Third Intermediate Period: breaks into small states
747–332 BCE	Later Period: invaded by Assyrians, then Persians
332–30 BCE	Ptolemaic Period: conquered by Alexander the Great and ruled by his general's family
30 BCE–395 CE	Roman Period: Egypt part of Roman Empire

FIND OUT MORE ▶▶ Ancient Religions 282 • First Scripts 369 • North and West Africa 240–241

Bull, symbol of god Addad

Dragon, symbol of god Marduk

▲ ISHTAR GATE
This gateway, named after the Babylonians' goddess of love and war, was the main entrance to the city of Babylon from around 600 BCE. It led to the Hanging Gardens of Babylon, built by King Nebuchadnezzar.

MIDDLE EASTERN EMPIRES

From around 2000 BCE, rival peoples in the Middle East fought to either conquer or defend land. Some, like the ►►BABYLONIANS and ►►ASSYRIANS, built great cities in Mesopotamia. Others, like the ►►HITTITES and ►►HEBREWS, settled and founded new kingdoms outside Mesopotamia.

WHY WAS THE MIDDLE EAST SUCH A RICH PRIZE?
Kings and peoples wanted to live in the Middle East because of its fertile farmland. The best land lay beside the Euphrates and Tigris rivers of Mesopotamia, but there were also fields, forests, and orchards in mountain valleys to the north and south. People also competed to control the long-distance trading routes that passed through the Middle East, linking Europe with Asia.

▲ CLAY MAP
Made by Babylonian scholars in around 600 BCE, this was one of the first maps of the world.

BABYLONIANS

Babylon became powerful around 1792 BCE, under King Hammurabi. From 1595 BCE, its people came under the rule of invaders. In 625 BCE, a general called Nabopolassar drove out the foreigners and became king. Under his son, King Nebuchadnezzar (r. 605–562 BCE), a great new empire emerged.

*KING HAMMURABI
r. 1792–1750 BCE*
King Hammurabi (pictured standing before the Sun god Shamash) conquered all of Mesopotamia to create a new kingdom, which was named after its chief city—Babylon. He introduced a strict code of law, and many crimes were punished by death. After he died, the empire weakened.

HOW DID THE BABYLONIANS MEASURE TIME?
Babylonians built mud-brick monuments and used them as sundials. They observed stars and planets, predicted their movements, and compiled calendars. They based their calculations on units of 60—which we still use today to measure minutes and seconds—and recorded all their findings in cuneiform writing.

HITTITES

The Hittites were people who settled in Anatolia (now Turkey), in around 1700 BCE. They could smelt iron, so they were able to make stronger weapons than their enemies. Around 1400 BCE, Hittite city-states joined forces to create a powerful kingdom.

HOW DID THE HITTITES FIGHT THEIR WARS?
Fast, two-wheeled war chariots—pulled by horses—were first used by Hittite warriors around 1800 BCE. Armed with bows and arrows, the charioteers would charge at ranks of enemy soldiers to scatter them. The Hittites also attacked enemy cities with the help of siege engines such as tall towers. The Hittites had two great enemies: the Ancient Egyptians and a war-like people from the state of Mitanni, in Mesopotamia.

◄ HITTITE GOD
This warlike god was carved on a gateway in the Hittite capital city of Bogazkoy (now in Turkey) in around 1300 BCE.

Battle-ax raised to strike enemies

WHY DID HITTITE POWER COLLAPSE?
The Hittites and their enemies fought to win the eastern Mediterranean region, with its forests, farms, and rich trading ports. In around 1200 BCE, the Hittites were also attacked by invaders from Mediterranean islands, known as Sea Peoples, and by nomad tribes from the east. These wars, plus famine, destroyed Hittite power.

HEBREWS

The Hebrews were shepherds and farmers in Canaan, at the eastern end of the Mediterranean Sea. Sea Peoples also settled there. Around 1020 BCE, the Hebrews conquered these peoples and founded a powerful new kingdom, led by great kings. Saul was the first king. He was succeeded by David, and then Solomon.

WHERE WAS THE PROMISED LAND?

The Hebrews believed that God had promised them a home in Canaan. According to the Bible, the prophet Moses led them to this land in around 1200 BCE. Later, in 922 BCE, the Hebrew kingdom of Canaan divided into two separate nations—Israel in the north and Judah in the south. Judah would give its name to the Jewish people.

Hebrews' valuable farm animals also taken into captivity

◄ HEBREW PRISONERS
The Assyrians besieged the town of Lachish, in Judah, in 701 BCE. This carving shows Jewish prisoners being led away by Assyria's King Sennacherib (r. 705–681 BCE). The picture once decorated the king's palace in the Assyrian city of Nineveh.

Crown is symbol of power

Human head represents intelligence

Wings of an eagle, the most powerful creature in the sky

Bull's legs and body symbolized strength

Middle Eastern empires

ASSYRIANS

The Assyrians lived in northern Mesopotamia. Their large empire, built around 1400 BCE, was destroyed by the Sea Peoples. In 900 BCE, the Assyrians conquered a new empire stretching from Egypt to the Persian Gulf. It collapsed after the Babylonians and Medes attacked in 612 BCE.

HOW DID THE ASSYRIANS FIGHT THEIR BATTLES?

The first Assyrian soldiers were farmers, who left their fields when called up to fight. But by around 740 BCE, the Assyrian kings had developed fierce new armies made up of captured foreigners. They fought with swords, spears, bows and arrows, and battering rams. They demanded tributes of lumber, metal, and horses from weaker peoples.

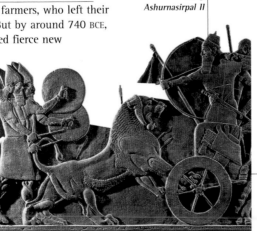

King Ashurnasirpal II

Wheeled war chariot copied from Hittite armies

PRACTICING FOR WAR ►
This stone carving shows the Assyrian King Ashurnasirpal II and his soldiers practicing combat skills by hunting lions. It comes from the king's palace at Nimrud.

GATEWAY GUARDIAN ►
This is one of a pair of huge stone figures that adorned the gateway of the palace of Assyrian King Sargon II (r. 722–705 BCE), at Khorsabad (now in Iraq). They represented the might of Assyria and guarded the palace.

FIND OUT MORE ►► Western Asia and the Middle East 264–265

MEDITERRANEAN SEAFARERS

From around 2000 BCE, people living close to the Mediterranean Sea, such as the ▸▸ MINOANS and ▸▸ PHOENICIANS, built strong wooden ships powered by sails and oars. They established long-distance sea routes linking Europe, Africa, and Asia, and became wealthy sea traders. Later, they sailed to explore and set up colonies.

WHAT MADE THE TRADERS SO PROSPEROUS?

Traders braved the stormy Mediterranean waters to earn as much as possible through overseas business. The most profitable cargoes included silver from Spain (used to make coins), tin from Britain, and copper from Cyprus. The tin and copper metals were smelted to make bronze. Phoenician cloth, colored purple with a dye made from shellfish, was so expensive that only kings and queens could afford to buy it.

◀ MYCENAEAN VASE

This jar, made some time between 1400 BCE and 1300 BCE, was found in a Mycenaean trading settlement on the Greek island of Rhodes. Traders used pots like this one to carry goods such as olive oil. Scholars believe that the Mycenaeans occupied many of the old Minoan palace sites around 1400 BCE but two centuries later their own

Octopus design shows importance of the sea for food

seafarers

MINOANS

From 2000 BCE to 1450 BCE, Minoan kings dominated the eastern Mediterranean area from the island of Crete. The kings grew rich by trading with other islands and demanding offerings from less powerful peoples. They lived in vast, elegantly decorated palaces.

WHY DID MINOAN POWER COLLAPSE?

In c. 1450 BCE, the Mediterranean island of Thera (now Santorini) was destroyed by a volcanic eruption. At nearby Crete, sea levels rose, dust blotted out the Sun, and the Minoans' crops died out. Then the palace at Knossos, Crete, was attacked by the Mycenaeans. By c. 1400 BCE, the Minoan civilization had disappeared.

▲ BULL-LEAPING

This fresco (wall painting) from the palace at Knossos, Crete, shows the sport of bull-leaping. Young Minoans vaulted over the backs of charging bulls as part of a religious ceremony. Afterward, the bull was sacrificed.

PHOENICIANS

The Phoenicians lived on the eastern shores of the Mediterranean Sea, and were powerful from around 1000 BCE to 500 BCE. They lived as farmers, foresters, and craftworkers who were highly skilled in woodworking, glass-making, and textile production.

◀ PHOENICIAN COIN

This silver coin shows a Phoenician warship, which was narrow in design to maximize speed. Phoenician cargo ships were much slower, due to their wider, heavier hull.

WHERE DID THE PHOENICIANS TRAVEL TO TRADE?

The Phoenicians sailed all over the Mediterranean Sea. A few ventured farther—to western Spain, southeast Britain, and western Africa—and built new cities in the regions where they traded. Their most famous city was at Carthage, in North Africa, which remained powerful until the Romans destroyed it in 146 BCE.

FIND OUT MORE ▸▸ Western Europe 252–253

PERSIAN EMPIRE

From 539 BCE to 331 BCE, the Persian Empire was the most powerful state in the world. Ruled from Persia (now Iran), it stretched from Egypt to India. It had rich resources of water, fertile farmland, and gold. The Persians worshiped their gods at fire altars.

▼ ROYAL PALACE
In 518 BCE, King Darius gave orders for a magnificent new palace to be built at Persepolis, in Persia. He commanded leaders from all over the empire to bring tributes (forced gifts) to him there.

GOLDEN ARMLET ▶
Persia was rich in gold. This armlet was found near the Oxus River, in modern Afghanistan.

Persians

Stairway carving of ambassadors from Media (north Iran) carrying tributes

HOW WAS THE PERSIAN EMPIRE GOVERNED?

Persian rulers claimed the proud title of "King of Kings" and demanded total obedience from their subjects. Under King Darius, the empire was divided into 20 provinces to try to stop any single region from becoming too powerful. Each province was ruled by a governor, called a **▶▶ SATRAP**.

Griffin, a monster from Persian mythology

WHAT WAS THE ROYAL ROAD?

This was the longest highway in the Persian Empire. It ran for more than 1,550 miles (2,500 km) from Sardis, in western Turkey, to the empire's capital, Susa, near the Persian Gulf. A giant network of roads linked the empire's provinces. Messengers traveled on horseback to deliver urgent royal commands or news, while merchants used camel trains to transport goods.

KING DARIUS I
r. 522–486 BCE
Known as Darius the Great, Darius I reorganized the Persian government, won great victories in Turkey, and led an invasion of Greece. But his army was defeated by Greek soldiers at the famous battle of Marathon in 490 BCE. This started a long-lasting war with the Greeks that eventually brought down the Persian Empire.

SATRAPS

Satraps were local rulers appointed by the king to govern individual provinces. Their job was to enforce law and order, and to collect taxes and tributes. They worked with Persia's army commanders to defend the empire's frontiers from enemy attack.

COULD THE SATRAPS BE TRUSTED?

Persian kings did not trust the satraps. They employed special spies, known as "the king's ears," to make sure that the satraps were not stealing taxes and tributes. But some satraps did become powerful, and plotted against the king. Some joined with enemies of the empire, such as Alexander the Great, the Macedonian leader who conquered the Persian Empire in 331 BCE.

FIND OUT MORE ▶▶ Western Asia and the Middle East 264–265

ANCIENT GREECE

Greece was home to a rich civilization that reached its peak between 500 BCE and 300 BCE. Its people lived by farming, fishing, crafts, and trading. They built 300 **▸▸ CITY-STATES** and settled in colonies. In 146 BCE, Greece was conquered by Rome, but many aspects of Greek culture still shape our world.

WHAT DO WE KNOW ABOUT MYCENAEAN KINGS?

Mycenaean kings were powerful from 1600 BCE to 1200 BCE. They were warrior chieftains who lived in fortresslike cities and ruled small kingdoms. Their name comes from the best-known of these—Mycenae, in southern Greece. They employed skilled artists and craftworkers to make fine pottery and magnificent gold jewelry. They owned fleets of trading ships that sailed to many ports.

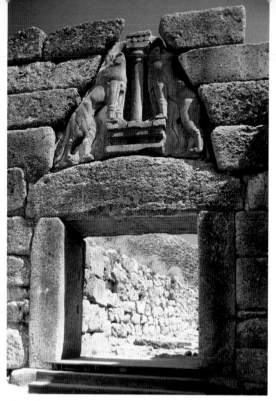

▲ LION GATE, MYCENAE
This gate, built in c. 1550–1100 BCE, formed part of a fortresslike wall that surrounded the ancient city of Mycenae. Mycenae was the center of the richest and most important kingdom of its time.

Ancient Greece

Gold decoration depicts lion hunt

▲ BRONZE DAGGER BLADE
This blade, made in around 1500 BCE, was found in a tomb in Mycenae. Mycenaean kings were often buried along with their weapons and dressed in their finest jewelry.

Hunters armed with spears and shields

Columns are 35 ft (11 m) tall and made of Parian marble

Scaffolding in place for renovation

WHO DID THE ANCIENT GREEKS WORSHIP?

The Ancient Greeks worshiped many different gods and goddesses. They believed that these gods had magic powers and that they were human in form, but more powerful and more beautiful. Each god or goddess controlled a different aspect of life. The supreme god Zeus led all other gods. His brother Poseidon ruled the sea, and another brother, Hades, ruled the underworld.

◀ SACRIFICE TO THE GODS
This marble carving is part of a frieze that decorated the Parthenon temple in Athens. It features Athenians leading a bull to be sacrificed to the goddess Athena. The Greeks regularly offered their gods and goddesses gifts of food, drinks, and flowers as sacrifices. They hoped for help in return.

Bull being led to a temple for sacrifice

WHAT WERE ANCIENT GREEK PLAYS ABOUT?

Greek tragedies and comedies told stories about gods and goddesses, or made fun of people such as politicians. Only men watched the plays. They thought women would find them too rude or upsetting. The plays of Sophocles, Aeschylus, and Euripides are still performed today.

THEATER ▶
This semicircular theater was built in Epidaurus, southern Greece, in c. 350 BCE. Greek actors (all male) wore masks to portray different characters, and recited their words to music. A chorus of junior actors sang, danced, and commented on the action.

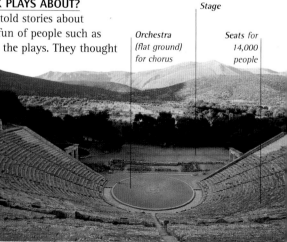

Stage

Orchestra (flat ground) for chorus

Seats for 14,000 people

▼ THE PARTHENON

Temples were homes for the gods and goddesses, and status symbols for cities. The Parthenon, Athens, was built between. 447 and 432 BCE, when Greek architecture was at its peak. It is one of the world's most famous buildings and was made from more than 24,000 tons (21,800 metric tons) of marble. This temple was dedicated to the goddess Athena. Inside stood a 40-ft- (12-m-) tall carved statue of Athena, with solid gold armor.

Frieze shows birth of Athena, and her battle with Poseidon over the Attica region

ALEXANDER THE GREAT 356-323 BCE

Alexander was ruler of Macedon, north of Greece. As a young man he conquered many lands, including some of the Greek city-states. When he died, his vast empire stretched from Egypt to Pakistan.

WHY DID THE GREEKS VALUE SPORTS?

Sports were good training for war, but city-states also organized sports competitions to form part of their religious festivals. The most famous was the Olympic Games, held every four years to honor the god Zeus. Competitors came from all over Greece. Victorious athletes won praise for themselves, and prestige for their families and towns.

GREEK DISCUS THROWER ▶
Greek artists often used top athletes as models. This statue, c. 450 BCE, depicts a discus thrower. Discus throwing was an early Olympic sport.

CITY-STATES

A city-state was made up of a town and all the land near it. Each one had its own government, laws, and way of life. City-states often fought each other, using troops of ▶ HOPLITES and warships.

HOW DID ATHENIAN DEMOCRACY WORK?

In Athens, all adult male citizens could listen to debates in the Assembly, which met on most days. Here, they could elect and expel city leaders, and vote to decide on government policies. Women, slaves, and foreigners were not able to vote. Three of the world's most famous philosophers—Socrates, Plato, and Aristotle—lived and taught in Athens.

◀ ATHENIAN COIN
This picture of an owl symbolizes Athena, the goddess of wisdom and guardian of Athens. Ancient Greek coins also showed many different local products or gods.

Olives and olive oil were valuable Greek exports

HOPLITES

Hoplites were trained foot soldiers who fought for their city-states using swords and spears. Their name came from the round hoplon (shield) that they carried for protection in battle. They also wore helmets, body armor, and plated greaves (shin guards).

HOW DID THE ANCIENT GREEKS FIGHT?

The Greeks used a battle formation called the phalanx. Soldiers stood in rows, overlapping their shields to make a solid wall of defence as they advanced. Hoplites fought agaisnt foreigners (in the Greek-Persian Wars) and other Greeks (in the Peloponnesian War between Athens and Sparta from 431 to 404 BCE). City-states also hired foreign experts, such as archers from Scythia..

HOPLITES IN CLOSE COMBAT ▶
This picture of hoplites in combat appears on a pottery vase made in Athens around 530 BCE. Only men from wealthy families could be hoplites. Poor men could not afford the weapons and armor.

Soldier dead on battlefield

FIND OUT MORE ▶▶ Ancient Rome 382–383 • Southeast Europe 256–257

CHINA'S FIRST EMPIRE

China was a collection of kingdoms ruled by rival dynasties (powerful families) until 221 BCE, when one king conquered the others and became the first emperor. The name "China" comes from his title, Qin Shi Huangdi, which means "first emperor of Qin."

▲ STANDARD WEIGHT
Weights like this were used by officials in the vast civil service set up by the Han dynasty, which ruled China after the Qin dynasty.

China's first empire

HOW DID THE FIRST EMPEROR UNITE CHINA?
Qin Shi Huangdi defeated his rivals and united China with the help of armies of soldiers like the ▶▶ TERRACOTTA WARRIORS who guard his tomb. China was also united by new laws enforcing the same system of writing, weighing, and measuring.

HOW DID CHINA FEED ITS PEOPLE?
In north China, farmers cut terraces on steep hillsides, to grow millet and wheat. In south China, they dug irrigation ditches and invented machines to carry water from rivers, to grow rice in flooded fields. By 2 CE, the Chinese population numbered 57 million.

Real gold wire joined the jade pieces together

Over 2,000 pieces of precious jade

▲ MODEL RIVER BOAT
This earthenware model of a sampan (river boat) is an artifact from an ancient Chinese tomb. For centuries, boats like this traveled along China's two great natural waterways, the Yellow and Yangtze rivers.

◀ FUNERAL SUIT
A princess of the Han dynasty was buried in this suit, which took 10 years to make. Jade was thought to have magical qualities that would preserve bodies after death.

WHAT WAS CHINA'S BEST–KEPT SECRET?
Around 2500 BCE, Chinese farmers discovered how to rear silkworms and unwind the fine thread of their cocoons. Women wove the thread into shimmering fabric and colored it with brilliant dyes. To preserve the value of silk, the Chinese government tried to keep the processes involved in making it a secret.

▲ BURIAL BANNER
This silk banner is from the tomb of Lady Dai of the Han dynasty, who died around 160 BCE. It is said to show her journey to heaven.

TERRACOTTA WARRIORS

When Qin Shi Huangdi died in 210 BCE, his body was buried with over 7,000 life-size warriors made of terracotta (baked clay). There were also foot soldiers, horses, and chariots. The underground tomb took 700,000 slave laborers many years to build.

WHY WERE THE WARRIORS MADE?
The terracotta warriors were designed to guard the emperor's body, and serve his spirit in life after death. The tomb entrance was defended by crossbows, set to fire automatically if robbers broke in. The Chinese buried all important people with food and drink, and killed servants to care for them.

Jade is carefully cut so pieces fit together

▲ TERRACOTTA GUARDS
Each clay soldier guarding Qin Shi Huangdi's tomb has an individual face, possibly copied from real members of the emperor's army. They all stand facing east in 11 rows, stretching for more than 650 ft (200 m).

FIND OUT MORE ▶▶ Imperial China 393 • Revolutionary China 429

MAURYAN INDIA

The Maurya dynasty ruled India from 268 BCE to 185 BCE. Its greatest king was Ashoka (273–232 BCE). He began his reign as a warrior, but after becoming a Buddhist, he tried to pursue peaceful policies.

Stupa

North gate carved with guardian spirits and scenes from Buddhist legends

WHAT WERE THE CITIES OF MAURYAN INDIA LIKE?
Mauryan cities were defended by steep banks of earth and timber walls. At Ashoka's capital, Pataliputra (near modern Patna), they stretched for 9 miles (14 km). Inside were temples, reservoirs, palaces, storehouses, and workers' houses.

HOW DID ASHOKA SPREAD BUDDHISM?
Ashoka set up tall stone pillars in important places, carved with Buddhist teachings and his own promises to rule well. He tried to make peace between different peoples in his empire, but after he died, the empire split into smaller states, until a new empire emerged under the Guptas.

LION PILLAR ▶
These lions stand at the top of the first carved pillar set up by Ashoka, at Sarnath, in north India. A wheel at each lion's feet symbolizes Buddhist teachings.

Mauryan India

GREAT STUPA AT SANCHI ▲
Ashoka encouraged his subjects to build stupas (domed monuments), like this one in central India, as reminders of the Buddhist faith.

FIND OUT MORE ▶▶ Buddhism 289 • Mughal India 407

GUPTA INDIA

Headdress with skull, sign of death

Trident, symbol of Shiva's destructive power

Nandi, a white bull, symbol of fertility

The Gupta dynasty was founded by the Hindu king Chandragupta I in 320 CE. From their home in northeast India, the Gupta kings won control of a large empire, which lasted for more than 200 years.

WHY IS GUPTA INDIA CALLED A GOLDEN AGE?
The art, architecture, science, music, literature, and dance of northern India flourished under the generous and tolerant Gupta kings. Gupta mathematicians developed the number system used all over the world today, and invented the concept of zero.

WHAT IS THE MAHABHARATA?
The *Mahabharata*, or "Great Epic of India," is the world's longest poem, and was developed into its present form in the Gupta age. It tells the story of five Hindu princes who lose their kingdom and struggle to win it back. Written in Sanskrit, it is one of the most important works of Hindu literature.

◀ SHIVA IN STONE
Fine sculptures, such as this statue of the Hindu god Shiva, were created during the golden age of the Guptas.

Gupta India

▲ CAVE MONKEY
Gupta artists decorated the walls of Buddhist temples in caves at Ajanta. They painted pictures of Indian animals and plants.

FIND OUT MORE ▶▶ Age of Empire 422–423 • Hinduism 286 • Mughal India 407

EARLY AMERICANS

The first Americans crossed the land bridge that linked Siberia with Alaska during the last Ice Age. Gradually, they spread through the continent. By around 8000 BCE there were people in almost every part of the Americas.

Gold headdress shaped like the Sun's rays

Large earrings of gold and turquoise

HOW DID EARLY AMERICANS LIVE?

The first Americans were hunters, gatherers, and fishermen, and this way of life continued in tropical rainforests and cold northern woods. Other peoples became farmers. In the Andes of South America they grew potatoes and herded llama. In fertile river valleys, ▶▶ MOUND BUILDERS grew corn, beans, and squash. In semideserts, the ▶▶ PUEBLO people farmed irrigated fields.

◀ CALUSA DEER HEAD
This wooden carving of a deer was made by the Calusa Indians, who lived in southwest Florida, perhaps as early as 1450 BCE.

Fine details made by pouring melted gold into a mold

HOW DID EARLY AMERICANS HONOR THEIR GODS?

The rituals of early Americans were closely connected with persuading the gods, or spirits, to continue to provide sunshine and rain. With gifts of blood and food, and sacrifices of animals and young people, they honored the gods on whom life depended.

◀ GOLDEN RITUAL KNIFE
This knife was made by the Sican people of northern Peru between 800 and 1375 CE. A powerful male figure, who was probably a Sun god, forms the handle.

◀ BURIAL OFFERING
This clay bowl from the Mimbres Valley, Arizona, was made around 1000 CE. It has been pierced to ward off spirits.

WHICH METALS DID EARLY AMERICANS TREASURE?

Around 1500 BCE, craftworkers in South America discovered how to shape nuggets of gold, silver, and copper by hammering them, stretching them into wire, or melting them and casting them in molds. They crafted jewelry, ritual objects, and images of gods.

Curved blade shaped like a Sun disk

PUEBLOS

From around 800 CE, in parts of southwest North America, rooms were stacked on top of each other to make villages called pueblos. People living in these apartments also became known as Pueblos.

◀ CLIFF DWELLING
The Mesa Verde pueblo, Colorado, was built in the alcove of a cliff. Pueblos were made of adobe (sun-dried mud bricks) and stone. They were abandoned, probably because of drought, by 1400 CE.

HOW MANY PEOPLE LIVED IN A PUEBLO?

Some pueblos, like that at Pueblo Bonito, in New Mexico, may have had as many as 650 rooms, and more than 30 ceremonial chambers (kivas). Each room could house a whole family, so the population of a pueblo could have been well over 3,000.

MOUND BUILDERS

Between 700 BCE and 550 CE, Adena and Hopewell peoples in the Ohio Valley built huge earth mounds. Some were meeting places for long-distance traders. Others were holy monuments or tombs.

WHERE WERE NORTH AMERICA'S FIRST CITIES?

Around 800 CE, mound builders by the Mississippi River also began to build cities. The largest was Cahokia, near St. Louis. It covered almost 6 sq miles (16 sq km) and had over 120 earth mounds. About 30,000 people lived there by 1200.

early Americans

Dead king and servants were buried deep inside

Royal palace and temple stood on top of the mound

CAHOKIA MOUNDS ▶
A king was buried under this mound at Cahokia, together with 250 men and women killed to serve him in the afterlife.

FIND OUT MORE ▶▶ American Indians 408 • Indian Wars 417

MAYA

The Maya lived in Central America and were powerful from around 250 to 900 CE. They built spectacular cities such as Palenque, Tikal, and Yaxchilan and developed a system of writing that used picture symbols called ▸▸ GLYPHS .

WHO RULED MAYAN KINGDOMS?
The Maya were divided into city states, constantly at war with one another, each of which had a ruler, acted as war-leader, law-maker, and chief priest. After 900 CE the civilization declined mainly because their farming methods led to exhausted fields and failing crops.

RAIN GOD ▸
This is a statue of Chac, the Mayan god of rain, who made all living things grow. According to myth, Chac broke open a giant rock to uncover the first corn plant.

Steep steps leading to the shrine on top of the pyramid

WHY DID THE MAYA BUILD PYRAMIDS?
Pyramids were the largest buildings in Mayan cities and were built as temples and royal tombs. Shrines where sacrifices were made to the gods were at the top, while burial chambers were hidden deep inside. The pyramids were built of stone, and covered with red-painted plaster, but this plaster has not survived.

Stairway (one on each of four sides)

Maya

◂ PYRAMID OF KUKULCAN
This temple was built in the city of Chichen Itza between 900 and 1200. It has a total of 365 steps, representing the solar year. The Maya were skilled astronomers and mathematicians.

In his left hand Chac carries a ceremonial bowl; in his right he has a ball of smoking incense

MAYAN GLYPHS

Mayan glyphs were painted on walls and pots, and carved into pieces of jade and monuments of stone. They were also written into books called codices, which were made out of long strips of bark paper that folded up like screens. This complex writing system was controlled by scribes of very high rank.

WHEN WAS THE RIDDLE OF THE GLYPHS SOLVED?
The study of Mayan hieroglyphs began 200 years ago. By the 1950s, scholars had worked out the glyphs for the names of rulers and animals. Then, in 1960, it became clear that most Mayan inscriptions are historical. They record important events, such as the births, marriages and deaths, and the victories in battle, of the godlike Mayan kings.

Glyphs stood for names, objects, or ideas

CALENDAR OF PREDICTIONS ▸
Four Mayan codices have survived. This codex was compiled between 1300 and 1400. It contains information that enabled priests to predict lucky and unlucky dates.

FIND OUT MORE ▸▸ Aztecs 403 • Conquistadors 405 • Incas 402

ANCIENT ROME

Rome began, around 800 BCE, as a settlement of farmers and shepherds in central Italy. Over the course of the next thousand years, it developed into a powerful city-state, and became the capital of an empire that stretched from Britain in the north to Arabia in the southeast.

HOW DID ROME EXPAND?
Gradually, the Roman Republic conquered its neighbors, until, by 260 BCE, it controlled all of Italy. Next, the Romans defeated the Carthaginians, which by 146 BCE gave Rome control of the Mediterranean. At the heart of the government of this expanding Roman Republic were the politicians called ▶▶ SENATORS.

MORTAL COMBAT ▶
In this Roman mosaic, made around 300 CE, a gladiator tackles a leopard. Gladiators were mostly slaves or criminals who had been trained in special schools.

WHAT WAS THE RELIGION OF ANCIENT ROME?
Jupiter, Minerva, Vesta, and Mars were among the chief gods and goddesses of Ancient Rome. On special occasions, animals were sacrificed to them in temples. Before going into battle, for example, a public sacrifice would be made to Mars, the god of war. Throughout the empire a wide range of non-Roman religions were tolerated, so long as they did not disrespect official Roman gods and the ▶▶ EMPERORS.

COLOSSEUM RUINS ▼
Opened by Emperor Titus in 80 CE, the Colosseum was the largest amphitheater in Rome. For the blood-thirsty "games" staged here, gladiators and animals were imported from every corner of the empire.

HOW WERE ROMAN SOLDIERS RECRUITED?
In the early days of Rome, every citizen had to be prepared to fight, but soldiers of the Roman imperial army were paid, highly trained professionals who signed on for 20-25 years of service. The ordinary foot soldier was equipped with a short sword, two javelins, and a heavy shield of leather and wood. When he was not at war, he was building forts and roads.

▲ ROMAN WOMEN
The grand ladies depicted in this Pompeii wall painting are having their hair dressed by skilled slaves. First and foremost, Roman women were expected to be mothers, but rich widows had some freedom.

SENATORS

The Roman Republic was ruled by the Senate, the council of noblemen that controlled all the top jobs in the government and army. After 27 BCE, when the Roman Republic was replaced by the Roman Empire, the Senate continued to play an important part in politics.

Ancient Rome

WHY WAS JULIUS CAESAR MURDERED?
In 44 BCE, five years after he had become the sole ruler of Rome, Julius Caesar was murdered in the Senate building. His assassins were a group of senators who thought he had become too powerful. They also resented the fact that Julius Caesar had rewarded hundreds of his supporters by making them senators. As a result, the Senate, which for most of its history had between 300 and 600 members, was packed with 900 senators.

◀ BRONZE COIN FEATURING JULIUS CAESAR
The profile on this coin is evidence of Julius Caesar's haughty style. He was much too kinglike for the proud Roman senators.

FIND OUT MORE ▶▶ Age of Migrations 384 • Byzantine Empire 385

EMPERORS

After Julius Caesar's death, Rome was divided by civil wars. By 27 BCE, his adopted son Octavian was master of the Roman world. Under the title Augustus, which means "revered" in Latin, he became the first Roman emperor. His reign brought peace and prosperity to a war-weary world.

WHY DID ROMANS GET BREAD AND CIRCUSES?

Rome was the largest city in the world. By 300 CE, it had a million inhabitants, many of whom were hungry and unemployed. To stop them from rioting, they were given "bread and circuses." The "bread" was the regular ration of grain issued to Roman citizens, and the "circuses" were the free entertainments and chariot races provided by politicians and emperors.

Canvas stretched over the top provided shade

STATUE OF FIRST EMPEROR ▲
Augustus reigned for nearly 50 years. He reorganized coins, laws, and taxation, and transformed the Roman army into a peace-keeping force, designed to protect the empire's expanding frontiers.

Stone and concrete made strong walls

Statues would have stood in arches

CELTS

The tribespeople who lived in western Europe before the Roman conquest were called Celts. Each tribe was made up of three main classes—druids, warriors, and farmers—and the largest settlements were hilltop forts.

GOLD TORC ▶
The Celts were skilled metalworkers. Weapons and tools were made of iron, but this torc (neck ring), found in Britain, was made from twisted strands of gold wire.

WHAT WERE CELTIC WARRIORS FAMOUS FOR?

Celtic warriors were famous for their love of feasting, fighting, and jewelry. They daubed their faces with a blue war paint made from woad (plant that produces a blue dye) and yelled at the tops of their voices as they rode into battle. But the terrible look and sound of a Celtic army was no match for the discipline of highly trained Roman legions.

Celts

WHO WERE THE DRUIDS?

After studying everything from herbalism to astronomy for up to 20 years, druids served Celtic society as priests and judges. At sacred pools, or groves of oak trees, they led religious rites that sometimes involved human sacrifice. Unlike most Celts, many druids could read and write.

▲ DUN AENGUS CELTIC FORT, IRELAND
Celtic tribes fought each other, and also battled against invaders. As refuges for themselves and their cattle, they built forts on easily defended sites such as hilltops and cliffs by the sea.

FIND OUT MORE ▶▶ First Metalworkers 367 • Holy Roman Empire 385

AGE OF MIGRATIONS

In 395 CE, the division of the Roman Empire became permanent, and the eastern and western parts, each had their own emperor. Despite this reorganization, the western empire could no longer hold out against waves of invading barbarian tribes from northeastern Europe. In 410, Rome itself was attacked.

Hun warriors practically lived in the saddle

▲ **ATTILA THE HUN**
This bronze plaque of a nomad warrior on horseback was found in Switzerland. It may represent Attila, the brilliant but ruthless leader of the Hun army.

migrations

WHO WERE THE BARBARIANS?
For the Romans, the Germanic tribes such as the Goths, moving across the empire were destructive, disorderly "barbarians." Over time, these migrant peoples did settle down, eventually giving their names to their new homelands such as the Franks in France and the ▶▶ ANGLES AND SAXONS in England.

WHO WERE THE HUNS?
The Huns were a nomadic people from today's central Asia. Mounted on swift ponies, and armed with bows and arrows, Hun armies rode deep into the Roman Empire in search of plunder. They were not interested in conquering land.

BARBARIAN ATTACKS	
235 CE	Germanic tribes start to invade
410	Goths capture Rome
435	Vandals take Roman North Africa
451	Hun invasions
455	Vandals sack Rome
476	Last western Roman emperor

ANGLES AND SAXONS

Angles and Saxons, who were later known as Anglo-Saxons, lived along the North Sea coast. They began to raid Britain while it was under Roman rule. After 410, when the Roman army left, they arrived in larger numbers to settle, and gradually took over much of eastern Britain.

WHO WAS BURIED IN SHIPS?
The Angles and Saxons were pagan, seafaring people, and ships played an important part in their culture. They believed that boats could ferry a dead person's spirit to the next world. People who had been wealthy when they were alive were buried in ships, together with the comforts and treasures they were expected to enjoy in the next world. Poorer Anglo-Saxons were sometimes buried with a few ship's planks.

WHY DID ANGLES AND SAXONS MOVE TO BRITAIN?
Around 200, the climate became warmer and sea levels rose, which made life more difficult for the Angles and Saxons living on the North Sea coast. At the same time, they were being squeezed by other westward-moving Germanic peoples. Some of the first Anglo-Saxons in Britain may have been soldiers, hired to protect villages against other raiders.

Strong iron base, decorated with gold, silver, and garnets

Bird of prey—its outstretched wings protect the wearer's brow

Side-pieces protect ears

◄ **KING'S HELMET**
This helmet was found in a ship grave at Sutton Hoo, in eastern England. It probably belonged to Raedwald, a powerful Anglo-Saxon king who died around 625. His grave treasures also included a sword, shield, gold coins, and silverware.

FIND OUT MORE ▶▶ Ancient Rome 382 • Normans 389

BYZANTINE EMPIRE

In 324 CE the emperor Constantine reunited the Roman Empire. By then Rome was too difficult to defend against barbarian attacks, so he moved his capital east to Byzantium, renaming it ▶▶ **CONSTANTINOPLE**.

▲ POPE AND PATRIARCH
In 1054, the Church in the west, led by the Pope, separated from the Church in the east, led by the Patriarch of Constantinople. The eastern, Orthodox Church used Greek rather than Latin.

WHO RULED THE BYZANTINE EMPIRE?
From Constantinople (now Istanbul), Constantine ruled over the entire Roman world, but eventually the empire split again. In 476, the western Roman empire was swept away. However, the eastern empire, which is called the Byzantine Empire, endured until 1453, when it was conquered by the Ottoman Empire.

CONSTANTINOPLE

In 330, Constantinople was proclaimed capital of the Roman Empire. The new city's splendid public buildings, which included a forum, were adorned with treasures from all over the empire.

WHY WAS CONSTANTINOPLE SO PROSPEROUS?
Constantinople was a meeting point for long-distance trade routes linking Europe, Asia, and the Middle East. Merchants brought silks from China, pearls and perfumes from Arabia, spices from southeast Asia, and fine wool and furs from Europe to sell in its markets.

Byzantine Empire

BYZANTINE ART ▲
This mosaic shows Christ washing the feet of his disciples. It is in the Hosios Loukas Monastery in Boeotia, Greece, which was built in the early 11th century. Christianity was central to Byzantine life, and the chief purpose of art and architecture was to glorify God.

FIND OUT MORE ▶▶ Christianity 288 • Ottoman Empire 397

HOLY ROMAN EMPIRE

On Christmas Day, 800, Charlemagne, the King of the Franks, was crowned Holy Roman Emperor by the Pope. Under Charlemagne, much of western Europe was ruled as one vast country, but within 40 years of his death, in 814, the Holy Roman Empire had fragmented.

WHY WAS THE EMPIRE FOUNDED?
Charlemagne was a brilliant leader, and his kingdom stretched from the North Sea to Italy. As Holy Roman Emperor, he was laying claim to some of the prestige of a Roman emperor, but with a new responsibility for the safety and prosperity of the Church and the Pope.

Holy Roman Empire

HOW DID CHARLEMAGNE WORK WITH SCHOLARS?
Charlemagne was a great patron of learning, inviting the most famous scholars of the day to his main court at Aachen. His advisers and friends included Peter of Pisa, Agobard of Lyons, and Alcuin of York. Under Charlemagne, rare manuscripts were collected, the text of the Bible was revised, and grammars, history books, and ballads were published.

WHAT HAPPENED TO THE TITLE?
By 843 Charlemagne's empire had split into three kingdoms, each of which was ruled by a member of his family. Following Charlemagne, there was no Holy Roman Emperor until Otto I was crowned in 962. After 1438, all but one of the holders of the prestigious title were Habsburg monarchs. In 1806 Napoleon abolished the title.

STAINED-GLASS WINDOW ▲
At Chartres Cathedral, France, Charlemagne is shown with Constantine (right).

ISLAMIC CIVILIZATION

In 610 CE, an Arab merchant called Muhammad founded a new religion called Islam. His teachings inspired the Arab peoples, and by 750 Muslims (followers of Islam) had conquered an area stretching from Afghanistan to ▶ AL ANDALUS in southern Spain. Trade, science, and culture thrived in this Islamic empire.

Islamic civilization

WHAT WAS LIFE LIKE IN MUSLIM LANDS?

Newly conquered lands were united by Islam, and by common tax systems, coinage, and laws. Jews and Christians sometimes paid higher taxes, but they were free to run their own religious affairs so long as they did not insult the Prophet Muhammad.

HOW DID ISLAM SPREAD SO QUICKLY?

Islam brought a new sense of unity and purpose to the traders and tribespeople of the Arabian Peninsula. Led by the ▶ CALIPH, Arab armies spread Islam in the Middle East and beyond. It helped that their main enemies, the Sassanids in Iran and the Byzantines in eastern Europe, were weakened by fighting each other. Islam was also spread by Muslim traders.

◀ QUTB-MINAR TOWER
This minaret, a slender tower used to call Muslims to prayer, was built in 1199 by a new ruling dynasty as a symbol of their victory. It is part of the Quwwat al-Islam (Might of Islam) Mosque, in Delhi, India.

Tower stands 238 ft (73 m) high

Carved inscriptions praise God and state greatness of Islam

Maps show the position of stars at night

Stars forming the constellations are shown in red

▲ THE BOOK OF THE FIXED STARS
This guide to the constellations was compiled by a famous Arab astronomer, Abd al-Rahman ibn Umar al-Sufi, in the 10th century. Arabic names for stars are still used today.

CALIPHS

After the death of Muhammad in 632, Muslims were ruled by caliphs. As Islam spread, the caliphs had great political as well as spiritual authority. After the reign of the fourth caliph, from 656 to 661, two rival traditions of Islam emerged: the Sunni and the Shi'a. This division meant it was no longer possible for the whole Islamic world to be ruled by a single caliph.

WHO WERE THE UMAYYADS AND THE ABBASIDS?

The Umayyads and Abbasids were dynasties of caliphs. From 661, Muslims were ruled by the Umayyads, based in Damascus (in Syria). In 750, a new dynasty, the Abbasid, seized power, although a branch of the Umayyad continued to rule Muslim Spain. The Abbasid caliphs were based at Baghdad, which became the prosperous center of a huge trading empire and the artistic capital of the Muslim world.

HARUN AND THE BARBER ▶
Harun-al-Rashid was the most famous Abbasid caliph. His court at Baghdad inspired many classic tales. This miniature painting illustrates a story in which Harun notices that his barber never moves from one spot. Harun has the floor removed and finds treasure beneath it.

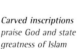

Delicate plaster, carved in Islamic geometric patterns

Roof supported by 124 columns of white marble

Cooling fountain at center of courtyard

◀ THE COURT OF THE LIONS
The Court of the Lions, part of the Alhambra palace, which was built in 1238–1354 for the ruling Nasrid family of Granada, the last Moorish kingdom in Spain. The central water basin is surrounded by 12 stone lions, each with a water spout. Soothing, cooling water was an essential ingredient of Islamic architecture.

WHERE DID MUSLIMS TRAVEL TO?
Muslim pilgrims, traders, soldiers, scholars, and government officials made long journeys across the Islamic empire and beyond. One of the most famous explorers, Ibn Battuta, set out on a pilgrimage to Mecca in 1325. He spent the next 25 years traveling, crossing the Sahara and even reaching China before returning to Morocco to write his story.

▲ RIDING THE MONSOON
For voyages of exploration and trade, Arab sailors used boats called dhows, which can be handled by a small crew. The voyages of real sailors inspired the imaginary adventures of Sinbad the Sailor.

WHY WERE TEXTILES SO IMPORTANT?
Many of the first Muslims were nomads, who needed to be able to pack up and move all their belongings quickly. Traditionally, woven cloth was used for tents, bags, clothes, cushions, bedding, and carpets. The art and craft of making textiles continued to be important in the Muslim world, which gave us the words for damask (from Damascus), muslin (from Mosul), and cashmere (from Kashmir).

AL ANDALUS

Muslim armies conquered southern Spain in 711. They called it Al Andalus, and it became the richest country in Europe. The Muslims, or Moors as they are sometimes called, brought new crops, such as oranges, almonds, and cotton, and new technology, such as water wheels. In 1492, Granada, which was the last surviving Islamic kingdom in Spain, fell to Christian rulers.

HOW DID AL ANDALUS LINK EAST AND WEST?
During the 10th century reign of Abd al-Rahman, Cordoba was the capital of Al Andalus. With its lavishly endowed libraries, it was a magnet for scholars and acted as the door through which the science of the East reached Christian scholars in western Europe. After 1031, when the ruling dynasty changed, Cordoba's golden age ended. In 1236 it was reconquered by Christian Spanish forces.

CORDOBA'S GREAT MOSQUE ▶
A mihrab is a niche that faces Mecca, the holiest city of Islam. This is the mihrab of the Great Mosque (Mezquita) of Cordoba, one of Islam's greatest architectural legacies to Europe. It was begun by the city's rulers in 785 and enlarged over the following two centuries.

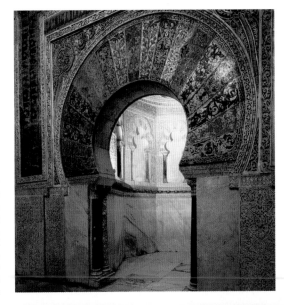

FIND OUT MORE ▶▶ Crusades 389 • Islam 290 • Medieval Africa 394–395 • Ottoman Empire 397

VIKINGS

Late in the 8th century, Viking raiders from Norway, Denmark, and Sweden began to sweep across Europe. In their versatile ▶▶LONGSHIPS, the Vikings sailed vast distances. Their golden age of trade, exploration, and colonization lasted until 1100 CE.

Tall prow stopped ship from diving into waves in rough seas

WHERE DID THE VIKINGS TRAVEL?

The Vikings raided and settled along the coasts of Britain, Ireland, and continental Europe. They crossed the Atlantic to reach Iceland, Greenland, and Newfoundland. Viking merchants traveled through Russia to Constantinople, exchanging the amber, furs, and whale oil of the north for wine, silks, spices, and silver coins from the Middle East.

HOW DID THE VIKINGS GET THEIR FIERCE REPUTATION?

The Vikings were not Christian, and they saw isolated monasteries and churches as easy targets for hit-and-run raids. But the first people to write about the Vikings were monks who had suffered in these raids. As a result, Viking atrocities were better recorded than Viking achievements.

HOW DID THE VIKINGS WORSHIP THEIR GODS?

The Vikings worshiped their gods in the open air, choosing natural landmarks such as big rocks, unusual trees, and waterfalls. Their most important gods were Odin, the god of knowledge, Thor, the god of metalwork and thunder, and Frey, the goddess of fertility. After around 1000, Viking peoples became Christian.

ROUND TOWER AT ARDMORE ▲
This tower stands in a cemetery in Ardmore, County Waterford, Ireland. It was built around 1100 by monks, as a refuge from Viking raiders. The doorway is 15 ft (4.5 m) above the ground, and was reached by a ladder that could be pulled inside.

▲ CARVED SILVER CHARM
This silver head of a bearded man, wearing a Viking helmet, was made to hang from a chain, probably as a good luck charm. The Vikings prized silver. We do not know whose face it is supposed to represent.

▼ VIKING WEAPON
This sword from Denmark has a double-edged iron blade. Viking warriors took great pride in their swords, which were handed down through families, and sometimes placed in graves.

Vikings

LONGSHIPS

Viking ships were the best in Europe. Besides the longships used for raiding and war, they had special fishing boats. For long-distance voyages, they built deeper, broader ships called knorrs.

HOW WERE VIKING SHIPS BUILT?

Viking ships were made of planks of oak or pine wood, nailed to a heavy central keel (supporting timber). This made them strong but flexible. The mast was made from a tall tree trunk and supported a huge square sail. There were oars for each crewman, to row the ship when there was no wind.

◀ REPLICA OF A VIKING LONGSHIP
The shallow hull of a longship made it less likely to capsize. It could be sailed in shallow water close to land, to make a surprise attack. Its planks overlapped for extra strength. Tarred wool was crammed between the planks to keep water out.

CARVED PICTURE STONE ▶
Stones like this, showing the brave deeds and epic voyages of Viking heroes, were raised by proud relatives.

FIND OUT MORE ▶▶ Byzantine Empire 385 • Exploration 400–401

NORMANS

The Normans were descended from Viking warriors who settled in Normandy, northwest France, in 911 CE. They conquered large areas of Europe, from England to southern Italy. Norman kings were strong rulers.

WHAT HAPPENED IN 1066?
The Normans invaded England in 1066. They were led by the Duke of Normandy, William the Conqueror, who became king of England. He removed English nobles, and gave their land to Normans. Norman nobles ran the government, and Norman priests led the Church. Norman rulers spoke French, and built castles. They imposed heavy taxes and harsh laws.

CATHEDRAL AT MONREALE ▶
This cathedral in Sicily was built in 1174–1189, in a mixture of Byzantine, Arabic, North African, and Norman styles. The Normans built castles and cathedrals in all the lands they conquered.

Normans

◀ **BATTLE OF HASTINGS, 1066**
The Bayeux tapestry is a record of William's conquest from a Norman point of view. In this scene, English foot soldiers are being trampled by Norman horses at the Battle of Hastings.

WHY WAS NORMAN SICILY SO REMARKABLE?
In 1060–1091, Sicily was conquered by Normans. The island's new rulers were tolerant of its Muslim inhabitants, and after the conquest it flourished as a multicultural center of art and learning. Norman Sicilian kings encouraged the work of Arab geographers and scientists, and sponsored the translation of Greek classic texts into Latin.

FIND OUT MORE ▶▶ Islamic Civilization 386–387 • Medieval Europe 390–391 • Vikings 388

CRUSADES

In 1095, Pope Urban II called for a war against the Muslim rulers of Jerusalem. This was the First Crusade. Over the next two centuries, Christian armies from Europe fought more crusades, but none was successful.

Crusades

WHY WAS THE FIRST CRUSADE CALLED?
For centuries, Christian pilgrims had been visiting the Holy Land, where Jesus had lived and which had been ruled by Muslims since 637. The First Crusade happened because, by the 11th century, the region's rulers were less sympathetic to Christian pilgrims.

WHAT DID THE CRUSADERS BRING BACK TO EUROPE?
Crusaders returned with apricots, lemons, rice, dyes, spices, perfume, soap, and glass mirrors. They also brought back a musical instrument, the ancestor of the modern guitar.

▲ **CRUSADERS ATTACK CONSTANTINOPLE**
In 1204, crusaders from western Europe sailed to Constantinople. Having captured and looted the city, they then ruled it for nearly 60 years. This Fourth Crusade never reached the Holy Land.

SOLDIER IN PRAYER ▶
This Crusader, featured on an English manuscript of around 1200, is kneeling in prayer before a battle.

FIND OUT MORE ▶▶ Islamic Civilization 386–387 • Medieval Europe 390–391

MEDIEVAL EUROPE

Between 1000 and 1500 CE, a lively society developed in Europe. Although most people still worked on the land, this was also the age of ▸▸CASTLES, cathedrals, and growing towns. Gradually, the traders and craftsmen of the towns began to have more influence on government.

Medieval queens were the mothers, sisters, and daughters of kings

Bishops were the local lords of the Church

medieval Europe

▲ MEDIEVAL CHESS PIECES
These chess pieces, made in Scandinavia around 1200, show the most important people in a medieval kingdom (from left to right): a queen, king, bishop (Church leader), and knight (who was always a nobleman).

CASTLES

A castle is a huge, fortified building, or set of buildings. The first castles, built around 900, were made up of a wooden fortress on top of an earth mound. Later, castles built of stone had towers, battlements, moats, and strong defensive walls. They also became prestigious homes.

WERE CASTLES ONLY USED IN WARTIME?
The first castles were built to shelter nobles, ▸▸KNIGHTS, and soldiers in a war. After around 1200, in times of peace, each castle had its own nobleman and his family living in it. Comfortable private rooms were added for important guests.

HOW DID GUNPOWDER AFFECT CASTLES?
From around 1300, gunpowder for firing cannons began to affect warfare in Europe. Cannon balls could smash through stone walls, making castles less useful as safe strongholds. Castles continued to be built, but for show. They were intended as impressive residences rather than indestructible fortresses.

▲ ROCHESTER CASTLE, ENGLAND
The main building of a castle was its keep (central tower). This one was built around 1130. Its stone walls would not burn, and were very hard to knock down.

WHAT WAS FEUDALISM?
Feudalism was the system of ownership of land in Medieval Europe from the 9th century. In theory the king was the owner of all land but he granted most of it to his nobles, who provided armed knights. The nobles too granted some land to lesser nobles and knights who also swore an oath of loyalty to their feudal overlord.

WHAT DID MEDIEVAL PEOPLE BELIEVE?
Medieval Europeans believed that God had made the world, and ruled it through his Church and the king. Few people, apart from priests and monks, could read and write. Ordinary people learned the stories of the Bible and the saints from preachers, and from the pictures painted in their churches.

TILLING AND SOWING ▶
This medieval painting shows an October scene outside Paris. Peasants are tilling the ground and sowing seed against the background of the French king's castle. The scarecrow is dressed as an archer.

HOW DID MEDIEVAL TOWNS DEVELOP?

Many towns grew up around markets, where farm produce was exchanged for the goods and services of specialized craftsmen, such as shoemakers and weavers. Through their guilds, traders and craftsmen regulated prices and organized the training of their apprentices.

WHAT WAS LIFE LIKE FOR PEASANT FAMILIES?

Most peasants worked on their local lord's fields in return for their own plots of land. Some, called serfs, were not free, and could not travel, or marry, without their lord's permission. Skilled men could be thatchers or carpenters. Women might weave cloth or brew ale.

Towers originally for defense, now for decoration

Plague victim, wrapped in shroud. Once infected, there was little hope of survival

▲ **THE BLACK DEATH**
This stained-glass window shows the impact of the Black Death, the plague that killed more than a quarter of Europe's population in 1347-1349. It was spread by fleabites and contact with infected people.

KNIGHTS

Knights were warriors on horseback. They came from noble families and were trained from boyhood to handle weapons, wear armor, and ride heavy war horses. Some knights owned castles and land, and kept local order. Others served in the private armies of great lords. Each knight had his own coat of arms, helping him to tell friend from foe in battle.

Metal helmet protects head

Metal breastplate and chain-mail tunic

Pointed sword digs between armor

HOW DID KNIGHTS FIGHT?

Knights charged into battle on horseback, spearing enemy soldiers with their long lances, or slashing at them with heavy swords, maces, and battle-axes. On foot, they fought with daggers and short swords.

WHAT WAS THE CODE OF CHIVALRY?

Knights were bound by a solemn promise to be loyal to their king. They were also supposed to respect women, protect the weak, and defend the Church. This code became known as chivalry.

Metal greaves (shin pieces)

Even the feet are protected by armor

▲ **ITALIAN KNIGHT**
This suit of armor, worn around 1380, gave good protection while the knight was on horseback, but was hot and heavy when fighting on foot.

Knight kneels in front of a noble lady

A TOURNAMENT SHIELD ▶
This ornamental shield was made for a tournament parade. Tournament contests gave knights a chance to practice their skills. Their lives and loves were celebrated in the songs and poems of traveling minstrels called troubadours.

FIND OUT MORE ▶▶ Crusades 389 • Normans 389 • Reformation 399 • Renaissance 398

MONGOLS

The Mongols were nomadic tribes from the steppes, or grasslands, of central Asia. In 1206 CE they declared Genghis Khan their supreme ruler. He led their conquest of an empire that, by 1279, included all of China and nearly all of Russia, as well as central Asia, Iran, and Iraq.

GENGHIS KHAN
r. 1206–1227

Genghis Khan began his career as Temujin, the brilliant, ambitious chieftain of one Mongol tribe. He was chosen as supreme ruler, and given the title Genghis Khan, by a gathering of all the Mongol tribes. After his death, in 1227, his empire was divided among his sons.

WHAT WAS SPECIAL ABOUT MONGOL ARMIES?
Mongol military might was based on the speed and ferocity of mounted archers. From galloping horses, Mongol archers let loose arrows that could pierce armor. The riders and the horses were tough, capable of covering more than 100 miles (160 km) a day.

WHO WANTED TO RULE THE WORLD?
Genghis Khan wanted to live up to his title, which means "universal ruler." He aimed to conquer the world and was proud of the fact that, eventually, it took almost a year to ride from one end of his realm to the other.

◄ **TIMUR IN INDIA**
In 1398, another Mongol warlord called Timur, or Tamerlane, invaded India and sacked Delhi.

Mongols

SAMURAI

Samurai were warriors from Japanese noble families, who served in private armies recruited by daimyo (local lords). Starting in 1180 with the Gempei Wars, they fought in civil wars that raged throughout Japan. In 1603, the Tokugawa ▶▶ SHOGUNS restored peace. Samurai then became officials and administrators.

WHAT WAS THE WAY OF THE WARRIOR?
Samurai swore a solemn oath of loyalty to their comrades and their lord. They aimed to follow a code, called the bushido (the way of the warrior). This called for self-discipline, skill, bravery, honor, obedience, and self-sacrifice. Many samurai also followed the teachings of Zen Buddhism.

samurai

NOBLE WARRIOR ▶
Samurai were expert horsemen and skilled with the sword, bow, and spear. They were paid not in money but in rice.

SHOGUNS

From 1192 to 1867, Japan was ruled by a series of powerful army commanders with the title of shogun. Japan's emperors had great prestige but little real power.

WHO WAS THE FIRST SHOGUN?
In 1192, the warlord Yoritomo, who was the head of the mighty Minamoto clan, defeated rival nobles to become the most powerful man in Japan. The emperor gave him the title of shogun, which means "great general." Yoritomo set up a new, military government, far away from the imperial court.

▲ **PORTRAIT OF YORITOMO**
Minamoto Yoritomo claimed to be descended from the Japanese imperial family. When he died, in 1199, he passed the title of shogun on to his sons, who ruled until 1219.

FIND OUT MORE ▶▶ Buddhism 289

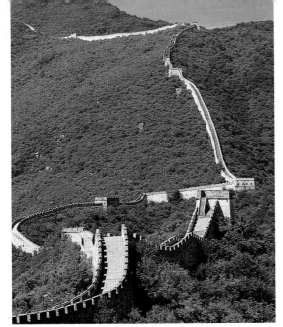

▲ GREAT WALL OF CHINA
The Great Wall snakes across the mountains north of Beijing. Defensive walls had been built since ancient times, but most of the Great Wall as it still stands was built under the Ming emperors.

IMPERIAL CHINA

For more than 2,000 years, from 221 BCE until 1912 CE, China was ruled by emperors. In that time, the capital city and the imperial dynasty (ruling family) changed. There were periods of unrest and of invasion by fierce tribes, including the Mongols, but the same system of government continued. Imperial China was a remarkably stable civilization, which led the world in art and technology, with inventions including paper, ►►PORCELAIN, and gunpowder.

CHINA'S RULERS	
221 BCE	Qin dynasty
206 BCE	Han dynasty
221 CE	Time of disunity
581	Sui dynasty
618	Tang dynasty
907	China divided into five dynasties
960	Song dynasty
1279	Yuan dynasty (Mongol)
1368	Ming dynasty (last Chinese dynasty)
1644 1912	Qing dynasty (Manchu dynasty from Manchuria)

WHY WERE EXAMS IMPORTANT IN CHINA?

The first Han emperor set up a civil service to run China. Before getting a job in the civil service, officials had to pass a series of difficult exams. Those who passed the top exams could expect jobs as government ministers, and marriage to princesses.

HOW DID BEIJING BECOME CHINA'S CAPITAL?

After invading China in 1279 CE, the Mongol (Yuan) emperors established their capital at Beijing, which was just inside the Great Wall, in what was then the far north of China. In 1368, a new dynasty, the Ming, came to power. They kept Beijing as the capital, rebuilding and expanding the city.

WHO LIVED IN THE FORBIDDEN CITY?

The imperial palace at Beijing is called the Forbidden City. Enclosed by a moat and high brick walls, this complex of palaces, halls, gardens, offices, and storehouses was built under the Ming dynasty. The imperial family lived there, along with nobles, servants, and officials.

Palaces and halls were surrounded by gardens

A red-robed senior official of the imperial household

An official greets others outside the gates

Imperial China

THE FORBIDDEN CITY ▲
A Ming painting on silk of the Forbidden City. The compound was closed (forbidden) to ordinary people, and the emperors hardly ever left it.

PORCELAIN

Porcelain is a translucent (semitransparent) ceramic material, made of fine white clay mixed with crushed stone. It can be shaped on a potter's wheel, or molded by hand. When fired (baked) at extremely high temperatures, it becomes waterproof, and so hard that steel cannot scratch it.

WHY WAS PORCELAIN SO PRECIOUS?

Porcelain was first made by Chinese potters during the Tang dynasty. It was a luxury product, for the use of nobles and emperors, and for centuries no one but the Chinese knew how to make it. Seventeenth-century Dutch sailors brought the first porcelain "china" to Europe, where it was a prized commodity.

Dragon design is painted with brush over smooth surface

◄ PORCELAIN BOWL
This delicate bowl was made during the Ming dynasty. Designs like this, in blue and white, became very popular. Millions of porcelain items were specially made to be sold overseas.

FIND OUT MORE ►► China's First Empire 378 • Revolutionary China 429

MEDIEVAL AFRICA

From around 750 to 1500 CE, lands to the south of Africa's Sahara Desert were home to many thriving civilizations. Muslim kings ruled in cities like ▶ TIMBUKTU, and chiefs called ▶ OBAS were powerful in rainforest kingdoms. ▶ SWAHILI peoples became rich through trade.

HOW DID TRADERS CROSS THE SAHARA DESERT?
Traders from North Africa crossed the Sahara together in a group called a caravan. They led as many as 10,000 camels, heavily laden with goods, in a long line known as a camel train. At the southern edge of the Sahara, the goods were transferred to donkeys or human porters, to be carried farther south.

WHICH AFRICAN GOODS WERE HIGHLY PRIZED?
Gold, ivory, ebony, and slaves from West African kingdoms such as Ghana, Mali, and Songhai were sold in North Africa and the Middle East. They were traded for salt and copper, mined in the Sahara. Later, European traders came for gold, ebony, and slaves.

◀ ELMINA CASTLE AND FORT, GHANA
This castle and fort were built by the Portuguese in 1482. Portuguese, and later Dutch and English, traders used it as a base for dealing in slaves, gold, and imported European goods. The Europeans set up many trading posts in West Africa.

Crown of Portuguese heads

medieval Africa

TIMBUKTU

Timbuktu (in central Mali) was one of the most important cities on the edge of the Sahara. After Muslim scholars brought the religion of Islam to the region, around 900, it became a great center of Muslim learning, with schools, a university, and a special market where valuable, handwritten books were sold.

Wooden scaffolding used by builders to repair walls

HOW DID TIMBUKTU BECOME WEALTHY?
Like a number of other cities on the edge of the Sahara, such as Gao and Jenne, Timbuktu was also on the banks of the Niger River. These cities were inland ports. Merchants from the south sent boatloads of gold, ivory, cotton, dried fish, and kola nuts upriver to them, to be sold to people living there, or to be carried to lands farther north. Timbuktu became a terminus (end point) for one of the main trading routes crossing the Sahara.

WHY DID MUSLIM PILGRIMS GO TO TIMBUKTU?
Many Muslim pilgrims traveled to Timbuktu to honor the city's 333 resident saints. These were celebrated Muslim scholars and teachers who taught their faith to people in the surrounding lands. Many beautiful mosques were built in Timbuktu.

◀ DJINGUEREBER MOSQUE
This mosque, built in 1327, is the oldest building in Timbuktu. It is made of mud bricks, a wooden frame, and mud-and-straw plaster.

SWAHILI

Swahili became the main language used by different peoples on the coast and islands of East Africa. Many of its words were taken from Arabic—the language of traders who sailed across the Indian Ocean, linking India and Arabia with East African ports such as Mogadishu, Gedi, and Kilwa.

WHO DID THE SWAHILI PEOPLES TRADE WITH?

East Africans produced valuable goods, such as leather, frankincense, leopard skins, ivory, iron, copper, and gold. They sold these to Indian Ocean traders. From around 1071, they sent ambassadors to trade with China, and, from 1418, welcomed Chinese merchant ships to East Africa's ports.

ZANZIBAR ▼
The island of Zanzibar, off the coast of East Africa, is where Swahili was first spoken. It became a major trading center for slaves, ivory, and cloves.

Elaborate metalwork collar

◄ OBA MASK
This mask of an oba is from around 1500. Cast in brass, it is decorated with a crown of small heads, portraying Portuguese people who first arrived in Yoruba lands around 1430. These look weak and unimportant, compared with the impressive size and proud expression of the oba.

OBAS

From around 1250 to 1800, a number of different kingdoms made up what is now southwest Nigeria, in West Africa. Each of these was ruled by an oba. The obas were both religious and political leaders. Their subjects, the Yoruba people, lived as farmers, and built city-states surrounded by massive walls of earth.

WHERE WERE MANY STATUES OF OBAS MADE?

People living in the rainforest kingdom of Benin, now in south Nigeria, were expert metalworkers and cast elaborate portrait heads of their obas, as well as decorative plaques and ceremonial objects. These were made from brass or bronze and were used for ancestor worship, or to decorate the rulers' palaces.

WHAT HAPPENED TO THE KINGDOMS OF THE OBAS?

The power of the obas and other African rulers was weakened by the arrival of Europeans. Portuguese, Dutch, and British traders took back news to their countries of the riches of Africa. Explorers were encouraged to travel there and, by 1900, almost all of Africa was ruled by European powers.

Oba's cap would have been made from beads

▲ STATUE OF OBA FROM BENIN
Most Benin bronzes, like this one, were in fact made of brass. Obas commanded large armies, and controlled trade in ivory, palm oil, pepper, and slaves.

FIND OUT MORE ▶▶ Africa 238–239 • Age of Empire 422–423 • Exploration 400–401 • Islamic Civilization 386–387

POLYNESIA

Polynesia is a group of scattered islands in the vast Pacific Ocean. Around 2000 BCE, families made long, dangerous journeys to settle there. The settlers arrived with pigs, dogs, and chickens. They built thatched wooden houses, gathered bananas, coconuts, and breadfruit, and fished.

▲ **THE POLYNESIAN TRIANGLE**
The islands of Polynesia cover an area of over 800,000 sq miles (2 million sq km). Roughly triangular in shape, New Zealand, Hawaii, and Easter Island are at its points. It took many days to sail between groups of islands. Settlers carried farm tools and food plants, to help them survive when they landed.

Polynesia

WHAT HAPPENED TO THE PEOPLE OF EASTER ISLAND?

The giant rapa nui statues were erected on Easter Island before 1200, cutting down numerous trees. Around 1600 the soil began to erode as the last trees were felled. The islanders could neither fish, as they had no wood for boats, nor farm. The population declined sharply, leading to social unrest.

WHY DID PEOPLE SET SAIL FOR POLYNESIA?

The islands in southeast Asia, where settlers traveled from, were probably overpopulated. This would have meant the farmland was exhausted, forests had been cut down, and the soil had eroded away. There may also have been wars between rival islanders, competing for food and land. But some sailors may have been adventurous, eager to explore new lands.

HOW DID THE SETTLERS NAVIGATE?

Settlers traveled in double-hulled canoes, which had sails made of matting. They observed stars, clouds, ocean swells, migrating birds, and te lapa (rays of light reflected underwater from land), and made maps from sticks, pebbles, and shells. Using these techniques, they reached distant islands like Hawaii, and also New Zealand, where settlers called themselves ▶▶ MAORIS.

STONE STATUES ►
Easter Island (also called Rapa Nui) was the furthest east that the settlers reached. They arrived in 500 CE. Using simple tools of stone and wood, they built many moai (stone statues). Some were 10 m (33 ft) high.

Statues portray ancestors or gods

MAORIS

Settlers first reached New Zealand around 800 CE. At first they lived in small, peaceful groups, but, as the population grew, they became more warlike. Around 1500, they began to build fortified hilltop settlements, called pa. They decorated buildings with woodcarvings, and tattooed their skins with swirling designs.

WHAT WAS LIFE LIKE FOR MAORIS?

The climate of New Zealand was colder and wetter than the settlers' home islands, so they had to adapt to their new environment. They hunted giant flightless birds, called moa, in the forests. They killed seals and gathered shellfish around the coast.

◄ **HEITIKI IN SHAPE OF HUMAN FIGURE**
This heitiki (greenstone neck ornament) was a sacred heirloom—it symbolized the mana (prestige) of the clan. It was also meant to link humans with gods.

FIND OUT MORE ▶▶ Exploration 400–401 • New Zealand 425

ASIAN TEMPLE KINGDOMS

Between 700 and 1300 CE, powerful kingdoms, including the Khmer, Pagan, and Sukhothai, emerged in different parts of southeast Asia. They grew rich from growing rice, selling valuable spices, and controlling merchants' sea routes. Their rulers built great temples.

Asian temple kingdoms

▲ BUDDHIST TEMPLE
This is one of over 5,000 temples built in 1000–1200 in the Pagan kingdom, now in Myanmar.

WHY DID ASIAN RULERS BUILD TEMPLES?
Rulers organized thousands of workers to build Hindu and Buddhist temples for worship. The Buddhist religion became much more popular, so many more Buddhist temples were built. The temples brought religious merit to rulers, prestige to their kingdoms, and displayed each ruler's wealth and power.

WHO INFLUENCED THE TEMPLE KINGDOMS?
Buddhist monks and Hindu holy men traveled from India to southeast Asia. They offered advice to kings and led religious rituals. Prayers, offerings, and festivals became an important part of people's lives.

BOROBUDUR MONUMENT ▼
This massive Buddhist temple was built on the island of Java (now in Indonesia) in 750–850 CE.

Stepped terraces were cut into a natural mound

Model of a stupa (Buddhist burial mound)

One of 500 statues of Buddha

FIND OUT MORE ▸▸ Buddhism 289 • Hinduism 286

OTTOMAN EMPIRE

Around 1300 CE, a new Muslim empire ruled by Turkish leaders called sultans was founded. At its largest extent, in 1700, it covered vast areas of Europe, Africa, and Asia. It lasted until the end of World War I (1918). Today's Republic of Turkey was founded in 1923.

Ottomans

▲ CERAMIC TILES FROM THE BLUE MOSQUE, ISTANBUL
The vibrant, tiled walls of the mosque of Sultan Ahmed, built in 1609–1619 and popularly known as the Blue Mosque. By endowing Istanbul with magnificent mosques and public buildings, the sultans aimed to surpass the achievements of the Byzantine emperors.

WHY WAS SULEIMAN I MAGNIFICENT?
The greatest of the Ottoman sultans was Suleiman the Magnificent. During his reign (1520–1566), the Ottoman Empire reached its greatest extent. He was also a poet and a patron of the arts, adorning Istanbul and other Ottoman cities with glittering mosques.

HOW DID CONSTANTINOPLE BECOME ISTANBUL?
In 1453, after a siege during which its walls were pounded by a battery of cannons, Constantinople was captured by Sultan Muhammad II. Renamed Istanbul, the old capital of the Byzantine Empire then became the new capital of the expanding Ottoman Empire.

WHERE DID JANISSARIES COME FROM?
Janissaries were elite soldiers who started as non-Turkish Christian boys from the Balkans. They were trained in Istanbul, where they converted to Islam.

SULTAN OTHMAN I ▲
The first sultan, Othman I (1259–1326), was the son of a Turkish chieftain. He led an army of ghazis (warriors fighting for the Muslim faith).

FIND OUT MORE ▸▸ Crusades 289 • Islamic Civilization 386–387

RENAISSANCE

One of the most creative periods in history occurred in Europe around 1350–1550. This cultural revival is known as the Renaissance (meaning "rebirth"). It was inspired by the civilizations of Ancient Greece and Rome.

WHERE DID THE RENAISSANCE TAKE PLACE?

Italy was the powerhouse of the Renaissance. At that time it was divided into independent states, where wealthy rulers offered ▶▶ PATRONAGE to great artists. The Renaissance also spread through southern France and Spain, and influenced northern Europe.

WHAT WAS THE RENAISSANCE VIEW OF THE WORLD?

There was a passion for knowledge. Scholars had mostly studied the teachings of the Church, but they now rediscovered ancient philosophers. Artists became fascinated by the human body. To celebrate its beauty, they turned away from the formal drawing style of the Middle Ages and adopted a more realistic, natural style.

LEONARDO DA VINCI
1452–1519

Leonardo was a genius. Writer, painter, sculptor, engineer, and architect, he left behind a wealth of sketches and what has become the world's best-known painting—the portrait of a mysterious, smiling woman known as Mona Lisa.

Muscle power operated a system of levers and pulleys

The wood, rope, and other materials available in Leonardo's day were too heavy for practical flight

▲ FLIGHTS OF FANCY
Leonardo da Vinci was a brilliant inventor. This reconstruction shows a flying machine that first appeared in his sketchbooks, alongside futuristic plans for a helicopter, tank, and diving suit.

Retinue includes portraits of the Medici family

Servants carry bows and spears for hunting

PROCESSION OF THE MAGI ▶
This painting from 1459 is by Benozzo Gozzoli. It is one of a series in the Medici family's private chapel in Florence, Italy. Although based on a Biblical scene, it shows the dazzling splendor of a Renaissance court.

FIND OUT MORE ▶▶ Artists 324 • Painting 320–321 • Philosophy 292–293

Wings are powered by pushing the pedals

Biblical king is shown as a Renaissance prince

▲ **NORTHERN FRINGES**
In Poland, rulers and merchants looked south to Italy and admired the architecture of the Renaissance. This classical facade is in the town of Zamosc, founded in 1579 by Jan Zamoysky, who had studied in Padua.

WHAT CAN WE SEE OF THE RENAISSANCE TODAY?
Many Italian cities still have splendid palaces, churches, libraries, and public squares built during the Renaissance. Visitors to Rome can wonder at the ceiling of the Sistine Chapel, created by Michelangelo, or the masterpieces painted by Raphael.

PATRONAGE

Patronage is the support given by the wealthy to artists, writers, and musicians. Renaissance patrons included the French royal family and powerful Italian nobles such as the Sforzas, the Medicis, and the Borgias.

WHY DID FLORENCE FLOURISH?
The Renaissance was a period of great social change, when more and more political power came from money and trade.
The Italian city of Florence was a European center of banking. Its leading family, the Medici, loaned money to popes and kings. It was the Medici fortune that paid the wages of artists such as Michelangelo and Leonardo da Vinci.

Renaissance

REFORMATION

The Reformation was a Christian movement of the 1500s. Its followers criticized the Catholic Church for corruption and called for radical reform. These protestors became known as Protestants.

WHO LED THE REFORMATION?
The Reformation began in 1517 when a German monk, Martin Luther, nailed a list of complaints to the church door in Wittenberg. Other preachers spread the Protestant message across northern Europe. They called for simpler forms of worship and personal faith.

WHAT WERE THE RESULTS OF THE REFORMATION?
The success of the Protestants aroused fear and anger among Catholics in Rome. A period of religious strife began that tore Europe apart for hundreds of years. Each side murdered its opponents. Churches and monasteries were destroyed. Civil and national wars caused devastation and streams of refugees.

▲ **PRINTED SCRIPTURE**
This Bible was printed by a German man named Johannes Gutenberg in about 1455. Printing with movable type made it possible to distribute the Bible and other works to large numbers of ordinary people. Martin Luther later translated the Bible from Latin into German.

Latin was rejected by Protestants because few could read it

Reformation

RELIGIOUS CONFLICT, EUROPE 1517–1568	
1517	German monk Martin Luther demands reform
1518	Swiss preacher Ulrich Zwingli calls for change
1541	John Calvin founds a Protestant Church, Geneva
1545	Catholics launch a Counter-Reformation
1560	John Knox founds Protestant Church of Scotland
1562	Wars between Catholics and Protestants in France
1568	Dutch Protestants begin revolt against Catholic Spain

FIND OUT MORE ▸▸ Christianity 288 • Printing 339

EXPLORATION

People have always set out to discover new lands and oceans. The greatest age of world exploration began in the 15th century and lasted over four centuries. The Arabs and Chinese had already made improvements in ship design and ▶◀NAVIGATION. These were now developed further by European seafarers.

Brazil, in South America, was discovered by accident in 1500—its coastline is not yet complete on this map

At Tordesillas in 1494 Spain and Portugal agreed to divide the newly discovered lands in the Americas between them

exploration

▲ MAPPING THE WORLD
This map was drawn up in 1502 and shows the world known to European seafarers at that time. The coasts of Europe, Africa, and western Asia have been charted, but those of the Americas are only just beginning to take shape.

Africa's interior remained unexplored by Europeans until the 1800s

WHY DID PEOPLE EXPLORE THE WORLD?
The most common reason was trade. The ▶◀OLD WORLD wanted Asian spices, African ivory, and gold. European traders were soon also seizing lands and trying to convert the local populations to the Christian faith. Many explorers, though, were driven by a sense of adventure or scientific inquiry.

HOW DID EXPLORATION AFFECT THE WORLD?
European countries brought many lands under their control. The world was opened up and new crops, including potatoes and tomatoes, were introduced from one land to another. However, there were some disastrous effects. In the ▶◀NEW WORLD, many native peoples died because they had no resistance to the European diseases that explorers and crews brought with them.

▲ POINTING THE WAY
This type of mariners' compass first came into use in about 1250. This one dates from the 16th century.

EXPLORATION	
1405–1433	Chinese fleets explore the Indian Ocean
1488	Diaz rounds southern Africa
1492	Columbus reaches the Caribbean
1497	John Cabot reaches Canada
1498	Columbus reaches South America
1498	Vasco da Gama sails to India
1500	Pedro Cabral reaches Brazil
1522	Magellan's crew sails around the whole world
1606	Willem Jansz reaches Australia

OLD WORLD

Europe, Asia, and Africa had been known to geographers since ancient times. They became known as the Old World after the European discovery of the Americas.

WHO EXPLORED THE OLD WORLD?
In the Middle Ages, the Venetian Marco Polo and the Moroccan Ibn Battutah traveled east to China. The Chinese admiral Zheng He sailed west to Africa in the 15th century. By the 16th century, Portuguese and Dutch ships were trading in southeast Asia.

TREASURES FROM THE EAST ▶
Silk reached Europe from China along the overland trading routes followed by Marco Polo. Porcelain became a major Chinese export as east–west shipping routes were opened up in the 15th and 16th centuries.

NAVIGATION

Navigation is any method used to find one's way or hold a ship on course. Sailors of the 16th century had various kinds of instrument to help them cross the oceans.

WHAT INSTRUMENTS WERE USED?
Sailors used a compass to see which direction they were traveling. They could also work out a ship's position by measuring the angle of the Sun or stars above the horizon. They did this with a metal plate called a quadrant, a disk called an astrolabe, or a simple stick called a cross-staff.

HOW WAS DISTANCE MEASURED?
Distances traveled at sea were calculated from speed and time. To measure these, a wooden log was thrown overboard. The crew called out the time it took for the log to pass between two measuring points on the ship. The ship's course and progress were measured on a pegboard.

HENRY THE NAVIGATOR
1394–1460
This Portuguese prince founded an observatory and a school of navigation on Cape St. Vincent, Portugal. Here, a new type of ship, called a caravel, was designed. Henry also sponsored voyages along the coast of West Africa.

NEW WORLD

"New World" was one of the terms that came to be used by Europeans to describe the newly discovered lands of North and South America.

WHY DID COLUMBUS SAIL WEST?
In 1492, Christopher Columbus persuaded King Ferdinand and Queen Isabella of Spain to sponsor a voyage westward. The goal was to find a new trading route to Asia. Columbus landed in the Bahamas, starting a new age of exploration and invasion.

◀ LANDFALL IN A NEW WORLD
Columbus and his crew meet the Taino people of the Bahamas, believing them to be Asians. The conquered Tainos had to give gold to the Spaniards as tribute. Columbus' discovery brought huge wealth to Spain, but spelled disaster for the native peoples of the Caribbean.

▲ FORTRESS ISLAND
Spain invaded Puerto Rico in 1508. Defenses were first built at San Felipe del Morro (above) in 1540. Spain's colonies soon came under attack from rivals such as the English.

Chimu goldsmiths from the northern part of the empire created this mask

The mask would be placed over the face of a dead nobleman as a funeral ritual

Beaten gold was a sacred metal to the Incas

Incas

▲ GOLD MASK
Craftsmen had privileged status in Inca society. Metalworkers from various parts of the empire made masks of shining gold. It was greed for such gold and treasure that lured Spanish invaders to Peru in 1531.

INCAS

The Inca people lived in the Andes mountains of Peru. Between the 12th century and 1532, they conquered an empire that stretched for 2,240 miles (3,600 km), from Colombia to Chile. The Inca empire collapsed after the Spanish invaded in 1531.

WHO RULED THE INCA EMPIRE?
The Incas formed a ruling elite. They were a small highland tribe who came to govern 12 million people, speakers of 20 different languages. Conquered chiefs were allowed to keep some local power, provided they adopted the Inca way of life.

HOW DID INCA SOCIETY FUNCTION?
Nobles who were loyal to the Sapa Inca (emperor) were made governors, generals, or priests. They wore golden earplugs as a badge of rank. Most citizens were poor farmers, but they also had to serve the state as soldiers, builders, or laborers.

WHO WAS DESCENDED FROM THE SUN AND MOON?
The Inca emperor claimed descent from Inti, the Sun god, and the empress from Mamakilya, the Moon goddess. Other gods and goddesses represented the sea, thunder, and the goodness of the Earth. The Incas also revered the holy places used by earlier Andean peoples.

A big square at the center of the town was for religious ceremonies

The town is 9,000 ft (2,743 m) above sea level

Inca walls were strong and earthquake-proof

◄ MACHU PICCHU
The Inca town of Machu Picchu was built on a remote mountain ridge in about 1450. Its buildings included a palace, housing, temples, army barracks, and craft workshops. The town was abandoned after the Spanish invaded and only rediscovered in 1911.

FIND OUT MORE ▶▶ Ancient Religions 282 • Conquistadors 405

AZTECS

The Aztec, or Mexica, people founded a powerful empire that ruled Mexico from around 1325 to 1521, when a Spanish invasion caused it to collapse. The Aztecs were farmers, warriors, and builders of great cities.

WHERE WAS THE CITY IN THE LAKE?

In 1325, a band of migrating Aztecs came to a large island in Lake Texcoco. When their priests saw an eagle land on a cactus there, they declared that this was the place to build a splendid new city, Tenochtitlán. This is now the site of Mexico City.

▲ AN AZTEC HISTORY
This is part of a codex, or manuscript, painted after the Spanish conquest. The blue square represents Lake Texcoco, and the eagle and cactus represent Tenochtitlán. The shield is a symbol of Aztec power.

Aztecs

Helmet shaped like an eagle's open beak

EAGLE WARRIOR ▶
This statue shows an Eagle warrior, a member of an elite military order, ready to fight for the Aztec god of war, Huitzilopochtli.

Wings like an eagle's are fixed to the arms

HOW DO WE KNOW ABOUT AZTEC LIFE?

After the Spanish invaded Tenochtitlán, they described many aspects of Aztec life, such as law, schooling, farming, and ▶▶ HUMAN SACRIFICE. Many artifacts from the Aztec Empire have also survived, including feather cloaks, jewelry, pottery, and knives.

TEMPLE OF DEATH ▶
The emperor or his priest cuts the living heart from the victim with a sharp knife. Blood pours down the steps of the temple pyramid.

HUMAN SACRIFICE

Human sacrifice is the killing of people for religious reasons. The Aztecs believed that the gods had sacrificed themselves for their people. They wished to repay that debt.

WHY DID BLOOD FLOW SO FREELY?

Being sacrificed was believed to be a great honor for the victims. Even so, the victims were often captured enemy troops who were taken to the capital to be killed on the pyramid of the Great Temple. At a four-day ceremony in 1487, tens of thousands of captives were sacrificed.

Shin guards represent eagle's talons

FIND OUT MORE ▶▶ Ancient Religions 282 • Conquistadors 405 • Maya 381

TUDOR AGE

The Tudors were a family of Welsh, French, and English descent. From 1485 to 1603 they ruled England, Wales, and rebellious Ireland. The Tudor kingdom became a powerful force in Europe and the New World.

HOW DID TUDOR MERCHANTS BECOME WEALTHY?
The Tudor economy depended on wool and the cloth trade, which was centered in the English region of East Anglia. To expand their trade, merchants and ships' captains began to seek new business in distant lands.

WHY DID HENRY VIII QUARREL WITH THE POPE?
King Henry VIII married his elder brother's widow, a Spanish princess called Catherine of Aragon. Although she had a daughter, Mary, she did not produce the male heir Henry wanted. The king fell in love with a beautiful courtier named Anne Boleyn. When the Pope refused to give him a divorce, Henry VIII made himself head of a ▶▶ CHURCH OF ENGLAND.

WHO WAS THE GREATEST TUDOR MONARCH?
Henry VIII was followed as ruler by his three children, Edward VI, Mary I, and Elizabeth I. Elizabeth was a strong and popular ruler, and a shrewd politician. She never married. Her reign saw battles with Spain, exploration of the New World, and a flowering of poetry and theater.

HENRY VIII
1491–1547

As a young man, Henry was handsome and intelligent. He loved hunting and dancing, and also composed music. As king, he became increasingly arrogant, selfish, and overweight. He married six times and had two of his wives executed. His reign was marked by political plotting, religious strife, and rebellion.

Spanish Armada is attacked by English ships and scattered by storms

◀ PORTRAIT OF POWER
This image of Elizabeth I shows her as a powerful and confident ruler. The background shows the defeat of the Spanish Armada in 1588, a fleet sent by the Catholic Philip II of Spain in a bid to overthrow Elizabeth and restore the Catholic church to England.

Spanish Armada, or war fleet, is shown nearing England in 1588

Crown is a symbol of royal power

Tudor age

Globe suggests England's growing role overseas

TUDOR MONARCHS	
1485	Henry VII wins throne from Richard III
1509	Henry VIII is crowned king
1547	Rule of the boy king Edward VI
1553	Reign of Mary I
1558	Elizabeth I becomes queen
1603	Death of Elizabeth I

CHURCH OF ENGLAND

Henry VIII finally broke with the Roman Catholic Church in 1534. However, he also rejected the Protestant teachings of Martin Luther. In 1559, after years of religious conflict, Elizabeth I created a reformed Church of England that contained both Catholic and Protestant elements. It was, and still is, headed by the monarch.

WHY DID RELIGION TROUBLE THE TUDORS?
Henry VIII's political quarrel with the Pope coincided with the bitter religious quarrels of the Reformation in Europe. Edward VI and Elizabeth I were both Protestant, while Mary I was an ardent Catholic. Many ordinary people were tortured and executed for having a different faith than the reigning monarch.

FOUNTAINS ABBEY, YORKSHIRE ▶
Roman Catholic monasteries and convents were closed down, or "dissolved," by orders of 1536 and 1539. Many were ransacked and today lie in ruins.

FIND OUT MORE ▶▶ Monarchy 410 • Reformation 399

CONQUISTADORS

In the 16th century, Central and South America were invaded by Spanish soldiers called conquistadors, who overthrew the Aztec and Inca empires. Many went in search of a rich land called ▶▶ EL DORADO.

HERNÁN CORTÉS
1485–1547
Cortés was born in Spain. In 1518 he was given command of a force of 550 soldiers. He landed in Mexico, and reached the Aztec capital in 1519. He was greeted peacefully, but soon there was bitter fighting. In 1521 Cortés destroyed the city, and in 1522 he became the Spanish governor of this newly conquered land.

WHO WAS THE GOD FROM THE SEA?

In 1517, Aztec spies saw conquistadors on the coast and relayed news of these pale, bearded strangers to Emperor Moctezuma II. He believed that their arrival marked the return of a long-departed god and king called Quetzalcoatl.

HOW DID THE CONQUISTADORS DEFEAT SO MANY PEOPLE?

The conquistadors were few in number, but they had ships, horses, armor, and deadly firearms. In Mexico they increased their numbers by joining up with native peoples rebelling against Aztec rule.

▲ SPANISH HELMET
Conquistadors were protected from the spears and clubs of native warriors by tough steel helmets and breastplates.

The Aztecs had no effective defense against steel swords and firearms

WHO KILLED THE INCA EMPEROR?

In 1532, a band of conquistadors led by Francisco Pizarro met the Inca emperor Atahualpa. They tricked him into being captured, and demanded a vast ransom of silver and gold for his release. It was paid, but in 1533 they executed him anyway.

TERROR UNLEASHED ▶
In 1520 Pedro de Alvarado was left in charge of Tenochtitlán. His brutality caused an uprising. The Spanish fled, but recaptured the city in 1521.

conquistadors

EL DORADO

El Dorado means "the golden one"—it is the Spanish name for a mythical land in South America, said to be rich in gold beyond all dreams.

WHY DID THE CONQUISTADORS SEEK EL DORADO?

Conquistadors were often brave, but they were also quarrelsome and violent, driven by a desperate desire for gold and power. Many died in remote jungles, still vainly searching for the riches of El Dorado.

Ornamental tweezers, made in Peru by a Moche goldsmith

GOLDEN TREASURE ▶
Conquistadors looted precious gold statues and ornaments from temples and palaces all over Central and South America. Many were melted down and shipped back to Spain.

FIND OUT MORE ▶▶ Aztecs 403 • Incas 402

THIRTY YEARS' WAR

The Thirty Years' War engulfed Europe between 1618 and 1648. It was a clash between Protestants and Catholics in Germany, which spread into a wider conflict involving Denmark, Sweden, and France.

THIRTY YEARS' WAR	
1618	Protestant revolt in Prague
1625–1629	Denmark enters war for the Protestants
1630	Sweden joins Protestant cause
1635	France joins the war as Sweden's ally
1646	France and Sweden invade Bavaria
1648	Treaty of Westphalia ends the war

WHO WAS THROWN FROM A WINDOW IN PRAGUE?
The Catholic Habsburg family ruled the Holy Roman Empire and Spain. When the Habsburgs tried to place a Catholic on the throne of Protestant Bohemia, their representatives were hurled from a window of Prague castle. Rebellion spread across Germany as Protestant princes within the empire challenged its authority.

WHO WAS THE LION OF THE NORTH?
The war was part of a wider struggle between the Holy Roman Empire and its enemies. Denmark, Sweden, and France all opposed the empire. The Swedish king Gustavus Adolphus, "Lion of the North", won many victories, but died in battle at Lützen in 1632.

Thirty Years' War

MAGDEBURG DESTROYED ▶
In 1631, the German city of Magdeburg was burned down by Holy Roman Empire forces. Peace brought more religious freedom and greatly weakened the Holy Roman Empire.

FIND OUT MORE ▶▶ Holy Roman Empire 385

ENGLISH CIVIL WAR

From 1642 to 1648 people in the British Isles were split by a war between King Charles I and Parliament. The king was said to be influenced by his wife, a French Catholic. He brought in unpopular taxes and tried to force his will on Parliament. This led to civil war.

WHO WAS "OLD IRONSIDES"?
Oliver Cromwell (1599–1658) was a farmer and Member of Parliament. In the English Civil War he proved himself to be a brilliant soldier. He and his armored troopers became known as Ironsides. He led a savage invasion of Catholic Ireland in 1649.

WHO WERE ROUNDHEADS AND CAVALIERS?
The forces of Parliament included many of the more extreme Protestants, called Puritans (also known as Roundheads, because of their short haircuts). The royalists were called Cavaliers (meaning "knights"). Their war ended with the capture of Charles I.

WHO WERE THE DIGGERS AND LEVELERS?
The leaders of the Parliamentary forces were mostly country landowners, squires, and merchants. Many of the poor people who fought for them wanted the land to be shared and equal rights for all. Cromwell crushed these Diggers and Levelers in 1649.

WHAT WAS THE COMMONWEALTH?
In 1649 a republic, or Commonwealth, was declared. There was now a Council of State instead of a king. However, the army was impatient for greater change, so in 1653 power was handed over to Oliver Cromwell, who was given the title "Lord Protector". Cromwell died and under his son the Commonwealth soon collapsed. In 1660 the monarchy was restored, but with limited powers.

Warrant to Execute King Charles the First. A.D. 1648.

Warrant authorizes the king's execution

Signatures and seals of the High Court

Signature of Oliver Cromwell

English Civil War

▲ DEATH WARRANT OF CHARLES I
Convicted as a traitor to his people, King Charles I was beheaded in Whitehall, London, on January 30, 1649, by order of the English Parliament. News of this event shocked the whole of Europe. Many people believed that kings ruled by divine right, or the will of God—so the execution was regarded as a terrible sin.

FIND OUT MORE ▶▶ Monarchy 410

MUGHAL INDIA

The Mughal Empire, founded in 1526, was the most powerful Islamic state to rule in India. It was at its most prosperous during the 17th century, when fine buildings such as the **▶▶ TAJ MAHAL** were constructed.

WHO WERE THE MUGHALS?

Mughal means "Mongol." Babur, the Asian invader who founded the empire, was descended from Mongol warlords. Under the Mughal emperors, roads were built, trade prospered, and the arts flourished.

Gold hilt studded with gems

WHERE WAS THE MUGHAL EMPIRE?

The Mughals governed northern India, and at times their rule extended from Afghanistan in the west to Bengal in the east. The emperor Shah Jahan moved the capital from Agra to Delhi in 1638, and pushed the empire's borders far to the south.

THE MUGHAL EMPIRE	
1526	Babur founds Mughal Empire
1556	Akbar the Great begins reign
1605	Jahangir becomes emperor
1628	Shah Jahan comes to power
1659	Aurangzeb seizes the throne
1675	Sikhs rise against Mughal rule
1707	Start of Mughal decline
1857	Last emperor

MUGHAL DAGGER ▶
The Mughal emperors owned magnificent daggers and swords, hunting weapons, precious jewels, gold, and ivory. They wore splendid silks and brocades. Their court was famed around the world for its luxury.

WHO CHALLENGED MUGHAL RULE?

The Mughals had to fight against Afghans and many regional Hindu rulers. The early Muslim emperors allowed all kinds of religious worship, but Aurangzeb offended Hindus and caused the Sikhs to rebel. He also clashed fiercely with the west coast kingdom of the Marathas and its ruler, Sivaji. However, it was the growing political power of British traders in India that brought about the final decline and collapse of the Mughal Empire in the 18th century.

Mughal India

▲ MUGHAL MINIATURE
This painting from about 1590 shows Akbar's palace being built. Mughal art was often in miniature, combining Persian and Indian styles.

TAJ MAHAL

The most famous monument of Mughal architecture is the Taj Mahal. It was built in the 17th century by Shah Jahan as a tomb for his beloved wife, Mumtaz Mahal, who died in childbirth.

HOW LONG DID IT TAKE TO BUILD THE TAJ MAHAL?

The Taj Mahal was begun in 1632 and completed 22 years later. About 20,000 people were employed, including Asia's finest craftsmen. Famous for its perfect symmetry, it is exactly as wide as it is high, and the dome is the same height as its façade.

◀ INSCRIPTIONS
Beautifully intricate inscriptions in the Persian style adorn the arches of the Taj Mahal. Many of them are verses from the Qur'an, the holy scripture of Islam.

TAJ MAHAL ▶
The domes, minarets, and arches of the Taj Mahal are reflected in still water. The walls of white marble are inlaid with over 43 varieties of precious stones.

FIND OUT MORE ▶▶ Gupta India 379 • Mauryan India 379

AMERICAN INDIANS

The lands of North America were originally occupied by a wide variety of American Indian peoples, each with their own language and culture. Ways of life varied from one region to another, according to the environment—some peoples lived in farming villages, while others hunted buffalo. Their worlds were changed forever by the European invasion.

Decorative bead headband

American Indians

WHAT WAS THE LEAGUE OF FIVE NATIONS?
Five American Indian nations in the northeast—the Seneca, Cayuga, Onondaga, Oneida, and Mohawk—made a powerful alliance, called the Iroquois Confederacy. It was founded in about 1570 by a prophet called Deganawida. The League's goals were cooperation and mutual defense. A council met each year to discuss their laws.

Resin made the canoe waterproof

▲ **EAGLE FEATHERS**
Among many hunters of the Great Plains, such as the Lakota (or Sioux), war bonnets indicated rank and bravery in battle. This one is made of eagle feathers, porcupine quills, buckskin, ermine tails, and horsehair.

Birch bark was stitched over a light timber frame

▲ **CANOE BUILDERS**
American Indians built all kinds of boats, using tree trunks, reeds, or buffalo hide. Birch-bark canoes were used on northeastern lakes and rivers.

HOW DID PEOPLE IN THE NORTHWEST LIVE?
The northwest (in what is now both the US and Canada) was an area with a large American Indian population. Many peoples there lived by salmon fishing or whaling, and by gathering fruits and berries. They lived in large houses, which were built of red cedar wood. Cedar was also used to make hats, boats, rope, cloth, boxes, and baskets.

WHY DID FARMERS BECOME HUNTERS?
As Europeans invaded the northeast, many American Indian peoples were forced to retreat westward. Some had to give up farming. Instead, they became buffalo hunters on the Great Plains, the grasslands that make up the prairie regions of the central part of the modern United States and Canada.

▼ **BUFFALO HUNTERS**
For generations, Plains Indians had hunted buffalo, both on foot and on horseback. In the 19th century, the great herds were almost completely destroyed by the arrival of the railroad, which prevented the free grazing of the herds and brought with it the guns of white hunters.

AMERICAN INDIANS	
1547	Horses introduced to North America by the Spanish
c. 1570	The Iroquois Confederacy is founded
1626	Manhattan Island is sold to the Dutch
1648	The Iroquois-Huron War
1722	The Tuscarora join the Iroquois Confederacy
1763	Pontiac, chief of the Ottawa, unites tribes against British troops

FIND OUT MORE ▶▶ Early Americans 380 • Indian Wars 417 • Western US 228–229

COLONIAL AMERICA

From the 16th to 18th century, European nations invaded and settled large areas of North America. The colonists often attacked and dispersed the American Indians, and fought each other for control of the territory.

WHO BUILT ST. AUGUSTINE?

The Spanish reached Florida in 1513, and in 1565 founded San Agustin (now St. Augustine), the first European settlement in what is now the US. They were the first Europeans to see the Mississippi River and to reach Kansas. The Spanish also extended Mexico northward into Texas, New Mexico, and California. These territories would become part of the US in the 19th century.

Indian control French control Spanish control British control

▲ **SAMOSET AND THE PILGRIMS**
In 1620, a ship called the *Mayflower* landed a group of settlers at Plymouth in New England. They were religious refugees from England and became known as Pilgrims. They nearly starved to death in their first winter, but a friendly Patuxet chief named Samoset helped them to survive. By 1625, they had taken over much of his land.

WHERE WAS LOUISIANA?

In 1682, the French explorer Robert de la Salle claimed all the lands around the Mississippi River for France. The region was named Louisiana, after King Louis XIV of France. Most of the eastern part passed to Spain and then to the US, while the western part was purchased by the US from the French in 1803.

WHERE DID THE BRITISH SETTLE?

The English seafarer Sir Walter Raleigh organized three expeditions to North America after 1584. He named Virginia after Elizabeth I of England, known as the "Virgin Queen" because she never married. In 1607, Jamestown in Virginia became the first British settlement on the Atlantic coast and became wealthy through the export of tobacco.

▲ **NEW WORLD ORDER**
This map shows early settlements around the Gulf of Mexico, as well as the 13 British colonies on the Atlantic coast, which later created the United States of America. There was European settlement on the Pacific coast, too, with the Russians settling Alaska in 1784.

colonial America

▼ **NEW AMSTERDAM**
In 1626, the Dutch purchased the island of Manhattan. Its port was named New Amsterdam. It was captured by the British in 1664 and renamed New York.

Buildings were in the Dutch style   Ships anchored at the mouth of the Hudson River

WHO WERE THE SETTLERS?

Europeans settled in the New World for many reasons. Some were religious refugees, such as the Quakers, who were unable to worship freely in their own lands. Some were convicted criminals, sent to work in the colonies as a punishment. Some were outlaws or pirates. Others were farmers or business people looking for good land and opportunities.

FIND OUT MORE ▶▶ American Revolution 414 • Indian Wars 417

MONARCHY

Monarchy means rule by a single person, such as a king or a queen. Normally, rule passes from one generation to the next within the same family, or ▶▶DYNASTY. In the 17th century monarchs held great power, but this power was increasingly being challenged, often with violence.

WHAT WAS THE DIVINE RIGHT OF KINGS?
This was the belief that monarchs were appointed by God to rule, and therefore had a right to impose their will on their subjects. This made it almost impossible to criticise or oppose the monarch.

WERE KINGS EVER ELECTED?
From 1573, kings of Poland were elected by an assembly of lords, called the Republic of Nobles. The great Polish soldier Jan Sobiewski was elected king in 1674, after defeating invading Turks. Many of those chosen as king were foreigners.

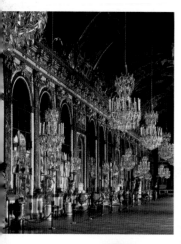

◀ HALL OF MIRRORS
This dazzling hall at Versailles was designed to reflect royal power and glory, impressing all visitors.

monarchy

COURTYARD AT VERSAILLES ▶
In 1682, the most luxurious palace in the world was Versailles, the glittering royal court of Louis XIV of France.

DYNASTIES

Dynasties, or royal families, often held power for hundreds of years. Many became hugely wealthy. Their rule came to an end if there were no children or relatives to inherit the throne, or if a monarch was overthrown by rivals or revolutions.

WHICH IS THE WORLD'S OLDEST DYNASTY?
The same dynasty has ruled Japan for 2,000 years or more. Legend states that it is even older, having been founded by Jimmu Tenno in 660 BCE. But, the emperors have not always held great power. Sometimes, real power was held by military governors called shoguns.

▲ HABSBURG 1273–1918
The Habsburgs ruled Austria and at times the Holy Roman Empire, the Netherlands, and Spain. Charles V reigned 1516–1556.

▲ STUART 1371–1714
The Stuarts ruled Scotland and, after 1603, England, Wales, and Ireland. Charles II reigned 1660–1685.

▲ BOURBON 1589–1830
The Bourbons ruled in France, Navarre, Naples, and Spain. Louis XIV (above, costumed as the Sun) was King of France 1643–1715.

▲ QING 1644–1912
The last dynasty of the Chinese Empire was founded by Manchurian invaders. Emperor Qianlong ruled 1735–1799.

▲ ROMANOV 1613–1917
The Romanovs were the last Russian dynasty. Catherine the Great married into the family and was empress 1762–1796.

FIND OUT MORE ▶▶ English Civil War 406 • Samurai 302 • Tudor Age 404

SCIENTIFIC REVOLUTION

The 18th century was a period of remarkable scientific breakthroughs. This began with the scientific advances of the 16th and 17th centuries, when people began to reject unproven theories and superstition in favor of careful observation, and carried out experiments to test ideas.

WHO DISCOVERED HOW BLOOD CIRCULATES?

In 1597, English student William Harvey went to Padua in Italy, which was then a center for studying the human body. He returned to become royal doctor, and in 1628 declared that blood was pumped around the body by the heart. Many doctors ridiculed his views, but Harvey was correct. His discovery changed our understanding of the human body forever.

NEW SCIENCE	
1609	Johannes Kepler works out how planets move
1638	Galileo Galilei publishes his theories of mechanics
1687	Isaac Newton publishes his three Laws of Motion
1753	Carolus Linnaeus works out a way of classifying species
1774	Joseph Priestley studies oxygen

WHO WAS THE FIRST PERSON TO SEE GERMS?

The first microscopes were made in the Netherlands in about 1590. Their design was improved by Robert Hooke and Anton van Leeuwenhoek. Van Leeuwenhoek made many important observations and in 1675 was the first person to see bacteria, or germs.

Can the bird survive without air?

The girls fear the worst

ROBERT BOYLE
1627–1691

Irish chemist and physicist Robert Boyle experimented with gases and with vacuums (in which gases are pumped out of a space). He introduced the idea of chemical elements, essential to the development of chemistry as a science.

THE EXPERIMENT ►
This 1768 painting by Joseph Wright of Derby is titled *Experiment with an Air Pump*. There was a growing public interest in science and the ways in which it could be applied to industry.

WHO WERE THE FIRST CHEMISTS?

From the Middle Ages to the early 18th century, alchemists believed they could turn ordinary metals into gold, and so find the secret of everlasting life. Although this was impossible, alchemy did provide a basis for useful experiments in chemistry, and inspired the genuine research of Robert Boyle.

◄ LAVOISIER'S LABORATORY
This the laboratory of Antoine Lavoisier, one of the founders of modern chemistry. He continued the research of Englishman Joseph Priestley into oxygen.

REFLECTING TELESCOPE ►
Telescopes were invented in the Netherlands in about 1608. In 1668, Isaac Newton was the first to use mirrors to improve the image seen through the telescope.

Scientific Revolution

FIND OUT MORE ►► Chemistry 162 • The Enlightenment 416 • Science 154

AGRICULTURAL REVOLUTION

The 18th and 19th centuries saw great changes across Europe and North America in the way people farmed. Scientific methods were used to improve crop yields and breed better livestock. ▶▶ **MECHANIZATION** made farming more efficient.

WHY DID CHANGES TAKE PLACE IN FARMING?

At this time there was a new interest in science and technology. Many old crafts were becoming modern industries, and farming was no exception. This was necessary, as cities were growing and their populations needed more food. In France, an inefficient farming system had resulted in famine and political unrest.

▲ BRINGERS OF CHANGE
Landowners wishing to improve their estates were at the forefront of change. They experimented with new breeds of cattle, and also learned how to change crops year by year to preserve the goodness of the soil.

◄ SEED DRILL
Seeds had been scattered by hand until Jethro Tull's seed drill (developed in about 1701) made it possible to plant seeds in rows, which could then be easily hoed.

Seed *placed here passed down the tube*

Agricultural Revolution

WHO WORKED ON THE LAND?

In many parts of Europe, farming had changed very little since the Middle Ages. Peasants labored in the fields in great poverty and often had little freedom to move away from their villages. In Britain, farm work was increasingly carried out by large numbers of low-wage laborers.

THOMAS WILLIAM COKE
1752–1842

Thomas Coke was one of the new landowners determined to improve agriculture. He replaced rye with wheat on his land in Norfolk, England, and bred cattle, sheep, and pigs. He also became a Member of Parliament.

MECHANIZATION

In the 1800s, new machines, such as reaping and threshing machines, were invented to do jobs that had previously been done by hand.

DID MACHINES REPLACE PEOPLE?

These new inventions were brought in to make farming easier and also to reduce costs. By the 1830s, English farm laborers were beginning to worry that mechanization would lead to loss of jobs. They protested by smashing new machinery and burning haystacks. Their fears were valid. In the next 150 years, the number of farmworkers declined rapidly.

AGRICULTURAL SHOWS ►
The Royal Agricultural Society meets at Bristol, England, in 1842. After 1838, the Society helped to spread knowledge of crops, livestock breeding, and new machinery among farmers.

FIND OUT MORE ▶▶ Early Farming 364–365 • Ecology 80–81

SLAVE TRADE

People have been bought and sold as slaves around the world through much of history. This trade reached new heights in the 16th to 19th centuries, as Arabs and Europeans plundered Africa. In the 18th century, it is believed that up to eight million Africans were shipped across the Atlantic Ocean.

TOUSSAINT L'OUVERTURE
1743–1803
Toussaint was a freed slave from the French colony of St. Dominique (Haiti). He joined a slave uprising in 1791. When revolutionary France abolished slavery, Toussaint became a respected leader. However, after a change of government, he was seized and imprisoned.

◄ **SLAVE CHAINS**
Slaves were transported to the Americas in chains. Many Europeans and Americans campaigned against slavery. It was abolished in the British Empire in the 1830s and in the US in 1865.

Iron chains could be fixed around necks or ankles

slave trade

HOW WAS THE SLAVE TRADE ORGANIZED?

West African slaves were normally captured by African raiders. At the coast they were exchanged for European guns or textiles. The European traders packed the slaves into ships and sailed for the New World. Once the Africans were sold, the European captains picked up cargoes before sailing home.

HOW WERE SLAVES TREATED IN THE NEW WORLD?

After the ordeal of the Atlantic crossing, the slaves were prepared for auction. Once sold, they were forced to work long hours on ▶▶ PLANTATIONS for no pay. Many slaves were treated with cruelty, and were chained and branded. Those who tried to escape were punished by whipping or even hanging.

◄ **AUCTIONED LIKE CATTLE**
Slaves are auctioned off to plantation owners in the southern US. They were examined to see if they were strong and healthy. Families might be split up, never to see each other again.

PLANTATIONS

Slaves in the Caribbean and the US were forced to work on plantations—estates where sugar cane, cotton, or other crops were grown. The owners paid workers no wages, so their profits were huge.

WHY WERE PLANTATIONS CREATED?

Plantations in the New World marked the start of farming on an industrial, global scale. Plantations produced "cash crops"—crops grown for sale and export rather than local use. The use of slave labor reduced costs.

PLANTATION IN GEORGIA ►
This is a cotton plantation in Georgia in 1895—thirty years after the abolition of slavery. The work is still exhausting in the heat of the day, the hours still long.

FIND OUT MORE ▶▶ American Civil War 424 • Medieval Africa 394–395

AMERICAN REVOLUTION

The period 1765-1788 saw great changes in North America. The 13 British colonies in the east demanded democratic government, and went to war against Britain in 1775. In 1776 they issued a ▸▸ DECLARATION OF INDEPENDENCE, and in 1781 the British command surrendered the fight.

American Revolution ⬉

WHAT WAS THE BOSTON TEA PARTY?
Taxes paid on imported goods were very unpopular. In 1773, colonists disguised as American Indians boarded an English ship in Boston Harbor and threw its cargo of highly taxed tea overboard. This became known as the Boston Tea Party.

WHO FOUGHT IN THE WAR?
British troops, including German mercenaries, were supported by colonial loyalists. The rebellious Patriots formed a Continental Army after 1775, defeating the British at Saratoga Springs in 1777. The French sent 6,000 troops to fight the British.

WHY DID THE COLONISTS REVOLT?
The people who had settled in North America valued personal freedom. Many of them had left Europe because of their strong religious or political views. They protested when the British government imposed taxes on them without consulting the local governing bodies of the colonies.

▼ SIEGE OF YORKTOWN, 1781
In 1781, George Washington and the French commander, the Comte de Rochambeau, besieged and finally defeated the British at Yorktown, Virginia.

DECLARATION OF INDEPENDENCE

In 1774, Patriots (the anti-British rebels) convened the first in a series of Continental Congresses in Philadelphia, Pennsylvania, to coordinate their struggle against the British. The 1776 Congress issued a Declaration of Independence, laying down its principles of freedom. A full United States government was founded in 1788.

◀ LIBERTY BELL
This bell hung in the Pennsylvania State House. It was rung to mark both the Boston Tea Party and the first public reading of the Declaration of Independence.

WHO CALLED FOR FREEDOM?
The 1776 Declaration of Independence was issued in Philadelphia, in the name of John Hancock, president of the Continental Congress. It was largely written by Thomas Jefferson, who later became the third US president. It declared that "all men are created equal" and have a right to "life, liberty, and the pursuit of happiness." These ringing words inspired revolutionaries around the world.

GEORGE WASHINGTON
1732–1799
Born in Virginia, Washington was a wealthy landowner and served with the British army. In 1775 he was chosen to command the rebel American army, which he led to victory in 1781. He oversaw the new constitution and in 1789 became the first US president.

FIND OUT MORE ▸▸ Colonial America 409

FRENCH REVOLUTION

The years 1789 to 1799 marked a turning point in European history. In France, calls for political reform were overtaken by a revolution that swept away the monarchy, the aristocracy, and the power of the Church. The revolution was followed by a **▸▸ REIGN OF TERROR**.

WHY DID THE FRENCH RISE UP?
In 1789, the French aristocracy and leading churchmen led privileged lives and had great power. However, the middle classes wanted more power for themselves. Taxes were high, the country was bankrupt, and the poor were starving. King Louis XVI failed to bring in reforms in time to stop a revolution.

WHAT HAPPENED ON JULY 14?
On July 14, 1789, the people of Paris were afraid that the army had been ordered to attack them. They armed themselves and marched to the Bastille, a royal fort used as a prison, in search of gunpowder. They attacked and captured the fort. The revolution had begun.

▲ DOOMED MONARCHS
King Louis XVI came to the throne in 1774, but failed to solve his country's problems. Queen Marie-Antoinette was disliked for her extravagance. She showed personal courage during the revolution, but was executed in 1793.

French Revolution

◀ MARCH TO VERSAILLES
In October 1789, the poor women of Paris led an angry mob to the royal palace of Versailles and demanded bread for their hungry families. The king agreed to their demands, but the crowd grew and fighting broke out. The next day the king was forced to return to Paris.

MAXIMILIEN DE ROBESPIERRE
1758–1794

Robespierre became one of the most radical leaders of the revolution. He whipped up a climate of fear, and soon his opponents were being sent to the guillotine. He himself was seized and beheaded without trial in 1794.

REIGN OF TERROR

The French Revolution succeeded in overthrowing a corrupt and unjust system of government, but it soon ran out of control. First, aristocrats were executed, and then the revolutionaries turned on each other in a bloodbath. The Reign of terror had begun, in which the state governed by fear.

◀ THE KING'S HEAD
King Louis XVI was accused of treason by the National Convention. He was executed in January 1793, ending over a thousand years of monarchy in France. The Revolutionaries' guillotines were claiming more and more victims.

HOW MANY PEOPLE DIED?
During the Reign of Terror (1793–1794), about 40,000 people were executed or murdered. A guillotine was set up in the Place de la Révolution in Paris. This wooden frame contained a sharp blade that dropped onto the victim's neck. Although it was supposed to be a humane method of execution, its efficiency meant that hundreds were dying every day.

WHEN DID THE TERROR END?
The creator of the Reign of Terror, Robespierre, was seized by his opponents in the National Convention and beheaded in 1794. In 1795 there were major uprisings. Order was restored by a soldier named Napoleon Bonaparte. Power passed to a five-man group called the Directory, and by 1799 Napoleon had seized power for himself. The revolution was over.

FIND OUT MORE ▸▸ Monarchy 410 • Napoleonic Wars 416

THE ENLIGHTENMENT

Scientific advances of the 17th and 18th centuries encouraged new ideas, and this led European philosophers to declare that humans progressed by using reason and logic, rather than faith or superstition. This period became known as the Enlightenment, or Age of Reason.

A statue of Wisdom replaced a statue of Atheism

Enlightenment

◄ A NEW RELIGION?
In 1794, Robespierre organized a festival of the Supreme Being. Although he was not an atheist, he disliked the rituals and doctrines of the Church.

WHO PUT TOGETHER A GREAT BOOK OF KNOWLEDGE?
New information systems were needed for this new age. Dictionaries began to appear, and a 28-volume encyclopedia, edited by Denis Diderot, was published in France in 1751–1772. Its contributors included thinkers such as Montesquieu, Rousseau, and Voltaire.

WHO ABOLISHED CHRISTMAS?
In 1793, the French National Convention passed a series of anti-Christian laws and forbade what it regarded as superstitious festivals. A new calendar was drawn up, one that began not with the birth of Christ but with a current human event, the French Revolution.

FIND OUT MORE ▶▶ Scientific Revolution 411

NAPOLEONIC WARS

During the French Revolution, France was at war with its neighbors in Europe. These wars resumed in 1799 under the leadership of Napoleon, who was crowned French emperor in 1804. A series of great victories soon brought much of Europe under his control.

Napoleonic Wars

WHERE DID NAPOLEON'S ARMIES MARCH?
Napoleon was a brilliant soldier. He defeated Austria. He invaded Spain in 1808 and his armies reached Moscow in 1812, only to be beaten back by the harsh winter weather. He made his relatives rulers in Spain, Italy, and the Netherlands. He was finally defeated by Britain and Prussia at Waterloo, Belgium, in 1815.

WHAT WAS NAPOLEON'S LEGACY?
Napoleon (1769–1821) died in exile. He is remembered as the man who brought the French Revolution to a close and as a military genius. He was a skilled administrator whose system of law, the *Code Napoléon*, gave the poor people of France some of the rights they had demanded in the revolution. The *Code* was also welcomed in many of the lands he invaded.

EUROPE AT WAR		
1805	●	French victory at Austerlitz
1805	●	British victory at Trafalgar
1808–1814	●	Peninsular War
1812	●	France invades Russia
1815	●	Napoleon defeated

A CORSICAN HERO ►
Napoleon Bonaparte came from the Mediterranean island of Corsica. He was a hero to his followers and his troops, but aroused fear among his enemies in countries such as Britain.

CANADA

European fishermen and fur traders visited Canada from the 16th century onward. They bought furs from the local people, who were related to the other native peoples of North America. France established colonies in Canada in 1608 (Quebec) and 1642 (Montreal), while the British claimed a vast territory around Hudson Bay after 1670.

JACQUES CARTIER
1491–1557

This French navigator made three voyages to North America between 1534 and 1541. He was the first European to see the St. Lawrence River and claimed the land for France.

▼ DEATH OF THE GENERALS
The British general James Wolfe lies dying in 1759, having captured Quebec and defeated the French. The French general, Montcalm, was also killed.

Canadian history

WHO FOUGHT TO CONTROL CANADA?
The French and British fought each other for Canada. Both wanted its furs, lumber, and rich fishing grounds. The French were defeated in 1759, and Canada became a British colony four years later. Many American colonists who had remained loyal to Britain during the American Revolution fled to Canada in the 1780s.

Both armies used native warriors as scouts and guides

WHEN DID CANADA BECOME A NATION?
In 1791, the areas of Canada settled by Europeans were divided between Upper (English-speaking) and Lower (French-speaking) Canada. These were reunited in 1841. Canada became a self-governing dominion of the British Empire in 1867. Settlement spread westward as Europeans arrived.

FIND OUT MORE ▶▶ Canada, Alaska and Greenland 224–225

INDIAN WARS

For much of the 19th century, especially between 1860 and 1890, a tragic conflict took place in the United States. Settlers and soldiers fought against American Indians. They seized their lands and herded the American Indians onto parcels of land known as reservations.

◀ GHOST DANCE
In 1890, many Indians on reservations had strange visions. They began to perform a magical "ghost dance," which they believed would return their land to them. It did not. Many were later gunned down or died of disease.

WHAT WAS THE TRAIL OF TEARS?
In the 1830s, gold was found in Cherokee territory in the southeastern US. About 16,000 Cherokees from the region were rounded up by the US army and forced to travel west in 1838 on a "Trail of Tears." Over 4,000 Cherokees died on the journey.

WHAT WAS CUSTER'S LAST STAND?
In 1876, General George Custer led the United States Seventh Cavalry into the prairie lands around the Little Bighorn River in Montana. Stumbling upon a big assembly of Sioux and Cheyenne warriors, Custer's force was defeated and killed. It was the last American Indian victory.

Indian Wars

INDUSTRIAL REVOLUTION

The Industrial Revolution changed the way things were made as new machines invented in the 1700s and 1800s meant it was possible to mass produce goods in factories. Starting in Britain and spreading through Europe and North America, a period of rapid social and economic change began, with widespread ▸▸URBANIZATION.

▲ STEAM HAMMER
During the 1830s and 40s, James Naysmith of Manchester, England, developed a massive steam-powered hammer.

▲ CITY SLUMS
The growth of cities during the 19th and 20th centuries meant many families in Europe lived in run-down, unhealthy housing.

▲ ON THE BRIGHT SIDE
Technology transformed public life after the 1880s. Electric street lamps lit up cities in Europe and North America.

▲ THE GREAT EXHIBITION
This international showcase for manufacture and trade was held in London in 1851, in a glass building called the Crystal Palace.

HOW WERE FACTORIES POWERED?

During the 18th century, water was an important source of power for industry, and many machines were driven by waterwheels. Steam power was also developed at this time. Steam engines were used to pump water out of mine shafts and to power new ▸▸TRANSPORTATION systems. Engines and furnaces were all fueled by coal. By the 19th century, coal was being transported to the factories by ship or rail.

WHY WERE GOODS MASS PRODUCED?

Before the Industrial Revolution, most goods were produced in small workshops or at home. Mass production in factories made it possible to manufacture goods more cheaply and quickly. Huge markets for these goods were opening up in the new cities, and in the lands that the European nations were conquering and settling overseas.

HOW DID WORKING CONDITIONS CHANGE?

The factory age meant that workers no longer owned the means by which they made a living. Some factory owners pushed up their own profits by pushing down the wages of their workers. Men, women, and children worked long hours for little pay, often in dangerous conditions. It took many years for wages and working environments to improve.

ISAMBARD KINGDOM BRUNEL
1806–1859
Brunel was born of a French father in Portsmouth, England. An engineering genius, he helped to shape the industrial age. He built tunnels, docks, and suspension bridges. He was appointed chief engineer of England's Great Western Railway and also designed steamships for crossing the Atlantic Ocean.

Work in a textile mill could be monotonous and noisy

Industrial Revolution

KING COTTON ▶
This photograph of a spinning mill in the United States dates from about 1890. New technology for spinning and weaving had marked the start of the Industrial Revolution in the 18th century. The 19th century saw cotton become the chief industrial textile. It was often produced in mills in Manchester, England, with raw cotton imported from the southern United States or India.

Children worked in factories and often went barefoot

▲ WORKERS UNITED
London dockers strike in 1889. The appalling working conditions of the early Industrial Revolution gradually improved as workers banded together in trade unions and campaigned for better wages. Some were socialists or communists, demanding political reform or revolution.

TRANSPORTATION

The Industrial Revolution depended on transportation to move materials, goods, and people. Canals were dug in the 18th century. In the 19th, it was the turn of the railroads.

WHEN DID THE RAILROAD AGE BEGIN?
The first steam locomotive to run on rails was seen in Wales in 1804. Designs were greatly improved in the 1820s by English rail pioneer George Stephenson. Railroads were soon opening up the world.

▲ ACROSS THE US
Locomotives belch smoke at a busy junction in the US in 1886. Railroads opened up new continents, crossing Europe, Asia, Africa, South America, and Australia. Railroad companies made huge fortunes.

URBANIZATION

Urbanization means the spread of towns. Between 1700 and 1900 the world's population grew from 679 million to 1.633 billion. Many people were city-dwellers.

WHAT KINDS OF CITIES WERE BUILT?
Cities grew up around coalfields or factories, at important seaports and railroad crossings. They provided cheap housing for the industrial workers. New British cities were often rows of row houses built of brick and slate, with small yards and alleys.

▲ GLASGOW SKYLINE
Smoke from factory chimneys darkens the sky in Glasgow. This Scottish city grew rapidly after the Clyde River was deepened in 1768, making it more accessible to shipping.

SOUTH AMERICAN INDEPENDENCE

The American empires founded by Spain and Portugal broke up in the 19th century. These European countries were no longer powerful, and their colonies struggled to break away. Wars brought liberation, but independence was often followed by strife between the new nations.

WHO WAS KNOWN AS THE LIBERATOR?

Simón Bolívar, "the Liberator," helped to free much of South America. He fought in Venezuela and ruled Colombia and Ecuador. He freed Peru, and Bolivia was renamed in his honor. Other freedom fighters included Bernardo O'Higgins and José de San Martín, who fought in Argentina, Chile, and Peru.

WHO ENDED PORTUGUESE RULE IN BRAZIL?

When Portugal was invaded by the French emperor Napoleon in 1807, the Portuguese royal family fled to their colony of Brazil. King John VI returned home in 1821, leaving his son Pedro to rule Brazil for him, but in 1822, Pedro declared himself to be emperor of an independent Brazil.

WHEN DID ARGENTINA BECOME INDEPENDENT?

The capital city of Argentina, Buenos Aires (meaning "fair winds"), was founded by the Spanish in the 16th century. In 1810, its people rose up against Spanish rule, gaining their independence in 1816. There followed a civil war between the city-dwellers and the ranchers of the provinces. The country was finally united in 1852.

WHAT WERE SOUTH AMERICA'S NEW ECONOMIES?

In the 19th century, South America's gold and silver mines began to run out. A new source of wealth was needed. In Brazil, plantations of coffee and rubber were set up, while Argentina's grasslands supported sheep and cattle. When refrigeration was invented, huge amounts of beef were exported from Buenos Aires.

▲ GAUCHOS OF ARGENTINA
The Gauchos were Argentine cowboys of part Spanish, part Indian descent. These daring, hard-living rogues opposed the new Buenos Aires government, backing their own leaders in a struggle for power.

The Spanish flag is given up to the victorious rebels

South American independence

◄ THE TURNING POINT
Bolivar was born in Venezuela. He defeated the Spanish at Carabobo in 1821. Venezuela, Ecuador, Colombia, and Panama all became part of an independent republic called Gran Colombia. Venezuela withdrew from this in 1829.

LIBERATION	
1816	Argentina declares independence
1818	San Martín liberates Chile
1819	Gran Colombia is founded
1821	Peru gains independence
	Venezuela and Ecuador are liberated
1822	Brazil annexes Uruguay
	Brazil breaks away from Portugal
1825	Bolivia is liberated

FIND OUT MORE ▶▶ South America 232–233

NATIONALISM

Nationalism means the wish of a people to govern themselves as a nation. This ideal reshaped the map of Europe in the 19th century. Later in the century, nationalism took on a second meaning—an exaggerated belief in the superiority of one's own nation.

WHY WAS POLAND IN REVOLT?
Between 1772 and 1795, Poland was divided among Russia, Prussia, and Austria. There were nationalist uprisings against the Russians in 1830 and 1863, but independence was not regained until 1918.

▲ THE GREEKS RISE UP
This postage stamp commemorates the 150th anniversary of the Greek uprising (1821-1827) against Turkish rule. The savage response of the Turks gained the Greek rebels sympathy across Europe.

WHEN DID GERMANY COME INTO BEING?
Since the Middle Ages, Germany had been a patchwork of free cities and small states within the Holy Roman Empire. In the 1800s, these gradually came together, economically, then politically. In 1871, Wilhelm I of Prussia became emperor of a united Germany.

NEW NATIONS	
1830–1831	Nationalist agitation; calls for democratic reform across Europe
1832	Greece recognized as independent from Turkey
1848	Nationalist and liberal uprisings across Europe
1871	Germany unites as an empire
1871	Italy becomes a single nation

IRISH BOMB BLAST ▶
Ireland became part of the United Kingdom in 1801. A nationalist organization, the Irish Republican Brotherhood (or "Fenians"), was founded in New York in 1857 to campaign for a free Ireland. It launched attacks in Manchester and London in 1867.

The red shirt became a symbol of freedom

WHO WERE THE REDSHIRTS?
Giuseppe Garibaldi (1807-1882) dreamed of uniting Italy and freeing it from foreign rule. In 1860 he assembled 1,000 volunteers, who wore red shirts as a uniform. They sailed from Genoa to Sicily and joined an uprising against that kingdom's French rulers. They then crossed to southern Italy. Garibaldi later tried to march on Rome, and fought against Austria.

◀ ITALIAN FREEDOM FIGHTER
Garibaldi leads his Redshirts into battle. As a young man, Garibaldi had joined the "Young Italy" movement. Forced to flee to South America, he fought against dictatorship and injustice there before returning to Italy in 1848.

OTTO VON BISMARCK
1815–1898
Bismarck was a Prussian politician, a conservative and a royalist. He opposed the liberal nationalists who demanded democratic change in Germany in 1848, but played a major role in creating the German Empire of 1871.

nationalism

FIND OUT MORE ▶▶ Holy Roman Empire 385 • Thirty Years' War 406

AGE OF EMPIRE

From the 19th century until the early 20th, much of the world was governed by a few very powerful European nations. The ▶ BRITISH RAJ controlled the riches of India. The ▶ FRENCH FOREIGN LEGION defended remote forts in the Sahara desert, and there was a ▶ SCRAMBLE FOR AFRICA by empire-builders.

WHY DID EUROPEANS WANT TO RULE THE WORLD?
The reasons were many. The factories of the newly industrialized lands needed resources, such as rubber. Some empire-builders wanted land for settlement; others were praying for converts to Christianity.

HOW WERE PEOPLE TREATED BY THEIR RULERS?
Most empire-builders claimed to be bringing civilization to peoples whom they believed to be inferior. Although the ruling countries did build towns, ports, and railroads, in some colonies the local peoples were treated little better than slaves.

THE WORLD IN 1900 ▶
The chief empire-builders were the French, British, Germans, Danish, Belgians, Dutch, Spanish, and Portuguese. The United States and Japan were also gaining overseas territories. The Russian Empire now ruled the whole of northern Asia. However, the Chinese Empire was losing territory to foreign powers.

BRITISH RAJ

By the 19th century, real power in India was held by the British East India Company. Following an uprising by Indian soldiers in 1857, British government rule, or Raj, was imposed on India in 1858.

WHO BECAME EMPRESS OF INDIA?
Queen Victoria (1819–1901) was declared Empress of India in 1876. Under her rule, Great Britain became the world's most powerful nation. Victoria had a shrewd grasp of politics and took a close interest in her government's foreign policy. India was one of the most important parts of the British Empire. The two countries had a great cultural influence on each other.

◀ VICTORIA AT WORK
Queen Victoria, Empress of India, is attended by her Indian servant as she writes letters and reads state papers in 1893.

SCRAMBLE FOR AFRICA

As explorers discovered new lands in Africa, European powers rushed in to take them over. The French clashed with the British in Sudan, and the Germans gained lands in East and West Africa.

WHAT HAPPENED IN BERLIN IN 1884?
In 1884–1885, the world's most powerful nations held a conference in Berlin, the capital of Germany. They divided between themselves vast regions of Africa. They knew little of these distant lands and did not consult the peoples living there. Borders were drawn up to serve their own political needs.

STANLEY FINDS LIVINGSTONE ▶
David Livingstone was a Scottish missionary and explorer who wanted to open trading routes through Africa. Held up by illness in 1871, Livingstone was found by H.M. Stanley, an explorer hired by the *New York Herald* paper.

THE WORLD IN 1900

	Ottoman Empire
	Britain and possessions
	France and possessions
	Denmark and possessions
	Spain and possessions
	Portugal and possessions
	Netherlands and possessions
	German Empire and possessions
○	Russian Empire and possessions
	Japan and possessions
	Italy and possessions
	US and possessions
	Independent nations
○	settlement symbol
◇	colonial possession

age of empire

EMPIRE 1800–1918

1824	Dutch and British divide southeast Asian territories
1883– 1885	Germany gains colonies in Africa and Pacific
1885	Belgian rule in the Congo
1887	French rule Indochina
1899– 1902	Second South African ("Boer") War
1904	Federation of French West Africa
1918	German and Ottoman empires broken up after defeat in World War I

◄ **SOLDIERS OF THE EMPIRE**
Foreign legionnaires and other foot soldiers serving in the great empires had to put up with harsh conditions, tropical fevers, and long absences from their home country.

FRENCH FOREIGN LEGION

Empires needed large armies to suppress rebellions or fight rival powers. The Foreign Legion was formed by the French in 1831 to fight in colonial wars. It was recruited from foreigners and gained a reputation for tough discipline.

WHERE DID THE LEGIONNAIRES FIGHT?
They fought wherever France needed them in their empire. The Legion was most famously associated with desert campaigns in North Africa. French territory stretched all the way from Algeria south to the Congo River. France also ruled Madagascar, French Guiana, and islands in the Caribbean, Indian Ocean, and South Pacific.

AMERICAN CIVIL WAR

In 1860 and 1861, a group of southern states, known as the Confederacy, withdrew from the United States. A civil war began when the Confederates attacked a federal fort in Charleston, South Carolina. In 1865, the Union defeated the Confederacy in this fierce conflict.

▲ BATTLE OF THE "IRONCLADS"
Armor-plated ships known as "ironclads" exchange fire off Virginia in 1862. The Union's goal was to stop ships from supplying the Confederacy.

WHY DID THE STATES FIGHT EACH OTHER?
The northern states were building an industrial economy. The agricultural southern states still relied on slave labor. They resented the increasing power of the north and feared that the federal government in Washington would impose reforms and end slavery.

HOW MANY PEOPLE DIED?
The US was reunited at a terrible cost. The northern troops lost 359,000 soldiers, while the southerners lost 258,000. Civilians suffered from looting and from the devastation of railroads, towns, and cotton plantations.

WHAT WAS THE UNDERGROUND RAILROAD?
This was a secret network of escape routes and hideouts for African American slaves. Between 1786 and 1861, activists such as Harriet Tubman (c. 1820–1913) helped about 50,000 slaves escape to freedom in the northern states and Canada.

DID THE CIVIL WAR END SLAVERY IN THE US?
Abraham Lincoln proclaimed an end to slavery in 1863, and it was finally abolished in the southern states after the war. African Americans remained poor, and the southern states passed laws that prevented them from voting or gaining equal status despite constitutional amendments guaranteeing these rights.

ABRAHAM LINCOLN
1809-1865

Lincoln was elected President in 1860 and again in 1864. He supported strong federal government and opposed slavery. Having led the Union to victory in the Civil War, he was assassinated at a theater in Washington, D.C., in 1865.

◄ UNDER FIRE
This howitzer (a short cannon) was the most common artillery piece used in the Civil War.

GRANT VERSUS LEE ►
In 1864, the Union general Ulysses S. Grant clashed with the Confederate general Robert E. Lee in a bid to capture Spotsylvania Court House in northern Virginia. Casualties were heavy. The battle was a draw.

American Civil War

AUSTRALIA

The coasts of Australia were first mapped by Dutch explorers in the 17th century and by the British in the 18th. In 1788, the British founded a colony in New South Wales and went on to settle the rest of this vast land.

JAMES COOK
1728–1779
Captain Cook was a brilliant English navigator who explored the coasts of Australia and New Zealand. He landed at Botany Bay in New South Wales in 1778 and claimed the land for Britain. Cook was killed in Hawaii by natives of the islands.

WHY WERE CONVICTS SENT TO AUSTRALIA?
From 1788 until 1852, the British sent criminals to Australia for punishment. The new country was built with forced labor. Free settlers were soon arriving also, to seek their fortune—especially after gold was discovered in 1851.

WHAT HAPPENED TO THE ABORIGINALS?
About two million Aboriginals lived in Australia in 1788. By 1900 only 50,000 survived. Many died of diseases introduced by the settlers. Others were murdered or driven off their land. Some worked as police trackers, or as laborers on sheep stations.

Australian history

WHEN DID AUSTRALIA BECOME A NATION?
The various colonies founded in Australia by the British were mostly granted self-rule in the 1850s. There was great rivalry between them, but they finally agreed to unite as states within a single federal Commonwealth in 1901.

ABORIGINAL FISHERS ►
Aboriginal hunters and fishers could survive in the harshest environments, but they only just survived the European invasion and the long years of suffering that followed.

FIND OUT MORE ►► Australia and New Zealand 274–275 • Exploration 400–401 • First Modern Humans 362–363

NEW ZEALAND

New Zealand is known to the Maoris as Aotearoa. Dutch and English navigators charted these islands, and by the 19th century, traders and whaling crews were landing there. The islands came under British rule in 1840.

New Zealand history

TREATY OF WAITANGI ►
In 1840, the British signed a treaty with a gathering of Maori chiefs on North Island. It guaranteed Maori rights to the land, but these were ignored by the settlers.

WHEN DID NEW ZEALAND GAIN SELF-RULE?
Britain granted the colonists self-rule in 1852. The country prospered from sheep farming and from the discovery of gold in 1862. In 1893, New Zealand became the first country to give women the vote. In 1907, it became a Dominion, a fully independent nation within the British Empire.

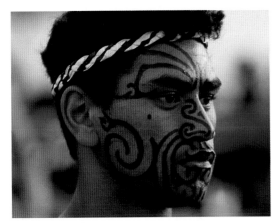

▲ MAORI TRADITION
The Maoris are descended from Polynesians who colonized Aotearoa about a thousand years before the arrival of the Europeans. They remain fiercely proud of their culture and its traditions.

WHAT BECAME OF THE MAORIS?
The Maoris had possessed firearms since the arrival of the first foreigners. After 1840, the settlers seized more and more land, so between 1845 and 1847, the Maoris rose up in revolt. A second war took place from 1860 to 1872. This won the Maoris representation in the New Zealand Parliament.

FIND OUT MORE ►► Australia and New Zealand 274–275 • Polynesia 396

WORLD WAR I

World War I (1914–1918) was the first war in history to be fought by many different nations around the world. About eight million men were killed, many in horrific ▶ TRENCH WARFARE, before the ▶ ARMISTICE in 1918.

Entente Powers and allies	Neutral Powers	Central Powers and allies	Greatest advance of Central Powers	xxxx Front lines November 1918	

▲ WAR ACROSS THE REGIONS
Europe lay at the center of the fighting. Troops came here from as far away as Africa, India, New Zealand, Australia, and Canada. The Western Front stretched from Belgium to Switzerland. The Eastern Front extended from the Baltic to the Black Sea. There was an Arab revolt against the Ottoman Empire in 1917, and Britain invaded most of the Middle East.

Guns fired from side turrets

▲ TANKS INTO BATTLE
Tanks were a British invention. They appeared in 1916 and were first used on a large scale in battle at Cambrai, France, in 1917. Tanks were armor-plated. Their treads could cross muddy trenches and crash through barbed wire.

WHY DID WAR BREAK OUT?
In the 20th century, European nations formed competing military alliances. War finally broke out in 1914 when a Serbian nationalist assassinated the heir to the throne of Austria. Austria went to war against Serbia, and many other countries joined in. On one side were the British, the French and Russian empires, Italy, and Japan (the Entente Powers). On the other side were the Germans, Austrians, Hungarians, Bulgarians, and Turks (the Central Powers).

WAR AND PEACE

1914	Germany invades Belgium in order to attack France
1915	Gallipoli offensive in Turkey; Italy joins the Entente
1916	Naval battle off Jutland, Denmark
1917	US enters the war on the side of the Entente; Russia leaves the war; Italy defeated by the Austrians; Arabs revolt against Turks
1918	Armistice ends the war

TRENCH WARFARE

In World War I, both sides dug long trenches as lines of defense, which stretched across Western Europe. These trenches filled up with stinking mud. Any order to go "over the top" and attack the enemy resulted in thousands of deaths.

WHERE WAS NO MAN'S LAND?
The territory between the two front lines was called "no man's land." It was a sea of mud, with broken stumps of trees and barbed wire entanglements. The area was raked by machine gun fire and pounded by heavy artillery, leaving craters big enough for soldiers to drown in.

DEATH IN GALLIPOLI ▶
The Gallipoli campaign between the Entente Powers and Turkey in 1915 included some of the worst trench fighting of the war. The campaign was a failure and cost the lives of many Australians and New Zealanders.

WHAT NEW WEAPONS WERE USED IN ACTION?

Various new technologies were available. In 1915, the German army used poison gas for the first time in warfare, and it was soon in general use. The British were the first to introduce the battle tank. Submarines were now able to torpedo enemy shipping, forcing ships to travel across the ocean in convoys. Aircraft and airships were used to drop bombs, spy on enemy positions, and attack enemy pilots.

WHAT WAS TOTAL WAR?

This was war on a scale never experienced before. It was not just fought by professional soldiers. Most of the troops were civilian conscripts, called up to serve in the armed forces. Ordinary homes in cities such as London were bombed from the air. Even ocean liners carrying passengers from neutral countries came under attack. Entire national economies were geared to the war effort.

▲ WOMEN GO TO WORK
A woman operates machinery at a munitions factory. In wartime, women had to take on work that only men had done before. Their proven abilities helped them to gain the vote after the war.

◄ "THE YANKS ARE COMING!"
On a poster, "Uncle Sam" calls on Americans to enlist in the army. Angered by German submarine activity, the US joined the war in 1917. The arrival of fresh troops at this point in the war hastened the defeat of the Germans.

World War I

WILFRED OWEN
1893–1918
Many young men on both sides of the conflict, who had been idealists in 1914, became horrified by the war and its cruelty. One of them was the English war poet Wilfred Owen, killed just a week before the Armistice.

ARMISTICE

An armistice is a laying down of weapons. The guns of World War I finally fell silent at 11am on the 11th day of the 11th month of 1918.

DID PEACE FOLLOW WAR?

No; in Germany there was street fighting and starvation. In 1919, the terms of the peace were agreed upon at Versailles, in France. The settlement was harsh on Germany, and this resulted in a sense of grievance that undermined any lasting peace.

▲ A LOST GENERATION
In war cemeteries across northern France, gravestones stretch as far as the eye can see. The war almost destroyed a whole generation. Of those who survived, many were left blind, disabled, or suffering from shock.

REVOLUTIONARY RUSSIA

By the 1890s, many European nations were bringing in democratic reforms, but not Russia. Angry about social injustice, many Russians looked to socialism, anarchism, or ▶▶ COMMUNISM for an answer.

▲ CZAR NICHOLAS II AND HIS FAMILY
Nicholas II (1868–1918) came to the throne in 1895, but occupied himself with family life and failed to deal with Russia's growing problems. After the October Revolution of 1917, he and his family were imprisoned and then shot.

WHEN WAS BLOODY SUNDAY IN ST. PETERSBURG?

In 1905, troops in St. Petersburg gunned down workers who wished to present a petition to the czar. This action resulted in strikes, mutinies, and uprisings all over Russia. As a result, a Duma, or parliament, was set up. However, the reforms it demanded were rejected by the czar.

WHO OVERTHREW THE CZAR?

In March 1917, strikes, mutinies, and protests brought Russia to a standstill. Russian troops fighting in World War I deserted the Eastern Front. The czar was forced from power and Russia became a republic. This became known as the February Revolution (Russia followed a different calendar than Western countries).

WHEN WAS THE OCTOBER REVOLUTION?

The republican Duma failed to bring the chaos in Russia under control. A communist group known as the "Bolsheviks" rejected attempts at liberal reform. They appealed directly to workers to rise up in a communist revolution. The Bolsheviks seized power in "October" (that is, November) 1917.

▲ LENIN'S CALL
Vladimir Ilyich Lenin (1870–1924) returned from exile in 1917. He called for power to be handed over to soviets (councils of revolutionary workers). After the October Revolution, he led the governing Communist Party.

COMMUNISM

Communists around the world were inspired by the writings of Karl Marx (1818–1883). Marx believed history was driven by economic forces and that a just and progressive society could only be created if the workers took control of the economic system.

WHEN WAS THE SOVIET UNION FOUNDED?

In 1918–1920, civil war raged through Russia as the communist Red Army fought opponents of the revolution ("the Whites"). The communists won, and a Union of Soviet Socialist Republics ("Soviet Union") was founded in 1922. Only the Communist Party held power. Most industries came under state ownership, and the economy was centrally controlled.

revolutionary Russia

◀ MAY DAY, 1920
A poster for International Workers' Day (or May Day) shows an idealized group of revolutionaries. At this time, communist parties were being founded in many countries.

WHO WAS STALIN?

Lenin's successor was Joseph Stalin (1879–1953). His secret police murdered many of his opponents and millions were sent to forced labor camps. Stalin was criticized after his death, but the Soviet system failed to reform and collapsed in 1991.

REVOLUTIONARY CHINA

By the late 19th century, the Chinese Empire was growing weak, and foreign nations were controlling its trade. In 1912 the last emperor, Puyi, was overthrown after a nationalist revolution. Many years of turmoil followed.

▲ MAO ZEDONG'S VICTORY
This poster dates from 1949, the year in which the People's Republic of China was founded. It shows the communist leader Mao Zedong in front of Beijing's Imperial Palace, with workers united together.

WHO CONTROLLED CHINA AFTER THE REVOLUTION?
Many forces fought to control China. First there were the nationalists, who founded a republic in 1912. Then there were the generals and regional warlords and, in 1921, the Chinese Communist Party. Finally, there was Japan, which gained Chinese territory in 1919.

CHINA 1912–1949	
1912	Chinese republic founded
1919	Japan gains Shandong
1931	Japan occupies Manchuria
1934–1935	The Long March
1937–1945	Japan invades China
1949	Communist victory

revolutionary China

◄ HARMONIOUS FIST SOCIETY
In 1900, this nationalist organization (also known as "the Boxers") attacked foreigners living in China. Lurid reports were used to justify intervention by an international force, which suppressed the rebellion.

WHO WON THE STRUGGLE?
After 1925, Chiang Kai-Shek became nationalist leader. Nationalists and communists became rivals but were forced into alliances as Japan overran China. Japan's defeat in 1945 was followed by civil war. By 1949, the communists had defeated the nationalists.

WHAT WAS "NEW CHINA"?
The nationalists fled to Taiwan, and the communist leader Mao Zedong proclaimed a people's republic. Its successes in the 1950s included better education, literacy, and health. However, unrealistic agricultural and industrial reforms caused hardship, leading to political chaos during the ▶▶ CULTURAL REVOLUTION.

CULTURAL REVOLUTION

Economic failures caused dispute within the Chinese Communist Party. Fearing that the ideals of the revolution would be lost, Mao Zedong called for a "cultural revolution," a change in public attitudes.

WHO WERE THE RED GUARDS?
Students and young people took up Mao's ideas with fervor. They declared themselves "Red Guards," dedicated to never-ending revolution. They tore down temples, denounced their teachers, and rooted out "traitors." The suffering was immense. By 1967, the regular army was clashing with the Red Guards, and Mao had little choice but to disband them in 1968.

DID CHINA REMAIN COMMUNIST?
When Mao died in 1976 there was a struggle for power. In the years that followed, China was still governed by the Communist Party, but it started to adopt some capitalist economic policies.

ALL TOGETHER NOW ▶
Chinese soldiers recite famous quotations of Mao Zedong. In the 1960s everything Mao did was publicly praised. There were pictures and statues of him everywhere. However, his political enemies were biding their time.

Red star represents communism

The Little Red Book of Mao's thoughts was brandished at mass rallies

FIND OUT MORE ▶▶ China's First Empire 378 • Imperial China 393

ASIAN CONFLICT

Asian conflict

The first half of the 20th century saw Great Britain, France, and the Netherlands being challenged by the peoples they ruled in south and southeast Asia. At the same time, Japan was trying to take the place of the Europeans and create its own Asian empire.

HOW DID GANDHI FIGHT FOR FREEDOM?

When Indian nationalists were demanding self-rule, one of the leading campaigners against the British was Mohandas K. Gandhi (1869–1948). Instead of calling for an uprising, Gandhi used nonviolent methods of protest. He lived very simply and called for India to return to the traditional values of village life. He became known as Mahatma or "great soul." With his influence, India became independent in August 1947. However, he was assassinated in 1948.

WHEN DID JAPAN BECOME POWERFUL?

After the restoration of the emperor's power in 1868, Japan turned itself into an industrial nation. It defeated Russia in 1904–1905 and annexed Korea in 1910. In 1919, it gained former German territories in Asia. During the 1930s, extremists and the military planned Japan's invasion of China. During World War II (1940s), Japanese armies finally swept through southeast Asia.

ASIA 1920–1942	
1920–1922	Gandhi leads Indian National Congress Campaign
1926–1942	Nationalist agitation in Indochina
1940	Japan occupies French Indochina
1941	The Vietminh founded

PEACEFUL PROTEST ▶
In 1930, Gandhi broke the law by marching to the sea to collect salt. Only the British were allowed to produce salt.

FIND OUT MORE ▶ Age of Empire 422–423 • Revolutionary China 429

THE DEPRESSION

An economic depression is a period of falling prices, low production of goods, and high unemployment. The Great Depression of 1929–1934 caused hardship in the United States, in the countries of Europe, and in their overseas empires. Banks closed and firms went out of business.

WHAT WAS THE WALL STREET CRASH?

In 1929, US investors found that their shares of stock had become worthless. All trading ceased on Wall Street, New York City's financial district, as the New York Stock Exchange crashed. Fortunes were lost overnight and factories laid off workers.

HOW WIDESPREAD WAS THE DEPRESSION?

The 1920s and 1930s were already desperate times in Australia and New Zealand, in Great Britain, and across Europe. When an Austrian bank collapsed, chaos spread to central Europe. Germany was struggling, too, as it tried to recover from World War I and pay money to France as reparation for the war.

▲ MONEY FOR PLAY
German children use wads of banknotes as toy bricks. The German currency lost value so quickly that one loaf of bread could cost millions of marks.

◀ BREADLINE
Hungry men line up for free soup at a public kitchen in New York City in 1931. By 1932 over 12 million Americans were out of work.

Depression

FASCISM

In 1922 a political movement called fascism grew up in Italy. It took its name from the fasces, an ax emblem that symbolized state power in Ancient Rome. Fascists believed in the authority of the state. Extremely nationalistic, they opposed democracy and communism.

FASCIST DICTATOR ▶
Benito Mussolini (1883-1945) marched on Rome in 1922 and became Italian dictator in 1925.

ADOLF HITLER
1889–1945

Austrian-born Adolf Hitler served in a German regiment during World War I. Embittered by defeat, he organized the Nazis and their seizure of power in Germany. As dictator, Hitler persecuted Jews and crushed opposition. His invasions of neighboring lands led to World War II.

WERE THERE FASCISTS IN OTHER COUNTRIES?

Fascism found supporters in many Western nations. It attracted people who were more worried about public order and unemployment than personal freedom. The National Socialist German Workers' Party was founded in 1920. The Falange, a fascist movement founded in 1933, took part in the ▶▶ SPANISH CIVIL WAR.

WHO WERE THE NAZIS?

Germany's National Socialists were known as Nazis. Their leader was Adolf Hitler. During the 1930s he provided work for the unemployed and built up Germany's forces illegally. Nazi thugs bullied, cheated, and murdered their way to power. They were extreme racists, consumed by hatred of the Jewish people.

▼ NUREMBERG, 1938
The Nazis staged huge political rallies, many of them in the city of Nuremberg. Here, soldiers march past carrying Nazi party banners bearing the words "Germany awake."

fascism

The swastika was an ancient symbol that the Nazis used to represent the "master race" of the "Aryan" peoples

SPANISH CIVIL WAR

▲ **FASCIST SALUTES**
Nazi salutes are given as Franco's troops take over the border town of Irún. German bombing of Spain outraged the world.

Civil war raged in Spain from 1936 to 1939. An alliance led by General Franco overthrew the elected government of the Spanish Republic. Franco's supporters were Falangists, conservatives, monarchists, and Catholics. Fighting for the government were socialists, communists, and regionalists.

WHO JOINED THE WAR?

Franco was backed by fascist Italy and Nazi Germany. Government forces received help from the Soviet Union and were backed by antifascist volunteers from all over Europe and the Americas. Many of these young idealists died fighting for Republican International Brigades. But the Republic fell, and Franco ruled Spain as dictator until his death in 1975.

▲ **"NO PASARÁN"**
"They shall not pass!" was the rallying cry of the Republic as Franco advanced on Madrid. Both men and women fought to the bitter end, but Franco did pass. This tragic war left Spain bitter and divided. Each town still remembers its suffering.

WORLD WAR II

In 1939, Nazi-ruled Germany invaded its neighboring countries, beginning a world war that left about 40 million people dead. Unlike World War I, this was high-speed warfare, or ▸▸BLITZKRIEG. It ended with the discovery of the terrible truth about the Nazi ▸▸HOLOCAUST and the unleashing of the ▸▸ATOM BOMB.

▲ EUROPE AND NORTH AFRICA INVADED
This map shows the advances of the Axis countries in the early years of the war. German troops overran much of Europe and North Africa. In many of the lands they occupied, such as France, the USSR, Yugoslavia, and Greece, there was ongoing resistance from nonmilitary fighters.

Axis territory 1939	Axis satellites	Non-Axis territory	Neutral states	— Axis advances

0 km 400 800
0 miles 400 800

HOW DID THE WAR BEGIN?
The military power of Germany grew unchecked, and in September 1939, it sent its tanks to invade Poland. Britain and France declared war against Hitler's Germany, but in 1940 he invaded the Netherlands, Belgium, France, Denmark, and Norway. Only a period of air warfare, the Battle of Britain, saved the United Kingdom from invasion.

World War II

Over 4,000 ships and landing craft took part in the operation

OPERATION OVERLORD ▶
The last phase of the war in Europe began on June 6, 1944 ("D-Day"). US, British, and Canadian troops landed by sea on the coast of Normandy, in occupied France.

▲ WAR IN THE PACIFIC
In 1941, Japan launched an unprovoked attack on Pearl Harbor, a US naval base in Hawaii. The US, the world's most powerful nation, entered the war. The Pacific conflict with Japan lasted nearly four years.

WHY WAS THIS A WORLD WAR?
The Allies included British, Australians, New Zealanders, Canadians, and South Africans, as well as exiled French and Poles. They were joined in 1941 by two giants—the Soviet Union and the US. The Axis alliance of Germany and Italy was extended to include Hungary, Romania, Bulgaria, and Japan.

WHEN DID THE TIDE TURN?
In 1942, the US smashed Japanese naval power at the Battle of Midway. Allied victories in North Africa allowed an advance through Italy in 1943. In heavy fighting on Europe's Eastern Front that year, the Russians defeated the Germans at Stalingrad. By 1945, the Allies were invading Germany from east and west.

A WORLD AT WAR	
1939	Germany invades Poland; Britain and France declare war
1940	Germany invades most of western Europe; Italy enters war
1941	Germany invades Yugoslavia, Greece, Soviet Union; Japan attacks USA
1942-1942	Japan invades southeast Asia and Pacific
1944	France liberated
1945	Allied victory

BLITZKRIEG

Blitzkrieg means "lightning war" in German. The term was first used in 1939 to describe the tactics of high-speed warfare that launched the Nazi invasion of Europe. It was made possible by new technology, weapons, and tactical thinking.

WINSTON CHURCHILL
1874–1965

Churchill had a long and controversial political career, which most people regarded as over in the years before the war. However, his outspoken opposition to Nazi Germany made him the ideal choice for prime minister in 1940. His determination, eloquence, and sense of humor made him a popular and successful leader.

WHAT WERE THE NEW WAYS OF WAGING WAR?

Blitzkrieg used fast tanks and aircraft to bypass ground defenses. Paratroops were dropped behind enemy lines. Civilians died in cities that were bombed. The British shortened blitzkrieg to "blitz" to describe the massive bombing of their cities. The Allies also adopted new tactics and bombed German cities into rubble. This war also saw the development of radar for detecting enemy aircraft, as well as flying bombs and rockets.

AIRBORNE TERROR ►
The German Ju-87 (Stuka) bomber was used to attack shipping, tanks, or fortifications. This terrifying machine could dive at an angle of 80°. It was used in the Battle of Britain and on the Eastern Front.

HOLOCAUST

The Holocaust ("sacrifice by burning") was an attempt to murder the entire Jewish people. German concentration camps had existed since the 1930s, but this act of genocide was accelerated by Nazi leaders at the Wannsee Conference in 1942. About six million Jews died.

156,000 troops crossed the English Channel

The assault was on five beaches along 50 miles (80 km) of coastal defenses

WHO DISCOVERED THE CONCENTRATION CAMPS?

In 1945, as Allied forces advanced, they found evidence of this monstrous crime. Jews from all over Europe had been rounded up, forced into cattle cars on trains, and taken to prison camps, along with other peoples the Nazis despised, such as Roma (Gypsies). Some victims were forced to work as slave labor; others were killed immediately in gas chambers.

▲ DEATH CAMP
From 1940 to 1945, Auschwitz, Poland, was the site of one of the worst death camps. Three to four million people, including Poles and Jews, were murdered there.

ATOM BOMB

Throughout the war, the US had secretly been developing the most destructive weapon ever known—the atom bomb. This produced energy by nuclear fission. In August 1945, US planes dropped two atom bombs on Japan which then surrendered.

WHY DID THE US DROP THE BOMB?

The United States government wished to bring the war to a rapid end and prevent the loss of any more troops. Critics of the bomb believed that the extent of its power, and the resulting loss of so many civilian lives, was morally unacceptable.

THE MUSHROOM CLOUD ►
Bombs were dropped on Hiroshima and Nagasaki. In Hiroshima, over 78,500 people died in one minute. Many victims died years later from the effects of radiation.

INTERNATIONAL ORGANIZATIONS

Nations have always formed alliances. In the 20th century, many new international organizations were set up worldwide for economic and political reasons, defense and peacekeeping, and health and welfare.

international organizations

WHY WAS THE UNITED NATIONS FOUNDED?
The League of Nations was founded in 1919 to keep the peace after World War I. But it failed to prevent World War II in 1939, so in 1945 the nations of the world set up a new organization, the United Nations (UN). Since then, the UN has encouraged international cooperation and worked to resolve conflict.

WHAT OTHER ALLIANCES WERE SET UP?
Some alliances have been political, such as the Arab League (1945) or the Organization of African Unity (1963–2002). The European Economic Community (1958) grew from a small trading alliance into the European Union. Military alliances included the North Atlantic Treaty Organization (1949–) and the Warsaw Pact (1955–1991).

THE OLIVE BRANCH ▶
The United Nations flag shows the world surrounded by olive branches, a symbol of peace. The UN has sent peacekeeping forces around the world.

FIND OUT MORE ▶▶ World War I 426–427 • World War II 432–433

DECOLONIZATION

After 1945, European nations began to give up their colonies. In some places, power was handed back to local people peacefully. White South Africans refused to share power, creating a system of ▶▶ APARTHEID .

WHEN DID WINDS OF CHANGE BLOW?
In 1960, the British Prime Minister Harold Macmillan made a speech in South Africa, declaring that a "wind of change" was blowing through the African continent. He meant that the age of empires and colonies was coming to an end. Today only a few colonies or "overseas territories" still exist.

FRENCH ALGERIA ▶
From 1954 to 1962, the French fought nationalist rebels in Algeria. This war caused great bitterness among the Algerians and French who lived in the colony. Independence was finally granted in 1962.

NELSON MANDELA
1918-

Nelson Mandela was a black lawyer who campaigned against apartheid. Imprisoned from 1964–1990, he became a symbol of resistance. After his release, he became South Africa's first black president.

APARTHEID

Apartheid is a word from the Afrikaans language that means "staying apart." It was the South African government's policy of racial separation from 1948 to 1994. White people, who made up only 14 percent of the population, refused to give the vote to black or Asian people. These peoples were denied basic rights and were not allowed to mix with the whites.

decolonization

WHAT WERE THE EFFECTS OF APARTHEID?
Black people were not permitted to live in areas reserved for whites. They were not even allowed to sit on the same benches. Many black people endured bad housing, poverty, and inadequate education. Black and white South Africans who protested against apartheid risked imprisonment or death.

WHEN DID APARTHEID END?
The end of apartheid came in 1994, when Nelson Mandela won South Africa's first democratic general election. This occasion marked the end of two centuries in which Europeans had attempted to rule the rest of the world. However, the newly independent nations of Africa still face many problems.

FIND OUT MORE ▶▶ Age of Empire 422–423

▲ PROTEST IN THE US
Protesters against the Vietnam War march through Washington, D.C., in 1969. Many people in the Western nations believed this war to be unjust, and large public demonstrations took place around the world.

COLD WAR

After World War II, allies who had fought fascism together became rivals for world power. From 1945 to 1990, there was a period of tension called the Cold War. Capitalist countries, led by the US, clashed with the communist countries of the Soviet Union and China.

CASTRO'S REVOLUTION ►
Revolutionary Fidel Castro overthrew the Cuban dictator Fulgencio Batista in 1959 and made Cuba a communist state.

Cold War

WHAT WAS THE CUBAN MISSILE CRISIS?
Both sides in the Cold War were heavily armed with nuclear weapons. In 1962, the Soviet Union secretly stationed missiles in communist Cuba. The US found out and demanded that the missiles be removed. The Soviet Union gave in, and the world narrowly avoided a nuclear war.

WHAT WAS THE IRON CURTAIN?
World War II had left communist governments in control of central and eastern Europe. They were opposed by the nations of western Europe and the United States. The two hostile sides, or "blocs," became isolated from each other. In a speech, British politician Winston Churchill said that it was as if an "iron curtain" had fallen across Europe.

WHAT WAS THE VIETNAM WAR?
In 1954, the French colonial army in Vietnam was defeated by communist rebels. The country was divided into North and South Vietnam, and the US intervened to support an anticommunist government in the South. During the 1960s, troops were sent to fight the communists. They failed to defeat them, and Vietnam united under communist rule in 1975.

FIND OUT MORE ►► Eastern Asia 268–269 • World War II 432–433

MIDDLE EAST

The Middle East saw much conflict during the last century. Its deserts contain the world's biggest oil fields, which have brought wealth to the area's rulers but also colonial interference and wars.

▼ THE SIX-DAY WAR
This war in 1967 was the third of many fought between Israel and its Arab neighbors. Israel won, occupying large areas of Arab territory. The war left 300,000 Palestinians refugees.

Middle East

WHAT IS THE PALESTINE PROBLEM?
In 1948, the UN made part of Palestine into the Jewish nation of Israel. Jewish people returned to their traditional homeland, but many displaced Palestinian Arabs became refugees. The struggle between Israelis and Palestinians for this land continues.

WHY HAS THERE BEEN FIGHTING IN IRAQ?
In 1979, Saddam Hussein became president of Iraq. Iraq invaded Iran and occupied oil-rich Kuwait, which was liberated by a US-led coalition in 1991. In 2003, the US and Great Britain claimed that Hussein remained an international threat and invaded Iraq. Hussein was overthrown but those opposed to the American presence in Iraq continued to fight the USA and its allies.

FIND OUT MORE ►► International Organizations 434 • Nations 312 • War 313

HISTORY OF THE UNITED STATES

Native peoples lived throughout the Americas for centuries—arriving from Asia by a land bridge—and they developed complex, diverse cultures. The arrival of Europeans completely changed their way of life. Soon after Columbus landed in North America, other European explorers followed. Within a century, European countries were planning permanent colonies in North America.

c. 1000 CE Leif Eriksson is the first European to set foot in North America

c. 1400 Native tribes move into the southwest

1492 Christopher Columbus sails from Spain for Asia and lands in the West Indies

1513 Ponce de León claims Florida for Spain

1519–21 Hernán Cortés conquers the Aztec Empire

1532 Francisco Pizarro conquers the Inca Empire

1585–87 Two unsuccessful attempts are made to colonize Roanoke Island

1607 Jamestown founded

1620 Mayflower compact; Pilgrims found Plymouth

1621 First Thanksgiving

1660 King Charles II of England assigns land to be sold to colonists

1692 Salem witch trials

1754 Outbreak of French and Indian War

1763 Treaty of Paris ends French claims in North America

1779 Boston Massacre

1773 Tea Act; Rebellious colonists stage the Boston Tea Party

1774 The 13 colonies form First Continental Congress

1775–83 American Revolution begins at Lexington and Concord; ends after British surrender at Yorktown

July 4, 1776 Declaration of Independence signed

1781 Articles of Confederation ratified

1787 Constitution signed

1789 George Washington elected first US president

1791 Bill of Rights ratified

1803 Louisiana Purchase doubles land area of US

1812–14 US at war with Great Britain; British burn Washington, D.C.; "Star-Spangled Banner" written

1820 Missouri Compromise signed in attempt to avoid crisis over slavery

1823 Monroe Doctrine

1830 Indian Removal Act creates "Indian territories"

1840 Telegraph first used

1841 Oregon trail opens

1846 US war against Mexico; US borders extended to Pacific Ocean

1849 California Gold Rush

1861 Civil War erupts when southern states secede from Union, forming Confederate States of America

1863 Battle of Gettysburg; Gettysburg Address; Emancipation Proclamation

1865 13th Amendment abolishes slavery

1865 Lee surrenders to Grant; President Lincoln assassinated

1867 Reconstruction Act

1868 14th Amendment grants citizenship to African Americans

1869 Union Pacific and Central Pacific railroads meet at Promontory Point

1870 15th Amendment gives African Americans the right to vote

1876 Alexander Graham Bell invents the telephone

1879 Thomas Edison makes the electric light bulb

1882 Chinese Exclusion Act

1886 Haymarket riot; American Federation of Labor organized

1890 Frontier closes; massacre of American Indians at Wounded Knee

1898 Spanish-American War; US acquires the Philippines, Puerto Rico, and Hawaii

1903 First flight by Wright brothers at Kitty Hawk

1913 16th Amendment places federal tax on income

1914 Panama Canal opens

1915 German U-boat sinks the *Lusitania*

1916 Child Labor Act

1917 US enters World War I; end of Progressivism

1918 End of World War I

Dec. 7, 1941 Pearl Harbor attacked; US enters war

1942 Relocation of Japanese-Americans begins; Bataan Death March; Battles of Coral Sea and Midway

June 6, 1944 D-Day

May 8, 1945 Germany surrenders

Aug. 6, 1945 US drops atomic bomb on Hiroshima

Aug. 9, 1945 US drops atomic bomb on Nagasaki

Aug. 15, 1945 Japan surrenders

1948 Marshall Plan implemented; Berlin airlift

1950 McCarthy hearings begin; start of Korean War

1954 Supreme Court ruling on *Brown* v. *Board*

US GOVERNMENT—A SYSTEM OF CHECKS AND BALANCES

The framers of the Constitution created a federal government with three branches so that any two could prevent the third from gaining too much power:
- The judicial branch consists of the Supreme Court and other federal courts.

- The legislative branch is the Congress, made up of the Senate (two senators per state) and the House of Representatives (numbers based on state population).
- The executive branch is the president and the Cabinet.

1919 18th Amendment begins Prohibition

1920 19th Amendment gives women the vote

1927 Charles Lindbergh makes flight across Atlantic; first "talkie" released

1929 Stock market crashes; Great Depression

1933 Great Plains become the "Dust Bowl"; President Roosevelt launches the New Deal

1939 Germany invades Czechoslovakia and Poland; Great Britain and France declare war on Germany

of Education

1955 Montgomery bus boycott

1957 *Sputnik I* launched

1958 First American satellite goes into orbit

1961 Bay of Pigs fiasco

1962 Cuban Missile Crisis

1963 March on Washington, D.C.; Dr. Martin Luther King, Jr. delivers "I Have a Dream" speech

Nov. 22, 1963 President Kennedy assassinated

1965 American troops sent to Vietnam

1968 My Lai massacre

Apr. 4, 1968 Dr. Martin Luther King, Jr. assassinated; violence erupts in 125 cities

1969 *Apollo 11* crew lands on the Moon

1972 Watergate break-in

1974 President Nixon resigns

1975 US personnel evacuated from Saigon; South Vietnam surrenders

1979 Global oil shortage; gas rationing

1979 Iranian rebels seize US Embassy

1981 Scientists identify Acquired Immune Deficiency Syndrome (AIDS)

Jan. 28, 1986 Space shuttle *Challenger* explodes

1986 Iran-Contra scandal

1991 US leads coalition in Operation Desert Storm

1992 US troops join UN mission in Somalia

1995 Oklahoma City bombing

1998 President Clinton impeached, later acquitted

Sept. 11, 2001 World Trade Center destroyed in terrorist attack

2001 US and Britain bomb Afghanistan; Taliban government collapses

2003 The US and combined forces invade Iraq to topple Saddam Hussein

2009 Barack Obama assumes office and becomes the first ever African American President of the United States

FIND OUT MORE ▸▸ American Civil War 424 • American Indians 408 • American Revolution 414 • North America 222–229

ACKNOWLEDGMENTS

DORLING KINDERSLEY would like to thank Jacqui Bailey, Kitty Blount, Laura Buller, Joe Elliot, Daniel Gilpin, Simon Holland, Jacky Jackson, Sarah Kovandzich, Esther Labi, Margaret Mulverhill, Margaret Parrish, and Nigel Ritchie for editorial assistance; Alyson Lacewing and Lee Simmons for proofreading; Sue Lightfoot for the index; Martin Copeland for picture research; Sheila Hanly, James Harrison, Clare Hibbert, Ian Probert, and Belinda Weber for link research.

Dorling Kindersley Ltd is not responsible and does not accept liability for the availability or content of any Web site other than its own, or for any exposure to offensive, harmful, or inaccurate material that may appear on the Internet. Dorling Kindersley Ltd will have no liability for any damage or loss caused by viruses that may be downloaded as a result of looking at and browsing the Web sites that it recommends. Dorling Kindersley downloadable images are the sole copyright of Dorling Kindersley Ltd, and may not be reproduced, stored, or transmitted in any form or by any means for any commercial or profit-related purpose without prior written permission of the copyright owner.

Picture Credits

The publisher would like to thank the following for their kind permission to reproduce their photographs:

Abbreviations key:
t-top, b-bottom, r-right, l-left, c-center

l. Getty Images: Phil Degginger br. **175** Associated Press AP: bl. Science Photo Library: Lawrence Livermore National Laboratory tr. **176** Corbis: Joe McDonald tl; Martin Harvey; Gallo Images bl; Roger Tidman claa; clbb. Getty Images: Photodisc Blue clb. N.H.P.A.: Kevin Schafer cla. **176–177** National Geographic Image Collection: Stephen G. St. John c. **177** Alamy Images: David Bishop/Phototake Inc br. Hulton Archive/Getty Images: ca. US Department of Defense tr. **178** PolaVisor, Copyright 2003 Winford Industries: cl. **178–179** Science Photo Library: Ted Kinsman. **179** Science Photo Library: Alexander Tsiaras br. Getty Images: Ashok Charles clb. **180** Science Photo Library: Alfred Pasieka tr. **181** Science Photo Library: John Walsh tr; K.H Kjeldsen tl. **182** Science Photo Library: Alfred Pasieka cl; David Parker bc. **182–183** Science Photo Library: Kent Wood c. **183** NASA: tr. **184–185** Corbis: Louis K. Meisel Gallery t. **185** National Grid Transco: br. Science Photo Library: Scott Camazine bl. **186** Ministry of Defence Pictures: Crown Copyright/MOD c. Science Photo Library: Alex Bartel l; Volker Steger/ Sandia National Laboratory br. **187** Corbis: Grafton Marshall Smith br; Getty Images: Photographer's Choice / Michael Dunning cl.; cra. Science Photo Library: Colin Cuthbert crb; Copyright W. T Sullivan cl. **188** Science Photo Library: D. Roberts. **189** Corbis: Stephen Grohe c. Science Photo Library: David Parker tr; Rosenfeld Images Ltd. tl. **190** Getty Images: Photodisc Green/TRBfoto clb; David Arky c. Zefa: Ausloser tl. **191** Associated Press AP: Elise Amendola tl; Loudcloud Inc cll. DK Picture Library: Science Museum bl. Getty Images: Roger Tully tl. Science Photo Library: Caida cr. **192** Corbis: Hulton-Deutsch Collection tc. Rex Features: Barry Greenwood bl. Science Photo Library: Roger Harris cl. **192–193** Courtesy of the BT Group plc 2003 c. **193** Alamy Images: Robert Harding Picture Library cra. Getty Images: Christian Lagereek crbb. Pa Photos: EPA crb; Martin Rickett cb. Science Photo Library: Mehau Kulyk tr. **194** Courtesy of Dyson: bl. Pa Photos: **194–195** Science Photo Library: Peter Menzel c. **195** Science Photo Library: Peter Menzel c; Victor Habbick Visions tr, bl. **196–197** Getty Images: Digital Vision c. **197** Science Photo Library: Richard T. Nowitz c. Getty Images: Sandra Baker tr. **198** ImageState/ Pictor: l. Porsche AG: r. **199** Alamy Images: Steve Allen tr. Corbis: Bettmann tl. Science Photo Library: Lineka tr. **200–201** ImageState/Pictor: First Light b. **201** Corbis: Lester Lefkowitz cl; tr. Getty Images: Wayne Eastep bc. **202** Courtesy The Microflat Company: Science Photo Library: Colin Cuthbert tl. **202–203** Arup: Colin Wade c. **203** Alamy Images: Andre Jenny tl; Doug Houghton tcr. Corbis: Grant Smith tcl; Massimo Mastrorillo tr; Sygma/Polak Matthew br; Tom Bean cr. **204** Corbis: Jeremy Horner ca. Getty Images: Chris Sattlberger bl; **204–205** Getty Images: Mark Segal c. **205** Corbis: Bettmann ca; Ted Horowitz cr. Getty Images: Jean Louis Batt bc. **206** Corbis: Lester Lefkowitz l. **206–207** Getty Images: Arnulf Husmo c. **207** Corbis: Mark Adams bc; Steve Chenn br. Science Photo Library: David Nunuk tc. **208** Corbis: Bettmann; Charles O'Rear bc; Layne Kennedy clb. Science Photo Library: bl; Andrew McClenaghan tl. **209** Science Photo Library: A. Barrington Brown cla; Dr. Tim Evans r; James King-Holmes clb; Tek Image bc. **210** Science Photo Library: Darque, Jerrican bl; Simon Fraser ca. **210–211** Science Photo Library: Tek Image c. **211** Rex Features: Jeremy Sutton. Science Photo Library: Andrew Leonard br; Mauro Fermariello c. **212–213** Corbis. **214** Alamy Images: Gus tl. N.H.P.A.: Martin Wendler bl. **215** Corbis: Firefly Productions tr; James A. Sugar br; Tibor Bognar tl. **216** Corbis: Tim Page bl. Alamy Images: Steve Allen t. **217** Corbis: Vince Streano t. Popperfoto: Reuters br. **218** Pa Photos: Toby Melville t. Pictures Colour Library: bl.

219 Alamy Images: ImageState/Randa Bishop tr. Corbis: SETBOUN br. **220** Corbis: clb; David Batterbury; Eye Ubiquitous claa; Macduff Everton bl; Stephen Frink tl; Stocktrek c. Getty Images: Daryl Balfour cla; Digital Vision tr. Science Photo Library: Bernhard Edmaier clbb. **222** Corbis: Terry W. Eggers bl. Getty Images: Harald Sund cl. **223** Getty Images: Bob Thomas cr; Sandra Baker tr. **224** Bryan and Cherry Alexander Photography: cr, b. Corbis: Doug Wilson tr. **225** Getty Images: Eric Meola r; Ron Thomas cl. Pictures Colour Library: eStock tl. **226** Corbis: Bob Krist cl. Getty Images: B & M productions b. Oxford Scientific Films: Philippe Henry br. **227** Corbis: Duomo cr. Getty Images: Bullaty-Lomeo tr; World Perspectives l. **228** Getty Images: Jack Dykinga bl. World Pictures: tr. **229** Getty Images: Chris Speedie l; Randy Wells cr. Robert Harding Picture Library: Photri tr. **230** Corbis: Joseph Sohm; ChromoSohm Inc ca. Getty Images: Brian Stablyk br; Photodisc Green bl. ImageState/Pictor: International Stock. **230–231** Nature Picture Library: David Noton. **231** Masterfile UK: Bill Brooks br. Zefa: M. Fiala tr. **232** Corbis: Gavriel Jecan l. Getty Images: Andrea Pistolesi cb; Digital Vision cla. South American Pictures: Tony Morrison ca. **233** Corbis: John Madere cr; Stephanie Maze bc; Theo Allofs tr. Getty Images: Hans Strand br. **234** Corbis: Jeremy Horner cr.; l. **235** Alamy Images: Tropicalstock.net tl. Getty Images: Michael Freeman br; Omar Bechara Baruque; Eye Ubiquitous cl; Roger Ressmeyer tr. **236** Corbis: Hubert Stadler ca; Michael Brennan bl. Lonely Planet Images: John Maier Jr br. **236–237** N.H.P.A.: Martin Wendler c. **237** Action Plus: Neil Tingle br. Corbis: Ricardo Azoury tr. Zefa: F. Damm cb. **238** Corbis: Yann Arthus-Bertrand. Impact Photos: Visa Image br. Still Pictures: G Hind/UNEP bl. **239** Corbis: Lindsay Hebberd cr. Getty Images: Glen Allison tl. Pictures Colour Library: br. **240** Getty Images: John Chard cr. Robert Harding Picture Library: B Schuster br. Panos Pictures: Mark Henley bl. **241** Getty Images: Geoffrey Clifford br; Glen Allison bl. Lonely Planet Images: Craig Pershouse cr; Geert Cole tl. **242** Corbis: Yann Arthus-Bertrand cr. N.H.P.A.: Martin Harvey b. Panos Pictures: Betty Press cl. **243** Corbis: Sygma/Campbell William c. Getty Images: Guido Alberto Rossi br. Pictures Colour Library: t. **244** Corbis: Roger de la Harpe; Gallo Images tl. Empics Ltd.: Mike Egerton c. N.H.P.A.: Nick Garbutt bl. **244–245** Pictures Colour Library: br. **245** N.H.P.A.: Martin Harvey t. Pictures Colour Library: cl. Rex Features: Richard Young cr. **246** Getty Images: David Norton bl; Louis-Laurent Grandadam cl. Impact Photos: Ray Roberts tr. **247** Corbis: Elke Stolzenberg tr. Getty Images: John Downer br. **248** Corbis: Hans Strand cl. Getty Images: Rick England br; Lars Hallén: bl. Still Pictures: Dylan Garcia tr. **249** Corbis: Hans Strand cl; William Findlay tr. Still Pictures: J Vallespir/UNEP bl. World Pictures: br. **250** Corbis: Geray Sweeney br; London Aerial Photo Library br; Sygma/Elder Neville tl. Getty Images: Jeremy Woodhouse cr. **251** Collections: Graham Burns cr; Paul Felix b. Getty Images: Stewart Bonney News Agency tl. Lonely Planet Images: Anne C. Dowie ca. **252** Action Plus: Franck Faugere/DPPI bl. Impact Photos: Gold Collection tr; Robin Laurance br. Pictures Colour Library: cl. **253** Corbis: Jose Fuste Raga/FMGB Guggenheim Bilbao Museoa. 2003 b; Roger Antrobus cl. Impact Photos: Gold Collection tr. **254** Getty Images: Suzanne & Nick Geary cr; Walter Bibikow b. Still Pictures: Magnus Andersson l. **255** Corbis: Ludovic Maisant cls. Getty Images: Anthony Cassidy cra; Hans Wolf b; Jorg Greuel tl. **256** Corbis: Michael Freeman cr. Getty Images: Robert Everts b. Lonely Planet Images: Paul David Hellander tl. **257** Corbis: Barry Lewis cl. Getty Images: Derek P. Redfearn cr; George Grigoriou t. Impact Photos: Peter Arkell bl. **258** Lonely Planet Images: Jonathan Smith tl. Panos Pictures: Clive Shirley cr. Rex Features: Tony Kyriacou br. Still Pictures: Bojan

Brecelj bl. **259** Getty Images: Douglas Armand b. Art Directors & TRIP: V. Shuba tl. **260** Photolibrary.com: Martyn Colbeck bl. Corbis: Tom Brakefield tr. Katz/ FSP: Van Cappellen/Rea br. Lonely Planet Images: Chris Mellor cl. **261** Corbis: Dallas and John Heaton tr. Getty Images: Andrea Pistolesi cb; Piecework Productions ca. **262** Hutchison Library: C. Nairn/GTV Disappearing World l; Trevor Page cr. Art Directors & TRIP: M. Lines br. **263** Alamy Images: Bryan and Cherry Alexander b. NASA: cl. Panos Pictures: Heidi Bradner tl. **264** Getty Images: David Hanson cr. Panos Pictures: Jon Spaull cl. Pictures Colour Library: b. **264–265** Corbis: Roger Wood tc. **265** Alamy Images: Ashfordplatt tr. Corbis: Peter Turnley clb. Pictures Colour Library: br. **266** Robert Harding Picture Library: T. Laird bl. Panos Pictures: Paul Smith tl; Penny Tweedie cr. **267** Alamy Images: Robert Harding Picture Library b. Corbis: Baldev/Sygma tl; James Davis, Eye Ubiquitous cl; Travel Pix tr. National Geographic Image Collection: David Edwards br. Pictures Colour Library: bl. **269** Alamy Images: Rex Butcher bl. Corbis: Bohemian Nomad Picturemakers tl; Tibor Bognar l. **270** Corbis: Torleif Svensson tr. Robert Harding Picture Library: T. Hall br. Pictures Colour Library: bl. **271** Corbis: Macduff Everton r. Impact Photos: Alain Evrard bl. Pictures Colour Library: bl. **272** Alamy Images: Jon Arnold Images br. **273** Corbis br. Getty Images: Kim Westerskov t. N.H.P.A.: Gerard Lacz cl. Pictures Colour Library: tr, cr, b. **275** Corbis: Peter Beck bl. Getty Images: John Lamb br. N.H.P.A.: A. N.T tl. **276** Getty Images: Johnny Johnson bl. Robert Harding Picture Library: Photri tr. **277** N.H.P.A.: Paal Hermansen. **278–279** Corbis: Dallas and John Heaton. **280** Corbis: David Cumming; Eye Ubiquitous l. The Art Archive: National Museum Bucharest/Dagli Orti tl. **281** Werner Forman Archive: Schindler Collection, New York br. Popperfoto: tl. **282** Ancient Art and Architecture Collection: bcl, l; R. Sheridan bl. Bridgeman Art Library, London/New York: Egyptian National Museum, Cairo cb. Corbis: Randy Faris tr; cr. The Art Archive: Musee du Louvre Paris/Dagli Orti c. **283** Corbis: Gunter Marx Photography bl; Yann Arthus-Bertrand tr. **284** Corbis: John Dakers; Eye Ubiquitous crb; Lindsay Hebberd tl. The Art Archive: Victoria and Albert Museum/Eileen Tweedy bl. **285** Alamy Images: Henry Westheim cl. Bridgeman Art Library, London/New York: Durham University bl. Corbis: Archivo Iconografico, S.A tr. **286** Bridgeman Art Library, London/New York: Ann & Bury Peerless/India Office Library, London bc. Corbis: Lindsay Hebberd tl. Pictures Colour Library: cl. DK Picture Library: Judith Miller & DK Picture Library – Sloans, USA cl. Rex Features: Geoff Dowen cr. **287** Corbis: David Reed tr. Getty Images: Photodisc Green/Michael Matisse bl. **288** Corbis: Andrea Jemolo tl. DK Picture Library: Glasgow Museum br. Sonia Halliday Photographs: l. **289** Alamy Images: Robert Harding World Imagery tr. Corbis: Adam Woolfitt tl; Geray Sweeney cr; Richard Bickel b. DK Picture Library: Powell Cotton Museum bl. **290** Bridgeman Art Library, London/New York: Giraudon/Musee Conde, Chantilly, France br. Panos Pictures: Karen Robinson cr; Marcus Rose cl. Rex Features: Sipa Press l. **291** Corbis: Blaine Harrington III t. Art Directors & TRIP: H. Rogers br. **292** Bridgeman Art Library, London/New York: Galleria dell' Accademia, Venice c. **292–293** Corbis: Alinari Archives b. **293** Getty Images: Michael John O'Neill cr. Ann & Bury Peerless: tl. **294** The Granger Collection, New York: tr. Rex Features: TDY cl. **294–295** Getty Images: Yann Layma b. **295** Corbis: Bettmann cr; Inge Yspeert cl. **296** Alamy Images: Joe Sohm cla, bl. Corbis: Peter Finger cr; Wendy Stone claa. Getty Images: Anthony Cassidy clb. Pa Photos: AFP Photo/Hector MATA tl. Rex Features: David Hartley clbb. **297** Alamy Images: Gianni Muratore bl; Wilmar Photography c. Corbis: Frank Leather; Eye Ubiquitous tr. Impact Photos: Javed A Jafferji br. **2**

98 Kobal Collection: Warner Bros/DC Comics cl. Rex Features: Nils Jorgensen bl. **298–299** Corbis: Ron Watts c. **299** Advertising Archives: 'Coca-Cola' and 'Coke' are registered trade marks of the Coca-Cola Company and are reproduced with kind permission from the Coca-Cola Company br. Courtesy Freeplay Foundation: c. ImageState/Pictor: Coccon tr. **300** Corbis: James A. Sugar bl. Hutchison Library: Eric Lawrie cl. **300–301** Corbis: Bob Krist c. **301** Corbis: Jennie Woodcock; Reflections Photolibrary br. Panos Pictures: Jeremy Horner cb. Popperfoto: br. **302** Robert Harding Picture Library: cl. **302–303** Rex Features: Sipa Press c. **303** Associated Press AP: Brian Branch-Price bc. Rex Features: Action Press b. **304** Corbis: Sygma/ Balaguer Alejandro br. Masterfile UK: Mark Tomalty bl. Popperfoto: Reuters tr. **305** Alamy Images: Rob Rayworth cr. Hulton Archive/Getty Images: Keystone bl. Science Photo Library: NASA tl. **306** Alamy Images: Gina Calvi cl. Pa Photos: EPA tr. Rex Features: Action Press (ACT) b. **307** Corbis: Peter Turnley tl; Roger Ressmeyer bl. Getty Images: AFP/Hotli Simanjuntak cr. Hulton Archive/Getty Images: Central Press cl. **308** Corbis: Richard Cummins cra. Getty Images: tr; China Tourism Press crb; Ken Ross br. Robert Harding Picture Library: E. Simanor l. **309** Corbis: Bettmann br. Popperfoto: cl. Science Photo Library: Astrid & Hans Frieder Michler cr. **310** Getty Images: V.C.L tr. Rex Features: Greg Mathieson b. **311** Corbis: Julie Dennis Brothers crb. Getty Images: bl. Pa Photos: tl. Rex Features: Sipa Press cra. **312** Corbis: Bettmann tr; Jay Syverson br. Magnum: Francesco Zizola cl. **313** Associated Press AP: Mark Richards, Pool cl. Corbis: Yogi, Inc c. Popperfoto: Reuters r. **314** Associated Press AP: Joe Marquette tl. Panos Pictures: Trygve Bolstad cr. Still Pictures: Hartmut Schwarzbach bl. **315** Science Photo Library: NASA br. UN/DPI Photo: t. **316** Alamy Images: Karen Robinson/David Hoffman PhotoLibrary br. Popperfoto: Rick Wilking/ Reuters l. **317** Panos Pictures: Piers Benatar cl. Popperfoto: Reuters/Haider Shah br; Reuters/Jerry Lampen cr. UN/DPI Photo: tr. **318–319** Photograph of Josette Bushell-Mingo as 'Rafiki' from the Original London Company of THE LION KING by Catherine Ashmore. **320** AKG London: Erich Lessing tr, cr. The Art Archive: Archaeological Museum Naples/Dagli Orti c; Archaeological Museum Naples/Dagli Orti tc; Palazzo Ducale Mantua/Dagli Orti br. Mark Roots Collection: Courtesy Michael Nelson Jagamara, from the collection of Mark Roots clb. **321** Bridgeman Art Library, London/New York: Mellon Coll., Nat. Gallery of Art, Washington DC tl, cl. The Art Archive: cb; National Gallery/Eileen Tweedy br. Réunion Des Musées Nationaux Agence Photographique: Gerard Blot tc, c. **322** Corbis: Christie's Images tl. Topham Picturepoint: HIP/British Museum c. **323** © The British Museum: Corbis: David Lees br. Hutchison Library: Carlos Freire cr. **324** Bridgeman Art Library, London/New York: Kunsthistorisches Museum, Vienna cl. Corbis: Bettmann cb; Nathan Benn bl. Topham Picturepoint: UPP cr. Christo and Jeane-Claude: Surrounded Islands, Greater Miami, Florida 1980-83. © Christo and Jeanne-Claude. Photo: Wolfgang Volz tr. **325** Bridgeman Art Library, London/New York: Stapleton Collection, UK tr. Magnum: Dennis Stock cl; Steve McCurry bl. Réunion Des Musées Nationaux Agence Photographique: Eugene Atget cr. **326** Alamy Images: Steve Allen cr. Courtesy Apple: c, background. © Christie's Images Ltd.: Charles Renni Mackintosh cl. The Art Archive: Villa la Pietra Florence/Dagli Orti tr. Kobal Collection: Paramount cll. Popperfoto: crr. Courtesy of the Trustees of the V&A Picture Library: ca. **327** Bridgeman Art Library, London/New York: Victoria & Albert Museum, London cbl. Cooper-Hewitt National Design Museum: Smithsonian Institution bcr. Corbis: Peter Harholdt br. DK Picture Library: British Museum tl; Cooper Hewitt cb; Judith Miller & DK Picture

Library – Lyon & Turnball Ltd. ca; Judith Miller & DK Picture Library – Gideon Hatch bcl. Marimekko: designed by Maija Isola 1965 bl. Vitra Design Museum: George Nelson c. **328** Corbis: Dallas and John Heaton cl; **328–329** Corbis: David Bell c. Getty Images: AFP br. **329** Associated Press AP: JAWOC tr. Corbis: Araldo de Luca crb; Dave Bartruff cr; Jim Winkley; Ecoscene c; Michael S. Yamashita br. **330** Lebrecht Collection: bc. Redferns: Elliott Landy cl. **330–331** Getty Images: Nick White tr. **331** Corbis: Paul A. Souders tr. Lebrecht Collection: David Farrell crb. Redferns: David Redfern bc. **332** DK Picture Library: Johnny Van Derrick br. Lebrecht Collection: br. **333** Getty Images: Thinkstock cl. Rex Features: Brian Rasic (BRA) tr. **334** Apple Corps Ltd.: br. Corbis: Europa Press/G.G/Sygma cr. Lebrecht Collection: Rue des Archives/BCA c. Rex Features: SNAP (SYP) l. **335** Lebrecht Collection: Wladimir Polak tr. Redferns: Graham Salter b; Odile Noel tl. **336** ArenaPAL: Hilary Shedel bl. DK Picture Library: Stephen Oliver cr. **336–337** Corbis: Sandro Vannini tc. **337** Lebrecht Collection: Laurie Lewis b; Ron Hill cl. Linda Rich: tr. **338** Kobal Collection: MGM b. Redferns: Henrietta Butler tr. **339** DK Picture Library: INAH cl. The Art Archive: Musee des Beaux Arts Dole/Dagli Orti bl; Victoria and Albert Museum/Eileen Tweedy tr. **340** Corbis: Philip Gould bl; Sygma br. Mary Evans Picture Library: tl. Kobal Collection: Joseph Shaftel Prods cr. **341** Mary Evans Picture Library: cr. Kobal Collection: 20th Century Fox/Tursi, Mario bc; Hammer cb; Selznick/MGM cbl. Moviestore Collection: 20th Century Fox cl. Reproduced by permission of Penguin Books Ltd.: tl. Topham Picturepoint: Heritage Image Partnership/British Library tr. **342** AKG London: bl. Bridgeman Art Library, London/New York: Leeds Museums and Galleries (City Art Gallery) UK tr. The Art Archive: British Library cl; Eileen Tweedy br. **343** Bridgeman Art Library, London/New York: Fitzwilliam Museum, University of Cambridge tr. The Art Archive: Lucien Biton Collection Paris cr. Mary Evans Picture Library: br. Pa Photos: Mok Yui Mok cl. **344** ArenaPAL: Colin Willoughby cl. Corbis: Michael S. Yamashita c. **345** ArenaPAL: Rowena Chowdry c. Photostage: Donald Cooper tr. Rex Features: Reg Wilson tr. **346** Kobal Collection: Damfx bl; Icon/Pathe/Bailey, Alex br; Universal cl. Moviestore Collection: Columbia bc. **346–347** Kobal Collection: Lucas Film/20th Century Fox c. **347** Corbis: Sygma bc. DK Picture Library: OSCAR statuette is the registered trademark and copyrighted property of the Academy of Motion Picture Arts and Science car. Katz/FSP: PH Westenberger/Liaison cr. Kobal Collection: 20th Century Fox/Paramount tr; TOHO bl. Moviestore Collection: Eon Productions br. **348** AKG London: bl. Corbis: Bettmann cl; Hulton-Deutsch Collection tr. Pa Photos: Stefan Rousseau cr. Popperfoto: Reuters crb. **349** Corbis: Barclay Graham/Sygma cl. Kobal Collection: Amblin/Universal cl; Dream Works/Allied Film Makers A. Ardmaan cr; Dreamworks LLC br. **350** Corbis: Michael Neveux br; cr. Courtesy of Oware Society: cb. Getty Images: Brand X Pictures tr. Rex Features: David Marsden cl. Courtesy Sony: tl. **351** Courtesy Apple: cll. Bang & Olufsen, AV Mediacenter 2003 cr, bl. Courtesy BlueroomStore.com: tr. Mary Evans Picture Library: tl. Moviestore Collection: Warner Brothers cl. Courtesy Nintendo: br. Pure Digital, a division of Imagination Technologies: c. Courtesy Sony: crr. **352** Action Plus: Glyn Kirk bl. Getty Images: Mark Thompson cl. **352–353** Sporting Pictures (UK) Ltd.: Huzilar c. **353** Associated Press AP: Bill Kostroun cr; Michael Conroy c. Corbis: Decamp Erik/Sygma br. Getty Images: David Rogers tr. **354** Bridgeman Art Library, London/New York: Marylebone Cricket Club, London, UK tl. Getty Images: Bob Thomas / Bob Thomas Sports Photography bc. **354–355** Getty Images: Pascal Rondeau c. **355** Associated Press AP: Mark J. Terrill tr. Topham Picturepoint: br. **356** Alamy Images: Popperfoto tl. The Art Archive: National Archaeological Museum Athens/Dagli Orti br. IOC/Olympic Museum Collections: tr. **357** Corbis: Sygma/Ruszniewski J.Y cl; Sygma/Seguin Franck cr. Getty Images: Clive Brunskill tc; Mike Powell/Allsport br; Scott Barbour/Allsport c. **358–359** Corbis: Neil Beer.

360 AKG London: tl. The Art Archive: British Library bl; **360–361** The Art Archive: National Archaeological Museum Athens/ Dagli Orti. **361** DK Picture Library: Mary Rose Trust tr. Werner Forman Archive: Ohio State Museum br. Silkeborg Museum, Denmark: cr. **362–363** AKG London: tr. **363** Bridgeman Art Library, London/New York: Lauros/ Giraudon tr. DK Picture Library: British Museum c. **364** Ancient Art and Architecture Collection: Ronald Sheridan tr. Sonia Halliday Photographs: cl. **365** Ancient Art and Architecture Collection: R. Sheridan tl. DK Picture Library: Arlette Mellaart br; Museum of London cr. **366** Werner Forman bc. Robert Harding Picture Library: Robert Estall tr; Simon Harris c. **367** Ancient Art and Architecture Collection: tr. The Art Archive: Archaeological Museum Cagliari/ Dagli Orti c. Genius of China Exhibition br; Musee Guimet Paris/Dagli Orti cl. **368** AKG London: Jean-Louis Nou br. **369** Ancient Art and Architecture Collection: cr. **370** Ancient Art and Architecture Collection: tl. DK Picture Library: British Museum tr. Werner Forman Archive: The Egyptian Museum, Cairo c. **370–371** Robert Harding Picture Library: George Rainbird Ltd. c. **371** DK Picture Library: British Museum tr. Werner Forman Archive: Luxor Museum, Egypt r. Robert Harding Picture Library: Nigel Francis tc. **372** AKG London: Erich Lessing cr. Ancient Art and Architecture Collection: tr, bc. Bridgeman Art Library, London/New York: Iraq Museum, Baghdad tl. **373** AKG London: Erich Lessing c, bc. The Art Archive: Musee du Louvre Paris/Dagli Orti r. **374** AKG London: cr; Erich Lessing bl. Ancient Art and Architecture Collection: Ronald Sheridan background. DK Picture Library: British Museum tl. **374–375** The Art Archive: Dagli Orti c. **375** Ancient Art and Architecture Collection: tr. The Art Archive: Dagli Orti cr. **376** AKG London: National Archeological Museum cl; Rainer Hackenberg tl. DK Picture Library: British Museum br. Sonia Halliday Photographs: br. **376–377** National Geographic Image Collection: Todd Gipstein c. **377** Ancient Art and Architecture Collection: tr. DK Picture Library: British Museum cr. The Art Archive: National Archaeological Museum Athens/Dagli Orti br. Sonia Halliday Photographs: tc. **378** Ancient Art and Architecture Collection: tr. Bridgeman Art Library, London/New York: Oriental Bronzes Ltd., London c. Corbis: Lee White br. DK Picture Library: British Museum cr. The Art Archive: Genius of China Exhibition l. **379** AKG London: Jean-Louis Nou tr, cr. Bridgeman Art Library, London/New York: Museum of Archaeology, History of Culture, Vadodara, India bl. The Art Archive: c. **380** Corbis: Michael S. Lewis br. DK Picture Library: American Museum of Natural History tl. The Art Archive: Archaeological Museum Lima/Dagli Orti tr. Werner Forman Archive: University Museum, Philadelphia tc. **381** AKG London: br. DK Picture Library: INAH tr. Corbis: bl. **382** AKG London: bl; Erich Lessing cl. The Art Archive: Galleria Borghese Rome/Dagli Orti bl. **382–383** Robert Harding Picture Library: Adam Woolfitt b. **383** AKG London: tc. Ancient Art and Architecture Collection: tr. Corbis: Michael St. Maur Sheil br. **384** DK Picture Library: British Museum l. Sonia Halliday Photographs: tr. **385** The Art Archive: Biblioteca Nazionale Palermo/ Dagli Orti tl; Dagli Orti tr. Sonia Halliday Photographs: c. **386** The Art Archive: British Library br; National Museum Damascus Syria/Dagli Orti cr. Sonia Halliday Photographs: cl. **386–387** The Art Archive: Dagli Orti c **387** The Art Archive: Dagli Orti br. Sonia Halliday Photographs: Biblioteque Nationale tr. **388** AKG London: br. Corbis: Richard Cummins tr. DK Picture Library: Danish National Museum cb; Statens Historika Museum, Stockholm tl; Viking Ship Museum, Norway bl. **389** AKG London: tr, bl, br. The Art Archive: Musee de la Tapisserie Bayeux cl. **390** Collections: Philip Craven bl. DK Picture Library: British Museum tl. **390–391** Ancient Art and Architecture Collection: bl. **391** AKG London: Jean-Francois Amelot tl. DK Picture Library: British Museum br. Sonia Halliday Photographs: tr **392** AKG London: tr, bl. The Art Archive: br; Victoria and Albert Museum/Eileen Tweedy tl. **393** AKG London: Erich Lessing br. The Art Archive: British Museum br. Robert

Harding Picture Library: T Waltham tl. **394** Werner Forman Archive: tl. Robert Harding Picture Library: J. Pate bl. **394–395** The Art Archive: Antenna Gallery Dakar Senegal/Dagli Orti c. **395** Werner Forman Archive: British Museum tr. Robert Harding Picture Library: N. Wheeler tr. **396** Werner Forman Archive: Courtesy Entwistle Gallery, London bl. Robert Harding Picture Library: Geoff Renner r. **397** AKG London: Jean-Louis Nou c. DK Picture Library: Robert O'Dea tl. The Art Archive: Turkish and Islamic Art Museum Istanbul/Dagli Orti br. **398** AKG London: Turin Biblioteca Reale ca. Scala Group S.p.A.: Palazzo Medici Riccardi, Firenze. **399** DK Picture Library: British Library cr. **400** Bridgeman Art Library, London/New York: Royal Geographical Society c. National Maritime Museum, London: b. **400–401** AKG London: c. **401** James Davis Travel Photography: br. DK Picture Library: British Museum tr, cra. Mary Evans Picture Library: cr. **402** AKG London: tl. Corbis: Galen Rowell b. **403** Scala Group S.p.A.: Biblioteca Nationale, Firenze. **404** AKG London: tr, c. Robert Harding Picture Library: P. Craven br. **405** AKG London: tr, c. The Art Archive: Bruning Museum Lambayeque Peru/Mireille Vautier br. **406** AKG London: tr. DK Picture Library: Wallace Collection bl. Mary Evans Picture Library: br. **407** AKG London: Victoria and Albert Museum tr. DK Picture Library: Wallace Collection c. Hulton Archive/Getty Images: Ernst Haas br. **408** DK Picture Library: Exeter Maritime Museum c. © Michael Holford: b. **409** Bridgeman Art Library, London/New York: Museum of the City of New York, USA b. Hulton Archive/Getty Images: Archive Photos cl. **410** AKG London: bcr. Corbis: Archivo Iconografico, S.A. tl; Gianni Dagli Orti bl. DK Picture Library: Etablissement public du musée et du domaine national de Versailles c. The Art Archive: Christ's Hospital/Eileen Tweedy bcl; Russian Historical Museum Moscow/Dagli Orti br. Mary Evans Picture Library: bc. **411** Bridgeman Art Library, London/New York: Bibliotheque des Arts Decoratifs, Paris/Charmet bl; National Gallery, London r. DK Picture Library: Science Museum br. Hulton Archive/Getty Images: cl. **412** Bridgeman Art Library, London/New York: Collection of the Earl of Leicester, Holkham Hall, Norfolk cr; Royal Agricultural Society of England, Stoneleigh br. Rural History Centre, University of Reading: b. **413** AKG London: tl, bl. Corbis: Bettmann cl. DK Picture Library: Wilberforce House/Hull City Museums and Art Gallery t. **414** Bridgeman Art Library, London/New York: New York Historical Society br. The Art Archive: Musee du Chateau de Versailles/Dagli Orti t. **415** Bridgeman Art Library, London/New York: Bibliotheque Nationale, Paris br. DK Picture Library: Wallace Collection tr, tcr. Mary Evans Picture Library: c. **416** Bridgeman Art Library, London/New York: Charmet/Musee de la Ville de Paris, Musee Carnavalet, Paris tl; Peter Willi/Louvre, Paris br. **417** AKG London: tc. Bridgeman Art Library, London/New York: Phillips, Fine Art Auctioneers, New York, USA c. The Greenwich Workshop: 2003 Howard Terpning, Courtesy of The Greenwich Workshop, Inc b. **418** Bridgeman Art Library, London/New York: Bibliotheque des Arts Decoratifs, Paris clb. Corbis: Bettmann tr. Hulton Archive/Getty Images: Rischqitz bc. The Salvation Army International Heritage Centre: cla. Science & Society Picture Library: tl, bl. **418–419** Hulton Archive/Getty Images: c. **419** Corbis: Gianni Dagli Orti cr. Mary Evans Picture Library: br. **420** Bridgeman Art Library, London/New York: Private Collection tr. The Art Archive: Museo Bolivar Caracas/Dagli Orti bl. **421** Bridgeman Art Library, London/New York: Archives Larousse, Paris br; Giraudon/Laurose/Bibliotheque Nationale, Paris bl. Mary Evans Picture Library: tr. **422** AKG London: br. Hulton Archive/Getty Images: cl. **423** Mary Evans Picture Library: br. **424** Corbis: Bettmann cr; Museum of the City of New York tr. DK Picture Library: Gettysburg National Military Park bl. Hulton Archive/Getty Images: MPI br. **425** Bridgeman Art Library, London/New York: Alexander Turnbull Library, Wellington, New Zealand br. Corbis: Anders Ryman bl; Dallas and John Heaton tr. DK Picture Library: Mitchell Library, State of New South Wales tl. **426** AKG London: cl. **426–427** AKG London: bc. **427**

AKG London: tc. Corbis: Hulton-Deutsch Collection tr, cr; Michael St Maur Sheil br. **428** AKG London: tr. Corbis: Bettmann tl. David King Collection: bl. **429** Bridgeman Art Library, London/New York: Private Collection cl. The Art Archive: William Sewell tr. Popperfoto. **430** AKG London: bl, br. Art Directors & TRIP: Dinodia tr. **431** Corbis: Swim Ink tr. Mary Evans Picture Library: tl. Hulton Archive/Getty Images: Fox Photos bl; Keystone br. Art Directors & TRIP: E Young c. **432** AKG London: cl. **432–433** The Art Archive: Imperial War Museum b. **433** AKG London: br. Corbis: Bettmann tl. The Art Archive: Domenica del Corriere/Dagli Orti tr. Mary Evans Picture Library: cr. **434** Corbis: br. Corbis: br; David Turnley bl. **435** Corbis: Francoise de Mulder cr; Wally McNamee tl. Hulton Archive/Getty Images: Three Lions br.

Jacket images:

Front: Alamy Images: Peter Horree fcrb. Corbis: Ralph Clevenger fcr; Franck Guiziou / Hemis c; Corey Hochachka / Design Pics fcl; Danny Lehman bl; Frank Lukasseck fbr; MedicalRF.com cr; Arthur Morris cl; Denis Scott br, clb; Keren Su fclb. Getty Images: Stone / Diane Cook and Len Jenshel crb. Science Photo Library: Professors P. M. Motta & S. Correr clb; Gustoimages cl; Claude Nuridsany & Marie Perennou fbl. **Back**: Getty Images: Taxi / Ian McKinnell c. Science Photo Library: Gustoimages cr; David Mack cl. **Spine**: Science Photo Library: Victor De Schwanberg b; Susumu Nishinaga cb.

All other images © Dorling Kindersley.
For further information see: www.dkimages.com